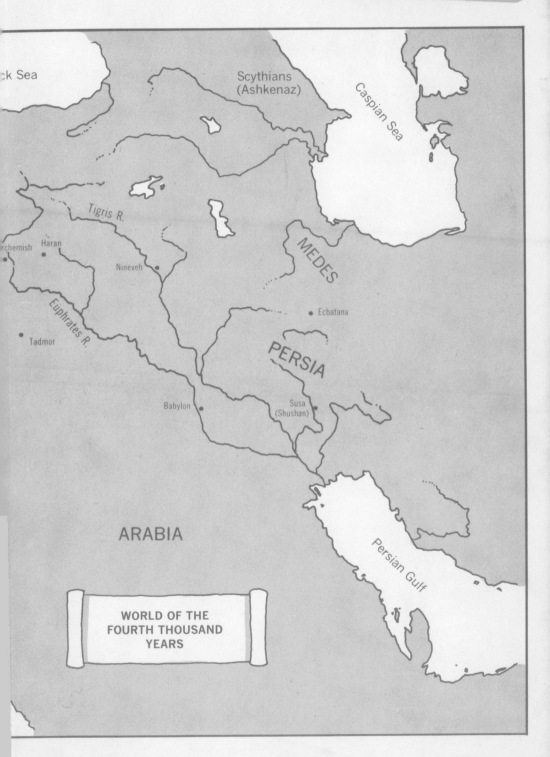

ck Sea

Scythians
(Ashkenaz)

Caspian Sea

Tigris R.

chemish Haran

Nineveh

MEDES

Ecbatana

Euphrates R.

Tadmor

PERSIA

Babylon

Susa
(Shushan)

ARABIA

Persian Gulf

WORLD OF THE
FOURTH THOUSAND
YEARS

THE FOURTH
THOUSAND YEARS

THE
FOURTH
THOUSAND
YEARS

by

W. CLEON SKOUSEN

BOOKCRAFT
Salt Lake City, Utah

LITHOGRAPHED IN U.S.A.
BY

PUBLISHERS PRESS

SALT LAKE CITY, UTAH

To My Father

ROYAL P. SKOUSEN

Born in Springerville, Arizona, in 1886, he lost his mother at the age of five. Most of his youth was spent with his father in construction camps where he began driving a team of mules on a slip-scraper at the age of twelve.

At eighteen he had charge of possibly the only stock drive ever attempted across the treacherous High Sierras of Old Mexico. Traveling with a younger brother and several natives, they swam the swollen rivers and scaled the ragged masses of the Rocky Mountains which stretch range upon range from the Pacific Ocean to the high, inland valleys of Mexico. Although long overdue and given up for dead, the party finally emerged safely in the state of Durango.

In 1908, at the age of twenty-two, he married Rita Bentley, daughter of Bishop (and later Stake President) Joseph C. Bentley of Colonia Juarez, Chihuahua, Mexico. Six weeks later he left for Norway on a thirty-month mission for the Church. Being of limited education and unable to learn the language, he sought divine assistance and overnight received the capacity to fluently express himself in the language of that land. This inspired gift remained with him throughout his mission.

Upon returning home he tried a variety of occupations, including selling, farming, and finally railroad construction and highway building in which he was notably successful. At various times he lived in Canada, Mexico, Utah, Nevada, California, Arizona, New Mexico and Texas.

He became an outstanding athlete, having equalled the world's record of his day for the fifty-yard dash. He was also a popular amateur dramatist and play director. In his later years he became an avid student of history. He also served a second mission, this one being in the Eastern States.

He died at San Bernardino, California, May 21, 1950, and at his funeral it was learned that he had been the quiet benefactor of many widows, orphans and needy persons about whom his family were unaware. In addition to the Golden Rule he had two favorite mottos:

"Make your word as good as your bond,"
"When you start a job, finish it!"

To this good and faithful man who was my father, this volume is gratefully dedicated.

Preface

Of all the writing projects I have ever undertaken, this one has been the most challenging and certainly one of the most gratifying.

For many years I have hoped there would be time and opportunity to make the spiritual and intellectual journey which I knew the preparation of this volume would require. Having completed the task I only hope I have been able to share with the reader a substantial measure of the thrilling adventure which the exploration of this subject matter provided for the author.

In the *Fourth Thousand Years* we are dealing with the most neglected area of all scriptural study. I have therefore tried to identify people and places sufficiently well so that the book is self-contained and does not require the student to do extensive outside reading in order to understand what we are discussing.

Too often the Old Testament has been relegated to what we might call "the child's interest level." However, no matter how interesting many of the stories in this part of the Bible may be to children, there is no doubt but what this part of the scripture is almost entirely adult-level reading and therefore it deserves the most serious and careful perusal by the mature student.

As I have indicated in the previous books of this series, the voluminous footnotes are salted into the text rather heavily just so the many interesting details which have been dug out will not get lost in the shuffle. After they have cooled off it is often difficult even for the author to remember the precise source from which many of these important nuggets were mined. Therefore it is as much for the benefit of the author as it is for the reader that the text is saturated with footnotes and reference material. These also help the reader appreciate that some of the most colorful and interesting material in the text comes from the scripture itself, and not from the imagination of the author.

In fact, wherever I have drawn personal deductions, or presented a suggested explanation which is not specifically spelled out in the scriptures, a deliberate attempt has been made to employ some type of signaling device so the reader can readily distinguish such passages. These signals consist of such phrases as "it would appear that," or "this would lead us to conclude," etc. Single words have also been used for this purpose such as "apparently," "probably," or "undoubtedly."

And because the King James translators sometimes used words which have now become obscure or obsolete, brackets have been used to enclose the author's suggested clarification.

The questions at the end of each chapter are specifically designed to encourage the student to make a more penetrating analysis of the subject matter. Most of the questions require specific factual answers rather than opinions. Some schools of modern pedagogy frown on the use of "memory" questions but thirty years of teaching have persuaded the author that students need a generous background of factual information in order to provide a better bedrock for their opinions. It gives them the intellectual tools with which to do precision thinking rather than indulge in rambling speculation. Too often "discussion classes" by inadequately prepared participants turn out to be what someone has called "the pooling of mutual ignorance."

The questions at the end of each chapter are designed so that a teacher of younger students can obtain rather simple answers whereas the teacher of more mature students can advise them in advance that they will be expected to know the answers in full bloom.

In this book I have tried to bring together the resources which seemed at the time to be the best available. For example, the more I have visited the Holy Land, the more it appears that no writer with whom I am familiar has come anywhere near Dr. Cunningham Geikie in equalling his elaborate and carefully documented description of historical Bible scenes. The results of his lifetime of study are set forth in a six-volume work published at the turn of the century called, *Hours With the Bible*. For modern developments in archaeology and historical research I have found one of the best non-technical resources to be the work of Dr. Emil G.

Kraeling in his new Rand McNally *Bible Atlas*. Contrary to what one might expect, this book is primarily text rather than maps, but the maps and illustrations which do appear are some of the finest in print. Another excellent book combining secular and Biblical resources is *The Story of the Bible World*, by Dr. Nelson Beecher Keyes. Both of these go well with the widely quoted volume, *The Bible as History*, by Dr. Werner Keller.

As for Bible commentaries, the student will find a surprising disparity in the quality of these books. One of the finest single-volume commentaries is by Rev. J. R. Dummelow of Cambridge. For analysis in depth, however, I have found nothing to equal the Old Testament portion of the six-volume commentary by Dr. Adam Clarke. Although published over a century ago, it still seems to come closer to filling the needs of the student than many of the more modern and less penetrating commentaries. *The Interpreters Bible* is a popular 12-volume work but its greatest value is in its preliminary treatises on specialized subjects.

Then, of course, there is nothing that can equal a careful study of the scriptures themselves. These must forever remain the major resources for a book such as this.

ACKNOWLEDGMENTS

Once again I wish to thank my friend Marvin Wallin who has endured the traumatic travails of a publisher by patiently encouraging this project until it has been completed. And no one could have asked for finer cooperation than that which has been provided by Paul Green and his able staff in mothering along the printing process from press to bindery. It was Howard Gerber and his brother, Harold, who drafted the most proficient members of their personnel at Twin Typographers to transfer the text from a voluminous manuscript to the neatness of the printed page. The maps, as usual, were done by my friend, Paul Hasegawa. I am grateful also for the fine work of Dale Bryner whose modern and intriguing vignettes enhance the beginning of each chapter.

Last of all may I say just a word about a special group for whom I am particularly grateful:

It is customary for an author to acknowledge his indebtedness to his family, but I am especially indebted to mine. With eight children, the time-consuming tasks of an author place an especially heavy burden on a wife. It is priceless treasure to have a companion who not only cheerfully shoulders the additional burdens but insists on staying up all kinds of hours proof-reading, indexing, checking references and performing a multitude of other necessary chores. To my children I am equally grateful. The tedious task of typing and retyping hundreds of pages of manuscript has been done exclusively by three of them—David, Julianne and Sharon. In addition David has done yeoman service in certain areas of specialized research as well as double-checking several thousand reference sources. It was he who discovered and brought back from England the extremely interesting article on James Bartley which appears in the chapter on Jonah. And while a father is busily involved in poring over manuscripts and pounding on a typewriter there are lawns to be cut, dishes and cars to be washed, errands to be run. This is where Harold, Kathy, Paul and Brent have made their most important contribution. Besides this, they have been good sports about patiently foregoing for a number of months many of the wonderful times we ordinarily spend together. And for the sake of completing this project they good naturedly gave up our usual summer vacation trip. All of this a father who writes appreciates beyond expression. Standing in the distance, but lending wonderful encouragement and support have been Rick, Cheryl and Glenn. For those who are statistically minded and realize I have listed more than eight children, let it be said that Cheryl and Glenn were acquired through fortunate marriages.

I close this attempted listing of acknowledgments with deepest trepidation for I cannot possibly name all who deserve a place here. One owes so much to so many. Nevertheless, to all who helped this project come to its final fruition I express my deepest, warm and personal appreciation.

W. Cleon Skousen
Salt Lake City, Utah

Contents

CONTENTS

CONTENTS xiii

CONTENTS

The Miraculous Defeat of the Assyrian Army
Isaiah's Last Appearance in Biblical History
The End of Isaiah's Ministry
The Fall of Assyria
The Fall of Judah
The Fall of Babylon
Isaiah Knew the Conqueror of Babylon Would be Cyrus
Isaiah's Historical Perspective

Prophecies Concerning America
Joseph Smith in Prophecy
Isaiah Addresses Himself to the Israelites in America
Isaiah and Nephi on the Coming Forth of the Book of Mormon
Twenty Prophecies in These Texts Have already Been Fulfilled

Isaiah Speaks of the Two Great "Zions" of the Latter Days
The Great Gathering
The Return of the Lost Ten Tribes
The Building of the New Jerusalem in America
The Gathering of the Jews and the Rebuilding of Old Jerusalem
Adolf Hitler and "The Protocols of the Learned Elders of Zion"
The Creation of a Modern Israel
The Building of a Temple in Jerusalem
The Second Coming of Christ
The Millennium

King Manasseh of Judah
Manasseh is Taken Captive to Babylon
King Amon of Judah
King Josiah of Judah
Josiah Cleanses the Temple and a Copy of the Ancient Law
      is Discovered
Josiah's Great Passover
The Raising Up of Prophets in the Land
The Prophet Zephaniah
The Prophet Nahum
The Fall of Nineveh and the Assyrian Empire
The Death of the Good King Josiah
The Prophet Habakkuk

Jeremiah Passes Through a Period of Intensive Preparation
The Lord's Controversy With Judah
Judah's Coming Calamity
The Lord's Message of Hope
Jeremiah Gets a More Realistic Perspective
The Reign of King Josiah, King Jehoahaz and King Jehoiakim
Jeremiah Flounders in the Mire of Persecution
Jeremiah Nearly Loses His Life
The Lonely Life of a Prophet
Jeremiah is Abused by Pashur, Son of a Priest
The Recorded Revelations of Jeremiah Are Burned by
      King Jehoiakim
The First Babylonian Captivity—598 B.C.

Jeremiah Receives a Revelation for the Captives
The False Prophets and Political Leaders Combine
      Against Jeremiah
The Prophet Lehi, Contemporary of Jeremiah
The Great Final Siege of Jerusalem Commences

Chronology
The Fourth Thousand Years

Down through the years there has been an extensive readjustment in the chronology of the Old Testament and this is still continuing. The following is an attempt to harmonize the most reliable information available as of this time. At best, however, it is only a "working" chronology, subject to future refinements, and the student must not be disturbed to find other chronologists using slightly different dating patterns. All of the following dates, of course, are B.C.

THE MONARCHY

1062 Birth of Saul
1032 Birth of David
1022 Saul anointed first king of Israel
1002 Saul slain. David becomes king of Judah
 995 David crowned king of all Israel. Captures Jerusalem and makes it his capital
 962 David dies after making Solomon his successor
 950 Temple of Solomon dedicated
 922 Solomon dies and the kingdom is divided

THE DIVIDED KINGDOM

Israel (Northern Kingdom)		Judah (Southern Kingdom)	
922	Jeroboam (no relation to Solomon)	922	Rehoboam, son of Solomon
		905	Abijam, his son
900	Nadab, his son	902	Asa, his son
898	Baasha (new dynasty)		
886	Elah, his son		
884	Zimri, usurper		
884	Omri (new dynasty)	861	Jehoshaphat, his son
876	Ahab, his son		
853	Ahaziah, his son		
852	Jehoram, his brother	849	Jehoram, his son
841	Jehu (new dynasty)	841	Ahaziah, his son
		841	Athaliah, his queen
		834	Jehoash, her grandson
814	Jehoahaz, his son		
798	Joash, his son	796	Amaziah, his son
782	Jeroboam II, his son		
		766	Azariah (Uzziah), his son
753	Zechariah		
753	Shallum, usurper		
753	Menahem (new dynasty)		
736	Pekiah, his son	739	Jotham, his son
735	Pekah, usurper		
		734	Ahaz, his son
732	Hoshea, usurper	727	Hezekiah, his son
723	No king		
722-721	Fall of Israel		

KINGDOM OF JUDAH

696 Manasseh, son of Hezekiah
642 Amon, his son
639 Josiah, his son
609 Jehoahaz, his son

609 Jehoiakim, his brother
598 Jehoiachin, his son
598 Zedekiah, son of Josiah
587-586 Fall of Judah

BABYLONIAN EXILE

586 Gedaliah, governor over Judah remnant
538 Cyrus of Persia takes Babylon, permits Jewish exiles to return
537 Zerubbabel and Joshua lead the first return to Judah (from Babylon)
520 Temple restoration begun, leaders are Haggai and Zechariah
516 Second temple completed
458 Ezra leads second large group of exiles to Judah
445 Nehemiah leads back third group of exiles (from Persia)
420 High Priests rule Judea from this point
332 Alexander the Great conquers Judea
320 Ptolemy I (Soter) of Egypt occupies Judea
264 Continues war in Judea between Egypt and Syria
250 Septuagint translation made in Alexandria of the Pentateuch
218 Palestine overrun by Antiochus III of Syria
175 Antiochus IV (Epiphanes) rules in Syria, provokes Jews

THE MACCABEAN REVOLT

167 Antiochus IV pollutes temple, Mattathits kills Syrian official
165 Judas Maccabeus victorious over Syria
164 The temple is purified
161 Jonathan Maccabeus continues revolt, overtures to Rome
142 Simon Maccabeus rules as High Priest, independence recognized by Syria and then Rome
135 John Hyrcanus I rules and expands Jewish territory
104 Aristobulus I rules, prosperity but internal strife
102 Alexander Janneus rules, favors Sadducees over Pharisees
76 Queen Alexandra, widow of Alexander, rules, favors Pharisees
66 Hyrcanus II and brother Aristobulus II rule as co-regents, their quarrel for power brings in Rome
63 Pompey captures Jerusalem, he and Julius Caesar rule Rome

IDUMEAN RULERS

46 Antipater of Idumea made procurator of Judea by Caesar. He appoints his son Herod as governor of Galilee
41 Mark Antony possesses Palestine, Herod and his brother Phasael are made his tetrarchs
33 Break between Antony and Octavian
31 Battle of Actium, Antony and Cleopatra defeated
30 Cleopatra and Mark Antony commit suicide
27 Octavian becomes Augustus Caesar

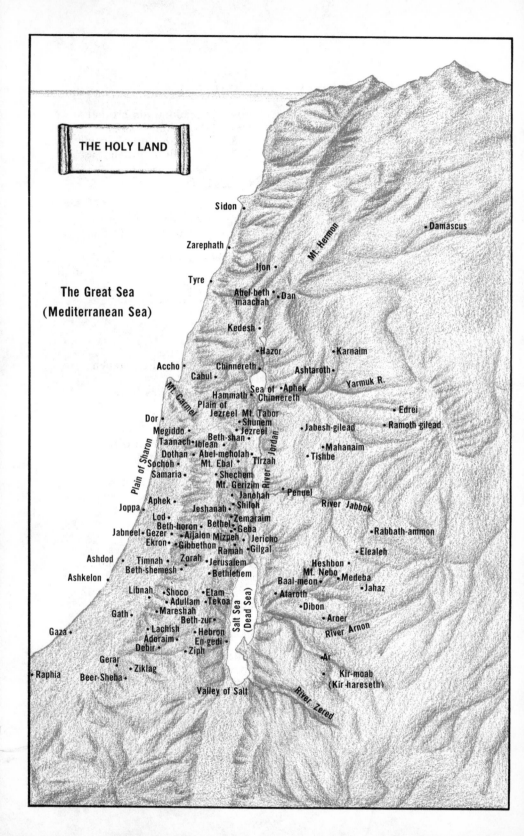

THE HOLY LAND

The Great Sea
(Mediterranean Sea)

Sidon

Damascus

Zarephath

Ijon

Mt. Hermon

Tyre

Abel-beth-
maachah

Dan

Kedesh

Hazor

Karnaim

Accho

Chinnereth

Ashtaroth

Cabul

Sea of
Chinnereth

Aphek

Yarmuk R.

Mt. Carmel

Hammath

Plain of
Jezreel

Mt. Tabor

Edrei

Dor

Shunem

Jabesh-gilead

Ramoth-gilead

Megiddo

Jezreel

Taanach

Beth-shan

Ibleam

Mahanaim

Dothan

Abel-meholah

Tishbe

Plain of Sharon

Sochoh

Mt. Ebal

Tirzah

River Jordan

Samaria

Shechem

Mt. Gerizim

Janohah

Penuel

Aphek

Shiloh

River Jabbok

Joppa

Jeshanah

Lod

Zemaraim

Beth-horon

Bethel

Geba

Rabbath-ammon

Jabneel

Gezer

Aijalon

Mizpeh

Jericho

Elealeh

Ekron

Gibbethon

Ramah

Gilgal

Ashdod

Zorah

Jerusalem

Heshbon

Timnah

Mt. Nebo

Medeba

Beth-shemesh

Bethlehem

Baal-meon

Jahaz

Ashkelon

Libnah

Etam

Ataroth

Shoco

Tekoa

Adullam

Dibon

Gath

Mareshah

Beth-zur

Salt Sea
(Dead Sea)

Aroer

Gaza

Lachish

Hebron

River Arnon

Adoraim

En-gedi

Debir

Ziph

Ar

Gerar

Ziklag

Kir-moab
(Kir-hareseth)

Raphia

Beer-Sheba

Valley of Salt

River Zered

Chapter One

How the Star of David
First Ascended

Somehow there radiates from the name of David a certain golden glow. The fascinating story of this turbulent, incredible life has bequeathed to the world a scintillating luster of imperishable renown which has enchanted the imagination of scriptural readers for nearly 3,000 years.

David was no ordinary specimen of humanity. He was born a son of Judah but today he is claimed by Jews, Christians and Moslems alike. In several ways he was the most important individual living upon the earth at the turn of the tenth century, B.C. He was the one single hope of a benighted people who had just passed through several centuries of apostasy but upon whom God was nevertheless depending to perpetuate the principles of freedom and truth in a heathen world. He was the maternal ancestor of Jesus Christ. In him was the royal genetic line which had been cloistered within the ranks of a covenant people and guarded by the prophets of God since the days of Adam.

As for the life of David, it was like a shooting star. It rose to heights of illuminating glory and then sank into depths of smothering darkness. In his triumphs he reflected the fruits of a supreme and inspired faith while in his failures he reflected the fallibilities of the flesh and the frailties of the race.

How Did We Get the History of David?

Before proceeding, however, we should say something about our Biblical text.

The tempestuous life and times of David were originally recorded by three prophets of God who knew David personally. They were Samuel, Gad, and Nathan. As the compiler of the book of Chronicles declares, "Now the acts of David the king, first and last, behold they are written in the book of Samuel the seer, and in the book of Nathan the Prophet, and in the book of Gad the seer."[1]

Tragically, all three of these magnificent scriptures have been lost. However, before they disappeared certain unknown compilers extracted material from them to create the six books known to us as:

The First Book of Samuel

The Second Book of Samuel

The First Book of Kings

The Second Book of Kings

The First Book of Chronicles

The Second Book of Chronicles

Nevertheless, it is extremely important to appreciate that these six books are *historical* compilations of a later date and are not the original writing of God's inspired prophets except as the compilers used their original material verbatim. Of course, two of the books do bear the name of Samuel and it is likely that much of the first and second books of Samuel was drawn from that prophet's writings; however, even these two books were originally called a part of the books of the kings. Not until long after their creation were they allowed to carry the name of the prophet Samuel.[2]

---

1. 1 Chronicles 29:29
2. Adam Clarke, *Bible Commentary*, Vol. 2, pp. 204-205

A careful study of these six historical books will disclose occasional tampering and editing by the ancient scribes. They were much more inclined to do this when copying "historical" books than when engaged in transcribing the inspired writings of a prophet who had originally recorded his material under the enveloping influence of direct revelation.[3] We shall identify and discuss these occasional textual problems as our story unfolds.

THE CAREERS OF SAMUEL AND SAUL WHICH PRECEDED THE RISE OF DAVID

An examination of the chronology at the beginning of this book will reveal that according to the latest compilations, David was born about 1032 B.C. when Saul was already thirty years of age. As of that moment no one could have guessed that both of these men would one day be kings of Israel. In fact, at that time the government of Israel was a theocratic government with the prophet Samuel at the head. Samuel had unified the nation, driven back the Philistines and established the longest period of tranquility and peace the Israelites had known for many generations.

Unfortunately, however, Samuel had two lecherous sons who caused a scandal and eventually brought about the downfall of his administration. Samuel had followed the natural inclinations of a father and had trained these sons to succeed him in the ministry. But the scripture says Samuel's sons "walked not in his ways, but turned aside after lucre, and took bribes, and perverted judgment."[4] The leaders of the various tribes apparently had been hankering for an excuse to abolish the theocratic form of government and they therefore used the corruption of Samuel's sons as the basis for their demands. They said to Samuel, "Behold, thou art old, and thy sons walk not in thy ways: now make us a king to judge us like all the nations."[5]

Samuel knew they were making a tragic mistake. He also knew that even though their complaints against his sons were true, their use of this scandal as a reason for demanding

---

3. Ibid., p. 269
4. 1 Samuel 8:3
5. 1 Samuel 8:5

a king was a ruse. Their own words had disclosed the real
basis for their demands. They had said they wanted a king
so they could be "like all the nations." It was not so much
a desire for governmental reform but *pride* that prompted
these princes of Israel to demand a king. Samuel was well
aware that if a king were appointed, his own lifetime of labor
to restore God's pattern of government would be practically
wasted. Nevertheless, he had to admit that his own sons
had not supported that pattern. It was aggravating, frustrating, discouraging. In a spirit of desperation Samuel went
to the Lord in prayer.

"And the Lord said unto Samuel, Hearken unto the
voice of the people in all that they say unto thee for THEY
HAVE NOT REJECTED THEE, BUT THEY HAVE
REJECTED ME, THAT I SHOULD NOT REIGN
OVER THEM."[6]

Nowhere in scripture is there a better example of God's
respect for human free agency than here. In the days of
Moses, God had given Israel a system of theocratic government which, if practiced conscientiously, could have created
another City-of-Enoch civilization. However, Israel had
rejected it. This latest generation of God's chosen people
wanted a king "like all the nations." Very well, they would
have one. The Lord said to Samuel, ". . . hearken unto their
voice: howbeit yet PROTEST SOLEMNLY unto them, and
shew them the manner of the king that shall reign over
them."[7]

What the Lord now had Samuel present to the Israelites
was a bill of particulars against the monarchial form of government. In essence He was telling them that liberty once lost
is regained only by the shedding of blood. Here is what
He told them to expect from a king no matter how carefully
he was chosen.

"This will be the manner of the king that shall reign
over you: He will take your sons, and appoint them for
himself, for his chariots and to be his horsemen; and some
shall run before his chariots. And he will appoint him

6. 1 Samuel 8:7
7. 1 Samuel 8:9

captains over thousands, and captains over fifties; and will set them to ear his ground, and to reap his harvest, and to make his instruments of war, and instruments of his chariots. And he will take your daughters to be confectionaries, and to be cooks, and to be bakers. And he will take your fields and your vineyards, and your oliveyards, even the best of them, and give them to his servants. And he will take the tenth of your seed, and of your vineyards, and give to his officers, and to his servants. And he will take your men-servants, and your maidservants, and your goodliest young men, and your asses, and put them to his work. He will take the tenth of your sheep; and ye shall be his servants. And ye shall CRY OUT IN THAT DAY because of your king which ye shall have chosen you; AND THE LORD WILL NOT HEAR YOU IN THAT DAY."[8]

This speech was an unveiled, naked prophecy. But it fell on their ears like thistledown instead of thunder. They spurned these words of warning and cried out, "Nay, but we will have a king over us; that we also may be like all the nations; and that our king may judge us, and go out before us and fight our battles."[9]

Samuel reported back to the Lord and received this instruction: "Hearken unto their voice, and make them a king."[10]

THE CALLING OF SAUL

So Israel was to learn through weeping, wailing and gnashing of teeth why human beings do not make good kings. No matter how carefully selected, it is rarely possible for any man to stand up under the tempting and corrupting weight of totalitarian authority. But Israel was determined to be like all the other nations and these, of course, were heathen nations. Israel was about to try man's age-old fantasy of pomp and pageantry and thereby create for herself a mirage of illusionary greatness as a substitute for God's reality of greatness. Nevertheless, the Lord was determined to give the people the best available candidate for king as of that moment.

8. 1 Samuel 8:11-18
9. 1 Samuel 8:19-20
10. 1 Samuel 8:22

If our chronology is accurate, the selection and coronation of King Saul under the hands of Samuel took place about 1022 B.C. At this time Saul was forty[11] and David therefore would have been about ten.[12]

There could be no doubt in the minds of the people that God had selected for them a noble and kingly fellow. The scripture says, "and there was not among the children of Israel a goodlier person than he: from his shoulders and upward he was higher than any of the people."[13]

We have dealt with the life of Saul during the early years of his reign in *The Third Thousand Years* (pp. 623-640). It will therefore be sufficient here to merely summarize the events which characterized this period of his life.

Saul had a brilliant and promising start as the first king of Israel. He commenced by winning a magnificent victory over the Ammonites after the Ammonite ruler, King Nahash, had conquered the territory east of the Jordan and was about to blind the right eye of every male in order to insure the complete subordination of the people. When Saul heard about it a spirit of righteous wrath rose in him. He took two oxen, dismembered them, and sent pieces of the butchered animals to all parts of Israel with this message: "Whosoever cometh not forth after Saul and after Samuel, so shall it be done unto his oxen."[14] Here was a novel way to recruit an army! A total of 330,000 Israelites rallied to the call and when Saul led this vast host across the Jordan in a forced march he caught the Ammonites early in the morning before they were even out of their beds. The scripture says they "slew the Ammonites until the heat of the day: and it came to pass, that they which remained were scattered, so that two of them were not left together."[15]

There had not been this much evidence of national unity among the Israelites in four hundred years!

---

11. Acts 13:21
12. See Chronology Table at the front of this book.
13. 1 Samuel 9:2
14. 1 Samuel 11:7
15. 1 Samuel 11:11

WHY THE LORD REJECTED SAUL

As might well be imagined, this magnificent victory made Saul very popular. Unfortunately, however, it was soon after this that Saul began to rebel. Neither Samuel nor the Lord could prevent him from exercising his free agency.

Saul's first mistake was during a military campaign against the Philistines. This war did not go nearly so well as the war with the Ammonites and during a moment of crisis King Saul found his army melting away and deserting the conflict. He therefore suspended action temporarily and went to Gilgal down by the Jordan river. He then asked the prophet Samuel to come and make sacrifices so the king could be told by revelation what the Lord wanted him to do.

This gesture was highly commendable, but Saul nullified it with a major blunder. Instead of waiting for Samuel to arrive, Saul became impatient and decided that he could offer sacrifices and get a revelation just as well as a prophet. He therefore pressed forward as though he held the office of a Priest and made the offerings.

Almost immediately afterwards Samuel arrived upon the scene and was sick at heart to discover that already a spirit of aggrandizement was consuming Saul. He cried out to him, "Thou has done foolishly: thou hast not kept the commandment of the Lord thy God, which he commanded thee: for now would the Lord have established thy kingdom upon Israel for ever."[16] Apparently the Lord was about to intervene and give the Israelites the opportunity for a smashing victory, but Saul's presumption in pretending to function as a Priest shortcircuited that great blessing.

In anguish the prophet Samuel declared to Saul, ". . . now thy kingdom shall not continue: the Lord hath sought him a man after his own heart, and the Lord hath commanded him to be captain over his people, because thou hast not kept that which the Lord commanded thee."[17]

Actually, Saul's kingdom was to continue to exist for several years, but not under the benediction of heaven. His

16. 1 Samuel 13:13
17. 1 Samuel 13:14

former blessings were cut off. Samuel's declaration anticipated the raising up of David but that was still in the future.
However, in the prophetic mind of Samuel it was already
a present, accomplished fact, therefore he spoke of it accordingly.

As for the king, from this moment on the spirit of
enlightenment and leadership faded in him. In fact, it was
only a short time after this that the blight of darkness which
had settled on Saul's mind became so oppressive that he
tried to kill his own son, Prince Jonathan. The armies of
Israel had to rescue the young prince from the resolute
wrath of his father.[18]

After that Saul blundered along for a period of time
and then aroused the anger of the Lord again by deliberately violating a divine commandment as he went into another war. This time it was with the Amalekites. Samuel
told Saul that it was the will of the Lord that this profligate
people be cleansed from that section of the land and that
their destruction was to be as complete as the destruction
of Jericho. Saul went forth but instead of fulfilling the
commandment he listened to his troops who thought they
should bring home the best of the flocks of the Amalekites.
Saul also decided to save the king of the Amalekites, whose
name was Agag.

When Samuel came down to meet the returning troops,
King Saul exclaimed, "Blessed be thou of the Lord: I have
performed the commandment of the Lord."[19]

Samuel looked solemnly at the king and said, "What
meaneth then this bleating of the sheep in mine ears, and
the lowing of the oxen which I hear?"[20]

King Saul tried to pass it off lightly. He said, "They
have brought them from the Amalekites: for the people
spared the best of the sheep and of the oxen, to sacrifice
unto the Lord thy God; and the rest we have utterly
destroyed."[21]

---

18. 1 Samuel 14:24-45
19. 1 Samuel 15:13
20. 1 Samuel 15:14
21. 1 Samuel 15:15

Even if this had been completely true, it once more reflected the stubborn habit which Saul possessed of rationalizing his own disobedience and continuously presuming to impose his own judgment over that of the Lord.

"Then Samuel said unto Saul, Stay, and I will tell thee what the Lord hath said to me this night. And he said unto him, Say on.

"And Samuel said, When thou wast little in thine own sight, wast thou not made the head of the tribes of Israel, and the Lord anointed thee king over Israel? Wherefore then didst thou not obey the voice of the Lord?"[22]

King Saul tried to argue with Samuel, saying, "Yea, I have obeyed the voice of the Lord, and have gone the way which the Lord sent me, and have brought Agag the King of Amalek, and have utterly destroyed the Amalekites. But the people took of the spoil, sheep and oxen, the chief of the things which should have been utterly destroyed, to sacrifice unto the Lord thy God in Gilgal.

"And Samuel said, Hath the Lord as great delight in burnt offerings and sacrifices, as in obeying the voice of the Lord? BEHOLD, TO OBEY IS BETTER THAN SACRIFICE, AND TO HEARKEN THAN THE FAT OF RAMS.

"For rebellion is as the sin of witchcraft, and stubbornness is as iniquity and idolatry. Because thou hast rejected the word of the Lord, he hath also rejected thee from being king."[23]

These final words penetrated the calloused conscience of Saul where all else had failed. He suddenly threw himself on the mercy of Samuel and pleaded for forgiveness. As Samuel turned away, Saul seized his mantle so that it ripped. Samuel used this as a sign and said, "The Lord hath rent the kingdom of Israel from thee this day, and hath given it to a neighbour of thine, that is better than thou."[24]

Shortly afterwards Samuel said to King Saul, "Bring ye hither to me Agag the king of the Amalekites."[25]

---

22. 1 Samuel 15:16-19
23. 1 Samuel 15:20-23
24. 1 Samuel 15:28
25. 1 Samuel 15:32

Apparently this Agag was a vicious and cruel ruler who above all his people deserved to die. We do not have a catalogue of his crimes but simply the judgment of God that he and his people had become so depraved and violent that the Supreme Judge had ordered them summarily returned to God.

When Agag was brought before Samuel, the Vulgate version says he came in "very fat and trembling."[26] The scripture says he exclaimed to Samuel hopefully, "Surely the bitterness of death is past."[27] But he knew better the moment Samuel spoke. The aged prophet replied with words which give us a suggestion of Agag's crimes, "As thy sword hath made women childless, so shall thy mother be childless among women."[28] With that the prophet Samuel took a weapon and dispatched the trembling Agag himself.

Samuel thereupon prepared to leave for Ramah, his home. This was the last time Samuel ever saw Saul.

King Saul, meanwhile, was left with the prophet's words which set the king's bile boiling. He was going to lose his throne to a "neighbour!" The prophet had not given Saul the slightest hint as to who the "neighbour" might be. In fact, as we shall see in a moment, even the prophet Samuel did not know who the new king was going to be. If Samuel had been able to reveal it, Saul would have found it hard to believe that this promised successor to his throne was going to be Saul's own future son-in-law. As of the moment the young man was merely a stripling teenager, but Saul was shortly going to meet him under circumstances which would cause the king to love him long before he learned to hate him.

THE RISE OF DAVID

In spite of the stormy session between Samuel and Saul, the Lord's prophet mourned for Saul.[29] After all, he had anointed this man king. And Saul was such a marvelous specimen of humanity, filled with so much promise in the

---

26. Clarke, *Bible Commentary*, Vol. 2, p. 257
27. 1 Samuel 15:32
28. 1 Samuel 15:33
29. 1 Samuel 15:35

beginning. How could a man of such natural kingly bearing behave so stubbornly and impulsively?

Suddenly the Lord shocked Samuel into his senses by
abruptly declaring, "How long wilt thou mourn for Saul,
seeing I have rejected him from reigning over Israel? Fill
thine horn with oil, and go, and I will send thee to Jesse
the Beth-lehemite: for I have provided me a king among his
sons."[30]

Samuel replied, "How can I go? If Saul hear it he will
kill me." The king had spies everywhere and Samuel had
seen enough of Saul to know that when the king was angry
he could commit murder. The Lord therefore said, "Take
an heifer with thee, and say, I am come to sacrifice to the
Lord. And call Jesse to the sacrifice, and I will shew thee
what thou shalt do: and thou shalt anoint unto me him
whom I name unto thee."[31]

Samuel kept his residence during these particular years
at Ramah, about three miles north of Jerusalem. Bethlehem
was only seven miles south of Jerusalem so in short order
Samuel made the brief journey and arrived in that famous
village where a little over a thousand years later the Savior
would be born. Samuel called the elders of the village to
assemble for a sacrifice and specifically invited Jesse and
his sons to come.

When the sacrificial ritual was finished and the crowd
had dispersed, Samuel apparently took Jesse and his sons
off to some private quarter. The prophet noted that Jesse's
oldest son was a tall, handsome man of maturity named
Eliab. The scripture says Samuel thought to himself that
surely he was looking at the next king of Israel. "But the
Lord said unto Samuel, Look not on his countenance, or on
the height of his stature; because I have refused him: for
the Lord seeth not as man seeth; for man looketh on the
outward appearance, but the Lord looketh on the heart."[32]

---

30. 1 Samuel 16:1
31. 1 Samuel 16:2-3
32. 1 Samuel 16:7

Samuel had Jesse call up each of his other sons. Altogether there were six.[33] As each one passed by, Samuel waited eagerly for the Lord's signal of endorsement, but each time the Spirit proclaimed, "Neither hath the Lord chosen this."[34] When all the sons had passed by, Samuel was filled with perplexity. Something was wrong. He finally said to Jesse, "Are here all thy children?" Jesse replied, "There remaineth yet the youngest, and, behold, he keepeth the sheep." This was a great relief to Samuel. He told Jesse to fetch the lad immediately.[35]

When the youthful David arrived Samuel noted that he was "ruddy, and withal of a beautiful countenance, and goodly to look to."[36] This was gratifying, but was he the one? Suddenly the Spirit enveloped Samuel and the Lord said, "Arise, anoint him: for this is he!"[37]

Up to this time Jesse and his sons probably had no idea what Samuel was trying to accomplish. It must have been especially curious that Samuel should demand that this teen-age David be brought in from tending the sheep. They must have been further puzzled as they saw the prophet suddenly bring forth a horn filled with sacred oil. A moment later they saw him walk over to the youngest son of Jesse, raise up the horn of oil and while calling upon heaven to witness the act, solemnly anoint the head of this boy and declare him to be the new king of Israel.

It was fantastic. Here was David, barely old enough to show a downy beard, sitting there in the crude and rustic garments of a hill-country shepherd and being blessed and anointed the king of God's people by the most famous prophet in Israel. The whole procedure raised a multitude of questions. How *could* David be king? He was too young, and anyway Israel already had a king. What would Saul do if he heard that David had been anointed king? Wouldn't there be a colossal civil war?

To all of these questions there were no immediate answers. The faith of this whole family was going to be

33. 1 Samuel 16:10 says seven, but 1 Chronicles 2:13 identifies each son by name and lists David as the seventh. This would lead us to conclude that only six were presented before David arrived.

34. 1 Samuel 16:8   36. 1 Samuel 16:12
35. 1 Samuel 16:11   37. Ibid.

tested as well as the faith of David. Even Samuel's faith was going to be tested.

It is interesting that the prophet Samuel made no attempt whatever to place David on the throne. So far as we know the anointing of David as king was kept a matter of deepest secrecy both by Samuel and the family of Jesse. And from Samuel's viewpoint everything the Lord had commanded him to do was now accomplished. The Lord wanted David anointed king? So be it, the deed had been done. Now it was up to the Lord to get him on the throne. Apparently Samuel felt completely satisfied that this was the Lord's problem, not his. Having done his duty as he saw it, "Samuel rose up and went to Ramah."[38]

THE BACKGROUND OF DAVID

In the veins of Jesse's son, David, ran the royal blood of the three great patriarchs, Abraham, Isaac, and Jacob. The line then passed from Jacob through his fourth son, Judah. This was the son upon whose head the dying Jacob had placed his hands and prophesied, "The sceptre shall not depart from Judah, nor a lawgiver from between his feet, until Shiloh come; and unto him shall the gathering of the people be."[39] Part of this prophecy was to be literally fulfilled in David, since he was the first Jewish ruler over Israel and from then on the custody of the scripture or the law remained with Judah until the coming of Christ.

David's more recent lineage included as his great grandfather, the well-to-do citizen of Bethlehem named Boaz.[40] And his great grandmother whom Boaz had married was none other than the famous Ruth in whose honor one of the books of the Old Testament was named.

The physical and personal qualities of David commended him as well as his lineage. Although not tall like Saul he became a magnificent specimen of athletic manhood as he grew to maturity. As for appearance, it will be recalled that even when a teen-ager, Samuel had noticed that David was "ruddy, and withal of a beautiful countenance." One

38. 1 Samuel 16:13
39. Genesis 49:10
40. Book of Ruth, chapters 3 and 4

of David's greatest assets was his humility coupled with a keen sense of practical problem-solving which eventually laid the foundation for the greatest kingdom ancient Israel would ever know. But he began his career as a sheep herder.

Too often those who have had to spend many years herding sheep allow themselves to get caught in the dull routine of dawdling away the dragging hours. They become absorbed in merely watching, waiting and dreaming. But not so with David. During these years when he was out with the sheep we know he developed at least three special skills to a polished peak of expert achievement. One was his skill with the harp or lyre which in those days usually had eight strings of one full octave. Not only could he play various kinds of music on this popular instrument, but he had also acquired or developed a great talent in putting words to the music. These lyrical expressions which David was able to pour out of his soul later made him famous as one of the world's greatest poets.

A third talent David developed was the ability to take two thongs of rawhide with a piece of sheepskin fastened between them and by using a rock for a missile, discharge the whirling weapon at a target with crack-shot precision. Although David never would have dreamed it, all three of these skills which were developed during his sheep herding days would one day play an important role in helping him become the king of Israel.

David Meets King Saul

In the Bible there are two different versions of how David met King Saul. The first is believed to be the authentic account and the one which we shall follow here. The second, unfortunately, appears to be a romantic fabrication which was mixed in with the first account as though the stories were somehow related. This created contradictions in the text and spreads confusion in the minds of Bible readers. Dr. Adam Clarke has identified 39 verses[41] which are scattered throughout 1 Samuel, chapters 17 and 18, as being suspect since they apparently did not appear in the original

---

41. 1 Samuel, chapter 17: verses 12 to 31 inclusive, also 41 and verses 54 to 58; chapter 18: verses 1 to 5; 9 to 11 and 17 to 19.

Hebrew text from which the Septuagint (earliest Greek translation) was taken.[42]

If the suspect passages itemized in footnote 41 are left out, the student will observe that the whole narration in

---

42. Concerning this problem, Dr. Adam Clarke states: "We are now happily in possession of an ancient version of these two chapters, which appear to have been made from a Hebrew copy, which had none of the thirty-nine verses which are here supposed to have been interpolated . . . This version is found in the Vatican copy of the Seventy [Septuagint], which, whoever reads and considers, will find the accounts there given regular, consistent and probable." (Clarke, *Bible Commentary*, Vol. 2, pp. 266-267)

The student will have little difficulty detecting the elements of contradiction which some ancient copyist created by mixing in a spurious story with what appears to be the true one:

A. After the scripture establishes that Saul arranged with Jesse to have David remain at Saul's court as an entertainer and armor-bearer (16:18-22), the suspect version has David back in Bethlehem tending his father's sheep (17:15).

B. After the scripture establishes that David has become a mature young man capable of being an armor-bearer and "a man of war," the suspect verses relegate him back to the role of a mere lad with only three out of six of his elder brothers old enough to fight the Philistines (17:12-13).

C. In the suspect version, the lad, David, is required to leave his sheep and take food to his three brothers at the front when the scripture has already established that there were six brothers other than David, and with three of them still at home besides David there would have been no need for David to leave his sheep and go.

D. The oldest brother, Eliab, who is known to have previously seen David receiving the great honor of being anointed king by the prophet Samuel (16:13), is represented in the suspect verses as treating him like a disgusting child, saying, 'Why camest thou down hither? and with whom hast thou left those few sheep in the wilderness? I know thy pride and the naughtiness of thine heart; for thou art come down that thou mightest see the battle." (17:28) Such a speech is out of harmony with previous events.

E. In the suspect version David is represented as being told that if he kills Goliath he will get to marry the king's daughter (17:25) which is completely inconsistent with the real reason given for David's marriage to her in a later chapter (18:20-27).

F. The suspect version presents David as still a lad, as previously indicated, and then immediately following the slaying of Goliath has King Saul making the lad supreme commander of all his armies (18:5).

G. The role of a mere lad is made even more inconsistent when the scripture states that shortly after slaying Goliath, David succeeded in slaying a hundred Philistines and receiving the king's daughter in marriage as a reward (18:20-27).

H. A bold and direct contradiction occurs where the scripture establishes that David became the much-loved entertainer and armor-bearer of Saul and depicts Saul as spending a long time getting David ready for the fight with Goliath and then turns around in the suspect verses and has David introduced to Saul immediately after the killing of Goliath as though Saul did not know who the young hero was and is meeting him for the first time! (17:55-58)

From all these facts it will be seen how obvious it is that some early copyists tried to intertwine two different versions of these events and in the process left a maze of confusion. For our purposes, we have followed what appears to be the original version and have eliminated from consideration the 39 verses which are believed to have been spuriously planted in the original Hebrew text.

these chapter fits together smoothly and sensibly. By making these suggested deletions nothing significant is sacrificed in the biography of David, but, on the contrary, some very irregular and incongruous matters are eliminated. Now back to our story.

The scripture is very clear that as soon as the Spirit of the Lord abandoned Saul, he frequently fell into ugly moods of morbid melancholy.[43] These neurotic states of abnormal depression were so profound that it alarmed the members of King Saul's court. Those attending him suggested that the king seek out some talented member of the kingdom who could play the harp and thereby employ the well-known therapy of music to lift up his spirits. To this Saul finally consented and immediately one of his servants advised the king that there was a young man in Bethlehem who had gained a reputation for such talents. Said he, "Behold I have seen a son of Jesse the Beth-lehemite, that is cunning in playing, and a *mighty valiant man,* and a *man of war,* and prudent in matters, and a comely person, and the Lord is with him."[44]

From these generous remarks it becomes immediately apparent that several years had passed since David, the lad, was first anointed king by Samuel. Apparently, by this time David had become a fully grown man with some military experience thereby proving him to be "a mighty valiant man, and a man of war." It is also obvious that while David's peacetime vocation continued to be the care and supervision of his father's flocks, he had nevertheless attracted the attention of notable people because of his "comely" appearance and musical talent.

The scripture says that Saul promptly sent messengers to Jesse who declared in the name of king: "Send me David thy son, which is with the sheep."[45]

Such a message to Jesse would naturally create a sense of anxiety, even alarm. Had Saul somehow learned that David had been anointed successor to the king's throne?

43. 1 Samuel 16:14-15
44. 1 Samuel 16:18
45. 1 Samuel 16:19

Was Saul intending to harm David? Jesse resolved to send along with David a quantity of food gifts in hopes that they would be accepted by Saul as a gesture of good will.[46] However, it turned out that there was really no need for Jesse's anxiety. When David came before the king he found the mighty Saul warmly receptive, friendly and cordial. The scripture says the king was so pleased with the young man that he dispatched a gracious message to Jesse saying in the most solicitous manner, "Let David, I pray thee, stand before me; for he hath found favour in my sight."[47]

To Jesse this must have come as both a compliment and a relief. Apparently David was not suspected by King Saul after all, nor resented. It would even appear that the king had taken a great liking to David. The Bible specifically says that King Saul "loved him greatly." After Jesse had consented to the arrangement, the king bestowed the great honor on David of having him as his personal aid and armor-bearer.[48]

DAVID AND GOLIATH

According to what we believe to be the most reliable text, it was while David was serving as armor-bearer for the king and *not* while he was still tending his father's flocks, that Goliath came upon the scene. The circumstances were as follows:

The Philistines had marched their conquering armies from the coastal plain and wound their way upward through the narrow valley of Elah,[49] which ascends into the highlands of Judah just west of Hebron. King Saul had mobilized his armies and confronted the Philistines at Shochoh (or Socoh) before they could reach the higher settlements.[50] Because the mountain spurs on each side of Elah valley are steep and close together, each army apparently scrambled to the top of opposite promitories, putting themselves well within shouting distance of each other. This arrangement was a

---

46. 1 Samuel 16:20
47. 1 Samuel 16:22
48. 1 Samuel 16:21
49. 1 Samuel 17:2. This valley is named after the streambed which flows down from the mountains of Judah and enters the Mediterranean just north of ancient Ashdod.
50. 1 Samuel 17:1

frequent stratagem in this area because it automatically provided security but at the same time furnished an excellent vantage point from which each of the opposing commanders could maintain a surveillance of his enemy.

It was under these conditions that the Philistines challenged the Israelites to a "duel of the champions." This was an ancient custom designed to avoid the bloodshed of a full-scale war by having each side represented in a duel. Under this procedure both sides agreed in advance to be bound by the outcome of the duel. It was the desire of the Philistines to lure Israelites into accepting such an arrangement because if the champion of the Philistines won the duel, all Israel would become a tributary to the Philistines without their having to wage an expensive campaign. For this purpose the Philistines challenged the Israelites with a giant-sized fellow named Goliath. The monstrous creature strutted up and down the front lines taunting the Israelites to raise up a champion and fight him in a duel.

It would appear that Goliath was a descendant of the famous Anaks which the Bible calls "giants." There was no doubt that this tribe of men must have made a formidable and frightening enemy. Several centuries earlier their gargantuan proportions had so frightened the spies of Israel that the people rebelled against Moses and refused to capture the promised land. It had to be left to the next generation. The words of the spies which put the Israelites in a frenzy of fear were the following: "We saw the giants, the sons of Anak, which come of the giants: and we were in our own sight as grasshoppers, and so we were in their sight."[51] These, it seems, were the ancestors of Goliath.

According to the Bible the mighty Goliath was "six cubits and a span" in height.[52] Using the minimum dimension of 18 inches for a cubit and six inches for a span, he would have been in the neighborhood of 9 feet, 6 inches tall.[53] If this were the case, it would place Goliath in the same physical category of enormous human specimens as the famous King Og of Moses' day whose iron bedstead is

51. Numbers 13:31-33
52. 1 Samuel 17:4
53. See Peloubet's *Bible Dictionary*, under "Cubit".

described as measuring around 13½ feet in length and 6 feet in width.[54]

The Bible gives the weight of Goliath's brass coat of mail as 5,000 shekels or approximately 156 pounds.[55] In addition, he carried a shield of brass on his back, a heavy plate of metal armor on his legs and a helmet of brass on his head.[56] In his hand he carried a spear with a shaft "like a weaver's beam," tipped with an iron, battering-ram type of head weighing in excess of 18 pounds.[57]

So this was the spectacle the Israelites beheld as Goliath came blustering out in full regalia to harangue and bully them. From a location where the armies of Israel could hear him, this mammoth man-creature bellowed out across the valley:

"Why are ye come to set your battle in array? Am not I a Philistine, and ye servants to Saul? Choose you a man for you, and let him come down to me [apparently the place of battle would be in the ravine between them].

"If he be able to fight with me, and to kill me, then will we be your servants: but if I prevail against him, and kill him, then shall ye be our servants, and serve us."

Goliath concluded his speech by crying out: "I defy the armies of Israel this day; give me a man, that we may fight together!"[58]

The scripture says that "When Saul and all Israel heard these words of the Philistine, "they were dismayed, and greatly afraid."[59] Of course, Saul was "from his shoulder and upward . . . higher than any of the people," so it would appear that the taunts of Goliath were aimed primarily at the king himself. In fact, the Jewish *Targum* quotes Goliath as having said to the Israelite army, "And ye, men of Israel, what noble exploit has Saul, the son of Kish, of Gibeah, done, that ye should have him made king over you? If he

54. Deut. 3:11
55. Clarke, *Bible Commentary,* Vol. 2, p. 261.
56. 1 Samuel 17:5-6.
57. 1 Samuel 17:7; Clarke, *Bible Commentary,* Vol. 2, p. 262.
58. 1 Samuel 17:8-10
59. 1 Samuel 17:11

be a hero, let him come down himself and fight with me; but if he be a weak or cowardly man, then choose you out a man that he may come down to me."[60]

The record is clear that Saul had no intention of volunteering for such a duel. Certainly it seemed a disgrace to let this giant braggart go unchallenged, yet there seemed to be too much at stake to risk the whole future of Israel on the fighting of any single Israelite, even Saul. It was at this point that Saul's armor-bearer spoke up.

DAVID ASKS PERMISSION TO FIGHT GOLIATH

Said David to Saul, "Let no man's heart fail because of him; thy servant will go and fight with this Philistine."[61]

But Saul objected. Obviously, if such a duel were too great a gamble for a veteran fighter like himself, how much more so for young David. Said the king, "Thou art not able to go against this Philistine to fight with him; for thou art but a youth, and he a man of war from his youth."[62]

David did not argue his military prowess although he was already known as "a mighty valiant man, a man of war;"[63] instead, he asserted that on previous occasions God had saved him from being destroyed by two ferocious wild animals, once when a lion came into his flocks and again when he was attacked by a bear. David declared, "Thy servant slew both the lion and the bear: and this uncircumcised Philistine shall be as one of them, seeing he has defied the armies of the living God. . . . The Lord that delivered me out of the paw of the lion, and out of the paw of the bear, he will deliver me out of the hand of this Philistine."[64]

Saul was impressed. He had seen enough of God's handiwork to know that such miracles were possible. Finally he decided to risk it. He said to David, "Go, and the Lord be with thee!"[65]

But David did not go. It seems the king quickly had second thoughts. He decided to reduce the risk as much as possible by putting his own stout armor on David.

---

60. Clarke, *Bible Commentary*, Vol. 2, p. 262.
61. 1 Samuel 17:32
62. 1 Samuel 17:33
63. 1 Samuel 16:18
64. 1 Samuel 17:36-37
65. 1 Samuel 17:37

It is interesting that David himself was apparently uncertain as to just how the Lord would bring Goliath into his power. He therefore went along with Saul in being girded up with the king's coat of mail, brass helmet, sword and shield. But the ordeal soon convinced him that this was not the way to do it. The big man's massive war gear was too much and David staggered under the load. He therefore said to Saul, "I cannot go with these," and took them off.[66]

Plutarch informs us that the ordinary weight of a soldier's full armor was around sixty pounds and that Alcimus in the army of Demetrius was considered a prodigious warrior because he could fight in armor weighing 120 pounds.[67] Since we know it required a great amount of practice to fight successfully even in ordinary armor, it was prudent of David to lay this encumbrance aside. Saul was such a huge man his armor must have weighed close to a hundred pounds.

It is significant that when David finally found himself confronted with the harsh necessity of deciding just exactly how he would fight the Philistine, he fell back on his years of experience with his sling. It apparently occurred to him that his own swift feet and his high-precision skill in the use of the sling could give him several strategic advantages. This would permit him to strike at Goliath from a brisk distance and by quickly shifting position he could out-maneuver this human tank as the heavily armored Goliath blustered about trying to get close enough to fling his 18-pound spearhead. So, having decided on his strategy, David picked up his staff and sling and headed for the nearby front lines. On the way he took from a brook five smooth stones.

THE BIG FIGHT

It must have looked ridiculous both to the Israelites and the Philistines as they saw this relatively miniature David stripped for action and running down the side of the mountain to meet Goliath. He carried nothing to defend himself save a shepherd's staff and a shepherd's sling. Even Goliath

---

66. 1 Samuel 17:39
67. Clarke, *Bible Commentary*, Vol. 2, p. 362.

was surprised. To a professional killer this was the deepest kind of insult. He bellowed out, "Am I a dog, that thou comest to me with staves?" Then the scripture says Goliath cursed David in the name of every heathen god to which he could lay his tongue. He closed his stream of violent invective with this snarling insult, "Come to me, and I will give thy flesh unto the fowls of the air, and to the beasts of the field."[68]

But David shouted back, "Thou comest to me with a sword and with a spear, and with a shield: but I come to thee in the name of the Lord of hosts, the God of the armies of Israel, whom thou hast defied. This day will the Lord deliver thee into mine hand; and I will smite thee, and take thine head from thee; and I will give the carcasses of the host of the Philistines this day unto the fowls of the air, and to the wild beasts of the earth; that all the earth may know that there is a God in Israel. And all this assembly shall know that the Lord saveth not with sword and spear: for the battle is the Lord's, and he will give you into our hands."[69]

Obviously, this speech was not just for Goliath, but for the gaping hosts of astonished Philistines. It was unbelievable that this cocky, half-witted Israelite would dare to challenge Goliath in the first place, and now, if by some stroke of fate or fortune he slew Goliath, that would be a miracle! Psychologically David scarcely could have created a better climate of psychosis to trigger mass hysteria than by this speech and the events which immediately followed it.

Without another word, David flung aside his shepherd's staff and ran full tilt toward Goliath. On the way his nimble fingers placed one of the stones in the pocket of the sling. As Goliath saw him coming, the grizzled old warrior whose hands had bloodied themselves in the slaughter of human beings for many years,[70] rose up and rumbled toward David

---

68. 1 Samuel 17:43-44
69. 1 Samuel 17:45-47
70. Jewish tradition has always depicted Goliath as having a long history of destructive terror in war. The Jewish *Targum* quotes Goliath as boasting: "I am Goliath the Philistine of Gath, who killed the two sons of Eli, Hophni and Phinehas the priests; and led into captivity the ark of the covenant of Jehovah, and placed it in the temple of Dagon my god; and it remained in the cities of the Philistines seven months. Also, in all our battles I have gone at the head of the army, and we conquered and cut down men, and laid them as low as the dust of the earth; . . ." (Clarke, *Bible Commentary*, Vol. 2, p. 262)

for the kill. But long before Goliath was even in striking distance, he saw the running Israelite unexpectedly stop, whirl his sling swiftly around his head, take a calculated aim, and suddenly let the missile fly.

The great Goliath probably never knew what happened. Quicker than his eye could follow it, the stone flew straight to its mark in the forehead of the giant and buried itself in his skull just below the helmet line. The monstrous Philistine dropped in his tracks as though he had been clubbed. Then the Bible says, "But there was no sword in the hand of David. Therefore David ran, and stood upon the Philistine, and took his sword, and drew it out of the sheath thereof, and slew him, and cut off his head. . . ."[71]

Instantly a cry of dismay went up from the hosts of the horrified Philistines, but a roar of triumph went up from the throats of the jubilant Israelites. In an instant all pandamonium erupted as the Philistines broke ranks and fled panic-stricken toward home. They had no intention of staying around to commit themselves to the outcome of this duel. It was not supposed to end this way. Like a wild pack of terrified animals they went stampeding toward the plain and the fortified cities which could protect them from the vengeance of Israel for the Bible says the Israelites lost no time in launching an immediate and devastating pursuit.

The slaughter of the Philistines continued across the plain and all the way to the gates of the nearest Philistine cities. When the mopping up was completed the tired but triumphant Israelites returned to the abandoned camp of the Philistines and gathered up the rich spoils from all their tents.

It had been a great day for Israel, a fantastic achievement for David, and a gratifying demonstration of pure faith in God which had allowed the forces of good to shatter the forces of evil.

---

71. 1 Samuel 17:51

Scripture Readings and Questions on Chapter One

Scripture Readings: 1 Samuel, chapters 16 and 17

1—What are the six "historical" books of the Bible? Were they written by prophets?

2—What was the basic reason for Saul's fall? How did this fulfill a previous warning of the Lord?

3—What was the prophet Samuel's personal reaction to Saul's fall? What did the Lord tell Samuel to go and do? Why was Samuel afraid to do it?

4—About how far from Jerusalem is Bethlehem? In what direction?

5—How many sons did Jesse have in addition to David? Who was the oldest one? How did he impress Samuel?

6—When David came in, what did Samuel note concerning him?

7—Why would it seem illogical to ordain David king at that particular time? Was any attempt made at this time to have David take over Saul's throne? What did Samuel do?

8—To which of the tribes of Israel did David belong? Who was his great-grandfather? Who was his great-grandmother?

9—What three skills did David learn while herding sheep? In what way did each of them help him in his career?

10—Who suggested to King Saul that he employ David to entertain him? Did this seem to give concern to David's father? What did he do?

11—What was King Saul's reaction when he saw David? What official assignment was David given?

12—In the spurious version of how David met Saul, name three contradictions which do violence to the rest of the scriptural account?

13—In what valley did the Philistines and Israelites meet for battle? Why were they able to shout back and forth to each other?

14—Why did ancient armies sometimes resort to the "duel of the champions?" What did each side promise to do?

15—According to the Bible, what was the height of Goliath? How much did his coat of mail weigh, approximately?

16—Whom did Goliath apparently want to fight? Why didn't Saul want to risk it?

17—What was David's role at this time? Why did Saul feel persuaded to let David fight Goliath?

18—In the beginning had David decided just how he would fight Goliath? What made him decide to use a sling?

19—What did Goliath say when he saw David? What did David reply?

20—What did the Philistines do after Goliath was killed? What did this indicate? What did the Israelites do?

CHAPTER TWO

Saul's Campaign
to Murder David

The unbelievable good news of David's magnificent heroism in challenging and killing Goliath swept through the cities and villages of Israel like a wild wind. As a result, great throngs of women went streaming down the roadways to meet the returning victors as they came trudging back up into the mountains of Israel.[1]

The sight of the welcoming multitude "with tabrets, with joy, and with instruments of music" must have been a particularly glorious spectacle for Saul. Perhaps it helped to dull the terrible pain of Samuel's doomsday prediction in which he warned that soon Saul would lose his throne. The prospect of being de-throned was such a nightmare to Saul that the slightest suggestion of rivalry from any source immediately sent his brain into convulsions of insane jealousy. It was a cruel turn of fate that in this present ecstatic moment of triumph Saul should be psychologically shot down by the one thing his stricken conscience could not endure, a possible rival.

---

1. 1 Samuel 18:6

It occurred just as the waving, cheering women drew close enough to sing their song of welcome and praise. They cried out: "Saul hath slain his thousands, and David his ten thousands!"[2]

Instantly, the king knew exactly what these women were saying. They felt that Saul, the big man and mighty king of Israel, had achieved a great military success, but it was the valiant David who deserved praise and honor in quantities ten times greater than Saul. With the prophet Samuel's doomsday prophecy searing his brain, Saul considered this song not only an insult to the dignity of his own person but a threat to his entire kingdom. The scripture says, "And Saul was very wroth, and the saying displeased him; and he said, They have ascribed unto David ten thousands, and to me they have ascribed but thousands; AND WHAT CAN HE HAVE MORE BUT THE KINGDOM?"[3]

In Saul's feverish mind there rapidly emerged a single, all-consuming obsession: this David was after his throne! Saul resolved that something had to be done immediately. The task was to somehow honor him so as to please the people but nevertheless consign him to some post or position which would quickly destroy him. The logical place was the field of battle. Saul knew that even though the Philistines had been beaten they would be back. Against Israel they waged a continuing war. Perhaps in some future engagements David would not be so fortunate. Soon after Saul returned to his headquarters at Gibeah he announced the removal of David from the intimate role of the king's body guard and armor-bearer. Instead, the heroic David would have the honor of serving as the "captain over a thousand."[4] Saul knew that in this new role David stood a far greater risk of being killed.

---

2. 1 Samuel 18:7
3. 1 Samuel 18:8
4. 1 Samuel 18:13. Notice that a previous passage (verse 5) which is not in the original Hebrew and is considered to be spurious, states that David was made commander in chief of all of Saul's armies. This, of course, would be the most foolish thing Saul could have done if he were worried about David seizing the throne. Making David captain over a thousand would be more logical since it would expose him to front line action but not give him control of the whole army. The contradiction between these two passages illustrates the confusion created by ancient scribes who sometimes tried to embellish the story with questionable material.

But David was not killed. As occasional skirmishes with the Philistines occurred, David dispatched them with alacrity. The scripture says, "David behaved himself wisely in all his ways; and the Lord was with him. Wherefore when Saul saw that he behaved himself very wisely, he was afraid of him. But all Israel and Judah loved David, because he went out and came in [victoriously] before them."[5]

DAVID FALLS IN LOVE

In between military ventures David stayed at Gibeah with his contingent of a thousand soldiers and was often in attendance at feasts or other formal affairs held at Saul's palace.[6] These occasions gave Saul's second daughter, the beautiful Michal, a chance to meet David and fall desperately in love with him.[7]

Apparently Michal made no attempt to hide her feelings and so this intriguing development made an enchanting and tidy morsel of court gossip. Soon the king's servants communicated the news to Saul thinking it would please him. It did. Saul looked upon his daughter's romantic excursion as a singular opportunity to kill David.[8] The Bible says, "And Saul commanded his servants, saying, Commune with David secretly, and say, Behold, the king hath delight in thee, and all his servants love thee: now therefore be the king's son-in-law."[9]

It would appear that the feelings between David and Michal were entirely mutual. Therefore when this proposition was secretly communicated to David he suspected no trap whatever but immediately began wondering how he could qualify for the hand of Michal. His great fear was that his humble origin would not allow him to meet the customary dowery for a king's daughter.[10] When this word got

---

5. 1 Samuel 18:14-16. "To go and come in" is an idiom usually referring to military ventures as it did to Moses in Deut. 31:1.
6. That such affairs were customary for David to attend is clear from 1 Samuel 20:5.
7. Verse 19 of 1 Samuel, chapter 18, indicates that David was expecting to receive Saul's oldest daughter, Merab, as his wife because she was promised to the soldier who killed Goliath. However, that alleged proposition together with verse 19 are part of the 39 spurious passages which did not appear in the original Hebrew and should therefore be ignored. See note 42, Chapter One.
8. 1 Samuel 18:21
9. 1 Samuel 18:22
10. 1 Samuel 18:23

back to the king he was exuberant. This situation fell in
perfectly with Saul's scheme. The king sent word to
David that no dowery would be required providing David
could present to the king evidence that he had personally
slain 100 of the king's enemies in the next encounter with
the Philistines. In an age of hand-to-hand combat this exorbi-
tant demand was even more fantastic than it would be today
with modern weapons. Nevertheless, David resolved to
attempt it. No doubt Saul felt certain that in such an undertaking David might become over-zealous, reckless, or exhausted and some stalwart Philistine could hew him down.

But Saul's elaborate scheme collapsed. In the very next
battle David performed so magnificently that the full tally
of one hundred Philistines[11] went down under the slashing
strength of David's mighty sling and sword arm. No doubt
Saul was as astonished as he was disappointed when the
fleshy foreskins of the full tally of one hundred Philistines
was thrown down before him. This left the king caught in
his own trap so that now he was without excuse and was
compelled to give "Michal his daughter to wife" without
receiving so much as a donkey for a dowery.[12]

It must have been a loathsome and disgusting predicament for Saul as he found himself forced to participate in the
formalities of a royal wedding which he had never intended
would occur. The congealing of the king's hatred now took
on a bitter homicidal fixation. The scripture says, "Saul became David's enemy continually."[13] What was most bedevil-
ling to the king was the fact that the more Saul hated David
the more the people loved him, and the more Saul tried to
ensnare David and smash his reputation the more successfully he behaved both in battle and civilian life. The scripture says David's name was "much set by" among all the
people.[14]

---

11. 1 Samuel 18:27. Note that this passage says *two* hundred Philistines which is
    obviously a copyist's error. David himself says the number was *one* hundred
    in 2 Samuel 3:14.
12. Ibid.
13. 1 Samuel 18:29
14. 1 Samuel 18:30

Saul's Second Attempt to Take David's Life

With the passing of time Saul finally became so desperate that he no longer made any attempt to keep his hatred of David a secret. He called in his sons and his top advisors to give them a specific order that it was the king's command that David should be destroyed.

However, within that closed confidential circle there was at least one man who had a higher regard for David than he did for the commands of the king. That man was Jonathan, the king's eldest son, and the heir-apparent to the throne of Israel. Before anyone could carry out the king's instructions Jonathan rushed out that very night to find his friend and brother-in-law. As soon as he could reach David, Jonathan gave him the latest report. Said he, "Saul my father seeketh to kill thee: now therefore, I pray thee, take heed to thyself . . . and I will go out and stand beside my father in the field where thou art, and I will commune with my father of thee; and what I see, that I will tell thee."[15]

David quickly hid himself while Jonathan went back to his angry father. Jonathan said to him, "Let not the king sin against his servant, against David; because he hath not sinned against thee, and because his works have been to thee-ward very good: for he did put his life in his hand, and slew the Philistine, and the Lord wrought a great salvation for all Israel: thou sawest it, and didst rejoice: wherefore then wilt thou sin against innocent blood, to slay David without a cause?"[16]

Strangely enough, this plea by Jonathan did shed a new light on the problem for Saul. He had been so intent on guarding his kingdom against the haunting phantom of an imaginary throne-snatcher that he had never quite gotten around to the ugly reality of recognizing that he would be destroying one of his most faithful servants and be guilty of shedding innocent blood. The old king's countenance gradually softened. Suddenly Saul exclaimed, "As the Lord liveth, he shall not be slain!"[17] This was the most sacred oath

---

15. 1 Samuel 19:2-3
16. 1 Samuel 19:4-5
17. 1 Samuel 19:6

a king or anyone else could take, and Jonathan relied upon it. With joyful exhilaration he hurried to the fields and hills surrounding the town in order to contact David and give him the great news.

"And Jonathan called David, and Jonathan shewed him all those things. And Jonathan brought David to Saul, and he was in his presence, as in times past."[18]

SAUL ATTEMPTS TO KILL DAVID HIMSELF

But the king's sacred oath, taken in the name of God, was completely in vain. The king could stand David only so long as he did nothing outstanding or praiseworthy. David, however, by nature and by heavenly endowment was not the kind of man who could maintain an extended status of commonplace mediocrity. The very next crisis orbited David into a whole new cycle of heroic achievement and popular acclaim.

The occasion was another war with the Philistines. The rulers of that predatory people just could not leave the mountains of Israel alone. After each defeat they would salve up their wounds, regroup their troops and charge up to the hills once more for battle. When the alarm was sounded in this latest attack, David had to leave his new bride and lead his soldiers swiftly down toward the maritime plain to cut the Philistines off. Whether other "captains of a thousand" participated in this particular battle we are not told. The scripture simply says that the man who emerged from the blood and fury of the contest as the hero of the day was David. It says "David went out, and fought with the Philistines, and slew them with a great slaughter; and they fled from him."[19]

Then David returned to Gibeah and innocently went to the king's house to be with him "as in times past." But things had changed. The word of David's valorous achievements was enough to quickly send the king into the depths of another psychopathic mood of morbid melancholy. After any successful battle it was customary to hold a feast of victory

---

18. 1 Samuel 19:7
19. 1 Samuel 19:8

and this was followed by various kinds of entertainment. It is thought to have been just such an occasion when David played his lyre and sang his famous songs so as to lift the "evil spirit" that was upon the king.[20] But while David was entertaining the king and his court, no one apparently noticed the look of insane fury which suddenly seemed to take possession of Saul. Before anyone could intervene or shout a cry of warning, the old king lifted his powerful war-javelin and flung it at David with all his might. Fortunately, the javelin missed its mark and went crashing into the wall behind him. But it was obvious to David that this was no time to reason with a madman. He therefore fled "away out of Saul's presence . . . and escaped that night."[21]

A NOTE ON THE PSALMS OF DAVID

Beginning at about this point in his life, the son of Jesse began recording the churning maelstrom of emotion which charged through his being as a result of the king's continuous campaign to murder him. It was undoubtedly providential that David possessed this inspired talent which permitted him to capture his feelings in some of the most poignant poetry ever written. Many of these are contained in the Book of Psalms and we will refer to some of them briefly as the story of David unfolds.

It is extremely unfortunate that one of the casualties in our modern, materialistic age has been the Psalms of the Bible. Past generations devoured them, memorized them, quoted them. This generation, for the most part, scarcely understands them. Their beauty and power need to be restored to their proper place in our literature and culture. Christians, especially, should realize that one of the very few places in the entire Old Testament where we can find an uninhibited, rapturous anticipation of the birth and mission of Jesus Christ is in the Psalms.[22]

The Hebrew title to the collection of Psalms as they appear in the Bible means "The Book of Praises," or "The

20. 1 Samuel 19:9
21. 1 Samuel 19:10
22. For a full discussion of prophecies concerning Jesus Christ in the Psalms see Chapter Five.

Book of God's Shining Forth."[23] Our title of "Psalms" comes from the verb "to sing" and is therefore translated "songs." In this case it refers specifically to songs designed to be sung with the accompaniment of a harp, the latter being known as a "psaltery." It also should be mentioned that the Jews refer to a psalm as a "mizmor," meaning "to be cut off" because when these poems were sung the individual syllables in each word had to be cut off from its neighbor so as to be assigned a particular note in the music.[24]

Most of the Psalms are credited to David, but the Biblical collection of 150 Psalms includes some which are specifically attributed to others.[25] The present collection is thought to have been made by Ezra around 445 B.C. Whoever the compiler was, he made no attempt to put them together chronologically, but some success has been achieved in doing it since.[26] Authorities also believe they are able to determine rather accurately when David wrote most of the Psalms about events in his own life since the cause of his various moods is often mentioned. Some of these we shall examine shortly.

---

23. Clarke, *Bible Commentary*, Vol. 3, p. 199
24. Ibid.
25. In this same source Adam Clarke gives on page 202 "A Classified Table of the Psalms" according to the accredited source:
    PSALMS WHICH HAVE NO INSCRIPTION OR SOURCE: 1, 2, 10, 33, 43, 71, 91, 93, 94, 95, 96, 97, 99, 104, 105, 107, 114, 115, 116, 117, 118, 119, 136, 137. TOTAL 24
    PSALMS CREDITED TO DAVID: 3, 4, 5, 6, 7, 8, 9, 11, 12, 13, 14, 15, 16, 17, 18, 19, 20, 21, 22, 23, 24, 25, 26, 27, 28, 29, 30, 31, 32, 34, 35, 36, 37, 38, 39, 40, 41, 51, 52, 53, 54, 55, 56, 57, 58, 59, 60, 61, 62, 63, 64, 65, 68, 69, 70, 84, 101, 103, 108, 109, 110, 122, 124, 131, 133, 138, 139, 140, 141, 142, 143, 144, 145. TOTAL 73
    PSALMS ATTRIBUTED TO SOLOMON: 72, 127. TOTAL 2
    PSALMS ATTRIBUTED TO THE SONS OF KORAH: 42, 44, 45, 46, 47, 48, 49, 84, 85, 87. TOTAL 10
    PSALMS ATTRIBUTED TO ASAPH: 50, 73, 74, 75, 76, 77, 78, 79, 80, 81, 82, 83. TOTAL 12
    PSALM ATTRIBUTED TO HEMAN: 88. TOTAL 1
    PSALM ATTRIBUTED TO ETHAN: 89. TOTAL 1
    PSALM ATTRIBUTED TO MOSES: 90. TOTAL 1
    PSALMS WITH TITLES BUT NO PERSON'S NAME: 66, 67, 92, 98, 100, 102. TOTAL 6
    HALLELUJAH PSALMS: 106, 111, 112, 113, 135, 146, 147, 148, 149, 150. TOTAL 10
    PSALMS OF DEGREES: 120, 121, 123, 125, 126, 128, 129, 130, 132, 134. TOTAL 10
    GRAND TOTAL 150
26. See Clarke, *Bible Commentary*, Vol. 3, pp. 203-208.

The Fourth and Fifth Attempts
Against David's Life

When David so narrowly escaped the speeding shaft of his father-in-law's war javelin, it sent him into the night shaken and perplexed. Nevertheless, he finally ended up at his own home with the apparent expectation that Jonathan and the king's servants could bring the king to his senses and the dawn of a new day would see cordial relations restored. He obviously did not think the king would follow up his attempted homicide with further immediate action, otherwise David would not have dared to return home.

It was during the night, however, that David discovered he was wrong. He found that his residence was being patrolled at every entrance by the king's guards. David's young wife was terrified. She pleaded with him to flee. Said she, "If thou save not thy life to-night, to-morrow thou shalt be slain!"[27] After what had happened the last few hours David could believe it. "So Michal let David down through a window: and he went, and fled, and escaped."[28] Neither Michal nor David realized it, but this was the end of their happiness together. Before long the king would strike down their marriage and while David would go on through the years secretly nourishing his love for Michal, nevertheless, their next meeting far in the future would reveal that their sweetheart days were past and their love had turned to ashes.

The anguish of spirit which David felt when he found his home completely surrounded is believed to be the source for the poetic outpouring which we now call the 59th Psalm.[29]

---

27. 1 Samuel 19:11
28. 1 Samuel 19:12
29. David's anxieties are reflected in the following words:
    Deliver me from mine enemies, O my God:
    Defend me from them that rise up against me.
    Deliver me from the workers of iniquity,
    And save me from bloody men.
    For, lo, they lie in wait for my soul:
    The mighty are gathered against me;
    Not for my transgression,
    Nor for my sin, O Lord.
    * * * *

The following morning when the servants of the king demanded admission to David's house, Michal showed them David's bed in which she said David was lying very ill. As a matter of fact, Michal had taken "an image, and laid it in the bed, and put a pillow of goats' hair for his bolster, and covered it with a cloth."[30]

When the king's servants reported back to Saul and told him they had not arrested David because he was sick, the king revealed the explosive degree of agitation in his mind by crying out, "Bring him up to me in the bed, that I may slay him!"[31]

The servants returned to David's house and only then did they discover that Michal had tricked them. They thereupon seized her and took the girl back to her father.

"Saul said unto Michal, Why hast thou deceived me so, and sent away mine enemy, that he is escaped?"[32] The frightened girl excused herself on the ground that David might have killed her if she had tried to prevent his escape. Of course, this did not jibe with her own complicity in placing an image in the bed and giving out the story that David was sick. But perhaps a distracted daughter of a half-mad king should not be expected to think rationally when she was frantically trying to prevent her father from murdering her husband.

As for David, he felt that remaining anywhere in the vicinity of Gibeah was virtual suicide and so he carefully made his way to Ramah, the nearby residence and headquarters of Samuel the prophet. After all, Samuel was the

---

29. (Continued)
> They return at evening;
> They make a noise like a dog,
> And go around about the city.
> Behold, they belch out with their mouths:
> Swords are in their lips:
> For who, say they, doth hear?
>
> * * * *
>
> Consume them in wrath, consume them,
> That they may not be;
> And let them know that God ruleth in Jacob
> Unto the ends of the earth. Selah!

30. 1 Samuel 19:13
31. 1 Samuel 19:15
32. 1 Samuel 19:17

one who had anointed him king and it certainly seemed expedient to now get counsel from the Lord's prophet in view of what was happening. And the trip was not in vain. Samuel immediately recognized the alarming extremity to which Saul's wild passion had pressed him. He therefore took David to "Naioth" which means a cluster of cottages and is believed to have been located in a suburb near Ramah.[33] It was at "Naioth" that Samuel had his sanctuary and a school of the prophets.[34]

Nevertheless, Saul's spies soon located David and a military guard was sent to haul him in. When the king's messengers arrived at Naioth they found Samuel presiding over the exercises of a Priesthood class with David apparently in their midst. As the soldiers moved in on the group a wonderful influence suddenly enveloped them so that they felt the spirit of prophecy coming upon them.[35] The guard decided to join the school of the prophets. Saul learned what had happened and sent two other groups of messengers but they likewise became so fascinated with the marvelous influence at the school of the prophets that they not only failed to capture David, but joined him.

This was too much for Saul. In a violent temper, he stormed down from Gibeah intending to wreak vengeance on the lot. First he went to Samuel's headquarters at Ramah, but failing to find the prophet or David there he stopped at a community well in Sechu and asked where Samuel could be found. The local rustics, being proud of the presence of the famous prophet in their community, had no compunction about revealing the location of Naioth, so Saul hastened to the cloistered sanctuary of Samuel's Priesthood school. As he drew near, however, a sudden dispensation of Heaven fell upon the benighted and unworthy Saul just as it had on his servants.[36] The king was so taken up with the glory of it all that he stripped off his royal garb and joined the prophets as though he were a commoner.[37] The local people watched

---

33. Cunningham Giekie, *Hours With the Bible*, Vol. 3, p. 169.
34. Clarke, *Bible Commentary*, Vol. 2, p. 274
35. 1 Samuel 19:20
36. 1 Samuel 19:23
37. 1 Samuel 19:24. This passage states that Saul was "naked" but all authorities appear to agree that the word means "disrobed" of his regal finery rather than completely unclothed. (See Geikie, *Hours With the Bible*, vol. 3, p. 169, note.)

Saul in amazement and then exclaimed, "Is Saul also among the prophets?" This was the second time Saul had enjoyed such an experience.[38] However, it was not a permanent endowment. It lasted only long enough for David to quietly remove himself and escape. And as soon as the light of Heaven departed from Saul, his murderous darkness returned.

Jonathan Tries to Save David's Life and Almost Forfeits His Own

As soon as David had left Samuel he went directly to the only other friend of national prestige who might help him. That was the crown prince of Israel, Saul's son, Jonathan. David's state of near despair is reflected in his plea to this trusted friend, "What have I done?" he cried, "What is mine iniquity? and what is my sin before thy father, that he seeketh my life . . . there is but a step between me and death . . . if there be in me iniquity, slay me thyself!"[39]

Jonathan loved David. He expressed the hope that he still might be able to appease his father as he had done before. He entered into a sacred covenant with David that he would do his utmost and then let David know. David therefore agreed to hide in the fields for three days while Jonathan tested the feelings of Saul. It was further decided that in order to avoid detection Jonathan would come into the field as though he were practicing archery. He told David to be somewhere in the vicinity of a stone pillar called Ezel. Jonathan said he would shoot three arrows near the stone and send a lad to fetch them. The prince said, "If I expressly say unto the lad, Behold the arrows are on this side of thee," it meant that all was well and the king was pacified. But if Jonathan shouted to the lad, "Behold, the arrows are beyond thee," that was the signal that David's life was in the greatest danger and he should flee in all haste.

The waiting period must have been three torturous days and nights for David as he waited in the nearby fields and crags like a criminal fugitive. But they were agonizing days and nights for Jonathan as well. All during the first day

38. 1 Samuel 10:9-11
39. 1 Samuel 20:1, 3, 8

and night he observed the king's behavior but nothing tangible emerged. On the second day, the king said to Jonathan, "Wherefore cometh not the son of Jesse to meat, neither yesterday nor to-day?"[40] Perhaps Jonathan should have avoided this question but he did not and thereby fell into a trap. He made excuses for David which instantly exposed the fact that he had been in direct contact with him.

That did it. King Saul howled at his son in a trembling rage, "Thou son of the perverse rebellious woman, do not I know that thou hast chosen the son of Jesse to thine own confusion. . . . For as long as the son of Jesse liveth upon the ground, thou shalt not be established, nor thy kingdom. Wherefore, now send and fetch him unto me, for he shall surely die."[41]

The intent of Saul's scathing rebuke was to suspend Jonathan's claim to the throne if he allowed David to continue living. However, Jonathan was not intimidated. He boldly declared to his father, "Wherefore shall he be slain? What hath he done?"[42] This honest question left Saul without an honest answer. He therefore responded the only way that a man in a blind, irrational passion knows how to answer. Saul seized his javelin and sent it hurtling toward his son. The heat of the king's rage probably dimmed his sight and crippled his aim because the bronze-tipped javelin missed its mark. In a spirit of righteous indignation the faithful Jonathan rose from his seat at the table and in "fierce anger" departed. This was the second time King Saul had tried to kill this distinguished and faithful son.[43]

Jonathan waited until the appointed time and then went out with his bow toward the stone pillar called Ezel. Somewhere up in the cliffs or hiding in the field was David. It must have been a heartbroken Jonathan who shot the three arrows toward the stone and then shouted to his attendant the fatal signal: "Is not the arrow BEYOND thee?"

Because of the great risk involved, no further contact was supposed to be made between them but perhaps Jona-

---

40. 1 Samuel 20:27
41. 1 Samuel 20:30-31
42. 1 Samuel 20:32
43. The first time was equally ridiculous. See 1 Samuel 14:24-25.

than realized that this might be the last time he would ever
see David. He therefore shouted to the lad who was with
him, "Make speed, haste, stay not." As soon as the boy
had gathered up the arrows, Jonathan handed him his bow
and quiver saying, "Go, carry them to the city."[44]

As soon as the boy was out of sight, David did exactly
what Jonathan hoped he would. He quickly came out of
hiding. But as David approached Jonathan the son of Jesse
lost complete control of his emotions. He fell to the ground
and bowed three times in grateful appreciation for Jonathan's
faithfulness in risking his own life to bring David the warning. Then the two men embraced each other and wept as
only strong men weep. Finally Jonathan said to David,
"Go in peace, forasmuch as we have sworn both of us in
the name of the Lord, saying, The Lord be between me
and thee, and between my seed and thy seed for ever."[45]
And so they parted.

David Gets Goliath's Sword

Events for David were now so perilous that the slightest misstep could bring instant death. He apparently was cut
off from his wife, his parents and all of his former friends
among the people of Israel. His slightest contact with them
could bring down the vengeance of Saul upon them.

In these desperate straits, David's greatest needs were
food and weapons. For this purpose he went to the least
likely place to get them — to the holy Tabernacle of Israel
which at that time was pitched in a place called Nob. The
High Priest in charge of the Tabernacle was Ahimelech[46]
who enjoyed this privilege by right of descent, he being the
great grandson of the High Priest Eli.[47]

Ahimelech recognized the famous son of Jesse but was
suspicious of the circumstances under which he came. No
doubt the son-in-law of the king presented a bedraggled
appearance after three days and nights hiding in the field,
but what seemed most strange to Ahimelech was the fact

---

44. 1 Samuel 20:40
45. 1 Samuel 20:42
46. Sometimes called Ahiah as in Samuel 14:3.
47. Ibid.

that David had no attendants. "Why art thou alone, and no man with thee?" inquired the priest.[48]

David's reply was not a normal one. It demonstrated that the king's fleeing son-in-law now considered himself in the midst of war, a war which Saul had declared against him. He therefore did not give the High Priest a straight-forward answer since that would have immediately made Ahimelech a party to David's problem. Instead he resorted to stratagem to protect Ahimelech and represented that he was actually on the king's business and needed food for himself and certain mysterious associates which he implied were working with him. The priest said he had nothing but unleavened bread from the golden shew-bread table in the Tabernacle and according to the Law of Moses this should only be eaten by priests. However, Ahimelech decided on his own responsibility that in view of the dire emergency he would give the bread to David.[49]

While these affairs were being transacted, David noticed a descendant of Esau, an Edomite, named Doeg, who apparently had been converted to the faith of the Israelites and was at the Tabernacle that day because he was "detained before the Lord."[50] David recognized Doeg as an officer of Saul's household, in fact, the chief herdsman for Saul.[51] Did the man know that Saul had ordered his servants to kill David on sight?

David quickly said to Ahimelech, the High Priest, "And is there not here under thine hand spear or sword?" Perhaps David was surprised when the priest replied, "The sword of Goliath the Philistine, whom thou slewest in the valley of Elah, behold, it is here wrapped in a cloth behind the ephod: if thou wilt take that, take it: for there is no other save that here." This weapon was undoubtedly a fine one. David said, "There is none like that; give it me."[52] So David took the sword of Goliath. However, he did not have to defend

---

48. 1 Samuel 21:1
49. 1 Samuel 21:6. This incident was cited by Jesus (Mark 2:25) to demonstrate from scriptural authority that in case of dire necessity the breach of a mere ritual or procedural regulation was not a sin.
50. 1 Samuel 21:7
51. Ibid.
52. 1 Samuel 21:9

himself against Doeg, the Edomite, because the king's servant had quickly left Nob. As soon as Doeg recognized
David he hurried back to Gibeah.

DAVID LEAVES ISRAEL

David anticipated that Doeg might betray him[53] and
so he fled with all haste from the mountains of Israel into
a self-imposed exile. Where he chose to hide, however, was,
next to Gibeah, the most dangerous and deadly place on the
face of the earth. For reasons the scriptures do not disclose, this completely audacious son of Jesse went straight
down the hills of Judah and up to the first main Philistine
city on the plain. That city turned out to be Gath, the home
of Goliath!

Of course, all of these Philistine cities on the maritime
plain catered to commercial trade so it was not uncommon
for them to have many strangers from surrounding areas
visiting them, even Israelites.[54] However, this singular man
David was not content to quietly slip into Gath and get
himself lost in the market-place crowds. He had to present
himself at no less a place than the king's palace! The king's
name or title was Achish and apparently David came to his
royal establishment under the impression that no one would
realize who he was. This almost turned out to be fatal.
Although probably few Philistines had ever seen David at
close range, there were undoubtedly those who did know
what the Goliath-killer looked like. "And the servants of
Achish said unto him, Is not this David the king of the land?
Did they not sing one to another of him in dances, saying,
Saul hath slain his thousands, and David his ten thousands?"[55]

David realized he was in the deepest kind of trouble.
If they found someone who could positively identify him
there would be a sacrifice to the god Dagon which would be
bigger than the rites celebrating the capture of Samson!

As we have already seen, David possessed an ingenious
capacity for various kinds of stratagems. In times of peace
men who employ such maneuvering often end up in jail, but

---

53. 1 Samuel 22:22
54. 1 Samuel 13:19-21
55. 1 Samuel 21:11

in times of war or special emergencies these are the devices that have saved nations. David now used a stratagem to save himself. He threw a fit of pretended insanity. The scripture says he "scrabbled on the doors of the gate, and let his spittle fall down upon his beard."[56] The 34th and 56th Psalms are said to have been written as a result of this fearful experience.

Nevertheless, David's subterfuge was such a persuasive demonstration of madness that the king decided this could not possibly be the great David. He therefore ridiculed his servants and said, "Lo, see the man is mad: wherefore then have ye brought him to me? Have I need of mad men, that ye have brought this fellow to play the mad man in my presence? shall this fellow come into my house?"[57]

To his great relief, David found himself thrown out of the city.

David Begins to Assemble a Military Force

From Gath, David fled into the deep canyons leading up to the mountains of Judah. At a point not far from the spot where he had killed Goliath, he took refuge in a grotto known as the "cave Adullam." Concerning this spot Dr. Geikie states: "About two and a half miles south of Shochoh, in the great Wady of the Terebinth [valley of Elah] where he had slain Goliath, there is a rounded hill about 500 feet high, almost isolated by valleys, and covered with ruins, shewing it to have once been a natural fortress strengthened by art. A well at its foot supplies water at all times, and near it are other ruins to which still clings the name of Aid el Ma — words identical in pronunciation with the Adullam of the Bible. To this spot David fled, seeking refuge in a cave known by that name. The sides of the lateral valley are, indeed, lined throughout with small caverns, which are still used for dwellings and folds, and there is, on the hill itself, a separate cave, low and blackened by smoke, in which a family now makes its home. There are still, moreover, in the wide valley below, clumps of terebinths, like those which gave it in Scripture times, the name of 'Elah,'

---

56. 1 Samuel 21:13
57. 1 Samuel 21:14-15

'the terebinth.' It may well be that this is the identical spot in which David hid."[58]

Caves and grottos are characteristic of this country due to rainwater or subterranean springs eroding away the soft limestone and gradually carving out caverns which have openings along the side of the steep cliffs where the water follows its natural escape route. Because of their location, these caves are easy to defend and nothing but a large army could rout a strong body of men from this location. Perhaps it was this element of security which permitted David to begin collecting a military force at Adullam. The scripture says, "And every one that was in distress, and every one that was in debt, and every one that was discontented, gathered themselves unto him; and he became a captain over them; and there were with him about four hundred men."[59]

All of this happened over a considerable period of time which meant that David was under the constant necessity of foraging food for himself and followers as well as training and organizing his new recruits until they were seasoned soldiers. During the struggle and travail of this period David is believed to have composed the Psalms now known as the 57th and the 142nd.

By this time David not only had a price on his head but so did the members of his family. This becomes apparent from the scripture which says, "And when his brethren and all his father's house heard it, they went down thither to him."[60] Perhaps it was about this time that David was joined by his three famous nephews — Joab, Abishai, and Asahel — all of whom would figure both prominently and tragically in David's career from this time hence.

THE FLIGHT TO MOAB

David could not afford to remain at Adullam too long. This spot was only twelve miles west of Bethlehem and barely two days' march from Saul's headquarters at Gibeah in Benjamin. David therefore led his family and band of followers down through the south country, passing around the

---

58. Geikie, *Hours With the Bible*, Vol. 3, p. 174
59. 1 Samuel 22:2
60. 1 Samuel 22:1

lower end of the Dead Sea and then climbing up into the heights of Moab on the eastern side.

The Moabites were descendants of Lot,[61] Abraham's nephew, but this remote relationship gave them little in common with the Israelites. The Moabites had completely capitulated to the heathen culture and heathen religion which inevitably made them look upon the Israelites as avowed enemies. David, however, was in the unique position of being a great-grandson of a Moabite woman. She was the beautiful and faithful Ruth who had married Boaz of Bethlehem.[62] It may have been for this reason that David felt a certain degree of security in fleeing to Moab. Moreover, the fact that Saul, the king of the Israelites, had declared David to be his enemy, was enough to ingratiate him with the Moabites since they would consider David a potential ally. All of these factors must have fortified David in his determination to seek asylum from these people. We further discover that he had a very special reason for seeking their friendship. The scripture discloses that David was extremely worried about his aged parents. This was no kind of life for them and he knew the constant running, hiding and fighting would eventually destroy them. Therefore David went before the Moabite king and said, "Let my father and my mother, I pray thee, come forth and be with you, till I know what God will do for me."[63] To David's great relief the king seemed perfectly willing to comply with this request so his parents made their home in Moab and remained there during all the time David was in hiding from King Saul.[64]

For David, however, this was only a temporary stop. Psalm 27, particularly verse 10, indicates that it was written while he was in Moab or shortly after he was separated from his parents.

Then David had the good fortune to be joined by Gad, an inspired servant of God who would remain with him for many years and become famous as "David's seer."[65] From

61. Genesis 19:30-37
62. Ruth, Chapter 4
63. 1 Samuel 22:3
64. 1 Samuel 22:4
65. 1 Chronicles 21:9

him David was able to learn "what God will do for me."
Gad instructed David to leave the Moabite country immediately and return to the mountains of Judah.[66] Although it
was a far more dangerous place for David to hide, nevertheless the Lord knew that Judah would be the first to
accept David as king and it was essential that he remain in
that vicinity as much as possible.

Leaving his parents, David gathered his followers together and migrated to an area where he would be in hiding
for a considerable period of time. The new place of refuge
was in the "forest of Hareth"[67] just a little above Adullum
near modern Kharas. This is about nine miles northwest of
Hebron.[68]

David had barely arrived in this new location when
he received news of an appalling tragedy which Saul had
committed against Israel. The aging king did not know it,
but the final, fearful climax to his disintegrating career lay
straight before him.

---

66. 1 Samuel 22:5
67. Ibid.
68. Geikie, *Hours With the Bible*, Vol. 3, p. 182

Scripture Readings and Questions on Chapter Two

Scripture Reading: 1 Samuel, Chapters 18 to 21 inclusive.

1—How did Saul interpret the plaudits which David received for killing Goliath?

2—What was Saul's purpose in changing David's official assignment? What did David become?

3—Why did Saul consent to his daughter, Michal, marrying David? Did he expect the marriage to actually take place? Why?

4—When Saul commanded his servants to kill David, who went out immediately to warn him?

5—What did Jonathan say which temporarily reconciled the king with David?

6—How did Saul happen to throw a war javelin at David?

7—What does the word *Psalms* mean? How many are attributed to David?

8—How did Michal save David's life? Do you think Michal should have gone with David?

9—To whom did David go for advice and protection? Why?

10—What happened when Saul sent messengers to arrest David? What happened when Saul came down himself?

11—What happened when Jonathan tried to save David's life and almost lost his own? Was this the first time Saul had tried to kill Jonathan?

12—Why did David flee to the Tabernacle? Did he get what he went after? Why was the High Priest a little suspicious?

13—What famous sword did David obtain for himself? Why did he think he might need it?

14—Describe what happened when David fled to the Philistine city of Gath. Why was this a dangerous place for him to go?

15—How did David escape from Gath? Where did he go next?

16—What kind of people began to attach themselves to David? How many belonged to his band before he made his next move?

17—Why did David go to Moab? How did he dare go up to a nation which had always been hostile toward Israel?

18—Who was Gad? Why was David pleased to have him along?

19—What did Gad tell David to do? Was there any good reason for it?

20—Where did David go next? What is its approximate location?

CHAPTER THREE

The Fall of Saul

While the most recent events described in the last chapter were occurring, a terrible blotch on the pages of Israel's history was being written with blood in the land of of Benjamin. This is how it came about.

At his capital city of Gibeah just north of Jerusalem, Saul received word that David, his son-in-law, had entrenched himself in the fortress-like cliffs of Judah and that the malcontents of the whole land were joining him daily. Saul immediately called his officers and servants together in an emergency meeting. Once assembled, the king launched into a tirade against them. He accused them of disloyalty, duplicity and distrust. He whimpered and moaned like a spoiled, churlish child claiming they had all conspired against him. He said they knew very well that Jonathan was in league with David but none had come forth with the necessary evidence so Saul could take action against Jonathan. He accused them of being ungrateful and said none of them felt sorry for the king in his present dreadful straits.[1]

This disgusting display of self-pity and paranoia suddenly brought forth an unexpected bounty of sensational

---

1. 1 Samuel 22:7-8

information. It came from none other than Doeg, the Edomite, who said he had some significant news for the king. "I saw the son of Jesse," said Doeg, "coming to Nob, to Ahimelech, the son of Ahitub. And he [Ahimelech, the High Priest] inquired of the Lord for him and gave him victuals, and gave him the sword of Goliath the Philistine."[2]

The tortured brain of the king assessed this news in the most grim and bitter terms. So the spirit of insurrection had spread to the very Tabernacle of God!

Saul ordered his servants to round up Ahimelech and all the priests at Nob for questioning. As they were hustled in before him, Saul focussed his attenion upon Ahimelech and angrily demanded, "Why have ye conspired against me, thou and the son of Jesse, in that thou hast given him bread, and a sword, and hast inquired of God for him, that he should rise against me, to lie in wait as at this day?"[3]

Ahimelech offered no defense for his actions but took the offensive by challenging the king. "And who," said he, "is so faithful among all thy servants as David, which is the king's son-in-law, and goeth at thy bidding, and is honourable in thine house?"[4]

Then, to put the record straight, Ahimelech declared, "Did I then begin to inquire of God for him? be it far from me: let not the king impute anything unto his servant, nor to all the house of my father: for thy servant knew nothing of all this, less or more [little or great]."[5]

But Saul was in no mood to argue or even investigate. The heated vitriol of his hatred toward David now boiled over on the High Priest and all his kindred. Cried the king, "Thou shalt surely die, Ahimelech, thou, and all thy father's house."[6]

Turning abruptly to his "footmen," Saul commanded, "Turn and slay the priests of the Lord; because their hand

2. 1 Samuel 22:9-10
3. 1 Samuel 22:13
4. 1 Samuel 22:14

5. 1 Samuel 22:15
6. 1 Samuel 22:16

also is with David, and because they knew when he fled, and did not shew it to me."[7]

But not one of the king's servants would raise his sword against the priests of God.

In his frustrated rage Saul turned to Doeg, the Edomite, saying, "Turn thou, and fall upon the priests!"[8] The dark mind of the Edomite apparently felt no compunction against the slaying of the Lord's servants if it were the king's orders, therefore he promptly drew his sword and set about the awful business. It was literally a cruel and senseless massacre. The Bible says eighty-five priests were ruthlessly hewn down that day.[9] Doeg then took his servants and fell upon the entire village of Nob where he killed everything that breathed; men, women and children, even the animals.[10] It was a horrible day for Israel.

Of the meager few who escaped this slaughter, one turned out to be the High Priest's son, Abiathar.[11] This frightened and grief-stricken priest fled southward hoping that somewhere in Judah he would find David and receive his protection. Abiathar's search finally ended in success and as soon as he stood before David he related the tragic news.

David's reaction was a mixture of sorrow for the dead and pity for the lone survivor. Said he, "I knew it that day, when Doeg the Edomite was there [at the Tabernacle in Nob], that he would surely tell Saul: I have occasioned the death of all the persons of thy father's house. Abide thou with me, fear not: for he that seeketh my life seeketh thy life: but with me thou shalt be in safeguard."[12]

This arrangement turned out to be a great boon to David, for Abiathar had succeeded in bringing with him the holy ephod of the High Priest to which the Urim and Thum-

7. 1 Samuel 22:17
8. 1 Samuel 22:18
9. Ibid.
10. 1 Samuel 22:19
11. 1 Samuel 22:20. He was the fourth in descent from Eli and was of the lineage of Ithamar, the youngest son of Aaron. He remained with David through the latter's life.
12. 1 Samuel 22:22-23

mim were customarily attached in their linen breastplate.[13]
We therefore discover David making use of Abiathar to
determine the will of the Lord in each new crisis.[14] No
mention is made of the Urim and Thummim, only the ephod,
but since Abiathar's ephod is specifically mentioned in connection with the receiving of revelation it is likely that those
sacred instruments were still with the High Priest's vestment.

Saul Sets up a New High Priest

Meanwhile, back at Saul's headquarters in Gibeah, the
king determined to create a new religious center for the
worship of the people. For reasons not revealed in the
scripture, Saul elected to build the new center in Gibeon
(a Canaanite town in Benjamin which must not be confused
with Saul's capital of Gibeah). The first step he took was
a fatal one. He ordered the driving out or killing of the
local Canaanite inhabitants of Gibeon.[15] The ancestors of
these people had obtained a sacred promise from Joshua
that Israel would always protect them.[16] Now Saul's soldiers
massacred them. It seems as though the very light of reason
had been extinguished in Saul. As we shall see later, this
stupid act by Saul became the cause for a subsequent reprisal
which wiped out nearly all of Saul's male descendants.[17] But
that remained for the future.

As of the moment Saul intended to call up a new High
Priest, named Zadok. This man was entitled to be a High
Priest but not as a result of Saul's appointment. Politicians
have no authority to select Priesthood leaders. Zadok's right
of appointment grew out of the fact that he was a direct
descendant of Aaron through Eleazor, Aaron's third son
(1 Chr. 24:3). Zadok was an honorable man and so devoted
to his Priesthood calling that when David became king he
had Zadok serve side by side with Abiathar.[18] This was an

---

13. Exodus 28:4-32; 39:8-21
14. See, for example, 1 Samuel 23:6, 9; 30:7; 2 Samuel 2:1; 5:19.
15. This terrible deed is not described in the scriptures but direct reference is
    made to it in 2 Samuel 21:1-2. Saul is said to have struck down this heathen
    city "in his zeal to the children of Israel and Judah." (2 Samuel 21:2) This
    was blind, reckless zeal and the kind of disobedience which had long since
    led the Lord to reject Saul.
16. Joshua 9:3-15
17. 2 Samuel 21:1, 2, 5
18. See for example, 2 Samuel 15:35-36; 19:11

unusual arrangement since only one High Priest should preside at any given time. However, circumstances beyond the control of either Abiathar or Zadok had brought them to their high offices and therefore David determined to honor them both.

Meanwhile, in Saul's day, Zadok presided at the Tabernacle in Gibeon, while Abiathar served with David.[19]

DAVID IS BETRAYED BY THE TOWN HE HAD SAVED

While David was staying in the "forest of Hareth" (near Hebron) he received word that a nearby town of Judah — called Keilah — was being attacked by the Philistines. The purpose of their attack was to steal grain and David was told that the new harvest was being seized by the Philistines directly from the threshing floor.

David immediately inquired of the Lord as to what he should do and the answer came back that he should defend the city. He therefore rallied his loyal forces and drove the Philistines down from Judah. But the next thing David knew he had become the target for a new attack by Saul. David's activities at Keilah had been communicated to the king and Saul promptly determined to take his army and go down to kill David and his whole cadre. David asked the Lord if the people of Keilah would betray him if he tried to make his stand at that place. The revelation came back that they would indeed betray him.[20] David therefore had no alternative but to leave that abominable and ungrateful community.

By this time David and his band numbered around 600.[21] With Saul's forces prowling on their heels continually, it was now necessary to move rapidly from place to place. However, David maintained the center of his operations "in a mountain in the wilderness of Ziph." It is believed that Ziph was "about four miles below Hebron, and about twelve miles, as the crow flies, south-east of Keilah. Here 2,882 feet above the sea, in a region full of caves in the limestone rocks, with two roads passing the hill on which the village

---

19. 1 Chronicles 16:39
20. 1 Samuel 23:11-12
21. 1 Samuel 23:13

stood . . . he could hope to elude his pursuers, at least for a time."[22]

Nevertheless, Saul hunted for David "every day" the scripture says,[23] and it was only when the elusive band seemed to have disappeared completely from sight that Saul became discouraged and returned to his capital city of Gibeah.[24]

However, there was one man in king Saul's entourage who did not return to Gibeah. It was David's beloved friend and brother-in-law, Prince Jonathan. Jonathan succeeded in remaining behind to discover for himself where David was hiding so he could make contact with him.

It must have been a joyful reunion. Not since David had first become a fugitive[25] were these great friends able to embrace each other. While they had been separated Jonathan had seen enough to convince him that Saul's hatred of David was driving the king to near insanity — lashing out one moment in a ruthless massacre of the priests of God[26] and then falling upon the nation's helpless heathen wards inhabiting Gibeon and slaughtering them.[27] So by this time Jonathan was completely convinced that it was only a matter of time until his father's kingdom collapsed. However, instead of being jealous of David as the prospective new king, this remarkable crown prince openly proclaimed his fealty to the son of Jesse, saying, "Fear not, for the hand of Saul my father shall not find thee; and thou shalt be king over Israel, AND I SHALL BE NEXT UNTO THEE. . . ."[28] The generosity of this noble crown prince, Jonathan, is without precedent in history. Jonathan told David that Saul already knew that he was allied in spirit with David and would support David as king rather than seek the throne himself.[29] The two men renewed their sacred covenant of friendship with each other and affectionately parted, David remaining at his stronghold and Jonathan hurrying back "to

22. Geikie, *Hours With the Bible*, Vol. 3, p. 187
23. 1 Samuel 23:14
24. This becomes apparent from 1 Samuel 23:19 indicating Saul had returned to Gibeah.
25. 1 Samuel 20:42
26. 1 Samuel 22:18-19
27. 2 Samuel 21:1
28. 1 Samuel 23:17
29. Ibid.

his house" at Gibeah.[30] It was the last time they would ever see each other in this life.

What a team Jonathan and David would have made as governors of Israel. But it was not to be. The torrent of tragedy which was soon to sweep Saul out of power would carry the magnificent Jonathan into oblivion on the same scarlet tide.

A NARROW ESCAPE

After this meeting with Jonathan, David moved his little band a few miles further south to Maon[31] where the highland wilderness of Judah sweeps down toward the Arabian desert. However, the people of Ziph had been keeping a close watch on David and his men with the intent of betraying them. Their leaders went up to Saul at Gibeah and said, "Now therefore, O king, come down according to all the desire of thy soul to come down; and our part shall be to deliver him into the king's hand."[32] Saul replied, "Blessed be ye of the Lord; for ye have compassion on me. Go, I pray you, prepare yet, and know and see his place where his haunt is . . . take knowledge of all the lurking places where he hideth himself, and come ye again to me with the certainty, and I will go with you: and it shall come to pass, if he be in the land, that I will search him out throughout all the thousands of Judah."[33]

These elders of Ziph carried out the order immediately and the next thing David knew, the military forces of Saul had completely surrounded him. In fact, they were on the very mountain where David and his men were desperately hiding.[34] Never before had David been so hopelessly at the mercy of Saul's vengeance. "And Saul went on this side of the mountain, and David and his men on that side of the mountain: and David made haste to get away for fear of Saul; and Saul and his men compassed David and his men round about to take them."[35]

Then a virtual miracle happened. A messenger from the north came frantically speeding into Saul's camp an-

---

30. 1 Samuel 23:18   33. 1 Samuel 23:21-23
31. 1 Samuel 23:25   34. 1 Samuel 23:26
32. 1 Samuel 23:20   35. Ibid.

nouncing that the land was being invaded by the Philistines![36] There was not a moment to lose.

Exasperated and no doubt enraged by this frustrating new development which would rob him of his prey, the disgusted Saul was compelled to abandon the capture of David at the very moment when success seemed assured. Reluctantly he assembled his troops and set off to join battle against the abominable Philistines.[37]

David Flees to En-gedi

This gave the frightened forces of David a chance to quickly move out of this treacherous territory. It was obvious that David was not safe even among the members of his own tribe!

His line of flight took him eastward across the famous "wilderness of Judeah." This is a desolate plateau approximately 15 miles wide. "This plateau is cut up by deep gorges, worn by the torrents and also by volcanic action. Nothing green refreshes the eye over the wide landscape. No stream waters it, except when the rains, for a time, fill the wadys with rushing torrents. Only the black tents of some poor Arabs who manage to find pasture for their goats in the cliffs and hollows of its almost bare rocks, give any human interest to the forbidding landscape."[38]

Crossing this plateau, David came to the two-thousand-foot cliffs which look down on the acrid waters of the Dead Sea as they stretch like a flashing sheet of burnished steel 1,300 feet below sea level. This is the lowest depression in the broken crust of the earth's surface, sinking as it does for another 1,300 feet below the surface of the Dead Sea. Around it lie the skeletons of barren eroding cliffs and the deadly wastes of total desolation.

David made his headquarters at about the only place where 600 men could survive. It was the rugged oasis of En-gedi lying part way up the cliffs on the west side of the sea. Today we call these cliffs the "Dead Sea Scrolls"

---

36. 1 Samuel 23:27
37. 1 Samuel 23:28
38. Geikie, *Hours With the Bible*, Vol. 3, pp. 192-193

country for the hundreds of limestone caves pocking these cliffs made excellent hiding places not only for David's men but for the sacred records of a people who would occupy these wastes several centuries after David.

As David and his band attempted to make a descent to En-gedi it was no easy task: "A winding track cut in the perpendicular rocks is the only means of descent; a single false step is death, for it would hurl one to the bottom, 2,000 feet below. A warm spring, from which the place takes its name, bursts from under a huge boulder 1,340 feet beneath the summit; the water goes streaming over the steep from amidst a thicket of canes and bushes, the home of thrushes, grackles, and warblers; its course marked by a fringe of vegetation as it falls. Six hundred feet below, outside the slope of debris from the heights above, a small oasis is reached, once famed for its palms, balsam, and wine. To this wild spot, well called the 'rocks of the wild goats,' since only they and the gazelle could find footing on the narrow ledges of the cliffs, David had to flee, hiding in the caverns with which the whole of the mountain [cliffs] are filled."[39]

DAVID HAS A CHANCE TO KILL SAUL

No sooner had Saul returned from driving back the latest wave of Philistine marauders than the spy report came to him that David was at En-gedi. Saul speedily took 3,000 "chosen" men and struck out for the barren and desolate region overlooking the Dead Sea. Apparently the movement of such a large military contingent gave advance warning to David for we are told that as Saul approached the area David and a troop of his men took refuge in a large grotto or cave.[40] There was a long period of painful waiting but finally they heard someone approaching. David and his men hid themselves well back along the sides of the cave and watched in amazement as the bulky frame of king Saul, himself, loomed up at the entrance.

The king was alone. It appeared that he was looking for some safe place to lie down and rest.

As soon as the exhausted Saul had fallen asleep, David's men urged their leader to creep forth and slay the

---

39. Ibid., pp. 193-194   40. 1 Samuel 24:3

king. It was an occasion of unbelievably good fortune and it must not be lost. David crept forward as they suggested, but instead of plunging his knife into Saul's throat David simply cut off a piece of the king's cloak and crept back to his men. No doubt they wondered what kind of stupid sentimentality had overcome their captain. David said, "The Lord forbid that I should do this thing unto my master, the Lord's anointed, to stretch forth mine hand against him, seeing he is the anointed of the Lord."[41] As long as a man still occupied the throne to which he had been anointed, it was not in David's nature to dishonor him. His men, however, were prepared to summarily dispatch the king, but David restrained them.[42]

In due time Saul awoke refreshed and departed from the cave to rejoin his troops. David followed him out. When Saul had gone a safe distance, David called to him, "My lord the king!" Saul turned about. He saw David humbly bow to the earth. Then the younger man cried out, "Wherefore hearest thou men's words, saying, Behold, David seeketh thy hurt? Behold, this day thine eyes have seen how that the Lord had delivered thee to day into mine hand in the cave. and some bade me kill thee: but mine eye spared thee; and I said, I will not put forth mine hand against my lord; for he is the Lord's anointed. Moreover, my father, see, yea, see the skirt of thy robe in my hand: for in that I cut of the skirt of thy robe and killed thee not, know thou and see that there is neither evil nor transgression in mine hand, and I have not sinned against thee; yet thou huntest my soul to take it."[43]

A glimmer of Saul's old, better nature gradually began to rise to the surface. The king shouted back up to David in a quisitive, friendly manner, "Is this thy voice, my son David?" Actually he knew without asking but his mind needed time to assimilate just what had happened. When the full impact of what David had just said and done rested upon his soul, the old king wept.[44] Almost as though he were suffering from what modern psychology calls schizophrenia, Saul now changed from his posture of hate and murder to a child-like and almost guileless humility. "Thou

---

41. 1 Samuel 24:6
42. 1 Samuel 24:7

43. 1 Samuel 24:9-11
44. 1 Samuel 24:16

art more righteous than I," he shouted up to David, "for thou hast rewarded me good, whereas I have rewarded thee evil. And thou hast shewed this day how that thou hast dealt well with me: forasmuch as when the Lord had delivered me into thine hand, thou killedst me not."[45]

Then Saul made a confession to David which confirmed what Jonathan had previously said about his father. Saul cried out, "And now, behold, I KNOW WELL THAT THOU SHALT SURELY BE KING. AND THAT THE KINGDOM OF ISRAEL SHALL BE ESTABLISHED IN THINE HAND."[46] He then asked David to make a promise to him. "Swear now therefore unto me by the Lord," he pleaded, "that thou wilt not cut off my seed after me, and that thou wilt not destroy my name out of my father's house."[47] This was not a difficult oath for David to make for among the king's children was Jonathan whom David loved as much and probably more than the king himself. And there was Michal, Saul's daughter and David's bride, from whom he had been separated.

Having heard David's oath, the humbled Saul seemed fully satisfied. He assembled his 3,000 troops and marched homeward. How different the history of Israel might have been had Saul found the strength to keep this better side of his personality predominant in his life. But as the future would reveal, the tortured mind of Saul would vacillate repeatedly from the rational angel of his own best self to the monstrous demon of a blood-thirsty and vengeful murderer.

David must have sensed that Saul's gesture of reconciliation was only a temporary apparition. The scripture closes the incident with the significant comment, "And Saul went home; but David and his men gat them up unto the [strong] hold."[48]

The Death of Samuel

It was at this juncture that news flew through the land that Israel's great and aged prophet Samuel was dead.[49]

---

45. 1 Samuel 24:17-18
46. 1 Samuel 24:20
47. 1 Samuel 24:21
48. 1 Samuel 24:22
49. 1 Samuel 25:1

He carried to the grave the sorrow that comes to the ordained servants of the Almighty who must serve in an age when the people are not worthy of their leadership. Nevertheless, he died with the joy that belongs to all those who know by the spirit of persuasive revelation that the purposes of God do not fail and that ultimately God's righteousness will prevail.

Samuel was loved by the Lord. His very conception was the reward of fasting and prayer.[50] He was blessed as a youth to be the companion of the High Priest, Eli, and to minister in the holy Tabernacle at Shiloh.[51] He was allowed to have revelations when Eli could not,[52] and when Eli was gone, Samuel rose to the position of prophet, seer and revelator to preside over the affairs of Israel in the same position Moses had held.[53]

At the height of his administration Samuel was able to unite Israel politically and spiritually to a far greater degree than at any time in the three previous centuries. He initiated a religious reform which for a full generation or more purged out the fertility cults with their immoral and obscene rituals.[54] And having cleansed the land of these heathen practices, he obtained permission from the Lord to drive out the heathen Philistines.[55] Under his Moses-like leadership the victory over the Philistines was so decisive that it established peace in the land for the remainder of Samuel's administration.[56]

However, in his later years, Samuel attempted to share the burden of the judgeship with his two sons, Joel and Abiah.[57] To Samuel's great sorrow, these sons took bribes and gifts.[58] They thereby corrupted the judgeship and destroyed the confidence of the people in theocratic government, meaning government under Priesthood leadership. In place of theocracy, the people demanded a king so they could be like the heathen nations around them with the visible glory of royalty, pomp and majestic pageantry.[59] Samuel warned them of the oppressive burden which they

---

50. 1 Samuel, ch. 1
51. 1 Samuel 2:11
52. 1 Samuel, ch. 3
53. 1 Samuel, ch. 7
54. 1 Samuel 7:3-4
55. 1 Samuel 7:9-10
56. 1 Samuel 7:11-14
57. 1 Samuel 8:1-2
58. 1 Samuel 8:3
59. 1 Samuel 8:4-5

would suffer under a monarchy, but the people were adamant.[60] The Lord therefore told Samuel to anoint Saul who had it within him to be a great king if he would just listen to the Lord's prophets. Samuel wrote a whole book of instructions for Saul and the other kings who would follow,[61] but it was of no avail. Unlimited power corrupted Saul as it has so many monarchs in world history. Therefore it was not long before the Lord rejected Saul and told Samuel to anoint David. Meanwhile the Philistines once more began to prey upon the land and it was all Saul could do to keep them from conquering Israel and putting the whole nation under tribute. Not at any time was Saul able to achieve the kind of overwhelming victory which would bring lasting peace to Israel the way Samuel had done.

Samuel did not live long enough to see David ascend the throne. He died at a time when David was a capital fugitive and Saul was bent on his murder. Under David there would be a temporary era of glory, but Samuel died knowing that the real triumph of Israel lay far in the future. His hope was in the coming Messiah and in the glorious epic of the latter days when Israel would finally come into her permanent inheritance of righteous power. It was the same hope which illuminated the vision and lightened the burden of the prophets who followed — Elijah, Isaiah, Ezekiel, Jeremiah, Lehi, Daniel and all those other valiant servants of God who were called to serve during the tempestuous centuries of the fourth thousand years.

Though Israel had not always obeyed Samuel, they knew that his death had torn from their kingdom one of its mightiest pillars. The scripture says that in deepest mourning "all the Israelites were gathered together, and lamented him, and buried him in his house at Ramah."[62]

David Marries Again

One of the heartbreaks of David's years in exile was not merely that he was separated from Michal, his wife, but that he learned somehow that Saul had outraged their

---

60. 1 Samuel 8:11-20
61. 1 Samuel 10:25
62. 1 Samuel 25:1

marriage by compelling Michal to be given in marriage to another man. The man's name was Phalti, the son of Laish of Gallim.[63] It is hard to measure the devastating feelings of David when this bitter news reached him. That it left a permanent scar and never really healed is obvious from subsequent events. Apparently David swore to himself that he would rescue Michal the instant he possessed the legal or military power to do so. For the moment, however, that prospect seemed extremely remote and the next series of events resulted in David getting married again.

The scriptures tell us that as soon as David felt there was going to be a truce between himself and Saul he did not remain at En-Gedi but assumed it would now be safe to return to the southern part of Judah where Gad, the prophet of the Lord, had told him he should try to remain.[64]

David seems to have arrived in the area at a time when it was being molested by bandits, thieves and night raiders from the lower desert. David therefore used his band of 600 to establish a degree of law and order in the region.[65] All that he asked in return was that the wealthier men of Judah support him so that he might keep his forces intact. Among the rich princes of Judah was a man named Nabal (the foolish one). He came from the royal line of Caleb but he proved to be a stiff necked "son of Belial."[66] He accepted David's protection, but was completely contemptible when David's men asked for supplies. As the future king of Israel, David decided to make an example of Nabal. He left 200 men to guard the camp and took 400 men to go up to the rich and extensive possessions of Nabal located in the town of Carmel of Judah.

Fortunately, however, the wealthy, obstreperous Nabal had a beautiful wife, named Abigail, who possessed more sense than her obnoxious husband. She learned through a servant what her husband had done to David and she also learned what David was about to do to her husband.[67] Abigail

---

63. 1 Samuel 25:44
64. 1 Samuel 22:5; 25:1-2
65. See the local herdsmen's description of these circumstances in 1 Samuel 25:15-16.
66. 1 Samuel 25:17. This is a term anciently used for worthless individuals who were believed to be servants of the devil. (See Peloubet's *Bible Dictionary* under Belial.)
67. 1 Samuel 25:14-17

immediately recognized that two headstrong men were about to propel themselves into an irreparable collision. Almost instinctively she seemed to sense that here was a situation where a beautiful woman could use her good offices to prevent a great disaster. Abigail therefore contrived a plan which would first undo the injury committed by her husband and then erase the mischief so resolutely planned by David.

First she prepared a great quantity of choice food stuffs and then hastened with her heavily laden pack train to intercept David and his men. When the son of Jesse and his band came into sight it was obvious that David was in a high temper and bent on sacking the nearby settlement. As David came near, Abigail suddenly threw herself on the ground before him and unburdened her soul with one of the most eloquent pleas ever attributed to a woman of antiquity.[68]

Abigail freely confessed the stupidity of her husband whom she said was appropriately called Nabal (the foolish one),[69] but then she appealed to David's sense of justice and honor. She reminded him that David was famous as a man of great virtue and goodness and that the shedding of blood in this helpless village would mar his record after he became king. She showed him the supplies she had brought and asked David to accept them and be satisfied.[70]

The sheer logic as well as the marvelous eloquence of Abigail's speech stopped David in his tracks. It brought him to his senses. After meditating a moment he said to her, "Blessed be the Lord God of Israel, which sent thee this day to meet me: And blessed be thy advice, and blessed be thou, which hast kept me this day from coming to shed blood, and from avenging myself with mine own hand."[71]

He accepted her stores with deepest appreciation and then said to her, "Go up in peace to thine house; see, I have hearkened to thy voice, and have accepted thy person."[72]

No doubt Abigail went home rejoicing. David had been impressed by her and she certainly had been impressed by him. Abigail had great news to tell her husband.

68. 1 Samuel 25:24-31
69. 1 Samuel 25:25
70. 1 Samuel 25:27
71. 1 Samuel 25:32-33
72. 1 Samuel 25:35

But when she reached home she couldn't even talk with her husband. She discovered that a great feast was in riotous progress and her husband was roaring drunk.[73] Obviously there was no opportunity to tell him the good news until he became sober. It was therefore not until the next morning when the bilious Nabal was trying to collect his senses that Abigail was able to tell him how close he had come to disaster. She assured him that all was well because David had listened to her pleas.

Nabal's reaction was amazing. Instead of being filled with relief and thanksgiving the enraged old man collapsed with a heart attack![74] He lingered for ten days and then died.[75]

When word reached David that Nabal was dead the future king of Israel decided that he had found a future queen. The scripture says Abigail was "a woman of good understanding, and of a beautiful countenance."[76] Apparently neither of these had escaped David's attention. "And David sent and communed with Abigail, to take her to him to wife."

Abigail did not hesitate a moment. The genuine possibility of a brilliant romantic awakening had suddenly come into her life. She took five maidens and went to meet David. They were married immediately.[77] As nearly as we can tell David was now twenty-eight.[78]

SAUL DECLARES A NEW WAR ON DAVID

These events had barely transpired when history began to repeat itself. The people of Ziph went up for the second time to try to betray David into the hands of Saul. In spite of the king's profound repentance at En-Gedi, he now

---

73. 1 Samuel 25:36
74. 1 Samuel 25:37
75. 1 Samuel 25:38
76. 1 Samuel 25:3
77. 1 Samuel 25:42. It is significant that while this beautiful woman already knew David would one day be king (see 1 Samuel 25:30) she did not become his wife because of queenly ambitions. She accepted David's proposal of marriage in the deepest of humility, saying, "Behold, let thine handmaid be a servant . . ." (1 Samuel 25:41)
78. 1 Samuel 25:39. We derive this from the fact that after his marriage to Abigail, David spent a year and four months at Ziklag (1 Samuel 27:7) before becoming king of Judah at the age of 30 (2 Samuel 5:4).

allowed his bitter jealously toward David to rise once again and overwhelm him.

Blind with resurging hate, Saul once more took three thousand chosen men and marched into Judah. His commander in chief was a man named Abner. This Abner was the son of Ner, Saul's paternal uncle, which would make Abner Saul's first cousin.[79] Abner was to have a long and singular influence in the career of David and therefore his name is one to be remembered.

The moment David received word that Saul was head-hunting again, he rallied his band and retreated into the south desert, but Saul followed him. In the vicinity of the wilderness area where David's forces were hiding, Saul decided to make camp. As was the custom during field operations, Saul had a trench dug and slept in it while his personal body guards and Abner, his commander, spread their bedrolls nearby to protect him.[80]

David watched these operations from his hiding place and then decided to attempt once more to reach the light of reason in Saul's mind. David said to his men, "Who will go down with me to Saul to the camp?"[81] Abishai, one of David's nephews,[82] volunteered to go. David didn't know it, but one day this young nephew would save David's life.

David took Abishai and crept down into the camp where they found the guards fast asleep. David and his nephew came up quietly beside the sleeping Saul and Abishai whispered, "God hath delivered thine enemy into thine hand this day: now therefore let me smite him . . ."[83] But David responded with the first complete explanation as to why he refused to slay Saul on this occasion or the previous one at En-gedi. "Destroy him not," said David, "for who can stretch forth his hand against the Lord's anointed, and be guiltless? . . . As the Lord liveth, THE LORD SHALL SMITE HIM: OR HIS DAY SHALL COME TO DIE:

79. 1 Samuel 14:50; 1 Chronicles 9:36, 39
80. 1 Samuel 26:5
81. 1 Samuel 26:6
82. Abishai was the son of David's sister, Zeruiah. She also had two other sons who figured prominently in the life of David named Joab and Asahel. (1 Chr. 2:16)
83. 1 Samuel 26:8

OR HE SHALL DESCEND INTO BATTLE, AND PERISH."[84] In other words, be patient, Saul's life is in the hands of God and everything will be worked out in the due time of the Lord.

Thereupon David and Abishai took Saul's spear and water cruse and departed.

The next day David ascended a high hill overlooking the camp of Saul and shouted to Abner, the commander of Saul's army, "This thing is not good that thou hast done. As the Lord liveth, ye are worthy to die, because ye have not kept your master, the Lord's anointed."[85] Then he taunted Abner by saying, "And now see where the king's spear is, and the cruse of water that was at his bolster."[86]

At this point Saul interrupted. He recognized the voice as being that of David and therefore cried out, "Is this thy voice, my son David? And David said, It is my voice, my lord, O king."[87] Saul immediately realized that since his spear and cruse of water were missing this must mean that during the night David had been close enough to the king to kill him and had taken these articles to prove it. Saul shouted up to David, "I have sinned; return, my son David: for I will no more do thee harm, because my soul was precious in thine eyes this day: behold I have played the fool, and have erred exceedingly."[88]

So David had reached the light of reason in Saul's mind the second time, even as he did at En-gedi. Holding aloft Saul's war javelin, David cried out, "Behold the king's spear! And let one of the young men come over and fetch it."[89]

Saul replied, "Blessed be thou my son David: thou shalt both do great things, and also shalt still prevail."[90]

The Bible closes the incident by saying, "So David went on his way, and Saul returned to his place."[91]

---

84. 1 Samuel 26:9-10
85. 1 Samuel 26:16
86. Ibid.
87. 1 Samuel 26:17
88. 1 Samuel 26:21
89. 1 Samuel 26:22
90. 1 Samuel 26:25
91. Ibid.

David Flees to the Philistines

In spite of these events, however, it was now clear to David that there was no hope of a permanent respite from Saul's persecution. No matter how determined Saul seemed to be to suppress his jealousy toward David, it was an obsession which he seemed unable to permanently control or purge from his soul. Therefore, "David said in his heart, I shall now perish one day by the hand of Saul: there is nothing better for me than that I should speedily escape into the land of the Philistines; and Saul shall despair of me, to seek me any more in any coast of Israel: so shall I escape out of his hand."[92]

David thereupon took his six hundred followers and went over to Gath, the home of Goliath. This was the city from which David had barely escaped some time earlier when he employed the stratagem of madness. At that time he "scrabbled on the doors of the gate, and let his spittle fall down upon his beard."[93] In disgust, the king had ordered David ousted. But now things were different. Perhaps king Achish of Gath did not even associate the previous lunatic fellow with David. In any event David and his band were welcomed. To Achish it was enough that David was a fugitive from Saul and had come seeking asylum. What was more important, David had a field-tested cadre of 600 troops which could provide a professional contingent of loyal mercenaries to implement the military might of Achish the next time he went to war.

Not only did Achish welcome David and his 600 soldiers, but he allowed them to bring down their families as well.[94] David brought with him Abigail and also a second wife, Ahinoam of Jezreel.[95] After a short time David asked permission to move his entire entourage to some area where they could have a city of their own. King Achish gave David and his band a village called Ziklag.[96] This settlement is

---

92. 1 Samuel 27:1
93. 1 Samuel 21:13
94. 1 Samuel 27:3
95. Ibid. Since Ahinoam was the first to bear David a son (Ammon) she is usually listed before Abigail when David's wives are named. However, 1 Samuel 25:43 would indicate that David married Abigail before he married Ahinoam.
96. 1 Samuel 27:5-6

believed to have been located partway between Gath and Beer-Sheba. It was therefore convenient to the desert country where Israel's ancient enemies still prevailed.

David and his band launched raids into this area and devastated the seats of power of the Geshurites, Gezerites and the Amalekites.[97] The latter were a remnant of those who were broken off from the main body of the people which the Lord had previously declared anathema.[98] By attacking these allies of the Philistines David was strengthening the future position of Israel but weakening the posture of the coastal federation of heathen warlords with which king Achish of Gath was identified. When Achish asked David what he had been doing David's reply indicated that he already looked upon himself as a fifth column in the camp of the Philistine enemy which had been so cruel to Israel in the past. David told Achish that he had been attacking tribes south of Judah.[99] King Achish assumed that these must be Israelites and he therefore declared to his court that David "hath made his people Israel utterly to abhor him; therefore he shall be my servant forever.[100]

The anxiety of Achish to have dedicated allies at this particular time was of paramount importance because the Philistines were preparing to launch the biggest attack against Israel in many years.

David surely must have been aware of all this and it undoubtedly accounts for the deceptive role he now deliberately played as he attempted to build his band into a sabotage unit or fifth column. Getting Achish to accept him was a most essential part of David's stratagem. As preparations continued, Achish assured David that he and his men would soon have an opportunity to avenge themselves on Saul. "Know thou assuredly," said Achish, "that thou shalt go out with me to battle, thou and thy men."[101] David could

---

97. 1 Samuel 27:8-9
98. 1 Samuel 15:2-3
99. 1 Samuel 27:10-11. This last verse demonstrates the fierceneess with which war was fought on these frontiers. The fact that David followed the barbaric customs of desert warfare is not to his credit. However, the spirit of desperate survival which existed at the time apparently moved the Lord to be more lenient in judging such actions than men of modern refinement would be inclined to allow.
100. 1 Samuel 27:12   101. 1 Samuel 28:1

only reply to Achish in an oblique manner by saying, "Surely thou shalt know what thy servant can do."[102] Achish saw nothing suspicious in the reply. Of course he knew what David could do. This son of Jesse was the mighty Goliath-killer. And he had spilled plenty of additional Philistine blood besides. Now, however, it was good to have him on the side of the Philistines, together with his 600 men. In a supreme manifestation of personal confidence the heathen king said to David, "Therefore will I make thee keeper of mine head for ever!"[103]

DAVID IS EXCLUDED FROM THE PHILISTINE WAR BUT GETS INTO ANOTHER ONE

The original rendezvous point for the Philistine troops was at Aphek[104] (located north of Joppa and a little inland). When the commanders looked over their forces they observed that Achish, king of Gath, had brought along with him that tough, hardy band belonging to David the Israelite.[105] The lords of the Philistines protested vehemently and severely chided Achish for taking such a ridiculous risk by having David, the notorious Goliath-killer, planted within their battle ranks.[106]

Achish stoutly defended David and expressed the utmost confidence in him. However, the lords of Philistine were adamant. There was not going to be any 600 Israelites bringing up the rear as the Philistines went into this war. Achish broke the news to David and the son of Jesse reacted the way Achish had feared he might. "But what have I done?" David said, "And what hast thou found in thy servant so long as I have been with thee unto this day, that I may not go fight against the enemies of my lord the king?"[107]

Achish assured David that he had nothing but the highest regard for him. Nevertheless the decision had been made and David must return. No doubt David had seen a monumental opportunity to spread chaos among the ranks of the Philistines as they launched their attack on Israel. His rear guard action might well have been the deciding factor

---

102. 1 Samuel 28:2
103. Ibid.
104. 1 Samuel 29:1-2
105. 1 Samuel 29:3
106. 1 Samuel 29:4-5
107. 1 Samuel 29:8

which could have tipped the outcome of the war. But the princes of the Philistines were too experienced in using this type of stratagem themselves. They refused to take a chance on David and told him he must go. So the scripture says "David and his men rose up early to depart in the morning, to return into the land of the Philistines. And the Philistines went up to Jezreel."[108] Little did David realize what was awaiting him back home.

When David and his men arrived at Ziklag they found their city in ashes![109] While they had been at Aphek a remnant of the Amalekites had come in from the desert and sacked the city. They had taken all their possessions, and, worst of all, kidnapped their wives and children. David soon learned that the Amalekites had also sacked other cities in southern Philistia since the mobilization for the war against Israel had left all of them virtually defenseless.

David asked Abiathar, the priest, to inquire of the Lord for guidance whereupon David received a promise that if he pursued after the Amalekites he would recover everything, including the wives and children.[110]

David immediately ordered his band to hurry forward, but they were already so weary from marching that by the time they reached the brook Besor, 200 of the men collapsed from exhaustion. David therefore left them behind with the heavier baggage while the remainder pressed rapidly forward. Enroute, David found a young Egyptian who had been a servant to one of the Amalekites but had been abandoned in the desert when he became ill. This young man heartily agreed to lead David to the encampment of the wretched Amalekites.

When David and his remaining 400 men finally reached the Amalekites they were able to move in on the camp with such ferocity that only those with camels were able to escape.[111] The women and children were found safe and all of the booty was recovered together with generous volumes of loot from other cities. David and his men gathered it all together and then, in company with their wives and children, joyously turned homeward.

---

108. 1 Samuel 29:11
109. 1 Samuel 30:1
110. 1 Samuel 30:8
111. 1 Samuel 30:17

Saul Panics as He faces the Great Last Battle of His Life

While all these events were transpiring in the south, the Philistine war against Israel was getting under way in the north.

In the past the Philistine hosts had usually made their attack by fighting their way up the rugged Sorek or Elah valleys and thereafter ascending directly into the mountainous region of Judah, Benjamin or Ephraim. This time, however, the Philistines had elected to fight the war in the open spaces of two northern valleys where they could use their chariots and avoid the guerilla tactics which the mountain men of Israel were learning to use so effectively.

A topographical map will show that beginning in the region of modern Haifa and Mount Carmel there is a broad valley which sweeps eastward. This is called the valley of Esdraelon. It extends beyond Meggido and then joins what is called the valley of Jezreel as it passes on down to the Jordan River. Through these two valleys there formerly ran one of the oldest and richest trade routes of the ancient world. It was the caravan route which joined Egypt to Mesopotamia. The Philistines therefore had this special reason why they wished to dominate the area and it seemed quite logical that this should be the place from which to launch a new war against Israel.

When Saul saw what massive preparations the Philistines were making he knew the Israelites were confronted with one of the greatest crises of their history. It was as great as the crisis which Samuel had encountered when he faced the forces of the Philistines at Ebenezer so many years before.[112]

But at Ebenezer the armies of Israel had been directed by the prophet of God. Furthermore, God had intervened to assure them a victory.[113] However, in this present trouble Saul found that the heavens were as brass. Zadok was the High Priest but, as we have previously noted, the Urim and Thummim apparently went with the ephod when Abiathar

---

112. 1 Samuel 7:12-14
113. 1 Samuel 7:10

fled from the massacre of the priests at Nob and joined David.[114] Saul could therefore get no divine guidance from any source whatever. Samuel was dead and the scripture says, ". . . the Lord answered him not, neither by dreams, nor by Urim, nor by prophets."[115]

Yet if ever Saul needed guidance from beyond the veil it was now. Saul finally resorted to a tactic of deepest desperation. He decided to try to get through to Samuel by means of a spiritualist medium. Saul himself had previously cleansed the land of sooth-sayers, wizards, and such[116] so he was not entirely sure that any who worked with familiar spirits were still in existence. His servants, however, told him of the witch "at En-dor."[117] En-dor turned out to be a short distance northward toward Nazareth. This meant Saul would have to cross the valley of Jezreel where the Philistines were camped in order to get to the witch. He decided to risk it and the dangerous journey was somehow negotiated.

The old woman received Saul, not knowing who he was. When Saul made his strange request she said, "Behold, thou knowest what Saul hath done, how he hath cut off those that have familiar spirits, and the wizards, out of the land: wherefore then layest thou a snare for my life, to cause me to die?"[118] But Saul replied, "As the Lord liveth, there shall no punishment happen to thee for this thing."[119]

"Then said the woman, Whom shall I bring up unto thee? And he said, Bring me up Samuel. And when the woman saw Samuel, she cried with a loud voice: and the woman spake to Saul, saying, Why hast thou deceived me? for thou art Saul. And the king said unto her, Be not afraid; for what sawest thou?"[120]

The woman claimed that she had seen Elohim ascending out of the earth.[121] Then she claimed she saw an old man

---

114. 1 Samuel 23:6, 9
115. 1 Samuel 28:6
116. 1 Samuel 28:3
117. 1 Samuel 28:7
118. 1 Samuel 28:9
119. 1 Samuel 28:10
120. 1 Samuel 28:11-12
121. 1 Samuel 28:13. The word, *Elohim*, in the original is translated "gods" in the King James translation of this verse.

coming up "covered with a mantle." Saul believed this must be Samuel so "he stooped with his face to the ground, and bowed himself."[122]

Then he heard a voice through the medium say, "Why hast thou disquieted me, to bring me up? and Saul answered, I am sore distressed; for the Philistines make war against me, and God is departed from me, and answereth me no more, neither by prophets, nor by dreams: therefore I have called thee, that thou mayest make known unto me what I shall do."[123]

The phantom voice then replied, "Wherefore then dost thou ask of me, seeing the Lord is departed from thee, and is become thine enemy? And the Lord hath done to him [Saul] as he spake by me: for the Lord hath rent the kingdom out of thine hand and given it to thy neighbour, even to David. . . . Moreover the Lord will also deliver Israel with thee into the hand of the Philistines: and to-morrow shalt thou and thy sons be with me: the Lord also shall deliver the host of Israel into the hand of the Philistines."[124]

This ugly doomsday prophecy with all its dark and bitter implications was too much for Saul. He went into a state of complete psychological shock and fell helplessly to the ground. The woman and the king's military aids raised him up and finally induced the king to eat a little for he had fasted all that day and night.[125] Finally, having recov-

---

122. 1 Samuel 28:14
123. 1 Samuel 28:15
124. 1 Samuel 28:16-19. The reader should keep in mind that this entire incident was typical of spiritual seances. One of the standard devices of "familiar" spirits is to pretend that they are some famous person (such as Samuel) and then deliver a message which, if it turns out to be correct, will give that spirit and its medium influence among men. Note that only the medium claimed to see anything. Saul heard only the medium's voice and the description of a spirit whom he assumed to be Samuel. While in the spirit world, Samuel would be under as strong a commandment to avoid the witch of En-dor as he was while alive. No member of the Priesthood beyond the veil would respond to the call of such a woman. Certainly God who had not allowed his prophets to give a revelation to Saul would not turn around to give credence to the witch of En-dor by authorizing Samuel to speak through her. What Saul heard was a deceptive communication from an imposter spirit pretending to be Samuel. Under the prevailing circumstances the spirit would not have required any particular genius to see that Saul was going to lose the coming battle. Hence the doomsday prophecy which was soon fulfilled.
125. 1 Samuel 28:20

ered a little strength, Saul "rose up, and went away that night."[126] Tomorrow would be the battle.

THE FALL OF SAUL

Perhaps if Saul had not spent so much of his time and energy trying to murder David he would have been better prepared to match the might of the Philistine armies. As it was, however, the numerical superiority, the advanced training and latest equipment, gave the Philistines a far superior fighting machine compared to Israel. Saul must have realized this right from the beginning. Perhaps his soldiers did too. In any event, their defense lines did not hold. Almost before the war was fully launched the ranks of Israel began to waver. The next thing Saul knew his mighty army had crumbled and left him with a heap of tactical ruins. Thousands of the Israelites were fleeing wildly in every direction trying to escape from threatened extinction.

When Saul realized that the war was lost, he frantically rallied his personal bodyguard and fled toward the mountains of Gilboa which border the valley of Jezreel along the south. Among those who gathered about the king in these last furious moments of his life were the three princes of Israel, the sons of Saul. The scripture says, "And the Philistines followed hard upon Saul and upon his sons."[127] We know that some of those who pursued them were Philistines in chariots,[128] but as Saul's entourage clambered into the ascending labyrinths of Gilboa's crags and forests the chariots would have found it impossible to follow. No doubt the chase was given over to the foot soldiers and archers.

Saul's valiant son, Prince Jonathan with his two brothers, apparently kept themselves between the king and the avenging pursuers, but it was in vain. One by one they were hewn down.[129]

Saul forced his heavily armored and exhausted body to plod on but the Philistines were not to be cheated of their prey. The pursuing archers sent a whole volley of arrows hurtling after the huge frame of the fleeing Saul. And

---

126. 1 Samuel 28:25
127. 1 Samuel 31:2

128. 2 Samuel 1:6
129. 1 Samuel 31:2

the scripture says "he was sore wounded."[130] Then followed the final frantic moments of clawing and climbing, trying to escape.

Finally, somewhere up there among the limestone ramparts of Mount Gilboa, the critically wounded, heartsick Saul pulled his armor-bearer with him into a hidden cloister offering temporary respite from the pestilence of the enemy. There, with the prophecy of the witch's phantom at En-dor echoing in the corridors of his haunted brain, and with the protruding, blood-spattered shafts quivering in his flesh, Saul came to a dreadful, desperate decision. These heathens would never take him alive! He would destroy himself.

Seizing upon this last companion, his armor-bearer, Saul commanded, "Draw thy sword, and thrust me through therewith; lest these uncircumcised come and thrust me through, and abuse me."[131]

But this frightened Israelite soldier who so often had offered his own life to save Saul's could not compel himself to perform the act. On Saul's command he would die for the king, but no command could induce him to kill the king. Disgusted, and blinded by pain, Saul seized a sword, probably his own, and thrusting the blade between the sheath of his armour, fell full-length upon it.[132]

"And when his armour-bearer saw that Saul was dead, he fell likewise upon his sword, and died with him.

"So Saul died, and his three sons, and his armour-bearer, and all his men that same day together."[133]

It was a fearful and devastating defeat. Not only were the armies of Israel decimated but many of the cities which the Israelites had occupied for centuries were now overrun and taken as the fruits of conquest by the Philistines.[134] The gruesome finale to the rout occurred the following day when the Philistines came back to strip the bodies of Israel's dead.

---

130. 1 Samuel 31:3
131. 1 Samuel 31:4
132. Ibid. Since we know from verse 9 that Saul was wearing his armor, he would be compelled to guide the blade between the plates before falling upon it.
133. 1 Samuel 31:5-6
134. 1 Samuel 31:7

Among the slain they found the bodies of Saul and his three sons.[135] Apparently the Philistines were unaware that the king of Israel and his sons had actually fallen. With the wildest exultation they cut off Saul's head as a trophy and stripped his armour for exhibition in their leading heathen temples.[136] Finally, they hung Saul's mutilated remains on the wall of Beth-shan, a nearby Philistine city. News of these sadistic proceedings reached some of the Israelites living in Jabesh-Gilead (a city in Trans-Jordan), which Saul had rescued from the Ammonites many years before.[137] These grateful people decided to rescue the body of Saul before it was further desecrated. Coming by night and with the greatest of stealth, they entered Beth-shan and found not only the body of Saul hanging on the wall, but the bodies of his three sons as well. They quickly removed all four of them and took their remains a safe distance from Beth-shan where they burned them. The bones and ashes were then gathered together and buried under a tree at Jabesh.[138]

Thus concludes the first book of Samuel and the last sad chapter in the torturous life of Saul, the first king of Israel.

---

135. 1 Samuel 31:8
136. 1 Samuel 31:9
137. 1 Samuel, ch. 11
138. 1 Samuel 31:10-13

Scripture Reading and Questions on Chapter Three

Scripture Reading: 1 Samuel, chapters 22 to 31 inclusive.

1—How did Saul find out that David had obtained food and secured the sword of Goliath from the Lord's Tabernacle?

2—What happened to the priests at Nob? Who was the lone survivor? What did he do? Was this helpful to David?

3—What great crime did Saul commit against the people of Gibeon? Who had promised that Israel would protect these people?

4—When Jonathan contacted David for the last time what remarkable statement did he make to David?

5—When the people of Ziph betrayed David, how did he happen to escape just as Saul was closing in?

6—What is the region of En-gedi famous for today? Describe the contact between David and Saul in the cave at En-gedi.

7—Did Saul know that David was going to replace him as king? How do we know?

8—Briefly summarize the life of Samuel. Where was he buried?

9—How did David happen to meet Abigail? What made it possible for David to marry her? What had happened to Michal?

10—Who was Abishai? What relationship was he to David? Who were Abishai's two brothers?

11—In spite of Saul's assurance, why did David flee to the Philistines?

12—What had happened when David visited Gath some time earlier? Why was he more cordially welcomed this second time?

13—Who was David's wife after Abigail? Why is she usually listed first?

14—When David moved his band to Ziklag what did he start doing to the tribes in the nearby desert? What appears to have been his reason?

15—Assuming David considered himself at war with the Philistines, was his conduct understandable?

16—Did Achish suspect David? What did he say?

17—Why didn't the lords of the Philistines want David to fight with them? How did Achish feel? What did they force David and his men to do?

18—Why did Saul seek out the witch of En-Dor? Was it dangerous to go there?

19—Do you think Saul actually talked with Samuel? Explain.

20—Describe the end of Saul's life. How did he die? What happened to his body when it fell into the hands of the Philistines?

21—Why did the people of Jabesh-Gilead feel impelled to rescue Saul's body? What did they do with it?

CHAPTER FOUR

David the Fugitive Becomes David the King

The news of Saul's death and Israel's military catastrophy reached David just three days after he returned to his sacked, fire-gutted headquarters at Ziklag.[1] It will be recalled that when David had discovered the ravaged settlement on his return from Aphek, he had pursued the Amalekite marauders to their desert haunts. There he had rescued the kidnapped wives and children from Ziklag, recovered the bounteous loot which the Amalekite raiders had obtained from all south Philistia, and then he had dispatched the raiders to the shades of limbo or scattered them to the four winds.

When David and his people returned to Ziklag they were confronted with the task of rebuilding the entire settlement. These operations had barely begun when there burst into camp a wild looking man "with his clothes rent, and earth upon his head."[2] He fell exhausted on the ground before David.

---

1. 2 Samuel 1:1-2
2. 2 Samuel 1:2. This practice of ripping one's clothes and putting soil or ashes on the head "were signs of sorrow and distress among all nations. The clothes rent, signified the rending, dividing, and scattering, of the people; the earth or ashes on the head, signified their humiliaton." (Clarke, *Bible Commentary*, Vol. 2, p. 220)

"And David said unto him, From whence comest thou? And he said unto him, Out of the camp of Israel am I escaped. And David said unto him, How went the matter? I pray thee, tell me. And he answered, That the people are fled from the battle, and many of the people also are fallen and dead; and Saul and Jonathan his son are dead also."[3]

The messenger probably had no comprehension of the explosive bolt which this alarming and dreadful news shot into the heart of David. It must have seemed incredible that the mighty Saul and Jonathan, that best-beloved and truest of all friends, were dead.

David demanded of the man, "How knowest thou that Saul and Jonathan his son be dead?"[4]

Had the messenger told the truth he would have saved his life. However, instead of stating simply that Saul had committed suicide he apparently hoped to ingratiate himself with David by pretending that he, himself, had killed the man who was David's professed enemy. Here is the story as the man told it. Note that the most important part was a lie.

"As I happened by chance upon Mount Gilboa, behold, Saul leaned upon his spear; and, lo, the chariots and horsemen followed hard after him. And when he looked behind him, he saw me, and called unto me. And I answered, Here am I. And he said unto me, Who art thou? And I answered him, I am an Amalekite. He said unto me again, Stand, I pray thee, upon me, and slay me: for anguish is come upon me, because my life is yet whole in me. So I stood upon him, and slew him, because I was sure that he could not live after that he was fallen: and I took the crown that was upon his head, and the bracelet that was on his arm, and have brought them hither unto my lord."[5]

Two things seemed immediately apparent to David. First, that Saul and Jonathan were indeed dead and secondly, that this impudent Amalekite had dared to kill Saul and rush

3. 2 Samuel 1:3-4
4. 2 Samuel 1:5
5. 2 Samuel 1:6-10

his crown to David thinking he might be rewarded with some rich bounty or a high office.[6] Because of David's own supreme estimate of the sanctity of the regal office this man's claim that he had killed Saul triggered an eruption of furious indignation in David. Under the emotional stress of the moment David turned to one of his band and cried, "Go near, and fall upon him!" As the Amalekite went down under the soldier's blow, David said, "Thy blood be upon thy head; for thy mouth hath testified against thee, saying, I have slain the Lord's anointed."[7]

The deceitful words by which the Amalekite had hoped to gain a fortune had cost him his life.

DAVID'S PSALM OF SORROW

Then David, in the most profound misery, rent his clothes and went into mourning. So did the members of his band. The scripture says, "they mourned, and wept, and fasted until even, for Saul, and for Jonathan his son and for the people of the Lord, and for the house of Israel; because they were fallen by the sword."[8]

Out of this moment of his soul's most oppressive sorrow David drained the emotional force to create one of his most notable compositions. It is called *Kadesh* or *The Song of the Bow*. In it David revealed the same devotion to Saul in death that he honored him with during life, and the same affection for Jonathan that he had expressed so often during their many years of closest friendship together. The gripping power and naked misery of this poem is felt most vividly in the original Hebrew, but certainly a sense of its torture and tears may be felt even in the translation. Here is what David sang:[9]

The Song of the Bow

The Beauty of Israel is slain
Upon thy high places:
How are the mighty fallen!
Tell it not in Gath,
Publish it not in the streets of Askelon;
Lest the daughters of the Philistines rejoice,
Lest the daughters of the uncircumcised triumph.

6. 2 Samuel 4:10
7. 2 Samuel 1:16
8. 2 Samuel 1:12
9. 2 Samuel 1:19-27

Ye mountains of Gilboa,
Let there be no dew,
Neither let there be rain upon you,
Nor fields of offerings:
For there the shield of the mighty
Is vilely cast away,
The shield of Saul,
As though he had not been anointed with oil.

From the blood of the slain,
From the fat of the mighty,
The bow of Jonathan turned not back,
And the sword of Saul
Returned not empty.

Saul and Jonathan were lovely
And pleasant in their lives,
And in their death they were not divided:
They were swifter than eagles,
They were stronger than lions.

Ye daughters of Israel,
Weep over Saul,
Who clothed you in scarlet,
With other delights,
Who put on ornaments of gold
Upon your apparel.

How are the mighty fallen
In the midst of the battle!
O Jonathan, thou wast slain
In thine high places.
I am distressed for thee,
My brother Jonathan:
Very pleasant hast thou been unto me:
Thy love to me was wonderful,
Passing the love of women.

How are the mighty fallen,
And the weapons of war perished!

DAVID WAITS UPON THE LORD

After the overwhelming defeat of Israel's army at Jezreel and Mount Gilboa, it was almost a miracle that the Philistines did not immediately take advantage of their victory by sweeping south along the mountains of Ephraim and Judah making bond servants out of the whole nation. But fortunately for Israel, they did not. This gave Israel time to recoup some of their loses, regroup some of their strength and prepare a new defense.

As for David, he waited on the Lord. For the moment the people of Israel were defeated, fragmented, demoralized and to a certain extent, apostate. They were not easily led, even by the Lord. David knew this and so he sought for guidance, probably through Abiathar, the High Priest, who was with him. The scripture says, "David inquired of the Lord, saying, Shall I go up into any of the cities of Judah? And the Lord said unto him, Go up. And David said, Whither shall I go up? And he said, Unto Hebron."[10]

Hebron was the capital city of Judah and straight up into the mountains from Ziklag, so the journey there was made quickly. The Lord already knew how the mood of the people had radically changed since the death and defeat of Saul. Earlier, some of the people such as the inhabitants of Keilah[11] and Ziph[12] had tried to betray David into Saul's hands, but now that Saul was gone this very man they had tried to betray seemed the logical choice for their king. No doubt the word also had been spreading that Samuel, the revered prophet so recently dead, had personally anointed David to be Saul's successor.

Therefore, no sooner had David arrived in Hebron than the Elders of Judah called a great convocation and anointed David their king.[13]

From these men David was able to learn more details concerning the death of Saul and his sons. One of the things they related was the fact that the men of Jabesh-Gilead had risked their lives to rescue the bodies of the king and his princes and decently dispose of them. David's first official act as king was to send a message to the men of Jabesh-Gilead thanking them for what they had done.[14] He also included a subtle suggestion designed to have them initiate a movement to get David properly recognized as the king of all Israel. This was extremely delicate and note how carefully David worded his veiled suggestion. Said he,

10. 2 Samuel 2:1
11. 1 Samuel 23:10-13
12. 1 Samuel 23:19-20; 24:1-2
13. 2 Samuel 2:4
14. 2 Samuel 2:5-6

". . . now let your hands be strengthened, and ye be valiant:
for your master Saul is dead, and also the house of Judah
have anointed me king over them."[15] But perhaps the suggestion was *too* subtle. At least nothing ever came of it.
In fact David had to wait more than seven years before the
northern tribes would accept him as king.[16]

The Northern Tribes Set Up a Separate King

The one subject on which human beings are least likely
to listen to God is with reference to politics. Just as Israel
had rejected God's prophets as their governors and demanded a king during Samuel's day, so now the majority
of them refused to accept David whom God had designated
as the one best fitted to serve them as king. The northern
tribes placed themselves under one of Saul's surviving sons.

The attempt to re-establish the house of Saul was initiated by Saul's cousin, the man named Abner, who had served
as Saul's commander-in-chief.[17] It will be recalled that Abner
was the man David had chided when that commander
was supposed to be guarding the sleeping Saul. David
and his nephew, Abishai, had been able to creep close
enough to the king to kill him, but instead they had merely
seized his spear and water cruse as proof of their feat.[18]
After such an incident it is understandable why Abner might
feel somewhat less than ecstatic about the prospect of David
becoming king, even though he knew the son of Jesse had
been designated by the Lord to that high calling.[19] And
equally understandable, perhaps, was Abner's fixed determination to preserve the dynasty of Saul and keep one of
his sons on the throne. After all, Saul's family were all
relatives of Abner. Certainly Abner would never have
guessed that one day he would be joining David!

The name of Saul's son whom Abner manipulated to
the throne of the northern kingdom, was Ishbosheth, and
he was forty years of age when the event took place.[20]
Subsequent history demonstrates, however, that it was Abner
and not Ishbosheth who was the real ruler of the northern
tribes. Ishbosheth was merely a figurehead or puppet king.

---

15. 2 Samuel 2:7
16. 2 Samuel 2:11
17. 1 Samuel 14:50

18. 1 Samuel 26:13-16
19. 2 Samuel 3:17-18
20. 2 Samuel 2:8-10

As already mentioned, Abner found it prudent to set up the capital for the ten northern tribes on the eastern side of Jordan (Trans-Jordan) since the Philistines, by virtue of their conquest, now had easy access to Ephraim and Benjamin where the former capitals of Israel had been located. The new capital was situated a short distance from the Jabbok river and was called Mahanaim.[21]

Hostilities Erupt Between the Forces of David and Abner

However, it would appear that after two years,[22] General Abner of the northern kingdom felt safe enough to take a body of men and make an excursion over to Gibeon of Benjamin[23] which was just a few miles from Saul's former capital at Gibeah. Abner ran into immediate resistance, however. It did not come from Saul's conquerors, the Philistines, but from General Joab, nephew of King David and the commander-in-chief of the territory of Judah. By coming to Gibeon as the military commander for the whole northern kingdom Abner was treading on thin political ice even though he was technically within his own tribal territory of Benjamin.

At first the two hostile parties appear to have met at the pool of Gideon and parleyed together.[24] Then it seems that Abner suggested that each side put up twelve men for a little sham battle to entertain them and show off their respective agilities. "Let the young men now arise, and play before us," said Abner.[25] This "play" may have been intended merely as a joust; however, when the twenty-four soldiers stood up and paired off, the "play" was abandoned in favor of premeditated mayhem. "And they caught every one his fellow by the head [the beard or long hair, no doubt], and

---

21. 2 Samuel 2:8
22. Reference to the "two years" is in 2 Samuel 2:10 where it is rendered in such a way that it sounds as though this is the duration of Ishbosheth's reign. However, Ishbosheth is later described as reigning as long as David was in Judah (7½ years according to 2 Samuel 2:11) and therefore Clarke believes this passage should have said that after Ishbosheth had reigned two years the following events transpired. This is the meaning ascribed to it above. (See Clarke, *Bible Commentary*, Vol. 2, p. 312)
23. 2 Samuel 2:12
24. 2 Samuel 2:13
25. 2 Samuel 2:14

thrust his sword in his fellow's side; so they fell down together. . . ."[26]

This spilling of blood was the signal for fierce and open warfare between the two forces. "And there was a very sore battle that day; and Abner was beaten. . . ."[27] So Abner fled from the scene with the survivors of his party. However, as he was endeavoring to escape he noticed a very fleet-footed young soldier following after him and "he turned not to the right hand nor to the left."[28] Abner shouted back at the young man to determine his identity and discovered that it was Asahel, the younger brother of Joab and Abishai, the nephews of David. Abner recognized this as a critical situation not only for himself but for all Israel. If he turned around and slew the young man it might very well start a blood feud between the house of Saul and the house of David. On the other hand, if he did not take some kind of action quickly, Abner knew he would be slain himself. The fleeing general therefore shouted back to young Asahel, "Turn thee aside from following me: wherefore should I smite thee to the ground? How then should I hold up my face to Joab thy brother?[29]

But Asahel paid no attention. He was catching up with Abner and closing in for the kill. "Wherefore Abner with the hinder end of the spear smote him under the fifth rib, that the spear came out behind him; and he fell down there, and died in the same place. . . ."[30]

This fatal incident inflamed a ferocious anger in Asahel's older brothers just as Abner had feared. Joab and Abishai chased after Abner and his men with increased fury and at sunset cornered them on a high hill. At this point Abner made a direct plea to Joab to call off his men. Cried he, "Shall the sword devour forever? . . . How long shall it be then, ere thou bid the people return from following their brethren?"[31] Joab replied that if Abner had not "spoken"

---

26. 2 Samuel 2:16. Authorities disagree as to the actual significance of this "play". Some believe it was a gladiatorial bout right from the beginning and was intended to settle matters between the two parties much like a duel. However, I believe this interpretation does violence to the word, "play", and it is better to accept the passage as rendered.

27. 2 Samuel 2:17   30. 2 Samuel 2:23
28. 2 Samuel 2:19   31. 2 Samuel 2:26
29. 2 Samuel 2:22

(possibly referring to the play or joust he had suggested) this whole thing could have been avoided.[32] Nevertheless, for reasons best known to himself, Joab decided to cease the slaughter. Wherefore, "Joab blew a trumpet, and all the people stood still, and pursued after Israel no more, neither fought they any more."[33] There is subsequent evidence that Joab was not giving up the fight; he was just postponing vengeance until another day.

Once the siege was lifted, Abner and his men felt free to depart. They marched all night in order to get safely across the Jordan. Meanwhile, Joab and his men marched all night in order to carry Asahel and the rest of their dead back to Bethlehem (their family home) for burial. Altogether this civil strife had cost Joab's party nineteen dead besides Asahel. Among Abner's forces, however, 360 had been killed.[34]

This was the first pitched battle between Judah and the northern kingdom. Conflict continued all through the remainder of the period that David was king of Judah. The scripture says: "Now there was long war between the house of Saul and the house of David: but David waxed stronger and stronger, and the house of Saul waxed weaker and weaker."[35]

DAVID RECOVERS HIS BELOVED MICHAL

When nearly seven and-a-half years had passed after the death of Saul, a series of events began to transpire which ultimately led to a united kingdom of Israel. In this connection the name of Michal suddenly looms up again in the record. It should be pointed out that while ruling as king of Judah in Hebron, David had expanded his royal household until it consisted of six families. The firstborn of each of these six wives is listed in the scripture.[36] Because of the prominence of some of them in the later history of Israel, we will list them here, beginning with the firstborn:

1—AMMON, born of Ahinoam the Jezreelitess.

---

32. 2 Samuel 2:27. This is a defective passage and its meaning somewhat obscure. However, it is believed the interpretation given above is the correct one. (See Clarke, *Bible Commentary*, Vol. 2, p. 313)
33. 2 Samuel 2:28
34. 2 Samuel 2:29-32
35. 2 Samuel 3:1
36. 2 Samuel 3:2-5

2—CHILEAB, born of Abigail, the widow of **Nabal the Car-**
melite.

3—ABSALOM, born of Maacah, daughter of King Talmai of
Geshur.

4—ADONIJAH, born of Haggith.

5—SHEPHATIAH, born of Abital.

6—ITHREAM, born of Eglah.

But in spite of this, there was one member of David's
family still missing. David longed for his beloved Michal,
the bride of his youth, whose vision of beauty had been his
main sustaining hope during all his terrible years of exile.
Of course, he knew that Saul had annulled their marriage
and given Michal to Phaltiel, the son of Laish,[37] but to
David this was a fraudulent transaction and one he had
intended to remedy the moment he had the political and
military power to do so. That opportunity now unexpectedly
arose.

It came about as the result of a marriage in the northern kingdom — Abner's. It seems that General Abner had
been attracted to one of the widows (a concubine) who had
belonged to the dead king Saul. The scripture says that
the puppet king, Ishbosheth, was very angry when he discovered that there had been a union between these two.[38]
Apparently it was not so much the marriage that worried
Ishbosheth, but the suspicious political implications. In
ancient times, the taking of a dead king's widow was often
the preliminary step to seizing the throne,[39] and Ishbosheth
appears to have taken this exact view of Abner's marriage
to Saul's concubine whose name was Rizpah.

Abner, however, refused to accept criticism from the
man he had made king. In fact, the next thing Ishbosheth
knew, this criticism had turned Abner violently against him.
The breach was so serious that Abner announced that he
would immediately use his influence to make a league with
David and unite the whole northern kingdom of Israel with
Judah![40] The scripture says, "And Abner sent messengers

37. 1 Samuel 25:44
38. 2 Samuel 3:7
39. Clarke, *Bible Commentary*, Vol. 2, p. 314
40. 2 Samuel 3:7-10

to David on his behalf, saying . . . Make thy league with me, and, behold, my hand shall be with thee to bring about all Israel unto thee."[41]

When David received this message there was no doubt in his mind that the powerful Abner could do exactly as he had proposed. However, David recognized that he, himself, had suddenly come into a very favorable bargaining position. It was the moment for which he had waited during many lonely years. To Abner's messengers David declared: "Well; I will make a league with thee [Abner]: but one thing I require of thee, that is, Thou shalt not see my face, except thou first bring Michal, Saul's daughter, when thou comest to see my face."[42]

No doubt the messengers from Abner were surprised at the injection of this personal and sentimental issue into the negotiation, but they accepted the instruction and returned to report. Meanwhile, David sent his own messengers directly to the puppet king, Ishbosheth, to make the same demand. He was leaving no stone unturned at this critical moment. Yet there was one last thing he did fail to do. He neglected to ask Michal what her feelings were.

This was a fatal error since time can change many things. It had changed Michal. Apparently she and her second husband were very happy together. Had Michal been asked about David's intentions she might have saved a flood of heartaches for all concerned. But she was not. As a result, Michal suddenly found herself being swept along on a tide of uncontrollable forces which was caused by David's love for her plus the use of unlimited power by her half-brother, King Ishbosheth, to make or break marriages. The Bible says, "And Ishbosheth sent, and took her from her husband, even from Phaltiel the son of Laish."[43]

The poor, distraught Phaltiel could scarcely believe the extent of the catastrophic misfortune which had so suddenly engulfed him. It was the same kind of bitter anguish David had suffered when Saul had angrily snatched this girl-bride

---

41. 2 Samuel 3:12
42. 2 Samuel 3:13
43. 2 Samuel 3:15

from his arms and given her to Phaltiel. Now Phaltiel was tasting of the same draft of gall administered by Saul's son.

As Michal was taken by the king's guard to be delivered to Hebron, the heartbroken Phaltiel followed the procession as though it were a funeral. The scripture says, "her husband went with her along weeping behind her. . . ."[44] When he had followed her as far as Bahurim, it was observed by Abner that Phaltiel was mournfully trailing along. No matter how Abner may have felt about the matter personally, he knew the presence of Phaltiel would become supremely embarrassing if the man continued with them to Hebron. Abner therefore summarily ordered the forsaken husband to return to his home. Reluctantly, Phaltiel obeyed.

No one can tell precisely what happened when Michal finally stood before David after all those long years of separation. The scripture does not say. But it does disclose her feelings toward David a short time later[45] and these were no doubt reflected to some extent at the time of their reunion. That David's love for Michal had not faded one iota is demonstrated by the very circumstances which he manipulated to assure her return, but as he took her in his arms he must have become immediately aware that this woman with the countenance and name of Michal was not the maiden-bride with whom he had shared the ecstacy of their honeymoon in Gibeah so many lonely, painful years before.

All during the haunting days of his flight from Saul, all during the maddening nights when the slightest misstep could have led to his murder, David had nourished the perfume-laden dream of the delicate, heavenly, beautiful Michal. Now, at the supreme moment of triumph in this, his thirtieth year, David unexpectedly found the essence of that vision turning to ashes within his grasp. What had once been a shrine of hope in a love-laden haven had suddenly transformed itself into a tomb of lost hopes and dead or dying memories.

Perhaps David thought the passing of time would heal the breach between them, but the plodding years merely

44. 2 Samuel 3:16
45. 2 Samuel 6:16

added to the burden. Michal's manifestations of resentment, and even open hostility produced a matwork of thorns in the pathway which separated them. No children were born to this union.[46] For Michal it was as though the harsh, confusing, cross-currents of life had robbed her of any reason for living. They had left her heart cold, her mind numb and her body barren.

DAVID IS TRAPPED BY A FEUD
WHICH NEARLY WRECKS THE KINGDOM

As far as Abner was concerned, his promise that Michal should be returned to David was now fulfilled. His next task was to hasten up and down among the northern tribes seeking a commitment from them that they would cease the current hostilities and work for the glorious rebirth of a united Israel under the vigorous leadership of King David. He reminded them of the prophecy wherein the Lord had said, "By the hand of my servant David I will save my people Israel out of the hand of the Philistines, and out of the hand of all their enemies."[47] We learn later that right while Abner was making these proposals a war was in progress between Joab and some of the northern tribes.[48] Nevertheless, Abner obtained sufficient support from the tribal leaders to justify a quick trip to Hebron with his proposals for a unified, pan-Israelite league.

David seemed highly pleased with this vigorous, determined cousin of Saul and sensed that Abner could indeed be the means of uniting the northern tribes with Judah. To show his pleasure, David provided a fine feast for Abner and his twenty men. At the conclusion of the festivities, Abner said, "I will arise and go, and will gather all Israel unto my lord the king, that they may make a league with thee, and that thou mayest reign over all that thine heart desireth."[49]

That was the last time David ever saw Abner alive.

It turned out that immediately after Abner had left, the tempestuous Joab, David's military commander, returned from the most recent war with the northern tribes.[50] When

---

46. 2 Samuel 6:23
47. 2 Samuel 3:18
48. 2 Samuel 3:22

49. 2 Samuel 3:21
50. 2 Samuel 2:22

Joab learned that Abner had been in the city and David had honored him with a feast, the general of Judah flew into a rage. He thundered into David and said he believed this old enemy had merely come to Hebron to get the lay of the land and use the knowledge for a massive attack[51]

There is no record of David's reply, but as soon as Joab came out of the meeting he sent messengers to ask Abner to return immediately to Hebron. The unsuspecting Abner gladly responded to this request and was soon back in Judah's capital. The Bible says that no sooner had Abner arrived at the city wall than Joab intercepted him. Under the guise of pretense, "Joab took him aside in the gate to speak with him quietly, and smote him there under the fifth rib, that he died, for the blood of Asahel his brother."[52]

When David heard the news of this treacherous act he was stunned. He saw the prospect of a united Israel crumbling into a heap of ruins. He knew the stupidity of Joab's rashness could easily catapult the tribes of Israel into a whole new cycle of fratricidal wars. David's task was to steady the ship. Somehow he must save his own good offices by appeasing the northern tribes. At the same time he must do nothing to destroy the confidence and support of Judah. He determined to fix responsibility for this murder on Joab but not perpetuate the feud by avenging it.

The first thing he did was to call in Joab and all his officers. To them he issued a regal command. "Rend your clothes," he sternly ordered, "and gird you with sackcloth, and mourn before Abner!"[53]

This was a bitter pill for Judah's general. He hated Abner. But now he had to publicly mourn for the death of the man whom he, himself, had killed. So did all his officers.

David then boldly issued a public disclaimer, certifying that this diabolical crime was not by any means of his making. Said he, "I and my kingdom are guiltless before the Lord for ever from the blood of Abner the son of Ner: Let it rest on the head of Joab, and on all his father's house. . . ."[54] When the body of Abner was taken out for burial "king

---

51. 2 Samuel 3:24-25
52. 2 Samuel 3:27

53. 2 Samuel 3:31
54. 2 Samuel 3:28-29

David himself followed the bier. And they buried Abner in Hebron: and the king lifted up his voice, and wept at the grave of Abner; and all the people wept."[55] David's manifestation of sincere sorrow for the death of Abner had an immediate, wholesome effect. The scripture says "all the people took notice of it, and it pleased them. . . . For all the people and all Israel understood that day that it was not of the king to slay Abner, the son of Ner."[56]

THE MURDER OF KING ISHBOSHETH

When the news of Abner's assassination crossed into Trans-Jordan and sped on the wings of hoarse whispers to the capital city of Mahanaim, there was one man who received it in terror. It was Saul's son, Ishbosheth. It was Abner who had made him the puppet king of Israel and it might have occurred to him to rejoice since now he would be able to rule in his own right and by his own strength. But Ishbosheth had no strength. The scripture says his "hands were feeble" on the reigns of government.[57]

The timidity of the king in the current crisis created a leadership vacuum. The people of Israel did not know whether to press forward in a league with David as Abner had suggested or remain loyal to the house of Saul. With Abner dead, perhaps Ishbosheth would start a new civil war.

But with David the problem was not that complicated. It is obvious that he was hoping the tribes would combine as Abner had suggested and then David could serve as their king in accordance with his anointing by Samuel. As for Ishbosheth, surely some accommodation could be arranged so that he might live out his life happily and receive the respect due to a son of the late king Saul.[58]

What David did not know was the fact that certain perfidious fellows from the tribe of Benjamin had already concocted a plot to end the dynasty of Saul with daggers and swords. They were going to undertake this scheme

---

55. 2 Samuel 3:32
56. 2 Samuel 3:36-37
57. 2 Samuel 4:1
58. That some such plan was in David's mind is clearly evidenced by his subsequent reaction to Ishbosheth's murder.

even though it meant assassinating a member of their own tribe.

The principal characters in the plot were two brothers, Rechab and Baanah, sons of Rimmon of Beeroth.[59] Both of these men were obviously well acquainted with the king for they came to his house seeking wheat from the king's stores and were casually allowed to come in to converse with Ishbosheth even though he was resting in his bed-chamber during the noon hour. But, in reality, they were not after wheat. They wanted the king's life.

"For when they came into the house, he lay on his bed in his bed-chamber, and they smote him, and slew him, and beheaded him, and took his head, and gat them away through the plain all night."[60]

What they intended to do with the murdered king's head soon became apparent. The scripture says Rechab and Baanah made their way frantically to Hebron. With their gruesome trophy in hand they marched straight into the presence of David. "Behold," they cried, "the head of Ishbosheth the son of Saul thine enemy, which sought thy life; and the Lord hath avenged my lord the king this day of Saul, and of his seed."[61]

But David had never asked to be avenged of Saul, his "enemy," nor of his seed. In fact, David had never treated Saul as an enemy but had honored him as the king of Israel and left the outcome of his mixed-up life to the providence of God.[62] The astonished Rechab and Baanah who undoubtedly had expected to be welcomed as heroic partisans for the house of David suddenly found themselves being treated as base criminals who were guilty of treason against their king.

David responded by sharing with these conspirators a page from the history of his own life. Said he, "When one told me, saying, Behold, Saul is dead, thinking to have brought good tidings, I took hold of him, and slew him in Ziklag, WHO THOUGHT THAT I WOULD HAVE GIVEN HIM A REWARD FOR HIS TIDINGS. How much more

---

59. 2 Samuel 4:5
60. 2 Samuel 4:7

61. 2 Samuel 4:8
62. 1 Samuel 26:10

when wicked men have slain a righteous person in his own house upon his bed? Shall I not therefore now require his blood of your hand, and take you away from the earth?

"And David commanded his young men, and they slew them, and cut off their hands and their feet, and hanged them up over the Pool in Hebron [a prominent place where all might see]. But they took the head of Ishbosheth, and buried it in the sepulchre of Abner in Hebron."[63]

DAVID BECOMES THE KING OF A UNITED ISRAEL

This decisive action by David was sufficient to assure the tribes of the north that the son of Jesse did not wish to come to power by assassination or by avenging himself upon any who might have opposed David in the past.

It must be remembered that the northern kingdom had been at war with Judah for several years and it was important for David to reassure some of these who had fought against his armies in the past that he had nothing vindictive in mind against his former enemies. Once this was fully manifest in David's treatment of Ishbosheth's assassins, the people of the northern tribes began to remember all kinds of good things about David which the war years had partially erased from their minds. After all, he was the magnificent Goliath-killer, and, as a captain over one of Saul's contingents of a thousand men, David had performed sensationally. They even remembered that Samuel, who was the greatest of the prophets since Joshua, had anointed this man to be king after the Lord had revealed that among all the children of Israel, this David was the one most likely to be a good ruler.[64]

Therefore, the mood of the people began to swell into a spirit of unity and jubilation. The scripture says, "Then came all the tribes of Israel to David unto Hebron, and spake, saying, Behold, we are thy bone and thy flesh."[65] Tribe by tribe and city by city, the leaders of the people of the

---

63. 2 Samuel 4:10-12
64. 2 Samuel 5:1-2. Since this was the substance of their speech when they came before David it is obvious that these were the same matters they had discussed among themselves in order to gain support for the new league with David.
65. 2 Samuel 5:1

northern kingdom made their way to Hebron to assure David
that he was their choice for king if he would be willing to
accept them as his people. ". . . and David made a covenant
with them in Hebron before the Lord; and they anointed
David king over Israel, according to the word of the Lord
by Samuel."[66] This was the third time David had been
anointed king — once by Samuel, once by Judah, and now
by the whole people of Israel.

We learn from Chronicles that this coronation was a
magnificent affair attended by vast multitudes from all over
the kingdom. This scripture says: "And these are the numbers of the bands that were ready armed to the war, and
came to David to Hebron, to turn the kingdom of Saul to
him, according to the word of the Lord."[67] It then lists the
tribal battalions which were represented at the coronation:

> Judah — 6,800
> Simeon — 7,100
> Levi — 4,600
> Aaron — 3,700
> Benjamin — 3,000
> Ephraim — 20,800
> Manasseh in Samaria — 18,000
> Issachar — 200 captains and "all their brethren."
> Zebulun — 50,000
> Naphtali — 37,000
> Danites — 28,000
> Asher — 40,000
> Trans-Jordan tribes (Reubenites, Gadites and half the tribe
> of Manasseh) — 120,000

The scripture concludes:

"All these men of war, that could keep rank, came
with a perfect heart to Hebron, to make David king over all
Israel: and all the rest also of Israel were of one heart to make
David King. And there they were with David three days,
eating and drinking: for their brethren had prepared for
them. . . . [They] brought bread on asses, and on camels,
and on mules, and on oxen, and meat, meal, cakes of figs,

---

66. 1 Chronicles 11:3
67. 1 Chronicles 12:23

and bunches of raisins, and wine, and oil, and oxen, and sheep abundantly: for THERE WAS JOY IN ISRAEL!"[68]

David had been only thirty years of age when he was anointed king over Judah.[69] Seven and a-half-years had passed since then,[70] so now he was nearing the age of thirty-eight as he took over the reigns of government to rule the united twelve tribes of Israel.

David Captures Jerusalem and Makes It His New Capital

One of the first things David did to unite his people was to give up the tribal capital of Judah at Hebron and move his headquarters to Mount Moriah where the city of Jerusalem now stands. No doubt David had many reasons for wishing to establish his capital in this place. For one thing, it was directly on the border between Judah and Benjamin and would therefore be more popular with the northern tribes than a capital further south such as Hebron. Secondly, this tiny piece of geography called Mount Moriah or Mount Zion was a very sacred spot to the Israelites.

In the days of Melchizedek, around 2,000 B.C., this spot had been called Salem or City of Peace.[71] After Melchizedek's people had achieved a remarkable degree of righteousness they were translated and joined the people of Enoch.[72] Thereafter the former site of Salem seems to have remained unoccupied. At least it was so when Abraham was told to go there and offer up his son on Mount Moriah.[73] That event occurred only a few years after the people of Melchizedek had been there, but the scripture is plain that when Abraham and Isaac arrived for the sacrifice it was an uninhabited region.[74]

---

68. 1 Chronicles 12:28-40
69. 2 Samuel 5:4
70. 2 Samuel 2:11; 5:5
71. Genesis 14:18; Hebrews 7:1-2
72. For an extensive discussion of Melchizedek's experience, see *The First 2,000 Years*, pp. 252-257.
73. Genesis 22:2
74. Genesis 22:4-13. Note that Abraham had to take all his supplies with him, implying an absence of resources at Moriah or the presence of any settlement. Note also that when he told his young men (verse 5) to remain behind he obviously intended that he and Isaac should be alone on Moriah when the sacrifice was made.

However, we know that by 1,500 B.C. people were again living in this place. This is proven by the famous cache of cuneiform tablets discovered in 1887 at Tell el Amarna on the Nile. Among these were "clay tablet letters sent between Jerusalem and Egypt, B.C. 1500, some of which show that the city at that time was called Jerusalem, sometimes shortened into Salem, and that Salem meant Peace."[75]

The Canaanite tribe which was in possession of this city at the time Joshua and the Israelites arrived (around 1,470 B.C.) was the Jebusites.[76] The tribe of Judah conquered and sacked the city during the period of early occupation, but the Jebusites rebuilt it. They possessed it continually down to the time of David, 1000 B.C.[77]

To reconstruct the capture of this city by David it is first necessary to visualize Jebus[78] or old Jerusalem as it then appeared. To begin with, it was not located on the summit of Mount Moriah where Solomon would later build his beautiful temple, but it occupied the lower spur running down from Moriah on the south called Ophel (or hill).[79] This spur is now completely outside the city walls of modern Jerusalem and seems like an illogical place to build the original city. However, this is due to a change in the topography since ancient times. Originally, this spur was a natural defense. On the east side of Ophel was the deep bedstream valley of Kidron or the valley of Jehosaphat. To the west was the valley of the Cheesemakers, the Tyropoeon. Finally, at its southern extremity, the terminus of this mountain spur peers down on the depths of the valley of Hinnom. Anciently, therefore, this area had excellent protection on three sides. It only remained necessary to merely build a stout fortress at the northern end of the spur and by adding the security of the usual city walls this whole area became an exceptionally well-protected sanctuary.

Today, these natural advantages are no longer apparent. Dr. Emil G. Kraeling explains why: "It seemed incredible

---

75. See Peloubet's *Bible Dictionary*, under "Jerusalem."
76. Numbers 13:29; Joshua 11:3
77. Judges 1:21
78. Judges 19:10; 1 Chronicles 11:4-5
79. For details see Peloubet's *Bible Dictionary* under "Ophel."

to scholars, until quite recently, that this small and seemingly
not very strong position could have been 'the stronghold of
Zion'. . . . However, in Biblical times the southeastern hill
[Ophel] was a good deal higher, relative to the valley-
bottom, than it is today. . . . The level of the Kidron Valley
has since antiquity risen from fifty-two to ninety-eight feet
[by being filled with debris]. . . . On the western side one
must dig from twelve to seventy-two feet down to reach
the natural rock. If one allows for this accumulation of
later ages, then the position was indeed very strong.
Josephus even claims that there was a further elevation on the
summit of the ridge which was shorn off in three years of
labor at the time of Simon Maccabeus (142-134 B.C.)."[80]

So, in ancient times, this area called Ophel was not
only the best natural sanctuary in this region, but it became
famous as the stronghold or fortress of Zion.[81] It is important to realize that in olden times it was Mount Moriah,
the Temple Hill, which was called Zion and not the more
western mountain which bears the name of Zion today. In
fact, archaeologists have found that the western mountain
was not settled extensively until six or seven centuries after
David. As Dr. Kraeling points out, "The soundings thus
far made on the western hill have not brought to light evidence of anything earlier than the Maccabean age."[82] It
was also on the Ophel of Mount Zion and not on the western
mountain that the tomb of David was originally built.[83] The
modern sightseer to Jerusalem will find his pilgrimage far
more profitable if some of these facts are known to him
before he is exposed to the traditional folklore which is sin-
cerely but erroneously dispensed by some (though not all)
of the local guides.

Another important reason why Ophel was the ideal
place for the establishment of a fortified city was the fact

---

80. Emil G. Kraeling, *Bible Atlas*. New York: Rand McNally & Company, 1964,
p. 196.
81. 1 Chronicles 11:5. "The east of the two hills on which Jerusalem stands was
originally known as Zion . . . the name Moriah is very seldom applied to it in
Scriptures, which almost always means the temple hill when it speaks of Zion."
(Geikie, *Hours With the Bible*, Vol. 3, p. 240 note)
82. Kraeling, *Bible Atlas*, p. 196
83. Nehemiah 3:15-16. Note that the original sepulchre of David was near the
Pool of Siloah (Siloam), the House of the Mighty and the king's garden, all of
which were located on the southern spur of Moriah called Ophel.

that an underground spring emerges here from the limestone rock in a deep recess which is today called, the Fountain of the Virgin Mary but was known in Old Testament times as Gihon.[84] From this place it flows underground and comes out a little lower at the famous Pool of Siloam. We know now that the ancient fortress of Zion was built in such a way that descending shafts and tunnels ran down to the main spring, thereby making it an indispensable asset as a source for water in time of siege. When these details are known, it is much easier to understand how David conquered this fortress which had defied the Israelites for so many centuries.

How David Conquered Jebus or Jerusalem

It was demonstrated at the time of David's coronation that a vast host of warriors were available to David now that the twelve tribes of Israel were united. However, even these were not sufficient to take the pagan capital of Jebus by direct assault. When the Jebusites saw David and his troops coming they apparently gathered all their people inside their fortress and then tossed down scoffs and jeers from the top of their battlements. David was required by the Law of Moses to first offer these people peace.[85] However, the Jebusites were not only defiant, but they placed their lame and their blind on top of their garrison walls and then taunted David by saying, "Except thou take away the blind and the lame, thou shalt not come in hither: thinking David cannot come in hither."[86] In other words, these walls are so high and so strong that our lame and our blind are all that are needed to defend them.

However, David had no intention of scaling these walls. He said to his men (apparently the famous 600) that, "Whosoever getteth up to the gutter [water way], and smiteth the Jebusites," should become the Commander-in-Chief of the new unified army of Israel.[87] Obviously, no man

---

84. Werner Keller, *The Bible as History*, p. 186.
85. Deuteronomy 20:10-12
86. 2 Samuel 5:6
87. 2 Samuel 5:8. Part of this passage implies that David hated the lame and the blind but authorities point out that the translation is defective. Dr. Kennicott says the verse should read: "And David said — Whosoever smiteth the Jebusites, and through the subterranean passage reacheth the lame and the blind who hate the life of David . . . shall be chief and captain." (See Clarke, *Bible Commentary*, Vol. 2, p. 319)

could accomplish this alone, so it was a combination effort with the 600 Davidian warriors apparently supporting their commander, Joab, in making this fantastic penetration into the interior of the fortress via the secret tunnel from the spring. This tunnel was rediscovered in 1867 by Charles Warren, a British Captain, and subsequent explorations established its antiquity back to the second millennium B.C.[88]

To appreciate the accomplishment of Joab and his men, the following description of this tunnel by Dr. Geikie will prove helpful: "After crawling through the Virgin's Fountain, when the water was unusually low, they [the modern explorers] had to pass through a tunnel fifty feet long, and then came on the 'new passage,' seventeen feet long, opening into the shaft. In this shaft they quickly reared a rough scaffolding to twenty feet above the bottom, and from this, a second, twenty-seven feet in all, above the bottom. A third landing made, was thirty-eight feet above the bottom. About six feet above this, the shaft opened out to the west into a great cavern, up an ascent at an angle of forty-five degrees, covered with loose stones a foot in cube [square] on an average. At about thirty feet up this came to a landing place in a cave twenty feet wide. Fifteen feet higher, they came to a level plateau. From this a passage, eight feet wide and from three to four feet high, ran for forty feet, where they found a wall, through a hole in which they squeezed. On the other side the passage sloped up again at an angle of forty-five degrees, the passage being two feet high. Pushing up this on their backs for fifty feet, they came to another wall, to block the passage, but getting through this, they came to a vaulted chamber, nine feet wide and twenty feet high and long. Next, came a pit, twenty feet deep, opening into a smaller one, eight feet deeper, and there all passage seemed to be blocked up. Lamps, jars, dishes ,and charcoal were found in the vaulted chamber, which had been used as a refuge. It was subsequently found that a shaft from the hill above communicated with these works below, giving access to them and enabling the citizens to go down to the water, even when an enemy lay outside. This upper shaft is in all forty-five feet deep. The whole

88. Keller, *The Bible as History,* p. 187

of the passages and chambers are cut in hard limestone rock. If, as seems possible, this was the way by which Joab scaled the city, he certainly deserved the reward he received."[89]

Having captured the fortress of the Jebusites, David set about building his new capital. He saved the highest summit of Mount Moriah (where Solomon's temple later stood) and constructed his walled city on the southern spur of the mount which we have already described. David apparently allowed the conquered Jebusites to remain in the area as demonstrated by subsequent events.[90] However, he had Joab build strong defenses around the whole city which at that time comprised only a few acres.[91] It was designated as "The City of David"[92] and even after the whole area was developed into a great metropolis and given the old name of Jerusalem, this area of Ophel continued to be called "The City of David," for he was buried there.[93]

DAVID'S MIGHTY ONES

To guarantee the security of his new capital, David moved his band of 600 into the precincts of this fortified city together with their families. Their main meeting hall or House of the Mighty is referred to by Nehemiah.[94] These valiant men who had gradually rallied to him through the years and who had repeatedly risked their lives to support David in his efforts to unite Israel were a great source of pride to David. The scriptures chronicle the names of the most important ones and we shall list them here together with a notation of their achievements so that the reader may better appreciate why David called them his Mighty Ones. Among these will be found names which have already figured prominently in our story and others will gain prominence as the rest of David's history unfolds.

JOAB — commander-in-chief under David. He was King David's nephew who murdered Abner but was rehabilitated in the

---

89. Geikie, *Hours With the Bible*, Vol. 3, pp. 230-231
90. 2 Samuel 24:18-24
91. 1 Chronicles 11:7-8. "In shape Jersusalem [when David took it over] was about three times as long as it was wide, and it may have covered an area of four to five acres." (Kraeling, *Bible Atlas*, p. 196)
92. 1 Chronicles 11:7
93. See note 83.
94. Nehemiah 3:16

minds of the people after going up the water way and capturing Jerusalem (Jebus) from the inside.

ABISHAI — elder brother of Joab (1 Chr. 2:16) and therefore
another nephew of David. He accompanied David on the
dangerous night mission into the camp of Saul (1 Sam.
26:6-9). Saved David's life when he was about to be killed
by Goliath's son (2 Sam. 21:16-17). In one battle he slew
300 Philistines (1 Chr. 11:20). He was loyal to David
during Absalom's rebellion.

JASHOBEAM — a Hachmonite who was chief of David's captains and famed for having taken on a large body of Philistines single-handedly (1 Chr. 11:11).

ELEAZAR — the son of Dodo, the Ahohite, who was with
David at Pasdammim, and when the other soldiers had fled
he was one of the few that stood his ground and drove the
Philistines away (1 Chr. 11:12-14).

BENAIAH — the son of Jehoiada. "He slew two lion-like men
of Moab: also he went down and slew a lion in a pit in a
snowy day. And he slew an Egyptian, a man of great
stature, five cubits high [7½ feet]." (1 Chr. 11:22-25)

ASAHEL — youngest brother of Joab and Abishai (1 Chr.
2:16), a nephew of David. He was extremely fleet-footed
and was overtaking Abner, commander of the northern Kingdom, when the latter thrust his spear into Asahel so that
the butt-end pierced him through and killed him. (2 Sam.
2:18-23).

ELHANAN — also a son of Dodo of Bethlehem and apparently
a brother of Eleazar (1 Chr. 11:26).

SHAMMOTH — the Harorite, sometimes spelled Shammah,
the Harodite (1 Chr. 11:27).

HELEZ — the Pelonite (1 Chr. 11:27).

IRA — the son of Ikkesh the Tekoite (1 Chr. 11:28).

ABIEZER — the Antothite (1 Chr. 11:28).

SIBBECAI — the Hushathite (1 Chr. 11:29), identified as
Mebunnai in 2 Samuel 23:27.

ILAI — the Ahohite (1 Chr. 11:29) identified as Zalmon in
2 Samuel 23:28.

MAHARAI — the Netophathite (1 Chr. 11:30).

HELED — the son of Baanah the Netophathite (1 Chr. 11:30),
identified as Heleb in 2 Sam. 23:29.

ITHAI — the son of Ribai of Gibeah in Benjamin (1 Chr. 11:31).

BENAIAH — the Pirathonite (1 Chr. 11:31).

HURAI — of the brooks of Gaash (1 Chr. 11:32), identified as Hiddai in 2 Samuel 23:30.

ABIEL — the Arbathite (1 Chr. 11:32), identified as Abialbon in 2 Samuel 23:31.

AZMAVETH — the Baharumite (1 Chr. 11:33).

ELIAHBA — the Shaalbonite (1 Chr. 11:33).

JONATHAN — the son of Shage the Hararite (1 Chr. 11:34).

AHIAM — the son of Sacar the Hararite (1 Chr. 11:35).

ELIPHAL — the son of Ur (1 Chr. 11:35), identified as Elephelet in 2 Samuel 23:34.

HEPHER — the Mecherathite (1 Chr. 11:36).

AHIJAH — the Pelonite (1 Chr. 11:36).

HEZRO — the Carmelite (1 Chr. 11:37), identified as Hezrai in 2 Samuel 23:35.

NAARAI — the son of Ezbai (1 Chr. 11:37).

JOEL — the brother of Nathan (1 Chr. 11:38).

MIBHAR — the son of Haggeri (1 Chr. 11:38).

ZELEK — the Ammonite (1 Chr. 11:39).

NAHARAI — the Berothite (1 Chr. 11:39), who served as the armor-bearer for Joab, the chief commander.

IRA — the Ithrite (1 Chr. 11:40).

GAREB — the Ithrite (1 Chr. 11:40).

URIAH — the Hittite (1 Chr. 11:41), husband of Bath-sheba and one of the most loyal soldiers David possessed.

SIGNS OF A RISING STORM

It was well that David had the nucleus of a well-trained military force constantly around him for the next several years were to be filled with continuous warfare and numerous surprise attacks. In fact, at this very moment news of David's ascension to the throne of a united Israel was spreading a frenzy of alarm throughout the whole Philistine federation along the coast. It had been over seven years since the Philistines had killed Saul and conquered Israel. Now it appeared that David, the Goliath-killer, was going to replace Saul.

To the lords of Philistines it seemed the right time to attack once more.

Scripture Readings and Questions on Chapter Four

Scripture Readings: 2 Samuel, Chapters 1 to 5 inclusive.

1—What were the circumstances when David first heard that Saul and Jonathan were dead? Was it an Israelite who brought the news?

2—What did the messenger bring to David? Why did he lie?

3—Who told David to go up to Hebron? Was he advised in advance what was going to happen to him or did he have to go in faith?

4—After being crowned king of Judah what did David do to start a movement among the nothern tribes to get them to accept him also?

5—Who promoted Saul's son to be the new king of the northern tribes? Was he related to Saul's son? In what way?

6—Why was the capital of the northern tribes changed to Mahanaim?

7—Was Abner foolish to bring an armed force to Gibeon? Describe briefly what happened.

8—Why was Abner afraid to kill Asahel? Then why did he do it?

9—Why was Ishbosheth angry at Abner when he married Rizpah?

10—Describe what Abner did because of his resentment. What was David's answer to Abner's proposal?

11—In arranging for Michal's return what mistake did David make? Who was Phaltiel? What did he do?

12—When Abner came to Hebron, was David pleased with him? How did he show it? What did Abner then say he would do?

13—When Joab found out what had happened, was he pleased? Describe what he did.

14—Why did this create serious complications for David? What did David do to keep the people favorable to him? Did Joab like it?

15—What were the motives of the men who murdered Isbosheth? What did David tell them? What did he do to them?

16—Why were some of the northern tribes afraid of David? Why did the punishing or Ishbosheth's assassin reassure them?

17—How old was David when he was crowned king of Judah? How old was he when he became king of a united Israel?

18—Name two important events which had occurred at the site of Jerusalem prior to the time David made it his capital.

19—How did Joab rehabilitate himself with David and the people? Was this a truly heroic accomplishment?

20—What was the reaction of the Philistines when they heard David was replacing Saul as king of Israel? What did they decide to do?

CHAPTER FIVE

The Rise of Israel to Greatness

By providential design David came upon the earth at one of those rare moments in history when the great empire nations of the world were temporarily at ebb-tide. Egypt had blunted her aspirations for territorial expansion by fratricidal civil war. Further north, the militant Hittite empire of Asia Minor and the cruel Assyrians from Mesopotamia had practically destroyed each other through a long series of violent struggles. In fact, the Hittites were so weakened and decimated that their empire was about to disappear from the stage of world power. The Assyrians, on the other hand, would survive as a national force, but their debilitated civilizations would be recuperating for nearly two centuries before the bite of their steel would be felt once again in the flesh of their neighbors.

Therefore, David, the Goliath-killer, emerged on the horizon of world events at one of those singular moments in history when it was possible for a chieftain-king of several rustic tribes to mobilize their resources and catapult to power from the Euphrates River to the Red Sea. And David accomplished this after little more than a decade of decisive military action.

THE PHILISTINES DECLARE WAR

However, David's neighbors, the Philistines, never intended that this should be so. Just as soon as they heard that David had become the king of a united Israel and had conquered the Canaanite city of Jebus, they vowed vengeance.

The first attack was straight up the Sorek valley, the gateway to Jerusalem. David heard that they were mobilizing but apparently expected that they would launch their attack up the main valley on the south (the valley of Elah) which opens up near Hebron, his former capital. David therefore "went down to the hold."[1] This is generally interpreted to mean Adullum,[2] David's old limestone cave fortress half-way down the valley of Elah toward the maritime plain where he had formerly hidden his band when he was a fugitive from Saul. However, the wily Philistines did not come up this route but marched up Sorek valley and emerged unexpectedly into the open vale called Rephaim (Valley of the Giants) which lies practically within sight of Jerusalem to the immediate southwest.[3]

But now the Philistines were in for a surprise. David had inquired of the Lord (probably through Abiathar) saying, "Shall I go up to the Philistines? wilt thou deliver them into mine hand? And the Lord said unto David, Go up: for I will doubtless deliver the Philistines into thine hand."[4] With this assurance David prepared to attack. As for the Philistines, they had not intended this to be anything like the all-out war which had defeated Saul at Jezreel, but nevertheless it was a major military thrust with "all the Philistines" represented.[5] They probably had expected David to come storming out of the fortress of Zion at Jerusalem and were just getting ready for a direct assault when the big surprise struck them.

David seems to have come crashing in upon them from the rear. It threw the Philistines into complete pandemonium. They not only lost the will to fight but fled from the field in such a panic that they did not even stay long enough to collect their idolatrous images.[6] The Philistines had carried

---

1. 2 Samuel 5:17
2. See Clarke's statement that this is the same occasion as the one referred to in 2 Samuel 23:14; Clarke, *Bible Commentary*, vol. 2, p. 374.
3. 2 Samuel 5:18
4. 2 Samuel 5:19
5. 2 Samuel 5:17
6. 2 Samuel 5:21

these monstrous idols before them hoping to insure their armies an overwhelming victory, but it was the living God of Israel whose prophecy was fulfilled. David celebrated this victory by burning the images as required by the law of Moses[7] and giving the area a new name. He called it Baal-perazim, meaning the place of breaches or defeat.[8]

THE SECOND ATTACK BY THE PHILISTINES

But this humiliating defeat at the hands of David was not something the Philistines intended to leave as a permanent scar on their military record. They regrouped their forces, strengthened their ranks and marched up Sorek valley once again. This time they were filled with an even stronger determination to avenge themselves on David.

But once again David waited on the Lord. Should he attack? The reply was a strange one. First, he was ordered to avoid a head-on collision with the Philistines, but somehow maneuver in "behind them and come upon them over against the mulberry trees."[9] The Lord said the army of Israel was to lie in ambush until "thou hearest the sound of a going in the tops of the mulberry trees . . . then thou shalt bestir thyself: for then shall the Lord go out before thee, to smite the host of the Philistines."[10] It would appear that perhaps some type of high wind or similar force in nature was to be used by the Lord to disturb the composure of the Philistines and therefore the signal for David to attack was "the sound of a going in the tops of the mulberry trees."

David followed these instructions carefully and as a result he was blessed with an even greater victory than before. In fact, when he saw how completely his forces were routing the Philistines he ordered them to chase after the enemy and destroy them all the way to the gates of their own cities. He wanted no more of these "return engagements." The scripture says "they smote the host of the

7. Deut. 7:5, 25
8. 2 Samuel 5:20; Geikie, *Hours With the Bible*, Vol. 3, p. 236
9. 2 Samuel 5:23. The exact specie of the tree is variously translated.
10. 2 Samuel 5:24

Philistines from Gibeon to Gazar."[11] The fact that the Philistines fled northward several miles to Gibeon before heading
homeward to the west reflects their terror in trying to escape
David's army.

This monumental defeat of the Philistines spread the
reputation of David to foreign nations. The Bible says, "And
the fame of David went out into all lands: and the Lord
brought the fear of him upon all the nations."[12]

DAVID GETS A NEW PALACE AS A GIFT
FROM KING HIRAM OF TYRE

Although Israel was surrounded on her western borders
by Canaanites and other Hamitic peoples, there was one
ruler among them who saw in David the possibilities of a
splendid ally. This was Hiram, king of Phoenicia, whose
domain included the wonderful Lebanon cedar forests and
whose capital was located at the world-famous seaport of
Tyre.

Authorities point out that Hiram had good reason to
associate himself with David, the conqueror of the Philistines.
Although Hiram's people, the Phoenicians, and the Philistines were both Hamitic peoples[13] and therefore of the same
racial origin, this did not prevent the Philistines from casting
greedy and covetous eyes towards Hiram's prosperous kingdom. Dr. Geikie comments on King Hiram's situation as

---

11. 2 Samuel 5:25. This text says "Geba" but is corrected in the marginal note to
correspond with 1 Chronicles 14:16 which says "Gibeon." As for Gazar (or
Gezer) this city was located a few years ago by Cermont Ganneau. It is
called, "Tell el Jeser, a ridge east of Ekron, rising seven hundred feet above the
Mediterranean, at a distance of fourteen miles inland, and standing in noteworthy isolation from the hills" nearby. Ganneau unearthed the facing of the
rocks on which was written the Hebrew words, "Boundary of Gezer." (Geikie,
Hours With the Bible, Vol. 3, p. 327)
12. 1 Chr. 14:17
13. The Philistines were descendants of Ham through Mizraim (Gen. 10:13-14;
Clarke, Vol. 1, pp. 84-85). The Phoenicians are believed to have been descendants of Ham through Canaan whose son was Sidon (Gen. 10:15). The
seaport of Sidon in Phoenicia is supposed to have been called after Canaan's
son of this name. Tyre was set up a few miles further south. (See Clarke,
Bible Commentary, Vol. 1, p. 85). These people were known anciently as
simply Canaanites, but the Greeks called them Phoenicians, meaning a brown
or dark people. (Donald Hardin, *The Phoenicians,* New York: Frederick A.
Praiger publisher, 1962, p. 22) It is interesting that the great Hamitic empire
of Egypt was through Mizraim (same as the Philistines) whereas the great
Hamitic empire of the Hittites in Asia Minor was through Canaan (same as
the Phoenicians). See Clarke, *Bible Commentary,* Vol. 1, pp. 84-85.

follows: "Among other motives for seeking the friendship of David, Hiram very probably had been anxious to secure his help against the Philistines, who had once before conquered Phoenicia, and were still dangerous neighbours."[14] Hiram sent envoys to David telling him of his desire to provide the king of Israel with a splendid palace made from the cedars of Lebanon.[15] This Hiram was no piker. He not only proposed to send the costly material for this palace but the masons and carpenters to build it.[16] This was a great compliment to David, regardless of Hiram's motives, and he appreciated its implications. The scripture says, "And David perceived that the Lord had established him king over Israel, and that he had exalted his kingdom for his people Israel's sake."[17]

The beautiful cedar palace was built in the "City of David." As mentioned earlier, this was the ancient center of Jerusalem located on Ophel, the southern spur of Mount Moriah or Mount Zion. These were days of intensive building activity in this area. The entire precinct of Ophel was being "repaired" and the thick, high walls of stone rebuilt at the same time Hiram's masons and carpenters were constructing the cedar palace.[18] Over it all brooded the mighty "Castle of Zion," which was the name of the Bastille-like fortress built by the Jebusites and captured by David when he took Jerusalem.[19] David lived in this fortified castle until his palace of cedar was completed.[20]

David Attempts to Bring the Ark of the Covenant to Jerusalem

When the magnificent cedar palace was completed and David had moved into it, he felt somewhat guilty that he should enjoy such pleasant surroundings while nothing had been done to honor the Lord with an appropriate place of worship. At the moment, the ancient tabernacle built by Moses was located in Gibeon[21] while the sacred Ark of the

14. Geikie, *Hours With the Bible*, Vol. 3, p. 236
15. 2 Samuel 5:11
16. Ibid.
17. 2 Samuel 5:12
18. 1 Chronicles 11:7-8. For a description of these same walls which had to be "repaired" after the captivity see Nehemiah, chapter 3.
19. 1 Chronicles 11:5
20. 1 Chronicles 11:7
21. 1 Chronicles 21:29

Covenant was at Kirjath-jearim situated on the border between Judah and Benjamin some twelve miles west of Jerusalem.[22] It apparently occurred to David to bring the Ark
of the Covenant to Jerusalem and then get the enthusiastic
support of the people in building a beautiful temple to
contain it.[23]

It will be recalled that during the last days of Eli the
Ark was taken into battle by Eli's sons and lost to the
Philistines.[24] However, it was not retained by the Philistines
because it proved to be a curse to them. They therefore
sent it back. For some strange reason, however, it was not
returned to the Tabernacle as it should have been, but was
retained in the house of a man named Abinidab living at
Kirjath-jearim.[25] Now, nearly two generations later, David
resolved to rehabilitate the Ark and give it the distinction
and dignity it deserved. He therefore said to the people,
"If it seem good unto you, and that it be [acceptable] of
the Lord our God, let us send abroad unto our brethren
every where, that are left in all the land of Israel . . . and
let us bring again the ark of our God to us: for we inquired
not at it [neglected it] in the days of Saul."[26]

This was a popular proposal. "And all the congregation said that they would do so: for the thing was right in
the eyes of all the people."[27] Therefore vast throngs assembled on the highway to see this great sight as the holy
ark of the Covenant was being transported to Israel's new
capital at Jerusalem.

To David this was a very sacred occasion. It was a
religious project rather than a political undertaking. We
therefore discover David presenting himself for the first time
in a new role. He appears as a Priest in addition to being
king. As we shall see later, David wore the ephod, blessed
the people and offered sacrifices which were accepted of
the Lord. Now, it was for just such an act that Saul was

---

22. 1 Chronicles 13:6. Note that the parallel passage in 2 Samuel 6:3 says "in
    Gibeah" but the marginal note states this should be translated "hill" rather
    than Gibeah, Saul's capital.
23. 2 Samuel 6:1-2. Note that 30,000 "chosen men of Israel" participated!
24. 1 Samuel 4:11. For a discussion of these events see *The Third Thousand
    Years,* pp. 607-612.
25. 1 Samuel 7:1   27. 1 Chronicles 13:4
26. 1 Chronicles 13:2-3

rejected of the Lord and told that his indiscretion would cost him his kingdom.[28] Was it not equally presumptuous for David to act in the office of a Priest as it was for Saul? This raises an extremely important question.

DID DAVID HAVE THE PRIESTHOOD?

In spite of the fact that there are more details concerning the life of David than any other individual in the Old Testament, his ordination to the Priesthood is not mentioned. Nevertheless, in connection with the events we are about to describe we do find him performing the functions of the Priesthood and doing it with God's sanction. The fact that this activity was authorized by the Lord and that David did indeed enjoy a portion of God's Priesthood has been verified in modern times. From what David is known to have done he would appear to have held the office of a Priest after the order of Aaron. However, he did not have any portion of the Melchizedek Priesthood.

As Joseph Smith stated, "Although David was a king, he never did obtain the spirit and power of Elijah and the fulness of the Priesthood; AND THE PRIESTHOOD THAT HE RECEIVED, and the throne and kingdom of David is to be taken from him and given to another by the name of David in the last days, raised up out of his lineage."[29]

This direct reference to David's "priesthood that he received" resolves the problem presently before us. It means that he did NOT presume to act as a Priest in the way Saul had done, but that he actually enjoyed the amount of divine authority needed to perform those functions.

It was a great compliment to David's integrity that he should have been ordained to such an office since at this time the Priesthood was not ordinarily entrusted to any except those who belonged to the tribe of Levi.[30] And the office of Priest was restricted to those Levites who happened to be descendants of Aaron.[31] This had been the procedure

---

28. 1 Samuel 13:7-14
29. Joseph Fielding Smith, *Teachings of Joseph Smith*, p. 339.
30. Numbers 18:1-6. For a discussion of the Levitcal Priesthood see *The Third Thousand Years*, pp. 404-406.
31. Numbers 18:7. For a discussion of the Aaronic Priesthood see *The Third Thousand Years*, pp. 400-404.

for nearly 500 years. David, of course, was of Judah, but it appears that because of his faithfulness, Zadok, Abiathar or some other person in authority conferred the Priesthood upon him.

A Violation of Priesthood Procedure Leads to the Death of Uzzah

In all the excitement connected with the moving of the Ark to Jerusalem the Levite Priests made a serious procedural mistake. Several hundred years of apostasy had so cluttered the pattern of ritual that they did not even remember how the Ark was to be carried. Instead of having certain Priests carry the Ark on their shoulders as required by the Lord[32] the sacred structure was put upon a "new cart" drawn by oxen.[33] Apparently David did not know an error of ritual had occurred. We conclude this from the fact that he later placed the blame for what happened on the shoulders of the Priests themselves.[34] Nevertheless, when all was thought to be ready the great procession commenced.

Apparently this journey was a rather boisterous, demonstrative and jubilant affair. "All Israel played before God with all their might, and with singing, and with harps, and with psalteries, and with timbrels, and with cymbals, and with trumpets,"[35] David was dancing and singing right along with all the rest.[36] It was a great day. As the people neared the city of Jerusalem they probably lifted the crescendo of their rejoicing to the highest volume possible. Psychologically, there scarcely could have been a better setting for God's shock treatment which they were now about to receive.

Apparently the Lord saw an opportunity to impress these people in a sudden and dramatic way that sacred patterns laid down by divine revelations should be respected and carefully followed. These were harsh days and the "schoolmaster" law was enjoined upon the people with a severe strictness calculated to serve as sort of a yoke to bind them to righteousness. God's purpose was not to shackle them but teach them a rhythm of obedience. In the name of unborn

---

32. Numbers 4:15
33. 2 Samuel 6:3, 6
34. 1 Chronicles 15:13-15

35. 1 Chronicles 13:8
36. 2 Samuel 6:5

millions who would be the victims of heathen practices if Israel failed to follow the "schoolmaster law," the Lord now reached out His hand to show these people just how close He really was.

It happened in connection with what appeared to be an accident. As the cart carrying the Holy Ark of the Covenant rumbled along the festive highway it neared the outskirts of Jerusalem. At a certain place it became necessary to leave the road and for some reason proceed into the City of David across the threshing floor of a man named Nachon or Chidon.[37] As the oxen attempted to make this ascent they stumbled and jerked the cart roughly. Immediately Uzzah, the son of Abinadab who had the Ark in custody, reached forth his hand to steady the Ark and prevent it from falling. The instant he touched the sacred structure he was seized by a paroxysm or convulsion and fell to the ground. When they examined him, he was dead.[38]

Israel Learns a Lesson

A great hush must have fallen over the multitude as the dancers stopped and the multitude of musicians fell silent. What kind of a curse was on this Ark? As soon as David could collect his wits he ordered the cart pulled into the nearest habitation. This turned out to be the house of Obed-edom, a friendly Philistine from Gath.[39] There the Ark was temporarily abandoned.[40]

As the crowds dispersed and went to their homes, the most perplexed among them was David. He was angry and he was afraid.[41] What kind of a personality was God, anyway? No doubt all Israel, as well as David, were asking some profound and soul-searching questions. Surely Uzzah had done this thing in perfect innocence. Indeed the law did say that none but the Priests of Aaron could lay hold of the Ark and that even a Levite could not touch it save upon pain of death.[42] Still, God is a rational being, an all-knowing

---

37. 1 Chronicles 13:9
38. 1 Chronicles 13:10
39. 1 Chronicles 13:13. This is generally considered to be the meaning of "Gittite." See Peloubet's *Bible Dictionary*, under "Gittite."
40. 1 Chronicles 13:14   42. Numbers 4:15-20
41. 1 Chronicles 13:11-12

being, a wise and loving being. Surely He must have known what was in Uzzah's heart as he reached out to steady the Ark. At the worst, could it be counted anything more than a technical violation? Yet Uzzah was dead.

There was no doubt but what this incident had sobered the nation. And it was high time. These people were scarcely a dozen years away from that terrible day when their former king whom they had demanded of God over the protest of His prophet, had massacred a whole community of God's faithful servants at Nob.[43] Ever since the days of Moses these people, even though blessed with almost continuous miracles, had rebelled, reviled God's commandments and broken their covenants. Was it worth it to have one of them suddenly transferred across the veil to shock them into the realization that God is something more than just a rational, wise, omniscient and loving being? That He is also a master scientist, adhering to principles of law? That He can establish order only when there is obedience to law? The incident of Uzzah was an object lesson.

If David could have completely absorbed the lesson, that alone would have been worth the stunned surprise which Uzzah must have experienced as he suddenly emerged into that more refined dimension of existence right next to us called the spirit world. A simple explanation by the Priesthood in charge would have been sufficient to completely reconcile Uzzah to an acceptance of what had happened. All that he would require would be an understanding that his part was a contribution and not a retribution. From the beginning, God has asked more of some men than others in order that the purposes of a great cause might be fulfilled.

It must also be remembered that Jehovah knew He was dealing here with His own maternal ancestor. He loved David. The coming Messiah who would be "God manifest in the flesh" was going to be born through the line of this same physically noble but spiritually fragile King David. This David needed to better appreciate that God's law is sacred ground, and that violations of divine procedures carry serious penalties. Unfortunately, what David did not learn from

---

43. 1 Samuel 22:18-19

Uzzah's experience he later learned through personal anguish in the precincts of what he, himself, described as "hell."[44]

THE ARK FINALLY ENTERS JERUSALEM

After three months had passed by.[45] David learned something which rekindled his courage and once more fired him with a determination to bring the dangerous but holy Ark within the capital city. The king was told that ever since Obed-edom the Gittite had given sanctuary to the Ark, his household had been blessed greatly. "And it was told King David, saying, The Lord hath blessed the house of Obed-edom, and all that pertaineth unto him, because of the ark of God. So David went and brought up the ark of God from the house of Obed-edom into the city of David with gladness."[46]

But this time David did it right. A whole chapter describing David's extreme caution in removing the Ark from Obed-edom is contained in 1 Chronicles, chapter 15, which greatly illuminates the briefer version in 2 Samuel.

"Then David said, None ought to carry the ark of God but the Levites: for them hath the Lord chosen to carry the ark of God, and to minister unto him forever."[47] He gathered together the descendants of Aaron and the princes of Levi and said: "Ye are the chief of the fathers of the Levites: sanctify yourselves, both ye and your brethren, that ye may bring up the ark of the Lord God of Israel unto the place that I have prepared for it. FOR BECAUSE YE DID IT NOT [properly] AT THE FIRST THE LORD OUR GOD MADE A BREACH UPON US. FOR THAT WE SOUGHT HIM NOT AFTER THE DUE ORDER."[48]

So David did get part of the lesson from Uzzah's tragedy. This time there was no "new cart" pulled by oxen. Instead, "the children of the Levites bare the ark of God upon their shoulders with the staves thereon, as Moses commanded, according to the word of the Lord."[49] This would mean that while other Levites attended, the actual transporting of the Ark was on the shoulders of the descendants of Kohath, Levi's second son.[50]

---

44. Psalms 16:10
45. 2 Samuel 6:11
46. 2 Samuel 6:12
47. 1 Chronicles 15:2
48. 1 Chronicles 15:12-13
49. 1 Chronicles 15:15
50. Numbers 4:15

And this chapter makes it clear that the singers and musicians who now went up before the ark were not a conglomorate mass of celebrants from "all Israel" but Levite choirs of well-trained singers with Levite instrumentalists who could play their orchestral arrangements with great skill.[51]

As for King David, he wore his linen Priesthood ephod over a "robe of fine linen"[52] and led the choirs and trumpets along the way. When the Levite Priests first lifted the Ark to their shoulders, David watched to see if God's anger would fall upon them, and when it did not, he stopped them after only six paces and made a sacrifice of thanksgiving and praise right on the spot.[53]

Now David's old joy returned to him and he danced among the common people with the utter abandonment of an exhilarated child. This amazing mixture of the poet, singer, dancer, soldier, priest and king was what endeared this David to the hearts of the people.

But there was one pair of eyes which watched the proceedings in utter disgust. The scripture says, "And as the ark of the Lord came into the city of David, Michal Saul's daughter looked through a window, and saw King David leaping and dancing before the Lord; and she despised him in her heart."[54] This scriptural reference clearly exposes Michal's true feelings toward David since she had been brought back into his household.

THE GREAT CELEBRATION IN JERUSALEM

Then the scripture continues, "And they brought in the ark of the Lord, and set it in his place, in the midst of the tabernacle that David had pitched for it: and David offered burnt-offerings and peace offerings before the Lord."[55] Of course, the "tabernacle" referred to here was not the famous Tabernacle which Moses had built and brought up out of the wilderness, for that ancient and sacred structure was at this particular time pitched in Gibeon.[56] It appears that

---

51. 1 Chronicles 15:16-24
52. 1 Chronicles 15:27
53. 2 Samuel 6:13
54. 2 Samuel 6:16
55. 2 Samuel 6:17
56. 1 Chronicles 21:29

the "tabernacle" set up in Jerusalem was some kind of magnificent tent which David had appropriately prepared for the Ark pending the time when he could build a permanent temple to protect it.

Meanwhile, he appointed door keepers and a whole entourage of Levites to make the temporary tent or tabernacle as sacred as possible.[57] Once the Ark was securely placed in its new resting place David participated in the offering of sacrifices and further functioned in his priestly role by blessing the people "in the name of the Lord of hosts."[58]

Then he exercised his prerogative as king by bringing out food and drink for the whole multitude.[59] It had been a satisfying and glorious day. "So all the people departed every one to his own house."[60]

But when David went to his house he had a surprise awaiting him. The scripture says, "And Michal the daughter of Saul came out to meet David, and said, How glorious was the king of Israel to-day, who uncovered himself!"[61] This embittered woman saw nothing beautiful in the simple

---

57. 1 Chronicles 15:23-24; 16:37-43
58. 2 Samuel 6:18
59. 2 Samuel 6:19
60. Ibid.
61. 2 Samuel 6:20. Concerning this incident the widely-used *Modern Interpreter's Bible* says: (Vol. 2, p. 1080) "The linen ephod was a small apron used for ceremonial occasions. There is no reason to suppose that its use was confined to priests and that David was acting as a priest. He obviously wore nothing else, for this was the cause of Michal's contempt." This is extremely reckless and faulty scholarship. It misleads the student and compounds four errors in three sentences. The first error is describing a linen ephod as "a small apron." There is little excuse for such an error since Exodus 28:6-8 describes the ephod as extending from the shoulder downward far enough to require a girdle about the waist thereby indicating that it was probably knee-length and certainly not an "apron." Verse 31 calls the ephod a "robe." The second error is the presumption that ephods were worn by people other than priests. Exodus 28:4 sets the ephod apart as one of the "holy garments" to be worn by "Aaron . . . and his sons." The third error is the claim that the ephod is no evidence that David was a priest. All evidence points to the exact opposite. Particularly when it is combined with the fact that David is known to have offered sacrifices and blessed the people (2 Samuel 6:17-18). The fourth error is the statement that David "obviously wore nothing else (besides the ephod), for this was the cause of Michal's contempt." This is directly contradicted by 1 Chronicles 15:27 which refers to this same incident, saying: "And David was clothed with a ROBE of fine linen . . . David ALSO had upon him an ephod of linen." So it was not literal nakedness which offended Michael but the fact that he had removed his kingly vestments and had thus "uncovered himself" as far as his royal office was concerned. Michal, it will be remembered, was a daughter of King Saul and therefore sensitive to the requirements of aristocratic manners.

linen ephod of the Priesthood. To wear it, David had stripped off his kingly robes and vestments of authority. Michal's aristocratic repugnance toward such unkingly behavior was only equalled by her already ripened revulsion toward this no-longer-loved husband of her youth.

David caught the full implication of her intended insult, but it did not leave him too shocked to retort. He told her that since the Lord had made him king over Israel he would humble himself even more deeply than she had seen him do that day. Then he assured her she was mistaken concerning her evaluation of the people's reaction to his behavior. He said those among whom he danced were pleased rather than offended.[62]

But now David was offended. As he spoke with Michal he evidently decided he had endured enough of this churlishness. The full implication of the shattered relationship between Michal and David is reflected in this simple scriptural conclusion, "Therefore Michal the daughter of Saul had no child unto the day of her death."[63]

DAVID IS FORBIDDEN TO BUILD A TEMPLE

As soon as possible David prepared to fulfill his ambition to build a sacred and beautiful structure for the Ark of the Covenant and the glory of God. David called in the prophet Nathan and said, "See now, I dwell in an house of cedar, but the ark of God dwelleth within curtains [of a tent]."[64]

Nathan understood this to mean that David wanted to build a temple to the Lord so he encouraged David, saying, "Go, do all that is in thine heart; for the Lord is with thee."[65] On a matter as important as this, Nathan should have presented the proposal to the Lord. But to Nathan this must have appeared to be such a magnificent idea that he never thought for a moment but what the Lord would approve of it.

Nevertheless, "it came to pass the same night, that the word of God came to Nathan, saying, "GO AND TELL DAVID MY SERVANT, THUS SAITH THE LORD,

---

63. 2 Samuel 6:23
62. 2 Samuel 6:21-22

64. 2 Samuel 7:2
65. 2 Samuel 7:3

THOU SHALT NOT BUILD ME AN HOUSE TO DWELL IN."[66] This must have come as a startling and embarrassing blow to Nathan. It made him look as though he did not know what he was talking about when he encouraged David. As a matter of fact, he didn't. That was why the Lord had to interfere. Nevertheless, the Lord deeply appreciated the sincerity of David's motives. He told Nathan to pass on to David a thrilling message. It was the great Messianic promise.

David was told that God would establish in David's house the very line through which there would one day arise "of thy sons" a princely person on whose shoulders God would establish his kingdom. "He shall build me an house and I will establish his throne for ever. I will be his father, and he shall be my son, and I will not take my mercy away from him, as I took it from him [Saul] that was before thee: but I will settle him in mine house and in my kingdom for ever. . . ."[67]

In a sense, some of these predictions seemed to be fulfilled in Solomon, David's son, for he did build the Lord's house or temple and he did inherit David's throne. However, he did not leave a kingdom "established for ever." Isaiah saw the full and deeper meaning of this prophecy being fulfilled in the second coming of Christ and employed this passage in his own writings as referring to the Christ.[68] Jeremiah also applied this prophecy to the coming of the Savior.[69]

David especially recognized the true intent of this message. He went in before the Ark and addressed the Lord in the most humble but animated praise. Among other things, he said, "Who am I, O Lord God? and what is my house, that thou hast brought me hitherto? . . . thou hast spoken also of thy servant's house FOR A GREAT WHILE TO COME."[70] It is apparent that David knew these things were not in the next generation but far in the future. At the height of his spirited contemplation of God's goodness,

---

66. 1 Chronicles 17:4
67. 1 Chronicles 17:12-14
68. Isaiah 9:7

69. Jeremiah 23:5-6
70. 2 Samuel 7:18-19

he exclaimed, "O Lord, there is none like thee, neither is there any God beside thee. . . ."[71]

DAVID RECEIVES THE PATTERN FOR THE TEMPLE

This was the period in David's life when he apparently reached the peak of his spiritual attainment. It will be noted that for almost his entire career it was necessary for him to reach the Lord through various prophets such as Samuel, Abiathar, Nathan or Gad. However, once he had received the great Messianic promise that through his descendants the very son of God would be born, David seems to have enjoyed the temporary power to receive one or more revelations in connection with the pattern for Solomon's temple.

At the close of his life David talked about these events. Here is how he described them to young Solomon. "My son, as for me, it was in my mind to build an house unto the name of the Lord my God: but the word of the Lord came to me, saying, Thou hast shed blood abundantly, and hast made great wars: thou shalt not build an house unto my name, because thou hast shed much blood upon the earth in my sight. Behold, a son shall be born to thee, who shall be a man of rest; and I will give him rest from all his enemies round about, for his name shall be Solomon, and I will give peace and quietness unto Israel in his days. He shall build an house for my name. . . ."[72]

But even if he were not allowed to build it, nevertheless David was given the exact pattern for the temple. The scripture says, "Then David gave to Solomon his son the PATTERN of the porch, and of the houses thereof, and of the treasuries thereof, and of the upper chambers thereof, and of the inner parlours thereof and of the place of the mercy-seat, and the PATTERN OF ALL THAT HE HAD BY THE SPIRIT, of the courts of the house of the Lord, and of all the chambers round about, of the treasuries of the house of God, and of the treasuries of the dedicated things: also for the courses of the Priests and the Levites, and for all the work of the service of the house of the Lord, and for all the vessels of service in the house of the Lord."[73]

---

71. 1 Chronicles 17:20
72. 1 Chronicles 22:7-10

73. 1 Chronicles 28:11-13

Not only did David receive a revelation on the pattern of the temple, the courses of the priests and the temple services, but he is specifically described as having reduced all the technical information to writing while under the influence of the Spirit. Notice these words, "All this, said David, the Lord made me understand IN WRITING by his hand upon me, even all the works of this pattern."[74]

DAVID ACQUIRES AN AMAZING KNOWLEDGE CONCERNING THE COMING MESSIAH

It also appears to have been at this very same time that David was given some of the most detailed knowledge in the entire Old Testament concerning the coming birth, mission, death and resurrection of Jesus Christ. In other words, nearly 1,000 years before Christ was born, his great maternal ancestor, David, knew some of the most intimate facts about his life.

In singing about the coming Messiah in his Psalms, David frequently looks upon his own suffering as a type of the misery and difficulty which the Savior would bear during his life. David therefore treats some of these matters in the first person as though he were talking about himself. Nevertheless, Peter and others point out that these passages had more specific reference to Jesus Christ.[75]

Here are some of the things David knew about the coming Messiah:

> PRE-EXISTENCE OF JESUS CHRIST: "Out of the womb, before the morning star, have I begotten thee." Psalm 110:3 as translated by Eusebius with the following comment: ". . . he [the Christ] came into existence from God himself before the morning star, that is before the organization of the world." (Eusebius, Church History, 3:16-18) If Eusebius is correct in his version of this passage, note the implication that in the pre-existence the Messiah was born of a heavenly mother before he was born of Mary in this life! That Eusebius was apparently correct in his version of this passage is supported by a number of authorities and several of the most ancient texts. (See Clarke, Bible Commentary, Vol. 3, p. 581)

---

74. 1 Chronicles 28:19
75. See, for example, Acts 2:25-34

CHRIST SIRED BY GOD: "The Lord hath said unto me [the Messiah], Thou art my Son; this day have I begotten thee." (Psalm 2:7)[76]

CHRIST TO BE A HIGH PRIEST AFTER THE ORDER OF MELCHIZEDEK: "Thou art a priest for ever after the order of Melchizedek." (Psalm 110:4)[77]

CHRIST TO BE BETRAYED BY A FRIEND: "Yea, mine own familiar friend, in whom I trusted, which did eat of my bread, hath lifted up his heel against me." (Psalm 41:9)[78]

CHRIST'S BODY NOT TO SEE CORRUPTION: In Acts 2:27 Peter quotes from David's Psalm 16:9-10: "Therefore my heart is glad, and my glory rejoiceth: my flesh also shall rest in hope. For thou wilt not leave my soul in hell; *NEITHER WILT THOU SUFFER THINE HOLY ONE TO SEE CORRUPTION.*"[79]

CHRIST'S SUFFERING ON THE CROSS: Many details concerning the crucifixion appear in the Messiah's lamentation which David wrote. We call it Psalm 22. Here are typical passages which the reader will immediately identify with the Savior's experience on the cross:

"My God, my God, why hast thou forsaken me." (Verse 1)[80]
"But I am ... a reproach of men, and despised of the people." (Verse 6)[81]

---

76. Concerning Jesus, the angel told Mary, "He shall be great, AND SHALL BE CALLED THE SON OF THE HIGHEST: and the Lord God shall give unto him the throne of his father David. . . . The Holy Ghost shall come upon thee, and the power of the Highest shall overshadow thee: therefore also that holy thing which shall be born of thee SHALL BE CALLED THE SON OF GOD." (Luke 1:32-35)

77. Paul wrote: "So also Christ glorified not himself to be made an high priest; but he that said unto him, Thou art my Son, to day have I begotten thee. As he saith also in another place, Thou art a priest forever after the order of Melchisedec." (Hebrews 5:5-6; see also 6:20)

78. Jesus said, "I know whom I have chosen: but that the scripture may be fulfilled, He that eateth bread with me hath lifted up his heel against me." (John 13:18) Later, at the Last Supper, the disciples wondered which one would betray him: "And they were exceeding sorrowful, and began every one of them to say unto him, Lord, is it I? And he answered and said, He that dippeth his hand with me in the dish, the same shall betray me. . . . Then Judas, which betrayed him, answered and said, Master, is it I? He said unto him, Thou hast said." (Matthew 26:22-25)

79. The body of Jesus was put into the cool, limestone tomb immediately after his death and remained there only three days. It was resurrected before the elements of corruption were operative.

80. "And about the ninth hour Jesus cried with a loud voice, saying, Eli, Eli, lama sabachthani? that is to say, My God, my God, why hast thou forsaken me?" (Matthew 27:46)

81. "And they that passed by reviled him, wagging their heads . . ." (Matthew 27:39)

"He trusted on the Lord that he would deliver him: let him deliver him, seeing he delighted in him." (Verse 8)[82]

Be not far from me; for trouble is near; for there is none to help." (Verse 11)[83]

"They gaped upon me with their mouths, as a ravening and a roaring lion." (Verse 13)[84]

"I am poured out like water, and all my bones are out of joint: my heart is like wax; it is melted in the midst of my bowels." (Verse 14)[85]

"My strength is dried up like a potsherd; and my tongue cleaveth to my jaws . . ." (Verse 15)[86]

"The assembly of the wicked have enclosed me." (Verse 16)[87]

"They pierced my hands and my feet." (Verse 16)[88]

"They part my garments among them." (Verse 18)[89]

"They . . . cast lots upon by vesture." (Verse 18)[90]

CHRIST RECEIVED VINEGAR TO DRINK: ". . . and in my thirst they gave me vinegar to drink." (Psalm 69:21)[91]

NONE OF CHRIST'S BONES WERE BROKEN: As the pascal lamb was to be slain without breaking any of its

---

82. "Likewise also the chief priests mocking him, with the scribes and elders, said, He saved others; himself he cannot save. If he be the King of Israel, let him now come down from the cross, and we will believe him. HE TRUSTED IN GOD: LET HIM DELIVER HIM NOW, if he will have him: for he said, I am the Son of God." (Matthew 27:41-43)

83. "Then all the disciples forsook him, and fled." (Matthew 26:56)

84. "And they spit upon him, and took the reed, and smote him on the head." (Matthew 27:30) "When the chief priests therefore and officers saw him, they cried out, saying, Crucify him, crucify him." (John 19:6)

85. "But one of the soldiers with a spear pierced his side, and forthwith came there out blood and water." (John 19:34)

86. "After this Jesus . . . saith, I thirst." (John 19:28)

87. "And from thenceforth Pilate sought to release him: but the Jews cried out, saying, If thou let this man go, thou art not Caesar's friend . . . they cried out. Away with him, away with him, crucify him." (John 19:12-15)

88. The Gospel writers describe Jesus as being "crucified" without furnishing the details (see Matthew 27:35; Mark 15:24; Luke 23:33; John 19:23, 37). However, Thomas refers to some of the wounds Jesus received when he said, "Except I shall see in his hands the print of the nails, and put my finger into the print of the nails, and thrust my hand into his side, I will not believe." (John 20:25) Earlier Jesus had appeared to the other disciples saying, "Behold my hands and my FEET." (Luke 24:39) indicating that the marks of his crucifixion were in his feet as well as his hands.

89. "Then the soldiers, when they had crucified Jesus, took his garments, and made four parts, to every soldier a part . . ." (John 19:23)

90. ". . . now the coat was without seam, woven from the top throughout. They said therefore among themselves, Let us not rend it, but cast lots for it, whose it shall be." (John 19:23-24)

91. "And the soldiers also mocked him, coming to him, and offering him vinegar." (Luke 23:36)

bones, so David said it would be of the Christ: "He keepeth all his bones: not one of them is broken." (Psalm 34:20)[92]

CHRIST TO SIT ON THE RIGHT HAND OF GOD. "The Lord [the Almighty] said unto my Lord [the Messiah]. Sit thou at my right hand, until I make thine enemies thy footstool." (Psalm 110:1)[93]

DAVID'S ADMONITION CONCERNING THE CHRIST: "Kiss the Son, lest he be angry, and ye perish from the way, when his wrath is kindled but a little. Blessed are all they that put their trust in him." (Psalm 2:12)

Having considered the spiritual and religious development of David, most of which occurred within those early years immediately following the conquest of Jerusalem, we now turn to his secular accomplishments as Israel's king.

DAVID EXPANDS HIS KINGDOM FROM THE EUPHRATES TO EGYPT

For a number of years, David was involved in almost continuous warfare as he expanded the influence of his kingdom on every point of the compass. We shall summarize these conquests for the sake of clarity but it should be remembered that they extended over a period of years.

The first foreigners to fall before the Israelites were the Philistines. In spite of the two defeats they had suffered soon after David came to Jerusalem, the Philistines still possessed the impudence to subjugate some of the border cities of Israel and force them to pay tribute. As soon as David was able to do so, he charged down to the maritime plain to teach the Philistines a lesson. And "David smote the Philistines, and subdued them: and David removed the bondage of the tribute which the Israelites paid to the Philistines."[94]

---

92. "Then came the soldiers, and brake the legs of the first, and of the other which was crucified with him. But when they came to Jesus, and saw that he was dead already, they brake not his legs . . . For these things were done, that the scripture should be fulfilled, A bone of him shall not be broken." (John 19:32-36)

93. Stephen, the martyr, saw this fulfilled: "But he, being full of the Holy Ghost, looked up steadfastly into heaven, and saw the glory of God, and Jesus standing on the right of God." (Acts 7:55)

94. 1 Chronicles 18:1 as rendered in the Vulgate text. (See Clarke, *Bible Commentary*. Vol. 2, p. 328)

The next territory to fall was Moab which had been abusing Israel off and on for several centuries. The Bible text describing this conquest is a difficult one involving faulty translation. The English version implies that David put two-thirds of the Moabite population to the sword, but Dr. Adam Clarke interprets this passage as referring to the destruction of two-thirds of their fortified cities rather than the actual killing of the people.[95] He states that David pulled down the walls of these cities so the residents could not rebel against him in the future. This fits the rest of the text wherein it says, "the Moabites became David's servants." Insurrection would be less likely if their cities were open and unprotected.

It will be recalled that David's great grandmother was Ruth, a Moabite and therefore a descendant of Lot. It will also be recalled that as long as David was a fugitive from Saul, the Moabite king was most friendly to him. Once David had become king of Israel, however, the Moabites looked upon him as an enemy just as they had looked upon Saul. This was the reason for completely subjugating them. However, it is not reasonable to believe that David would massacre two-thirds of the Moabite population when all of these factors are considered.

David next won a victory over the king of Zobah, named Hadadezer, who was a ruling potentate north of Israel, in Syria.[96] However, when the Syrians of Damascus heard about it they counter-attacked and David was obliged to fight one of the major battles of his entire career. This victory was won only after 22,000 Syrians had been slain.[97] "Then David put garrisons in Syria of Damascus; and the Syrians became servants to David, and brought gifts [paid tribute]."[98] The rich booty from these engagements was enough to swell the treasuries of Israel beyond anything they had ever known before. It included gold shields taken from the personal bodyguard of King Hadadezer[99] and also vast quantities of brass which were later used in Solomon's temple to make "the brazen sea, and the pillars, and the vessels of brass."[100]

---

95. Ibid., p. 329
96. 2 Samuel 8:3
97. 2 Samuel 8:5
98. 2 Samuel 8:6
99. 2 Samuel 8:7
100. 1 Chronicles 18:8

In northern Syria at the upper region of the Orontes Valley there was a great Hittite (Hamitic) city called Hamath.[101] Its king was named Tou[102] and he was delighted when he heard that David had subjugated the Syrian hosts since they had been waging persistent war against Hamath for many years. Therefore King Tou "sent Hadoram his son to king David, to inquire of his welfare, and to congratulate him because he had fought against Hadarezer [same as Hadadezer] and smitten him."[103] King Tou sent along a treasure of gifts for David consisting of "all manner of vessels of gold, and silver, and brass."[104] These were taken back to Jerusalem by David and dedicated along with his other treasure to the building of the great temple.[105]

David's next military conquest was to the south of Israel where he successfully conquered the pestilent Amalekites and the desert marauders, the Edomites, both of whom were descendants of Esau.[106] This particular campaign was under the direction of David's nephew, Abishai, who met the Edomites near the lower portion of the Dead Sea (in the Valley of Salt) and slew 18,000.[107] "And he [Abishai] put garrisons in Edom; and all the Edomites became David's servants."[108] So much for the people who had stubbornly refused to allow Israel to pass peacefully through their land when Israel came up out of Egypt![109]

The land of Edom became a great source of wealth for Israel during Solomon's reign because of the vast deposits of copper which were mined and manufactured into brass.

David's Kingdom Finally Fulfills a Prophecy

All of these mighty victories occupy but one short chapter in the Bible but it is obvious that they represent a whole series of monumental military campaigns involving tens of thousands of troops and the successful solving of

---

101. See Peloubet's *Bible Dictionary* under "Hamath."
102. 1 Chronicles 18:9
103. 1 Chronicles 18:10
104. Ibid.
105. Ibid. 18:11
106. See Peloubet's *Bible Dictionary* under these two subjects.
107. 1 Chronicles 18:12
108. 1 Chronicles 18:13
109. Numbers 20:18-21

extremely difficult problems in logisitics. It was therefore some 500 years after Moses that Israel ultimately dominated all of the domain originally promised by the Lord so many centuries before. It extended from the east branch of the Delta Nile (the river of Egypt) to the great river Euphrates in Mesopotamia. Abraham,[110] Isaac,[111] Jacob[112] and Moses[113] had all been promised that eventually Israel would occupy all this territory. Now it finally had been accomplished.

Our only regret is the fact that Israel's occupation or domination of this territory did not mean that righteous government was going to replace the heathen culture. Originally, the Lord had discussed with Moses the possibility of establishing a kingdom in this territory similar to the City-of-Enoch civilization. The Lord had promised that if the Israelites were righteous God would bless this people "AND MAKE THEE HIGH ABOVE ALL NATIONS. . . ."[114] He had said, "thou shalt lend unto many nations, but thou shalt not borrow; and thou shalt REIGN OVER MANY NATIONS, but they shall not reign over thee."[115]

To accomplish this it would have been necessary to cleanse the land of its heathen culture and establish the righteous law of the covenant. This was never done. As a result, David merely conquered these heathen peoples and placed them under tribute. They did not come under the law of the covenant nor did they abandon their heathen ways. Eventually this corrupted the whole kingdom of Israel. The policies of coexistence and compromise with evil during the days of David and Solomon had much to do with Israel's later downfall.

Nevertheless, to the extent God could reward Israel, He did. The scripture therefore closes the account of David's remarkable military conquests by saying, "So David reigned over all Israel, and executed judgment and justice among all his people."[116]

---

110. Genesis 13:14-17 but especially 15:18 which specifically describes Israel's inheritance as being "from the river of Egypt [east delta branch of the Nile] unto the great river, the river Euphrates."
111. Genesis 26:3   114. Deuteronomy 26:19
112. Genesis 28:4   115. Deuteronomy 15:5-6
113. Deuteronomy 34:1-4   116. 1 Chronicles 18:14

DAVID USES MULTIPLE MARRIAGES TO UNIFY THE KINGDOM

In order to unify his people and the royal families of conquered territories, David followed a policy characteristic of the times wherein he would take a wife from each of the leading families to establish political unity through the filial relationships of marital alignments.[117]

This is the reason political marriages in all countries and in all ages have been considered one of the most reliable procedures for the encouragement of a stable peace between nations. David therefore employed this device. Furthermore, since the principle of plurality of wives was acceptable under the patriarchal system of Israel, he saw no religious restriction to prevent the expansion of this policy wherever it might prove propitious. However, as we shall see later, the zeal of David and Solomon in carrying out this policy ultimately led them to become involved in all kinds of domestic turbulence. A strict adherence to the discipline of the order of marriage followed by the patriarchs could have avoided such difficulties.

In the first place, the Lord said that plurality of families was an abomination before him when undertaken for the selfish purposes of individuals. The Lord said that under ordinary circumstances "there shall not any man among you have save it be one wife. . . ." Then He added, "For if I will, saith the Lord of Hosts, RAISE UP SEED UNTO ME, I will COMMAND my people [to have plurality of families]; otherwise they shall hearken unto these things."[118]

A study of the lives of the patriarchs will show that when they had multiple families it was for the purpose of raising up a mighty posterity unto the Lord. In the specific cases of Abraham and Jacob, it will be noted that for the most part, their multiple marriages were entered into at the request of their wives who were either barren or wanted their husbands to ask other women to join with them in the task of bearing and rearing large families.

---

117. 2 Samuel 3:2-5 indicates the beginning of this practice and 2 Samuel 5:13 shows that it was a continuing policy.
118. Jacob 2:27-30

In the case of David, however, and to an even greater extent with Solomon, there was a combining of the righteous procedure which the Lord had invoked with the unrighteous procedure which men had invented. David and Solomon both began entering into their multiple marriages through the proper religious procedure and under the blessings of the Priesthood; but when they began branching out in all directions, taking on marriages which even included heathen princesses, the Lord was offended.

The Lord's point of view is expressed in the following passage: "David also received many wives and concubines, and also Solomon and Moses my servants, as also many others of my servants, from the beginning of creation until this time; and in nothing did they sin save in THOSE THINGS WHICH THEY RECEIVED NOT OF ME."[119] As we shall see later, multiple marriages which were not of the Lord were the ones which ultimately subverted the households of both David and Solomon. Therefore a prophet writing some four hundred years after David and Solomon said, "Behold, David and Solomon truly had many wives and concubines, which thing was abominable before me saith the Lord."[120] However, as the Lord elucidates His position in the more recent scripture we learn that this statement by Jacob is a little too broad. The Lord's position appears to be that He does not count multiple families abominable if He has COMMANDED them "to raise seed up unto me," but these practices are abominable in "those things which they receive not of me."

Nowhere is the contrast better illustrated than in the lives of David and Solomon.

David Establishes Elaborate Military and Administrative Machinery for His Kingdom

No doubt the complicated and extensive governmental machinery which David organized for the building of the kingdom evolved over a considerable period of time. We shall mention some of this structure of government in order

---

119. Doctrine and Covenants 132:38
120. Jacob 2:24

to appreciate both the skill of David as an administrator as well as the complexity of the kingdom's administrative requirements once it began to flourish.

At the head of the government stood David, "the anointed of the Lord." The calling of a king was sacred in the eyes of the people, but a ruler was never deified as so often happened in heathen kingdoms. David's power was limited by the constitution drawn up by Samuel, but by its very nature the monarchial type of government gave David tremendous arbitrary, personal power.

When traveling about the country or leading a procession, David rode his own royal mule.[121] The kings of Israel used the mule which symbolized tranquility and peace rather than mount a panoplied charger which represented war.

David functioned as a judge of civil and criminal matters and sat regularly at the gate of the palace to decide causes which the people felt necessary to bring to his attention.[122]

One of David's noblemen named Ahithophel functioned as the king's confidential advisor,[123] but in most national crises David relied upon the advice of the prophet Nathan. David had an official recorder or historian, a royal secretary, a treasurer and other necessary court functionaries.[124] The older sons of the king together with certain chosen dignitaries served as members of a privy council or cabinet.[125]

The army received David's special attention. The core of the military was the famous 600 who had been with him since the days of his exile and gained the name of the Gibborim or the "mighty ones" because of their bravery.[126] The main forces of the army were called "The Host" and consisted of 300,000 men divided into twelve sections.[127] Each section was required to serve for one month at its own expense and therefore the kingdom was constantly pro-

---

121. 1 Kings 1:33
122. 2 Samuel 15:2
123. 1 Chronicles 27:33
124. 2 Samuel 8:16; 17; 20:23-26
125. 2 Samuel 8:17, 18
126. See discussion in Geikie, *Hours With the Bible,* Vol. 3, p. 254.
127. 1 Chronicles 27:1-15

tected without subjecting it to heavy military budgets. Only when there was some major threat to the country were the other troops mobilized. Each of the twelve sections was divided into hundreds and into thousands and the principal commander was usually one of the Gibborim selected for that position by David.[128]

The supreme commander of the entire host was Joab, hero of the conquest of Jerusalem, and nephew of David. He was called "general of the king's army,"[129] and had an armor-bearer and ten attendants to carry his equipment and baggage.[130] Joab established a branch of the Jewish nobility which survived the captivity.[131]

Immediately around him, David gathered some of his most trusted warriors as a personal bodyguard. Surprisingly, many of these were foreigners. Some of these were Cherethites and Pelethites[132] under the leadership of a Levite Priest named Benaiah.[133] He was a tried and battle-scarred veteran who was son of Jehoiada, one of the chief Priests.[134] Since the days of Moses the Levites had been excused from military service in order to maintain the continuity of the religious and civic affairs of the nation. However, Benaiah had followed the example of his father Jehoiada, who, though a chief priest and the leader of the Aaronites, made 3,700 of his people available as warriors for David when the son of Jesse first became king in Hebron.[135] Benaiah afterwards elected to continue pursuing a military career and not only became the chief of David's personal bodyguard, but the commander of the third section of the host.[136] Later he replaced Joab as the commander-in-chief of the entire army of Israel.[137]

Other members of David's elite bodyguard were Philistines who came over to David from Gath, the home of Goliath. They were led by Ittai of Gath whose fidelity to David was so remarkable that David eventually placed him in charge of a third part of the whole army.[138]

---

128. Ibid.
129. 1 Chronicles 27:34
130. 2 Samuel 18:15
131. Nehemiah 7:11
132. 2 Samuel 8:18; 20:23
133. 1 Chronicles 11:24-25

134. 1 Chronicles 27:5
135. 1 Chronicles 12:27
136. 1 Chronicles 27:5
137. 1 Kings 2:35; 4:4
138. 2 Samuel 18:2, 5, 12

David Honors Jonathan's Only Son

As David settled down to the task of administering the affairs of Israel, it must have occured to him on countless occasions how gratifying it would have been if Prince Jonathan were yet alive. Together they would have made a great team. But since Philistine swords had hewn down that noble prince several years before, David wondered if he might not honor Jonathan's children. He sent for Ziba, the steward of Saul's property, and asked if Jonathan had left any sons.

Ziba answered in the affirmative. He had left a son named Mephibosheth who was living with a man named Machir in Lo-debar of Trans-Jordan.[139] However, he said the boy was lame in both feet. It was the result of an accident which occurred when news of Jonathan's death reached the capital. Mephibosheth was then five years of age and when the people panicked and began fleeing the city, the boy's nurse picked him up and fled with them. However, in her haste she stumbled and dropped the boy. He fell to the ground breaking or permanently damaging both of his legs so that it left him a cripple.

David immediately ordered Mephibosheth brought before him. The young man was apparently terrified lest David consider him a pretender to the throne and slay him. He threw himself at David's feet in the most abject reverence saying, "Behold thy servant."[140]

David said, "Fear not: for I will surely shew thee kindness for Jonathan thy father's sake, and will restore thee all the land of Saul thy father; and thou shalt eat bread at my table continually."[141] Mephibosheth could hardly believe this sudden bounty of good fortune, especially from a man whom his grandfather, Saul, had tried for so many years to kill. Mephibosheth exclaimed, "What is thy servant, that thou shouldest look upon such a dead dog as I am?"[142] It was very obvious that the cruelty of the past had left deep-seated scars in the soul of this crushed and crippled young

---

139. 2 Samuel 9:4. The location of Lo-debar is indicated in 2 Samuel 17:27.
140. 2 Samuel 9:6   142. 2 Samuel 9:8
141. 2 Samuel 9:7

man. David resolved to make it up to him and restore him to a status of proper dignity. He therefore commanded Ziba, Saul's steward, saying, "Thou, therefore, and thy sons, and thy servants, shall till the land [Saul's former estate] for him, and thou shalt bring in the fruits that thy master's son [and his family] may have food to eat: but Mephibosheth thy master's son shall eat bread always at my table."[143]

Ziba acquiesced to this command, nevertheless he resented it deeply. Ziba had 15 sons and 20 servants,[144] and apparently he had been operating Saul's estate like a lord of the manor since Saul's death. The new arrangement was not at all to his liking and years later he committed an outright fraud against both Mephibosheth and King David in order to get this estate back in his control. We shall deal with that event when it appears shortly.

---

143. 2 Samuel 9:10
144. Ibid.

Scripture Readings and Questions on Chapter Five

Scripture Readings: 2 Samuel chapters 6 to 9 inclusive.

1—What was the political status of the great empires at the time David came to power? How did this facilitate the building of Israel?

2—Why did the Philistines feel impelled to attack Davd immediately after he became king of a united Israel? What was the result?

3—Why did King Hiram of Tyre have a special reason for allying himself with David? What did he do to show his friendship for David?

4—When David became king of Israel, where was the Ark of the Covenant? Why wasn't it in the Tabernacle where it belonged?

5—Did David obtain popular support for the removal of the Ark to Jerusalem? Was the procession a solemn or jubilant affair?

6—Is there any record in the Bible of David being ordained to the Priesthood? How do we know he held the Priesthood? What level?

7—How far did the Ark have to travel before it reached Jerusalem? What happened when Uzzah reached out to steady the Ark?

8—Why did the Lord need to subject Israel to a shock treatment like this? What was the spiritual status of Israel at this time?

9—How long was it before the Ark was moved from the house of Obed-edom to Jerusalem? Where did David put it?

10—When David asked Nathan about building a temple what did Nathan say? Did the Lord agree? Why not?

11—Nevertheless, what good news did Nathan bring back to David? What does "Messianic" mean?

12—How did David find out about the pattern for the temple which Solomon would build? Was the information oral or written?

13—Name five things David knew about the life and mission of Jesus.

14—Which peoples did David permanently conquer as he expanded his kingdom?

15—Why was Tou pleased when David defeated the Syrians? What did he do to show his appreciation?

16—Was David's kingdom ever as large as the one promised by the Lord when he made covenants with Abraham, Isaac and Jacob? How far did it extend?

17—Why did David use multiple marriages to unify his kingdom? At what point did the Lord become displeased with this procedure?

18—Did David ever serve as a judge? Why did he ride a royal mule instead of a horse? What was unusual about Benaiah, the chief of David's bodyguard?

19—Did Jonathan leave any sons? How many? What did David do about it?

20—From whom did the Philistines descend? How about the Phoenicians? Where does the word, Canaanite, come from?

Chapter Six

The Ecstasy and the Agony

of David's Fall

The extent of the passing years as we enter the next period of David's life is difficult to measure. It would seem that after a substantial period of tranquility a whole new series of wars broke out as a result of a vindictive and insulting blunder committed by the heathen Ammonites living in Trans-Jordan. The Ammonites, it will be recalled, were the descendants of Lot but they had lost almost every fragment of the gospel and had been a pagan people for centuries. Nevertheless, David had succeeded in maintaining fairly good relations with them. Their king, named Nahash, had done many favors for David.[1]

When king Nahash, the Ammonite, died, David was grieved and sent a delegation from his court to express his sympathies to the people. But the princes of Ammon had already appointed Hanum, the son of Nahash, to be their new king and when David's ambassador arrived these princes of Ammon poisoned his mind with these words: "Thinkest thou that David doth honour thy father, that he hath sent comforters unto thee? Hath not David rather sent his

---

1. 2 Samuel 10:2

servants unto thee, to search the city, and to spy it out, and to overthrow it?''[2]

So it was decided to treat the men from David's court as contemptible spies. They were arrested, half of their beards were shaved off and their long robes were cut off at the waist.[3] In this embarrasing condition they were thrust back onto the street and forced to get home as best they might. When David heard of it he was outraged and he let it be known that the Ammonites had now become an evil odor in his nostrils.[4] Nevertheless, he made no attempt to avenge the wrong. It was the Ammonites who decided to make war. Either they assumed that David would soon be at their gates or the princes of Ammon wanted to use the newly created hostility as an excuse for mobilizing all of the nearby king-doms against Israel. They were even willing to pay their neighbors to fight againt David. The scripture says, ''. . . the children of Ammon sent and hired the Syrians of Beth-rehob, and the Syrians of Zoba, twenty thousand footmen, and of King Maacah a thousand men, and of Ish-tob twelve thousand men.''[5]

When David realized there was going to be war he sent Joab to lay siege to the Ammonite city of Medaba, apparently intending to conquer it before the Syrians arrived. However, when Joab reached Medaba the Ammonites boldly marched out of their gate to attack him and the next thing Joab knew he found that the Syrians had arrived and were closing in on him from the rear. This called for decisive and immediate action by the Israelites, since it was obvious they were about to be trapped. Joab therefore split his forces. He took one group and had them do an about face to con-front the Syrians. Meanwhile he told his older brother, Abishai to proceed with the remainder of the forces and attack the Ammonites.[6]

This strategy worked. As Joab and his host wheeled about and charged into the Syrians they panicked and fled. Then, when the Ammonites realized they were without sup-port, they ran from Abishai's army and locked themselves

---

2. 2 Samuel 10:3
3. 2 Samuel 10:4
4. 2 Samuel 10:6

5. Ibid.
6. 2 Samuel 10:9-10

inside their city. Perhaps they expected Joab to lay siege to Medaba and avenge himself, but Joab did not. Israel wanted no war with Ammon, merely a restoration of the status quo. Therefore Joab withdrew his forces and marched back to Jerusalem.[7]

All might have proceeded peacefully had not the pride of the Syrians been injured. When the Syrian kings learned what a miserable showing their soldiers had made after being paid to fight for the Ammonites, they decided to redeem their reputation. They mobilized a huge army and even obtained troops from "beyond the river," meaning the river Euphrates.[8] Then they headed back down toward Medaba, city of the Ammonites.

But they never reached it. When David heard what was happening he personally took command of the situation. David called for the combined forces out of every tribe in Israel, and pushed them across the Jordan and northward to Helam where he intercepted the Syrians. A fierce encounter followed and when the dust of battle had finally settled, the dead bodies of tens of thousands of the Syrians lay scattered across the terrain in every direction.[9] It was literally a rout. The Bible closes the incident by saying: "And when all the kings that were servants to Hadarezer [of Syria] saw that they were smitten before Israel, they made peace with Israel, and served them. So the Syrians feared to help the children of Ammon any more."[10]

DAVID LOSES THE MOST IMPORTANT BATTLE OF HIS LIFE

It seems that the final phase of the war with the Ammonites took place the following spring.[11] Joab was sent out to humble the Ammonites so there would be no further trouble. After conquering many of them the remnant fled to the walled city of Rabbah and there Joab besieged them. The campaign was proceeding with relative success so David

---

7. 2 Samuel 10:14
8. 2 Samuel 10:16
9. 2 Samuel 10:18. This scripture says the dead amounted to "forty thousand horsemen." However, 1 Chronicles 19:18 calls them "footmen" which is undoubtedly the correct version.
10. 2 Samuel 10:19
11. 2 Samuel 11:1 plus Clarke, *Bible Commentary*, Vol. 2, p. 334

"tarried" at Jerusalem.[12] It would have been better had he accompanied his troops. David did not know it but he was about to engage in the greatest contest of his life and lose it.

The scripture says David awakened in the late afternoon from a rest and decided to refresh himself by strolling along the parapet on the roof of his beautiful cedar palace. Directly below him were the homes of the Gibborim, the king's 600 "mighty ones" who were now leading the forces of Israel in the capture of Rabbah. One of these houses which was particularly close to the Cedar Palace was the home of Uriah, a non-Israelite, who had followed David with the devotion of a brother even though his own nationality was Hittite. Not only had Uriah distinguished himself as a soldier but he was on the top list of David's Gibborim commanders.[13] For a Hittite alien he had also accomplished something else distinctive. He had wooed and married an Israelite. She was Bath-sheba, the strikingly beautiful daughter of captain Eliam, another of David's commanders.[14] Apparently Bath-sheba had married Uriah only a short time before and as yet had no children.

The scripture says that on this late afternoon while David was strolling along the roof terrace of the palace he looked down and saw Bath-sheba bathing in the courtyard of her home. She "was very beautiful to look upon," the Bible says.[15] Had David known what this infatuating sight was going to mean to his career and his kingdom he might have fled from the temptation. But this he did not do. Instead, he sent messengers to discover the identity of this woman. They brought back the report that she was Bath-sheba, daughter of the noble Eliam, and wife of David's valiant warrior, Uriah.

This is all David should have required to banish from his mind the captivating charm of this beautiful woman. But he longed to make her acquaintance and therefore sent messengers to invite her to visit the palace. Although nothing need have come of it, the visit of Bath-sheba became more than merely a social call. It escalated from a pleasant visit between king and subject to an intoxicating and mad-

---

12. Ibid.
13. 2 Samuel 23:39

14. 2 Samuel 11:3
15. 2 Samuel 11:2

dening infatuation between a man and a woman. The physical magnetism which each felt for the other drove reason from their minds. The consequence was abject surrender to the fervor of the emotional hurricane which suddenly engulfed them.[16]

High on the battlements of Mount Sinai, the ancient prophet, Moses, had watched the finger of God engrave upon the tablets of stone the mandate of Heaven, "Thou shalt not commit adultery."[17] It became known as the Seventh Commandment and stood next to murder in the roster of serious offenses.[18] This was a crime against Heaven which now brought down upon the heads of David and Bath-sheba the vitriolic bitterness of inescapable judgment.

In several truly remarkable ways the affair between David and Bath-sheba was practically identical with the clandestine romance between Julius Caesar and Cleopatra. Caesar was 54 and married. He possessed a magnetic personality, was famous as a great soldier and general and at the moment was virtual ruler of a rising empire. Cleopatra was 21, married,[19] sensationally beautiful, and romantically capable of following a reckless inclination. The attraction between Caesar and Cleopatra was instantaneous and their affair began with their first meeting. It took place at the palace in Alexandria where Cleopatra had been brought at the command of Julius Caesar. Cleopatra had her first child as a result of this illegitimate adventure.

In all of these details the circumstances of David and Bath-sheba are in nearly perfect parallel. David was somewhere around 50, a handsome and magnetic personality and certainly much married. He was a heroic soldier, a great general and the ruler of a rising kingdom. From all we know of Bath-sheba she was young, fascinatingly beautiful, newly married and childless. She went to the king's palace on the king's invitation, became romantically involved and had her first child as a result of the affair.

---

16. 2 Samuel 11:4
17. Exodus 20:14
18. Alma 39:5-6
19. Cleopatra was married to her younger brother after the manner of the royal dynasties of Egypt.

There was one thing, however, which made a vast difference between the two cases. Julius Caesar and Cleopatra were both pagans who had been reared under the shadow of heathen amorality. David and Bath-sheba, on the other hand, were children of the patriarchs living under the discipline of God's revealed law. Both of them were aware that their act of indiscretion was something God had categorically forbidden and they also knew the penalty for adultery was of the severest kind.

Therefore as Bath-sheba returned to her house and David returned to his senses they must have both encountered the hollow agony of what they had done. A single moment of reckless passion had hurled them headlong into the hellfire of a soul-scorching furnace led by the terrifying fuel of their own mental anguish. Neither David nor Bath-sheba would ever be the same again. Not that it was the end of existence, nor the end of hope, but for each of them it was the end of an epic — the sudden, breathtaking and dizzy descent from a pinnacle of happiness down into the dark and deadly labyrinth of smothering darkness which can engulf a human soul with desolating despair. From that moment until the distant remoteness of the forseeable future, David and Bath-sheba would not be advancing to new heights of exhilarating happiness but simply seeking to recover the vast wastes of lost ground.

As for David, things would get infinitely worse before they got better.

Uriah Returns to Jerusalem

The scriptures tell us that after a few weeks had passed Bath-sheba communicated to David that she had conceived and was with child.[20] Because her husband, Uriah, had been gone so long at the front David knew that for Bath-sheba, at least, the disgrace of her involvement in adultery would soon become public knowledge. Then something occurred to David which offered a possible escape. He sent to Joab at the battle front and ordered Uriah back to Jerusalem. In his frantic state of mind David thought he could protect

---

20. 2 Samuel 11:5

Bath-sheba by having her husband home for a short time. When the child was born Uriah would then think it was his own. But the scheme failed.

Uriah returned well enough but his dogged loyalty to David and his comrades-in-arms made him unwilling to return to his own house. The scripture says:

"And David said to Uriah, Go down to thy house, and wash thy feet. And Uriah departed out of the king's house, and there followed a mess of meat [provisions] from the king.

"But Uriah slept at the door of the king's house with all the servants of his lord, and went not down to his house. . . . David said unto Uriah, Camest thou not from thy journey? Why then did thou not go down unto thine house?

"And Uriah said unto David, The ark and Israel, and Judah, abide in tents; and my lord Joab, and the servants of my lord, are encamped in the open fields; shall I then go into mine house, to eat and to drink, and to lie with my wife? As thou livest, and as thy soul liveth, I will not do this thing."[21]

David could see he was dealing with a stubborn man. But David was stubborn, too, and becoming increasingly desperate. He therefore determined to resort to stratagem. He determined to reduce Uriah's stubborness with a quantity of wine. David invited Uriah to dine in the palace. After indulging him in an excess of food and drink he hoped the man would exhibit a willingness to return to his home. However, to David's astonishment, Uriah "went out to lie on his bed with the servants of his lord, but went not down to his house."[22]

Now David seemed to drown the capacity to think rationally in the dregs of his own despair. If Uriah would not cooperate in saving the reputation of Bath-sheba then David would eliminate him and save her name by taking her unto himself. The original crime of adultery was now fertilizing the ground for the sowing and reaping of a far more atrocious crime, the shedding of innocent blood.

---

21. 2 Samuel 11:8-11   22. 2 Samuel 11:13

In the feverish frustration which so often overwhelms a guilt-ridden mind, David concocted a plot to do away with Uriah without getting himself involved. He would have Joab place Uriah where the battle was most dangerous and then have him abandoned to insure his being killed. It was ugly, vicious, depraved. David would spend the rest of his life cringing at the thought of this outrageous procedure by which he destroyed one of his most faithful and valiant warriors.

Uriah himself carried the letter of instructions to Joab but of course had no way of knowing or even suspecting that he was delivering his own death warrant.[23]

No doubt Joab was puzzled as to the reason David wished Uriah dead, but since it came as a royal command, Joab never hesitated. He decided to send Uriah out with a group of the king's most experienced fighters. They would attack the city wall. This military maneuver was carried out according to Joab's instructions but it backfired. Instead of Uriah alone being killed, a whole contingent of the king's top soldiers were wiped out.[24] Apparently they came too close to the wall and exposed themselves to missiles, rocks or scalding water being dumped on them from above.[25] For generations Israel's soldiers had been taught to avoid this kind of situation. They were instructed to remember the experience of Gideon's son, Abimelech, who was killed by a small millstone being throne from the top of a wall by a woman.[26] All of this explains Joab's careful instructions to one of his messengers following the debacle in which Uriah was killed. Joab said, "When thou hast made an end of telling the matters of the war unto the king, and if so be that the king's wrath arise, and he say unto thee, Wherefore approached ye so nigh unto the city when ye did fight? knew ye not that they would shoot from the wall? . . . then say thou, Thy servant Uriah the Hittite is dead also."[27] Joab hoped his bad tactics which led to the death of so

23. 2 Samuel 11:14
24. 2 Samuel 11:17
25. 2 Samuel 11:20
26. Judges 9:53. Note that Godeon is sometimes called Jerubbesheth or Jerubbaal (2 Samuel 11:21; Judges 6:32).
27. 2 Samuel 11:19-21

many good men would be forgiven after David learned that Uriah was among those who had died.

When David heard the news he reacted exactly as Joab had predicted. His relief over the death of Uriah was sufficient to ameliorate his anger over the way the project had been so badly bungled.

DAVID MARRIES BATH-SHEBA
BUT THE LORD REVEALS THEIR SINS

As soon as Bath-sheba heard that her husband was dead she went into the prescribed period of lamentation and mourning.[28] However, when this was past and David felt he could decently do so, Bath-sheba was brought to the palace and David made her his wife.

So far, David had the satisfaction of seeing everything work out according to plan. Uriah was out of the way, David had married his widow, and Bath-sheba's child could now be born at the palace under circumstances not likely to arouse suspicion. David knew it was a terrible thing he had done but at least the transgression was being kept a secret. In due time Bath-sheba's baby was born but then a bombshell fell. It caught David completely unawares and came upon him like an avalanche of wrath from a prophet of God just after Bath-sheba's baby arrived.

The scripture says, "The Lord sent Nathan unto David. And he came unto him and said unto him, There were two men in one city; the one rich, and the other poor. The rich man had exceeding many flocks and herds: But the poor man had nothing, save one little ewe lamb, which he had bought and nourished up. . . . And there came a traveller unto the rich man, and he spared [declined] to take of his own flock . . . to dress for the wayfaring man . . . but took the poor man's lamb, and dressed it for the man that was come to him."[29]

To David who often sat at the palace gate to pass judgments on just such problems, the rich man was guilty of a gross injustice. This was a simple case of abuse of power

---

28. 2 Samuel 11:26
29. 2 Samuel 12:1-5

and outright thievery. So David was angry and said to Nathan that the rich man should die unless he restored the stolen lamb fourfold.

Nathan looked at David and declared, "Thou art the man!"[30]

Without realizing it, David had condemned himself. Yet the worst was still to come. In a voice of doomsday, Nathan trumpeted a message which God had given him. "Thus saith the Lord God of Israel, I anointed thee king over Israel, and I delivered thee out of the hand of Saul. . . . Wherefore hast thou despised the commandment of the Lord, to do evil in his sight? THOU HAST KILLED URIAH THE HITTITE WITH THE SWORD, AND HAST TAKEN HIS WIFE TO BE THY WIFE AND HAST SLAIN HIM WITH THE SWORD OF THE CHILDREN OF AMMON."[31]

One can only imagine the smashing impact of this revelation on the mind of David. After all the clever plans, the risks and the subterfuge, the terrible truth was out. Not only would the people know of his sin with Bath-sheba but now they would know that the death of Uriah was deliberate murder.

Nathan followed this blast by pouring out on David the content of three terrible prophecies:[32]

1—"Now therefore the sword shall never depart from thine house."

2—"Behold, I will raise up evil against thee out of thine own house."

3—"I will take thy wives before thine eyes and give them unto thy neighbour, and he shall lie with thy wives in the sight of this sun [meaning it will be a matter of public knowledge]."

And all this, the prophet declared, "because by this deed thou hast given great occasion to the enemies of the Lord to blaspheme," meaning to curse God and denounce

---

30. 2 Samuel 12:7
31. 2 Samuel 12:7-9. Nathan's parable could not apply to David in all respects since David could never bring back Uriah, let alone restore "fourfold."
32. 2 Samuel 12:10-11

the work He was attempting to do through David's administration.

David did not know it, but the first prophecy would result in the violent death of three of his sons — Ammon, Absalom and Adonijah. Truly the sword and the assassin's dagger would not depart from David's house either in this generation or the next. The second prophecy was to be fulfilled in the not too distant future as David's best-beloved son tried to kill him and seize the throne. And this same son would partially fulfill the third prophecy by seizing ten of David's wives and violating them. A subsequent revelation revealed that eventually, after passing into the eternal worlds, David would be deprived of *all* his families![33]

David's reply to this apocalyptic judgment was to humbly confess, "I have sinned against the Lord."[34] Nathan then advised David that God was *not* going to require his life as might have happened in a case of this kind.[35] Nevertheless, he would pay for his sins to the uttermost farthing. To begin with, David was advised that he and Bath-sheba would not be allowed to keep the fruit of their offense. The child which had just been born to Bath-sheba would die.

David Pleads With the Lord

David's taste of a literal hell now commenced in earnest. First he went into the depths of humility with fasting and prayer to try to save Bath-sheba's child. Weeping and pleading, he "lay all night upon the earth."[36] It was to no avail. After he learned that the child was dead he ceased his fast and also his mourning. He had failed. He must be content. When he was asked why he had stopped mourning he replied, "While the child was yet alive, I fasted

---

33. Doc. & Cov. 132:39 which says: "David's wives and concubines were given unto him of me, by the hand of Nathan, my servant, and others of the prophets who had the keys of this power; and in none of these things did he sin against me save in the case of Uriah and his wife; and, therefore he hath fallen from his exaltation, and received his portion; and he shall not inherit them out of the world, for I gave them unto another, saith the Lord."
34. 2 Samuel 12:13
35. Ibid. Perhaps this was a technicality since David had not committed the murder with his own hand. Nevertheless, the Lord wanted David to know that he was personally responsible for Uriah's death and would be required to pay the full penalty for it.
36. 2 Samuel 12:6

and wept: for I said, Who can tell whether God will be
gracious to me, that the child may live? But now he
is dead, wherefore should I fast? Can I bring him back
again? I shall go to him, but he shall not return to me."[37]

From out of the mental torment and fierce anguish
which David now suffered came the passionate pleas contained in the 51st psalm:

> Have mercy upon me, O God,
> According to thy loving kindness:
> According unto the multitude
> Of thy tender mercies,
> Blot out my transgressions.
>
> Wash me thoroughly from mine iniquity
> And cleanse me from my sin.
> For I acknowledge my transgressions:
> And my sin is ever before me.
>
> Create in me a clean heart, O God,
> And renew a right spirit within me.
> Cast me not away from thy presence;
> And take not thy Holy Spirit from me.

The Meaning of Murder in the Sight of God

To appreciate the extremity of the problems in which
David had enmeshed himself, it is important to review all
that the Lord has said about the crime of murder. It is
defined by the Lord as being the deliberate shedding of
"innocent blood."[38] It is one crime which is not covered by
the atonement, meaning that the individual must pay the
penalty himself until the full measure of justice is met.[39]
This is what the Lord means in the scripture which declared,
". . . he that kills shall not have forgiveness in this world
nor in the world to come."[40] "Forgiveness" in this passage
is referring to the blotting out of sin by repentance and
baptism and obtaining forgiveness through the power of the
Atonement. The quoted passage means that this is not pos-

37. 2 Samuel 12:22-23
38. Deuteronomy 19:10-13. Note that the Lord has always defined a murderer
    as a person who, 1—with deliberate intent, 2—sheds innocent blood. The Lord
    makes it clear that murder does not include any of those situations where a person
    is killed, 1—accidentally, 2—in the heat of combat such as a war, 3—in the heat
    of passion arising during a fight, or 4—when a person kills in self defense. Only
    number 3 is considered a crime, but it is not considered murder.
39. Numbers 35:30-31; Joseph Felding Smith, *Doctrines of Salvation*, Vol. 1, p. 133.
40. Doctrine and Covenants 42:18

sible for a murderer.[41] One who has deliberately violated the sanctity of human life is on his own. The cosmic community of intelligences over whom the Father presides as God and Judge will not be reconciled to a murderer until he has personally suffered for his offense.[42] This is also true, of course, for any sins which are not brought under the Atonement. The Savior has warned that this suffering is so intense that God desires all to take advantage of the Atonement where possible. Declared the Christ, "For behold, I, God, have suffered these things for all, that they might not suffer if they would repent; but if they would not repent they must suffer even as I; which suffering caused myself, even God, the greatest of all, to tremble because of pain, and to bleed at every pore, and to suffer both body and spirit — and would that I might not drink the bitter cup, and shrink — nevertheless, glory be to the Father, I partook and finished my preparations unto the children of men. Wherefore, I command you again to repent, lest I humble you with my almighty power; and that you confess your sins, lest you suffer these punishments of which I have spoken, of which in the smallest, yea, even in the least degree you have tasted at the time I withdrew my Spirit."[43]

When David involved himself in an act of adultery it was indeed one of the most serious offenses against God. Nevertheless, with a confession of this sin and a perfect repentance (meaning that it would never be committed again) *there could have been complete forgiveness*.[44] Of course, there would be the loss of some extremely important blessings but the Atonement could still operate in his behalf.

David did not elect to follow this route. Instead of confessing his sin he tried to cover it up. He then com-

---

41. As Joseph Smith stated concerning those who had crucified Christ: "He [Peter] did not say to them, 'Repent ye and be baptized, for the remission of your sins,' but he said, 'Repent ye therefore, and be converted, that your sins may be blotted out, when the times of refreshing shall come from the presence of the Lord.' (Acts 3:19) This is the case with murderers. They could not be baptized for the remission of sins for they had shed innocent blood." (*Doc. History of the Church*, vol. 6, p. 253)
42. For a discussion on the Atonement and the principles which make it work, see *The First 2,000 Years*, pp. 352-362.
43. Doctrine and Covenants 19:16-20
44. Doctrine and Covenants 42:25-26 which reads: "But he that has committed adultery and repents with all his heart, and forsaketh it, and doeth it no more, thou shalt forgive; but if he doeth it again, he shall not be forgiven, but shall be cast out [of the Church]."

pounded his act of adultery by deliberately plotting the death of Uriah and taking Bath-sheba unto himself so that the birth of her son could be above suspicion. When David chose this course the Lord said, "thou hast despised me."[45] David had made the suffering of Jesus Christ of no effect in his behalf. He had thereby short-circuited the entire complex of elaborate machinery which God had so meticulously provided for the benefit of His children whom He loves. And He loved David. But David had taken himself outside of the plan of salvation. Only when his offense was exposed by a prophet of God did he finally face the reality of what he had done and try to repent. Joseph Smith said of him, "David sought repentance at the hand of God carefully with tears, for the murder of Uriah; but he could ONLY GET IT THROUGH HELL: he got a promise that his soul should not be left in hell."[46]

In other words, David would be required to balance the scales of justice with his own personal suffering. There is a point beyond which God cannot temper justice with mercy because it would make God unjust and He "would cease to be God,"[47] for the vast reservoir of independent intelligences in the universe would no longer voluntarily support Him.[48] This is an extremely important doctrine. It explains why human beings can commit certain offenses which carry them beyond the point where God and the Atonement of Jesus Christ can reach them. They must therefore balance the scales of justice on their own.

This is done in that much misunderstood place called, "hell." Hell is an isolated region or prison in the spirit world which is completely under the domination of Lucifer.[49] The suffering there is mental, not physical.[50] It is inhabited

---

45. 2 Samuel 12:10
46. Joseph Fielding Smith, *Teachings of Joseph Smith,* p. 339
47. Alma 42:13, 25; Mormon 9:19
48. Doctrine and Covenants 93:29-30
49. Alma 40:11-14; Doctrine & Covenants 76:73-74, 84-85, 103-106; 1 Peter 3:18-21, 4:6
50. Mosiah 2:38: "Therefore if that man repenteth not, and remaineth and dieth an enemy to God, the demands of divine justice do awaken his immortal soul to a lively sense of his own guilt, which doth cause him to shrink from the presence of the Lord, and doth fill his breast with guilt, and pain, and anguish, which is like an unquenchable fire, whose flame ascendeth up forever and ever." See also Mormon 9:3-5.

by those spirits who cannot come forth until the last resurrection, but are left subject to the abusive and misery-ridden
kingdom of Satan for a long period of time because, during
their mortal life, they elected to hearken to the will of Lucifer
rather than God.[51] Therefore, in the spirit world, Lucifer
has claim upon them and tries to hold them there as long as
he can.[52] The missionary work of the Priesthood beyond the
veil is to labor patiently among these people until they have
the strength to throw off the claim which Satan has imposed
upon them and walk forth free.[53]

The Lord promised David that ultimately, after much
suffering, he would finally achieve this freedom. This glimmer of good news was probably communicated to him by
Nathan. After receiving it, David exclaimed, "Therefore
my heart is glad, and my glory rejoiceth: my flesh also shall
rest in hope. For THOU WILT NOT LEAVE MY SOUL
IN HELL: neither wilt thou suffer thine Holy One to see
corruption. Thou wilt shew me the path of life: in thy
presence is fulness of joy; at thy right hand there are
pleasures for evermore."[54]

THE BIRTH OF SOLOMON

In all of this travail of soul, David appears to have done
what he could to comfort Bath-sheba and cushion the shock
of losing her first child. Even though David had taken the
initiative in the original offense of adultery and even though
Bath-sheba was not in any way a party to the ugly affair
which had destroyed Uriah, nevertheless she must have felt
bitterly aware that she was not at all blameless and could
have prevented this whole terrible chain of tragedy had she
played her own role of womanhood better instead of ignor-
ing the snare which her temptation of the king was bound
to create for him.

The scripture says that in due time Bath-sheba conceived again and was blessed with her second child.[55] But
now an interesting thing occurred. David had been told in

---

51. Doctrine and Covenants 88:100-101
52. Mosiah 2:33, 37; Alma 3:27, 40:13-14
53. See Joseph F. Smith, *Gospel Doctrine* (fifth edition), pp. 472-476..
54. Psalms 16:9-11
55. 2 Samuel 12:24

a revelation several years before his fall that he would have a choice son whose name would be Solomon.[56] He was further told that this son would be his successor and build a temple to the Lord.[57] How did David know that Bath-sheba's new baby was that special child of prophecy? The scripture says that David called in Nathan the prophet and Nathan disclosed that this baby was a "Jedediah," meaning a child "beloved of the Lord."[58] David therefore concluded that this must be the son which the Lord wanted to be known as "Solomon." This name means "peaceable"[59] and was prophetic since Solomon was the only king in Israel's history to have a long season of peace during his extensive, forty-year reign.

David told Bath-sheba that this infant would one day be his successor[60] and it must have brought peace to her troubled soul to know that the Lord would permit her to be the mother of this very special child.

THE FALL OF THE AMMONITES

It was probably while Bath-sheba was awaiting the birth of this second child that Joab sent news from Trans-Jordan that the siege of Rabbah, the royal city of the Ammonites, was in its final phase. Joab asked David to bring up reinforcements so that Rabbah and the rebellious Ammonites might be completely conquered. Joab said he had already "taken the city of waters"[61] but this is a bad translation. It should be, "I have intercepted, or cut off, the waters of the city."[62] David therefore rallied a large host and successfully took the city of Ramah. This was a rich metropolis so that as soon as Rabbah fell David "brought forth the spoil of the city in great abundance."[63] He also brought out the people and "put them under saws, and under harrows of iron, and under axes of iron, and made them pass through the brick-kiln."[64] On first reading this sounds

---

56. David disclosed this fact to the people in later years. See 1 Chronicles 22:9.
57. 1 Chronicles 22:10
58. 2 Samuel 12:25
59. Clarke, *Bible Commentary*, Vol. 2, p. 340
60. We learn this from a statement made by Bath-sheba many years later (1 Kings 1:17) and verified by David (1 Kings 1:30).
61. 2 Samuel 12:27
62. This is the translation given by Josephus in his *Antiquities of the Jews*, Book 7:7
63. 2 Samuel 12:30   64. 2 Samuel 12:31

as though he subjected the people to the most terrible tortures, but once again we have a poor translation. It really means that he employed them in various occupations such as sawing, harrowing the ground, cutting timber with axes and making bricks.[65]

The conquest of Rabbah was so impressive to the rest of the Ammonites that they readily saw the futility of further resistance and therefore capitulated. The whole people were then employed in a vast reconstruction program which David inaugurated to rebuild the country.[66]

The Rise of Evil in David's Own House

It was shortly after this that David came to understand the bitter reality of Nathan's prophecy concerning the raising up of "evil against thee out of thine own house."[67]

David appears to have been blessed with beautiful children and as they gradually matured, one of them, the attractive Tamar, became a source of temptation to her half-brother, Amnon. Now Amnon was the eldest of David's sons, having been born to Ahinoam while David was located at Hebron.[68] Amnon was therefore the crown prince and natural heir to David's throne. Tamar, however, was born of Maacah, a princess of Geshur whom David had married while at Hebron.[69] Tamar was therefore the half-sister of Amnon.

But the love Amnon felt for Tamar was not the love of brother for sister. It was an all-consuming, maddening infatuation which drove reason from his brain. His desire to possess Tamar was confided to a cousin named Jonadab, and this cousin contrived an insidious scheme which would allow Amnon to lure Tamar to him. Amnon was supposed to pretend illness and insist that Tamar be sent to him to

---

65. Clarke, *Bible Commentary,* Vol. 2, p. 341
66. 2 Samuel 12:31
67. 2 Samuel 12:11
68. 1 Chronicles 3:1
69. 2 Samuel 13:1 describes Tamar as Absalom's sister while 1 Chronicles 3:2 says Absalom was born of Maachah, daughter of the king of Geshur. This would give Tamar the same relationship and make her of royal blood on both sides of her ancestry.

make delicious cakes and nourish him so as to help heal
his sickness.[70]

The wretched scheme worked with diabolical perfection
and Tamar found herself trapped with Amnon and unable
to resist his strength. Tamar pleaded with Amnon for his
own sake as well as hers but there was neither reason nor
sympathy in him. Not until the contemptible plot contrived
by Jonadab had been allowed to fully run its tragic course
did Amnon come to his senses. The revolting thing he had
done filled him with hate for himself and for Tamar.

But, as so often occurs in such cases, the psychosis of
guilt ventilated itself in one direction only. The scripture
says: "Then Ammon hated her exceedingly; so that the
hatred wherewith he hated her was greater than the love
wherewith he had loved her. And Amnon said unto her,
Arise, be gone. And she said unto him, There is no cause:
this evil in sending me away is greater than the other that
thou didst unto me. But he would not hearken unto her.
Then he called his servant that ministered unto him, and
said, Put now this woman out from me, and bolt the door
after her. And she had a garment of divers colours upon
her: for with such robes were the king's daughters that
were virgins apparelled. Then his servant brought her out,
and bolted the door after her. And Tamar put ashes on her
head, and rent her garment of divers colours that was on
her, and laid her hand on her head, and went on crying."[71]

However, Tamar did not go to her own quarters, nor
did she go to her father, David. Instead she went to the
house of her brother, Absalom, and poured out her grief
to him. Strangely, the reaction of Absalom to all that she
related was not the normal reaction of a brother. Instead
of vowing vengeance he merely tried to comfort her. He
behaved as though the incident were really nothing serious
at all. Said he, "He is thy brother; regard not this thing."[72]
Tamar therefore endeavored to console herself and "remained desolate in her brother Absalom's house."[73] Little
would Tamar have guessed what this violence which she had
suffered from Amnon was doing to the brain of her brother.

70. 2 Samuel 13:2-6
71. 2 Samuel 13:15-19
72. 2 Samuel 13:20
73. Ibid.

Beneath his outward composure and apparent indifference Absalom was boiling with hate and rage.

And when David heard that Tamar had been ravished he was filled with rage also.[74] But what he did about it, we are not told. It must have been a bitter blow to David to realize that it was he who had insisted that Tamar go to Amnon.[75]

THE MURDER OF AMNON

Two whole years passed by[76] and then a new epic began to unfold. The scripture says Absalom invited King David and all of his sons to come several miles north to the mountains of Ephraim where Absalom's flocks were being sheared. It was customary at shearing time to have a feast since these occasions involved a gathering of the clan and often included merchants from the coastal cities who came to purchase the wool. David thought it would be too much of a burden on Absalom if he and his royal troop all went up to the feast and he therefore endeavored to excuse himself. Absalom accepted the excuse but insisted that if David did not come he should be represented by Amnon, the heir-apparent to the throne. Absalom had so completely disguised his feelings toward Amnon that King David had no suspicion that this request was part of a carefully contrived murder plot. David therefore consented.

It was customary in those days for the sons of the king to ride upon mules, the symbol of their royal station, and all of these arrived from Jerusalem in an impressive display of regal pageantry. The feast was accordingly held and it was an occasion of considerable indulgence both in eating and drinking.

Only when Absalom was certain that Amnon, the crown prince, was "merry with wine" did he give the fatal signal to his servants to sweep down on Amnon and hew him to death.[77] The suddenness of the attack caught the entire entourage completely by surprise, but when they realized that David's heir-apparent had been murdered, "all the king's

---

74. 2 Samuel 13:21
75. 2 Samuel 13:7
76. 2 Samuel 13:23
77. 2 Samuel 13:28-29

sons arose, and every man gat him up upon his mule, and fled."[78]

Someone rushed the news to David but it was a wild exaggeration of what had really happened. The unnamed scandal-monger cried out to the king, "Absalom hath slain all the king's sons, and there is not one of them left!"[79] David was beside himself. He arose and tore "his garments, and lay on the earth; and all his servants stood by with their clothes rent."[80] But David's nephew, the abominable Jonadab who originally invented the scheme which had led to the assault on Tamar, now came forth with the speculation that only Amnon had been killed because "by the appointment [or plan] of Absalom this hath been determined from the day that he forced his sister Tamar."[81] It almost sounded as though he had known of the plot in advance.

In any event, as David saw his sons gallop hastily into the city, he realized that the subtle shrewdness of Jonadab had accurately equated the situation. Absalom's passion for vengeance had not exploded into a general massacre of all the king's sons, but had vented itself exclusively on the head of Amnon. The scripture then says that in spite of the depravity of this crime, David's heart went out to Absalom.[82] He had always loved this son who was a handsome, kingly looking fellow.[83] Officially, he would have to treat Absalom's act of fratricide (the killing of a brother) as a serious crime, but in the secret recesses of his soul David sympathized with him. To David it was not difficult to rationalize what Absalom had done in view of the revolting depravity which Amnon had committed against his sister.

Nevertheless, time would disclose that this Absalom had more evil in his heart than Amnon. Though David did not know it, Absalom's dark mind was capable of moving from fratricide to patricide.

THE FLIGHT OF ABSALOM

Meanwhile, Absalom was taking no chances. He fled frantically northward and then passed over to the east side

78. 2 Samuel 13:29
79. 2 Samuel 13:30
80. 2 Samuel 13:31
81. 2 Samuel 13:32
82. 2 Samuel 13:39

of the Sea of Galilee where his maternal grandfather reigned as the king of Geshur. Absalom resolved to remain in this political sanctuary until he could determine his next strategic step.

It should be pointed out that with Amnon dead, Absalom was now the next in line as David's successor. At this point the scripture makes no mention whatever of Daniel (or Chileab) who was David's second son.[84] The authorities presume that he must have died sometime earlier.[85] This would therefore make Absalom, David's third son,[86] the heir to the throne. Before long this was precisely the role Absalom began to assume. An alert observer would have had no difficulty discerning that this man's intention was to become the next king of Israel, and soon.

These were the circumstances which precipitated Israel's terrible oncoming revolution, the opening subject of our next chapter.

83. 2 Samuel 14:25
84. 1 Chronicles 3:1
85. Geikie, *Hours With the Bible,* Vol. 3, p. 314
86. 1 Chronicles 3:2

Scripture Readings and Questions on Chapter Six

Scripture Reading: 2 Samuel, Chapters 10 to 14 inclusive.

1—Did David want a war with the Ammonites? What started it?

2—How did the Ammonites nearly succeed in trapping Israel's army? What happened? Did Joab lay siege to the Ammonites? Why?

3—Why did the Syrians return? Was their effort successful? What did this compel them to do for Israel in the future?

4—Why didn't David accompany Joab in the final siege of the Ammonites? Why did this decision change his life?

5—Who was Bath-sheba? How did King David happen to see her?

6—Did David know who Bath-sheba was when he invited her to the palace? Should this have made a difference?

7—In what ways was Bath-sheba partly to blame for what happened? Is it possible that she might have prevented David's fall as well as her own? How?

8—Name four parallels between the affair of David and Bath-sheba and that of Julius Caesar and Cleopatra.

9—What was the most important difference between these two cases?

10—What kind of person was Uriah? What was his nationality?

11—What was Joab instructed to do to get Uriah killed? How did it backfire? Was David angry?

12—What were the three prophecies pronounced by Nathan against David?

13—What happened to Bath-sheba's child? Did David try to prevent it? How?

14—What does the Lord mean when He says that a murderer cannot be "forgiven" in this world nor the world to come?

15—How would you define "hell"? What did the Lord mean when he said David's soul would not always remain in hell?

16—When can adultery be forgiven? What is nevertheless lost?

17—What was the name of Bath-sheba's second child? What name did the prophet Nathan give him? What did it mean?

18—What relation was Tamar to Absalom? To Amnon? To David?

19—How did Absalom succeed in murdering Amnon? What was David's reaction to this crime?

20—Where did Absalom flee? Why? How did the murder of Amnon elevate the status of Absalom?

CHAPTER SEVEN

The Closing Years

of David's Life

In spite of the fact that Absalom had murdered Amnon and fled to Geshur, the scripture is clear that David's "heart was toward Absalom."[1] This prince was "much praised . . . for his beauty"[2] and apparently had the qualities of personality which could have made him a popular successor to King David. Unfortunately, however, beauty and popularity are not the best means of measuring either character or ability. Time would disclose that this Absalom had political ambitions which not only called for the removal of Amnon but the destruction of David as well.

For three years Absalom remained exiled in Geshur,[3] then forces began to congeal which facilitated his return to Jerusalem. It was David's commander-in-chief, Joab, who first perceived that even though the king was reconciled with Absalom's self-imposed banishment and even though this was necessary because of the nature of his crime, the king nevertheless longed for Absalom's return.[4]

No doubt Joab also was anxious to do anything which he could to ingratiate himself with the man most likely to

1. 2 Samuel 14:1
2. 2 Samuel 14:25
3. 2 Samuel 13:38
4. 2 Samuel 13:39

be the next ruler of Israel. How shocked he would have been if someone had told him that one day he would kill Absalom with his own hands. As of this time, however, it fitted both the desires and purposes of Joab to wait for Absalom's return. His first task was to get David's tacit approval.

He did this through a very complicated ruse described in 2 Samuel Chapter 14. A woman was coached by Joab so that through her words David could discover a rational basis for allowing Asbalom to return in spite of what he had done. The ruse was successful and David did commit himself to Absalom's return; nevertheless, he suspected Joab may have had a hand in this whole affair. When David demanded that the woman tell him the truth, the woman admitted that Joab was responsible for what she had done. However, David was not angry. He knew Joab was simply trying to do him a favor. He thereupon said to Joab, ". . . go therefore, bring the young man Absalom again. . . . So Joab arose and went to Geshur, and brought Absalom to Jerusalem."[5] Nevertheless, David felt some compunction about having Absalom at court lest it bring his whole administration into disrepute by allowing a man who had killed his brother to be thus favored. Therefore, David instructed Joab, "Let him turn to his own house, and let him not see my face. So Absalom returned to his own house, and saw not the king's face."[6]

ABSALOM'S CONSPIRACY TO SEIZE THE THRONE

Another two years passed away,[7] and Absalom realized that unless he returned to the king's court and was granted the official approbation of King David it would be extremely difficult to carry out the plot which was rapidly evolving in his mind. Absalom was setting his face toward a course designed to bring about his father's death and the seizure of the throne of Israel.

---

5. 2 Samuel 14:21-23
6. 2 Samuel 14:24
7. 2 Samuel 14:28

To achieve the first step of this plan, that is, to get back into court circles, Absalom tried to employ the good offices of Joab, but Joab refused to come to him.[8] Finally, Absalom had his servants burn down Joab's barley field. This did bring Joab to the scene and in a high rage.[9] Absalom placated him, however, and said this was the only way he could get the Commanding General to visit him. Absalom then demanded, "Wherefore am I come from Geshur? It had been good for me to have been there still: now therefore let me see the king's face; and if there be any iniquity in me, let him kill me."[10] Joab was touched. He promised that he would intervene with the king. When the matter was taken to the throne, David, of course, suspected nothing. After hearing Joab's plea he decided that enough time had transpired so that he could, with propriety, bring Absalom back into his presence. David had not seen this son for five years and therefore when Absalom was ushered in before him David impulsively strode forward and kissed him.[11] It was apparent to all that the handsome, conniving prince had been restored to full filial status and was forgiven. This change of circumstances soon allowed Absalom to press his plan faster. He "prepared him chariots and horses, and fifty men to run before him."[12] He acted almost as though he were already king. He sat at the gate where David ordinarily held hearings and passed judgment, but when men would come with their cases Absalom would lie to them and say there was no one available to hear their cases. Then he would say, "Oh that I were made judge [meaning king, of course!] in the land, that every man which hath any suit or cause might come unto me and I would do him justice!"[13] And whenever any man bowed down in obeisance before Prince Absalom, he would raise him up, kiss him and treat him as a brother and an equal.[14] On the surface this seemed quite commendable, but the scripture says it was by this means that "Absalom stole the hearts of the men of Israel."[15]

---

8. 2 Samuel 14:29
9. 2 Samuel 14:30-31
10. 2 Samuel 14:32
11. 2 Samuel 14:33
12. 2 Samuel 15:1
13. 2 Samuel 15:4
14. 2 Samuel 15:5
15. 2 Samuel 15:6

Events similar to these transpired over a period of an-other four years[16] until finally Absalom felt confident that he could overthrow his father. Several things persuaded him that this was possible. First of all, the years which had passed since he had killed Amnon had allowed the crime to more-or-less fade from public consciousness. Sec-ondly, his father, David, was no longer the hero of the people that he had been before the prophet Nathan exposed and disgraced him. This had allowed a political vacuum to develop and the leaders of the various tribes were already much taken up by this handsome Absalom who had made elaborate promises as to how things would improve once he became king. Third, Absalom was encouraged in his seizure of the throne by Bath-sheba's grandfather, Ahithophel, who for years had been one of David's "mighty ones" and had eventually been made David's prime minister.[17] Apparently Ahithophel had come to hate the man who had consorted with Bath-sheba and arranged for the death of her husband. Ahithophel was looking for an opportunity for vengeance and therefore secretly joined Absalom's conspiracy against David.

The Rebellion of Absalom

To allay David's suspicions, Absalom asked for permis-sion to go to Hebron, capital of Judah, to offer sacrifices in fulfillment of an oath he claimed he had taken.[18] David consented and Absalom took with him 200 carefully selected men and proceeded to Hebron. He then "sent spies through-out all the tribes of Israel, saying, As soon as ye hear the sound of the trumpet, then ye shall say, Absalom reigneth in Hebron."[19] Absalom had been joined in Hebron by Ahithophel, David's "counsellor" or prime minister,[20] so when all was in readiness the signal was given. Immediately the leaders of the tribes began pouring down upon Hebron with all their military might ready to throw behind Absalom's revolution.

---

16. 2 Samuel 15:7. This passage says "forty" years which is obviously an error. The Syriac version is believed to have the original and correct wording which is "four" years. (Clarke, *Bible Commentary*, Vol. 2, p. 394.)
17. 2 Samuel 15:12
18. 2 Samuel 15:7-9
19. 2 Samuel 15:10
20. 2 Samuel 15:12

"And there came a messenger to David saying, The hearts of the men of Israel are after Absalom!"[21]

This blow to David was something for which he was not in any way prepared. And as if it were not enough to learn that Absalom was revolting, David soon received the equally shocking news that his prime minister, his trusted friend and comrade, Ahithophel, was directing Absalom. Later on, when David had time to record his feelings, he describes the thoughts which raced through his mind when he learned that Ahithophel had joined the revolt:[22]

> For it was not an enemy that reproached me;
> Then I could have borne it:
> Neither was it he that hated me that did magnify
>   himself against me;
> Then I would have hid myself from him:
>
> But it was thou, a man mine equal,
> My guide and mine acquaintance.
> We took sweet counsel together,
> And walked unto the house of God in company.
>
>   *   *   *   *   *
>
> He hath put forth his hands such as be at peace
>   with him:
> He hath broken his covenant.
> The words of his mouth were smoother than butter,
> But war was in his heart.
> His words were softer than oil,
> Yet were they drawn swords.

David Abandons Jerusalem

With so many of the hosts of Israel mobilized against him, David knew the city of Jerusalem would never withstand the all-out assault which Absalom undoubtedly intended to make upon it. He therefore ordered the immediate evacuation of the city in order to save both Jerusalem and its people from destruction. Practically the entire population prepared to accompany the king in his flight. Fortunately for David, Joab remained loyal in spite of his former friendship with Absalom. So did the 600 "mighty ones," the Gibborim. All these were there to march away

---

21. 2 Samuel 15:13
22. Psalms 55:12-14, 20-21

with David and his royal entourage when the signal was given to move out.[23]

This terrible day in David's life is given in greater detail than any day in the entire record of the Old Testament.[24] As he abandoned his beautiful cedar palace, David left no guards but simply assigned ten of his own concubines to watch over it and keep it in order until he could somehow return.[25] Had he known what was going to happen to these ten unfortunate women he would have taken them with him. David assumed that all Absalom wanted was the throne of Israel. Surely this son would not dare to mistreat the wives of his father.

David led the people out of the city and then took up a position where he could readily observe the throngs of both soldiers and civilians as they poured from the city gate.[26] This permitted him to calculate the strength of his following in this hour of threatening disaster. During this review several noteworthy events occurred.

First, he observed that when his valiant elite guard of 600 marched out with Joab, there was numbered among them a heroic fellow named Ittai whose loyalty to David had been demonstrated over a period of years and in a score of wars. But Ittai was a Philistine from Goliath's home town.[27] David saw no reason to involve this loyal foreigner in a civil war among the tribes of Israel. David therefore urged Ittai to return to his home (in Gath) and serve the king of that city. But Ittai replied: "As the Lord liveth, and as my lord the king liveth, surely in what place my lord the king shall be, whether in death or life, even there also will thy servant be."[28] David could not resist the warmth of such devotion. "And David said to Ittai. Go and pass over [with the 600]. And Ittai the Gittite passed over, and all his men, and all the little ones that were with him."[29]

23. 2 Samuel 15:18
24. Geikie, *Hours With the Bible*, Vol. 3, p. 326
25. 2 Samuel 15:16
26. 2 Samuel 15:17-18
27. 2 Samuel 15:19. See Peloubet's *Bible Dictionary* under "Ittai."
28. 2 Samuel 15:21
29. 2 Samuel 15:22

DAVID SENDS BACK THE ARK

The next thing that attracted David's attention was a great procession of Levites led by their two High Priests, Zadok and Abiathar. In their midst was a group of the descendants of Aaron carrying on their shoulders the sacred Ark of the Covenant. David contemplated the implications of this solemn sight and then said to Zadok, the High Priest who must have been closest to him, "Carry back the ark of God into the city: if I shall find favour in the eyes of the Lord, he will bring me again, and shew me both it and his habitation [the tabernacle]. But if he thus say, I have no delight in thee; behold, here am I, let him do to me as seemeth good unto him."[30] Here was a sudden flash of that humble David of old.

The king then instructed the two High Priests to carefully determine what Absalom intended to do after he occupied Jerusalem. It was important to know whether he intended to pursue his father or merely occupy the capital. David requested that they send him word through their two eldest sons, Ahimaaz (son of Zadok) and Jonathan (son of Abiathar).[31]

Now David prepared to ascend the Mount of Olives with his people. He was so overwhelmed with grief that the procession took on the appearance of a funeral. The scripture says, "and David went up by the ascent of Mount Olivet, and wept as he went up, and had his head covered, and he went barefoot: and all the people that was with him covered every man his head, and they went up, weeping. . . ."[32]

David was headed for Trans-Jordan and the wilderness beyond. He was not only leaving Jerusalem to save the blossoming capital from the scourges of civil war, but to win time. He needed to avoid a showdown with the supporters of Absalom until he could rally what might remain of his loyal hosts among the various tribes. The two-and-a-half tribes beyond the Jordan were not involved in the present revolt so he felt safe in fleeing there and mobilizing a resistance movement.

---

30. 2 Samuel 15:25-26
31. 2 Samuel 15:27-28
32. 2 Samuel 15:30

KEY ASSIGNMENT GIVEN TO HUSHAI

At the top of the Mount of Olives David stopped to worship God and no doubt include a fervent prayer for the success of the flight.[33]

He was just about to depart when one of David's aged friends and counsellors came trudging up the mount "with his coat rent, and earth upon his head."[34] It was Hushai — a new name in our story, but one to be remembered. It was obvious that Hushai, as old and feeble as he was, intended to join the ranks of David's supporters. The king suddenly thought of a better way in which Hushai might serve.

David pointed out to Hushai that his presence on this hazardous military venture could only prove a burden to the company but if he would return to Jerusalem and join himself solidly to Absalom he might counter-balance or nullify the schemes of the perfidious Ahithophel who was Absalom's principal strategist.[35] David further informed Hushai that the two High Priests, Zadok and Abiathar, were remaining behind as secret allies of David and any useful information obtained from Absalom's court could be forwarded to David through the courier service provided by the two sons of the High Priests.[36]

So Hushai, "David's friend," agreed to undertake this dangerous assignment and he thereupon returned to Jerusalem. As it turned out, this man probably saved David's life.

ZIBA DECEIVES DAVID

Now David once more prepared to leave the summit of Olivet but one final matter was pressed upon him. It involved Ziba, the former servant of King Saul who now served Jonathan's son, Mephibosheth.[37] Ziba suddenly showed up with 200 loaves of bread, 100 bunches of raisins, and 100 summer fruits together with a vessel of wine. All of these were loaded on two donkeys. When David saw Ziba and the bounteous supplies, he said, "What meanest thou by these?"[38] Ziba said they were gifts to sustain the king and

---

33. 2 Samuel 15:32
34. Ibid.
35. 2 Samuel 15:34

36. 2 Samuel 15:35-36
37. 2 Samuel 9:9-11
38. 2 Samuel 16:2

his household. David then asked him what had happened to Mephibosheth. Ziba had some distressing news. He said Mephibosheth had stayed in Jerusalem to welcome the armies of Absalom which he felt certain would restore the kingdom to him so that he could reign in the stead of his grandfather, Saul.[39] This development was disgusting to David. He had treated Mephibosheth like his own son and now in this hour of travail the young prince was deserting him. David had no way of knowing that this entire story was a lie. He therefore turned to Ziba and proclaimed that from this moment forward the property of Mephibosheth would belong to Ziba and his sons. With a sense of complete victory Ziba returned to Jerusalem. His scheme had worked. But if Ziba could have forseen the future he would have known that his triumph was painfully temporary. Meanwhile, David proceeded on his way.

SHIMEI ABUSES KING DAVID

In order to accurately visualize the specter of the desolate David retreating from his beloved Jerusalem, it is important to remember that he was now past sixty years of age.[40] The storms of life had battered both his soul and his magnificent athletic physique. But it was his soul which bore the more bitter burden as the king slowly made his way down the steep defiles leading to the Jordan river and the wilderness beyond. The prophecies of Nathan concerning the rising up of evil within the precincts of his own household were descending on David like an avalanche of vengeance. There had been incest, murder, and now Absalom, his best beloved son, was treacherously driving David from his throne. The unfathomable depths of David's misery were reflected by an incident which occurred as he was descending the tortuous road leading to Jericho. A man named Shimei of the family of Saul ran along the hillside overlooking the road and threw stones and clods of dirt at David. He cursed the king bitterly calling him a "bloody man," a murderer. When David made no move to have a soldier chase the fellow away, Joab's brother, Abishai, felt he could not tolerate

---

39. 2 Samuel 16:3
40. Available data indicates that David was approximately 64 years of age
   at the time of Absalom's revolution.

such abuse of his king. Therefore he said to David, "Why should this dead dog curse my lord the king? Let me go over, I pray thee, and take off his head."[41] But David said, "Behold, my son, which came forth of my bowels, seeketh my life: how much more now may this Benjamite do it? Let him alone, and let him curse. . . ."[42]

ABSALOM TAKES OVER JERUSALEM

Meanwhile, Absalom and his band of conspirators could hardly believe their good fortune as they came upon Jerusalem and found it virtually deserted. They took it over immediately and Absalom established himself in his father's palace. Now Ahithophel gave Absalom some depraved and pernicious advice. He wanted to create a permanent breach between father and son so that Absalom would not dare turn back from the abominable schemes Ahithophel had in mind for the new king. Ahithophel said to Absalom, "Go in unto thy father's concubines, which he hath left to keep the house; and all Israel shall hear that thou art abhorred of thy father; then shall the hands of all that are with thee be strong."[43] In other words, they would not fear that their new leader might get faint hearted and abandon the enterprise, therefore they would support him without reservation. Then the scripture says, "So they spread Absalom a tent upon the top of the house; and Absalom went in unto his father's concubines in the sight of all Israel."[44] It was considered the greatest possible insult a son could heap upon his father.

Then Absalom sought advice as to what they should do about the fleeing King David and his small and relatively weak band of followers. The traitorous Ahithophel now presented Absalom with a plan to have his father murdered. Said Ahithophel, "Let me now choose out twelve thousand men, and I will arise and pursue after David this night: And I will come upon him while he is weary and weak-handed, and will make him afraid; and all the people that are with him shall flee; and I will smite the king only: And I will bring back all the people unto thee . . . so all the people

41. 2 Samuel 16:9
42. 2 Samuel 16:11
43. 2 Samuel 16:21
44. 2 Samuel 16:22

shall be in peace."[45] This saying "pleased Absalom well, and all the elders of Israel,"[46] but fortunately for David, there was another voice to be heard.

When Absalom had first come into the city, David's friend, Hushai, was there, and Absalom was pleased when he learned that even this old friend of his father had seen the wisdom of taking up with the new order of things. It was therefore to Hushai that Absalom now turned to see what he thought of Ahithophel's plan. Hushai astutely and masterfully made Ahithophel's plan look like a colossal blunder.[47] By the time Hushai was finished he had not only convinced Absalom that he should abandon Ahithophel's plan but also that he should let his father flee unhindered. He argued that it was a better strategy not to challenge David just yet but proceed in all haste to mobilize additional forces from all the tribes so that Absalom, himself, could personally lead a strong and victorious army in conquering his famous father. In other words, why should Ahithophel have that honor? This tickled the egotistical mania of the profligate Absalom enormously. He smiled fatuously on the singular wisdom of the aged Hushai. Here was a counsellor worth having!

Ahithophel immediately perceived what was happening. He was being outwitted and out-maneuvered by this meddling old man. His well-laid scheme to be avenged on David was slipping from his grasp. With an almost fatalistic fixation this grandfather of Bath-sheba abruptly left the service of Absalom and made his lonely way back to his own city in Judah. There he placed his house in order and hanged himself.[48]

The Death of Absalom

The precious time which Hushai had won for David very probably saved his life. It gave him a chance to cross the Jordan, set up headquarters at Mahanaim[49] and rally the forces of Trans-Jordan for the great civil war which was coming. In due time Absalom likewise crossed the Jordan and pitched his camp in Gilead.[50]

---

45. 2 Samuel 17:1-3
46. 2 Samuel 17:4
47. 2 Samuel 17:7-14

48. 2 Samuel 17:23
49. 2 Samuel 17:24
50. 2 Samuel 17:24, 26

On the day of the battle David offered to lead the hosts personally but his three commanding generals urged him to remain in the city. These three commanders were Joab, Joab's brother, Abishai, and Ittai, the faithful Philistine who had insisted upon remaining with David in this hour of crisis.[51] To them David gave the solemn admonition that if they should happen to win they should "deal gently" with Absalom.[52] Then the forces of David marched out of the city by the hundreds and by the thousands and left the apprehensive David at headquarters to await the ultimate outcome of the conflict.

This great battle took place in the wood of Ephraim,[53] believed to have been above the Jabbock River and opposite the valley of Jezreel. If this were the case it is likely that Absalom had crossed the Jordan at the upper fords and entered Gilead directly from Jezreel. Ironically, Absalom's forces were led by Amasa, a nephew of David and a cousin of Joab.[54]

But the forces of David led by his battle-tested "mighty ones" were too much for Amasa and his newly mobilized troops from Israel. Before the day was finished the fierce hand-to-hand combat had taken the lives of 20,000 Israelites.[55] The fight was "scattered over the face of all the country" and as the heat of the battle increased, many of Amasa's men became frightened and mutinous. Finally, as the battle took on the appearance of a complete rout, thousands of the Israelites frantically fled away to hide themselves so that "the wood devoured more people that day than the sword devoured."[56] When the profligate Prince Absalom saw that his abysmal cause was entirely lost, he raced his mule through the forest in a frenzied attempt to escape. But with his long hair streaming out behind him disaster waited for him among those trees. As he plunged under the limb of an overhanging oak his head became tangled among the heavy branches and Absalom was jerked from his mule and left swinging helplessly in the air.[57]

51. 2 Samuel 18:2
52. 2 Samuel 18:5
53. 2 Samuel 18:6
54. 2 Samuel 17:25

55. 2 Samuel 18:7
56. 2 Samuel 18:8
57. 2 Samuel 18:9

A soldier recognized Absalom and quickly told Joab, whereupon Joab said, "And, behold, thou sawest him, and why didst thou not smite him there to the ground and I would have given thee ten shekels of silver, and a girdle."[58] The soldier replied, "Though I should receive a thousand shekels of silver in mine hand yet would I not put forth mine hand against the king's son: for in our hearing the king charged thee and Abishai and Ittai, saying, Beware that none touch the young man Absalom."[59]

In complete disgust, Joab seized three short javelins or darts and rushing to the place where Absalom was hanging, thrust all of them through his body "while he was yet alive in the midst of the oak."[60] Joab's ten attendants also smote Absalom to make certain the prince was dead and then they promptly cut him down.

"And Joab blew the trumpet, and the people returned from pursuing after Israel."[61] Joab ordered the body of Absalom cast into a deep pit in the wood and then instructed that it be covered with a great heap of stones.

Meanwhile, back at headquarters, a runner named Ahimaaz brought news to David that victory was assured and the enemy was in full flight. David immediately exhibited the deepest concern over what might have happened to Absalom, but the messenger could not tell him. When a second messenger arrived to report that Absalom was dead, David was shaken to the core of his soul with grief. In spite of all that this ungrateful son had done to him, David had never ceased to love him. The scripture says, "And the king was much moved, and went up to the chamber over the gate, and wept: and as he went, thus he said, O my son Absalom, my son, my son Absalom! Would God I had died for thee, O Absalom, my son, my son!"[62]

A Crisis Develops Between David and Joab

When Joab finally returned to the headquarters city of Mahanaim he could scarcely believe what he found. In-

---

58. 2 Samuel 18:11
59. 2 Samuel 18:12
60. 2 Samuel 18:14

61. 2 Samuel 18:16
62. 2 Samuel 18:33

stead of the usual rejoicing over their magnificent victory and the immediate possibility of returning to Jerusalem, he found the whole city in mourning. The people were creeping about in a confused dilemma almost as though they were ashamed of what had been accomplished.[63] Joab found that the king's morbidly emotional reaction over the death of his rebellious son was what had caused it all. For Joab this was the final straw. The commanding general was sick of the king's simpering distress over a son who had fully intended to murder him. Joab strode in before David seething with indignation. "Thou," he said, "hast shamed this day the faces of all thy servants, which this day have saved thy life, and the lives of thy sons and of thy daughters, and the lives of thy wives, and the lives of thy concubines, in that thou lovest thine enemies, and hatest thy friends. . . . for this day I perceive that if Absalom had lived, and all we had died this day, then it had pleased thee well."[64]

It is doubtful that any man had dared to address the king with such boldness, but Joab was not through. He threatened David. Said he, "Now therefore arise, go forth, and speak comfortably unto thy servants: for I swear by the Lord, if thou go not forth, there will not tarry one [of us] with thee this night: and that will be worse unto thee than all the evil that befell thee from thy youth until now."[65]

This speech seemed to arouse David from his stupor and so he went forth to the city gate to commend the people and encourage them for what they had done.[66] But while Joab had successfully imposed his will upon the irrational and grief-stricken David it was bought at a high price. He did not know it, but Joab was about to lose his life-long command over the hosts of Israel.

DAVID ONCE MORE RETURNS TO POWER

Just as soon as the alarm had spread among the various tribes that David's forces had prevailed and Absalom was dead there was a mad scramble among the leaders of the tribes to mend their political fences and realign themselves

---

63. 2 Samuel 19:2-3
64. 2 Samuel 19:5-6

65. 2 Samuel 19:7
66. 2 Samuel 19:8

with David.[67] The leaders sent over a ferry-boat to help
transport David and his family across the Jordan.[68] However, one of the first persons to attempt a reconciliation with
the king in person was none other than Shimei, the relative
of Saul, who had cursed David and run along the hills
throwing rocks at him as he was leaving the precincts of
Jerusalem. This man met David as he came across the
Jordan, and throwing himself at the king's feet, pleaded,
"Let not my lord impute iniquity unto me, neither do thou
remember that which thy servant did perversely the day that
my lord the king went out of Jerusalem, that the king should
take it to his heart. For thy servant doth know that I have
sinned: therefore, behold, I am come the first this day of
all the house of Joseph, to go down to meet my lord the
king."[69]

Abishai, a nephew of David and one of his commanders
who had wanted to destroy this Shimei when he first insulted
the king, angrily cried out, "Shall not Shimei be put to death
for this, because he cursed the Lord's anointed?"[70] But David
restrained him saying, ". . . shall there any man be put to
death this day in Israel? For do not I know that I am this
day king over all Israel?"[71] David wished to reconcile rather
than divide in this critical hour. The punishment of Shimei
could come later.

Another man who arrived on the scene and hoped David
would be in a forgiving mood was Ziba who came with his
fifteen sons and twenty servants to help ferry the household
of David across the Jordan.[72] This sudden expression of
solicitude was no doubt motivated by Ziba's anxiety over
the lie he had told the king in order to get the grant of his
master's property. However, his master, it will be recalled,
was Jonathan's son, Mephibosheth, and he also came down
to meet David. When the king saw him he said, "Wherefore
wentest thou not with me Mephibosheth?"[73] To Ziba's embarrassment Mephibosheth told the king the whole ugly
story. He said Ziba had deceived him. Mephibosheth had
wanted to join David but Ziba had pointed out that since

67. 2 Samuel 19:9-10   71. 2 Samuel 19:22
68. 2 Samuel 19:18   72. 2 Samuel 19:17
69. 2 Samuel 19:19-20   73. 2 Samuel 19:25
70. 2 Samuel 19:21

Mephibosheth was lame he would have to get a donkey on which he could ride. Instead of getting a donkey, however, Ziba had gone to David alone and slandered his master with lies.[74]

David could have become violently angry over this incident but he held his peace. After all, somebody had to take care of Mephibosheth all of his days so nothing would be gained by imposing a severe penalty on Ziba. It would only widen the gap between the two men. David therefore simply ruled that Ziba should go ahead tilling the land and when the harvest was in or the proceeds obtained, these should be divided equally with the crippled Mephibosheth.[75]

Mephibosheth held no grudge against Ziba, however, and said, "Yea, let him take all, forasmuch as my lord the king is come again in peace unto his own house."[76] Now that David had returned Mephibosheth knew that he could live at the palace as before. He therefore didn't seem to care whether he received anything from Ziba or not.

DAVID'S BID FOR A UNIFIED ISRAEL

David made one decision about this time, however, which had some disastrous consequences. When he saw that the leaders of the northern tribes were anxious to welcome him back to the throne he felt deeply hurt that the tribe of Judah (his own people) had not made a similar gesture. He therefore made a foolish but desperate bid to insure their support. He offered to allow his military forces to be taken away from the command of Joab and placed under the command of Amasa.[77] This was fantastic. Amasa was the man who had been in charge of Absalom's revolutionary forces! This was the man Joab had just beaten in the recent war. Nothing better demonstrated David's spiritual and intellectual stagnation as of this moment than this incredulous proposition. Nevertheless it did persuade Judah that David held no grudges against them and that there would be no vindictive recriminations for their recent rebellion. They therefore proceeded down to the Jordan to join the

---

74. 2 Samuel 19:26-27
75. 2 Samuel 19:29
76. 2 Samuel 19:30
77. 2 Samuel 19:13

leaders of the other tribes in escorting David over the river preparatory to his return to Jerusalem.[78]

Straggling along in the crowd, unhonored and unacclaimed, was Joab. He had been stripped of his command. The new commander was now Amasa, the recent treasonable leader of Absalom's insurrection. It was bizzare, bewildering.

But barely had this entourage crossed the Jordan when a violent quarrel broke out between Judah and the other tribes. The latter felt that Judah was monopolizing David. Said they, "Why have our brethren the men of Judah stolen thee away?"[79] Before David could answer, the leaders of Judah replied, "Because the king is near of kin to us."[80] But the other tribes were incensed. Said they: "We have ten parts in the king, and we have also more right in David than ye."[81] The debate grew hotter. Finally the scripture says "the words of the men of Judah were fiercer than the words of the men of Israel."[82] The whole thing had become ridiculous. Here were the conglomorate rebels from both groups who only a short time before had been bent on dethroning and killing David now quarreling madly over which of them had the greatest vested interested in the king and therefore the greatest right to lead him on his homeward march back to Jerusalem!

Suddenly a man of Benjamin named Sheba blew a trumpet and shouted, "We have no part in David, neither have we inheritance in the son of Jesse: every man to his tents, O Israel!"[83]

That did it. The other tribes arose and stormed off in high vexation leaving Judah alone to escort David back to Jerusalem. It was clear that a whole new revolution might erupt to divide Israel.

As soon as David reached Jerusalem and settled himself once more in the city he ordered Amasa to mobilize Judah and prepare to pursue Sheba's band.[84]

---

78. 2 Samuel 19:14-15, 40
79. 2 Samuel 19:41
80. 2 Samuel 19:42
81. 2 Samuel 19:43

82. Ibid.
83. 2 Samuel 20:1
84. 2 Samuel 20:4

THE MURDER OF AMASA

However, Amasa found the people of Judah slow to respond to the new call to arms.[85] David had given him three days to bring up his troops but when Amasa failed to appear, David ordered Joab's brother, Abishai, to take the Gibborim and what other forces he could muster and catch Sheba before he took up a position in some fenced city.[86] Joab also heard the order and apparently decided that he would go along as a common soldier. However, it appears that Joab didn't have time to put on his armor. He merely had time to fasten a sword to the girdle of his robe.[87] At Gibeon, just north of Jerusalem, this sword came out of its scabbard and fell in a clatter upon the roadway just as Amasa arrived breathlessly from Judah to take over his army. Joab casually picked up the sword and strode toward Amasa. Said he, "Art thou in health, my brother?" and with that he took Amasa by the beard as though to kiss him. Before the unsuspecting Amasa knew what had happened Joab had slit open his entire abdominal region.[88] The record says that while "Amasa wallowed in blood in the midst of the highway" one of Joab's soldiers shouted, "He that favoureth Joab, and he that is for David, let him go after Joab!"[89] So all the troops followed after Joab who now assumed command of the army once more.

THE DOWNFALL OF SHEBA

Joab pursued Sheba and his men through every part of Israel until Sheba barricaded himself behind the high walls of Abel, a city located clear up north near Dan-Laish. Joab laid siege to the city. To expedite its downfall he built an earthen ramp over the moat or trench and up to the wall where his men could commence battering down the wall.[90] It was apparent to the inhabitants of the city that Joab would soon be charging in upon them, so a certain "wise woman of the city" asked to communicate with Joab. When he came forward she cried out to him, "I am one of them that are peaceable and faithful in Israel: thou seekest to destroy

85. 2 Samuel 20:5
86. 2 Samuel 20:5-6
87. 2 Samuel 20:8

88. 2 Samuel 20:9-10
89. 2 Samuel 20:11-12
90. 2 Samuel 20:15

a city and a mother in Israel: why wilt thou swallow up the inheritance of the Lord?"[91] Joab shouted back that he had no desire to destroy the whole city if they would just deliver up Sheba, the man who "hath lifted up his hand against the king, even against David."[92] The woman promised to deliver the rebel up.

She was as good as her word. The woman did not deliver all of Sheba, but the most important part. The scripture says, "And they cut off the head of Sheba the son of Bichri, and cast it out to Joab."[93] Thus ended the revolution of Sheba. Joab "blew a trumpet, and they retired from the city, every man to his tent, and Joab returned to Jerusalem unto the king."[94]

David never challenged Joab's right to remain at the head of the army. His victory over Sheba seemed to settle that point. Nor was Joab punished for killing Amasa. David knew that Joab considered Amasa as great a traitor as Absalom and therefore worthy of death. Thus it appeared that these two old companions-in-arms were finally reconciled. Not until years later did Joab learn how David really felt.

THE THREE YEAR FAMINE

As the days of David were drawing to a close two additional events took place which we shall mention briefly. Some believe these occurred earlier in his reign but since the Second Book of Samuel presents them as occurring at this point of time we shall deal with them accordingly.

The first event was a three-year famine. David discovered (through a prophet, no doubt) that this was the result of God's displeasure against Saul and his house for slaughtering the Canaanite village of Gibeon when it had been a protectorate of Israel since the days of Joshua.[95] David therefore asked the Gibeonites what would satisfy them and they demanded that seven of Saul's sons be delivered unto them to be executed.[96] It is not clear why that number was designated nor why David selected the particu-

---

91. 2 Samuel 20:16-19
92. 2 Samuel 20:21
93. 2 Samuel 20:22
94. Ibid.
95. 2 Samuel 21:1-2; Joshua 9:3, 5, 15-17.
96. 2 Samuel 21:2-6

lar seven which he did, but it has been presumed that these
were seven of Saul's living descendants who participated in
the slaughter. Two of them were sons of Saul and five of
them were grandsons.[97]

The Gibeonites apparently placed the seven bodies of
the executed men in a field to be left exposed to the open
elements until rain finally came as a sign that the famine
was past. But even in the execution of justice, the innocent
suffer with the guilty. To this place came Rizpah, mother
of two of the men, who placed sack cloth on a rock for a
bed and watched day and night over the bodies to keep away
animals and vultures until the rains finally came. Just as
the season of moisture began David heard of Rizpah's faithful vigil and therefore had the bodies removed. They were
interred in the sepulchre of Kish, father of Saul. David also
had the remains of Saul and his sons (the scripture only
mentions Jonathan, but there is reason to believe the others
were included) brought to the same family tomb so that
all the family would have the same final resting place.[98]

The Ghost of Goliath Unexpectedly Arises

The second incident which now occurred was a series
of uprisings among the Philistines who had been quiet and
subservient for many years. Although David, now in his
sixties, was an old man insofar as military service was concerned, he nevertheless personally led his forces against the
Philistines. In the midst of the battle David found himself
confronted by none other than one of the sons of Goliath.
He was a gigantic fellow who immediately began bearing
down violently on the man who had slain his father.[99] For the
king of Israel it was a life-and-death struggle and the scripture says, "David waxed faint."[100] Fortunately, Joab's

---

97. 2 Samuel 21:8. This passage says the five grandsons of Saul who were executed were sons of Michal, wife of Adriel. This is an error. Michal had no
children (2 Samuel 6:23) and she was not married to Adriel. It was Merab,
sister of Michal, who was married to Adriel (1 Samuel 18:19) and Michal,
merely brought up her children. The Chaldee version is believed by Dr. Clarke
to be the correct translation: "And the five sons of Merab which Michal the
daughter of Saul brought up, which she brought forth to Adriel the son of
Barzillas." (Clarke, *Bible Commentary*, Vol. 2, p. 367)
98. 2 Samuel 21:10-14
99. 2 Samuel 21:16
100. 2 Samuel 21:15

brother, Abishai, was near, and seeing David's predicament he charged into the hulk of the Philistine giant and attacked with such ferocity that he finally killed him, thereby saving David's life.[101] When the battle was over, "the men of David sware unto him, saying, Thou shalt go no more out with us to battle, that thou quench not the light of Israel."[102] The fighting days of David were over.

But the wars with the Philistines were not over. The next encounter was at Gob and here another son of Goliath appeared on the scene. His name was Saph. He was slain by an Israelite named Sibbechai.[103] When the battle broke out again at Gob one of the notable events was the slaying of a brother of Goliath by an Israelite named Elhanan from Bethlehem.[104] Still another son of Goliath was killed in these wars but his name is not given. We are simply told that he had six fingers on each hand and six toes on each foot. He was slain by Jonathan, a nephew of David who was the son of David's older brother, Shimeah.[105] So the scripture closes this phase of the Philistine wars by saying that these four "fell by the hand of David, and by the hand of his servants."[106]

At last peace descended on the land and a semblance of peace came into the heart of David. Once more he found the power to sing a song of praise and thanksgiving to the Lord. The 18th Psalm is attributed to this period. It lacks something of the zeal of the earlier days, but nevertheless, David's aching heart could still reflect a little of the glory of the sweet singer of old.

> I will call upon the Lord,
> Who is worthy to be praised:
> So shall I be saved
> From mine enemies.

---

101. 2 Samuel 21:17
102. Ibid.
103. 2 Samuel 21:18
104. 2 Samuel 12:19. Since the words "brother of" are not in the original text this man may have actually been a son of the original Goliath and a namesake. Verse 22 indicates that all four of these men "were born to the giant of Gath" implying they were all sons of Goliath.
105. 2 Samuel 21:20-21
106. 2 Samuel 21:22

The sorrows of death compassed me,
And the floods of ungodly men made me afraid.
The sorrows of hell compassed me about:
The snares of death prevented me.

In my distress I called upon the Lord,
And cried unto my God.
He heard my voice out of his temple,
And my cry came before him, even into his ears.

*   *   *   *   *

Therefore will I give thanks unto thee,
O Lord, among the heathen,
And sing praises unto thy name.
Great deliverance giveth he to his king;
And sheweth mercy to his anointed,
To David, and to his seed for evermore.

A MILITARY CENSUS BRINGS A DEVASTATING PESTILENCE

The third incident which occurred during this final period of David's life was apparently the result of some secret military ambitions which David may have had to extend his influence beyond the existing boundaries. Ever since the days of Abraham, God had promised that the boundaries of Israel's domain would one day extend from the Euphrates to Egypt.[107] In David's day this had been achieved. Nevertheless, the scripture says Satan tempted David to make a military census.[108] Authorities have interpreted this to mean that David was about to launch his people into an imperialistic expansion and this was why God counted it a great evil.[109] Even Joab who was commanded to make the census objected.[110] Nevertheless, the rank of David prevailed and the census was taken.

The final tally is variously given, one being 800,000 fighting men[111] and the other 1,100,000.[112] But as soon as the census was completed David confessed, "I have sinned greatly . . . I have done very foolishly."[113] The Lord then revealed through Gad that three great catastrophies were headed toward Israel and that while the Lord would take away two of them, David and the people would have to

107. Genesis 15:18; Deuteronomy 34:1-4
108. 1 Chronicles 21:1
109. Clarke, *Bible Commentary*, Vol. 2, p. 377
110. 2 Samuel 24:3-4; 1 Chronicles 21:3-4

111. 2 Samuel 24:9
112. 1 Chronicles 21:5
113. 2 Samuel 24:10

endure at least one. Gad said the three oncoming plagues were seven years of famine, a great war or a three-day pestilence. David elected to have the land endure the pestilence. This turned out to be a violent sickness among the people and David saw a vision of the destroying angel standing on the summit of Mount Moriah where the threshing place of Araunah the Jebusite was located. David felt that the pestilence was entirely his own fault and that if it continued raging it might destroy all of Jerusalem. He therefore prayed to the Lord saying, "Lo, I have sinned, and I have done wickedly, but these sheep, what have they done? Let thine hand I pray thee, be against me, and against my father's house."[114] In reply, Gad, the seer, came to David and told him to purchase the threshing floor of Araunah over which the angel had stood and erect an altar upon it.[115] Then the pestilence would end.

When David told Araunah the Jebusite that he needed the threshing floor to build an altar and stop the pestilence, Araunah was in the greatest anxiety to help. He offered the threshing floor to David for nothing. He even told David to take the oxen which were treading out the grain and use them as the sacrifice. Then he urged David to use the wooden threshing equipment for the fire.[116] David was greatly moved by this overflowing generosity from a heathen neighbor, but he insisted on buying the site and paid Araunah fifty shekels of silver for it. Then David built an altar on the threshing floor and prepared the sacrifice.[117]

Since the Lord specifically designated the spot where this altar was to be built,[118] and since this later appears to have become the resting place for the Ark of the Covenant in the Holy of Holies of Solomon's temple,[119] it is believed that this might well have been the very spot on Mount Moriah where Isaac was offered as a sacrifice nearly 1,000 years before.[120] This spot is presently covered by the beautiful Moslem structure called, "The Dome of the Rock." The cave beneath this rock which was anciently used as a granary

---

114. 2 Samuel 24:17
115. 2 Samuel 24:18
116. 2 Samuel 24:21-23
117. 2 Samuel 24:25

118. 2 Samuel 24:18
119. See Geikie, *Hours With the Bible*, Vol. 3, p. 454
120. Genesis, Chapter 22

can still be seen. The Moslem faithful believe it was from this same spot that their prophet Mohammed ascended into heaven, therefore it is counted fully as sacred to them as it is to the Jews. The modern Moslem leaders have stated repeatedly that any attempt by the Jews to recover this ground will result in a full-scale religious war. The Jews, on the other hand, insist that they must have this sacred ground in order to build their great temple preparatory to the coming of the Messiah in the last days.[121]

In David's day, this spot was hallowed, not only by the Lord personally designating it as a place of sacrifice, but by manifesting His approbation in a miraculous way. The scripture says that as soon as David had prepared his sacrifice he called upon the Lord and immediately the Lord "answered him from Heaven by fire upon the altar of burnt-offering."[122] This divine manifestation stirred David to hasten with all his might in gathering together the material for the magnificent temple which would one day embellish this spot. He had seen the pattern of that structure in vision[123] and knew how beautiful and elaborate it must be. He therefore proceeded to gather all the necessary materials so that Solomon could construct it as soon as he became king.

Until that could be accomplished, David declared the summit of Mount Moriah to be a cloistered place for sacrifice and worship.[124] It would be like a temple beneath the open skies of heaven. Such a procedure has always been acceptable to the Lord pending the time when a temple could be built.[125]

David Spends His Last Years Preparing For the Building of the Temple

It will be recalled, that even back as far as the wars with the Syrians, Edomites, Moabites, Philistines, Amalekites and the Ammonites, David was consecrating all the precious

---

121. This issue has resulted in several heated debates in the United Nations between the governments of Israel and Jordan.
122. 1 Chronicles 21:26
123. 1 Chronicles 28:12, 19
124. 1 Chronicles 22:1
125. Joseph Fielding Smith, *Doctrines of Salvation*, Vol. 2, p. 232

metal which fell into his hands to the Lord for the building of His temple.[126]

During the last several years of his life, however, he went even further. He began expending vast sums to accumulate all of the building materials which Solomon would need to erect the temple. Here is the way the scripture describes it:

"And David commanded to gather together the strangers that were in the land of Israel [these were remnants of the heathen nations who were obligated to provide a certain amount of tribute or labor to Israel each year]; and he set masons to hew wrought stones to build the house of God.

"And David prepared iron in abundance for the nails for the doors of the gates, and for the joinings; and brass in abundance without weight.

"Also cedar trees in abundance: for the Zidonians [men of Sidon] and they of Tyre brought much cedar wood to David.

"And David said, Solomon my son is young and tender, and the house that is to be builded for the Lord must be exceeding magnifical of fame and of glory throughout all countries: I will therefore now make preparation for it. So David prepared abundantly before his death."[127]

It is apparent from this last passage that David felt he had the prestige and organizing ability to provide much of the material for the temple which young Solomon might find considerable difficulty in accumulating. At least it would take Solomon much longer. Therefore the father wished to expedite matters by using all his skill and good offices to assemble both the men and materials for the undertaking.

DAVID REORGANIZES THE AARONIC AND LEVITICAL PRIESTHOODS

Certain other things also had to be done in preparation for the temple. In earlier years when David had seen the

126. 1 Chronicles 18:11
127. 1 Chronicles 22:2-5

vision of the temple he was shown a new pattern for the organizing of the Aaronic and Levitical Priesthoods.[128]

It will be recalled that five centuries before when Israel had worshipped the golden calf at the foot of Mount Sinai, the tribe of Levi was the only one which had risen up and joined Moses when he called for an uncompromising commitment to God.[129] In consequence of this, the Lord had withdrawn the Priesthood from the other tribes and set up a hereditary Priesthood within the tribe of Levi.[130] However, even this tribe was not entirely without fault, and so the Lord had given them only the lesser portion of the Priesthood.[131] The fulness of the Priesthood was reserved for the High Priest[132] and certain others whom the Lord authorizes to have it from time to time.

The lesser priesthood enjoyed by the tribe of Levi was divided into two parts. That small segment of the tribe which were descendants of Levi through Aaron were allowed to be Priests and administer the ordinances such as the burning of incense and the offering of sacrifices.[133] They were comparable to the Priests who administer the ordinances in the Aaronic Priesthood today. The ordinances have changed but the calling has not.

The rest of the males in the tribe of Levi were called "Levites" and held the Levitical Priesthood which was comparable to the office of Deacon and Teacher today. Their task was to assist the Priests (descendants of Aaron) in preparing the sacrifices, keeping the precincts of the temple in order, teaching the people, and otherwise acting as assistants to the Priests.[134]

In the five centuries which had passed since the Aaronic and Levitical Priesthoods were organized, these orders had greatly increased in numbers. The Lord had therefore revealed to David that both Priesthoods were hereafter to be set up in "courses" or quorums.

---

128. 1 Chronicles 28:12-13
129. Exodus 32:26
130. Inspired Version Exodus 34:1; Numbers, Chapter 3
131. Doctrine and Covenants 84:24-26
132. For a full discussion of this matter see, *The Third Thousand Years*, pp. 400-401.
133. A full outline of the duties of the Priests of Aaron appears on pages 402-403 of *The Third Thousand Years*.
134. 1 Chronicles 23:28-32

The Aaronic Priesthood was divided into twenty-four quorums, sixteen of them being the descendants of Aaron's son, Eleazar, who were presided over by the High Priest, Zadok.[135] The other eight quorums were descendants of Aaron's youngest son, Ithamar, and were presided over by the High Priest, Abiathar.[136] Ordinarily, all of the Aaronic Priesthood would have been under one High Priest, but Saul had confused the whole matter at the time he massacred the Priests at Nob.[137] At that time Zadok had been elevated to High Priest in the northern tribes while Abiathar had become High Priest in Judah. When David united the tribes he accepted both men[138] (because they were both legitimate heirs to their offices) and they governed together until the days of Solomon when Abiathar was removed because of an unfortunate involvement in politics.[139] Thereafter, Zadok alone presided over the Aaronic Priesthood.[140]

These quorums of the Aaronic Priesthood each had a presidency and they drew lots to see which quorum would minister in the temple from week to week.[141]

The rest of the males in the tribe of Levi were also organized into courses or quorums.[142] The size of the quorum was determined by the type of assignment it received. Twenty-four quorums of 1,000 men each were assigned to assist the Priests at the temple and drew lots to see which week each quorum would serve.[143]

6,000 men were assigned to serve as "officers and judges" in Israel.[144] 4,000 men were assigned to serve as "porters" (port watchers) or keepers of the gates of the temple and guardians of the sanctuaries.[145] They were

135. 1 Chronicles 24:3-4
136. Ibid. Note that this passage says "Ahimelech" instead of Abiathar. Ahimelech was Abiathar's father who was long since dead. The insertion of his name here was either an error or another name by which Abiathar was known. We know from 1 Kings 4:4 that Abiathar was intended.
137. 1 Samuel 22:18-22
138. 2 Samuel 20:25
139. 1 Kings 2:26-27
140. 1 Kings 2:35
141. 1 Chronicles 24:5
142. 1 Chronicles 23:4-6
143. 1 Chronicles 24:31. It is interesting that the eighth course or quorum was that of "Abijah." (1 Chronicles 24:10) This is the group to which Zacharias, the father of John the Baptist, belonged. (Luke 1:5)
144. 1 Chronicles 23:4
145. 1 Chronicles 23:5

divided into four classes, each quorum of 1,000 having jurisdiction over one of the gates leading into the temple.[146]

In addition to all of these there were 4,000 Levites
chosen to be members of the tabernacle choirs and orchestras.[147] This last group is specifically described as being
divided into twenty-four quorums or courses just as those
who assisted the Priests in the temple.[148] They likewise drew
lots to determine when they would participate in the service.[149]
From this it seems reasonable to assume that all the officers,
judges, and porters or guardians were divided into courses
or quorums so that none of them was under the necessity
of serving continually but only as their specific assignments
came due. Thus, a good and efficient service was provided
without working an undue hardship on any of them.

In connection with the making of these assignments it
is interesting that in the days of Moses a Levite began serving at the age of thirty.[150] And because his duties in preparing the sacrifices, etc., were strenuous he was not required
to serve in that type of work beyond fifty.[151] However, even
during the administration of Moses the commencement age
was changed to twenty-five.[152] In the pattern revealed to
David, the Lord altered this age requirement by starting it
at twenty and no termination period is mentioned.[153] Today
the age factor has been reduced clear down to twelve. This
indicates that there is nothing rigid about the age element in
the Priesthood. It can commence at different ages as the
Lord wills it according to the requirements of the time and
the circumstances.

The Tabernacle Choirs and Orchestras

One further note should be added concerning the 4,000
Levite musicians which David established.[154] Since these
were included among the assigned "courses of . . . the
Levites"[155] and since these courses were given as a pattern

---

146. 1 Chronicles 26:13-18
147. 1 Chronicles 23:5
148. 1 Chronicles Chapter 25. Note that verses 5 and 6 clearly authorized women
    to participate in the musical organizations of the Priesthood.
149. 1 Chronicles 25:8
150. Numbers 4:3, 35
151. Ibid.
152. Numbers 8:24

153. 1 Chronicles 23:24, 27
154. 1 Chronicles 23:5 and Chapter 25
155. 1 Chronicles 28:13

"of all that he [David] had by the Spirit,"[156] it seems apparent that the Tabernacle choirs and orchestras were part of this revealed program.

We have already observed that while these musical organizations were made a Priesthood function, they included women. This is made clear from 1 Chronicles 25:5-6 where Heman's three daughters are specifically identified as being among those who provided "song in the house of the Lord, with cymbals, psalteries, harps, for the service of the house of God. . . ." One of the Psalms also talks about "the damsels playing with timbrels."[157]

The next thing to note is that David took a very strong personal interest in these choral and instrumental groups. David states that some of the instruments were those which he had "made"[158] and this is interpreted to mean that he either invented them or improved upon some of the instruments then in use.[159] We have already seen how David was famous himself in the use of the harp and the singing of original verse. Many of the Psalms were specifically created by him so they could be sung and played on special occasions.[160] Among the instruments used by the musicians were chiefly the following: harps, timbrels, flutes, cymbals and small drums.[161] Artists trained in the use of these individual instruments combined together to make an extremely impressive orchestral effect which gained great fame in ancient times.[162] The choral groups, sometimes referred to as "singing men and singing women,"[163] joined with the instrumentalists to present the musical part of the temple service. They also combined for festive occasions and provided martial music in times of war.

David considered this phase of Israel's culture so important that he assigned 268 skilled musicians to train the 4,000 Levites who had been designated as musicians and singers.[164]

---

156. 1 Chronicles 28:12
157. Psalms 68:25
158. 1 Chronicles 23:5
159. Geikie, *Hours With the Bible*, Vol. 3, p. 265
160. Ibid., p. 264
161. Peloubet's *Bible Dictionary* under "Music"
162. Ibid.   164. 1 Chronicles 25:6-7
163. 2 Samuel 19:35

THE ECONOMICAL MILITARY ORGANIZATION
SET UP BY DAVID

While the pattern for the religious organization described above applied exclusively to the tribe of Levi, the remainder of the tribes in Israel had also been placed under special obligation to serve the kingdom. As we have previously mentioned, the military forces from among all the other tribes were divided into twelve powerful armies of 24,000 each.[165] At the head of each army was one of David's mighty ones who had proven himself valiant in the wars of the past.[166]

Each of these armies served only one month out of each year. This made it possible for an individual to contribute his one month of military service without seriously disrupting the routine of his regular life and the requirements of his established occupation.

Furthermore, each army supported itself while serving during its assigned month thereby providing the nation with excellent protection without cost to the people.[167] In a day when arms and supplies were restricted to relatively simple requirements this procedure was a most equitable and economical division of labor.

Of course, David maintained his regular elite guard of 600, called the Gibborim, and there were other professional, full-time military leaders whose duty was to maintain a continuity of policy, up-to-date training tactics and specific standards of performance by all those serving in the twelve citizen's militia.[168]

So now David had performed all that God had required at his hand. The strength of Israel under David's leadership had established domination over 15,000 square miles of territory, the government had been instituted in all parts of the land, the Priesthood had been reorganized, preparations for a magnificent temple had been completed, and peace reigned from the Euphrates in the north to Egypt in the south.

David knew that for him the great climax of life lay just ahead.

---

165. 1 Chronicles, Chapter 27
166. Ibid.
167. See Clarke, *Bible Commentary*, Vol. 2, p. 627
168. See Geikie, *Hours With the Bible*, Vol. 3, pp. 254-258

Scripture Reading and Questions on Chapter Seven

Scripture Reading: 2 Samuel, chapters 14 to 24 inclusive

1—How long was Absalom in Geshur? After returning to Jerusalem, how long before he was allowed to see his father?

2—Give two reasons why Joab might want to help Absalom.

3—How long was Absalom engaged in preparing his revolution? What prominent official secretly supported him? Did Joab support him?

4—When Absalom's uprising occurred why did David decide to abandon the city of Jerusalem?

5—Did David take the Ark with him? The High Priests?

6—Who was Hushai? What did David tell him to do? Did it work?

7—Why did Ahithophel want to create a permanent breach between David and Absalom?

8—What was the motive for his hatred of David? How did he die? Why?

9—Did David fight in the war with Absalom? What instruction did he give his generals?

10—Who killed Absalom? What happened to his body?

11—What was David's reaction to the news about Absalom? Why was Joab shocked when he returned to David's headquarters at Mahanaim?

12—When David prepared to return to Jerusalem why did the leaders of the tribes quarrel over him? Who stormed off in disgust?

13—Who did David make his new commander? Was this a mistake? What happened to him?

14—How did Joab capture Sheba? About how far did he have to chase him?

15—Why did David have to be rescued during his war with the Philistines? What did his soldiers say about David fighting in the future?

16—Why did David make such a strenuous effort to gather materials for the building of the temple when he knew it would not be built in his lifetime?

17—How did David know how to reorganize the Aaronic Priesthood? What determined the size of a quorum or course in those days?

18—Has the Lord always had the same date for the ordination of the Aaronic Priesthood? Why?

19—What tribe was responsible for the setting up of Tabernacle Choirs and orchestras? Was it a Priesthood assignment? Could women participate?

20—What procedure did David provide for the military protection of the country from month to month? Why was this economical?

CHAPTER EIGHT

The Death of David and the Rise of Solomon

The well-deserved peace of David's old age was rudely disrupted one day by his oldest surviving son. It will be recalled that Amnon, David's original crown prince, had been killed by Absalom to avenge the assault on his sister. Then, when Absalom tried to seize the throne through violent revolution, he was slain by Joab. This left Adonijah as the next son in line for the throne.[1]

Unfortunately for Adonijah, however, the Lord had intervened several years before to disclose to David that Solomon was to be his successor and the builder of the temple.[2] It seems most improbable that this volatile information could have been kept hidden from all the curious interlopers who constantly maintain pipelines of secret communication throughout the environs of a royal palace. But if Adonijah knew of the Lord's preference for Solomon, he ignored it.

---

1. It will be recalled from 2 Samuel 3:2-4 that originally there was also a son between Amnon and Absalom named Daniel. However, the scriptures merely mention his birth and make no further reference to him. Authorities have assumed that he probably died before reaching maturity or for some other reason never became a contender for the crown.
2. 1 Chronicles 22:9-10

The scripture says, "Then Adonijah, the son of Hag-gith [a wife whom David had married in Hebron[3]] exalted himself, saying, I will be king: and he prepared him chariots and horsemen, and fifty men to run before him."[4]

It will be recalled that this was exactly the pretentious procedure which Absalom had followed just prior to his revolutionary effort to seize the throne.[5] One would have thought that David might have immediately detected the danger signal and reprimanded Adonijah. However, the scripture says he did not.[6]

There may have been good reason for this. King David was nearing the end of his life. As we shall see later, three-score and ten years were all that would be allotted to him,[7] and his physicians could already see that the palsy and chills of his last days were upon him.[8]

The physicians had prescribed a most unique remedy for these chills. They proposed that David allow them to select one of the most fair and attractive maidens in the land whom David would accept as a wife and companion and that while he would not know her as a wife he would have the comfort of her physical warmth and the tenderness of her care in his closing days. The maiden whom they selected was Abishag, a Shunammite from Jezreel, who was con-sidered the most beautiful girl "throughout all the coasts of Israel."[9] The scripture is plain that while she was mar-ried to David she was more of a nurse than a wife. It says, "And the damsel was very fair and cherished the king, and ministered to him: but the king knew her not."[10]

So these were the circumstances which prevailed at the palace when Adonijah decided to have himself proclaimed the new king. The young prince is described as "a very goodly man," meaning that he was handsome in appearance and attractive in demeanor.[11] Furthermore, he was encour-

---

3. 2 Samuel 3:4
4. 1 Kings 1:5
5. 2 Samuel 15:1
6. 1 Kings 1:6
7. This is the age given by Josephus for David's death (Josephus, *Antiquity of the Jews*, Book 7, ch. 15:2)
8. 1 Kings 1:1   10. 1 Kings 1:4
9. 1 Kings 1:3   11. 1 Kings 1:6

aged in his pretentions by Joab, commander of the armed forces, and by Abiathar, one of the High Priests.[12] The scripture says they followed him and "helped him."[13] Joab, of course, had done the same thing for Absalom when he had been the heir-apparent to the throne,[14] but Joab fought against Absalom and killed him when he saw that the prince's passion for power included the slaying of his own father, King David.[15]

One cannot help asking why Joab and Abiathar, the High Priest, would support Adonijah when the Lord had designated Solomon to be the new king. The only explanation is that perhaps they were unaware that the Lord had chosen Solomon. If they had such knowledge their conduct was particularly seditious, both against David and the Lord. But there is no direct evidence of this. To them it might have been nothing more than the necessity of making a political choice and they preferred the man whose seniority made him the heir-apparent rather than Solomon who was still in his early twenties.[16]

And it would appear that many of the people felt the same way about it. At least Adonijah later described the great popular support which he felt had gravitated to him in this hour when it looked as though King David would soon have to be replaced. Adonijah said, that "all Israel set their faces on me, that I should reign."[17] It is interesting, however, that this support did not include the prophet Nathan, nor Zadok, the High Priest, nor Benaiah, the commander of David's elite personal bodyguard.[18] Neither did it include the famous Gibborim, the valiant 600.[19] That these supported Solomon the king is the best proof that the Lord's preference for Solomon was known, at least to these men. And if to them, how could it have been kept a secret from the others?

---

12. 1 Kings 1:7
13. Ibid.
14. 2 Samuel, Chapter 14
15. 2 Samuel 18:14
16. The exact age of Solomon at this time is not given but since he was born when David was in his late forties, it is likely that he was now no more than 20 to 25 years of age.
17. 1 Kings 2:15　　　　　　　　　19. Ibid.
18. 1 Kings 1:8

In any event, Adonijah prepared to make himself king.

Just below the City of David (the Ophel of modern Jerusalem) and across the narrow valley of Kidron there was in ancient times a spring or well called Rogel.[20] It was marked by a prominent stone outcropping which had been named Zoheleth.[21] To this spot Adonijah invited all of his brothers except Solomon, all of the royal ministry of government, Joab, commander-in-chief of the army and Abiathar, the High Priest.[22] He had prepared a great feast for them there of "sheep and oxen and fat cattle."[23] Adonijah apparently made no secret of the fact that this occasion launched his campaign to be crowned the king of Israel and it was not long before the eating and drinking were interrupted by enthusiastic shouts of "God save King Adonijah!"[24]

The Ailing David Outwits His Ambitious Son

As soon as Nathan heard what was happening he caught the full implication of what would occur if Adonijah became king. Both Solomon and Bath-sheba would be slain. Nathan therefore hastened to find Bath-sheba and said, "Hast thou not heard that Adonijah . . . doth reign, and David our Lord knoweth it not?"[25] Apparently she did not know either, so Nathan said, "Now therefore come, let me, I pray thee, give thee counsel, that thou mayest SAVE THINE OWN LIFE, AND THE LIFE OF THY SON SOLOMON."[26]

There is no doubt but what Nathan believed the lives of Solomon and Bath-sheba would be forfeited if Adonijah came to power. He therefore suggested that Bath-sheba make a plea directly to David and then Nathan promised to come along afterward to support her contention so the king would appreciate the seriousness of the situation. As a result, the ailing David received the full benefit of a well prepared presentation. It appeared that for some time the king had been withdrawn from public life, even from his own family.[27] Therefore, Bath-sheba was somewhat apologetic

---

20. 1 Kings 1:9. En-Rogel means "well of Rogel." See marginal note.
21. Ibid.
22. 1 Kings 1:19
23. 1 Kings 1:9
24. 1 Kings 1:25

25. 1 Kings 1:11
26. 1 Kings 1:12
27. 1 Kings 1:15

as she came into his presence. She "bowed, and did obeisance unto the king. And the king said, What wouldest thou?"[28] Then Bath-sheba poured out her plea.

"My Lord," she said, "Thou swarest by the Lord thy God unto thine handmaid, saying, Assuredly Solomon thy son shall reign after me, and he shall sit upon my throne. And now, behold, Adonijah reigneth; and now, my lord the king, thou knowest it not."[29]

This approach was calculated to assist David in arousing himself from the lethargy of his old age so he would publicly declare who was to be the next king. Actually, this is something David should have done earlier, particularly when he knew the Lord had selected someone other than the heir-apparent to be his successor. To make her point decisively clear, Bath-sheba added:

"O king, the eyes of all Israel are upon thee, that thou shouldest tell them who shall sit on the throne of my lord the king after him. Otherwise it shall come to pass, when my lord the king shall sleep with his fathers, that I and my son Solomon shall be counted offenders."[30]

Now the prophet Nathan appeared on the scene and Bath-sheba judiciously withdrew. Nathan came right to the point. "My lord, O king, hast thou said, Adonijah shall reign after me, and he shall sit upon my throne?"[31] Before David could answer he poured on the fuel which would make David respond with positive action. Nathan declared that Adonijah had "gone down this day, and hath slain oxen and fat cattle and sheep in abundance, and hath called all the king's sons, and the captains of the hosts, and Abiathar the priest; and, behold, they eat and drink before him, and say, God save King Adonijah. But me, even me thy servant, and Zadok the priest, and Benaiah the son of Jehoiada, and thy servant Solomon, hath he not called."[32] Having completed his complaint, Nathan now carefully challenged the king in such a way that a direct answer was unavoidable. He asked, "Is this thing done by my lord the king, and thou hast not

28. 1 Kings 1:16
29. 1 Kings 1:17-18
30. 1 Kings 1:20-21

31. 1 Kings 1:24
32. 1 Kings 1:25-26

shewed it unto thy servant, who should sit on the throne of my lord the king after him?"[33]

David felt the ugly impact of all they were trying to tell him. And he was aroused. But instead of answering Nathan directly David said, "Call me Bath-sheba." When she came in before the king he rose to the occasion with the magnificence of his former regal self. Speaking as though he were laying down some eternal fiat, he declared, "Even as I sware unto thee by the Lord God of Israel, saying, Assuredly Solomon thy son shall reign after me, and he shall sit upon my throne in my stead: EVEN SO WILL I CERTAINLY DO THIS DAY."[34]

He immediately gave commandments as to the manner in which they should proceed to nullify the impudence of the pretentious Adonijah. "Take with you," he said, "the servants of your lord, and cause Solomon my son to ride upon mine own mule, and bring him down to Gihon. And let Zadok the priest and Nathan the prophet anoint him there king over Israel: and blow ye with the trumpet, and say, God save King Solomon."[35]

It was a mighty victory. Every person in the room knew they were witnessing a turning point in history. Benaiah, the commander of David's bodyguard, exclaimed "AMEN!"[36]

SOLOMON IS ANOINTED KING OF ISRAEL

A short time later Solomon came riding out of the palace area on king David's mule and was followed closely by the magnificent array of the king's personal bodyguard. It was no wonder that a great crowd quickly gathered to see what wonderful new thing was about to happen to Israel.

It was only a short distance outside the city wall to the famous oasis of Gihon where David had said the solemn anointing of the new king should take place. Today, Gihon is identified as the Fountain of the Virgin Mary.[37] Anciently, it was probably a popular meeting place and therefore ideal for the transacting of public business.

---

33. 1 Kings 1:27
34. 1 Kings 1:30
35. 1 Kings 1:33-34

36. 1 Kings 1:36
37. Geikie, *Hours With the Bible*, p. 355

Gihon is also but a short distance from the place where Adonijah was holding his feast. The place is called the well of Rogel and is identified as being across the Brook Kidron from Gihon and down a little to the southeast.[38] Therefore Adonijah and his party could not see what was taking place but were certainly within earshot when the trumpets began to blow.

But that did not occur until after the solemn anointing had taken place. The scripture says, "And Zadok the priest took an horn of oil out of the tabernacle, and anointed Solomon. And they blew the trumpet and all the people said, God save King Solomon."[39] As Solomon remounted his mule and began to make the short trek back into the city the enthusiasm of the people mounted with every step. "And all the people came up after him, and the people piped with pipes, and rejoiced with great joy, so that the earth rent with the sound of them."[40]

This was the din and clamor which first attracted the attention of Adonijah and his guests. They were just finished eating when the sound of the tumult reached them.[41] Joab, as commander-in-chief of Israel's army had reason to be genuinely alarmed. Said he, "Wherefore is this noise of the city being in an uproar?"[42] Just then Abiathar's son, Jonathan, came running up to broadcast the sensational news: "Verily, our lord King David hath made Solomon king! And the king hath sent with him Zadok the priest, and Nathan the prophet . . . and they have caused him to ride upon the king's mule: and . . . have anointed him king in Gihon; and they are come up from thence rejoicing so that the city rang again. This is the noise that ye have heard. And also Solomon sitteth on the throne of the kingdom."[43]

If a thunderclap with fire from heaven had rumbled down before them it scarcely could have left this party of merrymakers more dumbfounded. To Adonijah this was about the most shocking news he could have received. It meant the end of his plans, the end of his dreams, the end of his power, the end of his throne.

---

38. Ibid., pp. 353- 354
39. 1 Kings 1:39
40. 1 Kings 1:40
41. 1 Kings 1:41
42. Ibid.
43. 1 Kings 1:43-46

To the rest of the celebrants it meant something else. It was the chilling realization that a new king had been proclaimed by David while they were dawdling away their time at the festivities of a pretender. They were on the wrong side, and in ancient politics such a mistake might mean the difference between life and death. The scripture therefore says, "And all the guests that were with Adonijah were afraid, and rose up, and went every man his way."[44]

Adonijah fled also, but not back to his home. He appears to have headed for the heights of Mount Moriah just above the City of David where the altar of sacrifice had been set up by David in front of the temporary tabernacle which housed the holy Ark of the Covenant. The horns of the altar of sacrifice were always considered a sanctuary where a person could flee until his case was investigated and tried. There Adonijah clung in terror hopefully awaiting for some indication of Solomon's clemency toward him.[45]

Before long Solomon did hear of Adonijah's whereabouts and the desperate straits into which he had propelled himself. But Solomon now exhibited a generosity toward Adonijah which the latter in all probability would not have reciprocated had the circumstances been reversed. Said Solomon, "If he will shew himself a worthy man, there shall not an hair of him fall to the earth: but if wickedness shall be found in him, he shall die."[46]

With that, the new king sent his soldiers to bring Adonijah before him, and when they had done so Solomon looked down at his older brother and said simply, "Go to thine house."[47]

David Calls a Great Conference

Although David knew that his days were numbered, the challenging exhilaration of rising to the threat against Solomon and getting him anointed king appears to have resulted in a remarkable revival of David's vitality. An incident recorded in Chronicles clearly shows that this is what had happened.

---

44. 1 Kings 1:49
45. 1 Kings 1:51
46. 1 Kings 1:52
47. 1 Kings 1:53

King David sent forth a proclamation that all the princes of Israel, the military commanders, the administrators of the government and all the principal functionaries throughout the land should assemble in Jerusalem.[48] David had three things he wished to do before he died. It was on this occasion that they were accomplished.

Although David had been confined to bed for a long period with a lingering illness, he now gathered together sufficient strength to rise before the people and boldly address them. "Hear me," he said, "my brethren and my people: As for me, I had in mine heart to build an house of rest for the ark of the covenant of the Lord, and for the footstool of our God, and had made ready for the building: But God said unto me, Thou shalt not build an house for my name, because thou hast been a man of war, and hast shed blood. . . . Solomon thy son, he shall build my house and my courts: for I have chosen him to be my son, and I will be his father. Moreover, I will establish his kingdom for ever, IF HE BE CONSTANT TO DO MY COM-MANDMENTS AND MY JUDGMENTS, AS AT THIS DAY."[49]

David turned to young Solomon and said, "Solomon my son, know thou the God of thy father, and serve him with a perfect heart and with a willing mind . . . if thou seek him, he will be found of thee; but if thou forsake him, he will cast thee off for ever. Take heed now; for the Lord hath chosen thee to build an house for the sanctuary; be strong, and do it."[50]

Then David turned over to Solomon the written plans for the entire temple. This included the description of the actual temple and all that pertained to it, the porches, the treasuries, the upper chambers, the "inner parlours" and the place of the mercy seat. This also included a description "of the courses of the priests and the Levites, and for all the work of the service of the house of the Lord, and for all the vessels. . . ."[51]

---

48. 1 Chronicles 28:1
49. 1 Chronicles 28:2-7
50. 1 Chronicles 28:9-10
51. 1 Chronicles 28:11-13

David said to his son, "All this the Lord made me understand in writing by his hand upon me, even all the works of this pattern."[52]

Now David turned back to the vast congregation of generals, priests, ministers and leaders of the tribes. Said he: "Solomon my son, whom God alone hath chosen, is yet young and tender, and the work is great: for the palace [temple] is not for man, but for the Lord God."[53] He then outlined all that he had done to gather the necessary wealth and construction materials for this great project. He said that from his own personal treasury he had contributed 3,000 talents of gold and 7,000 talents of silver which in modern currency would be a fabulous amount of money running into tens of millions of dollars.[54] He then challenged this great congregation to support the temple project. He cried out, "And who then is willing to consecrate his service this day unto the Lord?"[55]

The aged king's plea touched the people. The scripture says, "Then the chief of the fathers and princes of the tribes of Israel, and the captains of thousands and of hundreds, with the rulers of the king's work, offered willingly."[56] They streamed forward to pour into the sacred treasury over 5,000 additional talents of gold, and 10,000 talents of silver.[57] They also arranged to contribute 18,000 talents of brass and 100,000 talents of iron. And all those who had precious stones came forth to contribute them in great quantities.[58]

"Then the people rejoiced, for that they offered willingly, because with perfect heart they offered willingly to the Lord: and David the king also rejoiced with great joy."[59] David blessed the vast conference in the name of the Lord and then burst forth in an eloquent psalm of praise and thanksgiving.[60]

The whole congregation caught David's religious spirit. They worshipped the Lord and offered numerous sacrifices

---

52. 1 Chronicles 28:19
53. 1 Chronicles 29:1
54. Clarke, *Bible Commentary*, Vol. 2, p. 632
55. 1 Chronicles 29:5   58. 1 Chronicles 29:7-8
56. 1 Chronicles 29:6   59. 1 Chronicles 29:9
57. 1 Chronicles 29:7   60. 1 Chronicles 29:10-19

and offerings.[61] Following this David entertained the conference with a great feast.[62]

At the height of this festive occasion David had his son, Solomon, brought forward. It will be recalled that when Solomon had been anointed king at Gihon it was an emerency situation and only the local people around Jerusalem had been available to hail him in his new calling. Now David had the proper assembly of dignitaries to do justice to a real coronation. Authorities believe Solomon to have been in his early twenties at this time,[63] and as he came before the multitude there was a great surge of patriotism and fervor. "And they made Solomon the son of David king the second time, and anointed him unto the Lord to be the chief governor. . . ."[64]

This was a time for rejoicing and unity. It was to demonstrate that the seditious pretentions of Adonijah which had threatened to split the kingdom were forgotten. The scripture says "And all the princes, and the mighty men, and ALL THE SONS LIKEWISE OF KING DAVID, submitted themselves unto Solomon the king."[65] This would have included Adonijah.

So David had accomplished three great projects at this historic conference. He had gained the support of the people for the completing of the temple project; he had publicly turned over to Solomon the plans for the temple and disclosed that they had been given to him by divine revelation; and finally, he had succeeded in having Solomon crowned and anointed a second time where the people of every tribe were officially represented and could declare their fealty.

For David this was a glorious way to end his reign of forty years duration.

David Dies

Apparently this great conference drained the last semblance of strength from David, and only a short time

---

61. 1 Chronicles 29:21
62. 1 Chronicles 29:22
63. Geikie, *Hours With the Bible*, Vol. 3, p. 405
64. 1 Chronicles 29:22
65. 1 Chronicles 29:24

later he lay on his bed breathing his last. In those moments while his spirit was hovering between two different spheres of reality, David undertook to give his final instruction to Solomon. His last words were, "I go the way of all the earth: be thou strong therefore, and shew thyself a man; and keep the charge of the Lord thy God, to walk in his ways, to keep his statutes, and his commandments, and his judgments, and his testimonies, as it is written in the law of Moses, that thou mayest prosper in all that thou doest, and whither soever thou turnest thyself."[66]

Then David imposed upon Solomon the responsibility of settling a number of old scores which the dying king felt were necessary before the scales of justice could extend their shadow of a balanced equity across the pages of his administration's history. First, there was Joab. Said David:

"Moreover thou knowest also what Joab the son of Zeruiah [David's sister[67]] did to me, and what he did to the two captains of the hosts of Israel, unto Abner the son of Ner, and unto Amasa the son of Jether, whom he slew, and shed the blood of war in peace, and put the blood of war upon his girdle that was about his loins, and in his shoes that were on his feet. Do therefore according to thy wisdom, and let not his hoar [gray] head go down to the grave in peace."[68]

David had never forgotten that terrible day in Hebron when he was just on the verge of uniting all Israel through the good offices of Abner, Saul's commander, and Joab had jeopardized the entire project by murdering Abner in cold blood. The incident of Amasa was less reprehensible since Amasa had previously been the leader of Absalom's rebel forces. Nevertheless, at the time Joab slew him, Amasa was the officially appointed commander of David's forces. David hadn't forgotten that either.

And there was the man from the house of Saul, a Benjamite, named Shimei, who had run along the hill throwing stones and dirt at David as he was retreating in sorrow from Jerusalem during Absalom's rebellion. Shimei had

66. 1 Kings 2:2-3   68. 1 Kings 2:5-6
67. 1 Chronicles 2:15-16

pleaded for clemency after he learned that David had won the civil war and David had granted it, but now David felt that the scales of justice and honor should be balanced against Shimei and he committed Solomon to the task of doing it for him.[69]

David commended others to Solomon who had helped him in times of distress. Concerning these he asked Solomon to "shew kindness."[70]

With these final words the aged David released his fragile grip on mortal life and slipped away into the vast, inviting adventure of the spirit world in the great beyond. He had reigned as king for forty years, seven years in Hebron and thirty-three years over all of Israel.[71] Josephus says he had reached the age of seventy years when he finally died[72] and his body was then laid to rest in his own private tomb located in the City of David.[73] Today the tomb of David is represented as being on the new Mount Zion or western summit in Jerusalem which was not even part of the city in David's day. This is merely a "memorial tomb" going back to the time of the crusaders.[74] The real tomb of David was built on Ophel, the southern spur of Mount Moriah (the original Zion).[75] The ruins of that tomb are probably buried today in the dust of that desolated eminence, mixed, perhaps, with the dust of his remains whose honor it was erected to proclaim.

Thus we come to the conclusion of that fantastically complex life which belonged to the great King David. In his veins ran royal blood, the finest of his time. He was a descendant of prophets and patriarchs clear back to Adam and through him was projected the maternal ancestry of Jesus Christ. The pattern of his personality was almost

---

69. 1 Kings 2:8-9
70. 1 Kings 2:7
71. 1 Kings 2:11
72. Josephus, *Antiquity of the Jews*, Book 15:2
73. 1 Kings 2:10
74. Geikie, *Hours With the Bible*, Vol. 3, p. 363
75. Nehemiah 3:15-16. Note that the original sepulchre of David was near the Pool of Siloah (Siloam), the House of the Mighty and the king's garden, all of which were located on the southern spur of Mount Moriah, called Ophel. It still existed in the days of Christ and was referred to by Peter (Acts 2:29). See also the comments of Dr. Geikie. (*Hours With the Bible*, Vol. 3, pp. 362-364)

encyclopedic — giant-killer, poet, singer, dancer, soldier, shepherd, Priest and king. He rose to heights and sank to depths that lesser men would never know. In a sense, he gained the whole world and then lost his own soul. After his fall he shook off his pride and through pleading "with tears" gained the promise his soul would not always remain in hell. So he fought, lived, loved, failed, suffered and yet succeeded on a scale rarely reached by any man. In David will be found the qualities of the best of us and the frailties of the worst of us. In a most remarkable way he epitomized the high and low, the width and depth, of the entire human race.

Although the Lord felt compelled to be very harsh in his judgment of David at the time of his offense, nevertheless, He held him up before the following generations as a well-nigh perfect example of integrity in all other respects. This attitude on the part of the Lord is epitomized in the following scripture: ". . . David did that which was right in the eyes of the Lord, and turned not aside from any thing that he commanded him all the days of his life, save only in the matter of Uriah the Hittite." (1 Kings 15:5)

Adonijah Makes Another Bid for the Throne

Soon after the aged David had been laid to rest, the cunning Adonijah apparently initiated a plot to destroy his younger brother, Solomon, and replace him on the throne. Being around thirty-five years of age and therefore twelve to fifteen years older than Solomon,[76] he perhaps thought himself shrewd enough to outmaneuver his less experienced brother. The Bible does not clearly define the elements of this plot except to verify that Solomon recognized it as a threat against his life and felt compelled to deal with it rigorously.

Adonijah began his conspiracy by attempting to take a single decisive step which would be recognized by all the people as a signal that Adonijah was the legal and rightful

---

76. These approximate ages may be derived from the fact that Adonijah was David's fourth son born in Hebron (2 Samuel 3:2-4) during the seven years David reigned there (1 Kings 2:11). Add this to the thirty-three years David reigned over Israel (Ibid.) and Adojinah would be somewhere in his middle thirties. As for Solomon, authorities generally agree he was around twenty when he first began to reign. (Geikie, *Hours With the Bible*, Vol. 3, p. 405)

heir to the throne of David instead of Solomon. In these times this could be achieved by taking in marriage one or more of the widows of the dead king. Why Adonijah thought he could get away with this is difficult to imagine, but perhaps he thought the inexperienced, young Solomon would fail to see through the intrigue until it was too late. Adonijah knew he was treading on thin ice. He therefore decided to get official approval for such a marriage and get it indirectly through the queen-mother. The scripture says:

"And Adonijah the son of Haggith came to Bath-sheba the mother of Solomon. And she said, Comest thou peaceably? And he said, Peaceably. . . . And he said, Thou knowest that THE KINGDOM WAS MINE, and that ALL ISRAEL SET THEIR FACES ON ME, THAT I SHOULD REIGN: howbeit the kingdom is turned about, and is become my brother's: FOR IT WAS HIS FROM THE LORD. And now I ask one petition of thee, deny me not. . . . Speak, I pray thee, unto Solomon the king, (for he will not say thee nay), that he GIVE ME ABISHAG THE SHUNAMMITE to wife."[77]

So there it was, a nice little piece of treachery neatly presented. Abishag, of course, was the beautiful girl from the Jezreel district who had cared for David during his final days, and while she was married to him, she had remained a virgin.[78] Surely it would seem a reasonable request that this beautiful maiden be allowed to marry Adonijah as a small appeasement to one who had seen the whole kingdom virtually snatched from his grasp. Certainly Solomon would understand that. . . .

But when the matter was presented to Solomon he understood more than Adonijah might have hoped. The scripture says Bath-sheba went into the throne room and was received with the greatest courtesy by her son. "And the king rose up to meet her, and bowed himself unto her, and sat down on his throne, and caused a seat to be set for the king's mother; and she sat on his right hand. Then she said, I desire one small petition of thee; I pray thee, say

---

77. 1 Kings 2:13-17
78. 1 Kings 1:4

me not nay. And the king said unto her, Ask on, my mother for I will not say thee nay."[79]

So having gained an advance commitment that Solomon would grant her request — a favorite tactic of feminine ingenuity — Bath-sheba shot home the missile: "Let Abishag the Shunammite be given to Adonijah thy brother to wife."[80]

Immediately Bath-sheba knew she had abused her good offices, for Solomon reacted as though assassins were suddenly at his door. He saw the full political implication of the whole scheme and demanded of his mother, "Why dost thou ask Abishag . . . for Adonijah? ASK FOR HIM THE KINGDOM ALSO . . . EVEN FOR HIM, AND FOR ABIATHAR . . . AND FOR JOAB. . . ."[81]

It may have been that Solomon was already aware through court informants that Adonijah, Joab and Abiathar were plotting some kind of *coup d'etat*; at least, the resolute action which Solomon now took would indicate that he possessed some type of advance knowledge which Adonijah's request for Abishag verified as an explosive reality. Solomon declared:

"God do so to me, and more also, if Adonijah have not spoken this word against his own life. Now, therefore . . . Adonijah shall be put to death this day."[82] A plot designed to achieve the overthrow of a government by violence has generally been regarded as totally subversive and punishable by death. Benaiah, the commander of the palace guard, was therefore sent forth immediately to find Adonijah and execute him, which he did.[83]

Solomon then had Abiathar the High Priest brought before him. The record is not at all clear concerning the true extent of Abiathar's implication in this whole disagreeable affair. Whether he was a victim of circumstances or genuinely guilty of plotting against Solomon whom the Lord had chosen, is not spelled out in the record. However, Solomon's treatment of Abiathar would imply the latter. He

---

79. 1 Kings 2:19-20
80. 1 Kings 2:21
81. 1 Kings 2:22

82. 1 Kings 2:23-24
83. 1 Kings 2:25

said to Abiathar, "Get thee to Anathoth,[84] unto thine own
fields; FOR THOU ART WORTHY OF DEATH: but I
will not at this time put thee to death, because thou barest
the ark of the lord God before David my father, and because thou hast been afflicted in all wherein my father was
afflicted."[85]

By this time the excitement caused by Adonijah's
execution had been communicated to Joab. He apparently
felt sufficiently guilty to cause him to flee to the sanctuary
of the altar of sacrifice and cling to its horns for protection.
However, the altar was only to serve as a sanctuary for
those whose guilt had not yet been determined. It was not
designed to protect a person after his crime had been established. As the Lord had said, "But if a man come pre-
sumptuously upon his neighbour, to slay him with guile;
thou shalt take him from mine altar that he may die."
(Exodus 21:14) This was Joab's situation. Not only
had he been a party to Adonijah's plot, but his two murders,
one of Abner and the other of Amasa, were publicly
known because they were committed openly with a cloud
of witnesses. Therefore when Solomon learned that Joab
was at the tabernacle[86] invoking the sanctuary of the altar,
he sent Benaiah to fetch him. "And Benaiah came to the
tabernacle of the Lord, and said unto him, Thus saith the
king, Come forth. And he said, Nay; but I will die here.
And Benaiah brought the king word again, saying, Thus
said Joab, and thus he answered me. And the king said
unto him, Do as he hath said, and fall upon him, and bury
him; that thou mayest take away the innocent blood, which
Joab shed, from me, and from the house of my father. . . .
So Benaiah the son of Jehoiada went up, and fell upon him,
and slew him: and he was buried in his own house in the
wilderness."[87]

---

84. Anathoth is believed to have been just three miles northeast of Jerusalem. It
   was the home of Jeremiah. (Jeremiah 1:1; Peloubet's *Bible Dictionary* under
   "Anathoth")
85. 1 Kings 2:26
86. It will be recalled that this was a temporary tabernacle to protect the Ark
   until the Temple was built. The ancient Tabernacle of the Wilderness was
   still pitched in Gibeon (1 Chronicles 21:29).
87. 1 Kings 2:30-34

This was a sad ending to another tempestuous life which had been energetically spent — sometimes for good and sometimes for evil. Fortunately, the element of time tends to efface the evil so that with the passing centuries no doubt Joab's posterity were proud of the fact that their great ancestor, Joab, had helped to win many victories for Israel and establish David in his Kingdom. After the captivity a branch of Judah's aristocracy traced their ancestry to Joab.[88]

The scripture says that when Benaiah had completed his task of executing Adonijah and Joab, he was given a new assignment. Solomon elevated him to the position of commander-in-chief over the entire armed services of Israel.[89] It was a reward for many years of faithful service by this Levite who was the son of Jehoiada, one of the chief prisets.[90]

Solomon also took action to clarify the lines of religious authority in the nation. He announced that since Abiathar had disgraced himself, hereafter there would be only one High Priest to preside over the Aaronic Priesthood and that would be Zadok.[91] Thus the high office once more returned to its original channel. It will be recalled that four generations earlier when Eli was High Priest the channel of authority was passing down through Aaron's youngest son, Ithmar.[92] Abiathar had been of this descent and was a great grandson of Eli.[93] However, even in Eli's day an unnamed prophet had said that the High Priest's office would one day depart from this house.[94] That prophecy now had been fulfilled as the office had once more reverted to the descendants of Aaron's older son, Eleazar, through whom Zadok traced his line.[95]

Solomon now had one remaining task to perform to fulfill the death-bed instructions of King David. What would he do about Shimei? This man had been a seditious

88. Ezra 8:9
89. 1 Kings 2:35
90. 2 Samuel 8:18 plus 1 Chronicles 12:27
91. 1 Kings 2:35
92. Peloubet's *Bible Dictionary* under "Eli."
93. Ibid., under "Abiathar."
94. 1 Samuel 2:27-35
95. Peloubet's *Bible Dictionary* under "Zadok."

individual in David's day and not only had thrown rocks and dirt at the king but cursed him as he was retreating out of Jerusalem during Absalom's rebellion. Solomon decided to move the man inside the City of Jerusalem and keep him under observation. Certainly he could do little harm so long as he was confined to the city limits. Therefore Solomon commanded Shimei, "Build thee a house in Jerusalem, and dwell there, and go not forth thence any whither. For it shall be, that on the day thou goest out, and passest over the brook Kidron, thou shalt know for certain that thou shalt surely die: thy blood shall be upon thine own head."[96]

Shimei declared this to be a most satisfactory arrangement and lived within these restrictions for "many days."[97] Eventually, however, he used the excuse of recovering two runaway servants from Gath as justification for leaving the city. Solomon heard about it and felt compelled to keep his word lest the orders of the king be considered of no consequence. So the king had Shimei brought before him and declared: "Thou knowest all the wickedness which thine heart is privy to. . . ."[98] The executioner then stepped forward and the life of Shimei was taken.[99]

This marked the end of internal tensions at the commencement of Solomon's reign. A period of tranquility now rested upon the domestic affairs of all Israel.

SOLOMON RECEIVES HIS FIRST VISION AND A MARVELOUS PROMISE

The scripture says, "And Solomon loved the Lord, walking in the statutes of David his father. . . ."[100] Nevertheless, he felt a deep compulsion to show the Lord how much he appreciated the marvelous privilege which had come to him in his youth to be anointed king and serve as the successor to the great David. To achieve his purpose Solomon resolved to take a great company of people with him to Gibeon where the ancient and famous Tabernacle of the congregation was located and where the great brazen altar stood ready to receive sacrifices just as it did in the wilderness for Moses.

---

96. 1 Kings 2:36-37
97. 1 Kings 2:38
98. 1 Kings 2:44

99. 1 Kings 2:46
100. 1 Kings 3:3

Being born to the purple, Solomon had a highly developed sense of regal magnificence and since this pilgrimage was to honor the Lord it had to be of superlative proportions and royal splendor. The solemn procession which advanced northward over the six miles from Jerusalem to Gibeon was lead by Zadok, the High Priest, followed by the musicians and the tabernacle choirs. Then came the king with his vast entourage of military officers, chiefs of state, judges, governors, and princes of all the tribes.[101] No doubt common citizens joined in where they could to swell the throng.

When they reached Gibeon the vast assembly was on historic ground. Here the heathen Hivites had lived as wards of Israel for more than four hundred years and here Saul had massacred them in one of his wild debacles of misguided zeal.[102] After that the ancient Tabernacle had been pitched here with its brazen altar and laver for washing which were both venerated relics from 500 years before when God was leading Israel with a cloud by day and pillar of fire by night.

At Gibeon, Solomon wished to show the Lord in some tangible way the extent of his appreciation and so he did it in the quantity of his sacrifices. A total of one thousand burnt-offerings[103] were sent up as a sweet savor to the heavens with all of the prayers and complicated ritual required for each one. Of course, to the Lord a sacrifice is only a teaching device designed to symbolize the Messianic mission and the submission of the worshipper to the ordinances of the Gospel.[104] In fact, as the Lord has so often emphasized through His prophets, a teachable and obedient heart is the truly acceptable oblation which the Lord rejoices to receive.[105] Only when this is presented to the Lord in company with the burnt-offerings is the purpose of the sacrifice fully achieved.

And apparently this is what the Lord found in Solomon's multitude of sacrifices. As a result, this youthful ruler of Israel was granted a marvelous blessing. "In Gibeon," the scripture states, "the Lord appeared to Solomon in a dream by night: and God said, Ask what I shall give thee."[106]

---

101. 2 Chronicles 1:2-3
102. This is referred to in 2 Samuel 21:1, 2, 5.
103. 1 Kings 3:4   105. Isaiah 1:19
104. Moses 5:6-7; Psalms 51:17   106. 1 Kings 3:5

The genuine humility of Solomon at this stage of his life is reflected in this admirable response to the Lord's query. Said he, ". . . I am but a little child: I know not how to go out or come in. And thy servant is in the midst of thy people which thou hast chosen, a great people, that cannot be numbered nor counted for multitude. Give, therefore thy servant an understanding heart to judge thy people, that I may discern between good and bad: for who is able to judge . . . so great a people?"[107]

The Lord was so pleased with this humble petition that He showered upon Solomon not only what he had requested but even the things he hadn't requested. Said the Lord: "Because thou hast asked this thing, and hast not asked for thyself long life; neither hast asked riches for thyself, nor hast asked the life of thine enemies; but hast asked for thyself understanding, to discern judgment: behold, I have done according to thy words: lo, I have given thee a wise and an understanding heart; so that there was none like thee before thee, neither after thee shall any rise like unto thee. And I have also given thee that which thou hast not asked, both riches and honour: so that there shall not be any among the kings like unto thee all thy days. And if thou wilt walk in my ways, to keep my statutes and my commandments, as thy father David did walk, then I will lengthen thy days."[108]

So Solomon was blessed by the Lord four ways — with wisdom, with riches, with honor and with long life. He gained all of them but the last. In his later years he failed to meet the requirements laid down by the Lord and forfeited this blessing, dying several years younger than David, his father.

Another point of interest is the statement of the Lord implying that David was a great king who administered the statutes and commandments of the Lord in such a commendable manner that Solomon should try to walk in his ways. This means, that in spite of the two great commandments which David broke — and they were the two most serious offenses in the whole decalogue — the Lord nevertheless

---

107. 1 Kings 3:7-9
108. 1 Kings 3:11-14

considered David a superb administrator and ruler over Israel in his day.

Solomon returned to Jerusalem filled with exuberance and appreciation. He went directly to Mount Moriah and straight in before the Ark of the Covenant where he expressed his thanksgiving to God for all that had happened.[109] Then he gave a great feast to all who were with him.[110]

SOLOMON'S WISDOM IS TESTED

However, Solomon had barely recovered from the excitement of his vision and the supreme satisfaction of his great religious pilgrimage to Gibeon when he was confronted by a problem which was a riddle wrapped in an enigma. No judge, regardless of his training or experience, would have cared to come to grips with the judicial decision which was now suddenly demanded of Solomon.

Two women who were keepers of an inn or tavern[111] came before Solomon to determine the custody of a child. The first woman spoke up and said, "O my lord, I and this woman dwell in one house; and I was delivered of a child with her in the house. And it came to pass the third day after that I was delivered, that this woman was delivered also: and we were together; there was no stranger with us in the house, save we two in the house. And this woman's child died in the night; because she overlaid it. And she arose at midnight, and took my son from beside me, while thine handmaid slept, and laid it in her bosom, and laid her dead child in my bosom. And when I rose in the morning to give my child suck, behold, it was dead: but when I had considered it in the morning, behold, it was not my son, which I did bear."[112]

This is as far as the first woman was allowed to go. The second woman roughly interrupted her and cried out, "Nay; but the living is my son, and the dead is thy son![113]

---

109. 1 Kings 3:15
110. Ibid.
111. The English version calls them harlots but Dr. Clarke points out there is no excuse for attaching this stigma to them when the word can be just as accurately translated "tavern-keeper." In the Chaldaic version the words "tavern-keeper" are specifically used. (Clarke, *Bible Commentary*, Vol. 2, p. 396)
112. 1 Kings 3:17-21
113. 1 Kings 3:22

The first woman protested and the second continued denying until the next thing Solomon knew he was right in the middle of a female verbal boxing match.

The king suddenly interrupted the debate with a startling command. He said to his servants, "Bring me a sword!"[114] The two women watched silently and apprehensively as the sword was brought forward. Then Solomon declared, "Divide the living child in two, and give half to the one, and half to the other."[115]

There must have been a tense moment, even among the king's servants, as they contemplated the cruel brutality of such a foolish command. What kind of justice was this? To the first woman it was no justice at all. It was sheer madness. She therefore cried out, "O my lord, give her the living child, and in no wise slay it!"[116] The second woman sneered, "Let it be neither mine nor thine, but divide it."[117]

That was all Solomon needed to hear. Before the sword could fall upon the infant the king pointed to the first woman and said: "Give her the living child, and in no wise slay it: SHE IS THE MOTHER THEREOF!"[118]

The first woman seized the tiny baby in her arms and ran forth rejoicing while the second woman cravenly stole away, completely shamed by the exposure of her despicable lie. To the king's servants this unexpected climax to the trial must have been almost stunning. Then came their realization of the brilliant maneuver by which Solomon had exposed the truth in this well-nigh impossible situation. It was superb, ingenious! "And all Israel heard of the judgment which the king had judged; and they feared the king; for they saw that the wisdom of God was in him, to do judgment."[119]

114. 1 Kings 3:24
115. 1 Kings 3:25
116. 1 Kings 3:26
117. Ibid.
118. 1 Kings 3:27
119. 1 Kings 3:28

Scripture Reading and Questions on Chapter Eight

Scripture Reading: 1 Kings, chapters 1 to 3 inclusive; 1 Chronicles, chapters 28 to 29.

1—What did Adonijah do which gave a clear signal that he intended to be David's successor?

2—What was David's status at this time? Did the public see him often?

3—How did David learn of Adonijah's campaign to have himself proclaimed king?

4—What did David tell Nathan to do in order to circumvent Adonijah's plan?

5—What happened to Adonijah's followers when they heard that Solomon had been anointed king? What did Adonijah do?

6—When Adonijah was brought before Solomon what did the king tell him?

7—When David called his great last conference what three things did he hope to accomplish? Was he successful?

8—Why did David say the Lord would not allow him to build the temple? Did the Lord say who should build it?

9—Was the temple to be built by private contributions as well as by the contributions of David and Solomon? How do we know?

10—Who did Adonijah want to marry after David's death? What was the significance of this request? Did Solomon so interpret it?

11—What happened to Adonijah? To Joab? To Abiathar?

12—Who was now the presiding High Priest? Was he from a different line than Abiathar?

13—Why did Solomon make his pilgrimage to Gibeon? What did he see in the vision there?

14—What four things was Solomon promised by the Lord? Did he get them all? Why?

15—In this vision what attitude did the Lord exhibit toward the recent administration of David? Is this surprising?

16—What was the first thing Solomon did when he returned to Jerusalem? What did he do to celebrate his successful pilgrimage?

17—Two women came to Solomon concerning a dead baby and a live baby. Were they harlots? Describe what happened.

18—Why would the members of Solomon's court be surprised with the outcome of this incident? What did it do for Solomon's reputation?

19—After this it says the people "feared the king." What does this mean? What does it mean "to fear the Lord"?

20—Describe in your own words the character and personality of David.

CHAPTER NINE

Solomon Builds the Great Temple

Having settled himself in his new role as ruler of Israel, Solomon now set upon the most important single project of his entire regal career. He would now construct the Lord's temple. The whole final phase of his father's life had been devoted to elaborate preparations for this magnificent edifice, the design and dimension of which the Lord had personally revealed to him. One of David's last mandates to Solomon had been, "Take heed now, for the Lord hath chosen thee to build a house for the sanctuary; BE STRONG, AND DO IT."[1] That time had come.

The actual initiating of this project occurred as a result of royal ambassadors arriving from King Hiram of Tyre. King Hiram ruled Tyre, Sidon and the remainder of Phoenicia which was approximately the same as Lebanon of today. The Phoenician ambassadors said King Hiram wanted to congratulate Solomon as the new king of Israel and also for being the son of such an illustrious father, "for Hiram was ever a lover of David."[2]

---

1. 1 Chronicles 28:10
2. 1 Kings 5:1

This friendly gesture gave Solomon a most propitious opportunity to ask Hiram to help him as he had helped David so that Jehovah's great temple could be built. In the greatest humility and supplication, he wrote to Hiram, "As thou didst deal with David my father, and didst send him cedars to build him a house to dwell therein [the cedar palace] even so deal with me. . . . Send me now therefore a man cunning to work in gold, and in silver, and in brass, and in iron, and in purple, and crimson, and blue, and that can [use] skill to grave with the cunning men that are with me in Judah and in Jerusalem, whom David my father did provide. Send me also cedar trees, fir trees, and algum trees, out of Lebanon: for I know that thy servants can [use] skill to cut timber in Lebanon; and, behold, my servants shall be with thy servants . . . and, behold, I will give to thy servants, the hewers that cut timber, twenty thousand measures of beaten wheat, and twenty thousand measures of barley, and twenty thousand baths of wine, and twenty thousand baths of oil."[3]

Hiram responded immediately. He wrote that he was sending a man who had the most exquisite skill in the construction and decorating of great buildings. This skilled artisan, known as Hiram, was no relation to the king but was of mixed nationality. His mother was from the tribe of Naphtali of Israel, and his father, a famous brass maker but now dead, was from Tyre.[4]

King Hiram further stated that if Solomon were willing to provide the food for the Phoenician workmen as well as a goodly number of Israelites to help them hew the timber, he would gladly make a gift to Solomon of the vast quantities of cedar and fir necessary to construct the temple and all its related buildings. Hiram said he would see that the logs were placed on rafts and floated from Tyre to Joppa where Solomon could then take possession of them and haul them up to Jerusalem.[5]

---

3. 2 Chronicles 2:3-10
4. 2 Chronicles 2:13-14. The name, Hiram, is given as Hurum in 2 Chronicles but as Hiram in 1 Kings. In this text we use Hiram. Note that the passage cited says this artisan's mother came from Dan, but 1 King 7:14 says she was actually of the tribe of Naphtali.
5. 2 Chronicles 2:16

The Manpower Required for the Temple Project

Unless one has visited Jerusalem and seen the temple site it is almost impossible to visualize the gargantuan proportions of the task involved in the building of this temple. The temple itself was not large, but the manmade plateau or square on which the temple eventually stood was an engineering task of fantastic dimensions.

In the first place, there was no practical accommodation for a temple on the summit of Mount Moriah as it existed in its natural state. It had a steep ascent on three sides and a peak to the north. The only flat surface was the threshing floor of Araunah and that was barely large enough to accommodate a good-sized room. Solomon's task was therefore to build a huge platform on top of this mountain and then erect the temple on top of that.

Solomon decided to get the timber on the way while the temple block was being built. He therefore requisitioned 30,000 men from the various tribes to cut timber. These men went up 10,000 at a time to Lebanon and worked one full month after which they returned for a rest while the other two contingents of 10,000 men, each put in a month.[6]

But the building of the acropolis or temple square was something else again. To furnish the manpower for this massive project, King Solomon requisitioned 70,000 men to "bare burdens" (meaning to haul stones for the walls and carry up broken fragments for the fill), and 80,000 "hewers in the mountains," (meaning those needed to quarry, square, face and place the huge stones).[7] These vast work forces may have also been divided into courses as were the wood cutters so that they did not have to work continually, but the Bible makes no mention of it.

In order to supervise such a mammoth undertaking, Solomon had 3,300 foremen, engineers and superintendents.[8] These included not only Israelites but "Hiram's builders" from Phoenicia,[9] who were far more experienced in elaborate projects of this kind than Solomon's builders.

---

6. 1 Kings 5:13-14
7. 1 Kings 5:15
8. 1 Kings 5:16
9. 1 Kings 5:18

In addition to providing all of the manpower itemized above, there was the equally important need to harness the entire economy of Israel so as to provide the food and other necessities for the workmen and meet the heavy tax levies which would unavoidably result from such a strenuous undertaking.

BUILDING TEMPLE SQUARE ON MOUNT MORIAH

Two modest passages in the scriptures[10] cover the gigantic task of building the acropolis of Jerusalem on which the temple could be erected. When it is realized that this was all done by hand labor and eventually encompassed an area constituting a fourth or more of old Jerusalem, the mind can begin to grasp the size of the effort. Some comprehension of the achievement may be gained from this description by Dr. Geikie:

"The hill (Mount Moriah) did not offer a level space sufficient for the building intended, and had to be cut away at one part and built up to the needed elevation at another. To enable this to be done, the central crest of Moriah was enclosed by huge walls reaching nearly to the level of the highest point, that which now forms the Dome of the Rock, originally the crown of Araunah's threshing floor. These supporting walls were of extraordinary thickness, and were formed of enormous blocks of stone fastened together by iron clamps, all the empty space between them and the living rock being filled up with stones, so as to form a level surface. At the northwest corner, however, the hill rose much higher than the level required, so that it had to be cut away, leaving a natural wall rising in the angle, to the height of 26 feet. On the northeast corner, on the other hand, the empty space which needed to be filled up with stones was no less than 123 feet deep; while, on the south side of the plateau, there was a labyrinth of vaults, cisterns, and chambers on which was heaped a mass of earth and stones. How great the labour required may be judged from the wall of the southeast angle having risen not less than 110 feet above the living rock, to secure the level needed. The result of this immense toil [plus the later enlargement by Herod] was

---

10. 1 Kings 5:17-18

the creation of a level space, in shape like a badly cut leaf
of a book, 1,520 feet on one side, 1,611 on the other, while
one end is 921 feet across, and the opposite one 1,017: a
trapezoid containing, altogether, about 35 acres. The defense
of this sacred space was easy on all sides but the north, the
ground falling steeply away except there. In that direction,
however, the hill extended outside the temple ground, and
hence to guard against attack from this point, a huge trench
was cut in the rock in the north-east, while on the north-west
there was a gigantic moat, known in our day as Birket Israel,
still measuring 104 feet broad and 65 feet deep. . . . It is
hard to imagine the grandeur of such an undertaking, in
such an age, for some parts of the vast walls are 143 feet
from the rock [up] to the old surface of the temple courts;
indeed, Sir Charles Wilson speaks of the south wall as
having been almost equal in height to the tallest of our
church spires."[11]

One of the major problems connected with the placing
of a temple on Mount Moriah was the fact that it had no
water there. Dr. Geikie comments on this as follows: "Before beginning the temple itself, moreover, provision had to
be made for the water supply, so essential for the innumer-
able sacrifices to be offered. There is no spring in the hill,
so that vast cisterns had to be hewn out, and a series of these
were therefore excavated, capable of holding over 10,000,000
gallons. All these were supplied with water brought by an
aqueduct from Solomon's pools [some 10 miles away beyond
Bethlehem] . . . a system of channels connecting the whole.
The final overflow, after they were filled, passed off by a
conduit into the Kidron. One cistern alone, that is known as
the Great Sea, the roof of which is supported by pillars of
rock, would contain nearly 3,000,000 gallons."[12]

One additional source of admiration and amazement
awaits the Jerusalem visitor and that is the quarries from
which the stone was cut for this project. Dr. Geikie says,
"The great source of the building material employed was,
however, the [underground] quarries near the Damascus
Gate of the city. I got into them through a low opening

11. Geikie, *Hours With the Bible*, Vol. 3, pp. 449-450.
12. Ibid. pp. 450-451

about a hundred yards east of that gate. . . . The roof is about thirty feet high, and remains as rough as when first created by the rude toil of the quarrymen. The ground is deeply bedded with fragments chiselled off the rough blocks by the masons, and with others fallen from the roof. . . . Five or six hewers seem to have worked together: each man cutting down into the rock perpendicularly, a chink four inches broad, to a fixed depth. Wedges of wood were then inserted, and these having been swollen by wetting them, split off the block required. Some such blocks still remain where the poor toilers left them nearly three thousand years ago. . . . The size of the quarries is very great: in some places not less than seven hundred feet from the entrance, and as broad, forming a vast confusion of rough pillars, rough footing, and rough sides and roof, all hidden in utter darkness, outside the little circle of the light of one's candle. One of the great stones at the southeast angle of the temple enclosure . . . is estimated to weigh a hundred tons, and this vast mass reached its place on the sacred hill only by being dragged from its bed in the quarries by the toil of great gangs of men! Another stone is over thirty-eight feet in length. . . . One huge stone that had been split, as it was being dragged out, still lies as it was left thirty centuries ago."[13]

In the light of these facts it can be readily understood why the preparation of the temple block and the collection of stone and timber required three years[14] before the construction of the temple could actually commence. This means that young Solomon began these preparations after being king only about one year. We conclude this from the fact that since we know he began the temple in the fourth year of his reign,[15] these three years of preparation would have had to commence during or shortly after his first year as king.

THE BUILDING OF SOLOMON'S TEMPLE

The scripture says, "Then Solomon began to build the house of the Lord at Jerusalem in Mount Moriah, where the

---

13. Ibid. pp. 447-448
14. The Septuagint text (1 Kings 5:18) says, "They prepared timber and stone, to build the temple for THREE YEARS." (See footnote in *Antiquities of the Jews*, by Josephus, Book 8, ch. 4:1)
15. 2 Chronicles 3:2; 1 Kings 6:1

Lord appeared unto David his father, in the place that David had prepared in the threshing-floor of Ornan (Araunah) the Jebusite. And he began to build in the second day of the second month, in the fourth year of his reign."[16]

The general plan for the temple of Solomon was identical with that of the ancient Tabernacle except that it was twice as long, twice as wide and three times as high.[17]

It was divided into a Holy Place 60 feet long and a Holy of Holies 30 feet long.[18] From this it will be seen that the structure was not large, but this permitted the most elaborate kind of decorating so that when the temple was completed it was like an architectural jewel, the fame of which spread throughout the nations of the earth so long as it stood.

As with the Tabernacle and temples in all ages, the front entrance was toward the east.[19] This entrance was very ornate and impressive, with a great porch as wide as the temple and extending fifteen feet out into the courtyard.[20] The high roof of the porch rested on two massive brass pillars each 27 feet high and 18 feet in circumference.[21] At the top of each pillar was an enlarged capital decorated with lily leaves. This was overhung with wreaths of 200 bronze pomegranates.[22] The pillar on the left (north side) was called Boaz while the one on the right (south side) was called Jachin.[23] It is assumed these pillars were hollow but even so, the casting of such massive metal structures would be a phenomenal task.

---

16. Ibid.
17. 1 Kings 6:2. This gives the dimensions of the temple as 60 cubits long, 20 cubits wide, and 30 cubits high. If we use the standard cubit length of 18 inches, it would make the temple 90 feet long, 30 feet wide, and 45 feet high. As indicated, these figures make the temple twice as long, twice as wide, and three times as high as the Tabernacle. We judge the height of the Tabernacle from the fact that the boards which formed its walls were 10 cubits or 15 feet high, (Exodus 26:16), this being only one-third the height of Solomon's temple.
18. 1 Kings 6:16-17, 20
19. Josephus, *Antiquities of the Jews*, Book 8, chapter 3:2
20. 1 Kings 6:3
21. 1 Kings 7:15
22. 1 Kings 7:19-20
23. 1 Kings 7:21. Josephus says "left" is the north side and "right" is the south side as though one were standing in the temple and facing east toward the front door. (*Antiquities of the Jews*, Book 8, chapter 3:6)

Hiram knew the casting would be difficult and he had to go clear up along the Jabbock river "between Succoth and Zarthan" before he could find the proper clay to make the cast.[24]

The floor of the porch was overlaid with gold[25] and constituted the approach to the two great doors which com-prised the entrance to the temple. These doors were made of thick planks of olive wood, elaborately carved, with gold foil carefully molded over the carving.[26] They swung on gold hinges.[27]

As one entered the Holy Place he would see the floor overlaid with gold[28] and the walls of carved cedar[29] magnifi-cently decorated with gold and precious stones.[30] Instead of a single candlestick with seven branches as was used in the Tabernacle, there were ten candlesticks of pure gold, five on the right and five on the left.[31] Along the side of the north wall was the golden table of shew bread just as it stood in the ancient Tabernacle.[32]

At the far end of the Holy Place was the partition which divided this room from the Holy of Holies. To one side of this partition was the golden altar of incense.[33] The parti-tion had two doors leading into the Holy of Holies. These, like the main doors of the temple, were made of heavy planks of olive wood, beautifully carved and overlaid with gold.[34] These doors also had gold hinges,[35] and were protected by a gold chain which hung across them.[36]

Inside the Holy of Holies there were two magnificent figures called cherubims which were 15 feet tall with 7½ foot wings spread out in each direction. The cherubims were placed so that their inside wings touch each other over the spot reserved for the Ark and their outside wings touched the north and south walls. The vast spread of these four wings therefore extended the full breadth of the temple or thirty feet.[37] Both of these huge figures were made of olive

24. 1 Kings 7:45-46
25. 1 Kings 6:30
26. 1 Kings 6:32
27. 1 Kings 7:50
28. 1 Kings 6:30
29. 1 Kings 6:18
30. 2 Chronicles 3:6-7

31. 1 Kings 7:49
32. 1 Kings 7:48; Exodus 40:22
33. 1 Kings 6:21-22; Exodus 30:1, 3, 6
34. 1 Kings 6:31, 34-35
35. 1 Kings 7:50
36. 1 Kings 6:21
37. 1 Kings 6:23-27

wood and were overlaid with gold.[38] The walls of the Holy of Holies were elaborately carved and then the entire interior was gold-plated, including the floor.[39] However, no source of light is mentioned. Since there were no windows, due no doubt to the three stories of "chambers" on the exterior, some type of candle or lamp light would have been necessary.

In the center of the Holy of Holies is believed to have been the outcropping of rock which was once the threshing floor of Araunah and on which the fire of the Lord had consumed David's sacrifice.[40] In due time the Ark of the Covenant would rest there beneath the over-shadowing wings of the two huge Cherubims.[41]

During the travail of completing the temple, the Lord gave Solomon a revelation of encouragement in which He said, "Concerning this house which thou art [engaged] in building, if thou wilt walk in my statutes, and execute my judgments, and keep all my commandments to walk in them; then will I perform my word with thee, which I spake unto David thy father. And I will dwell among the children of Israel, and will not forsake my people Israel."[42] This was the second time the Lord had spoken to Solomon in a direct revelation.

One thing worthy of note in connection with the building of this sacred structure is the fact that all parts of the building were pre-fabricated and then brought to the temple block where they could be quietly fitted together without disturbing the sanctity of this place. The scripture says, "And the house, when it was in building, was built of stone made ready before it was brought thither: so that there was neither hammer nor axe nor any tool of iron heard in the house, while it was in building."[43]

THE EXTERIOR OF THE TEMPLE

On the immediate exterior of the temple, there nestled against its walls on all sides but the front, three stories of chambers which might well be called the temple annex. No

---

38. 1 Kings 6:28
39. 1 Kings 6:29-30
40. 1 Chronicles 21:26
41. 1 Kings 8:1-7
42. 1 Kings 6:11-13
43. 1 Kings 6:7

doubt these chambers were used for the washings and
anointings, the accommodation of the ministering Priests and
the storage of temple clothing or other sacred ceremonial
equipment.[44] These chambers are described as three stories
high,[45] but since each floor was only five cubits or 7½ feet
in height,[46] the total height of all three stories would only
be somewhere in the neighborhood of 22½ feet. This means
that the chambers of the annex only extended half-way up
the wall of the temple. As we have already mentioned, the
height of the temple was 45 feet.[47]

Light was admitted into these chambers of the annex
by long, narrow windows[48] which were sufficient to illuminate the chambers but still not wide enough to permit an
intruder to invade these sacred precincts.

Each chamber on the first floor was only five cubits
(7½ feet) wide, while those on the second floor were six
cubits (9 feet) wide, and those on the third floor were seven
cubits (10½ feet) wide.[49] This may have been necessary
to accommodate the sloping wall of the temple which must
have been wider at the bottom than the top and buttressed
in order to give it support. This would make it necessary
to have the first-floor rooms smaller than those above.

All of these chambers had to be constructed so that
their beams were not fastened into the walls of the temple.[50]
The entrance to the annex section was through a doorway
on the right or "south" side of the temple. This opened onto
a spiral stairway ascending to the upper floors.[51] Each floor
had a hallway 7½ feet wide called "the place that was
left." The entrance to each chamber was off this corridor.[52]

44. 1 Kings 6:5
45. 1 Kings 6:6
46. 1 Kings 6:10
47. 1 Kings 6:2
48. 1 Kings 6:4
49. 1 Kings 6:6
50. Ibid.
51. 1 Kings 6:8. As previously mentioned in note 23, the right side of the temple
    would be on the south.
52. No mention of a corridor is found in the description of Solomon's temple, but
    when Ezekiel was shown the temple which the Jews would build in the last days,
    its specifications turned out to be exactly the same as Solomon's temple, and it
    does mention the existence of a corridor connecting these chambers (Ezekiel
    41:9, 11). Authorities have therefore felt justified in assuming that this was
    also characteristic of Solomon's temple. (See Clarke, *Bible Commentary*, Vol. 2,
    p. 539.)

Of course, not all of the Priests who served in the temple could reside in these chambers and therefore the majority of the Priests appear to have occupied quarters in the chambers which were built in the outer courtyard.

Actually, the temple had two courtyards[53] — an inner courtyard[54] for the sacrifices, oblations and probably the baptisms, and an outer courtyard[55] which encompassed the rest of the temple block and was considered the place of general assembly. We will take an imaginary look at the inner courtyard first.

The Inner Courtyard

This inner courtyard was called the courtyard of the Priests because it was in this place that they did most of their work. Here was the great altar of sacrifice, the great brazen sea and all the activities took place here involving the slaughter, washing and sanctifying of vast quantities of sacrificial animals. This courtyard was completely surrounded on all four sides by a high stone wall in three courses, topped by cedar coping.[56]

Because of the immense amount of butchering which took place within these walls it was extremely important that the disposal of refuse be immaculately arranged, and also that cleanliness be stringently enforced lest the temple area become so tainted that even the pleasant, pungent incense could not refresh the atmosphere. We have no description of these facilities in Solomon's day, but we are led to believe that Herod's reconstruction was simply an elaboration of what was already there. Dr. Alfred Edersheim gives us this description of the disposal facilities on the temple block after the reconstruction: "The system of drainage into chambers below and canals, all of which could be flushed at will, was perfect; the blood and refuse being swept down into Kidron and towards the royal gardens."[57] He later adds, ". . . the mouth of the main drain being the the valley

---

53. 2 Chronicles 33:5
54. See the discussion in Peloubet's *Bible Dictionary*, under "temple".
55. Ibid.
56. 1 Kings 6:36
57. Dr. Alfred Edersheim, *The Temple*, London: William Clowes and Sons, p. 55

of the Kidron, where the sewerage was probably used as manure for the gardens."[58]

All of this required great quantities of water and a most elaborate system of cisterns and aqueducts had to be built by Solomon for this purpose. Dr. Edersheim quotes Barclay's *City of the Great King*: ". . . the ground is perfectly honeycombed with a series of remarkable rock-hewn cisterns, in which the water brought by an aqueduct from Solomon's Pools, near Bethlehem, was stored. The cisterns appear to have been connected by a system of channels cut out of the rock; so that when one was full the surplus water ran into the next, and so on, till the final overflow was carried off by a channel into the Kidron. One of the cisterns — that known as the Great Sea — would contain two million gallons; and the total number of gallons which could be stored [in all the cisterns] probably exceeded ten millions."[59]

The altar of sacrifice in this courtyard was much larger than the one used in the wilderness, this one being 30 feet square and 15 feet high.[60] The one in the wilderness was only 7½ feet square and 4½ feet high.[61] Solomon's altar was probably built on the same design however. If so, it was constructed like a hollow box overlaid with plates of brass inside and outside and having raised horns at each of the four corners. The interior was filled with stones and earth on which the great fires were kept continually burning. A brass grating covered the fire so as to support the sacrifices placed upon it. Note that no sacrifices were burned inside the temple, but only incense which was burned on the golden altar.

The brazen sea was located in the southeast corner of the court of the priests.[62] It rested on the backs of twelve oxen, three facing each of the cardinal points of the compass.[63] The sea itself was 7½ feet high and 15 feet across.[64] Its edge was the thickness of the palm of the hand, or about four inches, and it was turned down like the lip of an ewer. This overhanging edge was beautifully decorated with lilies and rows of floral ornaments.[65]

58. Ibid. pp. 56-57
59. Ibid. p. 56
60. 2 Chronicles 4:1
61. Exodus 27:1
62. 1 Kings 7:39
63. 2 Chronicles 4:4
64. 2 Chronicles 4:2
65. 2 Chronicles 4:5

In conjunction with this huge reservoir of water or brazen sea there were ten large brass basins on wheels which could be moved around the courtyard and used for washing and cleansing in connection with the multitude of sacrifices.[66]

Because we now know that the ordinance of baptism was performed by the ancient Aaronic Priesthood,[67] it is most likely that the large brazen sea was used for baptisms just as similar fonts (on the backs of twelve oxen) are used in our temples today. Of course, the ordinance of baptism in ancient times could be done only for the living and not be performed vicariously for the dead as was done after the resurrection of Christ.[68]

The Outer Courtyard

The outer courtyard enclosed the entire temple ground and more or less formed a huge quadrangle. It had several gates, and was referred to as the place of general assembly. "The outer court was for the worshippers, who were intended to exercise the feelings suggested and symbolized by the ceremonies going on visibly in the court or unseen in the sanctuary but well known as to their meaning."[69]

Like the inner enclosure, this court had walls of stone topped by cedar.[70] The eastern side boasted a beautiful colonnade which was a favorite meeting place for the learned teachers.[71] When Herod rebuilt the temple during the Savior's era he duplicated this colonnade section which is referred to in scripture as Solomon's porch.[72]

It appears from several scriptures that this courtyard of the temple was planted in beautiful trees and shrubbery.[73]

---

66. 1 Kings 7:27-39
67. Doctrine and Covenants 84:26-27. In this citation the Lord states that the ordinance of baptism belonged to the Aaronic Priesthood during the days of Israel. The covenant of circumcision for boys at the age of 8 days was designed to remind parents of their responsibility to have all children baptized when they reached the age of accountability (Insp. Version, Genesis 17:4-11). See discussion in *The Third Thousand Years,* pp. 11-12.
68. Direct reference to baptism for the dead is found in the New Testament. See 1 Corinthians 15:29.
69. Peloubet's *Bible Dictionary,* under "Temple," p. 675.
70. 1 Kings 7:12
71. Peloubet's *Bible Dictionary,* under "Temple."
72. John 10:23; Acts 3:11; 5:12
73. Psalms 52:8; 92:12-13

What About the Mysterious Upper Rooms of Solomon's Temple?

One single verse in the Bible makes reference to "upper chambers." Nowhere else is there a description of this part of the temple, but it must have been a most important and sacred part because it says, "And he [Solomon] overlaid the upper chambers with gold."[74] What about these upper chambers?

Josephus partially assists us by stating that Solomon's temple had a second floor exactly like the first floor in all its dimensions. Josephus refers to the first floor of the temple (which is described so minutely in the Bible) as the "lower house." Then he calls the second floor the "upper house." Note the following interesting details which Josephus, alone, provides:

"There was another building erected over it [that is, over the first floor], equal to it in its measures. . . . He also built around the temple thirty small rooms. . . . Above these were other rooms, and others above them . . . so that these reached to a height EQUAL TO THE LOWER PART OF THE HOUSE: for the upper part had no buildings about it. . . . The king also had a fine contrivance for an ascent to the upper room over the temple, and that was by steps in the thickness of its walls; for it [the upper house] had no large door on the east end, as the lower house had, but the entrances were by the sides, through very small doors."[75]

From this it would appear that Solomon's temple which the Bible describes as 45 feet in height, was not one story, but two, and that the annex rooms built on the outside of the temple, only came half-way up the side of the temple wall or "equal to the lower part of the house." This fits the Bible's description of these rooms since they were only 7½ feet (five cubits) in height,[76] and all three stories of the annex would therefore amount to only 22½ feet (plus floor joists between stories) which would bring the roof of the annex just a little over half-way up the side of the temple's

---

74. 2 Chronicles 3:9
75. Josephus, *Antiquities of the Jews,* Book 8, chapter 3:2
76. 1 Kings 6:10

45-foot wall. The upper chambers could have had narrow windows for lighting just as the "chambers" of the annex.

Josephus further discloses that the entrance to the Upper House was not through the regular entrance to the temple but that there were doors on the sides, and stairways were built "in the thickness of the walls" (inside the walls themselves) which led to the upper chambers of the temple.

The next question which arises is concerning the use of the upper chambers. What was their purpose? There is not a word in either the Bible or Josephus concerning the use of the upper house nor the reason it had a special entrance separate from the lower house. We therefore turn to another source.

The modern student is extremely fortunate to have access to a more recent scripture which casts a completely new light on the ordinance work which was performed in Solomon's temple. Speaking of the importance of temples, the Lord declared, "And again, verily I say unto you, how shall your washings be acceptable unto me, except ye perform them in a house which you have built to my name? For, for this cause I commanded Moses that he should build a tabernacle, that they should bear it with them in the wilderness, AND TO BUILD A HOUSE IN THE LAND OF PROMISE [which, of course, would be Solomon's temple] THAT THOSE ORDINANCES MIGHT BE REVEALED WHICH HAD BEEN HID FROM BEFORE THE WORLD WAS."[77]

In the next verse (verse 39) the Lord reveals that He is talking about the ordinances relating to the Endowment. When it says that these ordinances have been kept hidden "from before the world was" it means simply that because of their extremely sacred character they have never been performed in public as were the animal sacrifices and the other ordinances belonging to the lower Priesthood. The Lord says (in verse 39) that "anointings" and "washings" and "solemn assemblies" and "holy places wherein you receive conversations" and the "endowment" all belong to "my holy house, which my people are always commanded to

---

77. Doctrine and Covenants 124:37-38

build unto my holy name." And, as the Lord had pointed out in verse 38, this included Solomon's temple.

Therefore, since the Lord clearly states in this revelation that somewhere in Solomon's temple the higher Priesthood ordinances or Endowment were performed, the question automatically arises, where was this work done? Now that we know from both the Bible and Josephus that there were upper chambers in Solomon's temple which were extremely sacred and overlaid with gold, we undoubtedly have the logical answer.

WHERE WAS THE VEIL IN SOLOMON'S TEMPLE?

The above information my also help to clear up another inconsistency in the Biblical description of Solomon's temple. The Bible says a beautiful and elaborate veil was prepared for the temple: "And he made the vail [Bible spelling] of blue, and purple, and crimson, and fine linen, and wrought cherubims thereon."[78] Where was this veil used?

In the Tabernacle of Moses (which was an improvised, portable temple[79]) the veil separated the Holy Place from the Holy of Holies.[80] But a completely different arrangement occurred in the more permanent temple structure built by Solomon. The scripture says that in the lower house of Solomon's temple, the Holy Place was separated from the Holy of Holies by a WALL or partition, overlaid with gold,[81] and that this wall contained DOUBLE DOORS[82] which were guarded by GOLD CHAINS.[83] As for the veil, there isn't a word about it, except to assure us that one was prepared. No statements are made as to where it was placed even though it is clear that it was no longer used to screen the Holy of Holies.

Authorities have thought that perhaps the veil was placed over the opening of the two doors whenever they were were left ajar,[84] but there is nothing in the record to indicate this.

---

78. 2 Chronicles 3:14
79. Doctrine and Covenants 124:38
80. Exodus 26:31-33
81. 1 Kings 6:21, 31
82. 1 Kings 6:31
83. 1 Kings 6:21
84. Josephus, *Antiquities of the Jews,* Book 8, Chapter 3:3

Because the veil is an important part of the Temple ceremony and not just a screen or partition, it is logical to assume that it would be used at the appropriate place in the temple service. If the upper chambers of Solomon's temple were used for the higher ordinances then its proper place would be between the terrestrial and celestial rooms just as it is in modern temples.

Furthermore, since Josephus informs us that the dimensions of the second floor were identical with the first, it would appear that the upper house consisted of a room sixty feet long (comparable to the Holy Place on the first floor), and a room thirty feet long (comparable to the Holy of Holies on the first floor). The veil then, rather than a wall could have been used to separate these two areas. Such an arrangement would have adapted itself to the exact requirements of the temple service or Endowment ceremonies.

As for the lower floor, its use, according to the Bible, was extremely limited, being set apart primarily for the Aaronic Priesthood to attend the altar of incense each day and renew the bounties on the golden table of shew bread. A little reflection will demonstrate the appropriateness of having a certain part of the temple ceremony pertaining to Aaronic Priesthood covenants performed on this floor, while covenants belonging to the higher or Melchizedek Priesthood would be more appropriately performed on the upper floor. This exact arrangement prevails wherever possible in L.D.S. temples today.

What Is the Endowment?

Because of its sacred character, the temple service is available only to those who have made the necessary preparations and proven their worthiness to participate. However, it is more sacred than secret. In 1912 the Church of Jesus Christ of Latter-day Saints published *The House of the Lord,* in which Dr. James E. Talmage gave this authorized description of the Endowment ordinances. These ordinances have been essentially the same since the days of Adam. Concerning them, Dr. Talmage wrote:

"The temple endowment, as administered in modern temples, comprises instruction relating to the significance and sequence of past dispensations. . . . This course of instruction includes a recital of the most prominent events of the creative period, the condition of our first parents in the Garden of Eden, their disobedience and consequent expulsion from that blissful abode, their condition in the lone and dreary world when doomed to live by labor and sweat, the plan of redemption by which the great transgression may be atoned, the period of their apostasy, the restoration of the gospel with all the ancient powers and privileges, the absolute and indispensable conditions of personal purity and devotion to the right in present life, and a strict compliance with gospel requirements. . . .

"The ordinances of the endowment embody certain obligations on the part of the individual, such as a covenant and promise to observe the law of strict virtue and chastity, to be charitable, benevolent, tolerant and pure; to devote both talent and material means to the spread of truth and the uplifting of the race; to maintain devotion to the cause of truth; and to seek in every way to contribute to the great preparation that the earth may be made ready to receive her King, the Lord Jesus. With the taking of each covenant and the assuming of each obligation a promised blessing is pronounced, contingent upon the faithful observance of the conditions.

"No jot, iota, or tittle of the temple rites is otherwise than uplifting and sanctifying. In every detail the endowment ceremony contributes to covenants of morality of life, consecration of person to high ideals, devotion to truth, patriotism to nation, allegiance to God."[85]

Preparing For the Dedication of the Temple

Altogether the temple required seven years and six months to complete. The foundations were laid in April of the fourth year in Solomon's reign and the temple was completed in October or November of the eleventh year.[86] However, the dedication did not take place until nearly eleven months later.[87] Authorities believe Solomon did this deliberately in order to wait for the great autumnal Feast

---

85. James E. Talmage, *The House of the Lord*, pp. 99-101
86. 1 Kings 6:37-38 plus Clarke, *Bible Commentary*, Vol. 2, p. 405
87. 1 Kings 8:2 plus notes in Clarke, *Bible Commentary*, Vo. 2, p. 412

of the Tabernacles or harvest festival when all of the people would be in a spirit of rejoicing and able to rest from their year's labor.[88]

The Feast of the Tabernacles lasted one full week and was designed to commemorate the days when Israel lived "in booths" or tabernacles of branches in the wilderness.[89] It was also to celebrate the ingathering of the harvest.[90] During the week of this particular holiday the people spent their time living apart from their homes and dwelling in improvised "booths" made of branches and thatch.[91]

The scripture says, "And all the men of Israel assembled themselves unto King Solomon at the feast [of the tabernacles] in the month of Ethanim, which is the seventh month."[92] We learn elsewhere, however, that the people actually assembled in Jerusalem seven days prior to the feast so that they could spend seven days preparing for the dedication of the temple which event was scheduled for the "eighth day" or the first day of the feast of the tabernacles.[93]

All of the available details concerning the pre-dedication ceremonies for Solomon's temple imply that exactly the same procedure was followed as that which attended the dedication exercises of the Tabernacle at the foot of Mount Sinai. On that earlier occasion the Lord gave Moses and Aaron elaborate ceremonies to be carried out over a period of seven days.[94] We know that this also occurred in Solomon's time for the scripture says, "Also at the same time Solomon kept the feast SEVEN DAYS, and all Israel with him, a very great congregation, from the entering in of Hamath [in northern Syria] unto the river of Egypt."[95]

To appreciate what happened during those seven days we refer back to the details furnished in the scripture concerning the dedication of the Tabernacle. There we learn that the High Priest and members of the Aaronic Priesthood serving at the dedication were required to remain within the precincts of the temple the entire seven days. The penalty

88. Ibid.
89. Leviticus 23:34-43
90. Leviticus 23:39
91. Leviticus 23:42-43

92. 1 Kings 8:2
93. 2 Chronicles 7:9
94. Leviticus 8:33
95. 2 Chronicles 7:8

for abandoning their calling during this period of consecration was death.[96]

The first ritual was the washings.[97] Then the High Priest was dressed in his sacerdotal robes. These consisted of six vestments. He first put on the embroidered coat which was like a frock that covered the upper part of the body.[98] Then came the blue robe which was a solid piece of blue linen with a hole in the middle which slipped over the head. At the hem of this robe were embroidered blue, purple and scarlet pomegranates and in between each one was a golden bell which tinkled softly as the High Priest performed the various rites.[99] Over the robe was worn the ephod which was a multi-colored half-robe with onyx stones on the shoulders from which hung woven gold chains to fasten to the breastplate.[100] A multi-colored girdle which matched the ephod was worn around the waist.[101] The breastplate was a colorful *linen* container about nine inches square.[102] On it were twelve jewels which represented each of the twelve tribes.

Inside the pocket of the breastplate were the famous transparent stones, the Urim and Thummim, which were used for revelation,[103] for the ascertaining of God's judgment in difficult cases,[104] and for the interpreting of ancient records.[105] Last of all, the mitre or head covering was placed on the High Priest which bore a shield declaring, "Holiness to the Lord."[106]

In Solomon's day, the High Priest was Zadok, a direct descendant of Aaron through Eleazar.[107] He was a man who had attained a heroic military reputation in his youth and had joined David in Hebron as one of his military leaders[108] even though his membership in the tribe of Levi

---

96. Leviticus 8:33-36
97. Leviticus 8:6
98. Exodus 28:4, 39
99. Exodus 28:33-35; 39:22-26
100. Exodus 28:6-14
101. Exodus 28:4, 8; 39:5
102. Exodus 28:15-30; 39:8-21
103. Numbers 27:21
104. Exodus 28:30
105. Doctrine & Covenants 10:1; Ether 3:23-24
106. Exodus 28:4; 39:27-31
107. 1 Chronicles 24:3
108. 1 Chronicles 12:28

could have exempted him from military service.[109] He had been made a High Priest in Saul's day,[110] and shared the ministry of High Priest with Abiathar in David's day.[111] After Abiathar's fall, Zadok became the presiding High Priest for the whole kingdom.[112]

After the investiture of the High Priest, the other "sons" or descendants of Aaron were attired[113] in their "holy garments" designed "for glory and for beauty."[114] The Priests wore much simpler clothing than the High Priest. Their vestments consisted of linen breeches and a "coat" or cassock of linen that came nearly to the feet. The cassock was held close to the body with a girdle.[115] Their linen bonnets were in the shape of a round, cup-shaped flower.[116]

This clothing was to keep these men comfortably attired while they performed their arduous labors and these vestments were not to be worn outside the precincts of the Tabernacle or temple: "And it shall come to pass, that when they enter in at the gates of the inner court, they shall be clothed with linen garments; and no wool [apparently because of the heat] shall come upon them, while they minister in the gates of the inner court and within. They shall have linen bonnets upon their heads, and shall have linen breeches upon their loins; they shall not gird themselves with anything that causeth sweat. And when they go forth into the utter [outer] court, even into the utter court of the people, they shall put off their garments wherein they ministered, and lay them in the holy chambers, and they shall put on other garments. . . ."[117]

The High Priest and his fellow members of the Aaronic Priesthood were now ready to function.

THE SEVEN DAYS OF SACRIFICE

Throughout the seven days of sanctification preparatory to the actual dedication, it was necessary for the Aaronic

---

109. When the Lord ordered a census of all Israelites available for war he specifically excluded the Levites because of their special calling. See Numbers 1:49.
110. 1 Chronicles 16:39
111. See, for example, 2 Samuel 15:35-36; 19:11
112. 1 Kings 2:27, 35   115. Ibid.
113. Leviticus 8:13   116. Ibid. plus Peloubet's *Bible Dictionary* under "Priest."
114. Exodus 28:40   117. Ezekiel 44:17-19

Priesthood to perform a daily routine of every major type of sacrifice belonging to the carnal commandments. Each sacrifice was executed in the most exacting manner and required the greatest physical exertion by the members of the Aaronic Priesthood.

The first ritual was called the Sin Offering.[118] This consisted of slaying a young bullock, skinning it, burning certain parts on the brazen altar and disposing of the rest of it according to the type of offense and the rank of the person committing it.[119]

The second ritual was making a Burnt-Offering which consisted of slaying the animal and disposing of its carcass by burning it in a prescribed manner.[120]

Then came the peace offering.[121] This involved the slaying of an animal chosen from among the cattle, sheep or goats. It was then divided between the altar of God, the priests and the donor. The kidneys and internal fat were burned on the altar, the breast and right thigh went to the Priests after having been waved toward the temple signifying that it had been given to God and was now conferred upon his servants; the rest of the meat was returned to the donor to be eaten by himself and family as part of a holy feast.[122]

In addition to these rituals there were Wave Offerings, the Meat (meal) Offerings and the Drink Offerings.[123]

All of this will emphasize to the modern student the tedious burden of the law of carnal commandments. Originally, God had required only the simple burnt-offering revealed to Adam to memorialize the coming sacrifice of Jesus Christ,[124] but now this wearisome weight of additional sacrifices had been added to emphasize the rhythm of obedience among these wayward descendants of the patriarchs.

All of these multitudinous rituals were carefully followed during the seven days prior to the dedication of Solomon's

---

118. For a full discussion see *The Third Thousand Years*, p. 339
119. Leviticus 1:3-17
120. See *The Third Thousand Years*, p. 339.
121. Leviticus 7:15-16, 28-34   123. Ibid. pp. 340-341
122. See *The Third Thousand Years*, p. 340.   124. Moses 5:5-7

temple. It was designed to sanctify and prepare the members of the Aaronic Priesthood who would now serve in this magnificent new sanctuary.

THE ANCIENT TABERNACLE IS REMOVED TO THE TEMPLE

Sometime during this period of preparation, Solomon planned to bring the Ark of the Covenant and the ancient Tabernacle of Moses to the great new temple.

When the temple block was first being constructed, the Ark of the Covenant had been necessarily removed from Mount Moriah together with the tent which protected it, and taken to the nearby "City of David." This was the suburb of Jerusalem which David had first occupied on the southern spur of Mount Moriah. There the Ark had remained in its tent or "curtains"[125] while the temple was being built.

The ancient Tabernacle of Moses, however, had remained at Gibeon[126] where Saul had ordered it moved when he established a religious center there under Zadok.[127]

The scripture gives us a great many details concerning the removal of the Ark of the Covenant to the temple but as for the Tabernacle of Moses, the record merely confirms that the Tabernacle was also taken there. No details are furnished. We are therefore left to conjecture concerning that rather dramatic moment when the Priests of Aaron carried their assigned portions of this ancient structure and its fixture from Gibeon to Mount Moriah, a distance of some six miles. Since the Tabernacle was now to be replaced by the beautiful new temple the Priests probably took the ancient fabrics, skins, boards and poles which had constituted Israel's center of worship for over 500 years, and stored them away within the cloistered sanctity of the new structure. The logical place for the storage of all these sacred relics would have been the chambers of the temple annex. However, this detail is not specified. The Bible simply says, "And they brought up the . . . tabernacle of the congregation, and all the holy vessels that were in the tabernacle, these did the priests and the Levites bring up."[128]

---

125. 2 Samuel 7:2
126. 1 Chronicles 21:29
127. 1 Chronicles 16:39
128. 2 Chronicles 5:5; 1 Kings 8:4

For those who wonder if this "tabernacle" might not have been the temporary tent or curtains covering the Ark at the City of David rather than the Tabernacle of Moses, the following may be helpful. Note that the structure which was brought to the temple for storage was the "TABER-NACLE OF THE CONGREGATION." This is the phrase which the scripture consistently uses in referring to the Tabernacle of Moses.[129] Note further the following scripture referring to the time when Solomon went up to Gibeon to worship shortly after his coronation: "So Solomon, and all the congregation with him, went to the high place that was at Gibeon; for there was the TABERNACLE OF THE CONGREGATION OF GOD, which Moses the servant of the Lord had made in the wilderness."[130] There should be no doubt as to the meaning of the scripture when it says the "tabernacle of the congregation" was brought to Solomon's temple by the Priests and the Levites.

And, having been stored safely away, this sacred portable Tabernacle which had witnessed the very presence of God on so many thrilling occasions, now completely disappears from history.

The Solemn Assembly on the Day of Dedication

The appropriate day for the dedication of the temple was on the "eighth day" after the one full week of preparation and sanctification which we have already described. The ancient Tabernacle had been dedicated on the eighth day at a "solemn assembly"[131] and precisely the same pattern was followed by Solomon. The scripture says, "And in the eighth day they made a solemn assembly: for they kept the dedication of the altar seven days and the feast [of the tabernacle] seven days."[132] This means that in the case of Solomon's temple, the solemn assembly took place on the eighth day if we count the previous week of preparation but on the first day of that week which commemorated the feast of the tabernacles.

As the solemn assembly convened, the High Priest and his associates in the Aaronic Priesthood duplicated the ritual

---

129. Exodus 39:32; 40:2, 22, 24, 26, 34, 35
130. 2 Chronicles 1:3
131. Leviticus 9:1, 5-6
132. 2 Chronicles 7:9

which the Lord had prescribed for Moses and Aaron on the "eighth day" when the Tabernacle was dedicated.

They commenced by sacrificing a young bullock for the High Priest and the Priesthood of Aaron as a Sin Offering.[133] Then followed the sacrificing of a ram for the High Priest and the Aaronic Priesthood as a Burnt-Offering.[134] The congregation was then called upon to make offerings in its own behalf. The people were required, as a body, to bring to the High Priest a young goat for a Sin Offering, then a calf and a lamb for Burnt-Offerings. This was followed by a bullock and a ram for Peace Offerings. Last of all came the Meat (meal) Offering.[135]

By the time all these offerings had been completed, the High Priest and his associates were no doubt exhausted. Furthermore, by this time the brazen altar was piled high with the animals and parts of animals which had been slain as offerings and laid upon it. In the case of Burnt-Offerings the whole carcass was placed on the altar, whereas the other offerings involved only the fat and certain parts of the animals. The fire on the 30-foot altar was not particularly extensive so the large quantity of sacrifices on an occasion like this would have been consumed very slowly.

This was the situation when the second great event occurred on this sacred eighth day.

The Ancient Ark of the Covenant Is Brought to the Temple

There was nothing among all the possessions of Israel which more directly connected them with God's glorious and miraculous manifestation of the past than the Ark of the Covenant. Originally the Ark had contained not only the stone tablets engraved by the finger of God,[136] but also a vessel filled with the miraculous manna which Israel received for 40 years,[137] and Aaron's staff which produced leaves, blossoms and almonds in a single night.[138]

Now, however, the only sacred items left in the Ark were the two stone tablets. The scripture says, "There was

---

133. Leviticus 9:2
134. Ibid.
135. Leviticus 9:3-4

136. Exodus 31:18; 34:28; Deuteronomy 10:5; Hebrews 9:4
137. Exodus 16:33-34; Hebrews 9:4
138. Numbers 17:8-10; Hebrews 9:4

nothing in the ark save the two tables which Moses put therein at Horeb when the Lord made a covenant with the children of Israel, when they came out of Egypt."[139]

What happened to the manna and Aaron's rod? The vicissitudes of this holy Ark had been multitude. It had been captured by the Philistines in the days of Eli[140] and even after its return to Israel it was not placed in the Tabernacle but left in the custody of several Levitical families.[141] When one considers its five centuries of turbulent history it is almost miraculous that the two tablets were still in it. And these, of course, made the Ark more sacred than anything else it ever contained.

Solomon was also well aware that God's commandments concerning the handling of this Ark needed to be respected and strictly complied with. In David's days a reckless and casual treatment of the Ark had cost one man his life.[142] Careful preparations therefore had gone into the transporting of the Ark to the temple. It was to be a highlight of the great convocation or general assembly on the eighth day.

Solomon had not only convened the great choirs and instrumentalists for this occasion, but all the "elders of Israel, and all the heads of the tribes, the chief of the fathers of the children of Israel, unto Jerusalem, to bring up the ark of the covenant of the Lord out of the city of David, which is Zion."[143]

As the great throng wound its way up the road leading to the temple grounds from Ophel or the City of David, it must have given the whole people sensations of rapture to realize that they were finally bringing the ancient, sacred Ark of God to its permanent home and ultimate resting place.[144]

---

139. 2 Chronicles 5:10
140. 1 Samuel 4:11-17
141. 1 Samuel 7:1; 2 Samuel 6:3, 11; 1 Chronicles 13:13; 15:24, 25
142. 2 Samuel 6:6-7
143. 2 Chronicles 5:2
144. The Ark appears to have remained in the temple of Solomon until the fall of Jerusalem in 586 B.C., when it was taken as a trophy or destroyed by Nebuchadnezzar. (2 Esdras 10:22) This is why there was no Ark in the second temple built after the captivity.

The processional entered the great gate (probably the east gate, though none is specified), and the Priests carried the Ark through the vast congregation, then through the court of the Priests, past the huge altar stacked with its heaps of sacrifices which its fires could only slowly consume, past the huge brazen sea established on the backs of twelve oxen, up the temple steps and onto the gold pavement of the great porch, through the beautifully carved, gold-plated doors, into the sixty-foot expanse of the Holy Place, through the open doorway of the gold-plated partition and then finally into the quiet, solemn sanctuary of the Holy of Holies.

There, beneath the symbolically protective wings of the two cherubims and surrounded by all the artistic beauty that the human heart and hand could contrive, this wonderfully historic, sacred Ark of God was brought to rest upon the outcropping of bare stone which had been the threshing floor of Araunah, the Jebusite.

For all who were permitted to witness this final, historic sequence, it must have been a thrilling and profoundly impressive moment. Once the Ark was in place, the Priests drew out the staves by which they had carried the Ark on their shoulders.[145] Then they reverently filed out through the Holy Place and into the Priests' courtyard. There the great choirs and instrumentalists were assembled "at the east end of the altar"[146] ready for their mighty acclamation. These consisted of the Levite singers "arrayed in white linen, having cymbals and psalteries and harps . . . and with them a hundred and twenty priests sounding with trumpets."[147] The signal for their musical accolade was the reappearance of the Priests from the door of the temple. This signified that the Ark was now in place. The burst of sound which arose from the massed choirs and multitude of musicians must have pierced the heavens and echoed throughout all the suburbs of Jerusalem. The Bible says, "the trumpeters and singers were as one, to make one sound to be heard in praising and thanking the Lord."[148]

Suddenly, a frightening thing happened.

---

145. 1 Kings 8:8
146. 2 Chronicles 5:12
147. Ibid.
148. Ibid., verse 13

There settled around the joyous multitude a vast vapor of darkness which increased in density until none could see what he was doing.[149] After five hundred years the cloud of God's presence which had guided Israel through the wilderness "with a pillar of cloud by day and a pillar of fire by night," had suddenly returned to comfort Israel.

THE DEDICATION OF THE TEMPLE

It was Solomon who seemed to realize before anyone else what a glorious thing was happening. He therefore cried out, "The Lord said that he would dwell in the thick darkness."[150] Then, addressing himself to the mighty unseen Personality before him, Solomon quietly said, "I have surely built thee an house to dwell in, a settled place for thee to abide in for ever."[151]

After these few words the king immediately "turned his face about" toward the great throng before him "and blessed all the congregation of Israel."[152]

The scripture says this took place while Solomon was standing "before the altar" but according to 2 Chronicles 6:13, the place where he stood was an 8-foot platform especially built for public assemblies. The scripture says, "For Solomon had made a brasen scaffold, of five cubits long, and five cubits broad, and three cubits high, and had set it in the midst of the court: and upon it he stood, and kneeled down upon his knees before all the congregation of Israel, and spread forth his hands toward heaven." Then began his dedicatory prayer. Said he, "Lord God of Israel, there is no God like thee, in heaven above, or on earth beneath. . . ."[153] He then poured out his heart in humble supplication.

"Behold," said he, "the heaven and heaven of heavens cannot contain thee; how much less this house that I have builded? Yet have thou respect unto the prayer of thy servant, and to his supplication, O Lord my God, to hearken unto the cry and to the prayer which thy servant prayeth before thee to day."[154]

---

149. 1 Kings 8:11
150. 1 Kings 8:12
151. 1 Kings 8:13

152. 1 Kings 8:14
153. 1 Kings 8:23
154. 1 Kings 8:27-28

Solomon first asked the Lord to hallow this temple as a center for worship and prayer.[155] He asked that the people's supplications emanating from this holy sanctuary or uttered from afar by those with their faces "toward this place,"[156] would be warmly received. He specifically asked that prayers be answered in forgiving sins of individuals as well as offenses of the whole people.[157] He asked that the Lord respond to their prayers in overcoming drouth[158] and ameliorating the ravages of famine or pestilence.[159] He prayed for the welfare of new converts,[160] for a righteous victory in time of war,[161] and for a special blessing upon any who fell into the hands of the enemy as captives.[162] He concluded by reminding the Lord that in spite of all their weaknesses as a people, the Lord "didst separate them [the Children of Israel] from among all the people of the earth, to be thine inheritance, as thou spakest by the hand of Moses thy servant, when thou broughtest our fathers out of Egypt, O Lord God."[163]

As Solomon closed his prayer and lowered his hands, a bolt of enveloping flame flashed out of the sky toward the great altar where the brazen grate was over-heaped with the sacrificial offerings of the people.[164] In an instant, as it were, the sacrifices were consumed just as they had been devoured by fire on the eighth day of the Tabernacle's dedication. In addition, the cloud of thick darkness suddenly became illuminated as the "glory of the Lord filled the house."[165] This was exactly the way the people in the days of Moses had been informed of God's personal presence at the Tabernacle.[166] So it was at the dedication of Solomon's temple.

"And the priests could not enter into the house of the Lord, because the glory of the Lord had filled the Lord's house. And when all the children of Israel saw how the fire came down, and the glory of the Lord [came] upon the house, they bowed themselves with their faces to the ground upon the pavement, and worshipped and praised

---

155. 1 Kings 8:29
156. 1 Kings 8:30
157. Ibid.
158. 1 Kings 8:35
159. 1 Kings 8:37
160. 1 Kings 8:41-43

161. 1 Kings 8:44-45
162. 1 Kings 8:46-48
163. 1 Kings 8:53
164. 2 Chronicles 7:1
165. Ibid.
166. Exodus 16:10

the Lord, saying, For he is good; for his mercy endureth for ever!"[167]

The great choirs broke forth again, as did the trumpets and other musical instruments, to unite in one great resounding acclamation of orchestral and choral praise.[168] In a very real sense this was Israel's mighty Hallelujah Chorus which she had waited so many centuries to sing.

SOLOMON'S GREAT FEAST

The majestic manifestations of divine approval had scarcely receded and the resounding response of the people had barely subsided when the jubilant crowds thronged forward to make additional sacrifices and oblations to the Lord.

So overwhelmed were the members of the Aaronic Priesthood in receiving these offerings that the whole middle section of the Priest's court had to be sanctified for the receiving of the avalanche of offerings. The scripture says, "The same day did the king hallow the middle of the court that was before the house of the Lord: for there he offered burnt offerings and meat offerings and the fat of the peace offerings: because the brazen altar [30 feet square] that was before the Lord was too little to receive the burnt offerings, and meat offerings, and the fat of the peace offerings."[169] And all this in spite of the fact that the great altar had just been cleared of its contents by the consuming fire of the Lord!

Furthermore, it would appear that not only on this eighth day but all during the week, Solomon had been contributing whole herds of oxen and flocks of sheep to celebrate the occasion. However, Solomon offered these thousands of animals to the Priests not as Burnt-Offerings but as Peace-Offerings. As Burnt-Offerings they would have been consumed, but as Peace-Offerings they could be distributed among the people for food.

Altogether Solomon contributed 22,000 oxen and 120,-000 sheep as Peace-Offerings.[170] It will be recalled that these sacrifices were to establish peace through sharing. The

---

167. 2 Chronicles 7:2-3
168. 2 Chronicles 7:6

169. 1 Kings 8:64
170. 1 Kings 8:63

sacrificial animal was divided between the altar (which received the kidneys and internal fat), the Priests (who received the breast and right thigh) and the donor who received the remainder of the meat for the feeding of those participating in the sacred feast.

It is almost impossible to visualize the physical labor involved in the ritualistic butchering of this number of animals. Nevertheless, the Bible is clear that a mighty host had descended on Jerusalem and if Solomon were to feed them it would require nothing less than the most extravagant kind of generosity. So the great feast was held, with King Solomon functioning as the unstinting host. It would appear that this gratuitous repast lasted during the entire seven days of the Feast of the Tabernacles. Since this particular festival was their thanksgiving holiday, no more appropriate occasion could have been selected for the dedication of the temple. Never before had this generation of Israel been blessed with so much for which to be thankful.

And on the "eighth day," meaning the day after the Feast of the Tabernacles had concluded (this being a full week after the previously mentioned "eighth day" when the temple was dedicated) Solomon "sent the people away: and they blessed the king, and went unto their tents joyful and glad of heart, for all the goodness that the Lord had done for David his servant [and for Solomon his son], and for Israel his people."[171]

From all that had happened the hosts of Israel knew that by fulfilling a divine commandment to build this beautiful temple they had achieved a wonderful new status with the Lord. Their problem now was to maintain it.

---

171. 1 Kings 8:66

Scripture Reading and Questions on Chapter Nine

Scripture Reading: I Kings, chapters 1 to 8 inclusive.

1—Why did Solomon seek the assistance of a pagan ruler in building the temple? What did King Hiram agree to do?

2—Give some indication of the amount of manpower required for the building of the temple.

3—Give three specific facts indicating the monumental nature of the task Solomon had in building temple square on Mount Moriah.

4—How did Solomon's temple compare with the ancient Tabernacle built in the wilderness? What was the large section called? What was the designation for the smaller section?

5—Which way did the temple face? How many floors did the temple annex section have? Where was their main entrance? How did one go from one floor to the other?

6—Was the altar of sacrifice inside the temple or out? Where was the brazen sea? Do we have any idea what it was used for?

7—Did Solomon's temple have upper rooms? Where was the temple veil?

8—What does it mean when the Lord says certain ordinances have been "kept hidden" since the foundation of the world?

9—Where was the ancient Tabernacle of Moses at this time? What happened to it after the temple was completed?

10—What was the Ark of the Covenant for? Where was it placed? What did it contain?

11—Describe the use of music in connection with the dedication of the temple.

12—What frightening event took place shortly after the Ark of the Covenant was taken into the temple?

13—What did Solomon do? Was this to comfort the people? Would a similar experience tend to frighten a modern audience?

14—Name three of the things Solomon asked for in his dedicatory prayer.

15—What exciting event took place immediately after Solomon had completed his prayer? Had this ever happened before?

16—What happened to the "thick cloud of darkness"? What did it represent to the people? Had this occurred at any time in the past?

17—Why couldn't the priests go into the temple for a short time?

18—What was the response of the people in sacrifices and oblations following the dedication? What did the priests have to do?

19—What is the principal difference between a burnt-offering and a peace offering?

20—How extensive was the great feast after the dedication? Who furnished the food? What does this indicate to you?

CHAPTER TEN

King Solomon's Golden Age

By the time the great temple was finished and dedicated, Solomon was in the twelfth year of his reign.[1] In terms of age, the king was now in his mid-thirties, but in terms of wisdom and administrative acumen he appears to have been gifted and mature to a degree far beyond the normal quotient for a man of those years. In a very literal sense the Lord had fulfilled His promise made to Solomon twelve years earlier: ". . . lo, I have given thee a wise and an understanding heart; so that there was none like thee before thee, neither after thee shall any arise like unto thee."[2]

During the years the temple was being built, Solomon was involved in a most intensive period of personal discipline and self-education. No matter how skillful Hiram, the artisan, might have been, and no matter how astute the king's 3,300 foremen and engineers might have been, the fact remained that the great majority of the more important administrative responsibilities involved in this mammoth undertaking necessarily fell upon Solomon.

The results of all of this was a tremendous broadening of Solomon's perspective and aspirations. Instead of the temple being the end of his achievements it turned out to be barely

---

1. 1 Kings 6:37 says the temple was finished in the eighth month of the eleventh year and 1 Kings 8:2 puts the dedication some eleven months later so this would make it the twelfth year. (See Clarke, *Bible Commentary,* Vol. 2, p. 412)
2. 1 Kings 3:12

the beginning. After twelve years on the throne of Israel, Solomon could see magnificent possibilities of glorious achievement for his kingdom. The building of the temple had illustrated three mighty forces working in his favor. First, was the manifest willingness of the people to sacrifice, both in labor and taxes, for the upbuilding of Israel. Second, there was practically no limit to the support Solomon could expect from his friend, the prosperous Hiram, King of Tyre, Sidon and all of Phoenicia. Third, there was a manpower potential of pyramid-building proportions emanating from the conquered nations around him which provided almost immeasurable quantities of workmen for any kind of construction project.[3] These heathen nations were under tribute to Israel and their annual indebtedness could be paid off in muscle power.

One other thing was boldly apparent to Solomon. That was the fact that the king of Israel was now a major symbol of power in the civilized world.[4] There was nothing petty or casual about the new image of Israel. She ruled from the river Euphrates to the borders of Egypt and that alone placed Solomon on a plateau of political respectability along side the great world powers of Egypt and Assyria. Although we have not mentioned it earlier, Solomon had already developed a very close working relationship with Egypt.

Solomon Allies Himself With the Pharaoh of Egypt

For over a thousand years the inhabitants of Palestine had been caught in the constant stream of cross-fire between Egypt and the forces to the north and east. Now that Israel had imposed its sovereignty over the western half of the fertile crescent it was extremely important for Solomon to neutralize any hostility on the part of Egypt so that she would not attempt to use Palestine as a base for military operations as she had in the past. Early in his career Solomon elected to achieve this through a political marriage. His haste may have been induced by the fact that the twenty-first dynasty of Egypt was already on the march and about the time Solomon ascended his throne the Pharaoh was advanc-

---

3. 1 Kings 9:20-21
4. 1 Kings 4:31; 10:24

ing up the maritime plain of Palestine where he had "taken Gezer, and burnt it with fire, and slain the Canaanites that dwelt in the city."[5]

Nevertheless, for Solomon to negotiate with the Pharaoh in terms of a political alliance sealed by a marriage between Solomon and the Pharaoh's daughter, was a hazardous business. In the first place, it might have had powerful repercussions among the spiritual leaders of Israel. The Lord had strictly forbidden intermarrying with the heathen Hamitic peoples. To Moses the commandment had been given: "Neither shalt thou make marriages with them; thy daughter thou shalt not give unto his son, nor his daughter shalt thou take unto thy son; FOR THEY WILL TURN AWAY THY SON FROM FOLLOWING ME."[6]

Abraham had also explained that the original Pharaohs of the earliest dynasties were of a lineage which could not receive the Priesthood[7] and intermarriage would therefore be unwise because it would frustrate God's program for both races. Then why did Solomon marry a daughter of Pharaoh?

Since the scripture does not deal with the question directly we can only evaluate it in terms of the historical setting and various secular sources. There, among other things, we learn that the twenty-first dynasty of Egypt may not have been Hamitic. Ever since the days of Abraham the Hamitic aborigines of Egypt appear to have been pushed further and further south by some of the aggressive waves of infiltrating Shemites and Japhethites. During one period of approximately 150 years (1730-1580 B.C.) the dynasties of Egypt's Pharaohs were the Shemite shepherd kings or Hyksos. They conquered the Delta and established a capital at Avaris which the Hebrews called Zoan and the Greeks called Tanes.[8] Later the traditional Egyptians had thrown the Shemites out and returned to power during the famous 18th, 19th and 20th dynasties.[9] But around 1100 B.C. Egypt was split in two and the southern region with its capital at Thebes went under

5. 1 Kings 9:16
6. Deuteronomy 7:3-4
7. Abraham 1:21-27
8. See Peloubet's *Bible Dictionary* under Zoan, p. 760.
9. Sir Alan Hardner, *Egypt of the Pharaohs*, London: Oxford University Press, 1961, chapters eight to eleven.

Hrihor while the Delta kingdom to the north was taken over by Smendes who set up the twenty-first dynasty.[10] The founder of this twenty-first dynasty established his headquarters at Tanis or Zoan, the old Hyksos capital of the Shemites. The descendants of Smendes continued to rule lower Egypt (the Delta region) from this place. This is the dynasty into which Solomon married. Since the dynasty which followed it (the twenty-second) is known tó have been non-Egyptian in origin,[11] it is suggested that the same may have been true of the twenty-first.

This is mentioned simply as a possible explanation for the fact that there appears to have been no initial objection to Solomon's political marriage to the daughter of the Pharaoh. In his later life, when Solomon entered into other marriages with heathen women there is a strong objection from the Lord because of their corrupting influence on Israel. On that occasion the daughter of Pharaoh is included as one of the "strange women" but this appears to be because of her idolatry rather than her race.[12]

In any event, we find the early career of Solomon marked by his marriage to the daughter of Pharaoh. The scripture says, "And Solomon made affinity with Pharaoh king of Egypt, and took Pharaoh's daughter, and brought her into the city of David, until he had made an end of building his own house. . . ."[13] All references to this Egyptian wife indicate that she was treated with the utmost deference and consideration, almost as though she were the symbol or personification of political amity between Egypt and Israel, which indeed she was. We also know that just as soon as possible Solomon built her a separate royal residence.[14] This was done not only for political reasons but out of religious considerations as well. At the time of their marriage, Solomon was living in David's cedar palace and since this structure (and later Solomon's own palace) were part of the sacred temple hill, he felt it might be presumptuous to

10. Encyclopedia Britannica, 11th edition (The older edition is called the "scholar's edition" and is used here because of its extensive coverage of Egyptology.) Vol. 9, p. 86
11. Gardner, *Egypt of the Pharaohs*, pp. 324-325.
12. 1 Kings 11:1-10   14. 2 Chronicles 8:11
13. 1 Kings 3:1

have a woman of alien faith living there. Solomon said, "My wife shall not dwell in the house [cedar palace] of David king of Israel, because the places are holy whereunto the ark of the Lord hath come."[15] This passage would further imply that the Ark and its tabernacle were situated within the protective confines of the palace courtyard while the temple was being built. This was all the more reason for the building of a separate residence for the daughter of Pharaoh.

SOLOMON BUILDS A KING'S PALACE AND A ROYAL COURT

The beautiful palace of cedars which had been such a source of pride to David was not sufficient to satisfy the needs of Solomon. The new demands for the administering of the kingdom plus the continuously expanding dimensions of Solomon's aspirations called for a palace which was virtually a city within itself. Solomon started a palace which took thirteen years to complete![16]

Incidental to the building of the king's private residence, Solomon constructed a royal court called "the house of the forest of Lebanon."[17] This structure was constructed of "costly stones . . . hewed stones, sawed with saws, within and without, even from the foundations unto the coping. . . ."[18] The decorations, pillars, beams, roof and flooring were of costly cedar given by the king of Tyre, hence the name, "the house of the forest of Lebanon."

This structure was 150 feet long, 75 feet wide and the same height as the temple, 45 feet high. It had three stories and "there were windows in three rows, and light was against light in three ranks."[19]

"And he made a porch of pillars; the length thereof was fifty cubits [75 feet] and the breadth thereof thirty cubits [45 feet]. . . . Then he made a porch for the throne where he might judge, even the porch of judgment: and it was covered with cedar from one side of the floor to the other."[20]

Solomon was occupied for a number of years completely fortifying the capital city of Jerusalem by building strong

---

15. Ibid.
16. 1 Kings 7:1
17. 1 Kings 7:2
18. 1 Kings 7:9
19. 1 Kings 7:4
20. 1 Kings 7:6-7

walls around it and refurbishing or repairing the one invincible castle of the Jebusites called the Millo.[21] This appears to have been the citadel or fortress of Zion.[22]

As we have previously seen, Solomon had a rich taste for expensive and lavishly brilliant decorations which demanded the most exquisite beauty in design. Therefore, with the Phoenician artists available, Solomon employed his rapidly increasing wealth to embellish the royal capital with the most magnificent and resplendent ornamentation.

Some idea of what a visiting dignitary would have seen as he came in to meet King Solomon might be gained from the following description of his throne: "Moreover the king made a great throne of ivory, and overlaid it with the best gold. The throne had six steps, and the top of the throne was round behind: and there were stays [armrests] on either side on the place of the seat, and two lions stood beside the stays. And twelve lions stood there on the one side and on the other upon the six steps: there was not the like made in any kingdom."[23]

There was no doubt about Solomon's sense of regal grandeur.

SOLOMON'S NAVY

Ever since David had conquered Edom, Israel had enjoyed access to the richest port of wealthy spice merchants and traders from the East. This was located on the eastern horn of the Red Sea at Ezion-geber. This is in the same general area as Eliatt of today and is easily found on the map at the tip of the Aqabah Gulf.

The Israelites, of course, were not seamen, they were shepherds. But they could learn. Therefore the unbounded generosity of the good King of Tyre once more asserted itself. He helped Solomon build a fleet of great ships at Ezion-geber.[24] These were not the ordinary little beachcoasting vessels, but mighty ships of the day copied after the Phoenician freighters which took to the open Mediterranean and

---

21. 1 Kings 9:15; 2 Samuel 5:9 plus Peloubet's *Bible Dictionary* under "Millo".
22. 2 Samuel 5:7, 1 Chronicles 11:5
23. 1 Kings 10:18-20   24. 1 Kings 9:26-27

sailed all the way to its western portals of Tarshish or Spain. This is what the scripture means when it says, "For the king had at sea a navy of Tharshish [Tarshish ships] with the navy [seaman] of Hiram."[25]

The scripture also gives further light on Solomon's new navy by stating, "And king Solomon made a navy of ships in Ezion-geber, which is beside Eloth, on the shore of the Red Sea, in the land of Edom. And Hiram sent in the navy his servants, shipmen that had knowledge of the sea, with the servants of Solomon."[26]

The Phoenicians, of course, were the world's greatest shipbuilders and sailors, and this new partnership with Solomon gave King Hiram an excellent opportunity to get Phoenician wares and Phoenician ships into the sea routes of the southern oceans. We now have the writings of a Phoenician priest which gives considerable details concerning this partnership bttween King Hiram and Solomon. The priest's name was Sanchuniathon and he described how King Hiram offered "to deliver to the prince of the Judaeans building materials for a new palace, IF HE WOULD CONCEDE HIM A PORT ON THE ETHIOPIAN SEA."[27]

Sanchuniathon states that as a part of this arrangement Hiram furnished the tremendous quantities of Lebanese lumber for the ships. He writes, "Although there were great palm forests in the neighborhood of this place, there was no timber suitable for building purposes, so Joram [Phoenician for Hiram] had to transport the timber there on 8,000 camels. A fleet of ten ships was built from it."[28] No doubt the timber was first floated to the port of Joppa before these camel trains picked it up. At least, this is the way the timber was brought down the coast for the buildings in Jerusalem.[29]

Sanchuniathon also knew the names of the three shipwrights who were sent from Phoenicia to supervise the building of the ten ships in Solomon's fleet. They were "Kedarus, Jaminus, and Kotilus."[30] As we have previously mentioned,

25. 1 Kings 10:22
26. 1 Kings 9:26-27
27. Werner Keller, *The Bible As History,* New York: William Morrow and Co., 1956, p. 198
28. Ibid.
29. 2 Chronicles 2:16

30. Werner, *The Bible As History,* p. 198

these ships were not skiffs or over-sized fishing crafts but large schooner-freighters which had proven themselves on rugged Mediterranean trips to Tarshish or Spain.

Of course, in order to trade with the merchants of foreign lands, Solomon would have to fill the holds of his ships with attractive wares and marketable raw materials. Tyre could furnish beautiful glassware and her famous purple dye and purple cloth while Israel exported the widely acclaimed healing ointment, the balm of Gilead. Then there were copper, bronze and iron wares for which the Mediterranean people were well known. But now we know there was something else. Only recently have we learned the amazing extent to which Solomon and the people of Israel were involved in the mining and refining of iron and copper ore for export and trade as well as for domestic use.

King Solomon's Copper and Iron Smelting Operations

A topographical map will show the deep Arabah valley which extends from the Dead Sea southward to the Aqabah Gulf of the Red Sea. This is actually part of a huge cleft in the earth's surface which begins in Asia Minor and cuts down through this territory, finally ending in Africa.

In the days of ancient Israel this Arabah valley belonged to the Edomites who had descended from Esau, brother of Israel (or Jacob). Hostility toward Israel had been manifest by the Edomites ever since the twelve tribes came up out of Egypt because the Edomites had become heathens and rough rustics of the desert. Nevertheless, David, in his day, had conquered them, placed them under tribute and taken advantage of this new relationship to build a seaport where the Arabah valley goes into the Aqabah Gulf. As we have already seen, it was called Ezion-geber.

In 1937, Dr. Nelson Glueck of the American Schools of Oriental Research, took a large expedition into the lower end of the Arabah valley and within three years the modern world knew a great deal more about King Solomon than it had ever known before.[31] Somewhat inland from the present

---

31. Ibid. pp. 192-201 provides a rather complete summary of this expedition.

port they found the remains of an extensive mining and smelting center dating back to 1,000 B.C.[32] The large complex of workshops was located right in "the middle of the scorching pitilessly hot plain."[33]

"Glueck tried to find an explanation for this strange fact. Why did the workshops have to be located right in the path of the sandstorms which almost incessantly sweep down the wadi [valley] from the north? Why were they not a few hundred yards further on in the shelter of the hills where there were also fresh-water springs? The astonishing answer to these questions was not forthcoming until the last excavation period.

"In the middle of a square, walled enclosure an extensive building came into view [as it was excavated]. The green discoloration on the walls left no doubt as to the purpose of the building. It was a blast furnace. The mud-brick walls had two rows of openings. They were flues; a skillful system of air passages was included in the construction. The whole thing was a proper, up-to-date blast furnace built in accordance with a principle that celebrated its resurrection in modern industry a century ago as the Bessemer system. Flues and chimneys both lay along a north-to-south axis. For the incessant winds and storms from the Wadi el-Arabah had to take over the role of bellows. That was 3,000 years ago. Today compressed air is forced through the forge.

"One question alone still remained unanswered: How was the copper refined in this ancient apparatus? Smelting experts of today cannot solve the mystery.

"Earthenware smelting pots still lie about in the vicinity. Many of them have the remarkable capacity of 14 cubic feet. In the surrounding hill slopes the multiplicity of caves hewn out of the rock indicate the entrances to the galleries [of the mines]. Fragments of copper sulphate testify to the busy hands that worked these mines thousands of years ago. In the course of fact-finding excursions into the surrounding country, the members of the expedition succeeded in identifying numerous copper and iron mines in the wadis of the Arabah desert.

---

32. Ibid. p. 194   33. Ibid.

"Eventually Nelson Glueck discovered in the casemated wall of the mound of rubble a stout gateway with a triple lockfast entrance. He was no longer in any doubt. Tell el-Kheleifeh was once Ezion-geber the long sought vanished seaport of King Solomon. . . ."[34]

Extensive comparisons between these new findings in the Arabah valley and other similar installations in the Near East led the experts to conclude: "Nowhere else in the Fertile Crescent, neither in Babylonia nor in Egypt, was such a great furnace to be found. Ezion-geber had therefore the best smelting facilities in the ancient Orient. It produced the metal for the ritual furnishings of the Temple at Jerusalem — for the 'altar of brass,' the 'sea' as a great copper basin was called, for the 'ten bases of brass,' for the 'pots, shovels, basins' and for the two great pillars 'Jachin and Boaz' in the porch of the Temple."[35]

As the digging in this area finally reached virgin soil and the scientists knew they had rounded out the story of this exciting find, Dr. Glueck said in his official report: "Ezion-geber was the result of careful planning and was built as a model installation with remarkable architectural and technical skill. In fact practically the whole town of Ezion-geber, taking into consideration place and time, was a phenomenal industrial site, without anything to compare with it in the entire history of the ancient Orient. Ezion-geber was the Pittsburgh of old Palestine and at the same time its most important seaport."[36]

So here is the answer to the mystery of how Solomon could send ships on a three-year journey and have them return laden with "gold and silver, ivory and apes, and peacocks."[37] These ships went out laden with wares on their upper decks and their holds bulging with copper, the rich malleable metal which, when mixed with a little tin, constituted the principal industrial ingredient for the great bronze age to which the whole civilized world of those centuries belonged.

34. Ibid. pp. 194-195
35. Ibid. p. 196
36. Ibid. p. 197
37. 1 Kings 10:22

The Israelites Who Went Down
to the Sea in Ships

Solomon's fleet sailed from Ezion-geber, out of the Aqabah Gulf, down the length of the Red Sea and out of the Gulf of Aden into the Arabian Sea. Then they could sail along the luxuriant, exotic coasts of equatorial Africa or across the Arabian Sea to the spice markets of India and the depots of oriental riches in Ceylon or Indo-China. We have reason to believe they explored the markets of all these areas.[38] The scripture says they took three years to make a voyage and as previously mentioned, they returned loaded to the gunnels with spices, almug (sandal) wood, precious stones, gold, silver, ivory, apes and peacocks.[39]

The great port of Ezion-geber became a populous place. When the large "Tarshish" ships came in with their precious spices, rare woods, strange animals and fabulous treasures in gold, silver, spices and jewels there were long lines of fast dromedary pack trains ready to rush the shipments to Jerusalem. The gold, silver and jewels went into the royal treasury while the merchandise was sold into the channels of commerce throughout the Mediterranean world.

And the sailors of Israel must have come home with some tall tales of high adventure. They had been to mysterious, typhoon-infested seas and beheld strange lands and stranger people. They had battled with the elements. The excitement of these Israelites who were the first of their people to go down to the sea in ships may be the inspiration for the 107th Psalm which says:

> They that go down to the sea in ships,
> That do business in great waters;
> These see the works of the Lord,
> And his wonders in the deep.
> For he commandeth, and raiseth the stormy wind,
> Which lifteth up the waves thereof.
> They mount up to the heaven.
> They go down again to the depths:
> Their soul is melted because of trouble.
> They reel to and fro.

---

38. Geikie, *Hours With The Bible*, Vol. 3, p. 426
39. 1 Kings 10:22

And stagger like a drunken man,
And are at their wit's end.
Then they cry unto the Lord in their trouble,
And he bringeth them out of their distresses.
He maketh the storm a calm,
So that the waves thereof are still.
Then are they glad because they be quiet;
So he bringeth them unto their desired haven.

Solomon Becomes One of the World's Richest Rulers

Among the places visited by Solomon's navy was the land of Ophir. The exact whereabouts of "Ophir" is no longer possible to determine, but Solomon's navy made regular stops there to secure the high grade gold for which it was famous. On the first trip the fleet brought back 420 talents of gold[40] and later "the weight of gold that came to Solomon in one year was six hundred three score and six [666] talents of gold."[41] At a value of $26,280 per gold talent, the sum of such a treasure would be $17,502,480.00 per year from this source alone.[42]

In addition to this, Solomon received a flood of treasure in tariffs and tributes from the "merchantmen, and of the traffick of the spice merchants, and of all the kings of Arabia, and of the governors of the country."[43] The Bible says further, "And they brought every man his present, vessels of silver, and vessels of gold, and garments, and armour, and spices, horses, and mules, a rate year by year."[44]

Such a fabulous store of gold and specie wealth began to accumulate around Solomon that he found great difficulty putting it all to practical use. The scripture says, "And all king Solomon's drinking vessels were of gold, and all the vessels of the house of the forest of Lebanon were of pure gold; none were of silver: it was nothing [to be] accounted of in the days of Solomon. . . . And the king made silver to be in Jerusalem as stones. . . ."[45]

---

40. 1 Kings 9:28
41. 1 Kings 10:14
42. A talent of gold was worth 3,000 gold shekels or $26,280. (See Dickeman's *Bible*, weights and measures, p. 1463)
43. 1 Kings 10:15
44. 1 Kings 10:25
45. 1 Kings 10:21, 27

Great quantities of gold were melted down and formed into the shape of arm-shields or targets and also body shields. This was Solomon's method of storing certain amounts of gold in some decorative form, (preferable, perhaps, to the modern device of storing it in the form of stubby bricks!). The scripture says, "And King Solomon made two hundred targets of beaten gold: six hundred shekels of gold went to one target. And he made three hundred shields of beaten gold; three pounds of gold went to one shield: and the king put them in the house of the forest of Lebanon."[46] These shields, we later learn, were used as part of the parade regalia, of the king's elite guard.

SOLOMON FORTIFIES THE LAND

Great quantities of wealth were spent by Solomon as well as stored. There was costly construction work on the temple, the king's new palace, the house of the forest of Lebanon, the Millo fortress and the walls of Jerusalem. But in addition to this Solomon set out to build up six fortress cities.[47] His object was to make these strategic centers his major points of defense in case of attack and also have them serve as patrol stations to guard the immense network of trade routes which Solomon now controlled throughout the western half of the Fertile Crescent.

The first of the six cities was Hazor, ancient capital of King Jabin, head of the northern Canaanite federation who had been defeated by Joshua five centuries earlier.[48] It had been the capital for a later King Jabin who was beaten in the valley of Jezreel by Deborah and Barak.[49] Hazor was now the principal city of all northern Palestine and was beautifully situated on a high place overlooking the waters of Lake Merom, feeder-source for Galilee.[50]

The second city fortified by Solomon was the famous Megiddo. This citadel guards the pass leading from southern Palestine to the north. It looks directly north upon the valleys of Esdraelon and Jezreel which sweep from the Medi-

---

46. 1 Kings 10:16-17
47. 1 Kings 9:15-18
48. Joshua 11:1-11
49. Judges 4:2-17
50. Peloubet's *Bible Dictionary* under "Hazor", p. 243

terranean to the Jordan river. Westward from Megiddo one looks across the pass which it guards toward Mount Carmel, some six miles away. Eastward are the mountains of Gilboa where Saul and Jonathan fought and died. South of Megiddo lay the rich maritime plains of the Philistines and the mountain heartland of Israel.

The third city rebuilt and fortified by Solomon was Gezer. This city had been recently sacked and burned by the Pharaoh of Egypt and its population massacred.[51] The Egyptian king had then presented the site to his princess-daughter who was married to Solomon.[52] This ancient city has been re-discovered by archaeologists.[53] It is located on a most advantageous high hill overlooking the whole Philistine plain. It is just off the road which comes down from Jerusalem to Jaffa (Joppa or modern Tel Aviv) so it occupied the most important spot possible for a military outpost between the Philistines and Israel. It guards Sorek valley leading up toward Jerusalem which was the route of attack the Philistines had used against David on several occasions.

Moving a little further north is the ancient route for the main road coming down from Samaria and Ephraim to the coast. This road is guarded by the twin cities of Beth-horan. One is called the Upper Beth-horan and the other the Lower or "nether" Beth-horan.[54] According to Chronicles, Solomon fortified both of them.[55]

Baalath is the fifth city mentioned in the scripture[56] which Solomon fortified but its precise location is not known.

The sixth city is called "Tadmor in the wilderness"[57] and all authorities appear to agree that Tadmor is the city which later became identified by its more famous Greek name, Palmyra,[58] the city of Palms, located in the Syrian desert 190 miles northeast of Damascus. Recently, however, there has been some discussion as to whether the word "Tadmor" or

51. 1 Kings 9:16
52. Ibid.
53. Geikie, *Hours With the Bible*, Vol. 3, pp. 237-238
54. 1 Kings 9:17
55. 2 Chronicles 8:5
56. 1 Kings 9:18
57. Ibid.
58. Clarke, *Bible Commentary*, Vol. 2, p. 420

Tamar was intended in the original text.[59] Tamar is an obscure city in Judah but because the other cities which Solomon fortified were fairly close together, a few critics have doubted whether Solomon would have gone so far afield as Tadmor (or Palmyra) to establish an outpost.[60] The revised version of the Bible has already inserted the word "Tamar" instead of Tadmor in 1 Kings 9:18. However, this is a dangerous practice where mere supposition is the basis for the change.

It should be kept in mind that Solomon is known to have gone much farther afield than Tadmor or Palmyra. His armies had conquered the great Hittite capital of Hamath way up to the north along the Orontes river.[61] The scripture also says, "And Solomon reigned over all kingdoms from the river [Euphrates] unto the land of the Philistines, and unto the border of Egypt."[62] Palmyra was right in the heart of the desert wilderness which Solomon is here described as having in his domain. In fact, Palmyra lay directly on the trade route which constituted the jugular vein of commerce between the Mediterranean markets of Arabia, Egypt, Philistia and Phoenicia, and those in the Mesopotamian kingdoms of Assyria, Babylon and Persia. Therefore, in terms of logic, Tadmor or Palmyra was the precise spot where a man with the wisdom of Solomon might have felt the need for a fortified outpost.

We point this out merely for the purpose of illustrating that the present Biblical text which says Solomon fortified Tadmor (Palmyra) has much more to support it in terms of both logic and historical circumstances than the poorly supported assumption that Tamar of Judah was intended.

SOLOMON'S CHARIOTS AND CAVALRY

Once Solomon had established peace throughout his domain he obviously intended to preserve it with a big stick. He therefore established fast, flexible, mobile military units throughout all of his kingdom. Because Israel had always looked upon horses and chariots as a symbol of conquest and

---

59. See Encyclopedia Brittanica, 11th (or classical) edition, vol. 20, p. 652
60. Rand McNally, *Bible Atlas*, p. 216.
61. 2 Chronicles 8:3
62. 1 Kings 4:21

oppression, it was a bold step for Solomon to presume to initiate the use of chariots and cavalry in his military outposts,
but this he did on an extensive scale. The scripture says, "And
Solomon had forty thouand stalls [sometimes rendered teams]
of horses for his chariots, and twelve thousand horsemen."[63]
In another place we learn that Solomon's chariots number
1,400 and that he had them distributed along with the cavalry
among the various cities which needed protection.[64]

Not only did Solomon use a great many horses and
chariots but he found the kings to the north and east so
anxious to buy a supply of these military resources that Solomon soon became the broker in the thriving business of selling
horses and chariots. It is interesting that Solomon made
no attempt to manufacture chariots or breed large numbers
of horses in Israel. Instead, he simply purchased the horses
and chariots from Egypt and then re-sold them. The scripture says, "And Solomon had horses brought out of Egypt
. . . And a chariot came up and went out of Egypt for six
hundred shekels of silver, and an horse for an hundred and
fifty: and so for all the kings of the Hittites, and for the
kings of Syria, did they bring them out by their means."[65]

The Egyptian horse was quite different from the fine-
boned and fleet-footed Arabian horse. Dr. Geikie says,
"Egypt was then famous for a breed of horses of unusual
size and strength, originally, it would seem, brought from
Asia to the Nile valley, the counterpart of the great war
horses of the middle ages, and these were in demand among
the various Hittite and Syrian kings."[66]

SOLOMON SEES THE LORD THE SECOND
AND LAST TIME

It was apparently at the height of his career as judge,
builder, industrialist, exporter and wealthy ruler of a great
kingdom, that Solomon was given the privilege of seeing the
Lord for the second and last time. In 2 Chronicles 7:11 a
quick reading would make it seem that this vision came to
Solomon immediately after the dedication of the temple, but

---

63. 1 Kings 4:26   65. 1 Kings 10:28-29
64. 1 Kings 10:26   66. Geikie, *Hours With the Bible*, Vol. 3, p. 423

from 1 Kings, Chapter 9, we are able to fix the timing of this vision more accurately.

It will be recalled that Solomon began building the temple in the fourth year of his reign,[67] and he completed it seven years later.[68] The scripture then says that he was thirteen years building his palace and all the other embellishments needed for the capital city of Jerusalem.[69] Therefore, by the time he was in the twenty-fourth year of his reign Solomon had been building for twenty years.[70] He apparently had reached a point in his career where the major aspirations of his heart had been achieved both for the government and the people. It was therefore an appropriate time for the Lord to give Solomon a vision and a warning.

The scripture says, "And the Lord appeared to Solomon by night, and said unto him, I have heard thy prayer, and have chosen this place for myself for an house of sacrifice. . . . And as for thee, if thou wilt walk before me, as David thy father walked,[71] and do according to all I have commanded thee . . . then will I establish the throne of thy kingdom, according as I have covenanted with David thy father . . . But if ye turn away, and forsake my statutes and my commandments, which I have set before you, and shall go and serve other gods, and worship them; then will I pluck them up [i.e. Israel] by the roots out of my land which I have given them; and this house, which I have sanctified for my name, will I cast out of my sight, and will make it to be a proverb and a byword among all nations. And this house, which is high, shall be an astonishment to every one that passeth by it; so that he shall say, Why hath the Lord done thus unto this land, and unto this house? And it shall be answered, Because they forsook the Lord God and their fathers, which brought them forth out of the land of Egypt, and laid hold on other gods, and worshipped them, and served them: therefore hath he brought all this evil upon them."[71]

---

67. 1 Kings 6:37
68. 1 Kings 6:38
69. 1 Kings 7:1-2
70. 1 Kings 9:1, 10

71. 2 Chronicles 7:17. The phrase, "walk before me, as David thy father walked," has reference to David's integrity as a public administrator, judge and king. The Lord compliments this aspect of David's public life on numerous occasions. If David had just been able to apply these principles in his private life as he met the crisis of Bath-sheba and Uriah he could have gone to his grave as one of God's greatest heroes.

No words could be plainer than these. A straight course demanding righteous obedience lay directly ahead for Solomon and his people. If they followed the path of righteousness they would be unbelievably blessed. If they forsook the path they would curse the day, for the consequences would be bitter.[72]

In view of this vigorous warning coming directly from the Lord in person, one would scarcely anticipate the amazing sequence of events which soon followed.

SOLOMON TRIES TO SHOW HIS APPRECIATION TO THE KING OF TYRE

The scripture says just about this same time, when Solomon was completing his extensive building operations, that he attempted to express his profound appreciation for the ardent friendship and extraordinary generosity exhibited by the good King Hiram of Tyre.[73]

It apparently occurred to Solomon that since Phoenicia was a relatively tiny country, the most precious gift he could confer on Hiram would be additional territory. He therefore ordered the inhabitants of "twenty cities in the land of Galilee" to be evacuated so that they could be presented together with their surrounding territory as a gift to Hiram.[74] In all likelihood they were located on the border between Phoenicia and Galilee so that this was quite a concession from Solomon's standpoint.

However, Solomon underestimated the tastes of Hiram. The king of Tyre was a typical urbanite whose city-minded tastes revelled in the concentration of power, wealth and population in a few major centers. He had little more than contempt for villages, towns and rustic hamlets even though they represented the acquisition of more territory. And Hiram already had more of the latter than he cared to develop. This, therefore, explains the passage which says, "And Hiram came out from Tyre to see the cities which Solomon had given him; and they pleased him not. And he said, What

---

72. 2 Chronicles 7:12, 17-22
73. 1 Kings 9:10-11
74. 1 Kings 9:11

cities are these which thou hast given me, my brother? And he called them the land of Cabul [displeasing or dirty] unto this day."[75]

But being a practical man of the world and accustomed to the subtle gestures of both politicians and merchants, he interpreted Solomon's gift as a delicate suggestion that the king of Israel needed a little more help. So, while King Hiram rejected the villages which Solomon offered him he turned right around and sent Solomon 120 talents of gold![76]

SOLOMON'S RESPONSIBILITY AS A STEWARD OF RICHES

When men become wealthy it is interesting to observe what they do with their newly acquired power. A few hoard their riches but most men of means eventually come to look upon their wealth as a stewardship to be employed in the building of industry, the improvement of the land, the beautifying of parks, or the creation of art centers, libraries and museums. In practically all ages, what communities could not afford, or taxpayers would not pay for, the wealthy have personally contributed. This has been notably true in the areas of culture, refinement and the arts.

The first commandment of God at the genesis time of the race was, "Be fruitful, and multiply, and replenish the earth, and subdue it: and have dominion over the fish of the sea, and over the fowl of the air, and over every living thing that moveth upon the earth."[77] And in the Tenth Commandment the Lord proclaimed the "Gospel of Work" wherein each man is commanded to labor and develop his own stewardship and not covet his neighbor's house and fields, or his neighbor's goods, or his neighbor's wife.

Furthermore, the Lord has always demanded that those who were gifted or fortunate enough to advance substantially beyond their neighbors in the accumulation of wealth were to be liberal in assisting others in acquiring the means of enjoying the good things of life as well as themselves.

---

75. 1 Kings 9:12-13
76. 1 Kings 9:14
77. Genesis 1:28

At the same time the Lord has vehemently rebuked the covetous poor who would steal or use violence to get that which belongs to others. A modern revelation reflects these views as the Lord declares:

"Wo unto you rich men, that will not give your substance to the poor, for your riches will canker your souls; and this shall be your lamentation in the day of visitation, and of judgment, and of indignation: The harvest is past, the summer is ended, and my soul is not saved!

"Wo unto you poor men, whose hearts are not broken, whose spirits are not contrite, and whose bellies are not satisfied, and whose hands are not stayed from laying hold upon other men's goods, whose eyes are full of greediness, and who will not labor with your own hands!"[78]

All of these principles were operative when Solomon found himself in possession of fabulous quantities of wealth. What did he do with this vast potential of power?

First, as we have seen, he built the temple, then the palace and the walls of Jerusalem. Next he fortified the land against invaders. He also engaged in developing copper and iron mines and smelters in the Arabah valley, building a seaport at Ezion-geber, constructing a fleet of ten large merchant vessels and promoting international trade with Egypt, the Hittites, the Syrians and the many countries reached by his navy in the Indian ocean.

In all of this Solomon and the entire nation of Israel prospered. The flavor of Solomon's reign is caught in the following passage: "And Judah and Israel dwelt safely, every man under his vine and under his fig tree, from Dan even to Beer-sheba, all the days of Solomon."[79] The scripture also speaks of "the merchantmen, and of the traffick of the spice merchants."[80] And there were the merchants and brokers who dealt in linen yarn, chariots, horses and other products out of Egypt.[81] The commercial trade in Jerusalem became so prosperous that the flow of gold "made silver to be . . . as stones."[82]

---

78. *Doctrine and Covenants* 56:16-17
79. 1 Kings 4:25
80. 1 Kings 10:15
81. 1 Kings 10:28-29
82. 1 Kings 10:27

Solomon also shared with his people the honors of government and administration which attended the rapid expansion of the kingdom. The scripture says, "But of the children of Israel did Solomon make no bondmen: but they were men of war, and his servants, and his princes, and his captains, and rulers of his chariots, and his horsemen."[83]

And all these who served him he appears to have rewarded profusely.

SOLOMON LAVISHES EXTRAVAGANT LUXURY ON HIS ROYAL COURT

Under a monarchy there is no pretense of "being equal," and therefore, as we have seen, the Lord looks upon it as an inferior method of government. Nevertheless, Solomon appears to have poured out the fruits of his kingdom on those who served him loyally. This is strikingly evident in the description of the way he provided for his royal court.

The scripture says, "And Solomon's provision for ONE DAY was thirty measures [660 gallons] of fine flour, and three-score measures [1,320 gallons] of meal, ten fat oxen, and twenty oxen out of the pastures, and an hundred sheep, besides harts, and roebucks, and fallowdeer, and fatted fowl."[84]

Authorities estimate that this was enough food to accommodate the sumptuous tastes of 14,000 people.[85] No doubt this would include not only the king's administrators, servants and stewards, but also their families. All of these appear to have been part of the official entourage or royal court of the king of Jerusalem. The proportions of such a gigantic regal community may appear to be completely out of reason until it is realized that only a century ago the Sultan of Turkey was feeding 10,000 similar courtiers three times a day at his palace in Istanbul.[86]

83. 1 Kings 9:22
84. 1 Kings 4:22-23; Geikie, *Hours With the Bible*, Vol. 3, p. 431
85. Geikie, *Hours With the Bible*, Vol. 3, p. 431
86. I have visited both the old and new palaces of the Sultan at Istanbul on several occasions. One cannot help but be impressed by the long wing of gigantic kitchens with cooking vessels sometimes four feet high and as many feet across. They give the appearance of belonging to the kitchen of some modern canning factory.

One may logically wonder, however, how Solomon provided such prodigious amounts of food every day. Early in
his career, Solomon divided the land of Israel into twelve
districts to facilitate the administration of government.[87] Apparently the division of the country according to the inheritances of the twelve tribes was no longer equitable since
population growth and available resources were at considerable variance with tribal alignments. One of the duties
of the governor in each of the twelve districts was to provide
the king's royal requisition of food for one month.[88] The
scripture says this is the means by which Solomon distributed
the responsibility of providing for the needs of his court and
the supplies of his royal cavalry: "And those officers [in
the twelve districts] provided victual for king Solomon, and
for all that came unto King Solomon's table, every man in
his month: they lacked nothing. Barley also and straw for
the horses and dromedaries brought they unto the place where
the officers were, every man according to his charge."[89]

SOLOMON GAINS FAME AS A PHILOSOPHER-KING

Plato could have envied Solomon. The Greek Philosopher believed the ideal form of government would be to have
a man with the unlimited power of a "king" but the wisdom
and judgment of a "philosopher" to guide him in his actions.[90]
Solomon is probably the closest thing the world has ever
come to providing a philosopher-king as Plato envisioned it.
But, as we shall see later, the arrangement had fallacies in
it which God perceived even if Plato did not.

Nevertheless, Solomon was a king and he was a philosopher. The scripture says, "And Solomon's wisdom ex-
celled the wisdom of all the children of the east country,
and all the wisdom of Egypt . . . and his fame was in all

87. 1 Kings 4:7
88. 1 Kings 4:27
89. 1 Kings 4:27-29
90. Plato lived 428-348 B.C. He said, "Until philosophers are kings, or the kings
    and princes of this world have the spirit and power of philosophy, and
    political greatness and wisdom meet in one, and those commoner natures who
    pursue either to the exclusion of the other are COMPELLED TO STAND
    ASIDE, cities will never have rest from their evils — no, nor the human race,
    as I believe — and then only will this our State have a possibility of life and
    behold the light of day." (*Plato*, Britannica Great Books edition, Vol. 7, p.
    369)

nations round about. And he spake three thousand proverbs: and his songs were a thousand and five."[91]

Much of the Book of Proverbs is attributed to Solomon as well as the Book of Ecclesiastes. However, only two of the Psalms bear his insignia so a thousand and three of these have been lost.

The Book of Proverbs is divided into five parts and is believed to contain the thoughts of Solomon in all but the last part.[92]

Part One consists of chapters 1 to 9 inclusive and represents a teacher giving wisdom and advice to a student. Authorities attribute the role of the teacher to Solomon although the text does not specifically identify him.

Part Two consists of chapters 10 to 22:17 and is described in the opening verse as simply, "the proverbs of Solomon."

Part Three extends from chapter 22:18 to chapter 24. This returns once more to the format of the tutor instructing his pupil.

Part Four covers chapters 25 to 29 and is described as the proverbs of Solomon "which the men of Hezekiah king of Judah copied out."

Part Five is not attributed to Solomon but is an appendix which contains "the words of Agur the son of Jakeh" in chapter 30 and the advice of an unnamed mother to her son, King Lemuel, in chapter 31 which closes the book of Proverbs. There is no way of identifying either of these individuals.

The Book of Proverbs is profoundly satisfying reading. Typical nuggets are found in the following:

> Trust in the Lord with all thine heart;
> And lean not unto thine own understanding.
> In all thy ways ackowledge him,
> And he shall direct thy paths.[93]

91. 1 Kings 4:30-32
92. The "Introduction to the Proverbs of Solomon," Clarke, *Bible Commentary,* Vol. 3, pp. 698-699.
93. Proverbs 3:5-6

Wisdom is the principal thing;
Therefore get wisdom.
And with all thy getting
Get understanding.[94]

These six things doth the Lord hate:
Yea, seven are an abomination unto him.
A proud look,
A lying tongue,
And hands that shed innoncent blood.
An heart that deviseth wicked imaginations,
Feet that be swift in running to mischief,
A false witness that speaketh lies,
And he that soweth discord among brethren.[95]

A soft answer turneth away wrath.[96]

Pride goeth before destruction,
And an haughty spirit before a fall.[97]

Even a fool, when he holdeth his peace,
Is counted wise.[98]

Train up a child in the way he should go;
And when he is old he will not depart from it.[99]

The borrower is servant to the lender.[100]

Where there is no vision, the people perish.[101]

As for the Book of Ecclesiastes, it is specifically identified as being written by "the Preacher" who "was king over Israel in Jerusalem."[102] The "Preacher" describes himself as "the son of David, king of Jerusalem,"[103] so there seems little doubt that Solomon is intended and the word "Preacher" is simply used out of a sense of literary modesty.

Ecclesiastes is the classical scripture deploring human vanity and emphasizing the need to replace it with a constant, humble trust in God. It was written at a time when Solomon had seen enough of life to realize that the helter-skelter "busy-ness" with which people occupy themselves is

---

94. Proverbs 4:7
95. Proverbs 6:16-19
96. Proverbs 15:1
97. Proverbs 16:18
98. Proverbs 17:28

99. Proverbs 22:6
100. Proverbs 22:7
101. Proverbs 29:18
102. Ecclesiastes 1:12
103. Ecclesiastes 1:1

often gratifying but not really important. He recognizes the limitations of the flesh and the necessity of adapting one's life to the realities of events as they unfold. Said he:

> To every thing there is a season,
> And a time to every purpose under the heaven.
> A time to be born, and a time to die;
> A time to plant, and a time to pluck up that which is planted.
> A time to kill, and a time to heal;
> A time to break down, and a time to build up;
> A time to weep, and a time to laugh;
> A time to mourn, and a time to dance;
> A time to cast away stones, and a time to gather stones together;
> A time to embrace, and a time to refrain from embracing;
> A time to get, and a time to lose;
> A time to keep, and a time to cast away;
> A time to rend, and a time to sew;
> A time to keep silence, and a time to speak;
> A time to love, and a time to hate;
> A time of war, and a time of peace.[104]

As in Proverbs, Solomon distills pearls of wisdom which have been repeated millions of times since:

> The sleep of a labouring man is sweet.[105]

> A good name is better than precious ointment.[106]

> Be not righteous [self-righteous] overmuch.[107]

> A living dog is better than a dead lion.[108]

> Whatsoever thy hand findeth to do,
> Do it with thy might.[109]

> The race is not to the swift
> Nor the battle to the strong.[110]

> Then shall the dust return to the earth as it was;
> And the spirit shall return unto God who gave it.[111]

> Let us hear the conclusion of the whole matter:
> Fear God, and keep his commandments;
> For this is the whole duty of man.[112]

---

104. Ecclesiastes 3:1-8
105. Ecclesiastes 5:12
106. Ecclesiastes 7:1
107. Ecclesiastes 7:16
108. Ecclesiastes 9:4

109. Ecclesiastes 9:10
110. Ecclesiastes 9:11
111. Ecclesiastes 12:7
112. Ecclesiastes 12:13

In addition to his proverbs and psalms, Solomon became widely known for his encyclopedic work on plants, animals, birds, fish and insects. The scripture says, "And he spake of trees, from the cedar tree that is in Lebanon even unto the hyssop that springeth out of the wall: he spake also of beasts, and of fowl, and of creeping things, and of fishes. And there came of all people to hear the wisdom of Solomon, from all kings of the earth, which had heard of his wisdom."[113]

Apparently to some extent Solomon anticipated Aristotle's (384-322 B.C.) encyclopedic work on the History of Animals and natural phenomenon by some 600 years. Unfortunately Solomon's works are no longer available for study. We simply have the assertion that he had a knowledge concerning all these things.

Solomon Is Visited by the Queen of Sheba

Fourteen hundred miles south of Jerusalem at the tip of the Arabian Peninsula was located one of the richest countries in Bible ages. It was called Sabaea or Sheba, and was particularly famous for its incense, balm and myrrh. This country was ruled at this particular time by a queen and she just could not believe all the extravagant stories she kept hearing about King Solomon. Her keen sense of female curiosity finally got the best of her and she set out with all the regal regalia her wealthy country could provide in order to show up this pompous potentate of Israel about which so many boasted. From her later acknowledgments, it is entirely clear that this queen made the 1400 mile journey from Sheba to Jerusalem with the full intent of embarrassing King Solomon by any means possible. What a sop to her own royal ego if she could return to Sheba knowing she had demonstrated both in wealth and intellectual powers that she was superior to this much vaunted Solomon!

Just in case things might prove otherwise, she took along some charming and extravagant gifts. Such is the wonderful, subtle and intriguing gift of intuition in womenkind — while expecting to win, she provided the means by which her departure from Israel would be almost as triumphant even if she lost! And this is exactly the way it turned out.

---

113. 1 Kings 4:33, 34

The scripture says, "And when the queen of Sheba heard of the fame of Solomon concerning the name of the Lord, she came to prove him with hard questions. And she came to Jerusalem with a very great train, with camels that bare spices, and very much gold, and precious stones: and when she was come to Solomon, she communed with him of all that was in her heart. And Solomon told her all her questions: there was not any thing hid from the king which he told her not. And when the queen of Sheba had seen all Solomon's wisdom, and the house that he had built, and the meat of his table, and the sitting of his servants, and the attendance of his ministers, and their apparel, and his cupbearers, and his ascent by which he went up unto the house of the Lord; THERE WAS NO MORE SPIRIT IN HER.

"And she said to the king, It was a true report that I heard in mine own land of thy acts and of thy wisdom. Howbeit I BELIEVED NOT THE WORDS, UNTIL I CAME, AND MINE EYES HAD SEEN IT: and, behold, the half was not told me: thy wisdom and prosperity exceedeth the fame which I heard!"[114]

Here the true nobility of the queen showed forth. Not only did she acknowledge defeat but she turned it around and made it such a humble testimonial that it gave stature to her own greatness. In an eloquent tribute to Solomon she turned to the magnificent entourage of the entire royal court and cried, "Happy are thy men, happy are these thy servants, which stand continually before thee, and that hear thy wisdom. Blessed be the Lord thy God, which delighted in thee, to set thee on the throne of Israel: because the Lord loved Israel for ever, therefore made he thee king, to do judgment and justice!"[115] From this last statement it is obvious that Solomon had not only answered her riddles but told her· a good deal about the history of Israel and the message of the Gospel.

To crown her tribute with a fitting climax the queen majestically presented as a gift to Solomon all of the luxurious exhibits she had brought from her own country to demonstrate its wealth and bounties. The scripture says,

---

114. 1 Kings 10:1-7   115. 1 Kings 10:8-9

"And she gave the king an hundred and twenty talents of gold [at a value estimated as being just over three million dollars[116]] and of spices very great store, and precious stones: there came no more such abundance of spices as these which the queen of Sheba gave to king Solomon."[117]

King Solomon was equally gracious in responding to the queen. He presented her with treasures from "his royal bounty"[118] and gave every personal attention and courtesy throughout her stay.

When the queen was completely satisfied that her trip had been successful and gratifying in every way "She turned and went to her own country, she and her servants."[119]

In the centuries that have passed since this distinguished meeting between Solomon and the queen of Sheba, much has been made of the romantic possibilities between these two as visualized both by fiction writers and traditional folklore. The kings of Ethiopia, for example, claim that the queen was not of Arab blood but an Ethiopian and that she had a son by Solomon named Menclik who started the royal line from which the present Ethiopian king is a descendant.[120] This, of course, contains not even a fragment of contemporary historical substance but is simply a tantalizing speculation by imaginative minds. The same is true of other bizarre stories which grew out of the famous meeting.

Solomon, as we shall see, soon had enough problems without being involved in a love affair with the queen of Sheba!

---

116. See note 42 of this chapter
117. 1 Kings 10:10
118. 1 Kings 10:13
119. Ibid.
120. Robert Coughlan, *Tropical Africa*, New York, Life World Library, 1966, p. 65. This tradition is based on the Abijssenian Chronicles written many centuries after the events described. (Encyclopedia Britannica, scholars edition [11th] p. 847)

Scripture Readings and Questions on Chapter Ten

Scripture Readings: 1 Kings, chapters 9 and 10. Extra credit assignment, the Book of Proverbs and the Book of Ecclesiastes.

1—Why would Solomon feel it was important to become allied with Egypt? What did he do to assure peace between the two nations?

2—Why did Solomon build a separate house for the daughter of Pharaoh?

3—How long did it take Solomon to build his palace and royal court? What other building did he do at the same time?

4—Describe in your own words what Solomon's famous throne looked like? What does this reflect concerning him?

5—How many ships are said to have been in Solomon's navy? Who built them for him? After what were they copied?

6—Why did King Hiram consider it an advantage to help build a fleet for Solomon? What was exported from Phoenicia? What from Israel?

7—What tribes occupied Arabah valley? Were they related to the Israelites? In what way? Why were they hostile toward Israel?

8—What was Ezion-geber? Where was it located? Why was it amazing?

9—Has Ezion-geber been located in modern times? Describe the blast furnace uncovered by scientists. Why was it amazing?

10—What two metals were mined in the Arabah valley in Solomon's day? Why was one of these particularly important during this age?

11—Approximately what was the value of a gold talent in Solomon's day? Would Solomon have been considered rich by modern standards?

12—What kind of wealth did the navy bring back to Israel? How long was each voyage? What areas did the ships appear to have visited?

13—Where did Solomon get the horses and chariots to guard his new fortified cities? How did this develop into a new business?

14—In what year of his reign did Solomon see the Lord for the second and last time? What warning was Solomon given?

15—How did Solomon try to show his appreciation for the help and friendship of King Hiram of Tyre? What happened?

16—Do people with riches have unusual responsibilities? What is the responsibility of the poor? Would you consider Solomon an exemplary custodian of riches from the Lord's point of view? Why?

17—What is a "Philosopher-King"? Why do you think Plato thought this was the best form of government? Would the Lord have agreed?

18—Is all of the Book of Proverbs attributed to Solomon? Can you recite two of Solomon's proverbs?

19—What was the basic theme of the Book of Ecclesiastes?

20—What was the purpose of the visit of the queen of Sheba to Israel? Was she wrong? What happened?

CHAPTER ELEVEN

The Fall of Solomon

Altogether Solomon reigned over Israel for a period of forty years.[1] We know that most of his reign was spent in peace and prosperity[2] and that up until the last few years he enjoyed the smiles of Heaven. As we have seen, it was in the twenty-fourth year of his reign and just sixteen years before the end of his life that the Lord favored Solomon with a wonderful night vision in which he was told that his tremendous efforts on behalf of the kingdom were completely acceptable to the Lord[3] and that if he continued his reign in righteousness his throne would be established "upon Israel for ever."[4] He was also warned, of course, that if he altered his course and did evil in the sight of the Lord both he and Israel would be rejected.[5] The important thing to observe, however, is that up until this time Solomon was in full fellowship with the Lord and appears to have done nothing to displease the powers on high.

From all we can tell, Solomon was approximately 49 years of age when he had this vision. It will be recalled that he was a very young man when he became king[6] but old enough to marry.[7] Authorities have therefore estimated his age at somewhere between 20 and 25 when he was crowned.

---

1. 1 Kings 11:42
2. 1 Kings 4:24-25
3. 1 Kings 9:3
4. 1 Kings 9:4-5
5. 1 Kings 9:6-9
6. 1 Kings 3:7; 1 Chronicles 29:1
7. 1 Kings 3:1

Taking the more conservative age of 25 he would be 49 when he received the vision which occurred in the twenty-fourth year of his reign. Furthermore, this would leave only 16 years more or age 65 for the time of his death since the scripture says the total duration of his administration was forty years.[8] It is important to keep these factors in mind as we now consider the final phase of Solomon's career.

We know that sometime between this estimated age of 49 and the time of his death at around 65, Solomon became involved in a series of tragic events. However, the scriptural details are extremely fragmentary and the compiler of Chronicles completely skips over this period almost as though he were embarrassed to mention it. Writing evasively he says, "Now the REST OF THE ACTS OF SOLOMON, FIRST AND LAST, are they not written in the book of Nathan the prophet, and in the prophecy of Ahijah, the Shilonite, and in the visions of Iddo the seer against Jeroboam the son of Nebat?"[9]

Unfortunately, we do not have any of these three inspired writings and so "the rest of the acts of Solomon, first and last," are not available to us from those sources. Our only other source is chapter 11 in the first book of Kings. From this information we learn that three important things occurred to Solomon during this period which led to disaster both for himself and Israel. These were first, the hundreds of political marriages with which Solomon encumbered himself; second, the severe impact of old age on Solomon, and third, the patronizing of heathen rituals by Solomon. Each of these deserve careful examination.

Solomon's Attempt to Maintain Political Unity Through Mass Marriages

According to I Kings, ch. 11, the first thing which occurred was a mad rush into a whole series of matrimonial engagements. Several things lead us to believe that this did not occur over an extended period of time but in a frantic period at the very end of Solomon's life.

---

8. 2 Chronicles 9:30
9. 2 Chronicles 9:29

For example, while nearly everyone is aware that Solomon acquired an assortment of 1,000 wives and concubines, many students miss the rather dramatic fact that he seems to have had practically no posterity. It is singular that the scripture identifies only one son for Solomon while it specifically mentions the large posterity of his father and those who followed after him.[10] This would strongly imply that Solomon did not marry any extensive number of wives until he was probably very old and in the very last stage of his life.

What would cause him to do this? Once we are aware of the importance of political marriages as a means of maintaining unity in his empire there looms up in 1 Kings, chapter 11, the probable explanation for much of what Solomon did. It states that as Solomon approached the end of his career he was threatened with widespread rebellion among his tributaries from Edom to Syria. Edom, of course, was the kingdom of the Arabah valley in which Solomon had developed his rich copper and iron mines, his smelting operations and the wealthy spice trade of Ezion-geber where the royal navy was docked. Syria, on the other hand, was rapidly coming under the domination of a rebel force from Damascus and Solomon knew this would destroy the rich trade routes which Solomon had controlled between the Mediterranean and Mesopotamia.

Although neither of these forces of insurrection succeeded in boiling over in triumphant separation until later, the text is clear that Hadad began his subversion of Edom shortly after Solomon ascended the throne,[11] and up in Syria a man named Rezon established himself in Damascus and continually sallied forth in excursions of conquest in Syria. Concerning Rezon, the scripture says, "And he was an adversary to Israel ALL THE DAYS OF SOLOMON, beside the mischief that Hadad did. . . ."[12] Solomon also had some worries about the great Hittite center of Hamath on the Orontes river which his troops had captured.[13] Then there was the continuing need to keep on good terms with the people

---

10. See for example, on David 2 Samuel 3:2-5; on Rehoboam 2 Chronicles 11:21; on Abijah 2 Chronicles 13:21. Dr. Adam Clarke emphasizes that Solomon apparently had only one son, namely Rehoboam. *Bible Commentary*, Vol. 2, p. 435.
11. 1 Kings 11:21   13. 2 Chronicles 8:3
12. 1 Kings 11:25

of Tyre and Sidon, especially after Hiram died. And there were the heathen peoples on the maritime plain and those within the confines of Israel proper. All of these appear to have provided the pressure which led Solomon to launch a campaign of political marriages. The scriptures say Solomon's marital alliances included "women of the Moabites, Ammonites, Edomites, Zidonians [people of Phoenicia] and Hittites."[14] The frantic campaign ended with some seven hundred "princesses" being joined to Solomon in marriage.[15] This word, "princesses" is interpreted to mean the daughters of royal houses or leading families with whom Solomon desired to establish political alliance. No doubt these families took pride in being able to boast that a member of their household was wife of the great king Solomon. In addition to these, Solomon also had three hundred secondary wives or concubines.[16]

It must be kept in mind that this procedure which we are suggesting as the only rational explanation for Solomon's strange conduct, was a customary device among kings in ancient times. In fact, it was counted as a status symbol among the more powerful rulers of the middle east to have all the leading families represented among their wives. Solomon would have been considered a third-rate marital politician in comparison with someone like King Chosroes of Persia who boasted 3,000 aristocratic ladies in his marital entourage.[17]

But even so, Solomon had risked the wrath of the Lord by taking this step. The scripture says, "But king Solomon loved many strange women . . . of the nations concerning which the Lord said unto the children of Israel, Ye shall not go in to them, neither shall they come in unto you: for surely they will turn away your heart after their gods: Solomon clave unto these in love."[18]

SOLOMON'S PROBLEMS COMPLICATED BY THE IMPACT OF OLD AGE

From this distance, the passing centuries make it well-nigh impossible to judge all that happened to Solomon in the

14. 1 Kings 11:1
15. 1 Kings 11:3
16. Ibid.

17. Geikie, *Hours With the Bible*, Vol. 3, p. 430
18. 1 Kings 11:1-2

last phase of his life. Nevertheless, there is considerable evidence that in addition to the political factors just mentioned Solomon suffered rather severely from the catabolical processes incident to old age.

Note the scripture specifically says that "when Solomon was old"[19] he began to behave in a manner which was completely out of character with the rest of his life. No longer was he the great man of much wisdom. No longer was he the epitome of encyclopedic astuteness which had so impressed the queen of Sheba. Nor was he any longer the guardian of the Gospel or the protector of the temple rites. Intellectually and spiritually, Solomon collapsed.

Today we are coming to understand a great deal more about geriatrics or the diseases and problems of old age. As we consider the pattern of Solomon's behavior in this period the premature collapse of his judgment and faculties seems to accurately correspond with the symptoms of *senile dementia*, one of the diseases of old age. This is a "permanent deterioration of the mental faculties as a result of disease or decay of the cerebral neurones."[20] It strikes earlier in some than others: "The age at which bodily and mental powers wane varies greatly with different individuals. One man may display unimpaired vigour at eighty, where another is an old man at sixty."[21] The latter appears to have been the case with Solomon.

Modern medicine has found that where chronic senility has become entrenched the post mortem examination of the victim has revealed serious brain damage through physical deterioration. Not all victims of *senile dementia* behave the same way, of course, but what we know of Solomon's conduct "when he was old" clearly harmonizes with the pattern of many people in this category.

For example, the person becomes at least partially irresponsible. He is deprived of good judgment, is easily influenced and easily prejudiced. However, the victim may think himself better than he used to be and is therefore in-

19. 1 Kings 11:4
20. W. S. Dawson, M.D., *Aids to Psychiatry*, London: Bailliere, Tindall and Cox, p. 191
21. Ibid. p. 192

capable of recognizing his own problems. He is described as sometimes being extremely "euphoric, and unduly confident of his bodily and mental powers" in which case, "Erotism may be marked."[22] This last quality tends to make the individual subject to romantic "hyperexcitability," and can result in embarrassing overt acts which were not characteristic of the person in his normal condition.[23]

In his earlier career Solomon appears to have used good judgment and propriety in his marriages. Only one of them appears to have been for political expediency, and that was his marriage to the Pharaoh's daughter. But toward the last he suddenly fell into that fantastic obsession which led to his acquisition of hundreds of wives. Even if he thought it were justified on political grounds this was not normal behavior for a man of Solomon's background. It did violence to the patriarchal order of plural families and shattered on a massive scale the Lord's commandments against intermarriages with heathen peoples. It carries strong overtones implying the ravage of *senile dementia*.

There is also the phenomenon which we shall consider next wherein Solomon violated the most fundamental teachings of his entire life and recklessly embraced practices which were abhorrent to him in his youth. This is another symptom often found in cases of senility. In fact, "the dementia may progress to a stage in which most of the instincts are lost. The patient loses regard for his person, becomes unclean and degraded in his habits. . . ."[24]

In an ordinary person such problems could be handled as part of the treatment of pathological senility, but what happens when the victim is a king with unlimited totalitarian authority? He can be capricious, pernicious and depraved without anyone having the power to interfere. Worse still, he can become the tool of avaricious people who know how to manipulate his non-discerning and non-discriminating mind by using flattery and coddling to induce him to act in a completely abnormal manner. Solomon's case history fits this possibility precisely.

---

22. Ibid. p. 193
23. Ibid. p. 192
24. Ibid. p. 194

Solomon Introduces Idolatry Into Israel

The scripture says, "For it came to pass, when Solomon was old, that his wives turned away his heart after other gods: and his heart was not perfect with the Lord his God, as was the heart of David his father [who, with all his faults, resisted every taint of idolatry]. For Solomon went after Ashtoreth the goddess of the Zidonians, and after Milcom the abomination of the Ammonites. And Solomon did evil in the sight of the Lord, and went not fully after the Lord, as did David his father."[25]

There were two characteristics of heathen worship which made them far more abominable than simply bowing down to images of wood and stone. One was the use of esoteric fertility rites in which drunkenness and acts of immorality were utilized as sacramental offerings by the heathen worshipper. The other was the slaughtering of human beings, particularly children and virgins, as forms of sacrifice. Only when these facts are understood will the Bible reader comprehend the vehemence with which the Lord and his prophets denounced "the groves," the phallic symbols and all other aspects of heathen worship associated with idolatry.

However, Solomon's sin appears to have been the building of heathen temples where these rites could be practiced rather than actually participating in them himself. And he appears to have built these heathen centers in response to the teasing and conniving of his idolatrous wives. The seriousness of his offense is spelled out in the following scripture, "Then did Solomon build an high place for Chemosh, the abomination of Moab, in the hill that is before Jerusalem [the Mount of Olives[26]], and for Molech, the abomination of the children of Ammon. And likewise did he for all his strange wives, which burnt incense and sacrificed unto their gods."[27]

From this it can be seen that even if Solomon were a victim of *senile dementia*, the Lord could not do otherwise than exhibit His absolute revulsion against what was hap-

---

25. 1 Kings 11:4-6
26. Clarke, *Bible Commentary,* Vol. 2, p. 427
27. 1 Kings 11:7-8

pening. Therefore the scripture says, "And the Lord was angry with Solomon, because his heart was turned from the Lord God of Israel, which had appeared unto him twice, and had commanded him concerning this thing, that he should not go after other gods: but he kept not that which the Lord commanded."[28]

We are not told which of the prophets the Lord used to communicate God's message to Solomon in this hour of judgment. Most likely it was Ahijah, since it was he who delivered a message almost identical in context to Jeroboam.[29] And the "prophecy of Ahijah" is referred to in Chronicles as having been given when Solomon was at this stage of his life.[30]

The edict which now fell upon Solomon was a prophecy of doom: "Wherefore the Lord said unto Solomon, Forasmuch as this is done of thee, and thou hast not kept my covenant and my statutes, which I have commanded thee, I will surely rend the kingdom from thee, and will give it to thy servant. Notwithstanding in thy days I will not do it for David thy father's sake: but I will rend it out of the hand of thy son. Howbeit I will not rend away all the kingdom; but will give ONE TRIBE TO THY SON for David my servant's sake, and for Jerusalem's sake which I have chosen."[31]

But who was Solomon's "servant" who was going to rend most of the kingdom from Solomon's son? Even before he died, Solomon learned who this "servant" was.

THE RAISING UP OF JEROBOAM

A man never knows when the finger of God will touch him on the forehead and designate him for a great new calling. It had happened to Samuel, Saul, David and Solomon. Now it happened to Jeroboam.

Jeroboam was one of those practical, hard-headed and efficient Israelites who had been made a servant or steward of the king. His father was Nebat, "an Ephrathite of Zereda," and his mother's name was Zeruah, who by this time

---

30. 2 Chronicles 9:29   28. 1 Kings 11:9-10
31. 1 Kings 11:11-13   29. 1 Kings 11:30-36

was a widow.[32] The scripture says Jeroboam had first come to the attention of the king several years earlier when Solomon was rebuilding the Millo fortress and repairing the city walls.[33] Young Jeroboam was observed to have been so "industrious" that Solomon made him the "ruler over all the charge of the house of Joseph."[34] This is interpreted to mean that he was made the king's royal governor to exact from the house of Joseph the charges or assessments in task work, food requisitions, taxes, tariffs and tributes. This required Jeroboam to make frequent trips from the mountains of Ephraim where he lived, to the capital city of Jerusalem.

On one of these journeys, and apparently at a time when the days of the aging Solomon were already numbered, a prophet stopped Jeroboam along the highway. This prophet's name was Ahijah from Shilo, the old sacred city of ancient Israel. Ahijah led Jeroboam off the highway and took him where they could be "alone in the field." There the prophet removed a new robe or garment which Jeroboam was wearing. No doubt Jeroboam was well acquainted with this prophet for Shilo was in his district. Nevertheless, he must have been alarmed when he saw Ahijah tearing his new robe to pieces.[35] The prophet divided the garment into twelve pieces and then declared:

"Take thee ten pieces; for thus saith the Lord, the God of Israel, Behold, I will rend the kingdom out of the hand of Solomon and will give ten tribes to thee . . . Howbeit I will not take the whole kingdom out of his hand: but I will make him prince all the days of his life for David my servant's sake . . . but I will take the kingdom out of his son's hand, and will give it unto thee, even ten tribes. And unto his son will I give one tribe [which was Judah, later joined by most of the tribe of Levi]."[36]

Then Ahijah delivered God's warning to Jeroboam. Said he: "And it shall be, if thou wilt hearken unto all that I command thee, and wilt walk in my ways, and do that is right in my sight . . . I will be with thee, and build thee a

32. 1 Kings 11:26
33. 1 Kings 11:27-28
34. Ibid.

35. 1 Kings 11:30
36. 1 Kings 11:31-36

sure house, as I built for David, and will give Israel unto thee."[37]

It is not difficult to visualize the startling impact of this message upon the mind of Jeroboam. It would not be surprising to hear the prophet say that God was displeased with Solomon, for as we shall see later, the whole administration of that aged king had now become a burden of apostasy and oppression in the eyes of the people; however, it would be a shock for any man to suddenly learn that it was God's will that he should receive ten-twelfths of the kingdom once Solomon had passed away.

We have reason to believe that while Jeroboam had the capacity to be a good king (otherwise God would not have chosen him) nevertheless he lacked the humility and patience necessary to satisfy the requirements for such a calling. In many respects he seems very much like Saul.

Ahijah had specifically stated that Jeroboam was not to receive his part of the kingdom until after Solomon had passed away but apparently the prospect was too much for the impatient Jeroboam for it says, "he lifted up his hand against the king,"[38] and he soon had reason to regret his impatience.

Up to this time Solomon had no way of knowing who was to get the vast majority of his kingdom for the Lord had merely disclosed that it was going to be one of his "servants."[39]

When Solomon heard that Jeroboam was the servant who was to rise up and succeed him, his fury knew no bounds. His childish deteriorating mind struck out at Jeroboam with lethal vindictiveness. The scripture says, "Solomon sought therefore to kill Jeroboam. And Jeroboam arose, and fled into Egypt, unto Shishak king of Egypt. . . ."[40] As we shall point out later, this Shishak is identified by authorities as being the founder of Dynasty Twenty-two. He had replaced the dynasty into which Solomon had married so Jeroboam found in Shishak a natural enemy of Solomon.

37. 1 Kings 11:38
38. 1 Kings 11:26
39. 1 Kings 11:11
40. 1 Kings 11:40

Solomon Dies

How much time transpired between these events and the last sad days when Solomon finally passed away around 922 B.C. cannot be ascertained. However, it could have been rather soon after Jeroboam fled to Egypt. The scripture simply says, "and Jeroboam . . . was in Egypt until the death of Solomon."[41]

In reflecting on the life of Solomon we cannot help but be puzzled by the amazing contradictions it contained. For one who began so brilliantly it cannot help but be a source of sorrow that it should end so tragically. Nevertheless, as we have seen, there is considerable reason to believe that there were mitigating circumstances associated with his spiritual and intellectual collapse of Solomon which significantly mitigate the harsh indictment which would otherwise be warranted against him.

We have noted that the weaknesses of Solomon were only associated with events which occurred "when Solomon was old."[42] In the vigor of his physical and spiritual prime he talked with the Lord, leveled the top of Mount Moriah, built a beautiful temple upon it, functioned in the Priesthood at its dedication, erected a palace and royal court, fortified the city of Jerusalem, organized an efficient civil service for the kingdom, built strong military outposts, launched a naval merchant marine, developed the world's largest copper smelting operation of his day, brought wealth and dignity to Israel and, during most of his reign, kept the peace for one of the longest periods in the entire history of the Palestinian area.

It was appropriate, therefore, that he should have been named Solomon — the peacable one — and that during most of his life the name which Nathan gave him was also appropriate and applicable. Nathan called him, "Jedediah" — beloved of the Lord.

Before the end came, however, there were certain storm warnings which erupted occasionally into symptomatic flurries of violence portending a rising insurgency. These were

---

41. Ibid.
42. 1 Kings 11:4

caused by several serious political schisms among Israel's tributaries which finally erupted into open rebellion. This led to the loss of Edom in the south,[43] and Syria in the north.[44] Nevertheless, by the time Solomon died, the rest of the kingdom seemed politically stable and it looked as though the crown would pass peacefully to Solomon's son, Rehoboam.

But prophecy had declared otherwise.

A Political Explosion Blows the Kingdom of Israel Apart

If Solomon had any other sons beside Rehoboam the Bible does not mention them. Nor does it mention any daughters.

Rehoboam was the son of Naamah an Ammonitess,[45] which means that he was half Israelite and half the descendant of Lot, Abraham's nephew. The Ammonites occupied the highlands east of Jordan and had been conquered by David. Though Shemites by descent, the Ammonites were rank heathens who had been a snare to Israel on several occasions in the past. Solomon must have married Naamah in his early twenties because Rehoboam was born about the time Solomon was 24 years old. We derive this from the fact that Rehoboam was 41 when Solomon died.[46]

All Israel seems to have recognized Rehoboam as the uncontested legitimate heir to the throne of Solomon. The scripture says, "And Rehoboam went to Shechem: for all Israel were come to Shechem to make him king."[47] The constitution of Israel provided that no king could take over the government without the consent of the people, and therefore this national convention for the procuring of a vote of confidence was an important event.

When Prince Rehoboam arrived at Shechem he undoubtedly noticed one person who was very prominent in the leadership of the northern tribes. It was Jeroboam. Here was the man whom the aged King Solomon had tried to kill because Jeroboam had "lifted up his hand against the king."[48]

43. 1 Kings 11:14
44. 1 Kings 11:23-25
45. 1 Kings 14:21
46. Ibid.
47. 1 Kings 12:1
48. 1 Kings 11:26

As previously indicated, Jeroboam had fled to Egypt and sought the protection of Pharaoh Shishak, but now he was back again. The scripture says that after Solomon died, the princes of Israel thought it was safe for Jeroboam to return so they "sent and called him."[49] Jeroboam had therefore arrived in time for this national convention, but, surprisingly, he made no attempt to launch a separation movement even though the prophet Ahijah had already told him that when Solomon died he would get ten of the tribes of Israel and Solomon's son (Rehoboam) would get only one.

Jeroboam simply assumed his previous role as one of the leaders of the northern tribes. In that role he joined with the tribal spokesmen in making certain demands upon Rehoboam before giving him their vote of confidence. The Bible says, "And Jeroboam and all the congregation of Israel came and spake unto Rehoboam, saying, Thy father made our yoke grievous, now therefore make thou the grievous service of thy father, and his heavy yoke which he put upon us, lighter, and we will serve thee."[50]

There was no doubt about the ominous tone of this demand, yet those who made it obviously felt it was just and reasonable. After all, the people had spent nearly 11 years enthusiastically building the great temple and the temple square. Then they had willingly spent an additional 13 years building the palace and royal court. But what had happened in the last few years of Solomon's life was something else again. The recent burden of supporting a thousand women and their lackeys, building heathen shrines and maintaining a regal bureaucracy in lavish extravagance was disgusting and intolerable.

As Rehoboam listened to these demands he knew they had deep implications for himself and his status with the haughty members of the aristocracy in Jerusalem. In order to comply with such requests Rehoboam would have to immediately inaugurate a severe austerity program. It would mean no more blatant extravagance, no more endless streams of gold, food, fodder and finery pouring into the royal treasury. There would be taxes, of course, but only for rea-

49. 1 Kings 12:3
50. 1 Kings 12:3-4

sonable, necessary services, not for the rich high life which the royal circles had been enjoying for the past several dissolute years. Rehoboam knew that if he consented to these demands there would be the shades of hades to face when he returned to Jerusalem. It was a critical decision. He needed time. Said he, "Depart yet for three days, then come again to me."[51] It was agreed.

Rehoboam immediately sought for the advice of the "old men" who had served Solomon. They were unanimous in their advice: "Speak good words to them, then they will be thy servants for ever."[52] The proud spirit of Rehoboam recoiled against them. The scripture says, "But he forsook the counsel of the old men, which they had given him, and consulted with the young men that were grown up with him, and which stood before him."[53] This is interpreted to mean the young men who belonged to Rehoboam's party and who expected to rise to eminence and power once their princely friend had been crowned king. When Rehoboam went to them, these men revealed themselves to be the spoiled and pampered sycophants of the "second generation" who were accustomed to enjoying the unearned fruits of first generation affluence. They could not visualize life without the perfumed apartments, luxurious gardens, the wine-filled goblets of gold, the pompous pageantry and all the lavish court life to which they had become addicted. They therefore gave Rehoboam advice which tickled his ears. They told him to crack the whip of authority over the people. Prepare them for greater burdens, not less. Rehoboam therefore used their very words as he went back to the princes of Israel and spoke "roughly" to them, saying, "My father made your yoke heavy, and I will add to your yoke: my father also chastised you with whips, but I will chastise you with scorpions [cat-o'-nine-tails]."[54]

The volatile reaction of the tribal leaders to this contemptuous affront was prompt and pronounced. Their bitter resentment exploded into a howling cry for revolution and independence. Said they, "What portion have we in David

51. 1 Kings 12:5
52. 1 Kings 12:7
53. 1 Kings 12:8
54. 1 Kings 12:14

. . . to your tents, O Israel!"[55] The vexed Israelites marched off in a high fever leaving Rehoboam unconfirmed and un-crowned. But Rehoboam apparently did not think they were actually so serious about it. Barely had the northern tribes-men reached their cities when Rehoboam ordered Adoram (or Hadoram), his chief tax collector, to go among them for the tribute. The next thing Rehoboam knew the sen-sational news reached him that Adoram had been stoned to death. "Therefore King Rehoboam made speed to get him up to his chariot, to flee to Jerusalem."[56]

The scripture closes the account of this historical crisis by saying, "So Israel rebelled against the house of David. . . . And it came to pass, when all Israel heard that Jeroboam was come again, that they sent and called him unto the congre-gation, and made him king over all Israel: there was none that followed the House of David, but the tribe of Judah only."[57]

REHOBOAM ACCEPTS THE ADVICE OF A PROPHET
AND AVOIDS A CIVIL WAR

In Jerusalem, meanwhile, Rehoboam was furiously mo-bilizing 100,000 troops. He would teach those rebels! Not only did he gather the sons of Judah but many came from the neighboring cities immediately to the north of Judah.[58] Rehoboam would now reunite his kingdom.

But suddenly there appeared at the palace a man who said he had received a revelation from God for the king. Rehoboam could not help but listen for the man was Shema-iah, one of the young prophets who had risen in the land. He said to Rehoboam:

"Thus said the Lord, Ye shall not go up nor fight against your brethren the children of Israel: return every man to his house; for this thing is from me."[59]

Although Rehoboam knew this undoubtedly meant the end of Israel's golden age and certainly the end of a united kingdom, he consented. He passed along the message of

---

55. 1 Kings 12:16
56. 1 Kings 12:18
57. 1 Kings 12:19-20

58. 1 Kings 12:21
59. 1 Kings 12:24

Shemaiah to his commanders and all his troops and "they hearkened therefore to the word of the Lord, and returned to depart, according to the word of the Lord."[60]

Thus a great civil war was avoided. By listening to the advice of a prophet, Judah escaped what would have been a useless blood-bath. Under the circumstances it is impossible to see how the contemplated military action could have been anything but a failure.

Israel Becomes Two Kingdoms

And so it was around 922 B.C. that the permanent division of the twelve tribes into two separate kingdoms became an accepted fact. In the beginning the kingdom of the south consisted almost exclusively of Judah while the tribes of the north were called, "Israel." However, the division left some fuzzy edges which need to be mentioned.

For example, the small tribe of Benjamin occupied a narrow strip of territory just north of Judah. In the past this tribe consistently attached itself officially to the northern tribes,[61] but on this occasion the cities along the southern border of Benjamin attached themselves to Judah. These included Mizpeh and Geba which a later king of Judah rebuilt.[62] We should also mention the territory of Dan. This was originally attached to Judah on the west, but later its people made their headquarters far to the north in Laish which they rebuilt and thereafter called Dan. The cities of their original inheritance in the south eventually attached themselves to Judah. These included Zorah (Samson's old hometown) and Ajalon (where Joshua commanded the sun to stand still).[63]

It also should be recalled that one tribe was located south of Judah in the desert uplands of the Negeb. This was Simeon. However, it had never amounted to much and consisted almost exclusively of nomadic families who dwelt in tents and maintained what economic ties they needed with Judah, but because they never participated in the governing of Judah they identified themselves politically with the federation to the north.

---

60. Ibid.
61. 2 Samuel 2:9
62. 1 Kings 15:23
63. 2 Chronicles 11:10

We are thus able to account for the political alignment of all the tribes in the two new kingdoms except the scattered tribe of Levi. When Ahijah had prophesied that the northern kingdom would be ten tribes and the southern kingdom would be one tribe he obviously left Levi unassigned because that tribe had never been given a geographical inheritance. The Levites were the custodians of the Priesthood and needed to be spread among all the tribes. However, this did not remain the situation for long. As we shall see shortly, the persecution of the Levites in the northern kingdom compelled practically the entire tribe (including the Priests of Aaron) to flee to Judah.[64] Later there was some intermingling again but not on a large scale. For all practical purposes, the northern kingdom consisted of Ephraim, Mannasseh, Reuben, Simeon, Dan, Naphtali, Gad, Asher, Issachar, Zebulun and Benjamin. The southern kingdom consisted of Judah and Levi.

Jeroboam Ignores the Warning of Ahijah

As soon as Jeroboam had been made king of the northern tribes and had begun to enjoy the fruits of Ahijah's prophecy concerning his calling from the Lord to rule over the ten tribes, he completely ignored the Lord's warning as to the manner in which he should conduct himself as king. The word of the Lord through Ahijah had been, "And it shall be, if thou wilt hearken unto all that I command thee, and wilt walk in my ways, and do that is right in my sight, to keep my statutes and my commandments, as David my servant did, that I will be with thee, and build thee a sure house, as I built for David, and will give Israel unto thee."[65]

Apparently Jeroboam became so fearful that his people would fall under the influence of Judah again, that he did not trust in the Lord but decided to use his own schemes. Like most human inventions they were a combination of some good and some evil. The good part consisted of establishing a national capital at Shechem where so many great events

---

64. 2 Chronicles 11:14
65. 1 Kings 11:38

had occurred in Israel's history,[66] and also in setting up a secondary capital at Penuel[67] to govern the tribes in Trans-Jordan.[68]

The second part of Jeroboam's plan to unite his people was a depraved abomination. This consisted of first making two golden calves. He set up one of them at a new religious center which he created in Dan while the other was set up for worship in the ancient shrine city of Bethel.[69] Jeroboam had been in Egypt long enough to see how infatuated the masses of people could become with calf worship when it was associated with the wild, licentious fertility rites of the heathens. He therefore committed his people to the very abomination which had robbed Israel of all but the vestiges of her inheritance at Sinai.

In addition to the fertility cults, Jeroboam introduced devil-worship at his shrine centers.[70] He made himself the head of this heathen cult and set up his own high priests.[71] He allowed any person who came forward with an offering of a young bullock and seven rams to be eligible for his priest-hood.[72] Often the lowest characters among the whole people thereby entered these heathen sacerdotal orders.[73] Jeroboam inaugurated a new date for the annual feast so the people

---

66. Shechem was located in the narrow valley between Mount Ebal and Mount Gerizim located 32 miles north of Jerusalem. Today it is called Nablus, being corrupted from Neapolis, a name given to it by Vespasian. Numerous springs originate here and flow down into attractive valleys which fan out both east and west. Abraham camped here when he first arrived in Canaan from Haran (Genesis 12:6). Jacob stopped here with his family and large herds as he came out of Haran. He liked it so well that he bought up a lot of the land on the east where Jacob's well is now located. Unfortunately, however, the prince of the city kidnapped and ravished Jacob's only daughter, Dinah, whereupon her older brothers without their father's knowledge, sacked and burned the town. When Israel came up out of Egypt they buried Joseph's bones here because this land was the patrimony of the tribe of Joseph (Joshua 24:32). It was here that the blessings and cursing were pronounced on Israel (Deut. 27:11-26, Josh. 8:30-35). Here Joshua assembled Israel and gave his final instructions (Joshua 24:1, 25). Shechem was made a city of refuge under the Levites (Joshua 21:20-21) but was completely destroyed by Abimelech (Judges 9:34-45) and had to be rebuilt. As we have seen, it became Jeroboam's capital for awhile and was the place where Israel declared its independence from Judah. The Samaritans took over the area after the conquest and made Mount Gerizim the center of their national religion. (See Peloubet's *Bible Dictionary* under Shechem, p. 613.)
67. 1 Kings 12:25
68. Penuel was located on the Jabbock river, a tributary to the Jordan. It was here Jacob wrestled with a heavenly messenger. See Genesis 32:24-32
69. 1 Kings 12:28-29
70. 2 Chronicles 11:15
71. 1 Kings 13:33; 2 Chronicles 11:15
72. 2 Chronicles 13:9; 1 Kings 12:31
73. 1 Kings 12:31

would not need to go to Jerusalem. He set up the 15th day of the 8th month,[74] instead of the 15th day of the 7th month which the Lord had designated, as the great harvest festival and Feast of the Tabernacles.[75]

As might have been expected, the Priests of Aaron and the Levites resisted this religious revolution with all their might but to no avail. A great persecution of the Levites spread throughout the northern tribes so that the cry went forth to flee to Rehoboam and Judah. The scripture says, "And the priests and the Levites that were in all Israel resorted to him out of all their coasts. For the Levites left their suburbs and their possession, and came to Judah and Jerusalem; for Jeroboam and his sons had cast them off from executing the priest's office unto to Lord."[76]

JEROBOAM REFUSES TO REPENT
EVEN AFTER A GREAT MIRACLE

Before long a "man of God" whose name is not given, came up to Bethel from Judah and began pronouncing a prophecy against Jeroboam's heathen altar. He declared, "O altar, altar, thus saith the Lord; Behold, a child shall be born unto the house of David, Josiah by name; and upon thee shall he offer the priests of the high places that burn incense upon thee, and men's bones shall be burnt upon thee. And he gave a sign the same day, saying, This is the sign which the Lord hath spoken; Behold, the altar shall be rent, and the ashes that are upon it shall be poured out."[77]

Jeroboam was apparently standing nearby and when someone told the king what the "man of God" had said to the altar, Jeroboam angrily reached out to grab the prophet. But his intention was never realized. All of a sudden his outstretched arm stiffened into a fixed position "so that he could not pull it in to him again,"[78] and his hand withered and "dried up."[79] At the same time Jeroboam's heathen altar began to quake and break apart so that "the ashes poured

---

74. 1 Kings 12:32
75. Clarke, *Bible Commentary*, Vol. 2, p. 437-438
76. 2 Chronicles 11:13-14
77. 1 Kings 13:2-3. Concerning this prophet being from Judah, see verse 14.
78. 1 Kings 13:4
79. Ibid.

out."[80] As Jeroboam looked at his afflicted hand he was shocked into temporary humility. He pleaded with the man of God, "Intreat now the face of the Lord thy God, and pray for me, that my hand may be restored me again!"[81] The prophet obliged him and the hand was healed. Jeroboam was so relieved that he wanted to reward this man who had genuine Priesthood power. "Come home with me," he said, "and refresh thyself, and I will give thee a reward."[82] But the prophet replied, "If thou wilt give me half thine house, I will not go in with thee, neither will I eat bread nor drink water in this place: for so was it charged me by the word of the Lord, saying, Eat no bread, nor drink water, nor turn again by the same way that thou camest."[83]

The scripture then takes a whole chapter to tell how this prophet later weakened in this resolution and while he would not eat with Jeroboam he did stop off to eat with a fellow prophet and, as a result. lost his life.[84] But that is incidental to the main historical thread we are now pursuing which is woven around Jeroboam. One would have thought that Jeroboam's encounter with the powers of the Priesthood exhibited by the prophet from Judah would have compelled him to see the error of his ways, but apparently the light had gone out in him. The Bible says, "After this thing Jeroboam returned not from his evil way, but made again of the lowest of the people priests of the high places: whosoever would [wish it], he consecrated him, and he became one of the priests of the high places."[85]

THE PROPHET AHIJAH PREDICTS JEROBOAM'S DOWNFALL

Now another incident happened to Jeroboam which certainly should have humbled him. This occurred after Jeroboam had begun a new capital city at Tirzah which is about 7 miles north of Shechem. It was there that his son, Abijah, fell desperately ill. When it appeared that he might die, Jeroboam sent his wife disguised as a poor peasant woman to see if the prophet Ahijah at Shiloh would tell her what was to become of her son. It will be remembered that this was the prophet who had first advised Jeroboam that he would

---

80. 1 Kings 13:5
81. 1 Kings 13:6
82. 1 Kings 13:7
83. 1 Kings 13.:8-9
84. 1 Kings, chapter 13
85. 1 Kings 13:33

become king of the northern tribes. By now, however, Ahijah was getting very old and was totally blind.[86] Nevertheless, the Lord revealed to him who the woman was before she had even reached the door. In fact, as she approached his house, the old prophet called out to her, "Come in, thou wife of Jeroboam; why feignest thou thyself to be another for I am sent to thee with heavy tidings. Go, tell Jeroboam, Thus saith the Lord God of Israel, Forasmuch as I exalted thee from among the people, and made thee prince over my people Israel, and rent the kingdom away from the house of David, and gave it thee: and yet thou hast not been as my servant David . . . but hast done evil above all that were before thee: for thou hast gone and made thee other gods, and molten images, to provoke me to anger, and hast cast me behind thy back."[87]

Ahijah now pronounced six prophecies which he instructed the woman to carry back to her apostate husband:

1—All of Jeroboam's descendants would be slain.[88]

2—Some would be left lying in the streets to be devoured by hungry dogs.[89]

3—Some would be left in the field and be devoured by vultures and other carrion birds.[90]

4—As she returned home, her son would die,[91] but because of his innocence and goodness he alone of Jeroboam's offspring would enjoy the blessing of a decent burial.[92]

5—A new king would thereafter reign over Israel.[93]

6—And because of the heathen practices introduced by Jeroboam, the ten tribes of Israel would eventually be rooted out of their entire inheritance in the promised land.[94]

The sad pronouncement was finally concluded "And Jeroboam's wife arose, and departed, and came to Tirzah, and when she came to the threshold of the door, the child died."[95]

Blindly stumbling on, Jeroboam continued his defiant, apostate course.

---

86. 1 Kings 14:4
87. 1 Kings 14:6-9
88. 1 Kings 14:10
89. 1 Kings 14:11
90. Ibid.
91. 1 Kings 14:12
92. 1 Kings 14:13
93. 1 Kings 14:14
94. 1 Kings 14:15-16
95. 1 Kings 14:17

What Had Happened to Rehoboam and
Judah During This Period?

It will be recalled that Rehoboam had started out his career as king of Judah by listening to Shemaiah, the prophet, and had thereby escaped becoming involved in a monstrous civil war. And by continuing to follow the prophet during the first three years of his reign, Rehoboam conducted himself in a most admirable manner.

The first thing he did was to attempt to overcome the massive military weakness which had resulted from the dividing of the kingdom. He knew Judah would be at a tremendous handicap in case of attack and he therefore launched a crash program to fortify the cities on the west and on the south of Jerusalem. It appeared that he was expecting an attack from the Egyptians or the Philistines rather than the northern tribes of Israel. We will list each of the fifteen cities which he fortified and fix its location in relation to Jerusalem so the reader may appreciate Rehoboam's plan of defense for the capital.[96]

Bethlehem and Tekoah were 7 miles south of Jerusalem.

Ethem was 9 miles south near Solomon's springs.

Socho was 18 miles southwest.

Adullum was 15 miles southwest in Elah valley. This will be remembered as David's former stronghold.

Bethzur was 17 miles south on the Hebron road.

Gath was at the mouth of Elah valley overlooking the Philistine plain. It was 25 miles west of Jerusalem.

Maresha, among the hills, was located 6 miles southeast of Gath.

Hebron, the former capital of Judah, was 23 miles south of Jerusalem.

Ziph was 4 miles south of Hebron.

Adoraim was 5 miles west of Hebron.

Lachish, now Tel el Hesy, was 22 miles west of Hebron.

Three cities which were directly west of Jerusalem were also fortified. These were Azekah, Zorah and Ajalon.

---

96. 2 Chronicles 11:5-12

Rehoboam wanted to guarantee the loyalty of these fortified cities in case of attack, and so he assigned his own sons to be in charge of them.[97] Rehoboam had a large family. The scripture says that by the end of his reign he had 18 wives and three times as many secondary wives or concubines. By these he had 28 sons and 60 daughters.[98]

Rehoboam's regime was further strengthened when practically the entire tribe of Levi including the Priests of Aaron migrated to Judah.[99] Rehoboam now had two tribes instead of one. And before long he needed far more than these.

EGYPT DECLARES WAR ON JUDAH

The twenty-first dynasty of Egypt into which Solomon had married was now out of power in the Delta, and Shoshenk I, the founder of the twenty-second dynasty, had elevated himself and his Lybian soldiers from mere non-Egyptian mercenaries to the rulers of the Lower Kingdom of Egypt. All available evidence indicates that this Lybian Pharaoh is the person identified in the Bible as Shishak.[100]

This Pharaoh had moved his capital from Tanis to Bubastus which was more toward the center of the Delta and his dynasty is therefore sometimes called the Bubastis dynasty.[101] He would be the one (if the experts have identified him properly) who had befriended Jeroboam, and it is easy to see how his hostility toward Judah may have stemmed from the biased stories Jeroboam told him.

The Bible says that after Judah had enjoyed three years of efficient and righteous administration under Rehoboam, the king began to imitate the worst part of his father's (Solomon's) reign. In short order the protective mantle of Heaven was withdrawn from Judah. During the fifth year of Rehoboam's reign the Pharaoh of Egypt suddenly thundered up into southern Palestine with 1,200 chariots and 60,000 horsemen. The scripture says "the people were without number that came with him out of Egypt; the Lubims

97. 2 Chronicles 11:23
98. 2 Chronicles 11:21
99. 2 Chronicles 11:13-14
100. 2 Chronicles 12:2 plus Sir Alan Gardiner, *Egypt of the Pharoahs*, pp. 329-330.
101. Ibid. p. 448

[Lybians], the Sukkiims [or Troglodytes who lived in caves along the Red Sea], and the Ethiopians [from Cush]."[102]

In a previous crisis Rehoboam had enjoyed the counsel of a prophet of God and that is exactly what he needed now. But when Shemaiah came to Rehoboam this time it was not with counsel but with a prophecy of doom. Said he, "Thus saith the Lord, Ye have forsaken me, and therefore have I also left you in the hand of Shishak."[103]

Immediately the king and the princes of Judah went into wails of mourning and pleading. And it touched the Lord. So He said to his prophet, "They have humbled themselves; therefore I will not destroy them, but I will grant them SOME deliverance; and my wrath shall not be poured out upon Jerusalem by the hand of Shishak. Nevertheless, they shall be his servants; that they may know [the difference between] my service, and the service of the kingdoms of the [foreign] countries."[104]

So Shishak and his mighty hosts successfully rammed their way through Judah's fifteen fortified cities and reached Jerusalem. And he "took away the treasures of the house of the Lord, and the treasures of the king's house: he took all: he carried away also the shields of gold which Solomon had made."[105] And of course the prize of the whole campaign would be Solomon's famous ivory and gold throne which was the envy of every royal house in the Middle East.[106]

Thus Shishak ravaged the previous treasures of the temple, the palace and the king's court which David and Solomon had so painfully collected. Shishak then put Judah under tribute and departed.[107]

But at least Rehoboam was left with his beautiful temple, his palaces and public buildings even though they had been stripped of their embellishments. He undoubtedly felt grateful they were not all burned to the ground. To restore some semblance of his former pageantry Rehoboam had his

102. 2 Chronicles 12:3; Clarke, Bible Commentary, Vol. 2, p. 655
103. 2 Chronicles 12:5
104. 2 Chronicles 12:7-8
105. 2 Chronicles 12:9
106. 1 Kings 10:18-20
107. We deduct this from the prophecy of Shemaiah, 2 Chronicles, 12:5

guard equipped with brass shields to replace the shields of gold.[108]

This is the last notable event of Rehoboam's reign. He ruled for a total of 17 years[109] which means he was only 58 years of age when he died.[110] The date would be approximately 905 B.C. The scripture says the details of his reign may be found in the "book of Shemaiah the prophet, and of Iddo the seer" but of course we have neither of these sacred books today. He was buried with his fathers in the royal tombs of the City of David.[111]

Abijah Succeeds Rehoboam as King of Judah

Although Rehoboam had many sons, Abijah was his favorite and was selected over his other brothers as the heir-apparent to the throne even during Rehoboam's lifetime.[112] Abijah was a great grandson of David on both his father's and his mother's side. Here is how that came about. Rehoboam was a grandson of David through Solomon and had married two granddaughters of David who were therefore his first cousins. The first marriage was to Mahalath, granddaughter of David through Jermoth[113] and the second marriage was to Maachah, granddaughter of David through Absalom.[114] It was this second wife, Maachah, who became the king's favorite consort[115] and when her first son was born the king decided to make him his crown prince. This was Abijah.

Before treating the life of Abijah perhaps we need to pause for a moment to clarify three names which are always confusing to Bible students. This Abijah we are now discussing who became king of Judah must not be confused with Abijah, the young son of Jeroboam, who fell sick and died. Nor must this Abijah (meaning "my father is Jehovah"[116]) be confused with the very similar name of Ahijah (meaning "my brother is Jehovah"[117]), who was the prophet of God from Shiloh and who pronounced prophecies concerning the rise and fall of Jeroboam. As we shall see later,

---

108. 2 Chronicles 12:10-11
109. 2 Chronicles 12:13
110. Ibid.
111. 2 Chronicles 12:16
112. 2 Chronicles 11:22
113. 2 Chronicles 11:18
114. 2 Chronicles 11:20
115. 2 Chronicles 11:21
116. Peloubet's *Bible Dictionary*, under Abijah
117. Ibid., under Ahijah

there are several other Biblical characters bearing these two names and each one must be carefully distinguished to avoid confusion.

As mentioned above, Abijah's mother was Maachah, daughter of Absalom, the infamous prodigal son of David who tried to murder David and seize the kingdom. This relationship was embarrassing to Maachah and the Jewish *Targum* therefore says: "Her name was changed into the more excellent name Michaiah, and her father's name into that of Uriel of Gibeatha, THAT THE NAME OF AB-SALOM MIGHT NOT BE REMEMBERED."[118] This explains why Abijah's mother is called "Maachah, daughter of Absalom," in one scripture,[119] and "Michaiah the daughter of Uriel of Gibeah" in another.[120]

Abijah only reigned three years over Judah.[121] According to the compiler of the Book of 1 Kings he started his career as abominably as his father's administration had ended. "And he [Abijah] walked in all the sins of his father, which he had done before him: and his heart was not perfect with the Lord his God, as the heart of David his father [literally, grandfather].[122] According to the compiler of 2 Chronicles, however, Abijah did not always remain a patron of heathen practices but finally repented sufficiently to commence a reform program of strengthening the Aaronic Priesthood and suppressing the impure cults which were becoming so prevalent. It remained for his son, Asa, to actually purge the heathen temples and centers of worship in Judah, but Abijah at least deserves credit for starting the reform.

Abijah's greatest concern during the reform was stopping the pattern of complete monopoly which heathen idolatry was attempting to achieve in all parts of the land. Therefore, when Abijah had attained a semblance of reform in Judah he decided to launch a reform project among the northern tribes as well. To achieve this he took a large army into that territory and forthwith called upon Jeroboam and the people to repent. Here indeed was a new way to do missionary work!

118. Quoted by Adam Clarke, *Bible Comemntary*, Vol. 2, p. 654
119. 2 Chronicles 11:20   121. 1 Kings 15:1-2
120. 2 Chronicles 13:2   122. 1 Kings 15:3

It also turned out to be a rather hazardous thing to do because when he arrived in the valleys of Mount Ephraim he discovered that Jeroboam was facing him with an army twice the size of his own.[123] Nevertheless, Abijah climbed to the top of a mount where he could shout down at the assembled hosts of Israel on the other side. This unusual acoustical phenomenon where a speaker from a high position can be clearly heard by those a long distance below made it possible for the king of Judah to deliver his message to a large host at one time.[124] Said he:

"Hear me, thou Jeroboam, and all Israel; ought ye not to know that the Lord God of Israel gave the kingdom over Israel to David for ever. . . . Yet Jeroboam the son of Nebat . . . is risen up and hath rebelled against his lord. And there are gathered unto him vain men, the children of Belial. . . . And now ye think to withstand the kingdom of the Lord in the hand of the sons of David; and ye be a great multitude, and there are with you golden calves, which Jeroboam made you for gods. Have ye not cast out the priests of the Lord, the sons of Aaron, and the Levites, and have made you priests after the manner of the nations of other lands? so that whosoever cometh to consecrate himself with a young bullock and seven rams, the same may be a priest of them that are no gods.

"But as for us, the Lord is our God, and we have not forsaken him; and the priests which minister unto the Lord, are the sons of Aaron, and the Levites wait upon their business . . . for we keep the charge of the Lord our God; but ye have forsaken him. And, behold, God himself is with us for our captain, and his priests with sounding trumpets to cry alarm against you. O children of Israel, FIGHT YE NOT AGAINST THE LORD GOD OF YOUR FATHERS, FOR YE SHALL NOT PROSPER!"[125]

---

123. 2 Chronicles 13:3. Authorities point out that there is good reason to believe that one cipher was added to all the military figures given in this chapter. Thus, Judah had 40,000 men (not 400,000), and Israel had 80,000 men (not 800,000), and the casualties were 50,000 (not 500,000). See Clarke, *Bible Commentary*, pp. 657-658.
124. I have spoken from the top of the Pyramid of the Sun near Mexico City and had my words clearly and distinctly understood several blocks away even though I was speaking at a level of projection appropriate for an ordinary assembly hall.
125. 2 Chronicles 13:4-12

This was a noble speech but it fell on deaf ears. In fact, it appears to have been a much longer speech than the version recorded in the Bible, and all the while Abijah was making his plea the cynical Jeroboam was redeploying his troops. He would teach Judah to call Israel to repentance! Jeroboam ordered half his men to quietly go around the mount and come up behind the forces of Abijah so as to cut them off from their homeland to the south. While Abijah was calling Jeroboam to repentance Jeroboam was preparing for a massacre.

The hosts of Judah had good reason to be terrified when they saw what was happening. The force in front of them was as large as their own and so was the force behind them. They were trapped by a host twice their size. If they had felt dependent on the Lord in the past, they certainly had reason to feel dependent upon Him now. The whole army of Judah cried out to the Lord to help them.[126] Then the priests blew their trumpets for attack and with a great shout they charged into the foe. Fortunately, they had not asked golden calves or other dumb idols for help, but had addressed themselves to the one source of power which could truly rescue them. As they pressed forward to do their best to fight their way out, the Lord more than made up for the odds which were against them. He intervened with divine power which smote "Jeroboam and all Israel." We have no idea what the Lord did that "smote" them but it must have been devastating for the number of the Israelites slain is given as being larger than the total number of Judah's whole army.[127]

In consequence of this victory, King Abijah of Judah declared the shrine city of Bethel as well as the cities of Jeshanah and Ephraim to be spoils of Judah.[128] For many years they were occupied as military posts of the southern kingdom.

As for Jeroboam, he never did recover his political strength nor his physical health after he was smitten. The scripture says "the Lord struck him, and he died."[129] However, he did not die suddenly. We know he lingered for

---

126. 2 Chronicles 13:14
127. 2 Chronicles 13:17. See note 123.
128. 2 Chronicles 13:19
129. 2 Chronicles 13:20

approximately four years before he finally passed away. The war with Abijah was in the eighteenth year of his reign[130] and he died after ruling twenty-two years.[131]

Meanwhile, as we have already mentioned, Abijah's life suddenly terminated after he had ruled Judah for only three years.[132] In fact Abijah died around 902 B.C. which was two years before the demise of Jeroboam. Abijah left a large family behind him. He had fourteen wives who gave him twenty-two sons and sixteen daughters.[133] The scripture says, "And the rest of the acts of Abijah, and his ways, and his sayings, are written in the story of the prophet Iddo."[134] As we have mentioned already, this scripture is lost.

Now we cross over into a new century. Great changes were in store for the people of Israel.

---

130. 2 Chronicles 13:1
131. 1 Kings 14:20
132. 1 Kings 15:2
133. 2 Chronicles 13:21
134. 2 Chronicles 13:22

Scripture Readings and Questions on Chapter Eleven

Scripture Readings: 1 Kings, Chapter 11 to 14. Extra credit assignment, 2 Chronicles, chapter 11 to 13.

1—What three things marred the final years of Solomon's reign?

2—What word in the Bible indicates that Solomon's 700 wives were primarily political marriages?

3—Name three characteristics of Solomon "when he was old" which are symptomatic of chronic senility.

4—Who was it induced Solomon to allow heathen temples and shrines to be built in Israel?

5—What were the two characteristics of heathen worship which made idolatry much more serious than merely bowing down to graven images?

6—What tribe did Jeroboam belong to? How did he come to Solomon's attention?

7—When the prophet Ahijah came to Jeroboam, what did he promise him? What was God's warning to Jeroboam?

8—Did Jeroboam patiently wait for the purposes of the Lord to be fulfilled as David had done? What action did he take? What was the result?

9—Approximately what year did Solomon die? Did he have a very large posterity? Why is this surprising?

10—Where did Rehoboam go to be crowned king of Israel? What did the northern tribes demand of him? What was Rehoboam's reply?

11—Who became the king of the northern kingdom? Who became king of Judah? How many tribes in the northern kingdom? How many in the kingdom of the south?

12—What happened when Rehoboam prepared to unite the kingdom by force of arms? Whose advice did he follow? Was this to his credit?

13—What did Jeroboam do to create political centers in the northern kingdom? What did he do to unite the people religiously?

14—Where did the "man of God" come from who warned Jeroboam? What did he say? What happened?

15—What did Jeroboam do to find out what would happen to his sick son? Did this fool Ahijah? What did Ahijah say would happen to the boy?

16—What are three of the things Ahijah said would happen to Jeroboam? What was Jeroboam's reaction to this warning?

17—Why would the Pharoah of Egypt attack Rehoboam and Judah when Rehoboam's father had married a daughter of Pharaoh? Was the attack successful? What did the Pharaoh do to Judah?

18—Who was King Abijah of Judah? How did he start his reign?

19—What was unusual about the way Abijah called the northern kingdom to repentance? What happened while has was giving his speech? Did the Lord appear to be with Abijah at this time?

20—After Jeroboam was stricken, how long did he live? Did he outlive Abijah?

CHAPTER TWELVE

The Struggle Between Reform and Apostasy

We are now entering the era of Biblical history which might be called the "No Man's Land" of the scriptures. All Bible students have difficulty with this era when they first begin. The difficulty grows out of the fact that the threads of Israel's history now divide themselves not only into the separate kingdoms of Judah and Israel but also into the administrations of different kings, different cultural levels, different political alliances, and different religious levels. Names of kings, priests, and prophets keep popping in and out of the story so fast that the reader loses contact with his former frame of reference and may therefore become discouraged. It will be our purpose here to take the story a period at a time and endeavor to keep the names and events of both kingdoms as closely in parallel as possible.

It will be recalled that as of approximately 911 B.C., the greatgrandson of Solomon became king of Judah. His name was Asa.[1] Two years later the great apostate King Jeroboam of the northern tribes passed away and his son Nadab took over the throne of Israel. So as of that moment we there-

---

1. His line of descent was Solomon, Rehoboam, Abijah, Asa.

fore have two new kings in power: Asa in Judah and Nadab, son of Jeroboam, in Israel. By far the most significant of the two was Asa, who reigned 41 years, so we will use his life as the chronometer for the next generation.

ASA PROVES THAT RIGHTEOUSNESS BRINGS UNITY AND PEACE

Asa came to the throne of Judah after seeing his father, Abijah, finally repent of his idolatry, start a reform but die after an abortive reign of merely three years. Asa therefore launched an all-out campaign to finish the job his father had commenced. He began with a nation-wide program of tearing down all the images and idolatrous altars.[2] He seemed particularly anxious to remove all those symbols of apostasy which had been erected in the days of his "fathers"[3] — meaning the last few years of Solomon's reign, all of Rehoboam's reign, and the opening portion of Abijah's reign before he repented. He also began eliminating the male and female prostitutes who attended the pagan temples, groves, altars and shrines.[4]

Asa noticed that this great reform resulted in a new spirit of peace among the people which not only made them more contented and happy, but more industrious and prosperous.[5] He also recognized, however, that the evil ambitions of the pagan peoples around about might someday bring a breach of the peace. He therefore decided to use this interval of peace to build up all his territorial defenses and fortify the principal cities. Said he, "Let us build these cities, and make about them walls, and towers, gates, and bars, while the land is yet [in a state of peace] before us; because we have sought the Lord our God . . . and he hath given us rest on every side."[6]

---

2. 2 Chronicles 14:3
3. 1 Kings 15:12
4. Ibid. The standard version says, "sodomites," but the original Hebrew says "consecrated persons" and refers to both men and women who prostituted themselves "in practices of the greatest impurity." (See Clarke, *Bible Commentary*, Vol. 2, p. 444.)
5. 2 Chronicles 14:7
6. Ibid.

Asa organized and trained the people so they could defend themselves in case of attack. Not only did this include Judah, but the southern cities of Benjamin as well.[7]

War With Zerah, the Ethiopian

After ten years of peace and prosperity[8] there suddenly appeared on the scene the huge army of "Zerah the Ethiopian."[9] He came with a host of 100,000 men and 300 chariots.[10] Some authorities feel that this Zerah was actually the crown prince O-serek-on (or Osorkon) of Egypt who was known as the "King's son of Cush" or Ethiopia, because this country was a tributary to the house of the Pharaoh. The title was similar to the "Prince of Wales" designation for the crown prince of England. And since he was called "the King's son of Cush" or Ethiopia it is easily understood how he and his men might be called Ethiopians.[11] It is believed that Zerah or Zerek in the Bible is taken from the central portion of O-serek-on's name. If this analysis is correct, then Asa was being attacked by the son of Pharaoh Shoshenk (or Shishak) who had raided Judah and taken all her magnificent treasures in the days of Asa's grandfather, Rehoboam.[12]

Asa had endeavored to prepare himself for this eventuality and he had also taught his people righteousness that they might be entitled to a special blessing in a time of crisis. Therefore Asa pleaded with the Lord, "Help us, O Lord our God; for we rest on thee, and in thy name we go against this multitude. O Lord, thou art our God; let not man prevail against thee."[13] There is no indication of any advance promise of victory from the Lord, nevertheless the king and his people went forth to do their best.

7. 2 Chronicles 14:8. As noted earlier, authorities have discovered that apparently a cipher has been added to the military statistics in this part of the record. Therefore, Judah had a standing army of 30,000 (not 300,000), and the cities on the border of Benjamin had an additional 28,000 (not 280,000). This fits more logically with earlier military statistics indicating that the standing army for ALL ISRAEL was 288,000. (1 Chronicles 27:1)
8. 2 Chronicles 14:1
9. 2 Chronicles 14:9
10. Ibid. Here again we believe one cipher has been added to the military statistics. the figure of 1,000,000 should be 100,000.
11. See Geikie, *Hours With the Bible*, Vol. 4, p. 39.
12. 2 Chronicles 12:2-4
13. 2 Chronicles 14:11

Asa apparently marched his troops down the spine of the mountains of Judah and swept down from Hebron to the maritime plain at Mareshah near Gath. Here Zerah could have used his chariots and seemingly would have been at the best possible advantage. Nevertheless, "the Lord smote the Ethiopians before Asa, and before Judah; and the Ethiopians fled. And Asa and the people that were with him pursued them unto Gerar: and the Ethiopians were over-thrown, that they could not recover themselves: for they were destroyed before the Lord, and before his host; and they [the armed forces of Judah] carried away very much spoil."[14]

Asa also attacked many of the Philistine cities nearby which were in league with Zerah. Asa's army "smote also the tents of cattle, and carried away sheep and camels in abundance, and returned to Jerusalem."[15]

ASA RECEIVES A COMMAND AND OBEYS IT

As he triumphantly returned to the capital, a prophet of the Lord named Azariah appears for the first and only time in scripture and declared to King Asa:

"Hear ye me, Asa, and all Judah and Benjamin: The Lord is with you, while ye be with him; and if ye seek him, he will be found of you; but if ye forsake him, he will forsake you."[16] The prophet then pointed out that whenever Israel had been "without the true God, and without a teaching priest, and without law,"[17] there had been war and vexations. He therefore urged Asa to completely purge the land of idol-worship (which he had vigorously begun to do at the start of his reign) and continue strengthening the administration of the Aaronic Priesthood. If they did this the Lord promised a special blessing would be available to them in a time of crisis similar to the one they had just received. In other words, when the people are righteous they can expect peace most of the time, but if occasionally there is war, God will be their helper.

---

14. 2 Chronicles 14:12-13
15. 2 Chronicles 14:15
16. 2 Chronicles 15:2
17. 2 Chronicles 15:3

So Asa cleansed the land of the Asherahs, which were the pagan shrines and groves;[18] and he also tore down and burned the Ashtoreths, which were the female images of the Phoenician "love goddess," known in other pagan nations as Ishtar, Venus, Aphrodite or Astarte.[19] In order to do this effectively, Asa had to search out the heathen haunts in the vicinity of every city, town and village under his jurisdiction. At this particular time his kingdom included all of Judah, part of Benjamin and certain cities in southern Ephraim.[20] Later on in this chapter we will discuss the sensual fertility rites which made Baal-worship and Ashtoreth-worship such an abomination before the Lord.

The scripture says that this reform movement had such a wholesome effect upon the southern kingdom that it attracted the attention of the faithful followers of Jehovah in the northern kingdom. And because many of these hungered after righteousness they flocked to Judah with their families in great numbers. The record says they came particularly from Ephraim, Manasseh and Simeon.[21] Such a migration might very well account for the fact that several generations later we find living in Jerusalem such men as Lehi and Nephi, descendants of Manasseh[22] and the family of Ishmael, descendants of the tribe of Ephraim.[23] In fact, Laban, the record-keeper for the entire tribe of Joseph, was found in Jerusalem[24] at that time.

King Asa apparently felt that there had been such widespread apostasy among the people that there should be a renewing of covenants. He therefore "renewed the altar of the Lord, that was before the porch of the Lord [at the temple]"[25] and called a great conference for the fifteenth day of the third month.[26] When they had convened together the king took 700 oxen and 7,000 sheep and offered them as sacrifices,[27] many, no doubt, as peace-offerings so they could be eaten by the people in a sacred feast during the confer-

---

18. Peloubet's *Bible Dictionary* under "Asherah."
19. Ibid. under "Ashtoreth."
20. 2 Chronicles 15:8
21. 2 Chronicles 15:9
22. Alma 10:3
23. 1 Nephi 7:2 plus *Journal of Discourses*, Vol. 23, p. 184.
24. 1 Nephi 3:2-4; 5:16   26. 2 Chronicles 15:10
25. 2 Chronicles 15:8   27. 2 Chronicles 15:11

ence. Then they entered into a covenant to "seek the Lord God of their fathers with all their heart and with all their soul."[28] They promised that anyone found practicing the heathen fertility cults, human sacrifices, and other idolatrous indulgences would be put to death as required by the law of Moses.[29]

And just to set a good example, Asa went out to a place which was apparently on the slopes of the Mount of Olives and tore down the personal shrine of the queen-dowager, his grandmother.[30] She was Maachah, daughter of the infamous Absalom. She seems to have erected a phallic symbol or image of a reproductive organ in the grove dedicated to Ashteroth.[31] King Asa "destroyed her idol, and burnt it by the brook Kidron."[32] He also "removed her from being queen"[33] or more properly, from being queen-dowager, for she was the widow of Rehoboam, Asa's grandfather.

Asa gathered together all of the treasures that were dedicated to the Lord from the spoils of his father's battles and added these to his own so they could be placed in the temple.[34]

Then the scripture says there was another period of peace in the southern kingdom.[35] When war finally came again it did not emanate from Egypt or the Philistines but came from the northern kingdom of Israel. Therefore let us shift our attention up to Israel and see what had been happening there.

NADAB IS MURDERED BY BAASHA WHO THEN BECOMES KING OF ISRAEL

It will be recalled that when King Asa took over in Judah, his coronation was followed two years later by a change in the northern kingdom as Nadab, Jeroboam's son, was crowned

---

28. 2 Chronicles 15:12
29. 2 Chronicles 15:13; Exodus 22:20; Deut. 13:6-9
30. 2 Chronicles 15:16. This passage says Maachah was Asa's mother but it seems obvious that this should read "grandmother" since Abijah was Maachah's son (1 King 15:2) and Asa was the son of Abijah (1 Kings 15:8).
31. 1 Kings 15:13 plus Clarke, *Bible Commentary*, Vol. 2, p. 446
32. Ibid.
33. Ibid.
34. 2 Chronicles 15:18
35. 2 Chronicles 15:19. This verse says the peace lasted until after the 35th year of Asa's reign but this would be impossible. See note 46 for the suggested explanation for this verse and also 2 Chronicles 16:1.

king.[36] But Nadab had barely buried his father and become established on his throne when a secret conspiracy began gestating among his military leaders headed up by a commander from the tribe of Issachar named Baasha.[37]

It was in his second year as king while Nadab was besieging the Philistine city of Gibbethon,[38] that a military mutiny occurred and Nadab was assassinated by Baasha and his band. The military cadre then raced back up to the capital at Tirzah and slaughtered all the "house of Jeroboam."[39] The scripture says it was done "according unto the saying of the Lord, which he spake by his servant Ahijah the Shilomite.[40] This prophecy had said that those which were slain would be left lying in the streets in their blood, to be devoured by the mongrel dogs of the town. And those who were slain in the field would not be buried but would be left for the vultures and carrion birds to feast upon.[41] So this is what Baasha and his band inflicted on the children and kinsmen of Jeroboam and Nadab.

But this man Baasha was certainly no improvement as a ruler when he made himself king. The scripture says, "And he did evil in the sight of the Lord, and walked in the way of Jeroboam, and in his sin wherewith he made Israel to sin."[42] Not only did Baasha glory in the power his murderous sword had brought him but he reveled in the vile and impure practices of the heathen debaucheries which had spread across the land. In such a state of mind it was inevitable that his lecherous attitude toward life would eventually gravitate toward war. He began plotting on the recapturing of certain cities from Judah and closing off the rich trade route which connected the two countries.[43]

It was at this point that an inspired prophet of God dared to come up out of Judah and call Baasha to an accounting. This prophet was Jehu, son of Hanani the seer.[44] Jehu told Baasha that if he continued the course he was following the same thing would happen to his posterity that had happened to the families of Jeroboam and Nadab. He said the

36. 1 Kings 14:20
37. 1 Kings 15:17
38. 1 Kings 15:27
39. 1 Kings 15:29
40. Ibid.
41. 1 Kings 14:11
42. 1 Kings 15:34
43. 2 Chronicles 16:1
44. 1 Kings 16:1; 2 Chronicles 16:7

word of God was as follows: "Behold, I will take away the posterity of Baasha, and the posterity of his house . . . Him that dieth of Baasha in the city shall the dogs eat; and him that dieth of his in the field shall the fowls of the air eat."[45]

The literal gruesomeness of this foreboding prophecy was something Baasha should have thoroughly understood for he and his men had just done the same thing to the seed of Jeroboam and Nadab. The question now was whether Baasha would risk bringing the same flood of blood on his own household. Amazingly, the answer was tantamount to a defiant "Yes!" Baasha bowed his neck and with the defiance of a mad bull charged down toward Judah. The scripture says, "Baasha king of Israel came up against Judah, and built Ramah, TO THE INTENT THAT HE MIGHT LET NONE GO OUT OR COME IN TO ASA KING OF JUDAH."[46] Ramah was about five miles north of Jerusalem flanking the main road.

As with East Berlin, there were many people fleeing from Israel to freedom and it was Baasha's intention to set up his own brand of Berlin wall to keep them from defecting to King Asa in Judah. As we have already noted, the scripture says, "for they fell to him [Asa] out of Israel in abundance, when they saw that the Lord his God was with him."[47] Among other things, this was a practice Baasha wanted to stop.

There is no doubt but what this political and economic embargo which Baasha now stubbornly enforced with the huge military resources of Israel, did indeed have a most serious impact upon Judah. This is borne out by the fact that King Asa of Judah did not dare to challenge Baasha directly nor did he even think to call on the Lord. In his excitement Asa used a most expensive and somewhat risky strategy. He attempted to divert Baasha from his Ramah project by

---

45. 1 Kings 16:3-4
46. 2 Chronicles 16:1. Note this passage says the event occurred in the 36th year of Asa's reign which would be impossible since by then Baasha would be dead. Dr. Clarke believes it should be 36 years since the "rending of the ten tribes from Judah," which would be the 16th year of Asa's reign or 859 B.C. and thereby brought into harmony with the rest of the account. See Clarke, *Bible Commentary*, Vol. 2, p. 663.
47. 2 Chronicles 15:9

having one of Baasha's allies attack him on the northern borders of the kingdom.

Asa achieved this political stratagem by first collecting together all of the remaining treasures from the temple and the king's palaces and then sending them by royal caravan to Ben-hadad, the king of Damascus, who was rapidly becoming a growing power in Syria. Of course Asa sent Ben-hadad a secret diplomatic dispatch along with the treasures. In the dispatch Asa said, "There is a league between me and thee, as there was between my father and thy father: behold, I have sent thee silver and gold; go, break thy league with Baasha king of Israel, that he may depart from me."[48]

Among the kings of those days there apparently was nothing which so persuasively demonstrated sincere friendship than a shipment of gold, silver and precious stones. Ben-hadad could remember no such gifts from Baasha. He therefore found no compunction whatever in suddenly turning against his neglectful friend Baasha and helping Asa, his cash-on-the-barrelhead friend from Judah. "And Ben-hadad hearkened unto King Asa, and sent captains of his armies against the cities of Israel; and they smote Ijon, and Dan, and Abel-maim, and all the store cities of Naphtali."[49]

This diversionary tactic worked precisely the way King Asa had hoped it would. The scripture says, "And when Baasha heard it . . . he left off building of Ramah, and let his work cease."[50] King Asa moved right in as Baasha moved out. The Bible says, "Then King Asa made a proclamation throughout all Judah, none was exempted: and they took away the stones of Ramah, and the timber thereof, wherewith Baasha had builded; and King Asa built with them Geba of Benjamin, and Mizpah."[51]

Asa Learns He Has Offended the Lord

After such an illustrious beginning one would wish that Asa could have continued his earthly biography under the smiles of heaven. However, the frailties of the flesh had been asserting themselves for some time and the next thing

---

48. 2 Chronicles 16:3
49. 2 Chronicles 16:4

50. 2 Chronicles 16:5
51. 1 Kings 15:22

Asa knew, Hanani (the seer and father of Jehu who had warned Baasha), appeared before him with a message from the Lord:

"Because thou hast relied on the king of Syria, and not relied on the Lord thy God, therefore is the host of the king of Syria escaped out of thine hand. Were not the Ethiopians and the Lubims a huge host, with very many chariots and horsemen? yet because thou didst rely on the Lord, he delivered them into thine hand. For the eyes of the Lord run to and fro throughout the whole earth, to shew himself strong in the behalf of them whose heart is perfect toward him. Herein [by sending extravagant gifts to King Ben-hadad of Syria] thou hast done foolishly: therefore from henceforth thou shalt have wars."[52]

In the past Asa had been humble when he heard the word of the Lord and had hastened to obey. This time, however, he took offense at the words of Hanani. He resented having a religious leader counsel him on politics and therefore treated Hanani as a subversive influence who should be locked up so he would not disturb the tranquility of the kingdom. The scripture says, "Then Asa was wroth with the seer, and put him in a prison house; for he [Asa] was in a rage with him because of this thing. And Asa oppressed some of the people the same time."[53] This last phrase probably refers to a persecution of those who respected Hanani's preachings.

All of this was a reversal of the king's illustrious and exemplary conduct in the past. Nevertheless, it was very real, and to its victims, very ugly and unfair. But as regrettable as this might have been for Judah, it was nothing compared to the violence and bad government which the ten tribes had been getting up in Israel. Let us leave Asa a moment and bring the northern kingdom up to date.

THE FALL OF THE HOUSE OF BAASHA AND THE RISE OF THE HOUSE OF OMRI

It will be remembered that King Baasha of Israel had come down and fortified Ramah just north of Jerusalem as

---

52. 2 Chronicles 16:7-9   53. 2 Chronicles 16:10

a means of harrassing Judah. Then he had been forced to give up the project when Syria began attacking his northern borders as King Asa had requested. We have reason to believe this occurred around 895 B.C.[54] About nine years later, in 886 B.C., the frustrated and unrepentant King Baasha finally passed away and the throne of Israel was filled by his equally wretched son, named Elah.[55]

But Elah only lasted a part of two years. He and his kinsmen were all murdered just the way the prophet Jehu had predicted they would be.[56] The deed was done by a man named Zimri who had charge of half the king's chariots.[57] The circumstances were amazingly similar to those which occurred at the time Baasha had seized the throne by murdering young King Nadab. On that previous occasion the armies of Israel had been engaged in fighting the Philistine city of Gibbethon and it was there that Baasha had started an army insurrection and struck Nadab down. Now the armies of Israel were again fighting at Gibbethon and once more there were ambitious military men who considered this to be a most propitious time to murder their young king. But on this occasion the role of Baasha was being played by Zimri and the young king who was about to be the victim of the planned assassination was Baasha's son, Elah! Such is the irony of history.

Young Elah, however, apparently suspected nothing. He had been on the throne nearly two years exactly as young Nadab had been king for two years prior to his assassination. The scripture says King Elah had not gone to Gibbethon to fight but had remained in the capital city of Tirzah. At the moment he was in the house of his steward "drinking himself drunk."[58] For Zimri this was a perfect setup. The army was occupied at Gibbethon and here was young Elah rapidly sinking into a helpless stupor over his wine cups. Zimri and his comrades moved in on Elah so swiftly that he probably never quite knew what happened.

---

54. See footnote no. 46.
55. 1 Kings 16:8. This passage says Elah became king in the 26th year of Asa's reign. Since 911 B.C. was the first year of Asa's reign this fixes Elah's regal inauguration at 886 B.C.
56. 1 Kings 16:3-4, 12
57. 1 Kings 16:9
58. Ibid.

In an instant Elah matriculated from being dead drunk to being just plain dead. Zimri slew him without mercy and then he and his gang raided every corner of the city slaughtering all of the king's "kinsfolks" and "friends."[59]

But one thing Zimri had not anticipated and that was the hostility of the army toward the thing he had done. When news of it was carried to Israel's siege troops at Gibbethon they were furious. They promptly rejected Zimri as king and crowned their own "captain of the host" as king. His name was Omri.[60] Then they angrily left off besieging the Philistines at Gibbethon and marched en masse to Tirzah where they laid siege to Zimri.[61] The city had few defenders so Zimri knew that under these circumstances his cause was doomed. As the gates and walls began crumbling away and Zimri knew "that the city was taken . . . he went into the palace of the king's house, and burnt the king's house over him with fire, and died."[62] His reign lasted exactly seven days.[63]

Of course, when this was accomplished Omri expected to replace Zimri as king but he suddenly found himself facing an ambitious competitor. The man's name was Tibni the son of Ginath who was very popular with about half the people. These supporters wanted to make Tibni king instead of Omri.[64] There was an immediate division among the people and it seems to have remained so for approximately five years.[65] Finally, however, Tibni was either killed or died a natural death and thereafter Omri became the king of all the ten tribes of Israel and the founder of a new dynasty which became the most evil of all the evil dynasties which

59. 1 Kings 16:11
60. 1 Kings 16:16
61. 1 Kings 16:17
62. 1 Kings 16:18
63. 1 Kings 16:15
64. 1 Kings 16:21
65. 1 Kings 16:23. This verse says Omri began ruling in the 31st year of Asa whereas 1 Kings 16:10 says the overthrow of Elah and Zimri (which led to Omri's becoming king) occurred in the 27th year of Asa's rule. This discrepancy is explained by Rabbi Jarchi as follows: "The division of the kingdom between Tibni and Omri began in the twenty-seventh year of Asa; this division lasted five years, during which Omri had but a share of the kingdom, which he held seven years; this was in the thirty-first year of Israel; twelve years in the whole." (Quoted by Clarke, *Bible Commentary,* Vol. 2, p. 450) Note that if the quarrel between Omri and Tibni began in the 27th year of Asa and extended to the 31st year it would constitute 5 years, i.e., the 27th, 28th, 29th, 30th and 31st.

cursed this period of Israel's history. Even foreign nations would carve on their tablets and obelisks specific references to the "House of Omri."

OMRI BUILDS A NEW CAPITAL AT SAMARIA

Omri maintained his capital at Tirzah for six years[66] but either because Zimri had burned down the royal palace or because of prospective political advantages, Omri decided to build a completely new capital called Samaria just a few miles west of Tirzah.[67] This latest venture completed a triangle of three capitals built thus far by Israel's kings. The first one was at Shechem, followed by Tirzah to the northeast, and now by Samaria to the northwest. All three are within a circumference of ten miles.

The newest capital was a hill bought by Omri from a man named Shemar.[68] Josephus points out that the city built on this hill was called by Omri "Semarion, but named by the Greeks Samaria; but he himself called it Semarion, from Semar, who sold him the mountain whereon he built it."[69] Today the city is called *Sebastia*, a name given to it by Herod the Great in honor of Augustus Caesar.[70]

Dr. Geikie describes the location of this new capital: "Six miles north-west from Shechem, a well-watered valley, which is, in fact, a continuation of that in which Shechem itself stands, opens out into a lovely plain, about five miles across, embosomed among green hills. In the centre of this there rises, like a boss on a great buckler, an oblong and almost entirely isolated hill, of white limestone, on the height of about four hundred feet. . . . The soft hills that surround it on all sides, beyond the velvet plain, are among the richest of Palestine, and are intersected by a network of fertile valleys, larger and smaller. . . . The palace and citadel occupied the top of the hill, and the town, hereafter the Samarina of the Assyrians, extended down its slopes; a strong wall, along the top of which ran a broad path, encircling the whole. From the palace above the town, Omri could look away to

---

66. 1 Kings 16:23
67. 1 Kings 16:24
68. Ibid.
69. Josephus, *Antiquity of the Jews*, Book 8, Chapter 12:5
70. Clarke, *Bible Commentary*, Vol. 2, p. 450

the Mediterranean on the west, the crest of the hill being more than 1,500 feet above its level. On the other sides there was a varied panorama of rounded hills and gentle valleys. On the south was the royal 'paradise' with its springs and rich gardens."[71]

The modern visitor to this site will have to use his imagination to resurrect the grandeur that once embellished the rugged nakedness of these hills and valleys which too often reflect the passing centuries of abject neglect. However, this author noted on a recent visit to this region that the conservation work by the Jordan Government is restoring some of its lost grandeur and it is now far less difficult to envision what it must have been like in the centuries of its glory.

PHOENICIAN PAGANISM GAINS A MONOPOLY IN THE NORTHERN KINGDOM

Omri gratified his personal pride by making his capital at Samaria a duplication of the extravagant palaces of the empire nations which were growing up around him. He was particularly taken up with the splendid architecture and opulence of the Phoenician cities of Tyre and Sidon. Not only did he adopt Phoenician architecture and embellishments but also her manners and ways. From here on the whole culture of northern Israel took on the pattern of pagan Phoenicia rather than the enlightened guidance of the Lord's chosen prophets. Conditions had been abominable before but now they became worse. The scripture says, "Omri wrought evil in the eyes of the Lord, and did worse than all that were before him."[72] The "statutes of Omri" (Micah 6:16) are supposed to refer to his laws favoring idolatry and opposing Jehovah-worship. By more extensively paganizing his own country, and thereby building a closer alliance with Phoenicia, Omri created a commercial partnership which launched northern Israel on the road to a decadent but plush prosperity boom. Omri died around the year 874 B.C. and his more famous son, Ahab, thereafter ruled in his stead.

Ahab, as it turned out, had a long reign of twenty-two years but the real ruler of the country during this perfidious

---

71. Geikie, *Hours With the Bible*, Vol. 4, pp. 46-47   72. 1 Kings 16:25

period was Ahab's wife, the notorious Jezebel. She was the daughter of Ethbaal, king of Tyre and Sidon (Phoenicia).[73] It must have pleased Ethbaal to get his country tied up with Israel since his own country had just gone through a period of turmoil. "King after king had been dethroned and murdered, till at last Ithobaal, or Ethbaal, A PRIEST OF ASHTORETH, had seized supreme power, after murdering his brother, Phalles.[74] Such was Ethbaal the father of Jezebel, so it is understandable why she came to Samaria hating Jehovah, despising Jehovah's prophets and determined to bind Israel so tightly to the fertility cults of Ashtoreth (the Venus Goddess of Phoenicia) that Jehovah-worship would be dead forever. For her own profligate purposes, Jezebel scarcely could have discovered a more responsive tool than the reprobate Ahab. He comes projected to us through history in the sad image of a spineless sop whose sponge-like character hungrily absorbed all the evil of his carnal wife, Jezebel, and made available to her the power of Israel's throne to execute the many venal schemes continually conjured up by this conniving woman.

Such appears to have been the situation in Israel when word came up from Judah that Asa, the ruler of the southern kingdom for 41 years, was dying.

The Last Days of Asa and
Rise of Jehoshaphat

Asa, the great grandson of Solomon, is said to have spent the last several years of his life suffering from a severe affliction in his lower limbs. The painful malady sounds as though it might have been some type of feverish inflammation caused by rheumatism or gout. The Bible says, "And Asa in the thirty and ninth year of his reign was diseased in his feet, until his disease was exceeding great: yet in his disease he sought not to the Lord but to the physicians."[75]

Two more years of misery elapsed and then, in his 41st year as the ruler of Judah, Asa passed away.[76] "And

---

73. 1 Kings 16:31 calls Ethball king of the "Zidonians" (people of Sidon) but Josephus says he was actually king of the whole country. (Josephus, *Antiquity of the Jews*, Book 8, chapter 13:2)
74. Geikie, *Hours With the Bible*, Vol. 4, p. 50
75. 2 Chronicles 16:12　　　　　76. 2 Chronicles 16:13

they buried him in his own sepulchres, which he had made for himself in the city of David, and laid him in the bed which was filled with sweet odours and divers kinds of spices prepared by the apothecaries' art: and they made a very great burning [of sacrifices] for him."[77]

For the most part this great grandson of Solomon had been a good king and Judah prospered under him. However, in his latter days he faltered like each of his famous progenitors and went to the grave a little less honored in history than he might have been otherwise.

Asa was fortunate, however, in having raised a son worthy of his own best self. This was Jehoshaphat who took over the throne on the death of his father around 870 B.C.[78] So while Ahab and Jezebel were ambitiously engaged in a campaign to corrupt the northern kingdom of Israel, Jehoshaphat was busy in the south endeavoring to duplicate the pattern of his father's earlier years in Judah. He fortified all of the principal cities,[79] bolstered the patriotic spirit of the people with military training,[80] and elevated the spiritual tone of the whole country.[81] Jehoshaphat's program was more extensive than his father's, however. It included a well organized system of education and a vast array of commercial undertaking similar to the program initiated by Solomon.

The king's educational program consisted of assigning many of the Levites to the role of "teachers" who organized themselves and began practicing in every city of Judah.[82] The basic text for this educational program was "the book of the law of the Lord"[83] and the teaching was done under the supervisory direction of two leaders of the Aaronic Priesthood identified as Elishma and Jehoram.[84]

The king's dynamic commercial enterprising was equally successful. Before long "he had much business in the cities of Judah"[85] and as the wealth of the country increased, "he built in Judah castles and cities of store."[86]

---

77. 2 Chronicles 16:14
78. 2 Chronicles 17:1 plus chronological chart at the front of this book.
79. 2 Chronicles 17:2
80. 2 Chronicles 17:13-19
81. 2 Chronicles 17:3-4
82. 2 Chronicles 17:7-9
83. 2 Chronicles 17:9
84. 2 Chronicles 17:8
85. 2 Chronicles 17:13
86. 2 Chronicles 17:12

The surrounding nations became increasingly astonished at this unexpected advance in the affluence and stability of Judah. They were impressed by her well-trained troops, her manifestation of growing prosperity and her internal unity. So, "the fear of the Lord fell upon all the kingdoms of the lands that were round about Judah, so that they made no war against Jehoshaphat."[87] Things improved even further. The king began receiving gifts from nearby princes who seemed anxious to maintain a mutually agreeable peaceful coexistence. The scripture says, "Also some of the Philistines brought Jehoshaphat presents, and tribute silver; and the Arabians brought him flocks, seven thousand and seven hundred rams, and seven thousand and seven hundred he-goats."[88] The people of Judah likewise seemed anxious to put more power in the hands of their king so "all Judah brought to Jehoshaphat presents; and he had riches and honour in abundance."[89]

At this point we observe an interesting phenomenon occurring. The southern kingdom of Judah is found to be prospering because of righteousness while the northern kingdom will be remembered as having prospered because of Ahab's alliances with wicked men in heathen nations. Obviously, there are different kinds of prosperity. From this we may gain an important lesson.

Ahab and Jezebel Completely Corrupt the Northern Kingdom

The prosperity of the northern kindgom of Israel was of the Gadianton variety. It was based on a corrupt king, a system of corrupt judges, a corrupt priestcraft and a close alliance with Ethbaal, a priest of Ashteroth who had won the throne of Phoenicia by murdering his own brother. Anyone who was not part of the system was outlawed. One can imagine the perfidy and intrigue which became rampant in such a society. The scripture says, "And Ahab the son of Omri did evil in the sight of the Lord ABOVE ALL THAT WERE BEFORE HIM."[90] It may be recalled that

---

87. 2 Chronicles 17:10
88. 2 Chronicles 17:11

89. 2 Chronicles 17:5
90. 1 Kings 16:30

his father Omri broke all the records for evil[91] and now the son had exceeded the father.

After he had married Jezebel, daughter of King Ethbaal, Ahab erected a "house of Baal" in the capital city of Samaria and placed an altar to Baal inside of it.[92] Then he made a grove in which the people could indulge in immoral practices around a phallic symbol dedicated to the love goddess, Ashteroth.[93] The scripture says, "And Ahab did more to provoke the Lord God of Israel to anger than all the kings of Israel that were before him."[94]

As one might expect, the few remaining servants of God who had not fled to Judah earlier could not refrain from emitting a cry of anguish at this institutionalizing of profligate degeneracy performed in the name of religion. And it appears that the Lord suddenly did something in Israel for the first time. He flooded the few righteous of Israel with revelation. Priesthood channels had so completely broken down that every man had to stand on his own witness rather than wait for divine direction to come through a presiding High Priest or some other person with the principal prophetic calling. The keys by this time were in the hands of a great prophet named Elijah who will appear on the scene shortly, but it is obvious that most of the time he was completely out of touch with whatever remnants of righteousness remained in the country for they all carried a death sentence on their heads.

We learn from a later scripture that this order to exterminate all prophets and Priesthood functionaries who protested the paganizing of Israel came from none other than Jezebel, Ahab's vulgar and sensuous queen.[95] No doubt she had Ahab issue the mandate so as to make it an official decree, but little did either Ahab or Jezebel realize that right in their midst was a man, of the royal palace, who bitterly opposed what they were doing to the country. When the king's mandate against God's servant went forth, this gov-

---

91. 1 Kings 16:25
92. 1 Kings 16:32
93. 1 Kings 16:33. This is the meaning of the word "grove" as translated in the King James Version. See Peloubet's *Bible Dictionary* under Ahab, p. 18.
94. Ibid.
95. 1 Kings 18:4. Note that it was she who "cut off the prophets."

ernor or king's steward named Obadiah, personally "took an hundred prophets, and hid them by fifty in a cave, and fed them with bread and water."[96] The bread, no doubt, came from the king's stores!

WHY IS THE LORD SO EASILY OFFENDED BY HEATHEN IDOLATRY?

One of the baffling things which can often puzzle Bible students is the vehement attitude which the Lord consistently takes against idolatry. The Lord told his ancient prophets that any person promoting or participating in such practices was to be dispatched back to the spirit world. Was this really necessary? Idolatry to most people simply means praying to a rock, a stone, an animal, a statue or some manmade image. And because this is so often done by ignorant, primitive peoples, the student may indeed get the impression that God is too harsh in denouncing such simple deviations from His First Commandments. After all, what real harm is there in it?

But God knows his children better than they know themselves. He is fully aware that simple deviations whereby men attribute good things to a rock, a statue, a rabbit's foot, a lock of hair, a golden calf, a relic, a saint, or a fairy, are not in and of themselves irreparably damaging. However, it is not the simple beginning but the tragic ending which the Lord has seen robbing men of their salvation by the millions down through the centuries. This is the reason for the great commandment resounding from Mount Sinai: "THOU SHALT HAVE NO OTHER GODS BEFORE ME!"[97]

It has been a serious mistake for secular scholars to attribute to Jehovah the petty jealousy of a pinched up tribal god who fears the competition of golden calves, rocks and images. God has said himself that he is a jealous God,[98] but this is not the jealousy of a Superior Being seeking blind adoration from the human race to feed a cosmic ego. Rather it is the anxiety of a Divine Parent who must zealously guard the well-being of these hundreds of millions of offspring whom He not only loves but in whom He has invested literally

96. Ibid.
97. Exodus 20:3
98. Exodus 20:5

aeons of effort to bring them to their present critical point of advancement. Of this He is *terribly* jealous, and idolatry is therefore not merely a simple deviation but a point of departure from the pathway of eternal progression onto the slippery slide of eternal retrogression.

What Was the Origin of Heathen Idolatry?

We are now able to trace in considerable detail the main tap root which produced the many branches of heathen philosophy and idolatrous practices. It had its beginning within three generations after the Great Flood and its principal architect was the grandson of Ham, a man named Nimrod. We have discussed this problem in an earlier book, *The First 2,000 Years*, but for the convenience of the reader we will repeat the highlights here.

Nimrod was the grandson of Ham through Cush.[99] He is described in the King James translation as "a mighty hunter before the Lord," [100] but the Inspired Version calls him "a mighty hunter *in the land*."[101] He gained this reputation, according to Josephus, because he was the leader in breaking away from the patriarchs, Noah and Shem, and building his cities and the Tower of Babel contrary to God's commands. Here is the way Josephus describes what happened in that early day, not at all unlike the spirit of the times engendered by Ahab and Jezebel:

"Now it was Nimrod who excited them to such an affront and contempt of God. He was the grandson of Ham, the son of Noah, a bold man, and of great strength of hand. He persuaded them not to ascribe it (their prosperity) to God as if it was through his means they were happy, but to believe that it was their own courage which procured their happiness. HE ALSO CHANGED THE GOVERNMENT INTO TYRANNY, SEEING NO OTHER WAY OF TURNING MAN FROM THE FEAR OF GOD, BUT TO BRING THEM INTO A CONSTANT DEPENDENCE ON HIS (Nimrod's) POWER. He also said he would be avenged of God, if He should have a mind

99. Genesis 10:8
100. Genesis 10:9
101. Inspired Version, Genesis 10:5-6

to drown the world again; for that he would build a tower too high for the waters to be able to reach! and that he would avenge himself on God for destroying their forefathers.

"Now the multitude were very ready to follow the determination of Nimrod, and to esteem it as a piece of cowardice to submit to God; and they built a tower, neither sparing any pains, nor being in any degree negligent about the work; and, by reason of the multitude of hands employed in it, it grew very high, sooner than anyone would expect; but the thickness of it was so great, and it was so strongly built, that thereby its great height seemed, upon the view, to be less than it really was. It was built of burnt brick, cemented together with mortar, made of bitumen, that it might not be liable to admit water."[102]

When the Tower of Babel was destroyed and the people were scattered abroad, Nimrod is given credit for expanding his grip on other major settlements until the Bible says, "the beginning of his kingdom was Babel, and Erech, and Accad, and Calneh in the land of Shinar."[103] By reading the marginal note it also will be observed that "he [Nimrod] went out into Assyria and built Ninevah, and the city Rehoboth, and Calah and Resen. . . ."[104] The land adjoining Assyria afterwards became known as "the land of Nimrod."[105] All this will give some idea of the tremendous political influence of this tyrannical personality in the early history of the world. The manner in which he accomplished his purposes is described in the Jewish Targum or paraphrased version as follows: "Nimrod began to be a mighty man in sin, a murderer of innocent men, and a rebel before the Lord."[106]

And just as Ahab and Jezebel later exploded emotionally when the servants of God opposed them, so did Nimrod. The Jerusalem Targum says he went up and down the land seeking to persuade "the children of men in their languages; and he said unto them, DEPART FROM THE RELIGION

---

102. Josephus, *Antiquity of the Jews,* Book 1, chapter 4:2-3
103. Genesis 10:10
104. Genesis 10:11, 12
105. Micah 5:6
106 .Quoted in Clarke, *Bible Commentary,* Vol. 1, p. 84

OF SHEM, AND CLEAVE TO THE INSTITUTES OF NIMROD."[107]

WHAT WERE THE INSTITUTES OF NIMROD?

As we have already seen, Josephus is the authority for saying that Nimrod did everything he could to belittle God as he endeavored to destroy man's confidence in Him.[108] He did not deny His existence. He just said God wasn't important in the lives of the people. He said men were their own benefactors and didn't need to thank God for the prosperity which they, themselves, had worked so hard to acquire.

Here is the cornerstone of heathen worship — *to place men above God*. This is done in two steps: first, deprecating either the existence or importance of God, and secondly, replacing the adoration of God with the worshiping of individual men.[109] This was exactly what Nimrod undertook to do. As a well-known Jewish scholar writes, "And not all this sufficed unto Nimrod's evil desire. Not enough that he turned men away from God, he did all he could to make them pay divine honors unto himself. HE SET HIMSELF UP AS A GOD, and made a seat for himself in imitation of the seat of God. It was a tower built out of a round rock, and on it he placed a throne of cedar wood, upon which arose, one above the other, four thrones, of iron, copper, silver and gold. Crowning all, upon the golden throne, lay a precious stone, round in shape and gigantic in size. This served him as a seat, and as he sat upon it, all nations came and paid him divine homage."[110]

Other conquerors imitated Nimrod. In due process of time the worship of these men completely obscured the existence of the Almighty insofar as the worshiping masses were concerned. The deifying of human beings is one of the chief characteristics of heathen religions whether in Egypt, Babylon, Greece, Rome, China or India. This was a major device in the "Institutes of Nimrod."

---

107. Ibid.
108. Josephus, *Antiquity of the Jews,* Book 1, chapter 4:2
109. The modern student will see these exact devices working today. It is exemplified in the professional cleric who uses his pulpit to preach, "God is Dead!" In the next breath he says, "Come follow me." It is the ancient routine of replacing the worship of God by the worship of man.
110. L. Ginzberg, *The Legends of the Jews,* Vol. 1, p. 178

Another factor which is known to have been introduced into pagan institutes from the earliest times is the fiction that human beings are somehow influenced or controlled in their daily actions by the sun, moon and stars. These astronomical bodies were credited with the power to bestow special gifts, tastes, tendencies and qualities of personality upon each person. If a person were born under a particular sign of the Zodiac he was told that throughout his life he would be under the influence of certain astrological forces and *there was nothing he could do about it!*

This destroyed the basic concept of "free agency" and personal responsibility for conduct. Whatever evil a person did he could always excuse himself by blaming it on the stars. As Jeremiah declared in his day: "Thus saith the Lord, Learn not the way of the heathen, and be not dismayed at the signs of heaven; for the heathen are dismayed at them."[111] On a number of occasions the prophets refer to the superstitious adherence of heathen nations to the principles of astrology.[112]

Another characteristic of heathen worship from earliest times was the elevating of animals above humanity. In the beginning the Lord had said to man, "The fear of you, and the dread of you shall be upon every beast of the earth, and upon every fowl of the air, upon all that moveth upon the earth, and upon all the fishes of the sea; *into your hand are they delivered.*"[113]

But the inventors of the heathen institutes delivered human beings over to the real or fancied whims of animals. In many cases animal life was made more sacred than human life, and humans were sacrificed to animal gods. Anyone who has visited the tombs of the sacred Apis-bulls in Egypt where these creatures were embalmed and buried in huge granite vaults at fantastic cost and human effort will realize what monstrous abuses the heathen animal cults have imposed on nations.

So Nimrod and others like him first destroyed the worship of the one true God, then they made themselves into

---

111. Jeremiah 10:2
112. For example, Isaiah 47:13; Daniel 1:20; 2:27; 4:7; 5:7.
113. Inspired Version, Genesis 9:8

gods, then they robbed the people of their sense of free will and finally they made them feel inferior to the dumb brutes of the animal world. In the process of inculcating these attitudes in the minds of the people every teaching aid possible was utilized. Image-worship was employed to represent God in stone and then the stone was worshipped. Other times self-appointed god-men like Nimrod had the people worship their images. The images of animals were worshipped, especially the golden bullock or calf. Images representing the sun, moon and stars automatically grew out of sun-worship and astrology. And in the case of Baal-worship and the Ashtoreth or goddess-love cults, the most obscene symbols were employed to promote the degraded immorality required in fertility worship. Such were the ramifications of so-called "idolatry."

WHAT MADE THE HEATHEN RELIGIONS SO POPULAR?

Nimrod, as we have seen, is alleged to have told his people, "Depart from the religion of Shem, and cleave to the institutes of Nimrod!" What would he conjure up to make his institutes the best possible means of seducing the masses away from the Priesthood under Shem and the practices of righteous living invoked by God? The answer was not so much in the philosophy or the images but in the *ritual*.

Heathen ritual was frequently devoted almost exclusively to the stimulating and satisfying of human passions. The words *adultery* and *idolatry* both come from the same derivation.[114] The heathen religions institutionalized immorality. As one authority points out, "Sacramental fornication was a regular feature of [their] religious life."[115]

Throughout the entire land of Canaan fertility worship centered around Baal and Ashtoreth. Dr. Geikie describes the significance of these two names:

"The supreme god among the Phoenicians was the sun-god Baal. His worship had been long established in Canaan before the Israelites entered it, and, indeed, as we have seen, they had been familiar with it among the Phoenicians

---

114. Enc. Britannica (1952 edition) Vol. 18, p. 596
115. W.O.E. Oesterly, *Hebrew Religion*, p. 167

and Asiatic tribes in the Egyptian Delta. The name was equivalent to 'lord' and 'ruler,' for Baal governed the material universe, but it seems especially to have referred to his relation to Ashtoreth, his feminine counterpart, as her husband. . . . Baal was the symbol of creative power, for the sun was the great generative force in nature. Originally worshipped without any image, and typified only by pointed stone pillars embodying an obscene symbol, he was ultimately represented in a human form, riding on a bull, with bunches of grapes and pomegranates in his hands. The loftiest names were given him. He was king of the universe, the light of the gods, their creator, and father."[116]

The student will have little difficulty detecting the satanical cleverness of the insidious priestcraft cult which operated behind such a religious monstrosity. By taking the power and excellence of the one eternal God and attributing these qualities to a depraved patron of alluring debaucheries reflects the most sophisticated tactics in moral and spiritual subversion.

Then, of course, there was Baal's evil female counterpart, the love-goddess Ashtoreth, whose shrine, symbol or grove are variously referred to as "Ashera." Dr. Geikie says, "Her symbol was the rough trunk of a tree with some twigs left on it, and this was raised alongside the pointed stone pillars of Baal, though stone obelisks of small size, consecrated to her, were also raised before his altar."[117]

Some idea of the gross cultural pollution involved in the ritual at Ashera shrines may be gained from the following: "The central idea of the worship of Ashera was lewdness. At the feasts of the goddess . . . the high places, the sacred groves, the very roads, became scenes of universal prostitution; its gains made over to the temple treasuries. Every temple had, besides, at all times, great bands of women and mutilated men consecrated to impurity."[118]

Such was the way of life Jezebel and Ahab imposed on the people of Israel.

116. Geikie, *Hours With the Bible,* Vol. 3, pp. 390-392
117. Ibid. p. 392
118. Ibid. p. 398

Human Sacrifices

In addition to immorality the rapacious heathen priests highlighted certain festivals with human sacrifices, especially of children. This included such fiendish practices as those followed in the worship of Moloch. The metal image of this god had a furnace inside with roaring flames which heated the 'metal statue to a glowing hue. When the metal was red hot the priest placed a tiny infant in the cradled arms of the image where it was instantly roasted. "The parents stilled the cries of the intended victims by fondling and kissing them — for their weeping would have been unpropitious — and their shrieks afterwards were drowned in the din of flutes and kettle drums."[119]

The Bible is plain that the curse of child sacrifices to Moloch was one of the abominations which Israel borrowed from the heathens. As early as the time of Moses the Lord was compelled to cry forth, "Thou shalt not let any of thy seed pass through the fire to Molech!"[120] Later the Lord said, "And they have built the high places . . . to burn their sons and their daughters in the fire; which I commanded them not, neither came it into my heart."[121] One of the Psalms mourns over those terrible days:

"And they served their idols which were a snare to them.
Yea, they sacrificed their sons and their daughters unto devils.
And shed innocent blood, even the blood of their sons and their
    daughters,
Whom they sacrificed unto the idols of Canaan:
And the land was polluted with blood.
Thus were they defiled with their own works,
And went a whoring with their own inventions."[122]

Not only were children sacrificed but so were some adults, especially virgins who refused to submit themselves to the vile immorality of the heathen ritual. Abraham speaks of these practices in his day:

"Now, at this time it was the custom of the priest of Pharaoh, the king of Egypt, to offer up upon the altar which was built in the land of Chaldea, for the offering unto these strange gods, MEN, WOMEN, AND CHILDREN. . . .

---

119. Ibid. pp. 400-401
120. Leviticus 18:21

121. Jeremiah 7:31; See also 2 Kings 17:17
122. Psalms 106:36-39

Now, this priest had offered upon this altar three virgins at one time, who were the daughters of Onitah, one of the royal descent directly from the loins of Ham. These virgins were offered up BECAUSE OF THEIR VIRTUE; they would not bow down to worship gods of wood or of stone, therefore they were killed upon this altar, and it was done after the manner of the Egyptians."[123]

Sometimes the volume of human sacrifices was astounding. Dr. Geikie says, "The numbers burned were sometimes very large. The Carthaginians [Phoenicians who migrated to north Africa] we are told, having lost a battle, it was ascribed to the anger of Moloch (Saturn), to whom boys from the noblest families had formerly been offered, instead of boys bought and fed up for the purpose, as had come to be the rule. An enquiry having been made, it was discovered that a number of parents had hidden away their sons, and therefore two hundred boys from the first families were offered at once together; three hundred others voluntarily giving themselves up afterwards, as free-will offerings for the good of their fatherland. . . ."[124]

Human sacrifices were associated with many of the principal gods in addition to Moloch. Concerning Ashtoreth, the heathen goddess to whom Jezebel and Ahab were consecrated, we read, "Children were thrown by their mothers from the top of the temple walls during the fast of Ashtoreth, to be afterwards burnt on the altar."[125]

The Calling of a Prophet in the Days of Ahab and Jezebel

When we consider the total depravity which existed in those days, who can conceive of a much more deplorable and desperate time to be called to the ministry? Who would dare go? God needed a man with the humility of a Samuel, the stamina of a Samson and the courage of a David. He needed a hit-and-run prophet; a man who could suddenly appear on the ramparts of a city or the court of a king and

---

123. Abraham 1:8, 11
124. Geikie, *Hours With the Bible*, Vol. 3, pp. 401-402
125. Ibid, p. 400

at the risk of his life deliver a scalding pronouncement and then disappear in the night like a phantom of doom.

The world was ready for Elijah.

Scripture Reading and Questions on Chapter Twelve

Scripture Reading: 2 Chronicles, chapters 14 to 17 inclusive; 1 Kings, chapters 15 and 16.

1—What happened to the people of Judah when Asa began tearing down the heathen idols and altars?

2—Why is Zerah thought to be an Egyptian rather than an Ethiopian? Why would the Egyptians be unlikely to allow an Ethiopian to attack Palestine?

3—When righteous people are attacked, what did the Lord say they could expect by way of a special blessing?

4—Why did some of the people in the northern kingdom begin moving down to Judah? What does this suggest with reference to Lehi, Nephi and Laban?

5—Why do you think the Lord put the death penalty on those who promote idolatry?

6—What did a prophet say would happen to the house of Jeroboam? Was it literally fulfilled?

7—What was the object of Baasha in fortifying Ramah? What caused him to abandon the project?

8—What happened to the descendants of Baasha and his son, Elah? Who did it? What happened to him?

9—What was Omri's new capital named? What were the names of the other two capitals built by the kings of Israel?

10—Was King Omri righteous or wicked? What did he do?

11—In what way did Ahab break his father's record? What did he do?

12—What three things did Jehoshaphat do to strengthen Judah?

13—As Judah became strong what did the surrounding heathen nations do? Did the people of Judah do the same thing?

14—Whom did King Ahab of Israel marry? What country was she from? What kind of a person was her father?

15—What did Jezebel try to do to all the prophets in northern Israel?

16—According to Josephus and other ancient writers, who invented and originally promoted heathen religious philosophy and ritual?

17—What line of reasoning was used to depreciate God? Is it used today?

18—What means were used to discourage the exercise of willpower in overcoming evil? Is it used today?

19—What means were used to reverse God's commandment concerning the relationship between the animal kingdom and man?

20—What was done to make heathen religious practices popular? Did they succeed? Does this explain why God has been so vehement in opposing idolatry?

CHAPTER THIRTEEN

The Coming of the
Prophet Elijah

At the peak of the apostate administration of Ahab and his heathen wife, Jezebel from Phoenicia, there suddenly appeared at the royal palace in Samaria a man who dared to risk his very life by coming to deliver a message to the king which would bring a curse upon the land. This man was Elijah.

At a time when the school of the prophets had been but recently drowned in a tidal wave of blood and when a royal edict made resistance to the new state religion a capital offense, Elijah strode into the presence of the king and cried, "As the Lord God of Israel liveth, before whom I stand, there shall not be dew nor rain these years, but according to my word."[1]

In this unheralded and unexpected manner the great prophet Elijah suddenly flashes into view on the pages of history. His background is obscure. The Bible simply says he was "Elijah the Tishbite, who was of the inhabitants of Gilead."[2] This means that he came from the pastoral territory of Israel on the east side of the Jordan. However, nothing is given to identify his parents, his tribe, his birthplace or his

---

1. 1 Kings 17:1
2. Ibid.

original calling. Someday we may be able to identify the significance of the word, "Tishbite," but as of the moment the ravages of the passing centuries have robbed it of its original intent and meaning. It may refer to a town or village but if so the exact location is not known.

Were it not for modern revelation we would be as much in the dark concerning the mission of Elijah as the secular world, but fortunately we do have many additional nuggets of knowledge which disclose Elijah to have been a man of far greater importance than many had supposed. Note that modern revelation does not furnish us any additional details concerning Elijah's biography, but only regarding his mission.

The Calling of Elijah

We now know that Elijah was the man who held the complete depository of Priesthood keys for the building of the Kingdom of God in his day.[3] These keys included all of the higher powers delegated to the Melchizedek Priesthood. They are sometimes calling the sealing powers.[4] He had the power to seal up unto condemnation those who blasphemed against the message of the Gospel, and he had the power to seal up the righteous who accepted the Gospel.[5] He had the authority to administer the full temple service with all the higher ordinances and ceremonies reserved for the most advanced members of the Kingdom.[6] This authority included the administering of the holy Endowment and the revealing of those whose calling and election are made sure.[7]

He had the power to seal together a man and woman in marriage for time and all eternity; and to seal their children to them so that through righteousness they could return to the presence of their Heavenly Father and enjoy their family relationship together forever.[8]

Elijah's Priesthood authority included the power by which the heavens could be sealed against rain,[9] the power to

3. The most comprehensive discourse on the calling of Elijah is found in the *Documentary History of the Church*, Vol. 6, pp. 249-254.
4. Ibid. p. 251; See the full discussion of this point by Joseph Fielding Smith in *Doctrines of Salvation*, vol. 2, pp. 116-117.
5. *Documentary History of the Church*, Vol. 6, p. 252
6. Ibid. p. 251
7. Ibid. p. 252
8. Ibid. pp. 251-252
9. 1 Kings 17:1

raise the dead,[10] turn rivers of water back from their courses,[11] call down consuming fire from heaven,[12] move mountains from their foundations[13] and cause peace to come upon a storm-tossed sea.[14]

From the most ancient times God has been willing to give to certain of his most distinguished Priesthood holders the power to control the organized intelligences in nature. However, this power was given with the instruction that it was to be used only when God commanded it.[15] This remarkable power over nature which Elijah received was identical with that which was given to Enoch[16] before the Great Flood and to Moses[17] after the Flood. It was also given to certain of the prophets in ancient America. As one of them exclaimed, ". . . we truly can command in the name of Jesus and the very trees obey us, or the mountains, or the waves of the sea."[18]

Had Elijah lived in a time of righteousness he could have been an Enoch or a Moses to his people. He had all the keys necessary to organize the Church and to serve as President of the Church.[19] But as we have already seen, there was no room for the Church of the Living God in the

---

10. 1 Kings 17:21-22
11. Although Elijah did not use this power we know his Priesthood included this capacity and was exercised by others having a similar degree of authority. See Moses 7:13
12. 1 Kings 18:37-38
13. This power was part of Elijah's authority though he did not have occasion to use it. For examples of those who did, see Helaman 10:9; Moses 7:13.
14. 1 Nephi 18:21
15. In giving similar power to one of His prophets the Lord said, "And now, because thou hast done this with such unwearyingness, behold, I will bless thee forever; and I will make thee mighty in word and in deed, in faith and in works; yea, even that all things shall be done unto thee according to thy word, FOR THOU SHALT NOT ASK THAT WHICH IS CONTRARY TO MY WILL." (Helaman 10:5.) The verses following itemize the powers of this prophet showing them to be the same as those given to Elijah. In modern times the Lord also said, "And if ye are purified and cleansed from all sin, ye shall ask whatsoever you will in the name of Jesus and it shall be done. But know this, IT SHALL BE GIVEN YOU WHAT YOU SHALL ASK. . . ." (Doctrine and Covenants 50:29-30)
16. Moses 7:13
17. The power of Moses over the elements was manifested all through his ministry. Acting under direction from the Lord it included such things as turning a rod into a serpent and a serpent into a rod, cleansing a leprous hand (his own), turning water into blood, bringing in plagues upon the land, dividing the Red Sea, providing manna for food, providing quail for food, causing water to spring from solid rock, causing the earth to open up and consume his enemies.
18. Jacob 4:6
19. *Documentary History of the Church,* Vol. 6, p. 251.

region where Elijah was called to serve. It was only by divine intervention that he could even escape with his life. As a result, his great powers over nature were usually reserved for the blessing and aid of the few who were near him.[20] Only in the case of the calling down of fire from heaven[21] were the unrighteous masses allowed to behold an exhibition of the phenomenal power which God had delegated to this man. But even then, as we shall see later, it failed to touch their apostate hearts.

For our modern insight into the monumental mission of the prophet Elijah, we are indebted to an important sermon given by Joseph Smith on March 10, 1844, just a few months before his martyrdom. In this sermon he revealed many of the exciting and important facts which he personally had received concerning the mission and calling of Elijah. Among other things, he stated, "The spirit, power, and calling of Elijah is, that ye have power to hold the keys of the revelation, ordinances, oracles, powers and endowments of the fullness of the Melchizedek Priesthood and of the kingdom of God on the earth; and to receive, obtain, and perform all the ordinances belonging to the kingdom of God, even unto the turning of the hearts of the fathers unto the children, and the hearts of the children unto the fathers, even those who are in heaven. . . . Then what you seal on earth, by the keys of Elijah, is sealed in heaven; and this is the power of Elijah, and this is the difference between the spirit and power of Elias and Elijah; for while the spirit of Elias is a forerunner, the power of Elijah is sufficient to make our calling and election sure. . . . The spirit of Elijah was manifested in the days of the apostles, in delivering certain ones to the buffetings of Satan, that they might be saved in the day of the Lord Jesus. They were sealed by the spirit of Elijah unto the damnation of hell until the day of the Lord, or revelation of Jesus Christ [when those who had paid the uttermost farthing could be brought forth]. . . . The spirit of Elias is first, Elijah second, and Messiah last. Elias is a forerunner to prepare the way, and the spirit and power of Elijah is to come after, holding the keys of power, building the Temple

---

20. See for example, 1 Kings 17:14-15, 22-25.
21. 1 Kings 18:20-40

to the capstone, placing the seals of the Melchizedek Priesthood upon the house of Israel, and making all things ready;
then Messiah comes to His Temple, which is last of all.
Messiah is above the spirit and power of Elijah, for He
made the world, and was that spiritual rock unto Moses
in the wilderness. Elijah was to come and prepare the way
and build up the kingdom before the coming of the great
day of the Lord, although the spirit of Elias might begin it."[22]

THE TWO LEVELS OF PRIESTHOOD

There has been a great quantity of confusion down
through the centuries as to the difference between Elias and
Elijah. This confusion is glaringly displayed in the translation of the New Testament where both names are given
as though they were the same person.[23] In the above remarks
of Joseph Smith we gain a far deeper insight into the fact
that Elias and Elijah represent different callings, different
persons and different levels of Priesthood.

With specific reference to Elias, Joseph Smith stated,
"The spirit of Elias is to prepare the way for a greater revelation of God, which is THE PRIESTHOOD OF ELIAS,
or THE PRIESTHOOD THAT AARON WAS OR-
DAINED UNTO. And when God sends a man into the
world to prepare for a greater work, holding the keys of
the power of Elias, it was called the doctrine of Elias, even
FROM THE EARLY AGES OF THE WORLD."[24]

The fact that the lesser Priesthood was apparently called
the Priesthood of Elias before it was called the Aaronic
Priesthood is interesting from a historical standpoint, and
the fact that the lesser Priesthood was called after Elias
"from the early ages of the world," would strongly imply
that the original Elias lived in the more ancient dispensations
which in all probability were before the Great Flood.

Not until the restoration of the Gospel did we have any
hint as to the identity of the original Elias. As indicated
above, if the work of the original Elias were known in "the
early ages of the world," he must have existed before the

---

22. *Documentary History of the Church*, Vol. 6, pp. 251-254
23. See, for example, Luke 1:17
24. *Documentary History of the Church*, Vol. 6, p. 250

Great Flood, but we know that he also lived after the Flood for the scripture says he conferred the keys of authority on Abraham for his dispensation.[25] These known criteria seem to limit our selection to either Noah or Shem. As we shall see in a moment, the Lord indicates it was Noah. Noah lived 600 years before the Flood and 350 years afterwards.[26] He died when Abraham was approximately 28 years of age[27] so he could easily have given Abraham the keys for his dispensation.

The Lord's disclosure that Elias was Noah is rather casually inserted in one of the modern revelations and could be easily missed on first reading. The Lord let the secret out when he revealed that it was "Elias" who appeared to Zacharias to announce the birth of John the Baptist.[28] The Bible, of course, does not identify the angelic messenger who visited Zacharias as "Elias" but calls him "Gabriel."[29] However, Joseph Smith had already been told that "Gabriel" was the unresurrected spirit of the great prophet, Noah.[30]

Thus, the mystery appears to be resolved. These modern sources help us understand that the prophet who closed the dispensation before the Great Flood and is known to us as Noah also opened the Gospel dispensation after the Flood as a restorer. He laid the preparatory foundation for all that was to follow and was called Elias. Since then all other "restorers" or ministers of God's preparatory work have been called Elias. An article in the Church News, dated April 23, 1960, by Joseph Fielding Smith is entitled "Elias Is Noah." This article comes to the same conclusion as the above.

Of course, the scriptures identify a number of other prophets as "Elias" such as John the Baptist[31] and John the Revelator,[32] but each of these came to earth long after the original Elias ministered among men and it is apparent that the use of "Elias" in connection with them has reference to

---

25. *Doctrine and Covenants* 110:12
26. Genesis 7:6; 9:28
27. See *First 2,000 Years*, p. 347, 349-351 and chronological table at the end of the book.
28. *Doctrine and Covenants* 27:6-7
29. Luke 1:19
30. *Teachings of Joseph Smith*, p. 157
31. Matthew 17:10-13
32. *Doctrine and Covenants* 77:14

their office and calling as "forerunners" or as men who launched the preparatory work of a new gospel dispensation. The Inspired Version says that even the first coming of Jesus Christ was preparatory to His coming in glory and was therefore a mission or calling in the spirit of Elias.[33] From this it becomes apparent that many people who have fulfilled the role of an Elias which relates to the lesser Priesthood were people who actually possessed the higher or Melchizedek Priesthood at the time of their Elias calling.

We have already noted Joseph Smith's statement that the Priesthood of Elias was identical with the Priesthood of Aaron although both Elias (or Noah) and Aaron held the higher Priesthood. Their missions, however, were primarily focused in the preparatory ordinances and the laying of a foundation for greater things to come. They therefore functioned on this preparatory level of their Priesthood authority.

The higher level or the realization of "the greater things to come" is represented by Elijah. Elijah personified the "greater revelation of God" or Melchizedek Priesthood and all the keys and powers necessary to establish the fulness of the Kingdom of God on earth. As we shall see later, this is why Elijah was not allowed to die.[34] He was translated so that he could join with Moses (who also was translated[35]) in conferring their respective Priesthood keys on the heads of Peter, James and John as they met with Jesus on the Mount of Transfiguration.[36] Jesus could have given these keys to the apostles Himself, since they originated with Him, but the Lord's respect for orderly processes impelled Him to perpetuate the continuous chain of authority from Adam down to these men by having them confer their keys upon Peter, James and John in person. To do this, Elijah and Moses had to be "in the flesh" and since this transfer of power had to take place before the resurrection, it was necessary to keep Elijah and Moses "in the flesh" as translated beings. During modern times, Elijah and Moses both appeared in the Kirtland Temple to transfer their keys to Joseph Smith and

---

33. Inspired Version John 1:27-28
34. Joseph Fielding Smith, *Doctrines of Salvation*, Vol. 2, pp. 110-111
35. Ibid.
36. Ibid. p. 110; Matthew 17:1-13; *Teachings of Joseph Smith*, p. 158

Oliver Cowdery.[37] This time they came as resurrected rather than translated beings.[38]

Some readers may wonder about the frequent reference to the ancient prophets possessing the Melchizedek Priesthood. The general impression is that this higher Priesthood was completely lost to Israel after the incident of the golden calf. However, the higher Priesthood was only taken away from the body of the Israelites as a people. We now know that the Lord's chosen leadership throughout this period possessed the Melchizedek Priesthood.

After the golden calf incident Moses retained the higher Priesthood,[39] so did Aaron[40] and Joshua.[41] We learn from modern revelation that this was true of *all* of the prophets which the Lord personally raised up. Joseph Smith states, "All of the prophets [of ancient Israel] had the Melchizedek Priesthood and were ordained by God himself."[42] They also appear to have had the endowment and the higher ordinances for which the Lord says the Tabernacle of Moses and the Temple of Solomon were expressly built.[43]

So this was the exclusive group of outstanding Priesthood leadership to which Elijah belonged. Knowing this, it becomes easier to grasp the true quality of greatness which Elijah possessed. However, during his earth-life, Elijah felt anything but great. Most of his lifetime was spent working out his salvation in fear and trembling.

ELIJAH IN FLIGHT

When Elijah told King Ahab that the land of Israel which had just made idolatry its state religion was no longer going to be blessed with its seasonal rains, he was actually predicting a devastating plague of drouth and famine. It was precisely the same kind of prophecy young Abraham

---

37. *Doctrine and Covenants,* 110:11, 14
38. Ibid. 133:55
39. *Doctrine and Covenants* 84:25
40. See discussion in *The Third Thousand Years,* pp. 400-401
41. This is evident from the fact that Joshua received personal revelations from the Lord (Joshua 1:2-7) rather than the ministering of angels under the Aaronic order (See *Doctrines and Covenants,* section 13).
42. *Teachings of Joseph Smith,* p. 181
43. *Doctrine and Covenants,* 124:38-39

had made against the land of Ur when its leaders rejected the Gospel and the Priesthood in order to indulge themselves in idolatry and priestcraft.[44] It was also the kind of prophecy the Lord had told Moses the people could expect if they turned to worshiping man-made images and practicing the abominable heathen cultist rituals. Said the Lord, "Take heed to yourselves, that your heart be not deceived, and ye turn aside, and serve other gods, and worship them; and then the Lord's wrath be kindled against you, and HE SHUT UP THE HEAVEN, THAT THERE BE NO RAIN, and that the land yield not her fruit; and lest ye perish quickly from off the good land which the Lord giveth you."[45]

King Ahab and Queen Jezebel undoubtedly had been proud of the rising prosperity in Israel since their alliance with Jezebel's father in Phoenicia. But beneath all prosperity there must be a foundation of abundant agriculture. No amount of wealth, industry or commercial activity is of much significance if people are starving. And that was exactly what Elijah said the wickedness of Israel would bring down upon them. It was enough to make the enraged King Ahab want to commit murder. So "the word of the Lord came unto him [Elijah], saying, Get thee hence, and turn thee eastward, and hide thyself by the brook Cherith, that is before Jordan."[46]

We do not know which of the Jordan tributaries the brook Cherith might have been, but apparently it was an obscure and isolated place where Elijah could hide safely without being accidentally discovered by soldiers, shepherds or passersby. It was also a desolate place where no animal life existed, therefore Elijah was completely dependent upon the Lord for his sustenance. The scripture says that during the time he was hiding at Cherith, "the ravens brought him bread and flesh in the morning and bread and flesh in the evening; and he drank of the brook."[47] Here was an existence on the most primitive, bare-subsistence level. The sluggish hours of each protracted day must have dragged by like slow-motion torment gnawing at Elijah's restless soul.

---

44. Abraham 1:29-30
45. Deuteronomy 11:16-17
46. 1 Kings 17:2-3
47. 1 Kings 17:6

Nevertheless, circumstances did change. They became worse. As the season wore on, the fugitive prophet realized that the hot, rainless days were reducing his brook to a diminishing trickle. Elijah therefore found himself confronted with the ugly prospect of death by thirst. Somehow he had to escape from this death-trap and find a new hideout. The question was, where could he go? At that very moment King Ahab was hunting everywhere for Elijah. The king was so determined to avenge himself on the prophet who had cursed his land that he had even extended the search into foreign countries.[48]

Finally, just as his water supply completely gave out, the word of the Lord came to Elijah, saying, "Arise, get thee to Zarephath, which belongeth to Zidon, and dwell there: behold, I have commanded a widow woman there to sustain thee."[49] Just why the Lord selected this particular woman is not disclosed. However, she appears to have been extremely remorseful over some sin she had committed and when she saw an opportunity to serve the Lord by ministering to one of His prophets she faithfully performed the service. Nevertheless, she was not psychologically conditioned to accommodate the prophet when he first came to her village which was located in the Sidon district of Phoenicia. What had brought this mother in Israel to live among heathens we can only guess. If it were to escape the famine she had certainly failed in her objective for she and her young son were preparing to eat their last morsel of food and die. Therefore, when Elijah first approached the woman she began by resisting his request for food. Only after Elijah had taken the appropriate initiative did the Lord touch her heart so that she felt the impelling "command" of the Spirit to render every assistance.

The strange and wonderful meeting between this woman and Elijah is related in the Bible as follows:

"So he [Elijah] arose and went to Zaraphath. And when he came to the gate of the city, behold, the widow woman was there gathering of sticks: and he called to her, and said,

---

48. 1 Kings 17:10
49. 1 Kings 17:9

Fetch me, I pray thee, a little water in a vessel, that I may drink.

"And as she was going to fetch it, he called to her, and said, Bring me, I pray thee, a morsel of bread in thine hand. And she said, As the Lord thy God liveth, I have not a cake, but an handful of meal in a barrel, and a little oil in a cruse: and, behold, I am gathering two sticks, that I may go in and dress it for me and my son, that we may eat it, and die.

"And Elijah said unto her, Fear not: go and do as thou hast said: but make me thereof a little cake first, and bring it unto me, and after make for thee and for thy son. For thus saith the Lord God of Israel, The barrel of meal shall not waste, neither shall the cruse of oil fail, until the day that the Lord sendeth rain upon the earth.

"And she went and did according to the saying of Elijah. And she, and he, and her house, did eat many days. And the barrel of meal wasted not, neither did the cruse of oil fail, according to the word of the Lord, which he spake by Elijah."[50]

ELIJAH ASKS FOR THE POWER
TO RAISE THE DEAD

It was during this interval of hiding and surviving on a bread and water diet that Elijah was unexpectedly accused of killing the son of his hostess. The boy was apparently quite young and when he became severely ill the widowed mother tried desperately to save him. But it was to no avail. As she finally saw the last breath of life go out of him she seized the boy in her arms and cried out against Elijah as though he had deliberately done this to punish her for some sin. In the most bitter anguish she demanded, "What have I to do with thee, O thou man of God? Art thou come unto me to call my sin to remembrance, and to slay my son?"[51]

If Elijah knew about her sin he did not comment on it but said simply, "Give me thy son."[52] What Elijah then did was rather amazing. Instead of anointing the child and praying to the Lord for his revival, he took the boy from his

50. 1 Kings 17:10-16　　　　52. 1 Kings 17:19
51. 1 Kings 17:18

mother's arms and carried the limp body up into the loft of the widow's humble home. It was in this loft, the Bible says, that Elijah had his own bed and there he carefully stretched the boy upon it.

For all Elijah knew this boy was permanently dead, and he wanted no witnesses as he earnestly pleaded with the Lord for the supreme blessing of restoring him to life. If the plea was not granted he could return the body to the distraught mother without having aroused her hopes needlessly. If the boy were brought back to life then it would be time enough to reveal to the mother his reason for taking the body to the privacy of the upstairs loft.

"And he cried unto the Lord, and said, O Lord my God, hast thou also brought evil upon the widow with whom I sojourn, by slaying her son?

"And he stretched himself upon the child three times, and cried unto the Lord, and said, O Lord my God, I pray thee, let this child's soul come into him again.

"And the Lord heard the voice of Elijah; and the soul of the child came into him again, and he revived."[53]

This was the miracle Elijah had sought. What joy must have flooded his being as he saw the first quivering signs of returning respiration and consciousness. And who can begin to understand the rapture of this grieving mother as she suddenly beheld that her son was alive again. "And the woman said to Elijah, Now by this I know that thou art a man of God, and that the word of the Lord in thy mouth is truth."[54]

Why Elijah followed the strange procedure of bending over the child three times as he prayed for his life we do not know. Later, Elisha did something similar in restoring the dead child of the Shunamite,[55] and Paul seems to have done the same thing in raising Eutychus.[56] However, the Savior did not do this when he raised the dead.[57]

---

53. 1 Kings 17:20-22
54. 1 Kings 17:24
55. 2 Kings 4:34
56. Acts 20:10
57. See for example, John 11:39-44; Matthew 9:25

Elijah Is Finally Authorized to End
the Terrible Famine

It was not until three years and six months[58] had passed away that the Lord said to Elijah, "Go, show thyself unto Ahab; and I will send rain upon the earth."[59]

We know from a later reference, that there was a lot more to this revelation than the simple statement quoted above. Elijah subsequently acknowledged that everything he did in connection with the dramatic events we are about to relate were carried out just as the Lord had instructed him to do it.[60] We therefore know that the revelations given to Elijah prior to the time he went to see the king were both detailed and comprehensive.

The forty-two months of continuous drouth had left deep and frightful scars on the face of Israel. The famine had forced King Ahab to temporarily transfer his headquarters from Samaria to his palace overlooking the rich fertile valley of Jezreel. But by this time even the valley of Jezreel was no longer fertile. The famine had become so severe that the king was about to lose the last of his royal mules and other livestock. The scripture says, "And Ahab called Obadiah, which was the governor of his house. . . . And Ahab said unto Obadiah, Go into the land, unto all fountains of water, and unto all brooks: peradventure we may find grass to save the horses and mules alive, that we lose not all the beasts.

"So they divided the land between them to pass throughout it: Ahab went one way by himself, and Obadiah went another way by himself."[61]

Fortunately, this Obadiah was a friend of Elijah. In fact, he was a friend of all the prophets. The scripture says that earlier, "when Jezebel cut off the prophets of the Lord, that Obadiah took an hundred prophets, and hid them by fifty in a cave, and fed them with bread and water."[62]

And now, as Obadiah passed along the road seeking feed for the king's livestock, who should he see but Elijah

---

58. Luke 4:25
59. 1 Kings 18:1
60. 1 Kings 18:36

61. 1 Kings 18:3-6
62. 1 Kings 18:4

whom everyone by this time must have thought was dead.
Obadiah fell to the ground in humble salutation, and said,
"Art thou that my lord Elijah? And he answered him, I am:
go, tell thy lord, Behold Elijah is here!"[63]

As Obadiah rose to his feet he acted as though Elijah
were trying to get him killed. Said he, "What have I sinned,
that thou wouldest deliver thy servant into the hand of Ahab,
to slay me? As the Lord thy God liveth, there is no nation
or kingdom, whether my lord [the king] hath not sent to
seek thee: and when they said, He is not there; he took [de-
manded] an oath of the kingdom and nation, that they found
thee not. And now thou sayest, Go, tell thy lord, Behold,
Elijah is here. And it shall come to pass as soon as I am
gone from thee, that the Spirit of the Lord shall carry thee
whither I know not; and so when I come and tell Ahab, and
he cannot find thee, he shall slay me: but I thy servant fear
the Lord from my youth. Was it not told my Lord what I
did when Jezebel slew the prophets of the Lord, how I hid
an hundred men of the Lord's prophets by fifty in a cave,
and fed them with bread and water? And now thou sayest,
Go, tell thy lord, Behold, Elijah is here: and he shall slay
me."[64]

This was quite a speech. It certainly revealed that Obadiah had learned from past experience that the prophets of
the Lord, especially Elijah, were like phantoms during these
treacherous days of murderous persecution. They appeared
suddenly and then vanished out of sight on the night wind
where not even the king could find them. Obadiah was taking
no chances on Elijah's proposed visit with Ahab. The Lord
might decide to take Elijah elsewhere, and then Obadiah
would be left alone to suffer the wrath of the king. However, Elijah asured Obadiah that this meeting was not his
own idea, but the Lord's. Said he, "As the Lord of hosts
liveth, before whom I stand, I will surely show myself unto
him [Ahab] to-day."[65]

Obadiah finally decided that Elijah really did intend to
face the king in spite of the risk involved. He knew Elijah

---

63. 1 Kings 18:7-8
64. 1 Kings 18:9-14
65. 1 Kings 18:15

would keep the engagement if the Lord had ordered it. Obadiah therefore agreed to deliver the message and bring the two men together.

Elijah and King Ahab Meet After Three-and-a-half Years

When this meeting took place King Ahab undoubtedly felt himself confronted by a most important decision. Here he was face-to-face with the very man whose words had brought disaster to the nation. The miserable situation of the country had to be remedied. Would this be accomplished by slaughtering Elijah on the spot or by appeasing him? Ahab's salutation reveals that he had not yet made up his mind just how he should deal with Elijah. Said he, "Art thou he that troubleth Israel?"[66]

God's prophet was taking no verbal abuse from this apostate monarch. Elijah replied, "I have not troubled Israel; BUT THOU AND THY FATHER'S HOUSE . . . ye have forsaken the commandments of the Lord, and thou hast followed Baalim."[67] Before Ahab could reply to the charge, Elijah boldly commanded him, "Now therefore send, and gather to me all Israel unto mount Carmel, and the prophets of Baal four hundred and fifty, and the prophets of the groves four hundred, which eat at Jezebel's table."[68]

Here was a command to assemble three different groups. First, there was to be a general conference of the people of Israel (usually represented by the leaders of the various tribes); second, the main body of priests belonging to Baal-worship were to be brought together and Elijah specified their number as being 450; third, the main body of priests who promoted Ashtoreth-worship in "the groves" and who were kept at the palace as Jezebel's personal holy men were to be assembled. This last group which Elijah numbered as 400 were self-mutilated men indoctrinated in all of the impure practices associated with the obscene Ashtoreth fertility cult.[69] Jezebel and her attendants worshipped at her shrines while King Ahab and his servants sponsored the

---

66. 1 Kings 18:17
67. 1 Kings 18:18
68. 1 Kings 18:19
69. Geikie, *Hours With the Bible*, Vol. 4, pp. 55-56

equally vile rites carried on in the castle-like temple which Ahab had built to Baal in Samaria.[70] Elijah had commanded the heathen prelates from both of these groups to assemble on Mount Carmel.

The scripture says, "So Ahab sent unto all the children of Israel and gathered the prophets together unto Mount Carmel."[71] However, the "prophets" referred to here were the phony priests of Baal. They were false prophets. Elijah was the only prophet of God at this vast assembly.[72] We also discover that Jezebel's 400 depraved priests of Ashtoreth did not show up. How Jezebel hated Elijah! No doubt there is an interesting facet of history which is unrecorded in the Bible but which would explain how Jezebel prevented her personal holy men from responding to Elijah's call. Only the 450 priests of Baal assembled on the heights of Carmel.[73] Later we will encounter the 400 priests of Jezebel which she retained at her palace in Jezreel.[74]

THE SCENE OF ELIJAH'S GREAT CONFERENCE

The visitor to the Holy Land will find Mount Carmel to be a whole range of luxuriant hills piled together half-way up the coast of Palestine. They have summits reaching altitudes of 1,700 feet above sea level. To the west the heights of Carmel rise abruptly out of the Mediterranean and look down on modern Haifa. Its great green hump then stretches eastward and slightly south along the entire length of the beautiful Esdraelon valley, thereby forming its southern border. The Carmel range is filled with springs and rich verdure which aways made it a popular retreat for special festivities whether religious or secular.

Dr. Geikie states that, "Its reputation as a sanctuary . . . led Pythagoras thither, while Tacitus tells us that Vespasian found on it, even in his time, an altar without image or temple. . . . This lovely chain of green and wooded heights dips at its west end, into the Mediterranean, by a steep bluff, known as Cape Carmel, while towards its east end there rises a prominent summit known immemorially as the scene

---

70. 1 Kings 16:32; 2 Kings 10:21
71. 1 Kings 18:20
72. 1 Kings 18:22
73. Ibid.
74. 1 Kings 22:6

of Elijah's sacrifice. The tradition is justified by the fact that it is the only spot in all the range where the Kishon is close enough to answer the requirements of the Scripture narrative. A steep path, from the plain below, leads to a hollow, sloping plateau, still called 'Mahrakah,' or 'the place of burning.' A peak rises, apart, to the south-east, facing the plain in a cliff about forty feet high, the descent afterwards being gradual. The nearly level plateau is dotted with olive trees, and there is a great cistern, now dry, dug out in the limestone rock. Below this, a short way off, is a well, or rather ancient reservoir, also cut out of the rock, overhung by some fine trees; a few broken stone steps now lead down to the water, which percolates through the limestone beds overhead, and is always more or less abundant, even in the dryest seasons. The water required for Elijah's commands, could thus be found even when the brooks and springs everywhere else had disappeared. . . . Fourteen hundred feet below flows the Kishon, when it does flow, which may be said to be only after such storms as that which closed the eventful day of Elijah's assembly. . . .

"Here, on the last prominent height at the east end of Carmel, where the last glimpse of the sea and the first of Esdraelon are offered, the four hundred and fifty prophets of Baal assembled on the appointed day: those of the Asherah appearing to have been kept from coming, by Jezebel, their special patroness."[75]

ELIJAH STAGES A CONTEST BETWEEN JEHOVAH AND BAAL

When the great crowd had assembled, Elijah took up a position where he could be most readily heard and shouted:

"How long halt ye between two opinions? if the Lord be God, follow him: but if Baal, then follow him."[76]

To this "the people answered him not a word. Then said Elijah unto the people, I even I only, remain a prophet of the Lord; but Baal's prophets are four hundred and fifty

75. Geikie, *Hours With the Bible*, Vol. 4, pp. 75-76
76. 1 Kings 18:21

men. Let them therefore give us two bullocks [apparently Elijah, in his poverty, did not have any!]; and let them choose one bullock for themselves and cut it in pieces, and lay it on the wood, and put no fire under: and I will dress the other bullock, and lay it on wood, and put no fire under. And call ye on the name of your gods and I will call on the name of the Lord: and the God that answereth by fire, let him be God."[77]

A great shout of approval went up from the assembled congregation.[78]

It is important to remind ourselves that ordinarily Elijah would never have dared to set up such a contest between Jehovah and Baal because the Lord is not an exhibitionist and does not give signs to the unbelieving. Only on rare occasions does he make an exception. This was one of them. As we shall see later, the Lord had authorized everything Elijah was doing, and one cannot help but notice how deeply Elijah enjoyed every precious second of it.

Turning to the prophets or priests of Baal, Elijah said, "Choose you one bullock for yourselves, and dress it first; for ye are many; and call on the name of your gods, but put no fire under."[79]

So the crowd watched as these haughty apostate priests killed a young bullock and after dressing it placed the several pieces on their heathen altar. Then they began their devilish chants. These were wild groans and moans as they cried out to Baal to show his power. "But there was no voice, nor any that answered. And they leaped upon the altar which was made."[80]

As time slowly crept by, Elijah decided to give a little zest to the affair. The scripture says, "And it came to pass at noon, that Elijah mocked them, and said, Cry aloud: for he is a god; either he is talking, or he is pursuing, or he is in a journey, or peradventure he sleepeth, and must be awaked."[81]

---

77. 1 Kings 18:21-24
78. 1 Kings 18:24
79. 1 Kings 18:25

80. 1 Kings 18:26
81. 1 Kings 18:27

This brought a howling reaction from the frenzied priests of Baal. "And they cried aloud, and cut themselves after their manner with knives and lancets, till the blood gushed out upon them."[82] Dr. Geikie watched antics very similar to this even in our own time at Gaza. He says, ". . . at last their excitement grows so great that they often cut themselves with knives and swords, till they faint with loss of blood, and pierce themselves with wooden or iron spikes, which they leave sticking in them, or lie on the sharp edge of a scimeter, or eat scorpions or prickly pear. . . ."[83]

But in spite of all this fantastic and exhausting chanting, praying, hacking and bleeding, the heavens were as brass. "And it came to pass, when midday was past, and they prophesied until the time of the offering of the evening sacrifice, that there was neither voice, nor any to answer, nor any [in the heavens] that regarded."[84]

Now Elijah was ready to act.

---

82. 1 Kings 18:28
83. Geikie, *Hours With the Bible*, Vol. 4, p. 78. The self-mutilated men or female impersonators who typified the priests of Ashtoreth have also had their counterpart in modern times. They are called Galli and the following description will give the student some idea of the sights which were common in ancient Israel: "A trumpeter went before them who proclaimed their arrival in the villages, the farmyards, or the streets of towns, by flourishes on his instrument — a twisted horn. The begging Galli followed in fantastic array, after a leader; an ass in their midst, carrying their begging bag and a veiled image of the goddess. They were dressed in women's clothes of different colours; their faces and eyes painted like those of women, and their head wound round with a linen or silk turban. Their arms were bare to the shoulders, and they danced along the streets to the sound of wild music, holding huge swords and bills, with whips for scourging themselves, in their hands, and making a hideous noise with rattles, fifes, cymbals or kettle drums. When they came to a farmyard they began their ravings. A wild howl opened the scene. They then flew wildly one past the other; their heads sunk low towards the earth, as they turned in circles; their loose hair dragging through the dust. Presently they began to bite their arms, and next to hack themselves with the two-edged swords they carried."

Then began a new scene. "One of them, the leader in this frenzy, commenced to prophesy, with sighs and groans, lamenting aloud his past sins, which he would now avenge by the chastisement of his flesh. He then took the knotted whip and lashed his back, cutting himself also with his sword till the blood ran down." (Quoted by Dr. Geikie in *Hours With the Bible*, Vol. 3, pp. 399-400)

At the close of these demonstrations the Galli always conducted a begging spree. "Some threw copper money to them, or even, in some cases, silver. Others brought wine, milk, or cheese, which was greedily accepted, and stuffed into the sack on the ass, beside the goddess. . . ." (Ibid.) Dr. Geikie closes by saying, "In the evening, when they reached a caravanserai, they made up for the bloody chastisements of the day by a debauch, and, if the opportunity offered, gave themselves up to every abomination." (Ibid.)

84. 1 Kings 18:29

The Miraculous Conclusion to the Contest

In the late afternoon, Elijah finally arose and said to the weary crowd, "Come near unto me."[85] As they pushed forward to get the best possible view of this final stage of the contest, the people saw Elijah repairing "the altar of the Lord that was broken down."[86] It had been many years since anyone had been allowed to use this Jehovah shrine. When the altar was repaired the crowd saw Elijah place twelve large stones or boulders on the crown of the altar. Each one represented a tribe of Israel. On these stones Elijah then piled the wood. Last of all he took a digging tool and excavated a trench completely around the altar. When all of this was prepared, Elijah was ready for the sacrifice. He took the young bullock, slew it, cleaned it, skinned it, cut the meat in pieces and then laid them on the wood after the pattern prescribed for a burnt-offering. Stepping back, he said to those nearby:

"Fill four barrels with water, and pour it on the burnt sacrifice, and on the wood."[87] When this was completed, he said, "Do it the second time. And they did it the second time. And he said, Do it the third time. And they did it the third time. And the water ran round about the altar; and he filled the trench also with water."[88]

This drenching of the sacrifice with water was undoubtedly intended as much for the heathen priests as it was for the people. It was not uncommon in those days for the wily priests to rig their altars with fires beneath them so that the sacrifices appeared to be ignited spontaneously. One authority says he "had seen under the altars of the heathens, holes dug in the earth with funnels proceeding from them, and communicating with openings on the tops of the altars. In the former the priests concealed fire, which, communicating through the funnels with the holes, set fire to the wood and consumed the sacrifice; and thus the simple people were led to believe that the sacrifice was consumed by miraculous fire."[89]

---

85. 1 Kings 18:30
86. Ibid.
87. 1 Kings 18:33
88. 1 Kings 18:34-35
89. Quoted by Clarke, *Bible Commentary*, Vol. 2, p. 459

Elijah used the twelve barrels of water to demonstrate that no secret fire or trickery was involved in what they were about to behold.

Finally everything was ready. At the precise time when the evening sacrifice was due to be offered at the temple in Jerusalem, Elijah stood before this improvised altar located high above the Mediterranean on Mount Carmel. Raising his voice so all might hear, he cried out, "Lord, God of Abraham, Isaac, and of Israel, let it be known this day that thou art God in Israel, and that I am thy servant, and that I HAVE DONE ALL THESE THINGS AT THY WORD. Hear me, O Lord, hear me, that this people may know that thou art the Lord God, and that thou hast turned their heart back again!"[90]

As the people waited tensely to see just what would happen, a frightening miracle suddenly occurred right before their eyes. The scripture says, "Then the fire of the Lord fell, and consumed the burnt sacrifice, and the wood, and the stones, and the dust, and licked up the water that was in the trench. And when all the people saw it, they fell on their faces: and they said, The Lord, he is the God; the Lord, he is the God."[91]

Immediately Elijah took command of the situation and with the voice of one proclaiming a divine judgment, cried out: "Take the prophets of Baal; let not one of them escape. And they took them: and Elijah brought them down to the Brook Kishon, and slew them there."[92]

This was the terrible finale to a contest which the heathen priests had undoubtedly expected to end with the death of Elijah. Instead they found themselves in the rough custody of their former disciples who jostled them down the mountain side to the Esdraelon valley 1,400 feet below. King Ahab followed the throng as they made their long descent down the northern slopes of Mount Carmel. He must have stood in numb bewilderment as he saw his heathen comrades, already splattered with their own blood from the sadistic self-torture throughout the day, now put to the sword by

90. 1 Kings 18:36-37   92. 1 Kings 18:40
91. 1 Kings 18:38-39

their former followers. No doubt the bodies were thrown into the channel of the Kishon where the churning flood water of the coming storm soon swept them out to sea.

With the execution of the 450 priests of Baal completed, Elijah prepared to return to the top of the mount. He said to King Ahab, "Get thee up, eat and drink; for there is a sound of abundance of rain."[93] In the prophetic mind of Elijah it was almost as though the rain were already there.

Apparently the gory sight of the massive executions did not spoil the appetite of the king. The scripture says "Ahab went up to eat and to drink."[94] Elijah went up, too, but neither to eat nor drink. He went up to pray.

Taking his servant with him, Elijah made his way to the high place not far from a spot which looked out over the Mediterranean. Elijah sat upon the ground and placed his face between his knees. Apparently engaged in earnest prayer, Elijah sought to have the Lord promptly fulfill his promise that rain would now fall upon the parched and desolate land. Finally Elijah said to his servant, "Go up now, look toward the sea."[95] The servant went up to the highest spot and looked carefully out into the darkening dusk across the Mediterranean. After awhile he returned and said to Elijah, "There is nothing." Elijah replied, "Go again seven times."[96]

"And it came to pass at the seventh time, that he said, Behold, there ariseth a little cloud out of the sea, like a man's hand. And he said, Go up, say unto Ahab, Prepare thy chariot, and get thee down, that the rain stop thee not."[97]

The warning to the king was barely in time. The wind came in from the Mediterranean carrying with it bulging billows of drenching moisture. The Bible says the "heaven was black with clouds and wind, and there was a great rain."[98]

Ahab's chariot rumbled down the steep slopes of Carmel seeking the main highway of the Esdraelon plain before the storm struck but running ahead of him was the sinewy servant

93. 1 Kings 18:41
94. 1 Kings 18:42
95. 1 Kings 18:43
96. Ibid.
97. 1 Kings 18:44
98. 1 Kings 18:45

of the Lord. We are told that "the hand of the Lord was on Elijah; and he girded up his loins, and ran before Ahab to the entrance of Jezreel."[99]

When Elijah gathered up his robe and tied it to his waist so he could race ahead of King Ähab he was strongly motivated. Some have thought that he did this to honor the king but this is unlikely. It seems far more probable that he wished to be immediately available to direct the inhabitants of the king's summer palace at Jezreel when the monarch came speeding in to relate the wonderful happenings of that day. No doubt Elijah had reason to hope that when they learned of the mighty manifestation of divine power which the king had witnessed the whole royal household might lead out in a nationwide reform movement. Judah had reformed under the leadership of her king without any miracle whatever. Surely Israel could do it after so great a miracle. Who could doubt the proximity of God's presence after seeing His consuming fire on Mount Carmel and then witnessing the termination of the three-year drouth exactly as His prophet had promised? Elijah was soon to find out.

The scripture says, "And Ahab told Jezebel all that Elijah had done, and withal how he had slain all the prophets with the sword."[100] But Jezebel's reaction was the very opposite of what Elijah earnestly hoped for. The diabolical mind of this evil woman masticated the words of her husband and turned them into fuel for a murder plot against Elijah. The feeble-spined Ahab stood meekly by watching developments but without making the least attempt to interfere.

Elijah, meanwhile, had not dared to come to the palace until he was certain it was safe. He remained available but at a respectable distance where he could get a good running start if things did not turn out right. News of the alarming direction which events were taking came to Elijah in a message from the queen herself. "Jezebel sent a messenger unto Elijah, saying, So let the gods do to me, and more also, if I make not thy life as the life of one of them [the dead priests of Baal] by to-morrow about this time!"[101]

---

99. 1 Kings 18:46   101. 1 Kings 19:2
100. 1 Kings 19:1

Why Jezebel warned Elijah in advance is difficult to comprehend. Perhaps she felt completely certain that he could not possibly escape and she wanted him to suffer the agony of a hunted fugitive until her elite guard cornered him and slashed him to pieces. But Elijah had no intention of being cornered and slashed to pieces. The scripture says that as soon as Elijah received the message, "he arose, and went for his life."[102]

ELIJAH BECOMES THE "WEEPING PROPHET"

In his flight the Lord left Elijah to his own devices. And Elijah did an amazing thing. He took his servant and headed for Mount Sinai!

Of course, the Horeb range of which Mount Sinai is the principal peak, is at the lower end of the Sinai peninsula and a long and wearisome journey for a man on foot. The shortest route would have been to follow the main highway along the spine of the Ephraim mountains to Jerusalem, Bethlehem and Hebron and then finally down to the wilderness outpost at Beer-sheba. But this would have been suicidal under the circumstances. Jezebel's soldiers would be lying in wait at every pass. It is more likely that Elijah and his servant proceeded down the valley of Jezreel toward the Jordan river and then traveled south along the Jordan gorge or Ghor to the Dead Sea. They could then take any of several routes to negotiate their way around that bitter sink hole and finally arrive at Beer-sheba.

The scripture says they eventually reached the outpost of Beer-sheba but it makes no reference to any incident or difficulty. At Beer-sheba Elijah commanded his servant to remain there while he proceeded to cross the desert alone. It is obvious that something of a most serious nature was taking place in the mind of Elijah.

Apparently the wonderful and exhilarating manifestation of God's power on Mount Carmel had generated in this prophet such a desperate but promising hope of possible reform among the apostate Israelites that Elijah had built himself up to expect as great a miracle at the summer palace in

---

102. 1 Kings 19:3

Jezreel as that which had occurred on Mount Carmel. And if Jezebel had repented, that would have been a miracle. But when Elijah saw that King Ahab was going to allow his foul-minded queen to revive the vendetta against the Lord's prophet and expunge from Ahab's mind the significance of the miraculous consuming of the sacrifice by fire as well as the sensational ending of the forty-two-month famine, it was too much. It was a devastating blow. Elijah's heart was broken, his morale was smashed, the joy of Mount Carmel had become wormwood and his hope for Israel had been annihilated.

But why would he go to Sinai? We later learn that this was the flight of a desperate man whose collapsing confidence in his personal capacity to fulfill a divine mission was driving him to make a final physical contact wth the touchstone of his faith. It was Elijah's admission that he was through. In his own estimation he had failed. Elijah was going to Sinai to die!

The lonely madness of discouragement which was eating out his soul seemed to compel Elijah to press southward toward that sacred mountain of the great prophet, Moses. There the glorious presence of God had created such a brilliant witness of the Creator's power and reality for ancient Israel. It seemed the final refuge where a broken prophet might make his report and die.

But somewhere out there on the desert, Elijah collapsed. Despondent, hungry and exhausted, he sat bent beneath the poor protection of a Juniper tree and pleaded with God to let him be released from life. "It is enough," he cried, "Now O Lord, take away my life; for I am not better than my fathers."[103]

The scripture says that "as he lay and slept under a juniper tree, behold, then an angel touched him, and said unto him, Arise and eat. And he looked, and, behold, there was a cake baken on the coals, and cruse of water at his head. And he did eat and drink, and laid him down again."[104]

Apparently at another place a little closer to Sinai "the angel of the Lord came again the second time, and touched

---

103. 1 Kings 19:4   104. 1 Kings 19:5-6

him, and said, Arise and eat; because the journey is too great for thee. And he arose, and did eat and drink, and went in strength of that meat FORTY DAYS AND FORTY NIGHTS UNTO HOREB, THE MOUNT OF GOD."[105]

ELIJAH AT MOUNT SINAI

This was the third time in sacred history that a human being had been animated sufficiently by the power of God to permit him to exist without food or water for approximately six weeks. The two previous occasions had both happened to Moses, and only a matter of a day or two apart.[106] A fourth occasion would be eight centuries hence when Jehovah, as Jesus the Christ, would duplicate the feat himself.[107]

When Elijah arrived at the "mount of God" — sometimes called Horeb after the forbidding volcanic range of which it is a part and sometimes called Sinai after its principal peak — he knew he was treading on sacred ground. Slowly he climbed the naked battlements of this almost completely lifeless and barren projection of wind-eroded rock. Somewhere up there among the solemn mystery of this mountain's silent peaks, Elijah came upon a cave. He entered and rested. Then the word of the Lord came to Elijah. Under the circumstances one would have expected a divine expression of warm reassurance and comfort but it was not. God loved Elijah and he knew this humble, valiant servant needed more than a mere morsel of spiritual sponge cake. He needed a stiffening of his spiritual spine. He needed a soul-charging challenge. Therefore the Lord said to His servant, "WHAT DOEST THOU HERE, ELIJAH?"[108]

Elijah thought he knew exactly what he was doing there, and so, without hesitation or apology, he told the Lord, "I have been very jealous for the Lord God of hosts: for the children of Israel have forsaken thy covenant, thrown down thine altars, and slain thy prophets with the sword; and I, EVEN I ONLY, AM LEFT: and they seek my life, to take it away."[109]

---

105. 1 Kings 19:7-8
106. See *The Third Thousand Years*, pp. 310, 325
107. Matthew 4:2
108. 1 Kings 19:9
109. 1 Kings 19:10

The Lord had already heard Elijah ask to die and now he was hearing the reason. Elijah felt that the higher order of Priesthood of which he was the final custodian was being rejected, discredited and desecrated by Israel. Apparently Elijah felt these apostates now deserved to be left to their doom. Why waste more years of suffering on their reprobate souls? They wanted to kill Elijah, but he had come here to deprive them of the pleasure by asking the Lord to let him pass peacefully into the spirit world.

From the Lord's point of view, however, this line of reasoning was the rationale of a humble servant suffering from the restricted vision of an earth-bound creature. The Lord was ready to illuminate his mind with the broader perspective of the Almighty. Therefore he said to Elijah, "Go forth, and stand upon the mount before the Lord. And, behold, the Lord passed by, and a great and strong wind rent the mountains, and brake it in pieces the rocks before the Lord; but the Lord was not in the wind: and after the wind an earthquake; but the Lord was not in the earthquake: and after the earthquake a fire; but the Lord was not in the fire: and after the fire a still small voice."[110]

To appreciate what actually happened here we must go to the Chaldee version. Our own version simply says "the Lord passed by," but the Chaldee version say, "And behold THE LORD WAS REVEALED."[111] Naturally, the moment Elijah was permitted to see the Lord he would expect Him to speak, but instead there came the rushing of a mighty hurricane roaring through the heights of Sinai. Then the earth shook with such violence that the ground quaked and the facing of the surrounding volcanic cliffs scaled off huge fragments of rock which went hurtling into the cavernous labyrinths below. Finally, from the splintered crags and seams of this barren mountain there shot forth flames of consuming fire. In all of these Elijah might have expected the Lord to deliver His mighty message, but the voice of God was in none of them. Only after the third phenomenon of billowing flames had spent itself did the Lord speak. Amazingly, it was not a loud, resonant, trumpeting proclamation,

---

110. 1 Kings 19:11-12
111. Clarke, *Bible Commentary*, Vol. 2, p. 402

but "a still small voice." It was the same still small voice which thousands of Nephites would hear in America after the resurrection of the Savior. Concerning it the scripture says, ". . . and it was not a harsh voice, neither was it a loud voice; nevertheless, and notwithstanding it being a small voice it did pierce them that did hear to the center, insomuch that there was no part of their frame that it did not cause to quake; yea, it did pierce them to the very soul, and did cause their hearts to burn."[112]

No wonder "when Elijah heard it, that he wrapped his face in his mantle, and went out, and stood in the entering in of the cave!"[113]

But what message did the Lord have for His prophet? He commenced by challenging Elijah with the same question He had asked before, "WHAT DOEST THOU HERE, ELIJAH?"[114] Once again Elijah repeated the bill of particulars in his indictment against apostate Israel. The Lord could have reminded His servant that such matters should be left to the judgment of God. He also could have reprimanded Elijah for abandoning his field of labor. Instead, He simply told him to return.

The scripture says, "And the Lord said unto him, Go, return on thy way to the wilderness of Damascus, and when thou comest, anoint Hazael to be king over Syria: and Jehu the son of Nimshi shalt thou anoint to be king over Israel: and Elisha the son of Shaphat of Abel-meholah shalt thou anoint to be prophet in thy room. And it shall come to pass, that him that escapeth the sword of Hazael shall Jehu slay: and him that escapeth from the sword of Jehu shall Elisha slay."[115]

What the Lord wanted Elijah to understand was the fact that great political upheavals were about to take place in the not to distant future and many of these who were presently persecuting the servant of God were about to taste the burning bite of devouring steel in their flesh. And those who escaped the sword would go down under a seven-year-famine which Elisha would be instructed to announce. Eli-

---

112. 3 Nephi 11:3
113. 1 Kings 19:13

114. Ibid.
115. 1 Kings 19:15-17

jah's despondency had grown out of his human tendency to assume that the hardships of the hour were likely to prevail permanently. The Lord wanted him to know that evil never prevails permanently. The task of a servant of God is to hold on.

The Lord also disclosed to Elijah that he was mistaken in assuming that he was the only one in Israel who had remained loyal to Jehovah. The Lord declared, "Yet I have left me seven thousand in Israel, all the knees [of] which have not bowed unto Baal, and every mouth [of] which hath not kissed him."[116]

Seven thousand! Where were they? This was what Elijah needed to know. He must find them.

So the Lord withdrew from Elijah and left him unto himself. The pilgrimage had been a success. The death-wish in Elijah's heart had been replaced by the passion to live and the will to work. No doubt it was a sober, humble and contemplative servant of God who slowly made his way down the steep precipices of Sinai to return to his field of labor. He must have sensed that he was about to enjoy the most exciting and satisfying part of his whole career.

---

116. 1 Kings 19:18

Scripture Reading and Questions on Chapter Thirteen

Scripture Reading: 1 Kings, chapters 17 to 19 inclusive.

1—Name five specific powers which Elijah possessed as part of the authority under the Higher Priesthood.

2—What was the Aaronic Priesthood called before the days of Aaron?

3—Who was the original Elias? On what is this conclusion based?

4—What Priesthood did the prophets of ancient Israel hold? Who ordained them?

5—What prophecy did Elijah make before King Ahab that nearly got him murdered? What did the Lord tell Elijah to do?

6—Why did Elijah leave his hiding place and flee to Phoenicia? Describe the meeting between Elijah and the widow woman.

7—When the widow's son died, why did Elijah carry the body of the boy up into the loft? What happened?

8—Who was Obadiah? What had he done to help the Lord's prophets? Why was he afraid to take Elijah's message to the king?

9—What three groups did Elijah tell Ahab to assemble on Mount Carmel? Which group failed to show up? Where is Mount Carmel?

10—Describe the highlights of the contest between Elijah and the priests of Baal.

11—What happened to the priests of Baal? Why does the Lord seldom exhibit his great power to the general public? How did Elijah dare to call for the manifestation of God's power on this occasion?

12—How long did the famine last which Elijah had predicted? When was it terminated? Describe the circumstances.

13—Why did Elijah run ahead of the king to the summer palace at Jezreel? What did King Ahab tell Jezebel? How did she react to the news?

14—How did Elijah learn that the Queen intended to kill him? What did he do? Was he alone when he left Jezreel? Was he alone when he reached Sinai? Who told him to go to Sinai?

15—Just why do you think Elijah felt compelled to go to Mount Sinai? What great historical events had occurred on or near this mountain? Would this be somewhat like returning to the Sacred Grove?

16—What happened to Elijah in the desert between Beer-sheba and Sinai? What did Elijah asked the Lord to do? How was the Lord's love of Elijah demonstrated during his crossing of the desert?

17—How long did Elijah go without food and water at Mount Sinai? Who else is known to have existed that long without food or water?

18—What question did the Lord ask Elijah when he spoke to him in the mount? What was Elijah's reply?

19—Why do you think the Lord revealed himself to Elijah and then exposed him to the wind, earthquake and fire before he spoke to him "by the still small voice?"

20—What did the Lord tell Elijah to do? What did the Lord say about the 7,000? Would this be helpful to Elijah?

CHAPTER FOURTEEN

The Last Days of Elijah

It must have been apparent to Elijah as he listened to the Lord's instructions on Mount Sinai that the earthly mission which God had given him was in its final stages. To a prophet such as Elijah, the most important part of those instructions would be the anointing of Elisha as his successor. In fact, this was the only instruction which Elijah had time to personally carry out. The anointing of Hazael to be king of Syria and of Jehu to be king of Israel had to be left for Elijah's successor.

As Elijah came down from Sinai he set his face toward Abel-meholah where Elisha lived.[1]

THE CALLING OF ELISHA

Passing only a few miles from Mount Sinai and the Horeb range was a camel caravan trail which constituted the ancient thoroughfare across the Sinai Peninsula. Elijah most likely followed this route as it led back up the Arabah valley, around the Dead Sea, then farther northward along the Jordan valley until he came to the opening of the Jezreel watershed about ten miles south of Bethshean. Directly across the Jordan and a short distance to the east is the place where

---

1. 1 Kings 19:16

Elisha's home of Abel-meholah is believed to have been located.[2]

The scripture indicates that Elisha belonged to a substantial family. He is described as the son of "Shaphat" and authorities point out that this word probably refers to the office of a local judge rather than a proper name.[3] The family possessed a relatively large estate and when Elijah crossed over the Jordan and came to Abel-meholah he found his future companion and successor "plowing with twelve yoke of oxen before him, and he with the twelfth."[4] This is interpreted to mean that eleven plows were being operated under Elisha's supervision while he, himself, drove the twelfth.

Everything connected with the meeting between Elijah and Elisha would indicate that the two men were already well acquainted. It will be recalled that Elijah originated from Trans-Jordan or Gilead,[5] which was the same territory where Abel-meholah was located, and Elisha conducted himself in a manner which would indicate that he was already familiar with the Lord's great prophet. When Elijah walked up to the plow where Elisha was standing the prophet simply removed his rough mantle and placed it across the shoulders of Elisha.[6] The astonished Elisha seemed to have known exactly what this emblematic gesture meant. He was being designated for the prophetic calling and being chosen as the understudy and future successor of Elijah. No lengthy discussion or art of persuasion was employed to induce Elisha to accept the call. It was not needed. He was one of the choice 7,000 referred to by the Lord who had not bowed the knee to Baal but respected the Holy Priesthood of God and accepted with enthusiasm the discipline and obedience required by such a calling.

After placing his mantle upon Elisha, the Lord's prophet apparently strode away almost as though he wished to test Elisha's fidelity and see if he would immediately follow. The scripture says Elisha promptly "left the oxen and ran after Elijah."[7] But Elisha was a practical man. He was fairly

---

2. Rand McNally, *Bible Atlas*, p. 235
3. Geikie, *Hours With the Bible*, Vol. 4, p. 85
4. 1 Kings 19:19
5. 1 Kings 17:1
6. 1 Kings 19:19
7. 1 Kings 19:20

young, apparently unmarried, and still living with his parents. It did not seem right to abruptly abandon his family without some explanation and farewell so he said to Elijah, "Let me, I pray thee, kiss my father and my mother, and then I will follow thee."[8]

Elisha was not like the man in the days of Jesus who wanted to postpone his calling to bury the dead and was told to let "the dead bury their dead."[9] Elisha was already amenable to the discipline of his calling and needed no such lesson. Therefore Elijah said to him, "Go back again: for what have I done to thee?"[10] This somewhat obscure reply seems to mean, "Go back, if you wish, but remember, your call is not from me but from God."[11]

While Elijah waited, his new companion hastened back to his family. He obviously appreciated that the rigors of his new assignment would separate him from his loved ones for long periods of time. He therefore "took a yoke of oxen and slew them, and boiled their flesh with the instruments of the oxen [using the wooden plow, and the wooden yokes for fuel], and gave unto the people, and they did eat. Then he arose, and went after Elijah, and ministered unto him."[12] At an early opportunity Elijah must have formalized the calling of Elisha by the laying on of hands and "anointing" him to be a prophet as the Lord had instructed.[13]

Another important thing Elijah was instructed to do while on Mount Sinai was to anoint new kings for both Syria and Israel. Political turmoil prevented this from being immediately accomplished and later chapters will cover this assignment. Meanwhile, Elijah and Elisha had the task of searching out the righteous 7,000.[14] It was also extremely important to ferret out and revitalize any remnants of the Melchizedek Priesthood or "prophets." Elijah had believed

---

8. Ibid.
9. Matthew 8:21-22
10. 1 Kings 19:20
11. See Clarke, *Bible Commentary*, Vol. 2, p. 463
12. 1 Kings 19:21
13. 1 Kings 19:16
14. The term 7,000 is sometimes used in Hebrew literature to depict "multitudes" rather than a specific number of 7,000. It is used in the same sense that we say "tens of thousands," "hundreds of thousands," and so forth. (See Clarke, *Bible Commentary*, vol. 2, p. 463)

these men were all extinct until the Lord had told him otherwise. In fact, some of these "men of God" began to appear before the public about this time so we presume Elijah and Elisha must have been busy behind the scenes working with them.

During this period one of their unnamed fellow workers who is called simply "a prophet" boldly appeared before King Ahab. For once in his life, the treacherous King Ahab was in a predicament where he was glad to see a true prophet of God. Disastrous times had fallen on Israel. To appreciate what was now about to happen it is necessary to take a brief look at secular history, particularly what was happening up in Syria.

THE RISE OF ISRAEL'S RELATIVES IN SYRIA

The territory northeast of Palestine is known to us as Syria but it used to be called the land of Aram. It started as "Aram between the rivers" or Mesopotamia and then gradually shifted its major axis toward the west, until by Elijah's day its capital was Damascus.

Originally, these people had been led by the immediate relatives of Abraham. In fact, around 2,000 B.C., Abraham and his brother, Nahor, had settled a region on the upper Euphrates which they called Haran, but eventually it assumed the name of Nahor's grandson, Aram.[15] When he was 62, Abraham and his nephew, Lot, moved down from Aram and eventually settled among the Canaanites in accordance with the commandments of the Lord, but his father, brother, and other relatives remained in Aram. Therefore, Abraham continued to call the upper Euphrates "my country" and "my kindred."[16]

A century later we find Isaac instructing Jacob to go to "Padan-aram [Plain of Aram[17]], to the house of Bethuel thy mother's father; and take thee a wife from thence. . . ."[18]

Even at that early date, however, Abraham's relatives in Aram were becoming apostate idolators. Concerning his own father, Abraham wrote, ". . . and my father tarried in

---

15. Genesis 22:21   17. Peloubet's *Bible Dictionary* under Padan-Aram
16. Genesis 24:4   18. Genesis 28:2

Haran and dwelt there, as there were many flocks in Haran:
and my father turned again unto his idolatry, therefore he
continued in Haran."[19] Later, when Jacob went up to this
country to find a wife he discovered that his relatives in
Haran or Aram kept "images" in their homes.[20] One of
Jacob's wives stole her father's idols so she could take them
with her to Palestine.[21] Herdsmen and others who accompanied Jacob insisted on taking their idols, and Jacob subsequently had to confiscate them.[22]

From all of this evidence it can be easily understood
why Aram or Syria became a land of rank apostates even
though they were relatives of the Israelites. A thousand
years later, when Elijah was ministering among men, the
people of Aram were already widely intermixed with other
peoples and, because of their apostasy, they apparently never
mentioned their original relationship with Israel. No doubt
they were much like the descendants of Lot, the Ammonites
and Moabites, who also refused to be identified with Israel,
but made themselves some of Israel's most persistent enemies.

However, there was one thing the people of Syria could
not help sharing with Israel and that was their language.
They had started out with Hebrew but changed it gradually
into a very popular dialect which swept from the Tigris to
the Mediterranean.[23] In the ancient world it emerged as
the universal language of this region and survived for centuries until it was largely replaced by Greek. Thus, we
find that in the days of Jesus the people of Jerusalem con-
versed in Aramaic, not pure Hebrew.[24] Hebrew was used
in the Temple and the Synagogue but Aramaic was the
language of the market, the home and the street.[25]

But returning to the people of Aram, it will be recalled
that David had subjected Syria to military conquest during
his day and forced its kings to pay tribute.[26] Even so, a
small band of free-booters under Rezon had set up headquarters at Damascus and harrassed Solomon during his

---

19. Abraham 2:5
20. Genesis 31:19
21. Ibid.
22. Genesis 35:4

23. See the *Interpreters Bible*, Vol. 1, p. 223
24. Alfred Edersheim, *The Life and Times of Jesus*, pp. 10, 130
25. Ibid.
26. 2 Samuel 8:6

entire reign.[27] Steps were never taken to suppress this source
of trouble so that a century later the king of Damascus had
become a formidable political power with 32 tributaries under
him.[28] It was almost inevitable that one day the avaricious
eyes of the rulers of Damascus would see great advantages
in launching a devastating attack upon Israel. That day
had arrived.

Syria Attacks Israel

The scripture says, "And Ben-hadad the king of Syria
gathered all his host together: and there were thirty and
two kings with him, and horses, and chariots, and he went
up and besieged Samaria, and warred against it."[29] It is
apparent from the record that King Ahab of Israel found
his country overrun before he scarcely knew what was
happening. All his garrisons and military outposts collapsed
and the capital city of Samaria was put under siege. The
strangulation of the city by such a huge military force soon
reduced it to desperate extremities so the king of the Syrians
began the customary routine of presenting a series of extor-
tionate demands.

"And he [Ben-hadad] sent messengers to Ahab king of
Israel into the city, and said unto him, Thus saith Ben-hadad,
Thy silver and thy gold is mine: THY WIVES ALSO AND
THY CHILDREN, even the goodliest are mine.

"And the king of Israel answered and said, My lord,
O king, according to thy saying, I am thine, and all that I
have."[30] It is unfortunate that we do not have an account of
Jezebel's reaction to all of this for she surely would have
been included in the booty!

But when Ben-hadad of Syria saw what a timid weak-
ling Ahab was, he decided to increase his demands. He sent
a message saying, "Yet I will send my servants unto thee
tomorrow about this time, and they shall search thine house,
and the houses of thy servants; and it shall be, that whatsoever is pleasant in thine eyes, they shall put it in their hand,
and take it away."[31] This latest demand to freely loot the

27. 1 Kings 11:23-25
28. 1 Kings 20:1
29. Ibid.

30. 1 Kings 20:2-4
31. 1 Kings 20:6

royal palace and the wealthy homes of the government officials was deemed intolerable. The king's advisors were perfectly willing to sacrifice the king's fortune and the king's
family but when it came to looting their own houses they
loudly protested: "Hearken not unto him, nor consent!"[32]
So Ahab sent back word that his first offer still stood but
rather than consent to the open looting of the royal palace
and the best homes of Samaria, the people would continue
to endure the siege.

This resistance filled the king of Syria with rage. He
sent a new message declaring, "The gods do so unto me,
and more also, if the dust of Samaria shall suffice . . . [with
adequate room following its conquest] for all the people that
follow me."[33]

However, the new spirit of resistance among his advisors gave Ahab courage so he replied, "Let not him that
girdeth on his harness [armor] boast himself as he that
putteth it off."[34] Obviously, this was an ancient version of
the proverb, "Don't count your chickens before they're
hatched."

The king of Syria commanded his general saying, "Set
yourselves in array."[35] He would teach these obstreperous
Israelites!

But the king of Syria had a low estimate of the extent
of the task before him. Before commencing that attack he
invited his generals and allied kings to join him at the festive
board with wining and dining. This turned out to be fatal.

At that very moment a "prophet" (not mentioned by
name but probably one of Elijah's fellow workers), was addressing himself to Ahab, king of Israel. He said that the
Lord had revealed to him that this vast multitude would be
delivered into Israel's hands if they went out of the city
immediately and attacked the Syrians. The astonished Ahab
said, "Who shall order the battle?" and the prophet replied,
"Thou!"[36]

---

32. 1 Kings 20:8
33. 1 Kings 20:10. On this verse see Clarke's *Bible Commentary*, Vol. 2, p. 465.
34. 1 Kings 20:11
35. 1 Kings 20:12
36. 1 Kings 20:14

Ahab attacked with a relatively small force at high noon[37] and caught the Syrians completely by surprise. When the Syrian soldiers saw the Israelites coming they attempted to rally but found themselves without leadership because "Ben-hadad was drinking himself drunk in the pavilions, he and the kings, the thirty and two kings that helped him."[38] The whole Syrian army was therefore routed and even Ben-hadad barely escaped. He had to mount his horse and race off with his wildly fleeing cavalry.[39]

King Ahab and the Israelites were jubilant and immediately felt justified in congratulating themselves, but the prophet of the Lord knew there was no time for boasting. "Go," said he, "strengthen thyself, and mark, and see what thou doest: for at the return of the year the king of Syria will come up against thee."[40]

Apparently for the second time in his life King Ahab had the good sense to heed the warning from a prophet of God. But in spite of his preparations Ahab was amazed at the vast host the Syrians were able to raise after their previous monumental defeat. They made the Israelites look "like two little flocks of kids; but the Syrians filled the country."[41]

However, once again in this moment of crisis the Lord was willing to give a special blessing even to so wicked a king as Ahab in order that God's righteous 7,000 might survive. So again "there came a man of God" who promised victory to Ahab and his hosts.

Ahab waited seven days[42] before he considered it the right time to join the Syrians in battle. When he attacked there was such a great slaughter that the Syrians once more madly retreated. They fled to the nearest walled city, called Aphek, which was located a few miles east of the Sea of Galilee. Thousands of the Syrians mounted the stout walls of Aphek prepared to make a stand. The Israelites, however, appear to have made no direct assault upon the city but seem to have worked day and night undermining the city walls. When these collapsed it was like the destruction of

---

37. 1 Kings 20:15-16
38. 1 Kings 20:16
39. 1 Kings 20:20

40. 1 Kings 20:22
41. 1 Kings 20:27
42. 1 Kings 20:29

Jericho. The falling barricades of brick and stone killed 27,000 Syrian soldiers.[43]

The shrewd Ben-hadad saw that his mighty war machine was virtually annihilated so he fled to an inner chamber of the city to work out a strategy of survival for himself and his top commanders. His advisers thought King Ahab would be flattered by a display of abject humility so "they girded sackcloth on their loins, and put ropes on their heads [probably around their necks] and came to the king of Israel, and said, Thy servant Ben-hadad saith, I pray thee, let me live."[44]

Ahab's reaction was exactly what the Syrians had hoped. His entire perspective as victor collapsed as he almost fawningly replied, "Is he yet alive? he is my brother."[45] Ahab was speaking of a man who only a short time before was demanding the king's wives for himself and officers and the king's children for his slaves. He had been on the verge of massacring the whole city of Samaria until the Lord intervened with directions to prevent it. Now Ahab had called this depraved creature "brother!"

It was obvious that Ahab saw in Ben-hadad a man of his own mold. The corrupt heart of Ahab went out to the king of Syria. And it so tickled Ahab's ego to have the mighty monarch from Damascus pleading for mercy that Ahab ignored the threat which Ben-hadad represented. He not only spared his life after the Lord had ordered his destruction but he honored Ben-hadad by having the vanquished monarch ride beside him in his chariot.[46]

The king of Syria was quick to exploit Ahab's gullibility. He pretended to offer a great concession. Said he, "The cities which my father [Ben-Hadad I] took from thy father, I will restore; and thou shalt make streets for thee [to contain bazaars for the sale of Israel's wares] in Damascus, as my father made in Samaria."[47] This minor concession was made the exclusive basis for a peace treaty between the two

43. 1 Kings 20:30
44. 1 Kings 20:32
45. Ibid.
46. 1 Kings 20:33
47. 1 Kings 20:34. See Clarke, *Bible Commentary*, Vol. 2, p. 467

countries and after Ahab had codified it in a covenant with the king of Damascus he "sent him away."[48] Ahab did not know it, but he had just signed his death warrant.

The prophet of the Lord intercepted the king as he was returning to Samaria. Being in disguise the king did not recognize him. The man pretended he had been fighting for the king as a soldier. He asked what the king would do to him for losing an important Syrian prisoner through sheer carelessness. The king said such malfeasance by a soldier was worthy of death. The prophet promptly removed his disguise and declared to Ahab, "Thus saith the Lord, Because thou hast let go out of thy hand a man whom I appointed to utter destruction, therefore thy life shall go for his life, and thy people for his people."[49]

Ahab had seen enough of God's prophets lately to recognize that they knew what they were talking about. This latest prophecy of doom sent him to Samaria "heavy and displeased."[50] Before long, however, he had more to displease him. News reached Ahab that the king of Damascus had returned home, mobilized another vast host and now defied Israel to try to get back the promised cities which Syrian troops continued to occupy. It was the old story of one criminally-minded king double-crossing another.

Ahab and Jezebel Commit a Murder

A short time after this, Ahab became involved in a vicious intrigue against a neighbor in Jezreel. This pleasant community overlooked the verdant Jezreel valley as it swept eastward toward the Jordan gorge. Here Ahab and Jezebel had built their summer palace. But it seems that a man of Israel named Naboth had a vineyard right next to the palace. Ahab wanted it. He therefore asked Naboth to sell it to him or accept another vineyard on a trade.

"And Naboth said to Ahab, The Lord forbid it me, that I should give the inheritance of my fathers unto thee."[51]

---

48. Ibid.
49. 1 Kings 20:42
50. 1 Kings 20:43
51. 1 Kings 21:3. Land was held among the Israelites as a trust for their posterity as required by the Law of Moses in Leviticus 25:23.

Instead of accepting the right of Naboth to make this decision concerning his own property, Ahab threw a childish tantrum. He "came into his house heavy and displeased, because of the word which Naboth the Jezreelite had spoken to him. . . . And he laid him down upon his bed and turned away his face, and would eat no bread."[52]

However, the treacherous Queen Jezebel induced Ahab to tell her the cause of his sorrow and when she had ascertained it she exclaimed, "Dost thou now govern the kingdom of Israel? arise, and eat bread, and let thine heart be merry: I will give thee the vineyard of Naboth the Jezreelite."[53]

What she had in mind was to murder Naboth. Jezebel engineered the scheme but nevertheless, from what we learn later, Ahab was apparently a knowledgeable party to the conspiracy and cynically allowed his wife to carry it out for him.[54] Jezebel's plot was to send a letter to the leaders of Jezreel (she and the king then being at the palace in Samaria), and tell them to hold a great public "fast" during which Naboth was to be especially honored. They were to "set Naboth on high among the people" and then at the height of the solemnities two "sons of Belial" or evil men were to emerge from the crowd and vehemently charge Naboth with committing blasphemy against "God and the king."[55] The elders of Jezreel were to promptly incite the people into mob violence with the intent of pulling Naboth from his place of honor and having him stoned to death.

When this corrupt communication was received by the elders of the city of Jezreel they made no attempt to protest against this shedding of innocent blood but went right ahead and carried it out to the last jot and tittle. Apparently Naboth's sons rose to the defense of their father for a later scripture discloses that not only was Naboth stoned to death but also his sons.[56] We further learn from the Septuagint

---

52. 1 Kings 21:4
53. 1 Kings 21:7
54. This becomes apparent from the Lord's subsequent condemnation of Ahab in 1 Kings 21:19.
55. 1 Kings 21:9-10
56. 2 Kings 9:26

version that the mangled bodies were left unburied to be devoured by prowling dogs and swine.[57]

The elders of Jezreel then sent a message to the capital saying, "Naboth is stoned and is dead."[58] Jezebel rushed into her husband with the news saying, "Arise, take possession of the vineyard of Naboth the Jezreelite, which he refused to give thee for money: for Naboth is not alive, but dead."[59] Josephus says, "Ahab was glad at what had been done, and rose up immediately from the bed whereon he lay."[60] Calling for his chariot, the king rode off to inspect his ill-gotten gains. Behind him followed two of his principal officers, Jehu and Bidkar.[61] Jehu is the man whom the Lord had identified to Elijah on Mount Sinai as a future ruler of Israel.[62]

Elijah Appears Before Ahab for the Last Time

But right while Ahab was reveling in his new acquisition, the word of the Lord came to Elijah saying, "Arise, go down to meet Ahab king of Israel, which is in Samaria: behold, he is in the vineyard of Naboth, whither he is gone down to possess it."[63]

There was no person or thing in all Israel which Ahab detested more than Elijah. It must have been a great shock to him in this hour of evil delight to suddenly see the rudely-clad prophet standing in the way. Ahab spat out at him, "Hast thou found me, O mine enemy?" Elijah replied, "I have found thee."[64] Then Elijah poured out on Ahab the condemnation of a divine judgment which Elijah had received from the Lord in the form of a prophecy. He said, "Thus saith the Lord, Hast thou killed and also taken possession? . . . In the place were dogs licked the blood of Naboth shall dogs lick thy blood, even thine."[65] Then Elijah announced the extermination of Ahab's house. Quoting the Lord, he said, "I will bring evil upon thee, and will take away thy posterity. . . .

---

57. The Septuagint version of 1 Kings 22:38 refers to this incident and says, "And the swine and the dogs licked his blood. . . ." See Clarke, *Bible Commentary*, Vol. 2, p. 478.
58. 1 Kings 21:14
59. 1 Kings 21:15
60. Josephus, *Antiquities of the Jews*, Book 8, chapter 13:8
61. 2 Kings 9:25
62. 1 Kings 19:16
63. 1 Kings 21:18
64. 1 Kings 21:20
65. 1 Kings 21:19

And will make thine house like the house of Jeroboam . . .
and like the house of Baasha. . . ."[66] But the worst condemnation was reserved for wicked Queen Jezebel. Said Elijah,
"And of Jezebel also spake the Lord, saying, The dogs shall
eat Jezebel by the wall of Jezreel."[67]

The literal fulfillment of all these prophecies was to become an ugly reality in the near future and the man who
would launch the bloodbath which would bring it about was
standing nearby right while Elijah was describing what would
happen. He was Jehu, commander of the hosts, who had
followed Ahab down to Jezreel in his chariot. As of this
moment it probably never occurred to Jehu that he would
be the instrument by which these things would be accomplished. They were horrible to contemplate. In fact the prospect of it was enough to shock the king, himself. For once
in his life, Ahab found the capacity to experiment with repentance. The scripture says that after hearing Elijah's
doomsday prophecy, Ahab ". . . rent his clothes, and put sack
cloth upon his flesh, and fasted, and lay [slept] in sackcloth
and went softly."[68]

Nor did the Lord ignore the gesture. Even from so
reprobate a person as Ahab, repentance received its reward.
The Lord said to Elijah, "Seest thou how Ahab humbleth
himself before me? because he humbleth himself before me,
I will not bring the evil in his days: but in his son's days
will I bring the evil upon his house."[69] And this was the way
it turned out approximately twelve years later.[70] Meanwhile,
however, Israel was to pass through some political crises
which originated in another sector.

In 853 B.C. Assyria Makes a Military Thrust Toward the West

For centuries Palestine had been in the cross-fire between the Egyptians and the Assyrians. First one would
push out in a military thrust and then the other. And more
often than not, the preliminary phases of the campaign by
either of these nations called for a conquest of Palestine since

---

66. 1 Kings 21:22. The posterity of both these kings was exterminated.
67. 1 Kings 21:23.   69. 1 Kings 21:29
68. 1 Kings 21:27   70. 2 Kings, Chapters 9 and 10.

this was part of the land bridge over which their conquering armies would have to pass. In 853 B.C. the Assyrians came down from Nineveh and launched the first of a series of campaigns which eventually propelled that nation into military dominance of the then known world. It was not achieved quickly, however, but required numerous campaigns and the most ruthless cruelty. Actually, Assyria had been practically dormant during the previous century trying to recover from its wars with the Hittites in Asia Minor. Now, however, Assyria was being mobilized under a new king named Shalmaneser III who boasted that he would restore the glories of the old Assyrian empire.[71]

Fortunately, the details of these wars were recorded on the famous monolith of Shalmaneser which was discovered by Henry Layard in 1845 while digging along the Tigris river at Tell Nimrud.[72] This archaelogical treasure is now in the British Museum and confirms a number of details contained in the Biblical history of this period. It also fills in some details which the Bible does not mention.

For example, from this source we learn that just as soon as the Assyrian juggernaut pushed across the Euphrates river and attacked Syria in 853 B.C., all the surrounding nations joined with Syria in resisting this common threat. Shalmaneser III recorded on his stone monolith that this included King Ahab of Israel. Up to this time Ahab had considered Syria the major threat, but once Assyria loomed up over the horizon Ahab rushed to Syria's support. In fact, the monolith says he provided half as much fighting power as the Syrians themselves.[73] The old saying that war and politics make strange bed-fellows certainly applies here.

Nevertheless, the coalition of little nations which helped Syria were successful in holding Shalmaneser. Shalmaneser III claimed a great victory in the major battle of this campaign which was fought at Qarqar on the Orontes River

---

71. Shalmaneser III reigned from 858-824 B.C. In the sixth, eleventh and fourteenth years of his reign he attacked the allied kingdoms of the west which covered Syria and Palestine. The monolith of Shalmaneser which is now in the British Museum describes these military events. (See Werner Keller, *The Bible as History*, p. 240.)

72. Ibid. p. 239

73. See comments of Dr. Emil G. Kraeling in the Rand McNally *Bible Atlas*, p. 280.

in Syria. However, he gained no new territory nor does "he claim to have carried off trophies, imposed tribute, or received submission."[74] All that came in later campaigns. There was some reason, therefore, why the coalition of smaller countries would have considered this battle a victory for them. After the battle at Qarqar, Assyria temporarily retired from the field and the little countries then went back to the business of fighting among themselves.

Israel was no exception. As soon as the Assyrians had gone home, King Ahab was determined to make the king of Syria give back the Israelite cities which he was still holding in spite of his "covenant" to return them. Ahab was especially anxious to recover Ramoth which lay in the uplands east of the Jordan river and was therefore called Ramoth-gilead, Gilead being the Trans-Jordan district of which Ramoth had been the seat of government under Solomon.[75]

To seize possession of Ramoth-gilead was no easy task. Ahab needed a substantial ally. All of a sudden he found one from a most unexpected quarter — Judah.

Ahab Acquires the King of Judah as an Ally

It appears that almost immediately after the war with the Assyrians,[76] Ahab was visited by Jehoshaphat, king of Judah. This was the first time since the division of these two kingdoms that there had been a visit by one royal house to the other. It seems rather astonishing that Jehoshaphat who had fought heathenism in Judah all during his reign would suddenly arrive in Israel expressing the greatest cordiality toward the heathen King Ahab. It is only when we realize that the shadow of Assyrian terror hung over all these nations that the political motives of Jehoshaphat can be understood. In a very few years the men of Nineveh would be back hammering on the gates of Judah, and King Jehoshaphat apparently anticipated this development and felt that, regardless of the cost, the need of the hour was a tight alliance between Israel and Judah.

---

74. See Geikie, *Hours With the Bible*, Vol. 4, p. 134
75. 1 Kings 4:13
76. The date of this battle is firmly fixed by archaeologists as June, 853 B.C. (See Dr. Kraeling in the Rand McNally *Bible Atlas*, p. 280), and since 853 marked the close of Ahab's reign we know the visit of Jehoshaphat would have had to be immediately after the battle of Qarqar.

As it turned out, the cost was greater than the good King Jehoshaphat had calculated. Nevertheless, this was a risk the king was willing to take. He did three things to assure a lasting partnership with King Ahab. First, as we shall see shortly, Jehoshaphat committed the military forces of Judah to fight with Israel in regaining Ramoth-gilead from King Ben-hadad of Syria.[77] Second, he agreed to an alliance between his own family and that of Ahab by having the daughter of Ahab and Jezebel betrothed to his own son, Jehoram, the crown prince of Judah.[78] The girl's name was Athaliah and she turned out to be a daughter of Satan, consecrated to total evil and following the same pattern of heathen immorality as her mother, Jezebel. Third, Jehoshaphat entered into a trade agreement with Ahab wherein they were to collaborate in the construction of two merchant fleets, one to sail the full length of the Mediterranean[79] and the other to embark from Ezion-geber[80] in an effort to duplicate the rich trade excursions of Solomon.

King Ahab, of course, was elated with the unexpected good fortune of having Jehoshaphat present himself at the capital in Samaria with the obvious intent of promoting good will between the two countries. Ahab promptly made a great feast for Jehoshaphat and his entire royal entourage. The scripture says he "killed sheep and oxen for him in abundance, and for the people that he had with him."[81] After the feasting and cordiality had created the proper atmosphere, Ahab felt sufficiently sure of himself to say to Jehoshaphat, "Wilt thou go with me to battle to Ramoth-gilead?"[82] Jehoshaphat replied with a fervor that must have surprised even Ahab, "I am as thou art, my people as thy people, my horses as thy horses."[83] There was no doubt about it, Jehoshaphat had come prepared to lay his whole kingdom on the line in order to show his good faith as a future partner of Israel.

MICAIAH, A NEW PROPHET, APPEARS ON THE SCENE

But having committed himself to support Ahab, Jehoshaphat then suggested that they make sure the project had the

---

77. 1 Kings 22:4
78. 2 Chronicles 21:6; 22:2
79. 1 Kings 22:48
80. 2 Chronicles 20:36

81. 2 Chronicles 18:2
82. 1 Kings 22:4
83. Ibid.

blessing of the Lord. Said he, "Inquire, I pray thee, at the word of the Lord to-day."[84] Ahab thought it was a splendid idea and the next thing Jehoshaphat knew, the apostate king of Israel had ushered in before them 400 of his motley palace "prophets."[85]

It will be recalled that the scripture had already spoken about 400 "prophets of the groves . . . which eat at Jezebel's table."[86] They were the self-mutilated priests of Ashtoreth who had failed to appear on Mount Carmel as commanded by Elijah.[87] From all we can tell, these were the same 400 professional palace prophets who now came parading in before Ahab and Jehoshaphat. Ahab said to them, "Shall I go against Ramoth-gilead to battle, or shall I forbear?"[88] They all chanted in perfect unity, "Go up, for the Lord shall deliver it into the hand of the king."[89] What these heathen prelates were accustomed to doing was telling the king exactly what he wanted to hear and then calling it "prophecy."

However, to the eyes of King Jehoshaphat there must have been sufficient evidence in the behavior, dress, and spirit of these men to clearly indicate that they were all uninspired hyprocrites. He said to Ahab, "Is there not here a prophet of the Lord besides, that we might inquire of him?"[90]

Ahab could have told Jehoshaphat about Elijah and Elisha, but instead, he chose to tell him about a prophet of Jehovah who was being held at that very moment in prison.[91] Said he, "There is yet one man, Micaiah, the son of Imlah, by whom we can inquire of the Lord."[92] Then, almost like a pouting child, he blurted out, "But I hate him; for he doth not prophesy good concerning me, but evil."[93]

Nevertheless, to please Jehoshaphat, Ahab sent an officer to fetch the imprisoned prophet from a nearby district.

---

84. 1 Kings 22:5
85. 1 Kings 22:6
86. 1 Kings 18:19
87. Ibid.
88. 1 Kings 22:6
89. Ibid.
90. 1 Kings 22:7
91. This is apparent from 1 Kings 22:26-27 where Micaiah is described as being taken "back" to prison.
92. 1 Kings 22:8
93. Ibid.

As Micaiah was being transported to Samaria, his custodial officer decided to give Micaiah a little practical advice. Said he, "Behold now, the words of the prophets declare good unto the king with one mouth: let thy word, I pray thee, be like the word of one of them, and speak that which is good."[94] But Micaiah replied, "As the Lord liveth, even what my God saith, that will I speak."[95]

For some reason King Ahab had decided to make Micaicah's appearance before him a public spectacle. He therefore set up improvised thrones for himself and King Jehoshaphat in an open place near the main gate of the capital.[96] When Micaiah arrived he saw the two kings dressed in their royal robes and giving audience to a large crowd. All the heathen priests were there including a certain arrogant fellow named Zedekiah. This priest had mounted iron horns across his forehead and was pushing about like a goring ox as a sign that Ahab, as the bull of Ephraim, would push Syria into the ground.[97] The other priests were also bellowing about in great gusto crying, "Go up to Ramoth-gilead and prosper: for the Lord shall deliver it into the king's hand."[98]

The arrival of Micaiah brought silence to the turbulent throng. King Ahab looked down from his temporary throne and said, "Micaiah, shall we go against Ramoth-gilead to battle, or shall we forbear?"[99]

Micaiah showed that he had a sense of humor and also a certain spirit of defiant bravado. He declared, "Go, and prosper: for the Lord shall deliver it into the hand of the king."[100] The sarcasm with which he parroted these exact words of the heathen priests revealed that he was making fun of the king. The exasperated Ahab who obviously had been the victim of the prophet's sharp barbs on previous occasions, cried out, "How many times shall I adjure thee that thou tell me nothing but that which is true in the name of the Lord?"[101]

Very well, so Ahab would truly like to hear the word of the Lord? Micaiah shot out at him, "I saw all Israel

---

94. 1 Kings 22:13
95. 1 Kings 22:14
96. 1 Kings 22:10
97. 1 Kings 22:11

98. 1 Kings 22:12
99. 1 Kings 22:15
100. Ibid.
101. 1 Kings 22:16

scattered upon the hills, as sheep that have not a shepherd: and the Lord said, these have no master: let them return every man to his house in peace."[102] Micaiah was predicting that if this war were undertaken King Ahab would be killed. Instead of being grateful for the warning, the simpering Ahab turned to Jehoshaphat and whimpered, "Did I not tell thee that he would prophesy no good concerning me, but evil?"[103]

But Micaiah was not through. He had something to say about these 400 wretched heathen priests. He proclaimed that a "lying spirit" had been put in the mouths of these phony prophets to persuade the king to go up to Ramoth-gilead where evil would befall him.

This was more than Zedekiah, the priest with the iron-horned headdress, could endure. He strode up and struck Micaiah across the face, saying, "Which way [or how] went the Spirit of the Lord from me to speak unto thee?"[104] Micaiah replied, "Behold, thou shalt see in that day, when thou shalt go into an inner chamber to hide thyself."[105]

King Ahab intervened at this point and ordered the guard to take the prophet away. "Take Micaiah," he commanded, "and carry him back unto Amon the governor of the city, and to Joash the king's son; and say, Thus saith the king, Put this fellow in the prison, and feed him with bread of affliction, and with water of affliction, until I come in peace."[106] Micaiah retorted, "If thou return at all in peace, the Lord hath not spoken by me." Then he turned to the people and cried, "Hearken, O people, every one!"[107]

The Fatal Battle at Ramoth-Gilead

It seems astonishing that Ahab would ignore the ominous prophecy of Micaiah in view of his past experience with the prophet of the Lord. But what seems even more amazing was the strange attitude exhibited by King Jehoshaphat. It was he who had asked for a prophet of the Lord in the first

---

102. 1 Kings 22:17
103. 1 Kings 22:18
104. 1 Kings 22:24
105. 1 Kings 22:25. The record does not disclose when nor under what circumstances this particular prophecy was fulfilled.
106. 1 Kings 22:26-27
107. 1 Kings 22:28

place. One would have expected Jehoshaphat to have heeded the warning of Micaiah even if Ahab did not. The fact that he ignored Micaiah's warning would seem to reflect the fear and confusion which the terror of Assyria had imposed on the minds of monarchs throughout the region. Jehoshaphat seemed determined to make "affinity" with Ahab at all costs.[108] So he sent for the armies of Judah and joined with Ahab in his campaign against the Syrians.

When the hosts of Judah and Israel had assembled at Ramoth-gilead, Ahab decided to resort to a strange strategy. He correctly assumed that the Syrians would concentrate their attack on him personally, so he disguised himself as a regular charioteer. However, his instructions to King Jehoshaphat were to "put thou on thy robes."[109] This was apparently intended as a military decoy, but for Jehoshaphat it could have been literal suicide. Nevertheless, he blithely consented, just as he had agreed to everything else.

The battle had barely begun when Jehoshaphat found himself in frantic straits. The king of the Syrians had told his officers to concentrate entirely on the capture of Ahab,[110] but "it came to pass, when the captains of the [Syrian] chariots saw Jehoshaphat, that they said, Surely it is the king of Israel. And they turned aside to fight against him: and Jehoshaphat cried out. And it came to pass, when the captains of the chariots perceived that it was not the king of Israel, that they turned back from pursuing him."[111]

This was a narrow escape. Had not the king of Syria been so dynamically emphatic about having his officers concentrate exclusively on the capture of Ahab, Jehoshaphat would have paid for this foolish farce with his life.

The Syrian officers never did discover Ahab but the Lord's prophetic declaration concerning him was fulfilled. One of the Syrian bowmen "drew a bow at a venture," meaning without aiming at any particular target.[112] "and smote the king of Israel between the joints of the harness: wherefore he

---

108. 2 Chronicles 18:1
109. 1 Kings 22:30
110. 1 Kings 22:31
111. 1 Kings 22:32-33
112. *The Interpreter's Bible*, Vol. 3, p. 184; Clarke, *Bible Commentary*, Vol. 2, p. 477.

said unto the driver of his chariot, Turn thine hand, and carry me out of the host; for I am wounded."[113] Nevertheless, Ahab determined to remain at least a symbol of leadership to his armies so, as "the battle increased that day . . . the king was stayed up in his chariot," and pretended to be in full command of the situation.[114] Eventually, however, he collapsed from the loss of blood which ran down his body and became a pool in the bottom of his chariot.[115] By evening he was dead.

"And there went a proclamation throughout the host about the going down of the sun, saying, Every man to his city, and every man to his country. So the king died, and was brought to Samaria; and they buried the king in Samaria."[116]

Then the scripture adds this final note, "And one washed the chariot in the pool of Samaria; and the dogs licked up his blood; and they washed his armour; according unto the word of the Lord which he spake."[117]

So, about the year 853 B.C., Ahab died and his son, Ahaziah, reigned in his stead.[118]

The Building of Two Maritime Fleets

King Ahaziah only ruled Israel during a part of two years (853-852 B.C.), but several important events occurred which gave prominence to his reign in Biblical history. He continued the alliance with Judah which Ahab, his father, had begun, and before long the two countries had worked out an agreement for the construction of two maritime fleets. One of the fleets was to be constructed on the Mediterranean with ships large enough to sail to Tarshish or Spain and the other fleet was to be built on the eastern gulf of the Red Sea to duplicate Solomon's naval excursions into the gold fields

---

113. 1 Kings 22:34
114. 1 Kings 22:35
115. Ibid.
116. 1 Kings 22:36-37
117. 1 Kings 22:38. The original prophecy was through Elijah who had said to Ahab, "Thus saith the Lord, In the place where dogs licked the blood of Naboth shall dogs lick thy blood, even thine." (1 Kings 21:19) Naboth was killed at Jezreel (1 Kings 21:15) whereas the incident of washing Ahab's chariot occurred in the pool of Samaria. There is surely some answer to this minor discrepancy but it cannot be found in the present incomplete account.
118. 1 Kings 22:40

of Opher and the spice markets of the Far East. It sounded like a magnificent venture but the Lord was displeased with it.

In 2 Chronicles 20:35-36 we read that "after this did Jehoshaphat king of Judah join himself with Ahaziah king of Israel who did very wickedly: and he joined himself with him to make ships to go to Tarshish [Spain]: and [also] they made the ships in Ezion-geber [located on the Akaba Gulf of the Red Sea]."

The next verse says that the Lord sent one of his servants named Eliezer to Jehoshaphat who said, "Because thou hast joined thyself with Ahaziah, the Lord hath broken thy works. And the ships were broken, that they were not able to go to Tarshish."

We further learn in 2 Kings 22:49, that prior to the destruction of the ships, Ahaziah had asked permission to send his sailors along with those from Judah. Jehoshaphat had refused. Perhaps it was because of the warning from Eliezer that Jehoshaphat thought he could save the fleet by refusing to let the apostate Israelites serve on the boats. But it was to no avail. Not only was the Mediterranean fleet of Tarshish ships destroyed, but so was the fleet at the port of Ezion-geber. (1 Kings 22:48)

THE MOABITE REBELLION

But King Ahaziah had more to occupy his mind than the loss of a few boats. He was on the verge of losing one of Israel's most valuable tributaries, Moab. These heathen descendants of Lot had been watching Israel gradually deteriorate and when King Ahab was killed at Ramoth-gilead, the king of the Moabites decided it was a good time to throw off the yoke of Israel. This king's name was Mesha and he turned out to be about the toughest enemy the Israelites had faced in that generation. The Moabites occupied the territory east of the Dead Sea. They were the people of Ruth and therefore, in part, the ancestors of David. Nevertheless, David had conquered them and placed them under tribute along with their distant relatives, the heathen Ammonites, who were also descendants of Lot and occupied the territory just north of Moab. Now, they were determined to break their connection with the Israelites.

King Mesha was so proud of his rebellion and administration that he wrote it up on a large black stone, beautifully
carved. More details concerning the early phase of the Moabite rebellion can be found on this Moabite Stone than in
the Bible. The recovery of this stone is one of the highlights
of Bible archaeology and should be of interest to all Bible
students.[119]

The king of the Moabites and the author of the Moabite
Stone had his capital at Dibon, or Diban, located about three

---

119. Dr. Werner Keller summarizes the story of its find: "In 1868 a German missionary, F. A. Klein, was visiting Biblical sites in Palestine. The route he
followed took him through Transjordan, through Edom, and eventually to
Moab. As he was riding in the neighborhood of Diban, the ancient Dibon on
the middle reaches of the Arnon, his attention was particularly aroused by a
large smooth stone. The yellow sand had almost completely drifted over it.
Klein jumped from his horse and bent over the stone curiously. It was un-
mistakably ancient Hebrew writing. He could hardly believe his eyes. It was as
much as he could do in the heat of the midday sun to stand the heavy basalt
stone upright. It was three feet high and rounded on top. Klein cleaned it
carefully with a knife and a handkerchief. Thirty-four lines of writing appeared.

"He would have preferred to take the stone document away with him,
then and there, but it was far too heavy. Besides, in no time a mob of armed
Arabs was on the spot. With wild gesticulations they surrounded the missionary, maintaining that the stone was their property and demanding from him
a fantastic price for it.

"Klein guessed that his discovery was an important one and was in despair.
Missionaries never have much money. He tried in vain to make the natives
change their minds. There was nothing for it but to mark the site carefully
on his map. He then gave up the idea of continuing his journey, hurried back
to Jerusalem and from there straight home to Germany to try to collect the
necessary money for the Arabs.

"But in the meantime other people got busy, which was a good thing;
otherwise, an extremely valuable piece of evidence for Biblical history might
well have been lost forever.

"A French scholar, Clermont-Ganneau, who was working in Jerusalem,
had heard of the German missionary's discovery and had set out at once for
Diban. It needed all his powers of persuasion to get the suspicious Arabs even
to allow him to examine the writing on the basalt stone. Surrounded by the
hostile eyes of the natives, Clermont-Ganneau took a squeeze (impression) of
the surface. Months later when Parisian scholars had translated the text, the
French government sanctioned the purchase without hesitation. But judge the
Frenchman's disappointment when he reached Diban, equipped with a caravan
and the necessary sum of money, and found that the stone had disappeared.
Only a patch of soot indicated the spot where it had been. The Arabs had
blown it to pieces with gunpowder — from avarice. They hoped to do a more
profitable trade with Europeans whose obsession with antiquity would make
them willing to buy the individual pieces.

"What could Clermont-Ganneau do but set out on the trail of the individual
pieces of the valuable document. After a great deal of trouble and searching,
and after endless haggling, he was successful in retrieving all the broken fragments. Two larger blocks and eighteen smaller pieces were reassembed in
accordance with the squeeze, and before the German missionary had even
collected the necessary money, the impressive stone from Diban was standing
among the valuable recent acquisitions in the Louvre in Paris." (Keller, *The
Bible As History*, pp. 235-237)

miles north of the Arnon river. On the Moabite Stone he describes his reign and his rebellion, how he added a hundred cities to his kingdom, how he built reservoirs and aqueducts and subjugated fortified Israelite towns such as Nebo. Concerning the latter he says, "And I went by night, and I fought against the city from the rising of the sun until noon, and I took it, and I killed all the people, seven thousand men and children, and the free women, and the young girls, and the slaves whom I consecrated [as temple prostitutes] to Astar-Chemosh. I carried away from there the vessels of Jahveh [Jehovah] and I dragged them on the earth before Chemosh."[120]

Mesha then says that the king of Israel, who was then Ahaziah, came with his army and occupied Jahaz, but for some reason not disclosed by Mesha, he returned to Israel without reconquering the land. Mesha rejoiced over this withdrawal and attributed his good fortune to the intervention of Chemosh his heathen god.[121]

We will continue our narrative about Mesha shortly, but for the moment, the thread of the Bible story now goes back to King Ahaziah of Israel who had left the Moabite campaign at Jahaz and returned to Samaria. There a fatal accident befell him.

ELIJAH'S MESSAGE TO KING AHAZIAH

The scripture says, "And Ahaziah fell down through a lattice in his upper chamber that was in Samaria, and was sick."[122] The upper windows of the houses in those days often projected out over the street, the bay forming a couch or seat for lounging. These windows were covered with lattices so that the occupants, particularly women, could not be seen by people passing below. Apparently one of the palace windows had a loose lattice or one which was not fastened properly and when King Ahaziah leaned against it from his couch it allowed him to fall through and land on the pavement or turf below.

---

120. Ibid., p. 108 (parenthesis in the original).
121. Ibid.
122. 2 Kings 1:2

When Ahaziah failed to recover from this fall he became worried lest he die, therefore he sent his servants to the heathen temple of Baalzebub located in Ekron, one of the five main Philistine cities. Baalzebub literally means the fly-god but is interpreted to mean "prince of devils."[123] Devil worship was so reprehensible to the Israelites that they often referred to Baalzebub as the dung-god.[124] Ahaziah instructed his messengers to go to the oracle or chief priest of Baalzebub and see whether the king was ever going to recover.

"But the angel of the Lord said to Elijah the Tishbite, Arise, go up to meet the messengers of the king of Samaria, and say unto them, Is it not because there is not a God in Israel, that ye go to inquire of Baal-zebub the god of Ekron? Now therefore thus saith the Lord, Thou shalt not come down from that bed on which thou art gone up, but shalt surely die."[125]

Elijah did just as the Lord had told him. He intercepted the king's messengers and conveyed to them exactly what the Lord had said. These men were so impressed that they decided to take the message back to the king rather than proceed to Ekron. However, it is apparent from the scripture that Elijah never identified himself to the messengers. Therefore, when the king had heard their story, he asked, "What manner of man was he which came up to meet you, and told you these words? And they answered him, He was an hairy man, and girt with a girdle of leather about his loins."[126] That's all Ahaziah needed to hear. Almost as though it were an oath he spat out the words, "It is Elijah the Tishbite!"[127]

Elijah's Life Is Saved by Consuming Fire

King Ahaziah hated Elijah. He did not look upon his words as a prophecy but more as a curse. He determined to teach Elijah what it meant to cross his king. Ahaziah sent out a captain and fifty men to find the prophet and haul him in. The soldiers finally located Elijah sitting quietly on top of a hill almost as though he were waiting for them. It must

---

123. Clarke, *Bible Commentary,* Vol. 4, p. 481
124. Ibid., Vol. 5, p. 65   126. 2 Kings 1:7, 8
125. 2 Kings 1:3, 4   127. Ibid.

have been a great relief to the captain of the guard when he spied the prophet, for Elijah had the reputation of being a most slippery and elusive quarry. With his prey practically in his hand, the captain arrogantly shouted up to the rustic figure, "Thou man of God, the king hath said, Come down!"[128] Little did the captain know what was about to happen to him and his men.

Elijah did not come down but proclaimed a divine judgment on this military band. As we have previously seen, such actions were always in accordance with a prior instruction from the Lord. Cried Elijah, "If I be a man of God, then let fire come down from heaven, and consume thee and thy fifty."[129] Immediately divine fire fell upon the captain and his guard and killed them.[130] As with the two eldest sons of Aaron, the fire from the Lord took their lives without destroying their bodies.[131] This would account for the sensational news which soon reached the palace in Samaria that the king's guard was lying dead beneath the hill where Elijah was camped.

King Ahaziah was thoroughly enraged. He would not be frustrated by a treacherous old man. So he sent out another guard of fifty men with a captain and told them to drag Elijah from his high perch and bring him before the king. But when they attempted to carry out their mission the same thing happened to them that happened to the first contingent.

If Ahaziah had not been on his death bed he probably would have risen up and taken out the next contingent himself. But since that was impossible he sent a third military guard to arrest Elijah. However, the captain of this third group was a humble man and greatly impressed by what had happened to his predecessors. Therefore, as he arrived at the foot of Elijah's hill, he made no arrogant demands of the prophet but meekly cried out, "O man of God, I pray thee, let my life, and the life of these fifty, thy servants, be precious in thy sight. Behold, there came fire down from heaven, and burnt up the two captains of the former fifties

128. 2 Kings 1:9
129. 2 Kings 1:10
130. Ibid.
131. Leviticus 10:1-4

with their fifties: therefore let my life now be precious in thy sight."[132]

Elijah would have no way of knowing of himself whether to trust the man or not. However, "the angel of the Lord said unto Elijah, Go down with him: be not afraid of him."[133] So Elijah went down to the captain of the guard and they took him before the king.

Whatever vows of vengeance Ahaziah may have made against Elijah prior to this time, he found himself unable to carry them out once he had seen the prophet of the Lord face-to-face and heard from his own lips the decree of God that the king was about to die. In fact, death may have come immediately after he heard these fatal words, "Thus saith the Lord, Forasmuch as thou hast sent messengers to inquire of Baal-zebub the god of Ekron, is it not because there is no God in Israel to inquire of his word? therefore thou shalt not come down off that bed on which thou art gone up, but shalt surely die."[134]

And the scripture says, "So he died, according to the word of the Lord which Elijah had spoken."[135]

Ahaziah had occupied a very short reign of less than two years and had no son to inherit his throne. He was therefore replaced by his brother whose name was Jehoram (or Joram).[136] Jehoram took over the throne of Israel around 851 B.C. and ruled until approximately 841 B.C.

THE TRANSLATION OF ELIJAH, THE PROPHET

Now it was time for Elijah to take leave of earth-life where his existence had been one of almost continuous hardship. For a number of years he had been working with Elisha to firm up the faith of the few valiant Priesthood holders and seek out as many as possible of the 7,000 in Israel whom the Lord had said were still loyal to Him. It appears that the Priesthood members or "sons of the prophets" had established centers at Gilgal, Jericho, and Bethel. Since the destruction of the priests of Baal at Mount Carmel the worship

---

132. 2 Kings 1:13-14
133. 2 Kings 1:15
134. 2 Kings 1:16

135. 2 Kings 1:17
136. 2 Kings 1:17; 3:1

of Jehovah had been more generally tolerated by the crown, and while the scripture makes no mention of the organizational mechanics involved, it seems obvious that Elijah and Elisha had been busy tutoring these brethren and helping them learn how to perpetuate the principles of righteousness under the government of the Priesthood.

These brethren had also learned to cultivate the spirit of revelation. Suddenly the light of Heaven poured out upon all of them the exciting but regrettable news that Elijah was about to be taken. As we shall see in a moment, Elijah knew about it, Elisha knew about it, so did the "sons of the prophets" at Bethel and Jericho.

The immediate reaction of Elijah to this revelation was a manifest desire to visit the brethren for the last time. In fact, the Lord commanded that this should be done. For some strange reason, however, Elijah wanted to make this final circuit alone. He therefore said to Elisha, "Tarry here, I pray thee; for the Lord hath sent me to Beth-el."[137] But Elisha would not hear of it. He knew that something tremendous was about to happen and he wasn't going to miss it even if he had to risk offending his beloved leader. Therefore he said, "As the Lord liveth, and as thy soul liveth, I will not leave thee."[138] So they went to Bethel.[139]

When they arrived, the local brethren could scarcely keep the great secret they possessed, so they took Elisha aside at the first opportunity and said, "Knowest thou that the Lord will take away thy master from thy head to-day?" And Elisha replied, "Yea, I know it; hold ye your peace."[140] In other words, keep it to yourselves.

Next, Elijah proposed to go Jericho, and once more he tried to get Elisha to tarry behind. But Elisha was as determined as ever to stay with him, so Elijah let him follow along.

---

137. 2 Kings 2:2
138. Ibid.
139. Ibid. This text says they "went down" to Bethel which has led some authorities to conclude that the Gilgal from which they were traveling was up in the mountains of Ephraim and not down near the Jordan river where we are accustomed to thinking of Joshua's original campsite of Gilgal.
140. 2 Kings 2:3

When they reached Jericho the "sons of the prophets" were as animated about their advance knowledge of Elijah's passing as the brethren at Bethel. They took Elisha aside to share the exciting news and, just as at Bethel, Elisha had to tell them, "Yea, I know it; hold ye your peace."[141]

Now Elijah was reaching a critical stage of his pilgrimage. The Lord had ordered him to cross the Jordan and he knew that somewhere over there on the other side he would be taken. Elijah therefore earnestly admonished Elisha, saying, "Tarry, I pray thee, here; for the Lord hath sent me to Jordan." But Elisha said with a sacred oath, "I will not leave thee!"[142] So the two of them proceeded down toward the river lying just three or four miles to the east.

However, they were not alone. Fifty of the "sons of the prophets" followed along as close as they dared.[143] This was just too wonderful to miss. As these men "stood to view afar off" they saw an almost unbelievable miracle. The elderly Elijah took off his rude mantle, rolled it up into sort of a staff and smote the waters of the river. "And they were divided hither and thither."[144] Not since the days of Joshua had such a thing happened.[145] The waters no doubt behaved in the same manner they did at that earlier date. If so, a clean break appeared in the midst of the torrent as though a huge, invisible dam had been instantly thrown up. The waters "rose up upon an heap,"[146] and the two servants of God walked over on dry ground.[147] Then the impeded flood roared back down into its channel.

The scripture says, "And it came to pass, when they were gone over, that Elijah said unto Elisha, Ask what I shall do for thee, before I be taken away from thee. And Elisha said, I pray thee, let a double portion of thy spirit be upon me. And he said, Thou hast asked a hard thing: nevertheless, if thou see me when I am taken from thee, it shall be so unto thee, but if not, it shall not be so."[148]

For Elisha there must have been some anxious moments as he waited in desperate anticipation to see whether or not

---

141. 2 Kings 2:5
142. 2 Kings 2:6
143. 2 Kings 2:7
144. 2 Kings 2:8

145. Joshua 3:9-17
146. Joshua 3:16
147. 2 Kings 2:8
148. 2 Kings 2:9-10

the Lord would allow him to witness the great drama of Elijah's departure. And he was not disappointed. In fact, when it came to pass it probably frightened him to the core of his being. The scripture says that as the veil parted there was a celestial chariot of such brilliant glory that it was afterwards called a "chariot of fire" and it had horses attached to it of similar glory. This vehicle swept in between Elijah and Elisha so that it separated them. The scripture does not specifically say so, but apparently Elijah entered the chariot and the next thing Elisha knew, his friend and patriarchal leader "went up by a whirlwind into heaven."[149] It must have been a marvelous, breath-taking sight, and as the full impact of the vision fell upon Elisha he impulsively cried out, "My father, my father, the chariot of Israel and the horsemen thereof!"[150]

When the heavens were closed and all nature seemed to have returned to its normal repose, Elisha felt a shadow of sorrow creep into his heart. The great Elijah was gone. Sadly he took off his cloak and rent it in twain.[151] Then he observed, lying on the ground, "the mantle of Elijah that fell from him."[152] Immediately he picked it up and strode back toward the river. Now he would discover whether or not he had a portion of Elijah's spirit. Wrapping the mantle together he smote the waters just as Elijah had done. At the same time he cried out, "Where is the Lord God of Elijah?"[153] And to his soul-satisfying gratification he saw the same magnificent miracle as that which had happened before. The waters "parted hither and thither."[154] Humbly but triumphantly he walked across on dry land.

When the fifty "sons of the prophets" saw the second dividing of the Jordan they exclaimed, "The spirit of Elijah doth rest on Elisha!"[155] They came running toward him, "and bowed themselves to the ground before him."[156]

However, these loyal disciples had not fully comprehended their revelation concerning Elijah. They knew he was going to be separated from Elisha, but apparently they

---

149. 2 Kings 2:11
150. 2 Kings 2:12
151. Ibid.
152. 2 Kings 2:13
153. 2 Kings 2:14
154. Ibid.
155. 2 Kings 2:15
156. Ibid.

did not realize that this was also going to be the end of Elijah's mortal mission. They appear to have interpreted the revelation as meaning that the Spirit would lead Elijah into the wilderness or some place where the aged prophet would need someone else to minister to him. They therefore said to the returning Elisha, "Behold, now, there be with thy servants fifty strong men; let them go, we pray thee, and seek thy master: lest peradventure the Spirit of the Lord hath taken him up, and cast him upon some mountain, or into some valley."[157]

Elisha appreciated this expression of their devotion, but he said, "Ye shall not send."[158] Had Elisha explained to them what had happened they no doubt would have been satisfied, but apparently he felt that this sacred vision was given to him as a personal sign just as Elijah had said. Therefore he did not share it with them at this time. The men, however, pleaded and pestered Elisha to let them hunt for their great leader until finally he consented in order to pacify them.

Elisha apparently let the sons of the prophets get across the river by whatever means they might. He made no attempt to facilitate their search with a miraculous crossing similar to the one he and Elijah had utilized. While they were away hunting, Elisha went on up to Jericho. There, after three days of fruitless, frantic searching, the fifty men returned to him. When they complained that they had failed to find the great prophet, Elisha chided them, saying, "Did I not say unto you, Go not?"[159] Later he must have told them what had really happened, however, because by the time Elisha proceeded on up to Bethel the word was out, and young non-believing hoodlums were challenging Elisha to "go up" the way his master had done. But this must wait for the next chapter. We will close this present chapter with one final question.

WHY WAS ELIJAH TRANSLATED?

As Elijah concluded one of the most difficult and strenuous Priesthood assignments in history, we pause to note the

157. 2 Kings 2:16   159. 2 Kings 2:18
158. Ibid.

purpose of the Lord in having this particular servant translated rather than pass through the change called death. It
is important to remember that a translated being is not resurrected nor the recipient of his final endowment of glory. He
must still pass through the portal of "death" but this will
happen in the twinkling of an eye rather than be precipitated
by disease or disaster. Translated beings remain "in the
flesh" but the seeds of death are temporarily suspended in
them so that they are not subject to the frailties of the flesh.
They are also endowed with tremendous powers over space
and time not ordinarily available to men in the flesh. So far
as we know all persons righteous enough to be translated
are allowed to make their residence with the people of Enoch.
They reside on a refined planet of their own and on a higher
dimension of glorified existence than mortal man. Concerning
the people of Enoch, Joseph Smith said,

"Now this Enoch God reserved unto Himself, that he
should not die at that time, and appointed unto him a ministry
unto terrestrial bodies, of whom there has been but little
revealed. . . . He is a ministering angel, to minister to those
who shall be heirs of salvation, and appeared unto Jude. . . .

"Many have supposed that the doctrine of translation
was a doctrine whereby men were taken immediately into the
presence of God, and into an eternal fullness, but this is a
mistaken idea. Their place of habitation is that of the terrestrial order, and a place prepared for such characters He
held in reserve to be ministering angels unto many planets,
and who as yet have not entered into so great a fullness as
those who are resurrected from the dead."[160]

So Elijah was made one of these choice ministering
angels to fulfill a special mission which the Lord had in
mind for him. So far as we know, the most important part
of that mission, and the reason why he had to be kept "in
the flesh" even though translated, was so that he could participate in the ministry of Jesus Christ prior to the Savior's
resurrection. Because Elijah was the last of Israel's prophets
to hold all of the sealing powers pertaining to the Higher
Priesthood, it was essential that he confer them on the heads

---

160. *Documentary History of the Church,* Vol. 4, pp. 209-210

of Peter, James and John at the Mount of Transfiguration.[161] Moses also appeared at that time and Joseph Fielding Smith explains why both of them had to come as translated beings.

". . . we understand why Elijah and Moses were preserved from death: because *they had a mission to perform,* and it had to be performed *before* the crucifixion of the Son of God, and *it could not be done in the spirit. They had to have tangible bodies.* Christ is the first fruits of the resurrection; therefore if any former prophets had a work to perform preparatory to the mission of the Son of God, or to the dispensation of the meridian of time, it was essential that they be preserved to fulfill that mission *in the flesh.* For that reason Moses disappeared from among the people and was taken up into the mountain, and the people *thought* he was buried by the Lord. The Lord preserved him, so that he could come at the proper time and *restore his keys* on the heads of Peter, James and John, who stood at the head of the dispensation of the meridian of time. He preserved Elijah from death that he might also come and bestow his keys upon the heads of Peter, James and John and prepare them for their ministry."[162]

We know from modern revelation that neither Moses nor Elijah continued in the status of translated beings very long after this event. They passed through the change and were resurrected with the Saints at the time of Christ's resurrection. In the Doctrine and Covenants 133:55 the scripture says, "And from Moses to Elijah, and from Elijah to John, WHO WERE WITH CHRIST IN HIS RESURRECTION . . ."[163] The New Testament gives several more details, saying, "And the graves were opened; and many bodies of the saints which slept arose, and came out of the graves after his resurrection, and went into the holy city, and appeared unto many."[164]

Among these, it would seem, were Moses and Elijah!

---

161. Matthew 17:1-3; *Teachings of Joseph Smith,* p. 158. Note that Elijah is translated "Elias" in the King James version.
162. Joseph Fielding Smith, *Doctrines of Salvation,* Vol. 2, pp. 110-111. (Italics in the original.)
163. Doc. and Cov. 133:55
164. Matthew 27:52-53

Scripture Reading and Questions on Chapter Fourteen

Scripture Reading: 1 Kings, chapters 20 to 22 inclusive; 2 Kings, chapters 1 and 2.

1—Approximately where did Elisha live? What kind of a home did he come from? Was he already acquainted with Elijah?

2—Who were the early leaders of Aram or Syria? Why does Abraham call it " my country" and "my people"?

3—What happened to Israel when Syria first attacked? Why did the Lord send a prophet to help a king as wicked as Ahab?

4—What did the prophet tell Ahab to do after winning the first battle? Did he do it? Where is Aphek?

5—When the king of Syria pleaded for his life what did Ahab do? Was it a mistake? What did the prophet say?

6—Why did Jezebel order the murder of Naboth? Who else was killed? Did Ahab consent? Who was sent to reprimand Ahab?

7—What did the prophet say would happen to Ahab? To Ahab's posterity? To Jezebel?

8—What apparently caused Jehoshaphat of Judah to seek an alliance with the wicked King Ahab of Israel?

9—What three things did Jehoshaphat agree to do in order to promote an "affinity" with Ahab?

10—When Jehoshaphat wanted to know the word of the Lord concerning the battle of Ramoth-gilead, how did Ahab try to obtain it?

11—Where was Micaiah when Ahab sent for him? What advice did the officer give the prophet? What did Micaiah say?

12—Did Micaiah's prophecy affect the plans of Ahab for his war? Did they affect the determination of Jehoshaphat to support Ahab?

13—Describe the events which led to the death of King Ahab.

14—Where did Jehoshaphat and Ahaziah build the two maritime fleets? Why was the Lord displeased? What happened to the ships?

15—Who led the rebellion of the Moabites? Why did he feel they could succeed?

16—What was King Ahaziah's fatal accident? Why did he send messengers to the oracle of Baalzebub in Ekron? What did Elijah tell them?

17—How did Elijah happen to call down fire from heaven to consume two contingents of the king's guard? What happened to the third?

18—Who had advance knowledge that Elijah would be translated? Who saw the dividing of the Jordan besides Elijah and Elisha?

19—Why did the "sons of the prophets" want to hunt for Elijah? How long did they search? What was the result?

20—Why was Elijah translated? When was he resurrected?

CHAPTER FIFTEEN

The Ministry of Elisha, the Prophet

After Elijah was translated the leadership of the faithful Saints fell to that unique and long-enduring prophet of the Lord who is known to us in history as Elisha. His ministry lasted approximately 65 years and extended from Damascus to Edom. Like Samuel of old, he visited the people on a continuous circuit. He was a counsellor to kings, an indefatigable traveler and a performer of great miracles. The latter included raising the dead, curing leprosy, causing leprosy, nullifying the effects of poison, purifying water, healing barrenness, raising an axe-head from the river bottom, abundantly increasing a supply of oil, causing blindness, curing blindness and feeding 100 men with 20 small loaves.

ELISHA BECOMES A HERO IN JERICHO

Barely had Elisha returned from witnessing the translation of his companion, Elijah, when the people of Jericho asked him to obtain a special blessing which would purify the local water supply. Jericho was located at one of the most pleasant sites in the fertile region lying west of the Jordan river.[1] However, it was several miles from the river and required its independent source of water. Something

---

1. The original Jericho was destroyed by Joshua, but a city built in that vicinity was afterwards given the same name.

had happened to the large spring at Jericho (believed to be the Sultan's Spring of today) so that those who drank from it became ill and died. The water also destroyed the plant life when used for irrigation so that it left the land barren.

Once the Lord had authorized Elisha to heal this water, he could have done it with a word, but to make the event more conspicuous, he said to those near him, "Bring me a new cruse, and put salt therein."[2] When they had brought it to him, "he went forth unto the spring of the waters, and cast the salt in there, and said, Thus saith he Lord, I have healed these waters; there shall not be from thence any more death or barren land."[3]

Some have wished to attribute this miracle to the chemical action of the salt rather than to divine intervention. However, any significant quantity of salt would have corrupted the water rather than cured it. Furthermore, a chemical reaction would have merely corrected the problem temporarily for the heavy flow of the spring would have soon replaced the treated water with a fresh supply requiring additional salt. The scripture is plain that the purifying of this water was of a permanent nature[4] thereby supporting the words of Elisha that the Lord had literally "healed these waters."

THE INCIDENT OF THE SHE-BEARS

As Elisha left Jericho he undoubtedly enjoyed the accolades of a local hero, but as he proceeded up into the mountains of Ephraim he found no such tribute awaiting him at Bethel. In fact, he was set upon by a mob of mature youths (erroneously called "little children" in our version[5]) who seem to have heard of Elijah's translation and therefore taunted Elisha saying, "Go up, thou bald head; go up, thou bald head."[6] Dr. Adam Clarke says the significance of this

---

2. 2 Kings 2:20
3. 2 Kings 2:21
4. 2 Kings 2:22
5. The word "naar" does not necessarily mean a child but is used to describe Solomon at his accession, when he was at least twenty years old. (Geikie. *Hours With the Bible*, Vol. 4, p. 127, note) Dr. Clarke says the word includes "a young man, a servant, or even a soldier, or one fit to go out to battle; and is so translated in a multitude of places in our common English version." He mentions many examples. (See Clarke, *Bible Commentary*, Vol. 2, p. 486)
6. 2 Kings 2:23

cry might be caught in the words, "Ascend, thou empty skull, to heaven, as it is pretended thy master did."[7]

Elisha at this time was still a rather young man.[8] He had been living with his parents just seven or eight years before when Elijah first called him and from all appearances was still unmarried. He also had nearly 65 years of active service ahead of him so at the time of this incident he was probably in his prime. The words, "bald-head" were often used in the old Hebrew vocabulary to imply leprosy since the disease often caused baldness. It was a term of hatred or derision.[9]

Undoubtedly Elisha was thoroughly accustomed to name-calling and was not likely to be offended by a youthful rabble like this one. But even if he were offended Elisha had no power to take action against the hoodlums unless the Lord commanded it. However if the Lord were offended that was another matter. It is therefore highly significant when the scripture says, "And he turned back, and looked on them, and cursed them IN THE NAME OF THE LORD."[10] Almost immediately there came from the nearby woods two ferocious she-bears which moved in among the pack of rabble-rousers at some point where they must have had difficulty getting away for the scripture says the maddened animals were able to "tare" 42 of them.[11] Whether any died from their wounds it does not say.

Certainly the news of what had happened created a fearful respect for Elisha at Bethel just as God's power had increased his community influence in Jericho. When directed by the Lord, this Elisha had power to hurt or to help according to the circumstances.

From Bethel, Elisha proceeded to Mount Carmel[12] where its springs and verdure offered many places of cloistered seclusion for one who wished to engage in prayer and meditation. Then he went down to his house in Samaria.[13]

---

7. Clarke, *Bible Commentary*, vol. 2, p. 486
8. Geikie, *Hours With the Bible*, vol. 4, p. 127
9. Ibid.
10. 2 Kings 2:24
11. Ibid.
12. 2 Kings 2:25
13. Ibid. Elisha's house at the capital of Samaria is referred to a number of times. See, for example, 2 Kings 5:9; 6:32.
    2 Kings 5:9; 6:32

THE GROWING THREAT OF THE MOABITE REBELLION

While Elisha had been participating in these recent events, war had been raging nearby at a distance of not more than two days journey. Elisha had been going serenely about the Lord's business but he undoubtedly knew that eventually the threat of the Moabite rebellion along the east side of the Dead Sea would require his attention.

Ever since the days of David, the Moabites had been tributaries of Israel. Their assessment for each year was "a hundred thousand lambs, and an hundred thousand rams, with the wool."[14] In 853 B.C., when King Ahab was killed, the Moabites saw that Israel was weakening, and so they refused to send any more tribute. In fact, the ruler of the Moabites, King Mesha, began capturing nearby towns and villages, overthrowing the military outposts of Israel and using Israelites to construct fortifications for the Moabites. King Mesha boasted of these things on his famous Moabite Stone. Ahab's son, King Ahaziah, had tried to reestablish the authority of Israel over Moab but had failed. This encouraged Mesha to launch a campaign to put Judah and Israel under tribute to him!

The first attack had been against Judah. A detailed description of this war is found in 2 Chronicles, chapter 20. However, no mention is made of this campaign in 2 Kings. According to Chronicles, Moab combined its strength with the Edomites to the south and the Ammonites to the north. The next thing King Jehoshaphat knew, his beauiful Jerusalem was threatened with a siege. Jehoshaphat ordered a general fast and prayed publicly to the Lord for deliverance. A Levite prophet named Jahaziel predicted victory without fighting and this literally came to pass. The Moabites, Edomites and Ammonites got to fighting among themselves just a few miles from Jerusalem. When the people of Judah marched out to the place they found the enemy camp abandoned with all of the rich spoils of these three armies scattered about in their tents. The Edomites made peace with Judah and once more became her tributary while the other two nations went back to their own territories to nurse the wounds they had inflicted on each other.

---

14. 2 Kings 3:4

ELISHA BECOMES A COUNSELLOR OF KINGS

It was some time after this that the new king of Israel, Jehoram, decided to ask Jehoshaphat of Judah to join him in completely smothering the volatile rebellion of the Moabites.

Having taken an inventory of his own forces,[15] Jehoram appealed to King Jehoshaphat of Judah, saying, "The king of Moab hath rebelled against me: wilt thou go with me against Moab to battle?"[16] Jehoshaphat replied, "I will go up: I am as thou art, my people as thy people, and my horses as thy horses."[17] It was the same kind of unqualified commitment the king of Judah had given to Jehoram's father.

King Jehoram of Israel wanted suggestions from the older man as to how they should attack. Said he, "Which way shall we go up?"[18] This was a good question since they either had to attack from the north as Ahaziah had done and been defeated or go clear down around the Dead Sea and attack from the south. The Moabite Stone mentioned in the last chapter makes it clear that King Mesha of the Moabites had thoroughly fortified the northern cities of his kingdom so there would be a stout resistance from that quarter. The southern approach, on the other hand, would be through the land of Edom which was a vassal kingdom of Judah. If the attack were directed from that quarter the king of Edom might feel obliged to join them, particularly if the king of Judah insisted. So, when Jehoram asked, "Which way shall we go up?" the king of Judah responded, "The way through the wilderness of Edom."[19]

When preparations were completed, the allied armies of Israel, Judah and Edom spent seven days marching to their rendezvous point near the southern part of the Dead Sea. But this proved to be a death trap. The only fresh water in this region was under the domination of the Moabites. The King of Israel said, "Alas! that the Lord hath called these three kings together to deliver them into the hand of Moab!"[20] But Jehoshaphat was not willing to jump to any such conclusion. Why not ask the Lord? He therefore said,

---

15. 2 Kings 3:6
16. 2 Kings 3:7
17. Ibid.

18. 2 Kings 3:8
19. Ibid.
20. 2 Kings 3:10

"Is there not here a prophet of the Lord, that we may inquire of the Lord by him?"[21]

Fortunately one of the Israelite soldiers was acquainted with Elisha and knew he was in the vicinity. Elisha was either on one of his ministerial circuits or he deliberately followed the armies on this Moabite venture. The Israelite therefore said, "Here is Elisha the son of Shaphat, which poured water on the hands of [ministered unto] Elijah."[22] Jehoshaphat was elated. Apparently he also knew Elisha even though that prophet's work was primarily in Israel. Said he, "The word of the Lord is with him."[23] So all three kings trooped down to the place where Elisha was staying.

However, when it came to kings, Elisha certainly had no special regard for the niceties of protocol. With him a wicked man was a wicked man and the fact that the wretch wore a crown made his sins just that much more reprehensible. Therefore, when he saw King Jehoram among the party Elisha aimed a verbal blast directly at this apostate king of Israel. "What have I to do with thee," he demanded, "get thee to the prophets of thy father, and to the prophets of thy mother!"[24] But King Jehoshaphat who was host of the group interceded to tell Elisha that not only Jehoram was in trouble but the King of Judah and the King of Edom as well. In response, Elisha still directed his remarks at Jehoram and said, "As the Lord of Hosts liveth, before whom I stand, surely, were it not that I regard the presence of Jehoshaphat the king of Judah, I WOULD NOT LOOK TOWARD THEE, NOR SEE THEE."[25]

Then Elisha made an unusual request. He called for a musician.[26] As the minstrel began to quietly play, "the hand of the Lord" touched the spirit of Elisha with revelation and told him what to do. As we get better acquainted with the prophetic calling we find that it is often a most difficult task for the Lord's servant to elevate his spirit to the threshold of direct revelation. Apparently Elisha had discovered that in his particular case, quiet music facilitated the transition. Very shortly he said to the three kings, "Make this valley

---

21. 2 Kings 3:11
22. Ibid.
23. 2 Kings 3:12

24. 2 Kings 3:13
25. 2 Kings 3:14
26. 2 Kings 3:15

full of ditches. For thus saith the Lord, Ye shall not see wind, neither shall ye see rain, yet that valley shall be filled with water, that ye may drink, both ye, and your cattle, and your beasts."[27]

That was a great relief. At least they would have water. Now what about the Moabites? Elisha almost chided them by saying, "This is but a light thing in the sight of the Lord: he will deliver the Moabites also into your hand."[28] Then Elisha commanded them to use the Lord's victory to completely break the strength of the Moabites.[29]

Immediately after this interview the armies of the three kings were put to work digging ditches, canals, and reservoirs to catch the water which was to flow through the Arabah valley. However, this northern end of the valley is a virtual wilderness and the stream beds are really desert wadies which carry a torrent during a rain storm and the next moment are bone dry. After a hard day's labor, the thirsty armies of Israel, Judah and Edom went to bed hopefully awaiting the outcome of this fantastic prophecy.

By morning the promise was fulfilled. Without visible wind, rain, or clouds, the water which apparently originated as a flash-flood far up in the Mt. Seir highlands, flowed down "by the way of Edom" just as Elisha had predicted.[30] Had they not caught it in their ditches and reservoirs this precious water would have soon disappeared as it flowed toward the nearby Dead Sea. Once the armies and their animals had quenched their thirst they were ready for the rigors of the day. Their battle had been made easy for them as a result of a mistake made by the Moabites.

The scripture says that when the Moabites arose in the morning and looked toward the Israelite camp they saw the pools and ditches of water. In the early morning sun the water looked blood red and they immediately assumed there

---

27. 2 Kings 3:16-17
28. 2 Kings 3:18
29. 2 Kings 3:19
30. In the vicinity of the Dead Sea it is possible even today to dig holes and have them fill with good underground water as it comes seeping down from higher levels. (See Werner Keller, *The Bible as History*, p. 238) In Elisha's prophecy, however, it is more likely that the fulfilment was by a distant flash flood since he specifically said it would come "by the way of Edom." (verse 20)

had been a conflict during the night and the people of Israel, Judah and Edom had apparently destroyed one another. Therefore, without adequate preparation or discipline the Moabites streamed down into the wadi to loot the enemy camp. Only when it was too late did they realize they were wrong, *dead* wrong. The Moabites turned and fled with the Israelites in hot pursuit. From then on the Moabites found themselves being hunted down from city to city and from refuge to refuge. Finally, King Mesha successfully entrenched himself with part of his army behind the high walls of a city called Kir-haraseth.

To appreciate the circumstances of this "last stand" resistance by King Mesha at Kir-haraseth we take the following description of Dr. Geikie concerning the traditional site of this city:

"A last despairing stand was made at Kir-haraseth . . . now known as Kerak, a town almost impregnable by its position. It stands on an isolated triangular plateau, of from 800 to 1,000 yards on each face, 3,720 feet above the sea, amidst heights still loftier, from which it is cut off on all points except one. Wadys from 1,000 to 1,350 feet deep, with precipitous sides, isolate it on the north and south, and a shallower ravine skirts its third side. The whole triangle has formerly been surrounded by a strong wall, and the rock is scarped a good way down. To an enemy, Kerak is utterly inaccessible except by winding paths on the west and northwest, and can be entered only at two points, on the northwest and on the south, by dark tunnels, cut for forty paces through the rock." (*Hours With the Bible,* Vol. 4, p. 116.)

At one time during the siege, King Mesha took 700 swordsmen and tried to cut his way out, but he was forced back.

As the siege continued, King Mesha decided that this terrible predicament was due to the anger of their Moabite heathen god, Chemosh. To save the country, he therefore called upon his eldest son, the crown prince, to submit himself to be burned alive as a sacrifice. As we have already seen, this type of summons "to death" was often counted a great privilege in heathen cultures. It was an honor to die as an appeasement to some national idolatrous deity.

Amazingly, it brought about the results intended. When King Mesha took his eldest son up on the high wall to be offered as a human sacrifice, he was in full sight of the opposing armies. No doubt these soldiers watched in fascinated abhorrence as the devil rites progressed to the sound of chants, moans, drums and fifes which continually lifted the emotions of the Moabites to that supreme moment when their crown-prince, the king's best beloved son, would die for his country in the sacred fires of the angry god, Chemosh. And as the dying screams of the victim reached the ears of the besieging troops, the armies of Judah and Edom suddenly lost their stomach for this entire war. Apparently they felt that when a nation had been pressed to such an extremity as this it was time to call a halt. So "there was a great indignation against Israel: and they [Judah and Edom] departed from him, and returned to their own land."[31]

As the attacking hosts melted away, a prayer of thanksgiving must have gone up to Chemosh from the benighted hearts of the Moabites. After this who would dare doubt the supreme power of the Moabite god when he had performed so great a miracle?

It would only be a short time before the people of Judah would vehemently regret this impetuous decision to retreat when God had said through Elisha that this evil political power should be smashed.

Elisha's Days of Miraculous Power

After the hosts of Israel had returned to their own country we find Elisha working out of Samaria and ministering among the northern ten tribes. It was about this time that word spread everywhere concerning the miracles which characterized every part of his work.

For example, a widow woman from the community of the faithful was about to have her sons sold into bondage to pay for their dead father's debts. When she appealed to Elisha he asked her what resources she had. It turned out to be nothing more than a small vessel of oil. Elisha had her obtain every empty jar, pot and vessel from the whole

---

31. 2 Kings 3:27

neighborhood and out of the one jar he poured out enough of this substance to fill everything she could set before him. When all of them were filled, he said, "Go, sell the oil, and pay thy debt, and live thou and thy children of the rest."[32]

Since Elisha proceeded frequently across the Jezreel valley to visit the faithful in Galilee, a certain woman of means urged him to stop by her house for food. This happened each time he passed that way until finally the woman induced her husband to fix a special chamber for him on the roof of their house. Elisha was so appreciative that he wondered what he could give her as a blessing. He offered to introduce her to the king or the captain of the host of Samaria (which shows the prestige Elisha had acquired at the capital), but the good woman had no such ambitions. Then Elisha's servant, named Gehazi, learned that the woman had never been blessed with children. Elisha obtained permission from the Lord to promise her a child the next year. She feared he was lying but the prophecy was fulfilled.

In later years, after the child had grown sufficiently to accompany his father into the field, the boy suffered an attack of what may have been sun-stroke. He cried out, "My head, my head," whereupon they carried him to his mother. The distraught woman carefuly rocked the child in her arms "till noon," and then he died.[33]

The frantic mother immediately took the body of the boy up to the chamber reserved for Elisha. She laid the limp form on Elisha's bed and then obtained a donkey and rode in all haste to Mount Carmel. Up there somewhere she found Elisha and threw herself at his feet. Gehazi, the prophet's servant, was going to thrust her away, but Elisha said, "Let her alone; for her soul is vexed within her: and the Lord hath hid it from me and hath not told me."[34]

As soon as he learned that her child was dead Elisha said to Gehazi, "Gird up thy loins, and take my staff in thine hand, and go thy way: if thou meet any man, salute him not; and if any salute thee, answer him not again: and lay my staff upon the face of the child."[35]

---

32. 2 Kings 4:7
33. 2 Kings 4:19-20
34. 2 Kings 4:27
35. 2 Kings 4:29

This strange procedure was not enough to persuade the mother. She swore she would not return with Gehazi but would remain with Elisha. Gehazi made the journey, did what he was told, and came back again. Said he, "The child is not awaked."[36] Elisha knew something was seriously wrong. We learn later that there was a weakness in this Gehazi which prevented the power of the Lord from functioning through him. Elisha therefore journeyed across the Jezreel valley in all haste with the mother no doubt following close behind. Upon arriving at the house, Elisha went up to the chamber where the child was lying. He closed the door "upon the twain" (meaning he shut out both the mother and his servant) and began fervently praying. In the process of pleading with the Lord he did what Elijah had done. The scripture says Elisha "lay upon the child, and put his mouth upon his mouth, and his eyes upon his eyes, and his hands upon his hands: and he stretched himself upon the child."[37]

The child had been dead so long that the body was cold, but now "the flesh of the child waxed warm."[38] Nevertheless, life did not return. The worried prophet "walked in the house to and fro" and then "went up, and stretched himself upon him: and the child sneezed seven times, and the child opened his eyes."[39] Elisha called for the mother and when she came running up, he said, "Take up thy son."[40]

When the grateful woman saw that her child was indeed alive, she fell at the feet of Elisha in gratitude. Then she ran to the bed, "took up her son, and went out."[41]

This blessing had not come easily. The Bible account would indicate that in all his career as a prophet Elisha never had to work so hard to bring about the manifestation of God's power.

ELISHA NEUTRALIZES POISONOUS GOURDS AND FEEDS 100 MEN WITH 20 SMALL LOAVES

During a period of famine, Elisha went down to meet with the faithful brethren at Gilgal again. Food was so short

---

36. 2 Kings 4:31
37. 2 Kings 4:34
38. Ibid.

39. 2 Kings 4:35
40. 2 Kings 4:36
41. 2 Kings 4:37

that one of the sons of the prophets went out to find something for a pottage or stew. In his search he came upon a vine of wild gourds and was so thrilled with his discovery that he picked the fruit of the plant until the lap of his robe was filled. He then hastened back to headquarters and "shred them into the pot of pottage" not knowing they were poison.

While the group was eating, several of them suddenly cried out to Elisha, "O thou man of God, there is death in the pot."[42] Elisha ordered them to bring him a sprinkling of meal whereupon "he cast it into the pot; and he said, Pour out for the people, that they may eat. And there was no harm in the pot."[43]

It was apparently during this same famine that a man came from Baal-shalisha (the location of which is no longer known), and presented Elisha with 20 small loaves of barley bread, and some ears of grain[44] still in the husk. These were the first fruits of this man's frugal harvest. Elisha did not hoard the supplies but ordered them served to the whole group of faithful brethren who were staying with him. The servant was astonished and said, "What, should I set this before an hundred men?" Elisha promised him that it would not only be enough but there would be a substantial amount left over. The servant followed the prophet's instructions and saw to his amazement that the supply was not only sufficient but there were quantities left over just as Elisha had predicted.[45]

As can be seen, many aspects of Elisha's ministry closely resembled certain aspects of the later ministry of the Savior. The Lord loved Elisha and in these troublesome days of persecution and apostasy He used Elisha to bless the righteous Saints of that day almost precisely the way He later did it for the people Himself.

---

42. 2 Kings 4:40
43. 2 Kings 4:41
44. 2 Kings 4:42. The text says "corn" but Indian corn, which flourished in America from the most ancient times, was not known among Biblical people of this period. Where the word "corn" appears in the text, it has reference to grains of various kinds, but most generally wheat. See Peloubet's *Bible Dictionary* under "corn."
45. 2 Kings 4:43-44

Elisha Gains a Blessing for the
Commander of the Syrian Army

We now come to one of the most notable chapters of the Old Testament. This is the story of Naaman, the leper, from Syria.

Naaman was the hero of the Assyrian war "because by him the Lord had given deliverance unto Syria."[46] He was captain of the entire army and considered "a great man with his master, and honourable . . . he was also a mighty man in valour."[47] Unfortunately, however, Naaman suddenly came down with the dreaded disease of leprosy.

In order to appreciate why this disease was so loathsome we will quote a letter written to Lord Lawrence, while Viceroy of India, which indicates how an educated native reacted to leprosy's living death. The man's name was Ram Buksh and he wrote, "Be it known to your enlightened mind that your devoted servant has been a leper for many years. My limbs [fingers and toes] have fallen off piece by piece; my whole body has become a mass of corruption; I am weary of life; I wish to die. My life is a plague and disgust to the whole village, and my death is earnestly longed for. It is well known to all that for a leper to consent to die, to permit himself to be buried alive, is approved of by the gods, who will never afflict another individual of the village with a similar malady. I therefore solicit your permission to be buried alive. The whole village wishes it. and I am happy and content to die. You are ruler of the land, and without your leave it would be criminal. Hoping that I may obtain your permission, I pray that the sun of prosperity may ever shine on you."[48]

Without personally experiencing it, this kind of human anguish would be impossible to comprehend. It is difficult to imagine the depths to which a mortal soul would sink before writing such a letter. Yet many thousands have endured it. Naaman was one of them, and while the extremity of his case was not yet so severe, it soon would have been. At the moment, the passion of Naaman was to live, not die.

---

46. 2 Kings 5:1; Geikie, *Hours With the Bible*, Vol. 4, p. 134
47. Ibid.
48. Quoted by Dr. Geikie in *Hours With the Bible*, Vol. 4, pp. 134-135

It was through a little slave girl captured during one of the skirmishes with Israel and who was then serving his wife as a maid, that Naaman learned about a prophet in Israel who could heal leprosy.[49] The fact that Naaman snatched onto this slender thread of hope with such great enthusiasm reflects the desperate state of his mind.

Disciplined to the protocol of working through government channels, Naaman obtained permission of his master, the King of Syria, to make contact with the king of Israel in order that he might be healed. Although Israel and Syria sometimes fought each other, they were allies when they faced their common enemy, Assyria, so the Syrian king felt no compunction about writing to Jehoram in Samaria and asking him to have Naaman healed. He assumed, of course, that the king above anyone else would know how such things were done in Israel.

To further assure a cordial reception Naaman took along a gift of gold, silver and raiment estimated from the figures in the Bible to have been worth a fortune.

Under the circumstances, however, the meeting between Naaman and King Jehoram was a delicate one. Here was a man who had taken Israelites prisoners and was undoubtedly a participant in the battle of Ramoth-gilead where Jehoram's father was killed. Nevertheless, he came with a magnificent gift for anyone who could cure him of leprosy. Being considered "unclean," Naaman did not actually go in before Jehoram but sent in a letter of introduction from the king of Syria. Jehoram read it and then exploded. "Am I God," he cried, "to kill and to make alive, that this man doth send unto me to recover a man of his leprosy?"[50] But as he reflected upon it he decided this whole thing might be a political or military trap. Said he, "See how he seeketh a quarrel against me!"[51] The angry king then began tearing apart his clothes to show his indignation.

Fortunately Elisha heard what was happening and quickly sent a message to King Jehoram in which he stated, "Wherefore hast thou rent thy clothes? let him come now to me, and he shall know that there is a prophet in Israel."[52]

49. 2 Kings 5:3
50. 2 Kings 5:7
51. Ibid.
52. 2 Kings 5:8

The king passed the word on to Naaman who immediately gathered his aids about him and proceeded to the house of Elisha which was not far away. "So Naaman came with his horses and with his chariot, and stood at the door of the house of Elisha. And Elisha sent a messenger unto him, saying, Go and wash in Jordan seven times, and thy flesh shall come again to thee, and thou shalt be clean. But Naaman was wroth, and went away, and said, Behold, I thought, He will surely come out to me, and stand, and call on the name of the Lord his God, and strike his hand over the place and recover the leper. Are not Abana and Pharpar, rivers of Damascus, better than all the waters of Israel? may I not wash in them, and be clean? So he turned, and went away in a rage."[53]

As Naaman drove his chariot angrily back toward Damascus he had to take a route which crossed the Jordan or use the alternate route which passed within a few miles of it. At some opportune moment his servants humbly approached the resentful commander whose hopes had been so rudely shattered and said unto him, "My father, if the prophet had bid thee do some great thing, wouldest thou not have done it? how much rather then, when he saith to thee, Wash, and be clean?"[54] So Naaman agreed to go through the silly ritual if only to satisfy his aides. It is understandable why the military leader might have felt contempt for the waters of the Jordan for they do not appear to be sweet, clear, healing waters. They are thick with rich silt from the uplands. Nevertheless, as he waded out into the dark current and plunged himself into the water seven successive times, something happened which was almost beyond belief. ". . . and his flesh came again like unto the flesh of a little child, and he was clean!"[55]

What a chatter of excitement must have occurred there on the banks of the Jordan as the whole party exclaimed in amazement over what they saw. The feelings of Naaman must have been more poignant and profound than words would express. He had found God, His prophet, and a complete restoration of health, all in one stroke. Moments later

53. 2 Kings 5:9-12   55. 2 Kings 5:14
54. 2 Kings 5:13

he was back in his chariot and driving furiously up toward the city of Samaria, some thirty-five miles away.

"And he returned to the man of God, he and all his company, and came, and stood before him [how glorious to be clean and respectable again!] and he said, Behold, now I know that there is no God in all the earth, but in Israel: now therefore, I pray thee, take a blessing of thy servant."[56]

By this, he meant the rich reward he had brought for anyone who could cure him. It could have kept Elisha in luxury for the rest of his life. But Elisha said, "As the Lord liveth, before whom I stand, I will receive none."[57] Naaman urged him further but Elisha firmly refused. This was the kind of situation which had tempted the notorious Baalam in an earlier century and caused him to lose his prophetic calling by accepting a reward for dispensing the powers of the Priesthood.[58]

Naaman then asked for two mule-loads of soil from Israel on which he apparently intended to build an altar and sacrifice to the true God, for he said, "thy servant will henceforth offer neither burnt-offering nor sacrifice unto other gods, but unto the Lord."[59] Of course, a true sacrifice could be made without any soil from Israel being required, but this would be one of the multitude of things this new convert to the Gospel would have to be taught.

Naaman next made a statement which sounds as though he were asking to be forgiven for any future occasion when he might be required to go in before his heathen god at Damascus and participate in the formalities of the Syrian state-religion.[60] Dr. Clarke and others believe this verse is defective and that the verb tense is wrong. They believe Naaman is asking forgiveness for *past* occasions when he had gone into the heathen temple of Rimmon to worship.[61] This would seem to make more sense because we have the clear implication that Elisha consented to his request by saying, "Go in peace."[62] He would certainly not have pronounced his

---

56. 2 Kings 5:15
57. 2 Kings 5:16
58. Jude, verse 11; See *The Third Thousand Years*, p. 438.
59. 2 Kings 5:17
60. 2 Kings 5:18
61. See Clarke, *Bible Commentary*, Vol. 2, p. 498.
62. 2 Kings 5:19

benediction on Naaman's return to heathen worship nor does the present text fit in with Naaman's previous declaration that hereafter he would offer "neither burnt-offering nor sacrifice unto other gods, but unto the Lord."

One final note of tragedy now enters into the Naaman story. As the jubilant Syrian commander once more set off for home he discovered someone running after him. It was Gehazi, Elisha's servant. The scripture indicates this man had watched with envy as he had seen Naaman offer Elisha the rich reward and had writhed with mental anguish as he had seen his master refuse it. Therefore, when Naaman had departed Gehazi said in his heart, "As the Lord liveth, I will run after him and take somewhat of him."[63]

As he came running up to Naaman's party he had already concocted a tall tale to cover his action. Said he, "My master hath sent me, saying, Behold, even now there be come to me from Mount Ephraim two young men of the sons of the prophets: give them, I pray thee, a talent of silver, and two changes of garments."[64] This, Naaman was delighted to do. In fact, he gave him *two* talents of silver, with the two wardrobes of clothing and sent along two servants to help carry the burden. Since two talents of silver are calculated by authorities to have weighed in excess of 116 pounds,[65] it is understandable why two servants were sent along to help carry them.

Gehazi had the servants unload the treasure at a certain "tower" (more literally "hill")[66] and then sent them back. Having hidden the fruits of his fraud in a house, Gehazi went in before his master. But Elisha had a big surprise for Gehazi. The Lord had shown the prophet every detail of the whole transaction. Said Elisha, "Whence comest thou, Gehazi? And he said, Thy servant went no whither."[67] But Elisha threw the lie back in his teeth by saying, "Went not mine heart [vision] with thee, when the man turned again from

---

63. 2 Kings 5:20
64. 2 Kings 5:22
65. See Webster's *New World Dictionary* under *Talent*: ". . . it varied widely in value at different times and in different places but was usually large, the lowest estimated weight being about 58 pounds."
66. *The Interpreter's Bible*, Vol. 3, pp. 214-215
67. 2 Kings 5:25

his chariot to meet thee? Is it a time to receive money, and to receive garments, and oliveyards, and vineyards, and sheep, and oxen, and menservants, and maid servants?"[68] There was no doubt about it, Gehazi had secured for himself a real treasure. But now his deception was exposed. It was humiliating and like hell-fire in his soul. But the next thing he knew, Gehazi had hell-fire in his flesh.

Elisha declared, "The leprosy therefore of Naaman shall cleave unto thee, and unto thy seed for ever."[69] This was like saying, "You have Naaman's silver, now you can have his leprosy." The terrible disease had passed from Naaman's house to his. And Gehazi did not have to wait long to see whether the prophecy would be literally fulfilled. The scripture says, "And he went out from his presence a leper as white as snow."[70]

ELISHA OVERCOMES THE POWER OF GRAVITATION

Not all of Elisha's miraculous powers were exhibited under such illustrious circumstances. Sometimes he used the power which the Lord had given him to solve routine problems for people living in the most humble circumstances.

For example, we next find Elisha ministering to the faithful brethren down at Gilgal. There they were attempting to enlarge their modest quarters by cutting and hauling logs up from the banks of the Jordan. In the process, one of the men engaged in cutting trees had an axehead fly off its handle and sink into the silt-laden waters of the river.

The man immediately ran to Elisha to report the loss and cried, "Alas, master! for it was borrowed."[71] Elisha accompanied the man to the water's edge and had him point out exactly where the axehead had disappeared. Elisha then took a stick and cast it over the spot, whereupon the heavy piece of iron came immediately to the surface and floated on top of the water, or, as the Bible says, "did swim."[72]

Elisha said to the man, "Take it up to thee. And he put out his hand and took it."[73]

---

68. 2 Kings 5:26
69. 2 Kings 5:27
70. Ibid.

71. 2 Kings 6:5
72. 2 Kings 6:6
73. 2 Kings 6:7

Here was another fascinating demonstration of the power that God had given Elisha. The incident soon took its place in the sacred literature of the people along with all the other marvelous things he had done.

ELISHA BECOMES A ONE-MAN ARMY AGAINST SYRIA

It was about this time that the king of Syria decided to fortify a certain place and ambush the king of Israel. As we have pointed out earlier, Syria and Israel were allies when threatened by Assyria, but in between times they skirmished with each other since the king of Syria at Damascus was attempting to expand his kingdom by making surrounding kingdoms pay tribute to him. As part of the program he concocted a clever scheme designed to capture King Jehoram and make him promise to pay an annual tribute before releasing him. Therefore an ambush was laid at a place often frequented by Jehoram.

The scheme failed, however, for the simple reason that the Lord told Elisha about it and Elisha told the king.

The king of Syria could not figure this out. Why did the king of Israel no longer pass that way? He decided there must be a spy in his camp who had warned Jehoram. He called a conference and said to his advisors and aides, "Will ye not show me which of us is for the king of Israel? And one of his servants said, None, my lord, O king: but Elisha, the prophet that is in Israel, telleth the king of Israel the words that thou speakest in thy bed-chamber."[74]

In the bed-chamber? Outrageous! This evil man must be liquidated at once. Whether the king believed Elisha operated by spies or by inspiration we do not know. But the scripture is plain that he firmly believed it was one or the other and forthwith dispatched a good-sized army to immediately find him and capture him. The soldiers had no difficulty locating the prophet. He was at Dothan, a few miles from Samaria, where Joseph had been sold into slavery nine centuries earlier. With complete contempt for the sovereignty of Israel the Syrian army marched into this territory and besieged the city with the intent of seizing Elisha and, from all indications, killing him.

---

74. 2 Kings 6:11-12

It was Elisha's servant who rose up early in the morning and found the city encompassed by "horses, and chariots and a great host." He cried out to Elisha, "Alas, my master! how shall we do? And he answered, FEAR NOT: FOR THEY THAT BE WITH US ARE MORE THAN THEY THAT BE WITH THEM."[75] Then, to encourage his servant, Elisha prayed that his eyes might be opened so that this faithful man could see the symbolic representation of God's support which surrounded them beyond the veil. "And the Lord opened the eyes of the young man; and he saw: and, behold, the mountain was full of horses and chariots of fire round about Elisha."[76]

Then Elisha went boldly out before the Syrians and as he did so he prayed that the eyes of this host might be blinded to a realization of where they were or who Elisha was. In other words, it was not literal blindness he wanted, but a confusion of mind. He thereupon said to the leaders of the Syrians, "This is not the way, neither is this the city: follow me and I will bring you to the man whom ye seek."[77]

Apparently the captain of the host thought he had found a secret friend and in his befuddled state of mind he led out behind Elisha, and the army followed him like sheep. When Elisha had led them to the destination he had in mind, he prayed that the Lord would open their eyes. "And the Lord opened their eyes, and they saw; and, behold, THEY WERE IN THE MIDST OF SAMARIA!"[78]

To the commander of the Syrians it must have seemed like a nightmare. He had followed this man into the strongest fortified city in Israel! When King Jehoram of Israel saw what had happened he was as jubilant as a child at the circus. One can almost see him jumping with excitement as he cried, "My father, shall I smite them? shall I smite them?"[79] Elisha replied, "Thou shalt not smite them: wouldest thou smite those whom thou hast taken captive? . . . set bread and water before them, that they may eat and drink, and go to their master."[80]

---

75. 2 Kings 6:16
76. 2 Kings 6:17
77. 2 Kings 6:19

78. 2 Kings 6:20
79. 2 Kings 6:21
80. 2 Kings 6:22

The puzzled king followed the instruction "and he prepared great provisions for them: and when they had eaten and drunk, he sent them away, and they went to their master."[81] It is doubtful that the Syrian commander realized exactly what had happened to him. Certainly it would have been difficult to give his king an objective report of this adventure. Nevertheless, the king of Syria learned enough to convince him that no more marauding bands should be allowed to go into the land of Israel at that time.[82]

The Starvation Siege of Samaria

The following year King Ben-hadad determined to lay siege to Samaria himself.[83] Even with Elisha at large he intended to risk it. And he had no intention of displaying the charity toward Israel that Elisha had generously exhibited toward the Syrian army. The siege was so long and so devastating that many of the people were reduced to the most depraved practices in order to survive. The scripture says the siege persisted until an "ass's head was sold for fourscore pieces of silver, and the fourth part of a cab of dove's dung for five pieces of silver."[84] But worst of all was the spreading of cannibalism. The people were eating their own dead.

One day as the king was walking along the top of the wall or on the flat roof of his palace a distressed woman shouted up to Jehoram, "Help, my lord, O king." He shouted back, "What aileth thee? And she answered, This woman said unto me, Give thy son, that we may eat him to-day, and we will eat my son to-morrow. So we boiled my son, and did eat him [with both families participating]: and I said unto her on the next day, Give thy son, that we may eat him: and she hath hid her son."[85]

King Jehoram could not stand to hear more. He ripped off his outer clothing and tore them to shreds to vent his

---

81. 2 Kings 6:23
82. Ibid.
83. The exact dating of this siege is uncertain. Dr. Clarke thinks it was the next year. (Clarke, *Bible Commentary*, Vol. 2, p. 502)
84. 2 Kings 6:25
85. 2 Kings 6:26-29. This is just what the Lord had told Moses would happen if Israel apostatized. (Deuteronomy 28:53, 57) There would be a similar resorting to cannibalism under the siege of Nebuchadnezzar (Ezekiel 5:10) and again under Titus in 70 A.D.

bitterness. Then he rushed into his palace and came out again wearing nothing but rude sackcloth.[86] The king was in a mood to do something violent. For some strange reason he had gotten the idea that this whole calamity was somehow attributable to Elisha. He therefore proclaimed, "God do so and more also to me, if the head of Elisha the son of Shaphat shall stand on him this day."[87] He then sent his messenger to Elisha's house to see if he were there so he could be arrested. But the Lord warned Elisha as he sat in his house with certain of the "elders." Elisha therefore said to his brethren, "See ye how this son of a murderer [son of Jezebel] hath sent to take away mine head? look, when the messenger cometh, shut the door, and hold him fast at the door, is not the sound of his master's feet behind him?"[88] Apparently Elisha wanted the messenger held until the king arrived in person.

The next verse is confusing in the King James Version so we use the Revised Version which says, "And while he was still speaking with them, the king came down to him and said, 'This trouble is from the Lord! Why should I wait for the Lord any longer?' "[89] In other words, if the Lord was not going to intervene to somehow terminate this terrible siege, the king was going to kill His prophet. The king must have been contemplating this action for some time. Now he would wait no longer.

FROM STARVATION TO ABUNDANCE IN TWENTY-FOUR HOURS

"Then Elisha said . . . Thus saith the Lord, To-morrow about this time shall a measure of fine flour be sold for a shekel, and two measures of barley for a shekel, in the gate of Samaria."[90] Such a prophecy, of course, was ridiculous. The king's chief aid sneeringly remarked, "Behold, if the Lord would make windows in heaven, might this thing be?"[91] Elisha looked at the king's officer and said, "Behold, thou shalt see it with thine eyes, but shalt not eat thereof."[92] No doubt the officer resolved that if there was any food around

---

86. 2 Kings 6:30
87. 2 Kings 6:31
88. 2 Kings 6:32
89. Revised Version, 2 Kings 6:33

90. 2 Kings 7:1
91. 2 Kings 7:2
92. Ibid.

he would definitely get his share. As for the king, he apparently concluded to wait at least one more day before avenging himself by killing Elisha.

It was early the next morning that four lepers came to the city gate to report that they had been to the camp of the Syrians and the camp was empty. They said the Syrians were nowhere to be seen. Originally, these lepers had gone to the camp hoping to beg some food but finding it deserted they were able to gorge themselves without any hindrance. The empty tents were not only laden with food and wine but also with an abundance of precious articles of gold and silver which ancient armies often carried with them so that their officers might fight the harder to protect their fortunes. All this had been abandoned.

But when King Jehoram heard about it he refused to believe. He decided it was a trap to lure the emaciated armies of the Israelites into the open so the city could be invaded and taken.[93] Nevertheless, he agreed to allow two of the last five horses left in the city to be harnessed to a chariot so that an exploratory party could go out and check on the leper's story. The chariot was driven clear down to the Jordan river, a distance of some thirty-five miles, and "lo, all the way was full of garments and vessels, which the Syrians had cast away in their haste. And the messengers returned, and told the king."[94]

It was hard to believe, but true, so the city gates were swung wide and the people swarmed out to gather food and loot from the Syrian camp. In the process, the King's chief officer who had sneered at Elisha was caught in the crush of the wild, famished crowd stampeding the city gate. The scripture says, "the people trode upon him in the gate, and he died."[95] So he had lived to see the imminence of this miraculous abundance in Samaria just as Elisha had predicted, but he had never lived to partake of it. Thus the strange prophecy was fulfilled. Meanwhile, "the people went out, and spoiled the tents of the Syrians. So a measure of fine flour was sold for a shekel, and two measures of barley for a shekel, according to the word of the Lord."[96]

---

93. 2 Kings 7:12
94. 2 Kings 7:15
95. 2 Kings 7:17
96. 2 Kings 7:16

But what had caused the Syrians to flee? Elisha must have been told by the Lord what had happened for no Syrian remained to disclose it. The scripture says, "For the Lord had made the host of the Syrians to hear a noise of chariots, and a noise of horses, even the noise of a great host: and they said one to another, Lo, the king of Israel hath hired against us the kings of the Hittites, and the kings of the Egyptians, to come upon us. Wherefore they arose and fled in the twilight, and left their tents, and their horses, and their asses, even the camp as it was, and fled for their life."[97]

This was the last major battle Ben-hadad of Syria would fight against Israel. He did not know it but his life was soon to end — by violence.

---

97. 2 Kings 7:6-7

Scripture Reading and Questions on Chapter Fifteen

Scripture Reading: 2 Kings, chapters 3 to 7 inclusive.

1—Describe the incident of the healing of the waters at Jericho. How tainted was the water? Was the cure temporary or permanent?

2—Tell about the incident of the young hoodlums and the two she-bears. Why does Dr. Clarke say these were probably teen-age ruffians and not children?

3—Briefly recite the interesting background on the finding of the Moabite stone.

4—Why was the attack against the rebellious Moabites launched from the south? Did Elisha assure Judah, Israel and Edom of victory?

5—How did the Moabite king try to break the siege? Did it work?

6—Recite the incident of the miraculous supplying of oil for the indebted widow.

7—Recite the highlights of the raising of the dead son belonging to the woman who had befriended Elisha.

8—Tell the principal facts in the healing of Naaman the leper. What nationality was he? Why did he first go to the king to be healed?

9—Tell of the events which led up to Gehazi, the servant of Elisha, getting leprosy.

10—Relate the incident of the recovery of the axehead from the river.

11—Why did the king of Syria want to capture the king of Israel? Why didn't he succeed? Why did he blame his servants? What did they tell the king about Elisha?

12—Where was Elisha when the Syrian army came after him? What do we remember most about this place?

13—What was the reaction of Elisha's servant when he saw the army? What did Elisha do to give him courage? What did Elisha ask the Lord to do to the Syrian army? Did it work?

14—What did the king of Israel want to do to the Syrian army? What did Elisha tell him? Did the king comply?

15—Did the king of Syria appreciate the generosity of Elisha in dealing with his troops the way he did? Did it make him friendly toward Israel?

16—How long was it before Syria launched an all-out war against Israel? How desperate did the people of Samaria become during the siege?

17—What was the incident which caused the king of Israel to resolve to kill Elisha? Was Elisha warned in advance? Did he flee?

18—Why was Elisha's prophecy concerning the turn of events within the next 24 hours so fantastic? What did the king's aid say? What was Elisha's reply?

19—How did the lepers happen to go to the camp of the Syrians? Why did the military leaders often bring great quantities of wealth into the field with them? What did the lepers find? What did they do?

20—What had caused the Syrians to flee? What happened to the king's aid when the gates to Samaria were flung open? Did this fulfill Elisha's prophecy?

CHAPTER SIXTEEN

The Latter Days of Elisha's Ministry

There is no attempt in the second book of Kings to maintain a chronological sequence of all the events reported. Elisha's activities in monumental political upheavals are fairly easy to follow because they are related to the orderly succession of the kings; however, faith-promoting incidents are interjected without necessarily referring to the events which precede or follow them. If the student keeps this in mind it may help avoid confusion since these incidents sometimes involve people or events of an earlier date. We now come to one of these.

The eighth chapter opens with a reference to a famine of seven years' duration which had occurred sometime earlier. The Bible says that after this famine was over, the king was conversing with Gehazi, the servant of Elisha, who was telling the king all of the marvelous things Elisha had accomplished. (The fact that the incident involved Gehazi indicates that this event occurred some years earlier before Gehazi came down with leprosy and left Elisha's service.)

The king had said to Gehazi, "Tell me, I pray thee, all the great things that Elisha hath done."[1] With the zeal of

---

1. 2 Kings 8:4

a missionary, this servant of the prophet proceeded to give the king a long recitation of Elisha's powers as the earthly ambassador of Jehovah. Of course, Gehazi undoubtedly knew it would require a virtual miracle to convert this king of Israel for he was Jehoram, son of Ahab and Jezebel! Nevertheless, Jehoram had not taken to the Baal worship of his father nor the Ashtoreth worship of Jezebel, his mother. In fact, he had thrown down the great Baal symbol at Samaria.[2] This did not mean he had turned away from idolatry, but he had rejected the more violent heathen cults for the milder calf-worship which Jeroboam had brought to Israel from Egypt a century earlier.[3]

Gehazi therefore had reason to respond warmly to the king's request. And he was just telling King Jehoram how Elisha had raised up the dead son of the Shunammite woman (the one who built Elisha a private room on top of her house), when this very woman came in before the king.[4] Gehazi was amazed. He said to the king, "My Lord, O king, this is the woman, and this is her son, whom Elisha restored to life!"[5]

It was quite a coincidence, but a fortunate one for the woman and her son because she came seeking help. From all appearances her husband was no longer living and when the famine had first commenced she took her son and went to the land of the Philistines because Elisha had told her the crop-failures in Israel would continue for a seven-year period.[6] Upon her return, however, she found her house and land in the hands of certain evil men who would not return it to her.[7] She therefore pleaded with the king to intervene for her.

"So the king appointed unto her a certain officer, saying, Restore all that was hers, and all the fruits of the field since the day that she left the land, even until now."[8] These "fruits" would not have been much during the seven-years drouth, but at least they would be enough to get her started again.

Gehazi's testimony concerning the prophet Elisha did not convert the king, but it softened his heart toward this

---

2. 2 Kings 3:2
3. 2 Kings 3:3
4. 2 Kings 8:5
5. Ibid.

6. 2 Kings 8:1
7. 2 Kings 8:3
8. 2 Kings 8:6

good woman who had been such a friend of Elisha down through the years.

THE END OF BEN-HADAD II, KING OF SYRIA

Northeast of Samaria about 125 miles lies the ancient city of Damascus, capital of Syria. For approximately thirty years a cruel and ruthless king named Ben-hadad had ruled from Damascus and kept the entire surrounding territory in an uproar.

Ben-hadad was the king who fought against Assyria in 853 B.C., and was supported in that campaign by Israel as well as most of the other kingdoms immediately east of the Mediterranean. This was the man whom the Lord had specifically rejected as a ruler among men. On Mount Sinai He had told Elijah to anoint Hazael in his place.[9] This was also the man whom the Lord had commanded King Ahab of Israel to destroy, but Ahab had failed to do so,[10] and this may account for the reason Elijah delayed in anointing Hazael to replace him. This Ben-hadad was the king of Syria who sent his commander, Naaman, to Israel to be cured of leprosy.[11] But he later sent his army to capture and kill Elisha so he would not disclose what the Lord had revealed concerning the secret strategies of the king.[12] Ben-hadad was also the king who besieged Samaria and held it so long the starving people resorted to cannibalism.[13]

But now this cruel king's reign was virtually over. Ben-hadad was critically ill.[14] What he longed to know above everything else was whether or not he would die. This was the situation when the word spread through Damascus that Elisha, the great oracle of Jehovah, had arrived in the city.[15] This news had the greatest significance for Ben-hadad. Elisha was the man who told Naaman how to be healed of leprosy;[16] Elisha was the man who single-handedly led a contingent of the Syrian army into certain captivity,[17] then voluntarily released them;[18] Elisha was the man who could read the most secret thoughts of the king, even in his bed-

9. 1 Kings 19:15
10. 1 Kings 20:42
11. 2 Kings 5:10-11
12. 2 Kings 6:12-14
13. 2 Kings 6:28-29

14. 2 Kings 8:7-8
15. 2 Kings 8:7
16. 2 Kings 5:10-11
17. 2 Kings 6:18-20
18. 2 Kings 6:23

chamber.[19] What luck of the stars had brought this oracle of Israel to Damascus?

As mentioned above, Elisha was fulfilling a commission given long ago to Elijah on Mt. Sinai when the Lord had stated that a man named Hazael was going to replace Ben-hadad as king of Syria.[20] No doubt Elisha had been told that this change was about to take place and he had therefore come to Damascus prepared to play his part in it.[21]

We discover that this Hazael whom the Lord had been talking about was a very high official among the councils of the king. In fact, he was the person whom Ben-hadad now sent as his royal delegate to see Elisha.

"And the king said unto Hazael, Take a present in thine hand, and go, meet the man of God, and inquire of the Lord by him saying, Shall I recover of this disease?"[22]

The gift which Hazael took to Elisha was no pittance or casual gesture. It consisted of "every good thing of Damascus forty camels' burden."[23] No further reference is made to this "gift" but we assume it was rejected by Elisha on the same basis he had rejected Naaman's gift. True prophets of God do not charge for dispensing the blessings of heaven.

When Hazael had been ushered in before Elisha, he said, "Thy son Ben-hadad king of Syria hath sent me to thee, saying, Shall I recover of this disease?" Hazael did not know it but he was in for a profound shock. He was about to discover that Elisha could not only hear conversations in bed-chambers, but he could read a man's mind. Hazael's!

Elisha said, "Go, say unto him, Thou mayest certainly recover: howbeit the Lord hath shewed me that he shall surely die!"[24] What kind of talk was this? Elisha was simply saying that the king was going to die but not from his disease. Then Elisha started staring accusingly at Hazael. Elisha

---

19. 2 Kings 6:11-12
20. 1 Kings 19:15
21. We deduct this from the fact that Elisha later reveals that the Lord had told him all about the future of Hazael. (2 Kings 8:12)
22. 2 Kings 8:8
23. 2 Kings 8:9
24. 2 Kings 8:10

knew already who was going to murder the king. Under the fixed glare of Elisha, Hazael became "ashamed."[25]

But then, to Hazael's amazement, he saw great tears form along the lashes of the prophet's eyes and drip down his cheeks. "And Hazael said, Why weepeth my lord? And he answered, Because I know the evil that thou wilt do unto the children of Israel: their strong holds wilt thou set on fire, and their young men wilt thou slay with the sword, and wilt dash their children, and rip up their women with child."[26]

Hazael bristled. It was obvious Elisha's verbal harpoons had hit home. Said he, "But what, is thy servant a dog, that he should do this great [horrible] thing? And Elisha answered, The Lord hath shewed me that thou shalt be king over Syria."[27]

Hazael promptly departed from Elisha's house and hurried back to the king. Ben-hadad was desperately anxious to hear the news. He asked, "What said Elisha to thee?" Hazael answered, "He told me that thou shouldest surely recover."[28] This was a lie. What Elisha said was that he COULD recover but that he would not. Hazael was going to kill him. Nevertheless, Ben-hadad took comfort from what he was told and no doubt spent his last hours hopefully encouraged by the asurrance that his illness was not fatal.

The next day Hazael came to visit the king as usual, but in his heart was a firm determination to immediately carry out the scheme which he must have had gestating in his mind for many months. He had come to murder the king. It was too dangerous having this oracle from Israel running around with his power to read men's minds. He might warn the king. So, pretending a gesture of solicitous help, Hazael went in privately to the chamber of the king where he "took a thick cloth, and dipped it in water, and spread it on his face, so that he died."[29]

Whether the people ever discovered how the king died we are not told, but Elisha knew that Hazael had murdered

---

25. 2 Kings 8:11
26. 2 Kings 8:12
27. 2 Kings 8:13

28. 2 Kings 8:14
29. 2 Kings 8:15

him. Hazael then seized power and ascended the throne of Syria to commence his harsh, brutal reign which did not terminate for 42 years.

We shall hear more of this Hazael later, but one final point requires notice before proceeding. Why was Hazael marked for anointing as king of Syria when he turned out to be a murderous reprobate? And a further question, why didn't the anointing ever take place?

The first question relates to the Lord's attitude toward all his children. He treats each individual in terms of his best potential, not his worst. Accordingly, he blesses, ordains, anoints, promotes and encourages a person right up to the very last moment his behavior will permit. With the coming of evil, of course, the Lord's blessings depart. But even when the Lord knows in advance that a person is going to ultimately fall, He honors the potential good in him as long as He can. Note the numerous examples of this in scriptural history.

It happened in the very beginning with Cain. The Lord knew that Cain had great qualities of leadership and potential good in him. He therefore honored Cain with the Priesthood, gave him personal revelations, and treated him every whit as graciously as Abel right up to the time that obstreperous son of Adam elected to plunge toward perdition. The Lord knew Cain would eventually choose that course, but until he did, THE LORD TREATED HIM AS THOUGH HE NEVER WOULD.

Notice the same principle operating in the calling of Judas, who betrayed the Lord; in the anointing of Saul who ended up massacring the Lord's priests and trying to murder David; in the anointing of Jeroboam who could not wait for his inheritance but decided to kill Solomon and take the kingdom immediately. All of these people had it within them to become distinguished leaders in their own right and the Lord honored that potential because He had known them in the pre-existence. He honored their best selves as long as He could even when He knew they would not. An omniscient and just God could not do otherwise.

We see the same principle operating in the case of Hazael. Years before, when Elijah was on Mount Sinai, the potential good in Hazael was deserving of recognition, and the Lord so honored it by instructing Elijah to anoint him king of Syria in place of Ben-hadad. At the same time Elijah was told to anoint Jehu king of Israel. As far as the record shows, Elijah never got around to anointing either one but left the assignment to Elisha. However, *time* was operating against one of these men. Elisha was able to have Jehu anointed as we shall see shortly, but when he came to Damascus the evil in Hazael had already manifest itself so that it was too late to anoint him. The Lord could not have a man anointed for his *potential* good after the conduct of his life had already assumed a pattern of very real evil. The same thing would have been true if there had been a delay in the anointing or the ordination of Cain, Judas, the two oldest sons of Aaron, Saul, David, Solomon, Jeroboam, and a host of others who fell. In these cases the anointing must be done in time or it cannot be done at all.

Such would appear to be the answer to our previous questions concerning Hazael. The anointing was delayed until the evil in Hazael's life made the bestowing of the blessing impossible.

How Jezebel Gained Control of Both Israel and Judah

Soon after Elisha participated in the epic events in Damascus he returned to Samaria, capital of Israel, where equally dramatic events were soon to transpire. The wicked house of Ahab had used the throne to corrupt the northern tribes and had recently acquired domination of the throne in Judah where it was corrupting that tribe as well. We need to remind ourselves how this came about so we can appreciate the catastrophic events which followed.

The widespread corruption of both Israel and Judah stemmed primarily from one source during this period. It was Jezebel. By 841 B.C. she must have been close to 60 years of age.[30] She was the daughter of Ethbaal, king of

---

30. We deduct this from the fact that by 841 B.C. she had a 22-year-old grandson. (2 Kings 8:26)

Phoenicia, who is described as "a priest of Ashtoreth, [who] had seized supreme power, after murdering his brother, Phalles."[31] Jezebel had married King Ahab of Israel and spread heathen idolatry throughout Israel because of her influence as queen.[32] When Ahab was killed she saw her son, Ahaziah, reign for two years, and after he died from an accidental fall through the lattice of a window, she saw her son, Jehoram, take over the throne. Meanwhile, she had succeeded in marrying her daughter Athaliah into the royal family of Judah and when Athaliah became queen of Judah she did to the people of David what her mother had done to Israel. It must have been a source of extreme gratification to the evil heart of Jezebel to realize that through politics she had been able to impose her heathen idolatry and her own personal brand of degenerate culture on the two nations of the world which were most vehemently opposed to such practices.

Jezebel probably knew she would gain a foothold in Judah when she consented to the marriage of Athaliah to the crown prince of Judah around 864 B.C.[33] This prince was named Jehoram and became king of Judah in 849 B.C. with Athalia as his queen. We call him "Jehoram OF JUDAH" to distinguish him from Jezebel's son, "Jehoram OF ISRAEL." These two men with identical names were kings of their respective countries at the same time![34] And because the king of Judah was married to Athaliah, sister of the king of Israel, they were also brothers-in-law.

JEHORAM OF JUDAH MURDERS ALL HIS BROTHERS TO COMMENCE AN EVIL REIGN

The father of Jehoram of Judah had been the "good king," Jehoshaphat, direct descendant of David. Just the moment he was dead, however, Jehoram and Athaliah as-

---

31. Geikie, *Hours With the Bible*, Vol. 4, p. 50
32. 1 Kings 21:25
33. This would appear from the fact that Ahaziah, son of Athaliah, was 22 years of age by 841 B.C. (2 Kings 8:26)
34. Beginning with 2 Kings 8:16 the Bible translators tried to distinguish between these two men by calling the king of Israel "Joram" while retaining "Jehoram" for the king of Judah. Many commentaries do the same. In this text we will retain their original names but distinguish them by calling one "Jehoram of Judah," and the other "Jehoram of Israel."

cended their royal thrones and lashed themselves to the helm of Judah's ship of state. They would brook no opposition whether threatened or real.

They began by having all six of Jehoram's brothers murdered.[35] These brothers had been made governors of principal cities in Judah and, so far as we can tell, were no threat to the throne whatever.[36] The blood purge was then expanded to include the "princes" or heads of principal families.[37] As it turned out, all this spilling of blood failed to secure the throne for Jehoram. He died a horrible death as a relatively young man after ruling only eight years.[38] The scripture says, "And he walked in the way of the kings of Israel, like as did the house of Ahab: for he had the daughter of Ahab to wife: and he wrought that which was evil in the eyes of the Lord."[39]

The nature of this evil is spelled out: "Moreover he made high places in the mountains of Judah, and caused the inhabitants of Jerusalem to commit fornication, and compelled Judah thereto."[40]

This dissolute destruction of the moral fiber of Judah brought rumbling thunder out of heaven. It came in the form of an epistle from the Lord's leading Priesthood authority on the earth at that time. 2 Chronicles attributes this epistle to Elijah which must be an error.[41] Authorities point out that this must have been done accidentally or because some scribe wanted to give the epistle greater authority in later generations. Since Elijah had been gone for at least thirteen years, his epistle was most probably authored by Elisha, the highest authority among the Israelites at this time. The document was loaded with foreboding disaster for Jehoram, king of Judah:

"Thus saith the Lord God of David thy father, Because thou hast not walked in the ways of Jehoshaphat thy father, nor in the ways of Asa king of Judah, but hast walked in

---

35. 2 Chronicles 21:4
36. 2 Chronicles 21:2-3
37. 2 Chronicles 21:4
38. 2 Chronicles 21:5, 18, 19. Note that his death came at age 40.
39. 2 Chronicles 21:6
40. 2 Chronicles 21:11
41. 2 Chronicles 21:12

the ways of the kings of Israel, and hast made Judah and the inhabitants of Jerusalem to go a whoring, like to the whoredoms of the house of Ahab, and also hast slain thy brethren of thy father's house, which were better than thyself: Behold, with a great plague will the Lord smite thy people, and thy children, and thy wives, and all thy goods: and thou shalt have great sickness by disease of thy bowels, until thy bowels fall out by reason of the sickness day by day."[42]

The plague which came upon the people was war — the infamous abomination of desolation. First, it began with the rebellion of the Edomites[43] who dominated the Arabah valley which was Judah's only link to Ezion-geber and the Red Sea. Then Libnah revolted and the scripture says the basic reason was "because he [the king] had forsaken the Lord God of his fathers."[44] Then things really broke loose as the Philistines and the Arabians combined together for an all-out assault directly on Jerusalem. They were not only successful in overcoming all resistance but looted the city and killed all of the king's children except his youngest son.[45] Many of the king's wives were also killed or captured,[46] but not the shrewd Athaliah, mother of the one child who escaped.[47] Her evil ways which had precipitated these fruits of apostasy were to survive and curse Judah for many years to come.

The king must have reflected frequently on the epistle from the prophet as he saw its words being literally fulfilled in the multitude of terrors around him. As for the king, however, his personal afflictions were just beginning. The raw sorrow over the loss of his wives and children and the ravishing of beautiful Jerusalem was still fresh in his mind when the lecherous disease predicted in the epistle began to attach itself to the vitals of his body. The exact nature of the affliction is difficult to determine, but the consequences were terrible. The scripture says, "And it came to pass, that in process of time, after the end of two years, his bowels fell out by reason of his sickness: so he died of sore diseases. . . . Thirty and two years old was he when he began to reign,

---

42. 2 Chronicles 21:12-15
43. 2 Chronicles 21:8-9
44. 2 Chronicles 21:10

45. 2 Chronicles 21:17
46. Ibid.
47. 2 Chronicles 22:2-3

and he reigned in Jerusalem eight years, and departed without being desired [regretted]. Howbeit they buried him in the city of David, but not in the sepulchres of the kings."[48]

KING AHAZIAH AND HIS MOTHER (ATHALIAH) RULE JUDAH

Thus ended the reign of Jehoram of Judah but not the consequences of his apostasy. These continued under the administration of his son, Ahaziah, and the influence of his surviving queen, Athaliah.

Ahaziah was the king's one son who had survived the massacre of the king's children during the war with the Philistines and Arabs. And his mother, the wicked Athaliah, had also survived. These two now combined their strength to further heathenize Judah. Concerning Ahaziah the scripture says, "He also walked in the ways of the house of Ahab: for his mother [Ahab and Jezebel's daughter] was his counseller to do wickedly."[49] Her influence over Ahaziah was no doubt facilitated by the fact that he was only 22 years of age when he ascended the throne.[50]

Under these circumstances it will be better appreciated how the 60-year-old Jezebel felt about this time as she beheld her son, Jehoram, on the throne of Israel, and her grandson, Ahaziah, on the throne of Judah.

EVENTS LEADING TO THE FALL OF THE HOUSE OF AHAB

But this royal monopoly lasted less than a year.

It will be recalled from the last chapter that the prophet Elisha had gone up to Damascus to be present when Hazael seized power by murdering Ben-hadad. Elisha was now back in Israel and ready to fulfill the Lord's assignment to

---

48. 2 Chronicles 21:19-20
49. 2 Chronicles 22:3; 2 Kings 8:27
50. 2 Kings 8:26. In 2 Chronicles 22:2 it gives his age as 42 when he began to reign. This is obviously an error of some scribe and all authorities recognize the age given in 2 Kings as the correct one. Dr. Clarke suggests that the error may have occurred as a result of the similarity of *caph* and *mem*, the single letters anciently used for twenty and forty, respectively. (See Clarke, *Bible Commentary*, Vol. 2, p. 675)

have Jehu overthrow the house of Ahab. Political and military developments facilitated the project as follows:

Since Hazael was now the new king of Syria it entered into the minds of Jehoram of Israel and Ahaziah of Judah that they might now go up and recapture Ramon-gilead. Years before Ben-hadad had promised to give this city back to Israel but had never done so. In fact, Ahab had been killed twelve years earlier trying to force Ben-hadad to give up this city. Jehoram and Ahaziah decided now was a good time to complete this unfinished business. They therefore marshalled the combined forces of both Israel and Judah and marched across the Jordan river at the Jezreel fords to attack Ramon-gilead.

According to Josephus the city was successfully occupied by the Israelites,[51] but Jehoram of Israel was severely wounded.[52] Further prosecution of the campaign was therefore suspended while Jehoram went to the summer palace at Jezreel to recover.[53] Ahaziah, king of Judah, came down to comfort and assist him during his illness.[54]

Meanwhile, the armies of Israel and Judah remained camped in the vicinity of Ramoth-gilead to protect it from any Syrian counter-attack. To this camp there now came "one of the children of the prophets" with instructions from Elisha. Elisha had said to him, "Gird up thy loins, and take this box of oil in thine hand, and go to Ramoth-gilead. And when thou comest thither, look out there [locate] Jehu [commander of the host] . . . and go in, and make him arise up from among his brethren, and carry him to an inner chamber; then take the box of oil, and pour it on his head, and say, Thus saith the Lord, I have anointed thee king over Israel. Then open the door, and flee. and tarry not."[55]

JEHU IS ANOINTED KING OF ISRAEL

"So the young man, even the young man the prophet, went to Ramoth-gilead. And when he came, behold, the captains of the hosts were sitting; and he said, I have an

---

51. Josephus, *Antiquities of the Jews*, Book 9, chapter 6:1
52. 2 Kings 8:28. Note the use of "Joram" for "Jehoram."
53. 2 Kings 8:29　　　　　　55. 2 Kings 9:1-3
54. Ibid.

errand to thee O captain, And Jehu said, Unto which of all us? And he said, To thee O captain. And he arose, and went into the house: and he poured the oil on his head, and said unto him, Thus saith the Lord God of Israel, I have anointed thee king over the people of the Lord, even over Israel. And thou shalt smite the house of Ahab thy master, that I may avenge the blood of my servants the prophets, and the blood of all the servants of the Lord, at the hand of Jezebel. For the whole house of Ahab shall perish . . . and I will make the house of Ahab like the house of Jeroboam the son of Nebat, and like the house of Baasah the son of Ahijah [both of which were exterminated]. AND THE DOGS SHALL EAT JEZEBEL IN THE PORTION OF JEZREEL, AND THERE SHALL BE NONE TO BURY HER."[56]

Having pronounced this declaration of prophetic calamity, the young Priesthood holder "opened the door, and fled."[57] He was not about to get caught in the revolutionary cross-fire which he knew for a certainty was now about to commence.

As Jehu came back into the place where "the captains of the host were sitting," they were burning with curiosity. One of them asked, "Is all well? wherefore came this mad fellow to thee?"[58] At first Jehu would not tell them because they had called him a "mad fellow," but finally he said, ". . . thus spake he to me, saying, Thus saith the Lord, I have anointed thee king over Israel."[59]

The commanders of the host were jubilant. They placed their military cloaks down before him to walk to the top of the stairs, and then "blew with trumpets, saying, Jehu is king!"[60] Jehu thereupon took a company of chariots and set out for Jezreel where King Jehoram of the house of Ahab was recovering from his wounds. As the chariots proceeded up the Jezreel valley the dust from the dry roadway could be seen several miles away by the watchman at the king's palace. A messenger was sent down by King Jehoram to see who this company might be and whether or not they

---

56. 2 Kings 9:5-10
57. 2 Kings 9:10
58. 2 Kings 9:11

59. 2 Kings 9:12
60. 2 Kings 9:13

came in peace. But when this messenger reached Jehu and found there was about to be a coup d'etat he did not return but fell in behind Jehu. A second messenger was sent but he also joined Jehu.

As the cavalcade drew closer to the palace the watchman noticed that the lead chariot was being driven "like the driving of Jehu the son of Nimshi; for he driveth furiously."[61]

Now the king was thoroughly alarmed. In spite of his half-healed wounds he ordered his chariot. His nephew, Ahaziah, king of Judah, ordered his chariot also.

THE FALL OF THE HOUSE OF AHAB

But barely had their chariots emerged from the palace courtyard when they met Jehu and his company near the vineyard that had belonged to Naboth. This was the very vineyard which Jezebel had committed murder to obtain for her husband, Ahab. And this was the spot where Elijah had appeared to Ahab years before and told him his posterity would be one day exterminated.[62] That day had come.

Of course King Jehoram scarcely suspected that Jehu had come as an avenger of the apocalypse and so he said, "Is it peace, Jehu?" The grim countenance of Jehu was probably as fierce as his answer. He replied, "What peace, so long as the whoredoms of thy mother, Jezebel and her witchcrafts are so many?"[63] Jehoram immediately turned to Ahaziah, king of Judah, and shouted, "There is treachery O Ahaziah!"[64]

Both of the kings suddenly wheeled their chariots around and frantically galloped away trying to escape. Jehu drove furiously close behind. "And Jehu drew a bow with his full strength, and smote Jehoram between his arms, and the arrow went out at his heart, and he sunk down in his chariot."[65] Jehu stopped abruptly, ordered the body thrown into the vineyard of Naboth so it could be buried there, and then proceeded at top speed after Ahaziah the King of Judah. Ahaziah had been seen fleeing "by the way of the garden

---

61. 2 Kings 9:20
62. 1 Kings 21:21-23
63. 2 Kings 9:22
64. 2 Kings 9:23
65. 2 Kings 9:24

house," so Jehu set out in hot pursuit.[66] However, this chase turned out to be an extended one, so Jehu delegated the capture of Ahaziah to his captains[67] while he returned to seize the summer palace. Apparently King Ahaziah escaped as far as Samaria[68] but was finally overtaken on the road to Gur and fatally wounded. He struggled on as far as Megiddo and died there.[69]

Meanwhile, Jehu charged toward the summer palace where he had his heart set on the destruction of that benighted daughter of Satan who had been the curse of Israel for two generations. He wanted Jezebel.

By this time Jezebel had already learned that Jehu had slain King Jehoram, her son.[70] She knew Jehu would be coming to the palace soon and that unless she could ingratiate herself with this avenging commander of the host, her own death was imminent. Therefore this murderess matron of the harlot cult of Ashtoreth spent her last moments beautifying herself. The scripture says she "painted her face and tired [adorned] her head, and looked out at a window."[71] This window faced directly toward the palace gate and as Jehu drove his chariot into the courtyard, she was up there where he could see her directly before him. "And as Jehu entered in at the gate, she said, Had Zimri peace, who slew his master?"[72]

Any Israelite would have known exactly what this strange salutation implied. Zimri was the Israelite general who slew King Elah around 885 B.C. and later slaughtered the dynasty of Baasha. But within a week he had been so overwhelmed with opposition that he rushed madly into the royal palace and burned the building over his head.[73] But even more significant was the fact that Zimri had been unseated by Omri, father of Jezebel's deceased husband, the unrighteous Ahab. So she hoped to shock Jehu and perhaps save her own life by reminding him what had happened to Zimri

---

66. 2 Kings 9:27
67. Ibid.
68. 2 Chronicles 22:9
69. 2 Kings 9:27
70. This becomes evident from her later salutation to Jehu.
71. 2 Kings 9:30
72. 2 Kings 9:31
73. 1 Kings 16:18

after he slew his master. But Jehu was not shocked. Zimri had no divine commission to cleanse the land. Zimri was as wicked as the man he slew. Jehu had been designated the executioner of the whole house of Ahab, and especially the heathen consort of Ahab, this Jezebel.

So Jehu shouted up toward the palace window, "Who is on my side? Who?"[74] Immediately several eunuchs who usually served in the harem quarter looked out of the window. Jehu said to them, "Throw her down!"[75]

She was promptly seized by these men and thrown to the courtyard below whereupon Jehu whipped his horses forward and the chariot wheels crushed out whatever life may have remained in the woman.[76] Jehu then pressed on into the palace with his troops to complete the *coup d'etat*. When affairs had settled down and the famished warrior had been fed, Jehu said, "Go, see now this cursed woman, and bury her; for she is a king's daughter."[77]

But a horrible thing had happened. The prophecies of Elijah and Elisha had been literally fulfilled. The scripture says, "And they went to bury her: but they found no more of her than the skull, and the feet, and the palms of her hands. Wherefore they came again, and told him. And he said, This is the word of the Lord, which he spake by his servant Elijah the Tishbite, saying, In the portion of Jezreel shall dogs eat the flesh of Jezebel: and the carcase of Jezebel shall be as dung upon the face of the field in the portion of Jezreel; so that they shall not say, This is Jezebel."[78] In other words, no one would be able to say, "Here is the grave of Queen Jezebel," for she would have none.

All of this seems extremely harsh, ugly and tragic, and so it was. But the cosmic eternities echoed with the screams of the children who had been burned alive in the heathen festivals sponsored by this woman, and there were the cries of God's servants as they had gone down to their deaths on this woman's command. Then there was Naboth

---

74. 2 Kings 9:32
75. 2 Kings 9:33
76. Ibid.
77. 2 Kings 9:34. She was the daughter of the king of Phoenicia (1 Kings 16:31).
78. 2 Kings 9:35-37

whom this woman had arranged to have murdered and in the process of which both he and his sons had been stoned to death and devoured by dogs and swine not far from the very spot where it had happened to Jezebel. So this was the woman whom Jehu smashed under the wheels of his chariot and upon whom the Lord had placed His prediction that dogs would one day devour her body.

JEHU ANNIHILATES THE HEATHEN DYNASTY OF AHAB

Jehu now sent a letter to the capital city, Samaria, and said to those who had custody of Ahab's seventy sons, "Now as soon as this letter cometh to you, seeing your master's sons are with you, and there are with you chariots and horses, a fenced city also, and armour; look even out [select] the best and meetest of your master's sons, and set him on his father's throne, and fight for your master's house!"[79]

But these officers of the royal family would not accept the challenge. They were "exceedingly afraid," and said to themselves, "Behold, two kings [Jehoram and Ahaziah] stood not before him, how then shall we stand?" So they wrote to Jehu saying, "We are thy servants, and will do all that thou shalt bid us; we will not make any king: do thou that which is good in thine eyes."[80]

Jehu said he wanted the seventy sons of Ahab destroyed and their heads delivered to Jezreel. This was done.[81] Jehu then cleansed the entire summer capital of Jezreel of all remnants of the house and administration of Ahab[82] and proceeded toward Samaria. On the way he found along the highway a whole party of travelers headed for Jezreel who were relatives of King Ahaziah of Judah, grandson of Ahab. Apparently they had not heard the news so they were blithely going to Jezreel "to salute the children of the king and the children of the queen."[83] These were all slain.[84]

Just before entering Samaria, one of the prominent national leaders named "Jehonadab the son of Rechab" came

---

79. 2 Kings 10:2-3
80. 2 Kings 10:4-5
81. 2 Kings 10:7

82. 2 Kings 10:11
83. 2 Kings 10:13
84. 2 Kings 10:14

out to meet Jehu.[85] Jehu said to him, "Is thine heart right, as my heart is with thy heart? and Jehonadab answered, It is."[86] Jehu thereupon took this man into his chariot and they rode together into the capital. The presence of a man like Jehonadab in Jehu's chariot undoubtedly helped gain popular acceptance of the new regime.

Jehu next cleansed Samaria of all taint of the Ahab dynasty. Then he turned to the problem of eliminating the Baal-Ashtoreth cult. This was done by subterfuge. He pretended he was going to have a mammoth solemn assembly honoring Baal. "And Jehu sent through all Israel: and all the worshippers of Baal came, so that there was not a man left that came not. And they came into the house of Baal and the house of Baal was full from one end to another."[87]

Jehu had them dress in their priestly robes[88] and then he said, "Search, and look that there be here with you none of the servants of the Lord, but the worshippers of Baal only."[89] So the great secret society of Baal was ready for its sacrifice and mystic ceremonies. Once they were under way, "Jehu said to the guard and to the captains, Go in and slay them, let none come forth. And they smote them with the edge of the sword. . . . And they brought forth the images out of the house of Baal and burned them. And they brake down the image of Baal, and brake down the house of Baal, and made it a draught house [public latrine] unto this day."[90]

Thus commenced the reign of Jehu as king of Israel which lasted 28 years,[91] from 841 B.C. to 814 B.C.

The dynasty of Ahab was now extinct except for Ahab's evil daughter, Athaliah.

AHAB'S DAUGHTER, ATHALIAH, RULES ISRAEL
SEVEN YEARS

It will be recalled that Athaliah had married the heir to the throne of David (Jehoram of Judah, son of Jehoshaphat), and when he ascended the throne, she became queen.

---

85. 2 Kings 10:15
86. Ibid.
87. 2 Kings 10:21
88. 2 Kings 10:22

89. 2 Kings 10:23
90. 2 Kings 10:25-27
91. 2 Kings 10:36

After his death, however, her son, Ahaziah, became king and Athaliah became the influential "queen mother." Now that Jehu had slain Ahaziah, the queen mother decided to seize the throne of David herself.

She commenced by having her guard kill all the other heirs to the throne of David so none would challenge her authority to wear the crown. This blood purge even included her own grandchildren.[92] But there was one little baby boy who was the latest and perhaps the only son of Ahaziah. He escaped from his grandmother through the good offices of Jehosheba, an aunt, who hid him with his nurse for seven years. They were both placed in the custody of Jehoida, the High Priest, who hid the little boy and his nurse in the temple.[93] This child is called Joash in II Kings, Chapter 11, but Jehoash in Chapter 12. And when he was in his seventh year, Jehoida, the High Priest, decided to make him king and oust the wicked Athaliah from the throne. In the annex of the temple there appears to have been an arsenal of spears and shields[94] so Jehoida instructed the military leaders to come disarmed to the temple on the Sabbath day so it would not arouse the suspicions of the queen. From the temple arsenal he furnished them with arms so that they immediately became a fully equipped guard, ready to resist any forces which might remain loyal to the queen. "And the guard stood, every man with his weapons in his hand, round about the king, from the right corner of the temple to the left corner of the temple . . . and he [the High Priest, Jehoida] brought forth the king's son, and put the crown upon him, and gave him the testimony [the book of the law]; . . . and they clapped their hands, and said, God save the king."[95]

For a seven-year-old boy this must have been an exciting experience. But it also turned out to be exciting for someone else — the queen. All of this caught her completely by surprise. "And when Athaliah heard the noise of the guard and of the people, she came to the people into the temple of the Lord. And when she looked, behold, the

---

92. This is apparent from the fact that Ahaziah's son had to be hidden from her in order to survive.
93. 2 Kings 11:3-4. They probably occupied the annex rooms built against the walls of the temple.
94. 2 Kings 11:10
95. 2 Kings 11:11-12

king stood by a pillar, as the manner was [when the king officially participated in state ceremonies], and the princes and the trumpeters by the king, and all the people of the land rejoiced, and blew with trumpets."[96]

This sight was more than Athaliah could stand. She tore her clothes and screamed at the people, "Treason! Treason!"[97]

"But Jehoida the priest commanded the captains of the hundreds, the officers of the host, and said unto them, Have [take] her forth without the ranges [temple courtyards]: and him that followeth her kill with the sword. For the priest had said, let her not be slain in the house of the Lord. And they laid hands on her; and she went by the way by the which the horses came into the king's house: and there was she slain."[98]

Jehoida, the High Priest, had good reason to rejoice over the termination of this woman's reign, for she had commanded her followers, the "sons of Athaliah,"[99] to break into the temple and take all the "dedicated things of the house of the Lord" and bestow them "upon Baalim."[100]

But after Athaliah was dead, "all the people of the land went into the house of Baal, and brake it down; his altars and his images brake they in pieces thoroughly, and slew Mattan the priest of Baal before the altars."[101]

It had been a bad year for Baal in Israel. Baal's temples were in ruins, his heathen prelates dead, and his great patron, the House of Ahab, was no more. The remnants of his cult would get their vengeance later on.

THE REIGN OF JEHOASH (OR JOASH) OF JUDAH

Jehoash was born around 842 B.C., and constituted the eighth generation down from David on his father's side. His mother was Zibia of Beer-sheba.[102] His grandmother

96. 2 Kings 11:13-14
97. Ibid.
98. 2 Kings 11:15-16
99. 2 Chronicles 24:7. The reference to "sons of Athaliah" is believed to indicate "followers" since Ahaziah is the only son she is known to have had. The Bible says she killed all the remaining heirs to the throne. (2 Kings 11:1)
100. Ibid.   102. 2 Kings 12:1
101. 2 Kings 11:18

was the wicked Athaliah who had tried to kill him along with all of the other "seed royal" so she could reign as queen.[103] As we have seen, he escaped by being taken to the temple with his nurse and being placed under the care of the High Priest, Jehoida.[104] When he was seven years of age Jehoida brought him forth, crowned him king, and had his grandmother, Athaliah, slain when she tried to interfere.[105]

The reign of Jehoash (or Joash) covered the years of approximately 834 to 796 B.C., inclusive, making his administration a total of forty years duration.[106] The early part of his reign was righteous and functioned under the direct supervision of the High Priest, Jehoida.[107] It was this king who started a drive to repair the Temple of Solomon. It had been assaulted, stripped, and broken into during many recent military raids and more recently by Queen Athaliah's followers who carried off anything which caught their fancy in order to decorate the temple of Baal.[108] But now that the wicked queen was dead, Jehoash determined to repair the building, so he had the people make donations for that purpose. However, after several years he noticed that the priests were making no attempt whatever to repair the temple. They had been using all the temple donations for themselves. So the king said to them, "Why repair ye not the breaches of the house?"[109] When they could give him no satisfactory answer he commanded them to collect no more money from the people unless they were going to use it for repairs. The lazy priests were completely apathetic about the whole affair. They announced they would refuse any donations in the future if they were going to be obligated to use them for the repairing of the temple.[110]

Jehoida, the High Priest, decided to get around the misappropriation of funds by having contributions made directly to him rather than to the lazy priests. So "Jehoida the priest took a chest, and bored a hole in the lid of it, and set it beside the altar, on the right side as one cometh into the house of the Lord."[111] He then had a trusted priest stand

103. 2 Kings 11:1
104. 2 Kings 11:2-3; 12:2
105. 2 Kings 11:12-16
106. 2 Kings 12:1
107. 2 Kings 12:2
108. 2 Chronicles 24:7
109. 2 Kings 12:7
110. 2 Kings 12:8
111. 2 Kings 12:9

by the box and place in it all the money which the people brought for the temple fund. Vast sums soon accumulated so "the king's scribe and the high priest came up, and they put [the money] up in bags, and told the money that was found in the house of the Lord."[112]

At last there was money to repair the temple. And the extent of the damage done to this beautiful building may be gathered from the following passages, "And they gave the money . . . into the hands of them that did the work, that had the oversight of the house of the Lord: and they laid it out to the carpenters and builders, that wrought upon the house of the Lord, and to masons and hewers of stone, and to buy timber and hewed stone to repair the breaches of the house of the Lord, and for all that was laid out for the house to repair it."[113]

Jehoida and the king did not allow any of the original money to be used for expensive equipment in the temple, but employed all of this money to pay the workmen who did the repairs.[114] Only later, when they were sure all the bills had been paid for necessary labor, did they embellish the temple with vessels of silver and gold.[115] The scripture also says that any contributions which properly belonged to the priests were immaculately handled so that they received whatever was due them.[116] Earlier, the priests had been guilty of "mingling funds." Jehoida and the king were not going to make the same mistake.

JEHOIDA DIES AND JEHOASH APOSTATIZES

The most important single factor in the entire career of King Jehoash of Judah was the wise advice and support he received from the aged High Priest, Jehoida. Jehoida was already an old man by the time Jehoash was born, so when he finally passed away Jehoida had lived longer than any person of record since the days of the patriarchs. He had reached 130 years![117]

Jehoida had been a great spiritual leader of the people and for all practical purposes served as ruler of the country

---

112. 2 Kings 12:10
113. 2 Kings 12:11-12
114. 2 Kings 12:13-4

115. 2 Chronicles 24:14
116. 2 Kings 12:16
117. 2 Chronicles 24:15

during the reign of the weak King Jehoash. Therefore, when he died, "they buried him in the city of David among the kings, because he had done good in Israel, both toward God and toward his house."[118]

But no sooner was the High Priest buried than Jehoash, the king, became unanchored. Some of his princes flattered and influenced him until he agreed to allow the heathen rituals to be practiced again.[119] The abominations spread like a plague across the land and the spirit of the Lord began departing from the people. The new High Priest was Jehoida's son, named Zechariah, and when he saw that the king was in a state of apostate rebellion, he proclaimed, "Thus saith God, Why transgress ye the commandments of the Lord, that ye cannot prosper? Because YE HAVE FORSAKEN THE LORD, HE HATH ALSO FORSAKEN YOU."[120]

King Jehoash rejected the message from the Lord by sending his men out to form a murderous conspiracy against Zedekiah. "And they conspired against him, and stoned him with stones at the commandment of the king in the court of the house of the Lord. Thus Joash [Jehoash] the king remembered not the kindness which Jehoida his father had done to him, but slew his son."[121]

This slaying of a High Priest at the precincts of the temple of the Lord became a long-remembered blot on the history of Judah. When Jesus was ministering to the people in his day he referred to "the blood of Zacharias son of Barachias, whom ye [your ancestors] slew between the temple and the altar."[122] This passage has caused much speculation since Zacharias, son of Barachias was the well-known prophet and was not slain in this manner so far as is known, but only Zecharias, the son of Jehoida. Dr. Clarke and others believe the New Testament scribes somehow confused the two when recording the words of Jesus, and that it was the

---

118. 2 Chronicles 24:16
119. 2 Chronicles 24:18
120. 2 Chronicles 24:20
121. 2 Chronicles 24:21-22
122. Matthew 23:35

example of Zecharias, son of Jehoida, to whom Jesus was referring, rather than Zacharias, the prophet.[123]

In any event, the prophecy of the martyred Zechariah soon came down like a pestilence on the head of King Jehoash. It began in the form of a threatening attack by Hazael, king of Syria. That assassin who had gained his throne by smothering Ben-hadad, was on the march. He came down the Mediterranean coast as far as Gath (Goliath's old hometown) and, after conquering it, headed up the valley of Sorek toward Jerusalem.[124] Terror seized the heart of King Jehoash in Jerusalem so he resolved to bribe the Syrian king in hopes he would pass Judah by and make his conquests elsewhere. "And Jehoash king of Judah took all the hallowed things that . . . kings of Judah had dedicated, and his own hallowed things, and all the gold that was found in the treasures of the house of the Lord, and in the king's house, and sent it to Hazael king of Syria: and he went away from Jerusalem."[125]

But very shortly the Syrians were back again. Perhaps they thought the king may have replenished his treasuries by this time and another shake-down would be in order. Judah met the invading hosts of Syria with a large force, but their resistance collapsed, and the demoralized hosts of Judah were beaten down by the smaller task force of Syrians.[126] The enemy "destroyed all the princes of the people . . . and sent all the spoil of them unto the king of Damascus."[127]

After this great disaster, two servants of King Jehoash decided to avenge the death of the High Priest Zechariah. The scriptures say they slew the king while he was in his own bed.[128] So around 796 B.C. the forty-year reign of Jehoash (or Joash) came to an end and his son became the new king of Judah. His name was Amaziah.[129]

Amaziah was 25 years old when he began to reign.[130] The first important thing he did after being securely settled

---

123. Clarke, *Bible Commentary*, vol. 5, p. 132. It should also be noted that Zecharias and Zacharias are alternative spellings for the same name.
124. 2 Kings 12:17
125. 2 Kings 12:18
126. 2 Chronicles 24:24
127. 2 Chronicles 24:23
128. 2 Kings 12:21; 2 Chronicles 24:25
129. 2 Kings 14:1
130. 2 Kings 14:2

on the throne was to execute the two palace servants who had slain his father.[131] Thus began the 29-year reign of Amaziah.

The House of Jehu Undertakes the Government of Israel

The Bible narrative now jumps back about 35 years to tell us what had been happening up in Israel. It will be recalled that Jehu, the commander of the armies of Israel, had been anointed under the direction of Elisha to destroy the house of Ahab and cleanse the land of Baal-worship. Having killed the king and his mother, Jezebel, and having wiped out all the known kinsmen of this family, Jehu started a new dynasty. He personally reigned as king for 28 years,[132] from around 841 to 814 inclusive.

In the beginning Jehu had the blessing of the Lord because of his integrity in cleansing the land of all those heathen cults which promoted the esoteric fertility rites and human sacrifices. Eventually, however, Jehu compromised by allowing calf-worship. This was an Egyptian cult first introduced by Jeroboam and therefore called "the sins of Jeroboam, which made Israel to sin."[133] Jehu found that as the support of the Lord withdrew from him, so did his good fortune. The same Syrian military force that had been such a plague to Judah likewise devoured large regions of Israel and her tributaries. The whole Trans-Jordan territory from the Sea of Galilee to the borders of Moab fell to Syria. This included not only several heathen tributaries but the entire inheritance of the tribes of Gad, Reuben and half of Manasseh.[134]

This was the situation in 814 B.C. when Jehu finally died and his son Jehoahaz took over as king.[135] Jehoahaz reigned from around 814 to 798 inclusive, a total of 17 years.[136] All during these years he suffered continuous raids and harrassment from Syria[137] until finally "Jehoahaz besought the Lord, and the Lord hearkened unto him: for he saw the

---

131. 2 Kings 14:5-6
132. 2 Kings 10:36
133. 2 Kings 10:31
134. 2 Kings 10:33

135. 2 Kings 10:35
136. 2 Kings 13:1
137. 2 Kings 13:3

oppression of Israel, because the king of Syria oppressed them."[138] It is implied that because of his prayers some type of assurance was given to the king that the tide would begin to turn.[139] We later learn that Jonah appeared on the scene about this time and prophesied that ultimately the bounds of Israel would be as great as they were in the days of David and Solomon.[140] All things considered, it will not be surprising if we ultimately learn that it was Jonah who gave the assurance to Jehoahaz that Israel would one day throw off the prodding harrassment of Syria.

Jehoahaz died around 798 B.C., and his son, Joash, then took over the throne of Israel.

Joash ruled Israel from 798 to 782 inclusive, a total of 16 years,[141] and it was during his reign that the tide began to turn in favor of Israel and against Syria. Joash learned that this would be the case as a result of his last visit with Elisha just before the old prophet died.

THE DEATH OF ELISHA

For either personal or political reasons, Joash allowed the calf-worship of Egypt to continue throughout his reign just as his father had done, but nevertheless, he had great regard for Elisha, the prophet of the Lord. His feelings were vividly demonstrated when he heard that Elisha was deathly ill. He hurried down to the place where Elisha was staying and when he came into the presence of the dying prophet he moved close beside his bed. The scripture says, "And Joash the king of Israel . . . wept over his face, and said, O my father, my father, the chariot of Israel, and the horsemen thereof"[142] This was like saying, "O my father, thou art the only defense of Israel!"

"And Elisha said unto him, Take bow and arrows. And he took unto him bow and arrows. And he said to the king of Israel, Put thine hand upon the bow. And he put his hand upon it: and Elisha put his hands upon the king's hands. And he said, Open the window eastward. And he

138. 2 Kings 13:4
139. 2 Kings 13:5
140. 2 Kings 14:25. The king who would achieve this was to be Jeroboam II, the future grandson of Jehoahaz.
141. 2 Kings 13:10   142. 2 Kings 13:14

opened it. Then Elisha said, Shoot. And he shot. And he said, The arrow of the Lord's deliverance, and the arrow of deliverance from Syria: for thou shalt smite the Syrians in Aphek, till thou have consumed them."[143]

What a great farewell message from this renowned prophet of God. So Israel would prevail after all! Then Elisha told the king to take the remaining arrows in his hand and shoot them into the ground.[144] For some reason the king shot three arrows and then stopped. Elisha told him he should have shot five or six because the arrows were victory symbols and each one represented a victory over Syria.[145] In any event, Joash had the assurance that he would win at least three great battle over the Syrians.

It was shortly after this that Elisha died. Since his original calling on that exciting day when Elijah came to visit him, Elisha had served during the administration of six kings of Israel — Ahab, Ahaziah, Jehoram, Jehu, Jehoahaz and Joash. He died the year before the Moabites invaded Israel[146] which is believed to have been during the tenth year of the Joash administration, or 788 B.C. If so, this would mean that Elisha had presided in his prophetic calling for a period of approximately 65 years![147]

Although governing primarily in spiritual affairs Elisha was a key figure in making many critical political decisions. He was loved of the Lord and allowed to exercise practically all of the miraculous powers later employed by the Savior. As mentioned earlier, by God's power he raised the dead, caused and cured leprosy, nullified the effects of poison, purified deadly water, healed barrenness, raised an axehead from a river bottom, abundantly increased a supply of oil and fed a multitude. Not a scrap of this great man's writings are in existence and only a few morsels of his spoken words. Nevertheless, he stands out in sacred history as one of the greatest of God's spiritual leaders.

---

143. 2 Kings 13:15-17
144. 2 Kings 13:18. The text says "smite upon the ground," but since the king was shooting from inside the house this is interpreted to mean "shooting" the arrows into the ground. (See Clarke, *Bible Commentary*, Vol. 2, p. 524)
145. 2 Kings 13:19
146. 2 Kings 13:20
147. Clarke, *Bible Commentary*, Vol. 2, p. 523

The War Between Joash and Amaziah

King Joash of Israel deeply mourned the death of Elisha. Soon, however, his attention was dragged back to the bristling problems of politics. The latest threat to peace came from the most astounding of places — Judah.

In the third year of the reign of Joash (around 795 B.C.), a 25-year-old descendant of David had come to the throne of Judah.[148] His name was Amaziah, son of Jehoash who was murdered in his bed by two of his servants.[149] The new young king therefore commenced his reign by executing the two servants who had killed his father[150] and then launched forth in a military campaign to increase the influence of Judah.

Amaziah first declared war on Edom which occupied the Arabah valley south of the Dead Sea. Edom had been independent for about 50 years.[151] These descendants of Esau were an enterprising people and had carved a new capital out of solid rock on a mountain 70 miles down the valley from the Dead Sea. It was an impregnable fortress 4,000 feet above sea level which the Edomites called Selah or Petra, meaning "the Rock." The king of Judah was determined to humble this proud capital. In a war marked by terrible ferocity he killed 10,000 Edomites in the "Valley of Salt" and marched 10,000 more to Petra where they were hurled over the cliff and "broken in pieces."[152] Amaziah then plundered the Edomites and returned home with everything he could lay his hands on, including the Edomite gods.[153] The latter he was soon worshipping and the shadow of disaster followed almost immediately.

The cause of his calamity was a sequence of events which eventually involved Amaziah in a war with Israel. The scripture says that prior to the war with the Edomites, Amaziah had hired a vast number of Israelites to fight alongside his own troops and had advanced a large sum of money as compensation.[154] However, he was warned that since these

---

148. 2 Kings 14:1; 2 Chronicles 25:1
149. 2 Kings 12:21; 2 Chronicles 24:25
150. 2 Kings 14:5-6
151. Since the reign of Jehoram of Judah.
152. 2 Chronicles 25:12   154. 2 Chronicles 25:6
153. 2 Chronicles 25:14

Israelites were mostly idolators they would undoubtedly corrupt the armies of Judah.[155] Amaziah therefore discharged these Israelites and forfeited the earnest money he had already paid.[156] But this did not satisfy the mercenaries from Israel who expected to make themselves rich from the looting of Edom. They therefore avenged themselves enroute to their homes by raiding numerous cities of Judah. Josephus says 3,000 Jews died defending their homes.[157]

The king of Judah blamed all this on Joash, king of Israel, and was determined to avenge himself. King Joash tried to avoid a showdown by saying, "Why shouldest thou meddle to thy hurt, that thou shouldest fall, even thou, and Judah with thee?"[158] But Amaziah was adamant and therefore sent back a message which declared, "Come, let us see one another in the face."[159] That is exactly what happened and Amaziah lived to regret it. The battle took place at Bethshemesh some 15 or 16 miles west of Jerusalem. The armies of Judah were vanquished and Amaziah was mortified by being taken prisoner. He was then hauled back to Jerusalem where Joash made a 600-foot breach in the outer wall and looted the city.[160] He sacked the temple and palace, carried away hostages, and plundered the principal suburbs.[161]

Joash allowed Amaziah to go back on his throne but took the hostages to make sure that Amaziah and the people of the southern kingdom would now keep the peace. Amaziah lived 15 years longer than Joash[162] but continued in such disgrace with his own people that they finally conspired against him. When Amaziah saw that they wanted to kill him he fled southward and the assassins chased him clear to Lachish, 18 miles west of Hebron, before they finally caught up with him and hewed him down. The body was then brought back to Jerusalem for burial.[163] The people then acclaimed Amaziah's son as the new king. His name was Uzziah (or Azariah) and he was only 16 when he ascended the throne.[164] Nevertheless, he proved to be one of the best kings Judah had produced in 200 years.

155. 2 Chronicles 25:7
156. 2 Chronicles 25:9
157. Josephus, *Antiquities of the Jews*, Book 8, ch. 9:1
158. 2 Kings 14:10
159. 2 Chronicles 25:17
160. 2 Chronicles 25:23
161. 2 Chronicles 25:24
162. 2 Chronicles 25:25
163. 2 Chronicles 25:27-28
164. 2 Chronicles 26:1

THE RISE OF JEROBOAM II

Meanwhile, up in Israel, Joash had completed a series of military campaigns to the north in which he had thrown back the forces of Syria as Elisha had promised. He then died about 782 B.C. and was succeeded by his son whom he had named Jeroboam after the first king of the northern tribes. He is therefore known in history as Jeroboam II.

Jeroboam II was fortunate in that he came to power while the Assyrians were occupied for an extensive period of time with their own affairs at home. Immediately before this, however, they had greatly weakened Syria, Hamath, Phoenicia and the Philistines by pummeling them off and on for several decades. Therefore, when the Assyrians temporarily retired from the arena for some 40 to 45 years, Jeroboam II found himself in a particularly strong position to march forth and pick up the political pieces. He returned the boundaries of the kingdom to the same dimensions (in length, at least) that Israel had enjoyed in the days of David and Solomon.[165] They extended from the Orontes river in the north to Edom in the south and from the Philistines on the west to the Moabites and Ammonites on the east. It included everything but Judah and the Arabs of the Negeb.

All of this was a literal fulfillment of the prophecy made a short time earlier by the famous prophet Jonah.[166] It is appropriate therefore that we next consider one of the most extraordinary epics in the entire Bible — the amazing ministry of Jonah which occurred about this time.

---

165. 2 Kings 14:25
166. Ibid.

Scripture Reading and Questions on Chapter Sixteen

Scripture Reading: 2 Kings, Chapters 8 to 13 inclusive.

1—What story was Gehazi relating to the king of Israel when the Shunammite women came in with her son? How did this help the woman?

2—List three outstanding events in the life of Ben-hadad of Syria which are mentioned in the Bible.

3—Why was Ben-hadad glad Elisha had come to Damascus? Whom did he send to confer with Elisha? What was sent along with him?

4—What did Elisha tell the messenger about the king? What did Elisha do that made the messenger feel "ashamed"?

5—Whom had the Lord previously designated as the successor of Ben-hadad? What were the circumstances?

6—Then why was the man never anointed king of Syria?

7—What nationality was Jezebel? Give a brief history of her life.

8—How did Jezebel's daughter become queen of Judah? What kind of influence did she have on Judah?

9—What happened to Jehoram, king of Judah? Was this a fulfillment of prophecy?

10—Did Elisha anoint Jehu to be the new king of Israel? Describe the circumstances of Jehu's anointing.

11—Briefly relate the meeting between Jehu and the king of Israel at Jezreel. What happened to the king?

12—Describe the circumstances leading to the death of Jezebel. Who had predicted these circumstances?

13—How did Jezebel's daughter succeed in seizing the throne of Judah and reigning for seven years?

14—Who replaced her on the throne? Describe the circumstances.

15—How old was the High Priest, Jehoida, when he died? Where was he buried? Was this significant?

16—What happened to King Jehoash after the High Priest died? What did Zechariah, the son of the High Priest, do? What happened to Zechariah? What happened to the king?

17—After Jehu had annihilated the house of Ahab what was his attitude toward idolatry? Where did calf-worship originate?

18—Was King Joash of Israel a disciple of Elisha or just an admirer? What did he do when he heard Elisha was dying?

19—What was Elisha's last prophecy? What did he do to dramatize it for the king?

20—How long is Elisha believed to have served as a prophet? What miracles did he perform which were similar to those later performed by the Savior?

CHAPTER SEVENTEEN

The Ministries of Jonah and Amos

Of all the multitude of prophets whose lives flash across the panorama of the Old Testament, there are few who have aroused more exciting discussion than Jonah.

Jonah's entire history is condensed into approximately three pages of the average Bible, but those pages have been scrutinized by Bible readers down through the centuries with a certain sense of astonishment if not outright disbelief. Even though Jesus referred to Jonah's experience as a historical fact,[1] and even though other sources give full credence to it,[2] many scholars have found this account of Jonah a baffling stumbling block which defies rational comprehension.

In the following pages we will present some rather recent information which may be of considerable interest to those who have pondered in puzzled wonderment over the many questions raised by the story of Jonah. Perhaps the experiences of Jonah will turn out to be more rational than many people have thought.

---

1. Matthew 12:38-41; Luke 11:29-32
2. See Clarke's *Bible Commentary*, Vol. 4, pp. 669-670. John Taylor discusses the ministry of Jonah in the *Journal of Discourses*, Vol. 14, pp. 260-261.

Jonah came from a town called Gather-hepher, which is believed to have been located in the lower portion of Galilee and belonged to the tribe of Zebulun.[3] His exact ancestry is not known but the scripture describes him as "the son of Amittai."[4]

Jonah seems to have appeared on the scene shortly after Elisha's death. It will be recalled that Elisha's last official act was to confirm to King Joash that Israel would begin to prevail over Syria and its brutal monarch, Hazael.[5] Jonah then came among the people confirming this prophecy and going even further, Jonah predicted that Israel would one day dominate the length of the land from Hamath in northern Syria to the heathen tributaries down along the Dead Sea. At the time this must have seemed like a most wild and extravagant prophecy since its fulfillment would require the revival of Israel's strength comparable to the days of David and Solomon. Nevertheless, the prophecy stood. In fact, it was within that same generation which we will be discussing shortly, that this prophecy was literally fulfilled. It was accomplished under the reign of Jeroboam II who was king from 782 to 753 B.C.

It should be noted in passing that Jonah's *original* prophecy promising the revival of Israel, is no longer found in the scriptures. It was only after the inspired prediction was fulfilled that the ecclesiastical historians referred to it.[6] Were it not for this reference we would never have known that Jonah had ever made such a prophecy. This reference is also valuable as a means of fixing the time of Jonah's ministry. From this source we know that he was prophesying prior to the time Jeroboam II launched his conquest of Syria which is estimated to have occurred around 775 B.C.[7] However, Jonah's ministry must have been only a few years prior to this time since his prophecy, mentioned above, correlated with that of Elisha who proclaimed it just before he died

3. 2 Kings 14:25; Peloubet's *Bible Dictionary* under Gather-hepher.
4. Jonah 1:1
5. 2 Kings 13:14-19
6. 2 Kings 14:25
7. The exact date is not given but since it no doubt took Jeroboam II several years for such an extensive campaign, 775 B.C. would be a reasonable approximation.

around 788 B.C.[8] This would therefore mean that Jonah was probably preaching sometime between 788 and 775 B.C. These are only approximations but they will give the reader some general frame of reference which is all that we presently have to guide us.

After Jonah comforted Israel with the promise that her boundaries would soon be restored to the dimensions she had known in the days of Solomon, there is no further scriptural reference to Jonah until we come to the book bearing his name. The Book of Jonah opens with a startling commandment from the Lord. "Arise," said the Lord to Jonah, "go to Nineveh, that great city, and cry against it; for their wickedness is come up before me."[9] It was obvious that the Lord was not only concerned about wickedness in Israel and Judah but about the problems of other people as well.[10] And it was no wonder that the wickedness of Nineveh had "come up before" the Lord. For approximately 100 years the Assyrians had been terrorizing the entire Middle East.

SEEING ASSYRIA THROUGH THE EYES OF THE PROPHET JONAH

The resurgence of Assyrian power after a long period of incubation emerged in the ninth century B.C. This came

---

8. We know Joash was the king of Israel when Elisha died (2 Kings 13:14). Joash began to reign about 798 B.C. and Elisha's death is believed to have occurred in about the tenth year of his reign. This would make it 788 B.C. (See Clarke, *Bible Commentary.* Vol. 2, p. 523)

9. Jonah 1:2

10. Students of the Old Testament often gain the impression that the Lord was exclusively interested in His "chosen" people and had no concern for other nations whatever. Cynics cite this as proof that Jehovah was only a tribal god, not the eternal God. However, the Bible itself refutes this claim. Modern revelation further refutes it. For example, we can start back even before the Great Flood where the Lord gave a commandment to the ancient patriarchs to preach to all nations. The scripture says, "And they were preachers of righteousness, and spake and prophesied, AND CALLED UPON ALL MEN, EVERY-WHERE, TO REPENT: AND FAITH WAS TAUGHT UNTO THE CHILDREN OF MEN." (Moses 6:23) Among these great teachers was Enoch who preached to the various nations of his day (Moses, ch. 7); and Noah was sent on a special mission of 120 years' duration to warn all nations of the coming Flood (Moses 8:17-20). After the Flood the patriarchs were used to warn the various nations continuously. They warned Nimrod and his people concerning the building of the Tower of Babel (Ether, ch. 1). Abraham preached to the Chaldeans (Abraham 1:5, 7), and to the people in Haran (Abraham 2:15). Later, Abraham taught the Gospel of Jesus Christ and the principles of divinely revealed astronomy and mathematics to the Egyptians (See *The First 2,000 Years*, pp. 285-291). The Lord told Abraham that he and his descendants were to "bear the ministry and Priesthood UNTO ALL NATIONS." (Abraham 2:9) Certainly one of the most dramatic examples of God's concern for other nations is the one we are now considering — the mission of Jonah to Nineveh, capital of Assyria.

about as a result of the passionate political ambitions of a king named Assurnasirpal who reigned from around 884 to 860 B.C. Assurnasirpal launched his armies out toward the four points of the compass and by using the most depraved forms of barbaric terror he succeeded in crushing resistance on all fronts. His own stone carvings boast of his sadistic cruelty. It included the prolonged torturing of captives, blinding children before the eyes of their parents, flaying (skinning) men alive, roasting them in kilns, chaining them in cages where the populace could torture and torment them for their amusement, then have the survivors sent off for execution.[11] He boasted in one place that, "All the chiefs who had revolted I flayed, with their skins I covered the pillar, some in the midst I walled up [buried alive], others on stakes I impaled, still others I arranged around the pillar on stakes. . . . As for the chieftains and royal officers who had rebelled, I cut off their members."[12]

This cold-blooded savagery became traditional with the Assyrian. Two hundred years later its kings were still gloating over similar atrocities. One reads, "I burned three thousand captives with fire, I left not a single one among them alive to serve as a hostage."[13] And again, "These warriors who had sinned against Ashur and had plotted evil against me . . . from their hostile mouths have I torn their tongues, and I have compassed their destruction. As for the others who remained alive, I offered them as a funery sacrifice . . . their lacerated members have I given unto the dogs, the swine, the wolves. . . . By accomplishing these deeds I have rejoiced the heart of the great gods."[14] Still another blurts out his folly, "My war chariots crush men and beasts. . . . The monuments which I erect are made of human corpses from which I have cut the head and limbs. I cut off the hands of all those whom I capture alive."[15]

Stone carvings in Nineveh show men being impaled, their skin being torn from their living bodies, their tongues being torn from their throats and others being trodden to

11. Will Durant, *Our Oriental Heritage*, p. 275
12. Ibid.
13. *Cambridge Ancient History*, Vol. 3, p. 13
14. Will Durant, *Our Oriental Heritage*, p. 276
15. Ibid.

death. "One shows a king gouging out the eyes of prisoners with a lance while he holds their heads conveniently in place with a cord passed through their lips."[16]

Such was the character of the people who were striving to conquer the world in Jonah's time. The people of Israel had already had a taste of these blustering mad men. The son of Assurnasirpal was the famous Shalmaneser III[17] whose reign is said to have lasted from 860 to 824 B.C. The reader may recall that King Ahab of Israel joined with the king of Syria and many other neighboring states to stop this Shalmaneser III at Qarqar (Karkar) on the Orontes river in 853 B.C. On his statues Shalmaneser III boasts that he obtained heavy tribute not only from Ahab of Israel but in later years from Jehu.[18]

Shalmaneser III was followed by his son, Shamshi-Adad V who ruled from 823 to 810 B.C. Shamshi-Adad V was then succeeded by his son named Adad-nirari IV who held all of the eastern Mediterranean states in subjection from 810 to 781 B.C. This constituted a total of exactly 100 years that Assyria had bullied and brutalized the nations around her. As far as we can tell, this last king of Assyria, Adad-nirari IV, was a contemporary of Jonah and may very well have been the one who was in power when Jonah was ordered to go to Nineveh and warn that city of its coming destruction.[19]

THE CITY OF NINEVEH

From earliest times the capital city of Assyria had been Nineveh. It had been built on the upper Tigris shortly after the Great Flood epic by the famous King Nimrod,[20] so by the time of Jonah this city was already more than 1,200 years old. The scripture says that its size compassed "three days' journey,"[21] which is interpreted to mean that the city and

---

16. Ibid.
17. Called Shalmaneser II in older texts.
18. Werner Keller, *The Bible as History,* pp. 240-241
19. If Jonah began his ministry shortly after 788 B.C. and Adad-nirari IV reigned over Assyria until 781 B.C., their lives would be contemporary.
20. The Revised Version gives Genesis 10:10-11 as follows: "And the beginning of his [Nimrod's] kingdom was Babel, Erech and Accad, and Calneh, in the land of Shinar. Out of that land he went forth into Assyria and builded Nineveh . . ."
21. Jonah 3:3

all its surrounding districts required three days of walking to cross them. The population is variously estimated from 300,000 to more than a million. Ancient writers describe the city as a fortress capital with walls 100 feet high and wide enough at the top to permit three chariots to be driven abreast around its battlements.[22]

Little did the the proud inhabitants of Nineveh know that within three centuries this gigantic complex of luxurious fortified magnificence would be a pile of broken rubble. Around 500 B.C., the site of this ancient city was visited by the Greek historian, Herodotus, and he found nothing remaining but mounds of slumbering ruins. However, Jonah lived when Nineveh was at the height of her violence and glory. She was proud, powerful, and licenciously wicked. The prophet Nahum later described the crimes of these people, particularly the way the Assyrians treated those whom they captured:

"Woe to the bloody city! It is all full of lies and robbery; the prey departeth not; the noise of a whip, and the noise of the rattling of the wheels, and of the prancing horses, and of the jumping chariots. The horseman lifteth up both the bright sword and the glittering spear: and there is a multitude of slain, and a great number of carcases; and there is none end of their corpses; they stumble upon their corpses: Because of the multitude of the whoredoms of the well-favored harlot, the mistress of witchcrafts, that selleth nations through her whoredoms, and families through her witchcrafts."[23]

Who would dare call such a violent city to repentance? To Jonah it must have seemed preposterous, even insane, that any one person would have the audacity to call such a monstrous metropolis as Nineveh to an accounting, especially a humble servant of God such as himself. When the Lord told Jonah to go up to Nineveh and "cry against it," the scripture leaves no question as to Jonah's personal reaction. He was absolutely terrified.

22. Clarke, *Bible Commentary,* Vol. 4, pp. 701-702; Geikie, *Hours With the Bible,* Vol. 4, pp. 304-306.
23. Nahum 3:1-4

Jonah Attempts to Run Away From His Mission

No one can guess the mental torture Jonah must have endured before his feverish, desperate mind finally latched on to a decisive course of action. And once he had reached that frantic decision he lost no time in executing it. The map will show that his mission to Nineveh was toward the east, but to our amazement we discover that Jonah girt up his skirts and begat himself forthwith toward the west. Jonah was running away!

This was not the first time the Lord had found one of his prophets frantically frightened by the prospects of an unexpected assignment. It had happened to Enoch,[24] to Noah,[25] to Moses,[26] and would later happen to Jeremiah.[27] However, Jonah was the first and only prophet on record to actually flee from an assignment. With each of His other prophets, the Lord was able to discuss the matter and reassure them, but this Jonah didn't stay around for any discussion. He just rose up and departed.

The cruel and wicked city of Nineveh held such terrors for Jonah that he decided to propel himself speedily in the opposite direction. He raced down toward Joppa, the main Mediterranean seaport lying west and a little north of Jerusalem. There he took passage on a freighter destined for the most distant land he could reach — Tarshish! This is believed by many authorities to have been located at the other end of the Mediterranean Sea on the Spanish Peninsula.[28] Tarshish was a rich land, famous for its precious metals which the Phoenicians shipped back to the commercial centers for the Egyptians, Assyrians, Babylonians and other peoples of the Middle East. But to Jonah, Tarshish was the end of the world, and that is exactly where he wanted to be. Even at the risk of offending the Lord, he was determined to get himself removed so far from the scene of this awful assignment that the Lord might get someone else to

---

24. Moses 6:31
25. Moses 8:26
26. Exodus 3:11; 4:10-14
27. Jeremiah 1:6
28. Geikie, *Hours With the Bible*, Vol. 3, p. 383; Peloubet's *Bible Dictionary*, under "Tarshish."

do it. His idea was to get himself out of sight and out of mind — the Lord's mind.[29]

But no matter how terrified Jonah may have been as a result of this call to Nineveh, it was certainly no worse than the nightmare he was now about to endure.

THE TERRORS OF THE SEA

Joppa was the only creditable harbor in southern Palestine. Today, Israel's magnificent modern metropolis of Tel Aviv incorporates this ancient port. Once Jonah's ship had departed from the shelter of this harbor it was at the mercies of the open Mediterranean which often swallowed vessels large and small during the violent storms of those days. How far Jonah's freighter progressed before the storm struck we are not told, but the experienced seamen in charge of the craft knew they were in desperate straits. The force of the smashing hurricane threatened to swamp the ship and rip its timbers apart. The sailors at first thought they could save her by heaving their "wares" overboard so as "to lighten it,"[30] but they soon found this was not enough. The fury of the gale became so ferocious that the sailors became afraid that "the ship was like to be broken."[31]

The shipmaster had ordered all his mariners to pray, "every man to his own god,"[32] but Jonah did not pray with them. While all this excitement was going on the run-away prophet was down in the hold of the ship fast asleep. Whether from exhaustion and fatigue or just sheer relief of mind, we are not told, but he was sleeping the slumber of total oblivion. Through some happenstance the ship's captain found him. He was angry with his passenger and immediately cried out, "What meanest thou, O sleeper? Arise, call upon thy God, if so be that God will think upon us, that we perish not!"[33]

But by the time Jonah struggled up on deck the sailors were in the process of drawing lots and Jonah drew lots with them. They felt this storm must be the result of some offense by one of them which had aroused the wrath of that man's

29. Jonah 1:3
30. Jonah 1:5
31. Jonah 1:4
32. Jonah 1:5
33. Jonah 1:6

god. Ironically, the lot accidentally fell to Jonah and he
decided this was as good a time as any to confess that he
had indeed offended his God. In fact, no matter who might
have gotten the token or lot, it is likely that Jonah would have
interrupted the drawing to assume responsibility for what
was happening. Now that he was awake and refreshed he
felt the most profound sense of guilt. Said he: "I am an
Hebrew: and I fear the Lord, the God of heaven, which
hath made the sea and the dry land."[34] Then he told them of
the Lord's revelation to him and his missionary call to go
to Nineveh. The sailors believed him and asked Jonah what
should be done to appease his God. Jonah was so depressed
and downcast that he was ready to give up. In absolute de-
jection he said to them, "Take me up and cast me forth into
the sea; so shall the sea be calm unto you; for I know that
for my sake this great tempest is upon you."[35]

However, something about Jonah aroused the pity of
the sailors. Instead of throwing him into the sea they decided
to try once more to save themselves by rowing to the shore.
The scripture says: "the men rowed hard to bring it to
the land; but they could not; for the sea wrought, and was
tempestuous against them."[36]

Only at long last, when their strenuous efforts had completely exhausted them, did the sailors finally agree that
perhaps their only hope was to throw Jonah overboard. But
they didn't feel good about it. They decided to say a prayer
to Jonah's God and asked Him to forgive them for what
they were about to do. Said they, "We beseech thee, O
Lord, we beseech thee, let us not perish for this man's life,
and lay not upon us innocent blood: for thou, O Lord, hast
done as it pleased thee."[37] Then they cast him into the sea.

Jonah disappeared in the crashing, billowing waves behind the heaving vessel and for all the mariners knew, he
was quickly swallowed up and sank to a watery grave. The
sailors watched apprehensively to see what the storm would
do, and to their relief and amazement they saw that almost
immediately after the ejection of Jonah into the briny deep,

34. Jonah 1:9   36. Jonah 1:13
35. Jonah 1:12   37. Jonah 1:14

the "sea ceased from her raging."[38] The sailors were certainly impressed by Jonah's God and "they feared the Lord exceedingly."[39] They did not know anything about this powerful Deity but they decided to get lined up with Him right away. The scripture says they "offered a sacrifice unto the Lord, and made vows."[40]

JONAH AND THE WHALE

Now the unbelievable thing happened.

In spite of the fact that Jonah had felt that his time had come and asked the sailors to throw him overboard, he did not die easily. In fact, the moment he was submerged in the roaring tide of frothy waves he began struggling with all his might, mind and muscle to save his gasping life. It was a horrifying experience and Jonah describes in his own words how he felt as he plunged downward into the pounding depths of this cold, smothering sea. He wrote, "The waters compassed me about, even to the soul; the depth closed me round about, the weeds were wrapped about my head. I went down to the bottoms of the mountains; the earth with her bars was about me forever."[41]

Then it happened. There was a sudden rushing of water, a monstrous mouth gaped wide, and almost before Jonah could discover what was happening he had been plucked from the water and was slithering down into the gastric cavity of some large sea animal which the Bible says the Lord had "prepared."[42] The Book of Jonah says it was a "fish"[43] but Jesus called it a "whale."[44] The distinctions between the two are enormous and would have been the difference between life and death insofar as Jonah was concerned. In a gill-breathing creature such as a fish, Jonah would have been immediately smothered by the lack of air. The whale, on the other hand, is an air-breathing mammal. At regular intervals it rises to the surface for oxygen. The amount of air in the stomach would be minimal but apparently enough to keep Jonah alive.

---

38. Jonah 1:15
39. Jonah 1:16
40. Ibid.
41. Jonah 2:5-6

42. Jonah 1:17
43. Ibid.
44. Matthew 12:40

What was it like in the gullet of this mammoth creature? Who could possibly fathom the feelings of a human being floundering in the slippery, slimy viscera of a mammal as big as a medium-sized boat? What of the terrible opaque darkness, the maddening suspense, the absolute silence, the hot, humid air, and the contant menace of being bathed in the acid-laden digestive juices?

Until the days of the great whaling expeditions, no one had recorded what it was like to be swallowed by a whale; probably because none had ever lived to tell about it. Today, however, we have what appears to be a completely creditable account of a man who did just that. He experienced Jonah's nightmare and lived to describe what it was like.

The Story of a Modern Jonah

A short time ago a newspaper in England reminded the public that the experience of Jonah had been largely duplicated by a man named James Bartley. This feature article by David Gunston appeared in the Ipswich Evening Star on August 21, 1961, an original copy of which I have on file. The article carries the headline, "Man Was Swallowed By Whale — Emerged Alive." Because of the many interesting facets of this account it is being set forth in full text. Mr. Gunston writes:

"Although in the old days of whaling, when ferocious sperm whales were the main quarry, more than one staunch seaman met death through being swallowed by an enraged monster, the instances where the man survived and lived to tell the tale are rare indeed.

"To be tossed into the sea from a frail whale-boat by a leaping, tail-thrashing sperm in agony from the first harpoons, bitten and, maybe even swallowed, was not an infrequent fate of these intrepid whalers.

"But to emulate the ancient miraculous experience of the Hebrew prophet Jonah and emerge from the whale's belly later alive and unharmed is an adventure at once unbelievable and fantastic. Yet it has undoubtedly occurred.

"In a long and close study of the subject I have discovered only one instance completely corroborated by reliable authorities, and its details are so remarkable that it is worth recounting.

"It was February, 1891. The English whaling ship Star of the East was cruising near the far southern Falkland Islands, then a great whaling base. She was after sperm whales, or cachalots — the great barrel-headed, 60-70 ft. long kin of Moby Dick which were at that time still the mainstay of the industry. (Nowadays, the rather larger blue and fin whales are the chief commercial prize, there being far fewer sperms remaining to be caught.)

"The look-out on the mainmast suddenly spotted a large sperm about three miles away; two whale-boats were lowered and eventually one of the harpooners was able to sink his first lance in the creature's side.

"As so often happened, the sperm curved to dive, its 12-foot wide tail rearing out of the water and upsetting the second boat and its crew. One man was drowned and a later check of the rescued revealed another unaccounted for.

"He was Seamon James Bartley, a youngish, very tough and hardy whaleman of great value to his ship; but after this fateful encounter with a sperm, he was given up for lost like so many before him.

"The whale in question was finally killed by the first boat and in a few hours its great carcass was lying alongside the Star of the East, waiting to be flensed. The crew set to work and spent the rest of that day and part of the night dismembering their haul and 'trying out' or rendering down into oil, its thick underskin of blubber.

"Next morning they resumed their gruesome task and attached lifting tackle to the whale's stomach, now exposed, and hoisted it on to the deck for cutting up. The men were startled by what they thought was a slight, spasmodic movement within. Being well acquainted with the voracious appetites of the sperm and doubtless expecting to see a large fish, maybe a shark, still alive, they immediately slit open the great paunch.

"Inside, to what must have been their immense horror, was Bartley, doubled up, drenched, but still alive, though deeply unconscious.

"He was at once laid out on the deck and treated with a crude but effective dousing of sea water.

"After some minutes of this, he began to come round, but his mind was not clear and he was put to bed in the captain's own quarters. The entire ship's company, from the master downwards, doubtless appalled and overwhelmed by his fate, treated him with a kindness and solicitude that must have been rare in those rough, uninhibited days.

"For two weeks Bartley remained under lock and key in the captain's cabin — only a half-human, gibbering lunatic whose recovery was more than once despaired of.

"However, he gradually regained possession of his senses and at the end of the third week had almost entirely recovered from the psychic shock of his experience. His physical condition seemed unimpaired, and he soon resumed his normal duties.

"During his stay in the whale's stomach his unclothed parts were exposed to the merciless acid of the animal's gastric juices, and his face, neck and hands were bleached and shrivelled to a deadly whiteness with the look and feel of old parchment.

"When he was able to talk coherently of his ordeal he said he clearly remembered the sensation of being thrown from the boat into the sea. Then followed a tremendous rushing sound he believed was the swirling of the whale's tail through the water, and he was soon 'encompassed by a great darkness.'

"He said he felt he was slipping along a smooth passage that itself seemed to move along and carry him onward. This sensation lasted only a short while, and then he realized he had more room. As he groped about him he touched the walls of his prison: they were thickly slimy and yielding.

"Slowly it dawned on the fellow's bemused mind what had in fact happened to him, and he confessed he was overcome with horror and fright. He asserted he could breathe easily but that the heat was terrific — not a scorching heat like that of the sun, but a close, oppressive heat that seemed to open up the pores of his skin and draw out his vitality.

"In time he became very weak and sick and began to realize there was no way of escape. He admitted trying to face death calmly, but the knowledge of his predicament, the complete darkness, the intense heat, his growing weakness and, oddest of all, the terrifying quiet, finally overcame him. He claimed he could remember nothing more until he came round in the captain's cabin — which for a lowly seaman must have been the final touch to his nightmare!

"His mental and physical condition were not harmed, however, and when interviewed on his ship later he was reported to be 'in splendid spirits, and enjoying life,' as well he might, for he must then have been one of the luckiest men alive.

"Of James Bartley's subsequent fate nothing seems to be known other than he continued at sea. With the typical modesty of the mariner he appears deliberately to have avoided publicity, but after the Star of the East's return home both her captain and one of her officers issued separate detailed descriptions of the incident.

"The case was later taken up and investigated very thoroughly by M. de Parville, scientific editor of the 'Journal des Debats' of Paris and a scientist of authority and repute. In spite of his initial scepticism, de Parville was eventually so convinced of the truth of the thing that he closed his long account published in the journal in 1914 with these words: 'I believe that the account given by the English captain and his crew is worthy of belief. There are many cases reported where whales, in the fury of their dying agony, have swallowed human beings, but this is the first modern case where the victim has come forth safe and sound. After this modern illustration I end by believing that Jonah really did come out from the whale alive as the Bible records.'

"De Parville died during World War I and the Bartley case was later re-investigated by Sir Francis Fox, a well-known and respected British civil engineer who was associated with the construction of the Mersey tunnel at Liverpool and the Victoria Falls bridge.

"From his personal interest in the story of the original Jonah he again went into the 1891 story, checking de Parville's records and drafts. In his book of memoirs, 'Sixty-three Years of Engineering,' published by John Murray, London, 1924, he recounts the story very fully and examines it with detachment, reaching a firm conviction of its complete veracity.

"Since then a number of natural history writers have asserted in often garbled or fourth-hand stories of Bartley's experience — without checking its original sources.

"There is no doubt that sperm whales can swallow a man with ease, and have in fact done so many times. One old-time whaling captain described the sperm whale as having an 8 ft. swallow,' and instances of sharks both 10 ft. and 16 ft. long have been reliably recorded as found in the stomachs of sperms cut up on whaling ships.

"These creatures have a V-shaped trapdoor of a mouth lined with 18-28 conical teeth 8 inches long, and this formidable equipment is mainly used for biting and eating large chunks of giant squid that form their main food.

"However, complete, unbitten food is sometimes taken, usually fish, and there is some evidence that when attacked, enraged and in pain, these whales will attack man deliberately in self-defense, occasionally swallowing their victims whole.

"It is noteworthy that Bartley bore no teeth-marks, and his unvarnished description of the swallowing and after fits in with known biological facts. The gullet would aid his progress stomach-wards, the wall of the belly would be soft and mucous-covered, and the insulation from outside sound there would be complete. The great heat is explained by the fact that the normal body temperature of a sperm whale is around 104 degrees F. — to a human being high fever heat.

"The greatest stumbling-block some modern scientists have encountered in this case is just how Bartley managed to breathe sufficient air during his many hours' incarceration when the creature's digestive juices were present and eating into his uncovered skin. But according to the man's own testimony he found no difficulty in breathing whilst still conscious, and he also asserted that he felt he would have finally died from starvation rather than other causes, and in fact he collapsed from fright and shock, not from lack of air.

"The explanation seems to be that contrary to later beliefs based on only partial knowledge of the case, the whale's belly was not full, or indeed even partly full, of gastric juices at the time, and as shortly afterwards the animal was in fact killed, its stomach secretions ceased altogether from that time. Bartley was never completely immersed in fluid and there was sufficient air within to keep him alive.

"Nevertheless, the case remains remarkable and quite miraculous. From my own researches into it I am satisfied that this modern Jonah really did endure this bizarre adventure, an adventure that certainly lends credence, in an age of scepticism, to the age-old story of Jonah.

"Bartley did not equal the prophet in the duration of his ordeal, for Jonah was in the whale's belly 'three days and three nights.' It is rarely mentioned also, that Our Lord Himself corroborated the Jonah story in a passing reference (Matthew, xii, 40). Those who, in spite of this, condemn the Biblical tale of Jonah and his whale as 'just another fish story' cannot have heard of James Bartley and his."

JONAH IS LIBERATED

The shock which Seaman James Bartley encountered when he fully comprehended that he had been swallowed by a whale was undoubtedly very similar to the traumatic effect which it had upon Jonah. Jonah describes the panic which preyed upon him during the endless hours which he spent wondering what his fate would be. He wrote, "Out of the belly of hell cried I," and "when my soul fainted within me I remembered the Lord: and my prayer came in unto thee, into thine holy temple."[45]

At the appropriate time and under circumstances which would not further endanger the prophet's life, the Lord brought about the liberation of Jonah. The Bible says, "And the Lord spake unto the fish, and it vomited out Jonah upon the dry land."[46] This regurgitation from the stomach of the

45. Jonah 2:2, 7   46. Jonah 2:10

whale was probably as frightening as being swallowed in the first place, but it must have seemed miraculous beyond belief when Jonah finally looked about him and realized that he was actually free and safe. His nightmare was over.

But the Lord allowed Jonah very little time to sit around commiserating with himself. Barely had the prophet gathered his wits about him when a new revelation broke through upon him. The Lord said, "Arise, go unto Nineveh, that great city, and preach unto it the preaching that I bid thee."[47] Jonah consented. He had endured enough. He was completely reconciled, even to such a preposterous assignment as going to Nineveh. Humbled and resolute he set out for the capital of the Assyrian empire.

Of course, his first task was to get himself cleaned up, obtain some new clothes and secure some badly-needed nourishment. Afterwards the journey before him would be a little less formidable. Even so, it was far from a pleasant trip. No matter where the whale might have cast Jonah upon the shore line, he would still have to travel several hundred miles to reach Nineveh. Striding out across the deserts, plains and stone-faced mountains, Jonah slowly and carefully made his way toward the capital of Assyria.

Jonah Denounces Nineveh

The scripture says "Nineveh was an exceeding great city," and when Jonah finally reached its borders on the banks of the Tigris he braced himself for the ordeal which lay before him. He did not commence his message immediately but proceeded into the labyrinth of this vast human beehive "a day's journey." Only then did he deliver his proclamation of a coming calamity. Cried he:

"Yet forty days, and Nineveh shall be overthrown!"[48]

"Yet forty days and Nineveh shall be overthrown!"

As he repeated the warning over and over Jonah watched for the reaction of the people.

Undoubtedly Jonah must have filled his night dreams with expectations of the most terrifying acts of barbarous

47. Jonah 3:2   48. Jonah 3:4

cruelty as he imagined what these people would do to him as soon as he fixed the curse of the Almighty on their wicked city. But whatever Jonah may have anticipated in the way of flaying, dismemberment, stoning or burning, it never came. To his undoubted astonishment he noted that as he cried out against the people a strange sorrow settled upon his listeners. When he bore witness against their immorality, their violence, cruelty and crimes, they made no attempt to arrest him, punish him or persecute him. Instead, the people slowly began to leave the streets and go into their houses to mourn and to pray. Instinctively, they seemed to sense that Jonah was right. Nineveh was living on borrowed time and no one could blame God if He decided to wreak vengeance on the whole wretched metropolis. Contrary to everything Jonah had expected, the Bible says, "The people of Nineveh believed God, and proclaimed a fast, and put on sackcloth, from the greatest of them even to the least of them."[49]

Not only were the people universally touched by Jonah's message, but even the proud and haughty king listened intently when the message was brought to him. His officers quoted the Hebrew prophet as saying, "Yet forty days, and Nineveh shall be overthrown!"

Even to him it was enough. Down came the king from his throne. He threw off his royal vestments and went into mourning with sackcloth and ashes. Then he sent out a decree to all the people. It was an absolute command issued jointly by the king and his nobles. It declared, "Let man and beast be covered with sackcloth, and cry mightily unto God; yea, let them turn every one from his evil way, and from the violence that is in their hands. Who can tell if God will turn and repent, and turn away from his fierce anger, that we perish not?"[50]

Such words from the lips of wicked men who had lived by the sword and corrupted their lives, was rewarding indeed. The people of Nineveh wept and wailed out their pleas to the Lord as they sought strenuously to obtain His pardon for their violent sins and abomination. Before long the whole

---

49. Jonah 3:5
50. Jonah 3:8-9

city was thrown into a state of the most abject sorrow and repentance.

The People of Nineveh Reverse a Prophecy

One of the greatest lessons from the scriptures is to learn that prophecy can be reversed. In fact, the purpose of prophecy is to warn people what will happen if certain trends are allowed to continue. The hope of Heaven is that the people WILL TAKE HEED AND REVERSE THE TREND AND THEREBY REVERSE THE PROPHECY. That is exactly what the people of Nineveh did. The scripture says, "And God saw their works, that they turned from their evil way."[51] The Lord therefore resolved to suspend the terrible destruction which He had prepared for them.

Somehow this was communicated to Jonah. He learned that the Lord was not going to execute His judgment on Nineveh at the end of forty days after all. The obstreperous prophet exploded. Instead of shouting a loud Hallelujah that his mission had been a total success, he became so angry with the Lord that he wanted to die. He told the Lord he suspected all the time that He might go soft and back down on His promise to smash this city. The scripture says, "And he prayed unto the Lord, and said, I pray thee, O Lord, was not this my saying, when I was yet in my country? Therefore I fled before unto Tarshish: for I knew that thou art a gracious God, and merciful, slow to anger, and of great kindness, and repentest thee of the evil [that was predicted for Nineveh]. Therefore now, O Lord, take, I beseech thee, my life from me; for it is better for me to die than to live."[52]

The Lord made no direct response to Jonah but simply said, "Doest thou well to be angry?"[53] Prophets can have tantrums just like ordinary people and there was no doubt about Jonah's state of mind. The scripture says he was "very angry."[54] If God was appeased, so be it, but Jonah was not. After all he had gone through — being practically drowned, swallowed whole by a whale, heaved up after three days and nights — and then having traveled several hundred miles to pronounce judgment on Nineveh, what did the Lord mean

---

51. Jonah 3:10   53. Jonah 4:4
52. Jonah 4:2-3   54. Jonah 4:1

by backing down? It just wasn't the way to treat a man. Better to kill him or let him die than to be frusrated this way! It is likely that Jonah had built himself up to expect some spectacular fire and brimstone, Sodom-and-Gomorah finale when the forty days were up. To be told now that nothing would happen was downright provoking.

Anyway, Jonah decided to go up a safe distance from the city and wait out the forty days just to see if the Lord might not come through with a little something or other. "So Jonah went out of the city, and sat on the east side of the city, and there made him a booth, and sat under it in the shadow till he might see what would become of the city."[55]

But this day and night vigil turned out to be more than Jonah had expected. The blistering sun beat down on him with such fury that he could scarcely stand it. One night the Lord had a gourd plant grow up suddenly so that the following day Jonah had shade for his booth. For this the prophet was grateful indeed. But the next night a worm destroyed the plant and it withered away as rapidly as it had grown. In the broiling heat and a desolating desert wind Jonah fainted. When he revived, God was ready to communicate with him.

Said the Lord: "Thou hast had pity on the gourd, for the which thou hast not laboured, neither madest it grow: which came up in a night, and perished in a night . . ."[56] This was to teach Jonah that the decision concerning the destruction of Nineveh was not the prophet's prerogative, but the Lord's. And just as the Lord gave Jonah the blessing of the gourd plant and took it away, so also He could do what He considered best for Nineveh. It was Jonah's task to support the Lord, not rebel against Him. Jonah had pity on the gourd plant because it was a blessing to him but he was greatly distressed when it was taken away even though he was in no way responsible for its being there originally. Neither was Jonah responsible for the growth of Nineveh. Then why should he concern himself with the Lord's decisions concerning it? The Lord gave Jonah His basic reason for wanting to save the city. Said He, "And should I not spare Nineveh

---

55. Jonah 4:5   56. Jonah 4:10

that great city, wherein are more than sixscore thousand persons that cannot discern between their right and their left hand. . . ?" (Jonah 4:11)

Here was the lesson of God's continuing, immeasurable mercy. Jonah was thinking only of the wicked men and women who had debauched the great Nineveh. God was thinking of their children, 120,000 of them, who were innocent and knew not their right hands from their left. Why condemn them? Their parents had repented, why not spare the city?

Thus the ministry of Jonah to Nineveh comes to a conclusion. With it Jonah disappears from the panorama of Biblical history. However, he had carved a place for himself among men, which made his personal epic an immortal part of the sacred annals. From the life of Jonah the student of the Bible garners a host of valuable lessons.

The Reign of Jeroboam II of Israel

Although the scripture doesn't say so, it is very likely that Jonah lived long enough to see his prophecy fulfilled concerning the expansion of Israel's boundaries to the same length the kingdom had enjoyed under David and Solomon. As we have previously pointed out, this occurred during the reign of Jeroboam II.

Jeroboam was fortunate in that he ascended the throne of Israel around 782 B.C. just as the Assyrians were retiring from their field of conquest. For three administrations[57] the royal house of Assyria was involved in quarrels at home and this allowed Israel a free hand in recovering her lost tributaries. It would be interesting to know whether or not the temporary reform which Jonah had initiated in Nineveh had anything to do with the suspension of Assyrian aggressions during the several decades which followed. In any event, the scripture says, ". . . Jeroboam the son of Joash king of Israel . . . reigned forty and one years. . . . He restored the coast of Israel from the entering of Hamath unto the sea of the Plain [Dead Sea], according to the word of the Lord God of Israel which he spake by the hand of his servant Jonah. . . ."[58]

---

57. Shalmaneser IV, Assur-dan III and Assur-nirari   58. 2 Kings 14:23-25

In order for Jeroboam II to reach clear up to Hamath on the Orontes river it was necessary for him to subdue Syria. From a military standpoint this represented a double victory. Syria had been molesting Israel for many years so there was the immediate task of defeating this old enemy. But then Assyria had also coveted this same territory and had placed it under heavy tribute, so when Jeroboam II invaded Syria he ran the risk of a "war of intervention" from Nineveh. Had not the Assyrians withdrawn their extended talons of conquest during this period, Jeroboam II might have found his armies annihilated by a wave of chariots and infantry from across the Euphrates.

Circumstances were propitious, however, for a victory over Syria. It will be recalled that Jeroboam II's father, King Joash, was promised by Elisha that he would commence the driving back of the Syrians. It thereafter remained for Jeroboam II to finish the job.

After Israel had conquered Syria on the north and all of the Trans-Jordan territories clear down past the Dead Sea, King Jeroboam II settled down to the task of administering this rapidly expanding domain. Prosperity began to return to the cities of Israel almost immediately. Samaria, the capital, soon abounded in wealth and commerce which revived the luxuries and extravagant living of the days gone by. They also revived the corrupt abominations and immoral practices of the past. Prophets began rising up in Israel which warned the people that unless they returned to the God of their fathers the bloom of Israel's prosperity would fade and the nation would be swept into oblivion. One of these mighty voices which came crying repentance was that of Amos. He had a whole roster of sins checked off against Israel. These are worth noting because they are the same offenses which plague the affluent nations in modern times.

THE PROPHET AMOS

Amos was not tutored for his role as a prophet. He was a shepherd and a keeper of sycamore trees. He came from Tekoa which is a town located a short distance south of Bethlehem.[59] In the utmost humility he came through Israel de-

---

59. Amos 7:14; 1:1

nouncing the sins of the people. In fact, to make his message more palatable he began by denouncing the sins of Israel's traditional enemies — the Syrians, the Philistines, the men of Tyre and Phoenicia, the Edomites, Ammonites and Moabites.[60] Finally he got around to Israel and Judah. His main theme was, "Woe to them that are at ease in Zion."[61] He accused them of sacrificing their souls as they dishonestly attempted to secure for themselves material pleasures. Their courts were mercenary and corrupt. They took bribes and "sold the righteous for silver, and the poor for a pair of shoes."[62] The poor were neglected and abused and those who were blessed with abundance "turn aside the way of the meek."[63] There was a rising tide of immorality. Both fathers and sons were profaning themselves with the same women.[64] Money-lenders were illegally dealing with items pledged to them by the poor.[65] Amos compares the people to fat cows feeding in the lush meadows of Baashan in Trans-Jordan.[66] He speaks of those "that lie upon beds of ivory, and stretch themselves upon their couches, and eat the lambs out of the flock, and the calves out of the midst of the stall; that chant to the sound of the viol . . . that drink wine in bowls, and anoint themselves with the chief ointments: but they are not grieved for the affliction of Joseph."[67]

The people attempted to cover up their sins committed during the week by offering generous sacrifices to the Lord on the sabbath day, but the Lord would not be thus mocked. Through Amos He declared: "I hate, I despise your feast days. . . . Though ye offer me burnt-offerings and your meat-offerings, I will not accept them: neither will I regard the peace-offerings of your fat beasts. Take thou away from me the noise of thy songs; for I will not hear the melody of thy viols. But let judgment run down as waters, and righteousness as a mighty stream."[68]

Amos declared that unless Israel repented she had a shocking calamity awaiting her and the prophet said he would tell them exactly what they could expect. "Surely," he cried,

---

60. These comprise the first two chapters of Amos.
61. Amos 6:1
62. Amos 2:6; 5:12   65. Amos 2:8
63. Amos 2:7   66. Amos 4:1
64. Ibid.   67. Amos 6:4-6
                                      68. Amos 5:21-24

"the Lord God will do nothing but he revealeth his secret unto his servants the prophets."[69] He then proclaimed that "An adversary there shall be even round about the land; and he shall bring down thy strength from thee, and thy palaces shall be spoiled."[70] Amos quoted the Lord as saying of Israel, "Therefore will I cause you to go into captivity BE-YOND DAMASCUS."[71] The only threatening power "beyond Damascus" was Assyria and no doubt the people understood exactly what Amos was saying. Amos also said that when that day came there would be a long period without revelation, without prophets and without the expressed will of the Lord. Said he, "Behold the days come, saith the Lord God, that I will send a famine in the land, not a famine of bread, nor a thirst for water, but of hearing the words of the Lord. And they shall wander from sea to sea, and from the north even to the east, they shall run to and fro to seek the word of the Lord, and shall not find it."[72]

The Apostate Priest, Amaziah, Challenges Amos

In connection with one of his revelations, the Lord said to Amos, ". . . the high places of Isaac shall be desolate, and the sanctuaries of Israel shall be laid waste; and I will RISE AGAINST THE HOUSE OF JEROBOAM WITH THE SWORD."[73] When Amos began to preach this message the apostate priest at the shrine in Bethel named Amaziah saw a chance to snare Amos. He therefore twisted the above message to make it sound like a personal threat against the life of the king. He wrote to Jeroboam II saying, "Amos hath conspired against thee in the midst of the house of Israel: the land is not able to bear all his words. For thus Amos saith, JEROBOAM SHALL DIE BY THE SWORD, and Israel shall surely be led away captive out of their own land."[74] Note how carefully and maliciously Amaziah changed the word of the Lord.

This apostate priest then went directly to Amos and said, "O thou seer, go, flee away into the land of Judah, and there eat bread, and prophecy there: But prophesy not

---

69. Amos 3:7
70. Amos 3:11
71. Amos 5:27

72. Amos 8:11-12
73. Amos 7:9
74. Amos 7:10-11

again any more in Beth-el: for it is the king's chapel, and it is the king's court."[75] In other words, if Amos must ventilate his queer ideas he should go down to Judah or at least away from Bethel for it is offensive to those royal personages who frequent the king's chapel and the king's court.

In reply, Amos seized Amaziah by his intellectual beard and declared, "I was no prophet [before this mission], neither was I a prophet's son; but I was an herdsman, and a gatherer of sycamore fruit: And the Lord took me as I followed the flock, and the Lord said unto me, Go, prophesy unto my people Israel. Now therefore hear thou the word of the Lord: Thou sayest, Prophesy not against Israel, and drop not thy word against the house of Isaac. Therefore, thus saith the Lord, Thy wife shall be an harlot in the city, and thy sons and thy daughters shall fall by the sword, and thy land shall be divided by line, and thou shalt die in a polluted land: and Israel shall surely go into captivity forth of his land."[76] The actual fulfillment of Israel's conquest was approximately three decades away. Amos was telling Amaziah that he would live to see it and suffer in it. So would his family.

For the rest of Israel Amos left a message of distant hope. He first described the dispersion, then the gathering.[77] Quoting the Lord, he said, "For lo, I will command, and I will sift the house of Israel among all nations, like as corn is sifted in a sieve, yet shall not the least grain fall upon the earth [or be lost]."[78] And, in due time, "I will bring again the captivity of my people of Israel [a captivity by the Lord], and they shall build the waste cities, and inhabit them; and they shall plant vineyards, and drink the wine thereof; they shall also make gardens, and eat the fruit of them. And I will plant them upon their land AND THEY SHALL NO MORE BE PULLED UP OUT OF THEIR LAND WHICH I HAVE GIVEN THEM, saith the Lord thy God."[79]

---

75. Amos 7:12-13
76. Amos 7:14-17
77. The prophet Joel was preaching the same message about this time. However, Joel's emphasis was more like that of Jeremiah and Ezekiel, therefore we will consider Joel's writing in conjunction with these later prophets.
78. Amos 9:9
79. Amos 9:14-15

But all that would be in the twentieth century A.D. Meanwhile, Israel was on the brink of an apocalyptic disaster. By the end of Jeroboam II's reign in 753 B.C. the people were only 32 years away from a reign of terror emerging once again out of Assyria.

Scripture Reading and Questions on Chapter Seventeen

Scripture Readings: The Book of Jonah and the Book of Amos

1—Is it true that the Lord was only interested in His "chosen people" during Old Testament times and ignored other nations? Support your answer with three examples.

2—Name four types of atrocities which the Assyrian kings boast of committing against conquered people.

3—How old was the city of Nineveh by this time? How big? How many people approximately?

4—When Herodotus saw the site of Nineveh around 500 B.C. what was it like? What do you deduct from this as a moral lesson?

5—What would you give as the explanation for Jonah's conduct when he was sent on a mission to Nineveh?

6—Where did Jonah decide to go? Where do authorities believe this was located? What was Jonah trying to do?

7—Recite the circumstances which led to Jonah being thrown overboard. Did the sailors want to do it? What did they do first?

8—Did Jonah quietly surrender himself to the sea to be drowned? What does he say happened to him before the whale saved him?

9—Would it have made any difference whether Jonah had been swallowed by a fish or a whale?

10—Recite the highlights of James Bartley's experience as reported recently in the British press.

11—How long did Jonah say it would be until Nineveh was destroyed? What was the people's reaction? What was the king's reaction?

12—Was Jonah's prophecy fulfilled? Why not? What does this teach us?

13—What was Jonah's reaction to the Lord's decision? How did the Lord teach Jonah that he was wrong? What was in this wicked city that the Lord was particularly anxious to save?

14—Did the prophets know that the wicked Jeroboam II would restore the ancient boundaries of Israel? Who specifically predicted it?

15—Was Amos a polished scholar and trained Priesthood holder? Where did he come from? What was his occupation?

16—Name three offenses Amos attributed to Israel during these prosperous days.

17—What did Amos say was going to happen to Israel if she did not repent? What did "beyond Damascus" mean?

18—How did the apostate priest, Amaziah, twist the word of the Lord in reporting it to the king? What did Amaziah say to Amos?

19—What did Amos tell the apostate priest about his own calling as a prophet? What did he tell Amaziah about himself? About how long before this was going to be fulfilled?

20—How did Amos end his message? Should all reprimands and warnings be concluded with a positive alternative or a note of hope?

Chapter Eighteen

Fall of the Ten Northern Tribes

Anyone living in Israel during the reign of Jeroboam II (782-753 B.C.), must have felt a radiant surge of national pride as he watched the armies of the king return from one battle after another with bright victory streamers flying from their helmets. Whole nations became tributaries to Israel and lush prosperity returned to the precincts of Samaria. It was something the country had not known for over a century.

But in spite of these material achievements which produced such abundant temporal blessings there were far too many factors of evil in evidence. These symptoms of social and spiritual decadence created profound sorrow among the faithful followers of God. For several years Amos had been rebuking the nation. As we pointed out in the last chapter, the poor among the Israelites were being mistreated and exploited, the affairs of government were being manipulated and corrupted with bribery and intrigue, merchandising was being carried on with practices which were both dishonest and an affront to the law of Moses, and the social fiber of the people was being shredded into fragments by flagrant immorality and cult practices which were as depraved as the heathens.

The Task of the Faithful in Times of Apostasy

Scattered among the people, however, were those who cloistered themselves against the decadent taint of corruption and sought with all their might to prevent their children from becoming enveloped in the milieu of vice and blasphemy. The prophets were not being purged as they had been during the days of Ahab and Jezebel, but they were continually exposed to ridicule and persecution. Certain of the Psalms which were sung during this period strongly reflect the soul-stirring anxiety of the followers of the Lord to keep the faith. Any generation caught in a turbulent period of apostasy would be likely to cry out with sentiments such as these:[1]

> Help, Lord; for the godly man ceaseth;
> For the faithful fail from among the children of men.
> They speak vanity every one with his neighbor:
> With flattering lips and with a double heart do they speak.
>
> *   *   *   *   *
>
> For the oppression of the poor, for the sighing of the needy,
> Now will I arise, saith the Lord;
> I will set him in safety
> From him that puffeth at him.
>
> The words of the Lord are pure words:
> As silver tried in a furnace of earth,
> Purified seven times.
> Thou shalt keep them, O Lord,
> Thou shalt preserve them from this generation for ever.
> The wicked walk on every side,
> When the vilest men are exalted.

Another Psalm which carries the spiritual message of longing by the chosen of the Lord during days of despondency is the 62nd Psalm:

> Truly my soul waiteth upon God:
> From him cometh my salvation.
> He only is my rock and my salvation;
> He is my defense; I shall not be greatly moved. . . .
> In God is my salvation and my glory:
> The rock of my strength, and my refuge, is in God.
> Trust in him at all times; ye people,
> Pour out your heart before him:
> God is a refuge for us. Selah.

---

1. Psalm 12

Surely men of low degree are vanity,
And men of high degree are a lie:
To be laid in the balance,
They are altogether lighter than vanity.
Trust not in oppression,
And become not vain in robbery:
If riches increase, set not your heart upon them.

God hath spoken once; twice have I heard this;
That power belongeth unto God.
Also unto thee, O Lord, belongeth mercy:
For thou renderest to every man according to his work.

Such were the quiet, prayerful murmurings of the faithful in those ugly, profligate days of apostasy just before the fall of Israel.

The Ministry of the Prophet Hosea

One of the powerful personalities raised up by the Lord during this period was that persuasive proponent of the Gospel named Hosea. He preached both before and after the fall of Israel so his ministry is said to have extended over a period of at least 23 years and possibly as much as 80.[2] He received his call during the height of the apostate period under Jeroboam II, king of Israel. Hosea was apparently a young man at that time and the Lord told him to go out and marry a girl from among the common people even though they were in a state of apostasy.[3] In accordance with this strange commandment, Hosea married a girl named Gomer. By her Hosea had first a son,[4] then a daughter,[5] and finally another son.[6] Each one of them received a name which was symbolic of the future history of Israel. From this symbolic element in the account, some authorities have tried to con-

---

2. Hosea 1:1 says his ministry extended from the days of King Uzziah to King Hezekiah. Since King Uzziah began to reign in 766 B.C. and Hezekiah concluded his reign 686 B.C. there is a maximum spread of 80 years. On the other hand, Uzziah finished his reign in 739 B.C. while Hezekiah commenced his reign in 716 B.C., making a minimal spread of 23 years.
3. Our present text says, "Go, take unto thee a wife of whoredoms . . . for the land hath committed great whoredom, DEPARTING FROM THE LORD." (Hosea 1:2) This is metaphorical language meaning that the infidelity of the people toward the Lord was like a loss of chastity since this was part of the established ritual under the fertility rites of the heathen cults which Israel was following.
4. Hosea 1:3-4
5. Hosea 1:6
6. Hosea 1:8-9

clude that the whole story is a parable and did not really happen. However, the text itself would indicate otherwise.

Apparently the Lord was putting Hosea through a rigorous training discipline designed to give him (and through him, the people of Israel), some conception of God's feelings as His chosen people continually rebelled and prostituted themselves by running after heathen debaucheries. In moments of repentance and remorse they always hastened back, seeking to be accepted as the intimate companion of the Lord. Hosea's marriage to Gomer was a powerful teaching device apparently designed to help him convey to the people of Israel the feelings of the Lord on these occasions when they clamored for acceptance. The Lord had put Abraham through a similiar discipline at the time He commanded the great patriarch to offer up his son as a sacrifice. That experience permitted Abraham to better appreciate the feelings of his Heavenly Father on that terrible night of Gethsemane when the Father felt compelled to allow the betrayal and sacrifice of His Only Begotten Son in order to provide the great Atonement for the human race. The role of Godhood is fantastically complex and prophets like Abraham and Hosea were given a taste of its inner substance.

Hosea was next put through a second marriage, even more difficult than the first. He was instructed to take unto himself a companion whom he would have ordinarily considered repulsive because of her impure life.[7] Perhaps his first wife represented apostate Judah while his second wife represented the far more immoral Israelites of the northern ten tribes. Now Hosea would really know how the Lord felt when His depraved and debased people sought acceptance after having completely corrupted the Lord's plan of life. The scripture says Hosea *bought* this second wife[8] just as the Lord had been compelled to pay a high price so many times for His own apostate people of Israel. Hosea then said to the woman, "Thou shalt abide for me many days; thou shalt not play the harlot, and thou shalt not be for another man: SO WILL I ALSO BE FOR THEE."[9] In other words, Hosea was saying to this woman what the Lord had

---

7. Hosea 3:1
8. Hosea 3:2

9. Hosea 3:3

said to each generation of Israel — that in spite of the past, if she would be true to him, he would faithfully perform his covenant with her.

Incidental to this experience Hosea learned from the Lord that Israel was about to go into a long history of "many days" when she would be unwed, unclaimed, and without inspired leadership,[10] but that in "the latter days," the Lord would take Israel to Himself and honor her even as Hosea had promised to honor with fidelity this woman whom he had reclaimed from a fallen state.[11]

Hosea thereafter used the symbolism of Israel as an impure woman in much of his preaching. In fact, he appears to have received his information from the Lord in this precise form. Note passages like this one in chapter 2: "Plead with your mother [Israel], plead: for she is not my wife, neither am I her husband: let her therefore put away her whoredoms out of her sight, and her adulteries from between her breasts; . . . [otherwise] I will not have mercy upon her children: for they be the children of whoredoms. For their mother hath played the harlot: she that conceived them hath done shamefully: for she said, I will go after my lovers, that give me my bread and my water, my wool and my flax, mine oil and my drink. Therefore, [saith the Lord] behold, I will hedge up thy way with thorns, and make a wall, that she shall not find her paths. . . . For she did not know that I [Israel's true husband and Lord] gave her corn, and wine, and oil. . . . And she shall follow after her lovers, but she shall not overtake them . . . then shall she say, I will go and return to my first husband: FOR THEN WAS IT BETTER WITH ME THAN NOW."[12]

OTHER TEACHINGS OF HOSEA

Hosea did not always speak in parables. Often his accusations were blunt and direct. For example:

"Hear the word of the Lord, ye children of Israel: for the Lord hath a controversy with the inhabitants of the land, because there is no truth, nor mercy, nor knowledge of God

10. Hosea 3:4
11. Hosea 3:5

12. Hosea 2:2-8

in the land. By swearing, and lying, and killing, and stealing, and committing adultery, they break out, and blood toucheth blood."[13] When murder becomes so prevalent that the blood of one victim flows along the cobblestone gutters to combine with the blood of another, a society has indeed sunk to a level of the most infamous depravity.

Hosea held out a little more hope for Judah as of that moment than he did for apostate Ephraim and the northern ten tribes. Said he, "Though thou, Israel, play the harlot, yet let not Judah offend."[14] Later he added, "Ephraim compasseth me about with lies, and the house of Israel with deceit: but Judah yet ruleth with God, and is faithful with the saints."[15] The entire context of chapter 5 is an indictment against Ephraim and chapter 6 is an urgent petition by the prophet that the people repent of their evil and seek the forgiveness of the Lord. "Come," cried Hosea, "and let us return unto the Lord."[16] Hosea quotes the Lord as saying, "I desired mercy, and not sacrifice; and the knowledge of God more than burnt offerings."[17]

Through Hosea the Lord denounced the apostate priests who had "dealt treacherously" against Him. They had organized secret murder cults similar to the Gadiantons in ancient America. Said He: "And as troops of robbers wait for a man, so the company of priests murder in the way by consent: for they commit lewdness."[18]

The people at large were not much better. They were a motley mob of fawning sychophants who "make the king glad with their wickedness, and the princes with their lies."[19] And the princes played their own part in contributing to the corruption of the king. Hosea said, ". . . the princes have made him sick with bottles of wine; he stretched out his hand with scorners [being too drunk to know they were making fun of him!]."[20]

The dissolute administration of affairs in Israel was something from which the Lord wished to completely detach Himself. He therefore issued a disclaimer saying, "They

13. Hosea 4:1-2
14. Hosea 4:15
15. Hosea 11:12
16. Hosea 6:1
17. Hosea 6:6
18. Hosea 6:9
19. Hosea 7:3
20. Hosea 7:5

have set up kings, but not by me: they have made princes, and I knew it not."[21] And the Lord left no doubt as to how it was all going to turn out. He predicted that they would go back into bondage, become a prey to their heathen enemies and end up eating "unclean things in Assyria."[22] There it was, bold and clear! At last the Lord had revealed exactly who it was that would one day conquer Israel. And he told them that their magnificent, ornate, bejewelled images of gold were going to be hauled off and presented as gifts to the king of Assyria.[23] All that Israel counted precious and delicious in her sight was going to be summarily swept away.

Nevertheless, the Lord longed for these people. The tender feelings of a bereaved Parent spill out across the pages of the thirteenth chapter. He cried, "O Israel, thou hast destroyed thyself; but in me is thine help."[24] The only way He could help this generation and the multitude of apostate generations to follow, would be in the spirit world. The Lord therefore looked forward to the day when all of these choice but rebellious Israelites would have paid the uttermost farthing for their sins, learned obedience, and prepared themselves for a worthy resurrection. In contemplation of that great day the Lord exclaimed: "I will ransom them from the power of the grave; I will redeem them from death: O death, I will be thy plagues; O grave, I will be thy destruction: REPENTANCE SHALL BE HID FROM MINE EYES."[25]

This last phrase, "repentance shall be hid from mine eyes," has great significance. It refers to that far distant time when the redemption and resurrection will have been completed and the probationary estate of man will be finished. Then mankind will once more be subject to the immediate consequences of their acts just as they were before they came here. The principle of "repentance" only operates in a cosmic environment where judgment is temporarily sus-- pended and men are allowed a certain period of time to "turn back." In fact, this is what repentance means. Such a time of tolerance for sin and evil is not possible in the

---

21. Hosea 8:4
22. Hosea 9:3
23. Hosea 10:5-6

24. Hosea 13:9
25. Hosea 13:14

presence of God for there He "cannot look upon sin with the least degree of allowance."[26] This may be the very reason why the Lord had to remove us from His presence in order to give us a chance to learn from personal experience why sin and disobedience destroy happiness and how they cut us off from the blessings of Heaven. If in this life we were struck down for even the slightest deviation from righteousness we would probably learn little but tread timidly down the pathway of life in a state of terror, continually fearing lest we accidentally slipped and brought down the wrath of punitive judgment upon us.

The Lord therefore set up a cosmic laboratory for the Second Estate in which men could actually exist in a state of suspended judgment, a place where they could look evil full in the face, even taste of it if they wished, and then have time to turn away from it and escape the penalty through the efficacy of the Atonement. This is what the prophet was talking about when he said, ". . . there was a space granted unto man in which he might repent; therefore this life became a probationary state; a time to prepare to meet God; a time to prepare for that endless state which . . . is after the resurrection of the dead."[27]

And that "endless state" after the resurrection is when the Lord says "repentance shall be hid from mine eyes." No longer will men enjoy the luxury of tasting sin (being disobedient) and still have time to turn back without suffering any penalty. They will be able to turn back, of course, but the penalty will be decisive and immediate. Perhaps at that time mankind will appreciate far more than they do now the genius of the plan which provided a space of time in the Second Estate for repentance. It has allowed us time to recognize our errors, repent, reform, bring our sins under the Atonement and HAVE THEM BLOTTED OUT![28] Hosea wanted us to realize that this is only a temporary luxury. The Lord has warned that there will sometime come a day when "repentance shall be hid from mine eyes!"

---

26. Doctrine and Covenants 1:31
27. Alma 12:24; 42:4
28. Isaiah 1:18; 43:25; Doctrine and Covenants 58:42; Ezekiel 33:14-16; Alma 7:13

THE COLLAPSE OF THE NORTHERN KINGDOM COMMENCES

All the time Amos and Hosea were solemnly predicting the harsh realities of Israel's coming catastrophe it must have sounded perfectly ludicrous to Samaria's "men of affairs." They had reason to feel that they had everything going their way on a magnificent scale. They believed the reign of Jeroboam II had changed the whole future historical prospect for Israel. Not in a hundred years had the gross national product been so sensationally high, the standard of living so fastidious, nor the economic outlook so supremely prosperous. Why listen to a couple of odd-ball eccentrics who were no longer in the main stream of Israel's current intellectual thought but were going about describing their dismal visions and preaching sermons saturated with sour grapes. This was no time for pessimism. It was a time to rejoice, to celebrate, to live it up!

But around 748 B.C., Jeroboam II died and that is all it took to prick the bubble of illusionary grandeur in which Israel had been extravagantly living. It is true that Jeroboam's son, Zechariah, assumed the throne in proper order, but he had held the crown for no more than six months when the sinister hand of an assassin pulled him from his throne and spilled his blood upon the ground. The royal house of Jehu thereby came crashing down into oblivion during the fourth generation just as the Lord had predicted.[29] The man who murdered Zechariah was Shallum. He must have had the temporary support of the army since he was able to ascend the throne without serious interference.[30] However, only one month later, a man named Menahem murdered Shallum,[31] and the throne of Israel changed hands for the third time in a single year!

Now the pompous "men of affairs" in Samaria must have felt a growing sense of panic and apprehension as the whole fabric of stability and prosperity in Israel began to tremble on its foundations. Distrust and hate seemed to infest the very atmosphere. The new King Menahem found that even his own home-town of Tirzah closed its gates

---

29. 2 Kings 10:30; Amos 7:9
30. 2 Kings 15:10
31. 2 Kings 15:14

against him and nearby cities added their defiance. Menahem was so enraged that he launched a war against this segment of his own people with a wanton ferocity that was more befitting a savage barbarian than a king of Israel. The scripture says, "Then Menahem smote Tiphsah, and all that were therein, and the coasts thereof from Tirzah: because they opened not to him, therefore he smote it; and all the women therein that were with child he ripped up."[32]

All of this civil war and murder with its continuing struggle for political power was a signal to Israel's tributaries to immediately strike for independence. As fast as they broke away, however, Judah picked them up. While Israel was falling apart, something rather phenomenal had been happening in Judah.

THE REIGN OF UZZIAH IN JUDAH

Clear back in 766 B.C., a young son of Judah had ascended the throne of David named Uzziah (or Azariah). His father, King Amaziah, had spent the last years of his reign as a vassal of Israel and was finally killed by the people as a protest against his policies.[33] Young Uzziah, however, was a king after the pattern of Solomon. He wanted peace, order, and obedience to God. He was only sixteen when he began his reign,[34] and his first important task was to gently extricate himself from the domination of Israel. This could have brought immediate military reprisal had it not been for the fact that Jeroboam II was engaged in a series of conquests to the north. The gradual assertion of independence by Uzziah therefore went more or less unnoticed. At the same time Uzziah was vigorously fortifying Judah and pressing his people toward material security, he was campaigning with equal enthusiasm for a return to the ways of the Lord. This was the marvelous formula of "spiritual-material-balance" which had always brought prosperity and the blessing of Heaven to God's people whenever they have had the good sense to follow it. It was also true with Uzziah. The scripture says, "and as long as he sought the Lord, God made him to prosper."[25]

---

32. 2 Kings 15:16
33. 2 Kings 14:19

34. 2 Kings 14:21
35. 2 Chronicles 26:5

Uzziah reconquered Edom and restored the naval base at Elath (sometimes called Eloth or Ezion-geber).[36] This permitted the rich commerce to start flowing into Palestine from Africa and the spice markets of the Far East. He then conquered the Philistines[37] who were still a plague to Judah, and this was followed by a conquest of the Arabs who occupied the borders to the south.[38] About this time Jeroboam II died up in Samaria and Israel began its sequence of murders, civil war and political disintegration which we have previously described. So as fast as the Trans-Jordan nations broke away from Israel during this period of confusion, Uzziah picked them up as tributaries of Judah. The Ammonites therefore began paying tribute to Judah,[39] and eventually nineteen districts of northern Syria, including Hamath, entered into an alliance with Uzziah.[40]

A wholesome, new respect soon gravitated to Uzziah from all the surrounding nations. It resulted primarily from his policy of military preparedness combined with a just and efficient administration. Had Judah remained weak while growing in prosperity it would have been an irresistible bait to the armies and predatory politicians of nearby neighbors. By combining righteousness, justice, prosperity and military strength, Uzziah inspired their respect and preserved the peace.

To protect his country from avaricious or bellicose potentates on Judah's borders, Uzziah built an army of 307,500[41] and gave them the best equipment and logistical support possible.[42] This includes "engines, invented by cunning men, to be on the towers and upon the bulwarks, to shoot arrows [pole-sized] and great stones withal."[43] Uzziah had fortified Jerusalem with high towers,[44] and had built military outposts in the desert.[45] He dug many new wells in the Negeb [called the low country], and built oases in the "plain" or valley of the Jordan. The scripture says that by this means the king was able to maintain vast flocks and rich vineyards.[46]

36. 2 Chronicles 26:2
37. 2 Chronicles 26:6-7
38. 2 Chronicles 26:7
39. 2 Chronicles 26:8
40. See discussion by Geikie, *Hours With the Bible*, Vol. 4, p. 227
41. 2 Chronicles 26:13   44. 2 Chronicles 26:9
42. 2 Chronicles 26:14   45. 2 Chronicles 26:10
43. 2 Chronicles 26:15   46. Ibid.

The spiritual leadership of Judah during this period came through the inspired mind of a prophet named Zechariah. We know nothing of this man save that which is found in the fragment of scripture which says, "And he [Uzziah] sought God in the days of Zechariah, who had understanding in the visions of God: and as long as he sought the Lord, God made him [Uzziah] to prosper."[47] This particular prophet must not be confused with the Zechariah who lived 300 years later and whose Biblical writings are contained in the Book of Zechariah.

Next we come to a new and important epic in history which suddenly threw a menacing cloud of threatening destruction over the whole Mediterranean civilization. It was while Uzziah was ruling in Judah and Menahem was king of Israel that there unexpectedly appeared on the horizon of eastern Syria the fierce fighting forces of Assyria. That cruel, tyrannical people of the upper Tigris had recovered from their temporary season of respite from conquest and were once more charging across the Euphrates to reconquer all of their former tributaries.

THE REVIVAL OF ASSYRIAN IMPERIALISM

It will be recalled that Jonah had gone to Assyria some 40 years earlier and shaken the Assyrian capital with a thundering judgment of total destruction if that people did not repent. We have already seen that this had a solemn and sobering impact on Nineveh and its seems to have been followed by a period of complete withdrawal from imperialistic expansion. There were military forays to be sure, but restricted to the Mesopotamian area. During that period of relative tranquility three kings had reigned: Shalmaneser IV (781-771); Assur-dan III (771-753); and Assur-nirari (753-745). Then the prevailing dynasty had been suddenly overthrown and a powerful personality of unknown origin seized the crown. In the Bible he is called, Pul,[48] but in the Assyrian chronicles he took the renowned name of Tiglath-pileser. He was the third king to bear that name and he is therefore called Tiglath-pileser III to distinguish him from his predecessors.

---

47. 2 Chronicles 26:5

48. 2 Kings 15:19

Tiglath-pileser III or Pul was the founder of the so-called Second Assyrian Empire. By the time of his death the holdings of Assyria were equal in dimension to the empire built by his great namesake four centuries earlier. This new king also initiated for the first time in history a policy of true empire building. Conquerors of the past had usually sallied forth in military raids and terrorized neighboring nations just enough to make them pay tribute. Tiglath-pileser III, however, intended to impose the whole complex culture of Assyria upon all conquered people. His plan for political homogenization was worthy of a Roman caesar. He made royal provinces out of all defeated nations and placed in each one of them a satrap or governor to collect taxes and maintain order. He intended to impose on all of these provinces a single system of law — Assyrian law; a single system of government — the Assyrian government; and a single form of religion — the worship of Assur.

As soon as Tiglath-pileser III had secured the throne around 745 B.C., he set out from Nineveh to subdue Babylon and Chaldea to the south. After fierce fighting, he finally succeeded in putting a king of his own choice on the throne of Babylon and then he captured and crucified the princes of Chaldea. Chaldea, it will be recalled, was Abraham's native country and he lived in Ur, which was Chaldea's principal metropolis.

By 743 B.C., Tiglath-pileser III had solidified his grip on Assyria and was ready to head out toward the west. His vast array of fighting men presented such a show of force that the king thought the monarchs of the smaller nations might capitulate without a struggle. Tiglath-pileser therefore held a "durbar" at Arpod, north of Aleppo, to give the Mediterranean states a chance to bring "gifts" and thereby avoid a terrifying massacre by the Assyrians. The Phoenicians and many other minor kingdoms in northern Syria promptly responded. However, Hamath and nineteen districts in that region decided to mobilize a resistance movement and build it around the army of Judah which boasted over 300,000 men. Tiglath-pileser III finally broke up this alliance but he did not care to attack Judah with its large standing army.

In 742 B.C. the Assyrians returned for another "durbar" and this time 17 royal personages rushed forward with their gifts and treasures which they earnestly hoped would placate the Assyrians sufficiently to assure another year of peace. This time there was found among those who came on bended knee with chariots of treasure none other than Menahem, king of Israel. His gifts were so gratifying to Tiglath-pileser that the Assyrian tyrant confirmed Menahem on the throne. of Israel and promised military aid if Israel were ever attacked. Little did Menahem realize that this was the very nation which before long was going to sack Israel and carry off her people into permanent exile and servitude.

For several years, however, the Assyrians were directly involved in extensive campaigns in Armenia and Chaldea. While they were thus occupied many changes took place in both Judah and Israel.

The Throne of Judah Passes from Uzziah to Jothan to Ahaz

It will be recalled that the good King Uzziah had reigned over Judah ever since about 775 B.C. He had built a righteous kingdom, restored the Lord's true pattern of worship, and built a powerful and prosperous nation. Just before the Assyrians reappeared on the scene his prestige was unequalled by any of the surrounding monarchs. But around 748 B.C., Uzziah did a very foolish thing. The book of 2 Kings charitably passes over the offense by merely mentioning his punishment,[49] but 2 Chronicles gives us the details. It says, "But when he was strong, his heart was lifted up to his destruction: for he transgressed against the Lord his God, and went into the temple of the Lord to burn incense upon the altar of incense."[50] As with King Saul three centuries earlier, Uzziah just could not resist the temptation to function as though he held the Priesthood. "And Azariah the priest went in after him, and with him fourscore priests of the Lord, that were valiant men [members of the king's guard as well as priests]. And they withstood Uzziah the king, and said unto him, It appertaineth not unto thee, Uzziah,

---

49. 2 Kings 15:5
50. 2 Chronicles 26:16.

to burn incense unto the Lord, but to the priests the sons of Aaron, that are consecrated to burn incense: go out of the sanctuary [the portion of the temple called the Holy Place], for thou hast trespassed; neither shall it be for thine honour from the Lord God."[51]

This infuriated the aging king and he stood defiantly before the altar with "a censer in his hand to burn incense."[52] Suddenly a bright, feverish spot appeared in the king's forehead which both he and the priests recognized as leprosy. With a cry of "Unclean!" the priests rushed forward to "thrust him out," but Uzziah needed no persuading or pushing. A surging pang of self-condemnation enveloped the king so that he "hasted also to go out, because the Lord had smitten him."[53] Uzziah continued to suffer from leprosy the remainder of his life. The scripture says, "And Uzziah the king was a leper unto the day of his death, and dwelt in a several [separate] house, being a leper; for he was cut off from the house of the Lord: and Jotham his son was over the king's house, judging the people of the land."[54] In other words, Jotham began serving as regent somewhere around 750 B.C. and continued in that capacity until his father's death, whereupon he became king in his own right. Jotham's ascension to the throne after Uzziah's death is calculated to have been between 734 and 739 B.C.[55]

The next verse of scripture in Chronicles has some interesting implications. It says, "Now the rest of the acts of Uzziah, first and last, did Isaiah the prophet . . . write."[56] If this is so then we do not have all of Isaiah's writings for he barely mentions this king. In the opening passage of his book Isaiah says his calling as a prophet began "in the days of Uzziah" and in the first verse of the sixth chapter he says the great vision in which Isaiah saw the Lord occurred the year King Uzziah died. But these two meager references

---

51. 2 Chronicles 26:17-18
52. 2 Chronicles 26:19
53. 2 Chronicles 26:20
54. 2 Chronicles 26:21
55. The student of the Bible will find it impossible to reconcile the conflicting figures appearing in our modern Bible. Scholars have developed a working chronology which approximates the known facts of history, both Biblical and secular, and this is the chronology we are using here.
56. 2 Chronicles 26:22

certainly do not constitute "the rest of the acts of Uzziah, first and last." Obviously, some of the writings of Isaiah must still be unavailable.

After Uzziah died of leprosy and Jotham took over the throne, the people of Judah probably expected the new king to enjoy a long and prosperous reign. After all, Jotham had served as regent during his father's long illness and had exhibited excellent capacity. But a long reign for this king was not to be. Jotham only outlived his father by a couple of years. He died between 733 and 735 B.C. and was succeeded to the throne by his son, Ahaz, who turned out to be one of the worst kings Judah ever had. Ahaz apostatized and lost nearly every vestige of greatness which his father and grandfather had garnered for Judah. He abandoned the Lord, abandoned his prophets, and promptly found himself involved in a disastrous war with Israel and Syria. In order to understand how this came about we have to see what had been happening up north during the past several years.

The Throne of Israel Passes from Menahem to Pekahiah and Then to Pekah

It will be recalled that Israel had become wealthy and powerful under Jeroboam II but after he died in 748 B.C., his son, Zechariah, only ruled six months when he was assassinated by Shallum.[57] Shallum then ruled one month and was assassinated by Menahem.[58] After all of this spilling of blood, Menahem finally entrenched himself on the throne and ruled until about 736 B.C. It was during his reign that the Assyrians appeared on the scene again and Menahem paid tribute to them in order to avoid being pulverized by the Assyrian juggernaut. When Menahem died, his son Pekahiah, took over the throne of Israel but he lasted only two years. It seems that a captain of the royal guard named Pekah conspired against the king and with 50 men from Trans-Jordan (Gileadites), invaded the king's palace at Samaria and slew Pekahiah in his own house.[59]

---

57. 2 Kings 15:8-10
58. 2 Kings 15:13-14
59. 2 Kings 15:25

Pekah then became king of Israel around 735 B.C. and had been on the throne only one or two years when the Assyrians returned and once more threatened to smash the vassal kingdoms of Palestine if they did not pay regular tribute. After all, Israel's former king Menahem had paid tribute and enjoyed peace with Assyria. Why not Pekah? But Pekah was of a different stamp than Menahem. He wrote to King Ahaz of Judah and also to the king of Syria recommending the formation of a strong alliance between all of the bigger kingdoms of Palestine and upper regions of the Mediterranean. He felt that a mighty federation of western powers could stop Tiglath-pileser. The king of Syria agreed but King Ahaz of Judah did not. Ahaz was for placating the Assyrians rather than fighting them. Pekah was furious. He could not forgive Ahaz for thus destroying his plan. Pekah therefore decided to take a combined host from Israel and Syria and pound on Judah until she agreed to come into the alliance. Judah was in a genuine predicament.

The Prophet Isaiah

It was at this stage that one of the greatest prophets in the Old Testament suddenly emerged upon the scene. It was Isaiah. He had been receiving revelations for several years before[60] but now the Lord instructed him to take part in the national life of the kingdoms. Isaiah was told to meet King Ahaz "at the end of the conduit of the upper pool in the highway of the fuller's field."[61] We shall hear of this public meeting place several times in the Bible. This conduit is identified as being the channel which carried water from the famous Gihon spring to the gardens and orchards on the western side of Kidron valley.[62] At the end of the conduit was a pool which was used by the public to replenish their water supply and apparently much public business was transacted in this area.

When Isaiah met the king he told the monarch that the word of the Lord was as follows: "Take heed, and be quiet; fear not, neither be fainthearted. . . ." The Lord promised

---

60. Isaiah 1:1, 6:1
61. Isaiah 7:3
62. See observations of Dr. Emil G. Kraeling, Rand McNally *Bible Atlas*, p. 300.

Ahaz that "the two tails of these smoking firebrands" [Israel and Syria] were about to be conquered themselves and therefore Judah should not undertake to fight them lest it provoke a completely unnecessary calamity.[63] Ahaz was warned that unless he accepted this advice he was in for some dark days indeed.

Isaiah soon perceived that Ahaz considered himself a "practical" politician who was not going to be diverted from his war plans by a religious leader who was improperly dabbling in politics. Isaiah was therefore authorized by the Lord to tell Ahaz he could test the validity of the promise by asking for some proof that God's integrity was behind it. After all, Gideon and others had asked and received for themselves such proof. But Ahaz wanted none of it. He sanctimoniously announced that he did not wish to "tempt the Lord."[64] This turned out to be pure hypocrisy for, as we shall see later, Ahaz was getting ready to not only tempt the Lord, but insult Him.

Isaiah was so frustrated by this turn of events that he finally determined to give Ahaz a sign whether he wanted it or not. But in order not to cast pearls Isaiah gave Ahaz a sign which must have gone completely over the king's head. Nevertheless it was the greatest proof of prophetic reliability that Judah would ever know. Isaiah told Ahaz about the sign of "a virgin" bearing a child who would be the very Son of God. Said he, "Therefore the Lord himself shall give you a sign; Behold, a virgin shall conceive, and bear a son, and shall call his name Immanuel [God is with us]."[65] Even though Ahaz undoubtedly missed the whole implication of this magnificent prophecy, nevertheless, it gave Isaiah a chance to get it on the record. And while he was at it, Isaiah unloaded on the king a whole avalanche of prophecy, most of it relating to events 2,700 years thence!

Undoubtedly all of this left the king puzzled, stupified, and without the least comprehension. However, once he had rejected the advice of the Lord, startling things began to happen which jolted his comprehension thoroughly. Almost

63. Isaiah 7:4-8
64. Isaiah 7:10-12
65. Isaiah 7:14

overnight the massed armies of Israel and Syria thundered to his gates! They had reacted to the war-making preparations in Judah and swarmed across the land. The Lord knew that if Ahaz had taken heed and kept quiet these two nations would have prepared more leisurely for their attack on Judah and before they could have launched their campaign they, themselves, would have been attacked by Assyria. This would have kept them from bothering Judah in the least degree. But this kind of divine wisdom was what the "wisdom" of Ahaz had haughtily rejected. So Ahaz now reaped the whirlwind.

During their lightning campaign Israel and Syria had poured down out of the mountains of Ephraim and captured over 200,000 people in Judah.[66] About the same time an attack came from the Edomites,[67] and another came from the Philistines.[68] Judah was under the most serious threat to her political existence since the war against her by Pharaoh Shishak two centuries earlier.

THE VIOLENT APOSTASY OF AHAZ

Nevertheless, King Ahaz thought he knew how to save Judah. He stripped the temple of its treasures, imposed assessments on all the leading families, and sent this accumulated loot to Tiglath-pileser III to bribe him to rescue Judah.[69] The Assyrian monarch took the wealth from Ahaz but for the time being, at least, "helped him not."[70] Tiglath-pileser had plans of his own involving the conquest of Syria and Israel but he expected to attack them from the north, not down around Jerusalem where Judah was fighting for survival.

Ahaz next turned to the heathen gods for help — the gods of his enemies! Said he, "Because the gods of the kings of Syria help them, therefore will I sacrifice to them, that they may help me."[71] If the frenzied and superstitious Ahaz could not bribe the Assyrians to help him, he would bribe his enemy's gods! Such was the mentality of this king.

---

66. 2 Chronicles 28:6-8
67. 2 Chronicles 28:17
68. 2 Chronicles 28:18

69. 2 Chronicles 28:20-21
70. Ibid.
71. 2 Chronicles 28:23

In order to achieve this last objective, Ahaz closed the temple in Jerusalem, "cut in pieces the vessels of the house of God,"[72] and built heathen altars to the gods of Damascus "in every corner of Jerusalem."[73]

Then Ahaz committed a terrible offense against his own family. The scripture says, "Moreover he burnt incense in the valley of the son of Hinnom, AND BURNT HIS CHILDREN IN THE FIRE, AFTER THE ABOMINATIONS OF THE HEATHEN whom the Lord had cast out before the children of Israel. . . . Wherefore the Lord his God delivered him into the hand of the king of Syria; and they smote him, and carried away a great multitude of them captives. . . ."[74]

These captives were not mere hostages but constituted the entire population from some of the conquered regions in northern Judah. They were herded up into the mountains of Ephraim along with cart-loads of booty and treasure. Only through the intervention of one of the Lord's prophets at Samaria were they rescued.

This prophet's name was Oded and when he saw the "two hundred thousand women, sons, and daughters" and the vast quantity of spoils which were being hauled up from Judah, he cried out to the commanding officers, "Behold, because the Lord God of your Fathers was wroth with Judah, he hath delivered them into your hand, and ye have slain them in a rage that reacheth up unto heaven. And now ye purpose to keep under [you] the children of Judah and Jerusalem for bondmen and bondwomen unto you: but are there not with you . . . sins against the Lord your God? Now hear me therefore and deliver the captives again which ye have taken captive of your brethren: for the fierce wrath of the Lord is upon you."[75]

This was a direct command from the prophet of the Lord. Certain civilian leaders who were "heads of the children of Ephraim" responded to this injunction and "stood up against them that came from the war."[76] There was a heated debate which obviously took place while Pekah, the

---

72. 2 Chronicles 28:24
73. Ibid.
74. 2 Chronicles 28:3-5

75. 2 Chronicles 28:9-11
76. 2 Chronicles 28:12

king, was absent fighting at Jerusalem. The military men finally backed down and the civilian Ephraimites assumed command of the situation. The Bible says they "took the captives, and with the spoil clothed all that were naked among them, and arrayed them, and shod them, and gave them to eat and to drink, and anointed them, and carried all the feeble of them upon asses, and brought them to Jericho, the city of palm trees, to their brethren: then they returned to Samaria."[77]

To the starving, bedraggled prisoners of Judah, this magnanimous manifestation of humanitarian generosity must have seemed like manna from Heaven. But, when King Pekah returned from the battle-front and discovered what had happened to all his prisoners and spoils he probably consigned his own leaders to the shades of hades. However, it would have done him little good because he was soon to go there himself. Pekah did not know it, but he was about to lose both his life and his throne.

TIGLATH-PILESER III CONQUERS SYRIA AND PART OF ISRAEL

We have already mentioned that Tiglath-pileser, king of the Assyrians, had refused to go down to Jerusalem to rescue King Ahaz, but apparently, after some delay and many pleas by Ahaz, he "hearkened unto him."[78] Actually Tiglath-pileser merely did what the Lord knew he had been planning to do all along. He opened up a northern campaign against Damascus in Syria. This Assyrian assault on Damascus completely diverted the Syrians from continuing their war in Judah and sent them wildly rushing back up to Damascus to save their capital. But in this attempt they failed. Tiglath-pileser III captured Damascus, killed the king, impaled his noblemen on stakes and sacked the city.[79]

King Ahaz, undoubtedly feeling delirious with joy, rushed up to the Assyrian camp near Damascus to bask in the glory of Tiglath-pileser's devastating victory.[80] It was while he

---

77. 2 Chronicles 28:15
78. 2 Kings 16:19
79. Ibid., plus the Assyrian chronicles which describe what took place. The latter is summarized by Keyes in his *Story of the Bible World*, pp. 82-83.
80. 2 Kings 16:10

was there that he noticed an ornate heathen altar which immediately struck his fancy. He had a duplicate skillfully made to replace the great altar Solomon had built.[81] When Ahaz returned to Jerusalem he removed Solomon's altar from the front of the temple and place it on the north side. He then substituted the altar copied from the heathen shrine of Damascus as the main altar of the temple. At the same time he took away the mobile bases for the ten small lavers which were used in connection with the preparation of sacrifices. He also took the huge brazen font or "sea" from off the backs of the twelve oxen and "put it upon a pavement of stones."[82] He continued to keep the temple closed.[83]

But while Ahaz was doing all of this in Judah, Tiglath-pileser III had not remained in Damascus. Shortly after his victory over the Syrians he had ordered his massive war machine to make a direct assault on Israel. The scripture says, "In the days of Pekah king of Israel came Tiglath-pileser king of Assyria, and took Ijon, the Abel-beth-maachah, and Janoah, and Kedesh, and Hazor, and Gilead, and Galilee, all the land of Naphtali, and carried them captive to Assyria."[84]

This meant that the whole region north and east of Samaria was conquered and the Israelite population forced to migrate to Assyria. This left King Pekah with Samaria (the capital city) and the territories of Ephraim, Benjamin and Simeon, but little else.

It was almost inevitable that a conspiracy to overthrow King Pekah would eventually emerge from such a train of disaster. It did. A man named Hoshea organized an assassins' band with full determination to seize the throne. At an opportune moment Hoshea succeeded in getting near to the king, "and smote him, and slew him, and reigned in his stead."[85]

---

81. 2 Kings 16:10-14
82. 2 Kings 16:17
83. This becomes apparent from 2 Chronicles 29:3 which states that the temple was opened by the son of Ahaz, King Hezekiah.
84. 2 Kings 15:29
85. 2 Kings 15:30. Note that the text states that this happened in the twentieth year of the reign of Jotham, but that would be impossible. Much of Pekah's activities occurred during the reign of Jotham's son, King Ahaz (see 2 Kings 16:5). This is further supported by 2 Kings 17:1 which says that the man who slew Pekah began his reign in the days of Ahaz.

So the law of retribution took its toll. As King Pekah had come to the throne of Israel by assassination,[86] so now he lost it the same way. Chronologists have put the date of his death at approximately 732 B.C.

The Last of the Ten Tribes Are Conquered and Led Off to Assyria

Once Tiglath-pileser III had conquered northern and eastern Israel, he went on to subdue the Philistines, the Arabs, and carry his conquest to the very gates of Egypt. But there he stopped. In fact, he spent all the remaining years of his administration solidifying his empire. Not until his death did any significant changes occur. However, when death did come to Tiglath-pileser, it was around 727 B.C., and the Assyrian grip on the vassal kingdoms was temporarily weakened as the passion for independence burned brightly in the provinces of the empire. The dead king was succeeded on the Assyrian throne by his son who took the name of Shalmaneser and is identified in history as Shalmaneser V. Almost immediately after his coronation Shalmaneser set out to hold the provinces and tributaries of the empire in check.

The king of Israel (King Hoshea) who had come to power by assassinating King Pekah, was anxious to maintain cordial relations with the new monarch from the Tigris. Therefore, the Bible says that when Shalmaneser V visited the territory "Hoshea became his servant, and gave him presents."[87]

But these gifts and presents were merely to buy time. Hoshea had already entered into secret negotiations with the Pharaoh of Egypt (named "So") to set up a permanent alliance against Assyria.[88] A short time later, when the alliance had been ratified, Hoshea began treating the Assyrians with defiant contempt. Shalmaneser received word that Hoshea refused to pay tribute "as he had done year by year," and therefore the Assyrian king set out to settle the matter once and for all.

---

86. 2 Kings 15:25
87. 2 Kings 17:3

88. 2 Kings 17:4

498 THE FOURTH THOUSAND YEARS

Whether by his governor of the territory or in person we are not told, but by some effective means Shalmaneser secured custody of King Hoshea of Israel and thrust him into prison.[89] The Assyrian army then arrived soon afterwards and placed the whole city of Samaria under siege.[90] To Hoshea's bitter disappointment, the Pharaoh of Egypt apparently made no attempt whatever to redeem his pledge of assistance, and Hoshea must have finally realized that the Pharaoh had drawn Israel into this alliance simply to create a temporary buffer between Egypt and her most dangerous enemy, Assyria.

The Israelites did not capitulate, however, and the siege of Samaria continued for three whole years.[91] It is impossible to imagine how the people could have survived so long unless the siege was rather loosely managed. In any event, the Samarians lasted longer than Shalmaneser V.

In 722 B.C. Shalmaneser died suddenly after ruling only five years and Dr. Emil G. Kraeling suggests that it seems to have been by assassination while he was campaigning in Palestine or Syria.[92] The throne of Assyria was immediately seized by an aggressive personality who is known to us as Sargon II. He ruled from 722 to 705 B.C. For many years Sargon was considered a mythical character since no trace of him appeared in any monuments of antiquity. Only Isaiah 20:1 made mention that such a person ever existed. In 1843, however, a French consular agent and scholar, Paul Emile Botta, uncovered the remains of Sargon's great palace at Khorsabad just north of Nineveh. On the walls of the palace were inscriptions which fully verified what the Bible had said about him. One of these palace inscriptions reads: "At the beginning of my rule, in the very first year I reigned . . . I set siege to and conquered Samaria . . . I carried away into captivity 27,290 persons who lived there; I took fifty fine chariots for my royal equipment."[93] Later the evacuation of the Israelites continued until this region was almost denuded of population. We deduct this from the fact that even though Sargon brought many displaced persons in from

---

89. Ibid.
90. 2 Kings 17:5
91. Ibid.

92. Kraeling, Rand McNally *Bible Atlas*, p. 297
93. Keyes, *Story of the Bible World*, p. 83

other conquered territories,[94] the land nevertheless remained
so lightly populated that lions and other wild animals began
to take over the region.[95] This was interpreted by the new
settlers as a sign that they were not properly worshipping
the God of this land. They asked the king of Assyria to
send back a priest who could teach them how to worship
the God of Israel. He did so and the priest set up his headquarters at Bethel. The scripture says he "taught them how
they should fear the Lord."[96] However, they went right ahead
worshipping the heathen deities at the same time. So the
scripture summarizes this paradoxical situation by saying,
"They feared the Lord, and served their own gods."[97]

THE ISRAELITES IN ASSYRIA

Meanwhile, the original Israelite inhabitants of Samaria
had been dragged off to Assyria and consigned to the same
cities where the earlier captives of Israel had been settled.
It will be recalled that some ten years earlier Tiglath-pileser
III had captured the Israelites around Galilee as well as
those in Trans-Jordan and had compelled them to travel by
forced marches to "Halah, and Habor, and Hara, and to
the river Gozan."[98] When Sargon II conquered Samaria
and the rest of Israel he pushed the captives together and
marched them off to the same places. As the scripture says,
"In the ninth year of Hoshea, the king of Assyria [Sargon
II] took Samaria, and carried Israel away into Assyria, and
placed them in Halah and in Habor by the river of Gozan,
and in the cities of the Medes."[99]

Dr. Emil G. Kraeling makes this comment concerning
the region where the Ten Tribes were taken:

"According to the Biblical account, he [Sargon II]
settled them in Halah on the Habor, the river of Gozan,
and in the cities of the Medes. Halah lay northeast of
Nineveh, which city at a slightly later day had a gate named
the 'gate of the land of Halah' (*Halahhu*). Since there is
reason to believe that the city lay between Nineveh and Sargon's new capital (*Khorsabad*), the large mound of *Tell*

---

94. 2 Kings 17:24
95. 2 Kings 17:26
96. 2 Kings 17:28

97. 2 Kings 17:33
98. 1 Chronicles 5:26; 2 Kings 15:29
99. 2 Kings 17:6

'Abassiyeh has been nominated for it. Excavations there might give us traces of the ten lost tribes.

"The Habor region, which is mentioned next, is that of the river which to this day bears the same name, *Khabur,* and enters the Euphrates from the north. If this is the river described as 'the river of Gozan,' it has become more vivid through the rediscovery of the ancient city of Gozan. This city (Guzana in the cuneiform texts) is at *Tell Halaf,* where interesting finds were made in excavations carried on by Baron M. von Oppenheim in 1911-13. It lay near *Ras el 'Ain* at the source of the *Khabur* River. . . . Other Israelites were taken much farther to the northeast, to 'the cities of the Medes.' These people (the Medes) had only recently entered the world picture, and *Agbatana* (*Ecbatana*), today called Hamadan, was their capital. However, the reference to 'cities of the Medes' remains vague. Cities under Assyrian control must be meant, and these will hardly have been very far to the north. As the Medes later inherited northern Mesopotamia, the phrase may refer to cities around the *Khabur* sources."[100]

THE TEN LOST TRIBES

Thus the remnants of these apostate Israelites disappeared into the mysterious limbo of the great unknown. It has been thought by many authorities that they completely lost their identity by mixing with other peoples,[101] and it is true that we seem to find fragments of them scattered across the face of the earth. Nevertheless, the Lord has assured us in modern revelation that eventually their location and identity will be revealed and we will find that in spite of the mixing process, the majority have maintained their integrity as a distinct people.

Concerning their return the Lord has said, "And they who are in the north countries[102] shall come in remembrance

100. Kraeling, Rand McNally *Bible Atlas,* pp. 297-298
101. Ibid.
102. There is no doubt that this is referring to the Ten Tribes for in section 110, verse 11, of the Doctrine and Covenants the Lord says "the ten tribes from the LAND OF THE NORTH" will be led to Zion.

before the Lord; and their prophets[103] shall hear his voice, and shall no longer stay themselves; and they shall smite the rocks, and the ice shall flow down at their presence. And an highway shall be cast up in the midst of the great deep. Their enemies shall become a prey unto them, and in the barren deserts there shall come forth pools of living water; and the parched ground shall no longer be a thirsty land. And they shall bring forth their rich treasures unto the children of Ephraim, my servants. And the boundaries of the everlasting hills shall tremble at their presence. And there shall they fall down and be crowned with glory, even in Zion, by the hands of the servants of the Lord, even the children of Ephraim. And they shall be filled with songs of everlasting joy. Behold, this is the blessing of the everlasting God UPON THE TRIBES OF ISRAEL, and the richer blessing upon the head of Ephraim and his fellows."[104]

From this remarkable statement we would be led to assume that the return of the Lost Ten Tribes will be no casual affair but a spectacular demonstration of God's power. Jeremiah verifies this and implies that it will be more amazing than Israel's miraculous crossing of the Red Sea. After this great event the seed of Jacob will no longer say, "The Lord liveth, that brought up the children of Israel out of the land of Egypt; but, the Lord liveth, that brought up the children of Israel from the land of the North."[105]

When these people come with their records, histories and fabulous wealth to help embellish the New Jerusalem, they will also bring a knowledge concerning matters of which the world is presently unaware. For example, they will be able to relate the exciting circumstances surrounding that occasion when the resurrected Christ appeared to them shortly after He appeared to the Nephites in America. Were it not for the Book of Mormon we would be ignorant of the event. This much did Jesus reveal to His Saints in America around 34 A.D. Said He, "But now I go unto the Father,

---

103. During a conference of the Church in June, 1831, Joseph Smith stated that "John the Revelator was then among the ten tribes of Israel" and was working "to prepare them for their return from their long dispersion." (Joseph Fielding Smith, *Essentials of Church History* [1937], p. 126)
104. Doctrine and Covenants, 133:26-34
105. Jeremiah 16:14-15

and also to show myself unto the lost tribes of Israel, for they are not lost unto the Father, for he knoweth whither he hath taken them."[106] The Nephites apparently wondered why Jesus had not told His disciples in Jerusalem about the lost tribes and the remnants of Israel in America. Jesus said, "Neither at any time hath the Father given me commandment that I should tell unto them concerning the other tribes of the house of Israel, whom the Father hath led away out of the land. This much did the Father command me, that I should tell unto them: That other sheep I have which are not of this fold [the Jewish fold]; them also I must bring, and THEY SHALL HEAR MY VOICE; and there shall be one fold, and one shepherd. And now, because of stiff-neckedness and unbelief they UNDERSTOOD NOT MY WORD; therefore I was commanded to say no more of the Father concerning this thing unto them."[107]

Many thought that this passage meant that Jesus would take the Gospel to the gentiles, but that was Paul's mission. The gentiles did not hear the voice of Jesus. They only heard a testimony from those who had known Him. It was the remnant of Israel in America and the lost tribes who were to hear His voice and receive the Gospel of Christ's personal ministry.

It is interesting that just before the Ten Tribes disappeared in the human labrynth beyond the Tigris river, the preoccupation of all their prophets was the message of hope which pointed to the great restoration of Israel in the last days. Joel was the first one to spring the flood-gate of revelation concerning this great event and Amos, Hosea, Micah and Isaiah followed immediately after. Joel focused on a single theme which we shall consider later, and since we have already discussed the revelations recorded by Amos and Hosea, it now remains for us to cover briefly the scriptural jewels recorded by Micah. We are saving Isaiah for a special treatment in the chapters to follow.

THE PROPHET MICAH

Once the student establishes in his mind a historical frame of reference for each of the Old Testament prophets,

---

106. 3 Nephi 17:4   107. 3 Nephi 15:15-18

their writings become richer and far more meaningful. This is certainly true of Micah. In the opening verses of his writing Micah says that he began his ministry during the time Jotham was king of Judah. Jotham, you will recall, was the son of King Uzziah. He served as regent during the 11 to 12 years that his father had leprosy. At his father's death he took over the throne in his own right but only survived an additional five years when he was succeeded by his son, Ahaz, who apostatized, defied the prophet Isaiah, and made an alliance with the Assyrians. Micah was active all during this period and even continued preaching clear down into the next reign which belonged to the good King Hezekiah. He therefore saw the fall of the northern tribes and many of the crises which assailed Judah soon afterwards. In his writings we will therefore find references to both Judah and Israel with correlary prophecies and warnings concerning their bombastic and turbulent future.

The first chapter of Micah contains God's witness against the evil and idolatrous Israelites who have been behaving like heathens. Micah lashes out at their extravagant images or idols which have been paid for out of "the hire of an harlot."[108] This has reference to the immorality of the fertility cults wherein the women devotees performed immoral acts and contributed the revenue derived from such practices to the embellishment of their heathen temples and gaudy images. Micah says very shortly all these manmade objects of worship shall be "beaten to pieces."[109]

Chapter two is a verbal blast against the men of affairs in Israel who stayed awake nights concocting schemes to cheat their neighbors. Micah cries out, ". . . they covet fields, and take them by violence; and houses, and take them away: so they oppress a man and his house, even a man and his heritage."[110]

In chapter three Micah talks about the great famine of revelation that is coming. As Israel goes into gentile captivity Micah says they will be victims of the most vicious atrocities. "Then shall they cry unto the Lord, but he will

---

108. Micah 1:7
109. Ibid.
110. Micah 2:2

not hear them: he will even hide his face from them at that time, as they have behaved themselves ill in their doings."[111]

Micah strikes out at the apostate priests and public officials both in Israel and Judah: "Hear this, I pray you, ye heads of the house of Jacob, and princes of the house of Israel, that abhor [true] judgment, and pervert all equity. They build up Zion with blood, and Jerusalem with iniquity. The heads thereof judge for reward, and the priests thereof teach for hire, and the prophets thereof divine for money: yet will they lean upon the Lord, and say, Is not the Lord among us? none evil can come upon us."[112]

Micah then placed the seal of divine retribution and prophetic judgment on all of them. Said he, "Therefore shall Zion for your sake be plowed as a field, and Jerusalem shall become heaps, and the mountain of the house [of the Lord] as the high places of the forest."[113] It was a prediction of total devastation for both kingdoms.

In chapter 4, Micah abandons the contemplation of ugly things and leaps down the corridors of time to our day. Some of the most famous prophecies in the scripture concerning the work of the Lord in the last days will be found in Micah. Here is how he starts:

"But in the last days it shall come to pass, that the mountain of the house of the Lord shall be established in the top of the mountains, and it shall be exalted above the hills; and people shall flow unto it.

"And many nations shall come, and say, Come, and let us go up to the mountain of the Lord, and to the house of the God of Jacob; and he will teach us of his ways, and we will walk in his paths: for the LAW SHALL GO FORTH OF ZION, AND THE WORD OF THE LORD FROM JERUSALEM.

"And he shall judge among many people, and rebuke strong nations afar off; and they shall beat their swords into plowshares, and their spears into pruninghooks: nation shall

111. Micah 3:4
112. Micah 3:9-11
113. Micah 3:12

not lift up a sword against nation, neither shall they learn war any more.

"But they shall sit every man under his vine and under his fig tree; and none shall make them afraid: for the mouth of the Lord of hosts hath spoken it."[114]

The reader will recognize immediately that these verses pertain to the Second Advent of the Savior and the ushering in of the Millennium. When this is accomplished there will be two world capitals, one the City of Zion in America, and the other in ancient Jerusalem. No student of the Bible could possibly know that this was what Micah had in mind unless he had the additional resources which God has revealed in modern times and which we will be discussing later.

Micah tells the Israelites that some of them will be taken to Babylon, but they will be delivered.[115] This, of course, is referring to the Jews. Then Micah sweeps down to our modern day and says these same daughters of Zion (the Jews) shall be compassed by "many nations" but the Lord says, "I will make thine horn iron, and I will make thy hoofs brass: and thou shalt beat in pieces many people: and I will consecrate their gain unto the Lord. . . ."[116]

The Arab nations of this generation can already testify that this prophecy has been literally fulfilled insofar as they are concerned. With the greatest apprehension the Arab leaders have watched the return of the Jews to the Holy Land. The Jews said they wanted to buy the land from the Arabs and establish a national homeland as required by the scriptures. They promised to create a government where every nationality and religion would be treated equally. The Arabs, however, said the prophetic "return of the Jews" had already been fulfilled when the Jews returned from Babylon. They said the Lord never intended to gather the Jews anymore because they allowed themselves to be driven from Palestine by the Romans; therefore the Arabs had become the chosen people of the Lord as evidenced by the fact that they have occupied the Holy Land ever since.

---

114. Micah 4:1-4
115. Micah 4:10
116. Micah 4:11-13

However, in spite of these divergent points of view, the Jews continued to come. In fact, the emigration was greatly accelerated by the Nazi extermination orders during World War II. A crisis occurred in 1948 when six Arab nations representing around 40,000,000 people, decided to drive the Jews (who were then less than a million) into the Mediterranean. The Arabs violated a United Nations mandate in order to launch the attack, but after a few months of ferocious fighting it became fully apparent that the small band of Jews was going to be able to hold their ground. Finally, an armistice was reached and the Jewish homeland became a recognized political reality.[117] From a military standpoint it was precisely the kind of latter-day miracle Micah had predicted.

THE BIRTHPLACE OF JESUS CHRIST

It is also within the confines of the modest little book of Micah that the birthplace of Jesus Christ is designated. Micah said it would be in Bethlehem. Some 735 years later, Herod asked his "wise men" where the Messiah was supposed to be born and they quoted Micah 5:2. The New Testament version of this passage is very similar to the more ancient text, but the Messiahship of the coming Jesus is clearer in Micah's version. Micah wrote:

"But thou, Beth-lehem Ephratah, though thou be little among the thousands of Judah, yet out of thee shall he come forth unto me that is to be ruler in Israel; whose goings forth have been from of old, from everlasting."

The New Testament version says simply, "And thou Bethlehem, in the land of Juda, art not the least among the princes of Juda: for out of thee shall come a Governor, that shall rule my people Israel."[118]

A PROPHECY CONCERNING AMERICA

Then Micah describes a situation in the last days which the Lord specifically identifies as a prophecy concerning America. Micah said that in that great day of Israel's res-

---

117. For a more detailed account of what is happening in modern Israel see the article in the Appendix entitled, "A Modern Miracle in the Holy Land."
118. Matthew 2:6

toration, ". . . the remnant of Jacob shall be among the Gentiles in the midst of many people as a lion among the beasts of the forest, as a young lion among the flocks of sheep: who, IF HE GO THROUGH, both treadeth down and teareth in pieces, and none can deliver."[119]

When Jesus appeared to the people in America following His resurrection He pointed directly to these words of Micah as referring to "this people" — the Nephites and Lamanites — "who are a remnant of the house of Jacob."[120] Jesus went on to say that the Gentiles would develop into a mighty people on the American continent in the last days and that He would restore the Gospel among them.[121] Then would come their time of testing. They would either remain righteous and help build the New Jerusalem,[122] or they would defiantly rebel against the Lord's work of the last days and have to be "cut off from among my people who are of the covenant."[123] Jesus said that if they chose this latter course and became unrighteous then He would allow the powerful "remnant of Jacob," or the Lamanite-Nephite nations of the American continent to destroy the mighty gentile civilization which had risen up to dominate the land.[124]

It is interesting to observe that the Gentile nations on this continent are primarily the United States and Canada in North America, and Venezuela, Brazil, Paraguay, Uruguay and Argentina in South America. The peoples of Mexico, Central America, and the nations on the western side of South America are the ones which carry a heavy strain of Lamanite-Nephite blood. Until very recently they have all been relatively weak nations, but the Lord has said they will become so powerful that if the circumstances warrant it they will hang over the Gentile nations like a sword of Damocles. As long as the Gentiles do not fight the work of the Lord, all will be well, but if unrighteousness prevails and the American gentiles become immoral, apostate and anti-Christ, then these nations who are a remnant of Jacob will "treadeth down and teareth in pieces, and none can deliver."

119. Micah 5:8
120. 3 Nephi 21:2
121. 3 Nephi 16:10; 21:1-11
122. 3 Nephi 21:20-24
123. 3 Nephi 21:11
124. 3 Nephi 21:11-21

The Savior also quoted Micah's prediction that if this became necessary the great gentile cities would become defenseless.[125] Their chariots and other vehicles would be destroyed.[126] Their preachers and purveyors of false doctrine would be destroyed,[127] and the workmanship of gentile achievement which the people worship as a source of pride and accomplishment will all be cast down.[128]

Jesus then quoted Micah 5:15 differently than it appears in our modern Bible. The King James version says, "And I will execute vengeance in anger and fury UPON THE HEATHEN, such as they have not heard," but Jesus gave this differently and included it with two other verses which are not even in the Bible. We therefore assume that this is what Micah originally wrote before scribes and translators mutilated it: "And it shall come to pass that all lyings, and deceivings, and envyings, and strifes, and priestcrafts, and whoredoms, shall be done away. For it shall come to pass, saith the Father, that at that day whosoever will not repent and come unto my Beloved Son, them will I cut off from among my people, O house of Israel; and I will execute vengeance and fury upon them, EVEN AS UPON THE HEATHEN, such as they have not heard."[129]

Immediately after the above information was given by the Savior to the ancient American Saints He hastened to explain that the destruction of the American Gentiles was not inevitable. In fact, He said, "But if they will repent and hearken unto my words, and harden not their hearts, I will establish my church among them and they shall come in unto the covenant and be numbered among this the remnant of Jacob, unto whom I have given this land [America] for their inheritance; AND THEY SHALL ASSIST MY PEOPLE, the remnant of Jacob, and also as many of the house of Israel as shall come [the Ten Tribes], that THEY MAY BUILD A CITY, WHICH SHALL BE CALLED THE NEW JERUSALEM. And then shall they [the Gentiles] assist my people that they may be gathered in, who are scattered upon all the face of the land, in unto the New Jerusalem."[130]

125. Micah 5:11; 3 Nephi 21:15
126. Micah 5:10; 3 Nephi 21:14
127. Micah 5:12; 3 Nephi 21:16

128. Micah 5:13; 3 Nephi 21:17
129. 3 Nephi 21:19-21
130. 3 Nephi 21:22-24

Some students of prophecy tend to treat the destruction of the Gentiles on the American continent as an inevitable and irrevocable prediction of disaster. This is an error. It spreads discouragement and apathy among the modern Saints who would be striving with all their might to bring to pass the promise of the Lord that the Gentile nations of America can be saved and used to help the restored Church of Jesus Christ perform its great labor of building the New Jerusalem, gathering God's people from across the earth, and building a pre-Millennial civilization of the highest order. All this is possible. The Lord has declared it so, and all should be striving mightily to bring it about. That is why both the Savior and Micah describe the powerful "remnant of Jacob" or the Lamanite-Nephite nations, as only a potential threat to the Gentiles. Jesus specifically said, ". . . if the Gentiles will repent and return unto me, saith the Father, behold they shall be numbered among my people, O house of Israel. AND I WILL NOT SUFFER MY PEOPLE, WHO ARE OF THE HOUSE OF ISRAEL, TO GO THROUGH AMONG THEM, AND TREAD THEM DOWN, saith the Father."[131] This is why Jesus and Micah both referred to the destructive power of the remnant of Jacob as conditional. Note the phrase, "IF he go through, both treadeth down, and teareth in pieces, and none can deliver."[132] This means that the destruction of the Gentiles is not predestinated any more than the destruction of Jonah's Nineveh. The future of the Gentiles in the Western Hemisphere depends entirely on how they respond to God's mighty trumpet of warning which is now being sounded among them. No worker in the Kingdom is entitled to take a pessimistic view and say that the task is impossible, for the Lord has proclaimed the very opposite. As in every dispensation, the outcome depends largely on the degree of enthusiastic dedication among those who carry the message. The rest is up to the Gentiles. As of the moment of this writing they are responding better than at any time since the Gospel was restored. If this trend continues there is an excellent chance that the United States, Canada, Brazil, Argentina and the other Gentile nations of the Americas can go into the Mil-

---

131. 3 Nephi 16:13-14
132. Micah 5:8; 3 Nephi 21:12

lenium intact. If this trend collapses, they will reap a whirl-wind.

THE LORD'S CONTROVERSY WITH ANCIENT ISRAEL

In the last two chapters of Micah, he reiterates the same message as his great contemporary, Amos. Amos had already itemized the crime of Israel for which she was about to be punished. Micah does the same thing and includes an eloquent denunciation of the dissolute princes, the apostate priests and the corrupt people in general. Said he:

"Hear ye now what the Lord saith . . . for the Lord hath a controversy with his people, and he will plead with Israel. O my people, what have I done unto thee? and wherein have I wearied thee? testify against me. For I brought thee up out of the land of Egypt and redeemed thee out of the house of servants [slavery]. . . . Will the Lord be pleased with thousands of rams, or with ten thousands of rivers of oil? shall I give my first-born for my transgression, the fruit of my body for the sin of my soul?"[133]

No doubt this last statement was a verbal whiplash against King Ahaz of Judah who had recently committed the terrible crime of sacrificing his own children as burnt offerings to heathen gods.[134]

Micah continues, "He [the Lord] hath shown thee, O man, what is good; and what doth the Lord require of thee, BUT TO DO JUSTLY AND TO LOVE MERCY, AND TO WALK HUMBLY WITH THY GOD?"[135] ". . . Shall I count them pure [who transact their business] with the wicked balances, and with the bag of deceitful weights? For the rich men thereof are full of violence, and the inhabitants thereof have spoken lies, and their tongue is deceitful in their mouth."[136] ". . . For the son dishonoureth the father, the daughter riseth up against her mother, the daughter-in-law against her mother-in-law; a man's enemies are the men of his own house."[137]

Micah then closes his writings with an expression of faith in the final exaltation and triumph of the Lord. Despite

---

133. Micah 6:1-4, 7
134. 2 Chronicles 28:3
135. Micah 6:8
136. Micah 6:11-12
137. Micah 7:6

the bitter persecutions he was apparently suffering, he declared, "Therefore I will look unto the Lord; I will wait for the God of my salvation: my God will hear me. Rejoice not against me, O mine enemy: when I fall [in death], I shall arise [in the resurrection]; when I sit in darkness [in prison], the Lord shall be a light unto me.[138] . . . Who is a God like unto thee, that pardoneth iniquity, and passeth by the transgression of the remnant of his heritage? he retaineth not his anger for ever, because he delighteth in mercy. He will turn again, he will have compassion upon us; he will subdue our iniquities; and thou wilt cast all their sins into the depths of the sea."[139]

Thus the prophet Micah, stalwart contemporary of Amos, Hosea and Isaiah, passes into history.

Now we come to that greatest of all the prophetic Old Testament writers — Isaiah.

Scripture Readings and Questions on Chapter Eighteen

Scripture Readings: 2 Kings, chapters 14 to 27 inclusive; 2 Chronicles, chapters 26 to 28 inclusive; The Book of Hosea and the Book of Micah.

1—How would you describe the task of the faithful in a time of apostasy?

2—How did the Lord try to teach Hosea what it was like to be the God of Israel? Did Hosea do as he was instructed?

3—Name five offenses with which Hosea charged the Israelites.

4—Explain the phrase, "repentance shall be hid from mine eyes."

5—Why do you think the "men of affairs" in Samaria would ridicule the prophets like Amos, Hosea and Isaiah and consider them "impractical"? Who turned out to be the most practical?

6—How did the throne of Israel happen to change hands three times in a single year?

7—How would you characterize the reign of King Uzziah of Judah? What caused him to get leprosy? What happened to the kingdom?

8—Who created the second Assyrian empire? What is his name in the Bible? What was his feeling toward Israel? Why did he have a different attitude toward Judah?

---

138. Micah 7:7-8
139. Micah 7:18-19

9—Why did Syria and Israel attack Judah? What was Isaiah's advice to King Ahaz? Did he respond? What was his substitute program?

10—What happened to the 200,000 people of Judah who were captured by Israel?

11—What happened to compel Syria and Israel to discontinue their attack on Judah? What happened to Damascus? What happened to northern Israel?

12—What did the king of Assyria do with the captured Israelites from Galilee and Gilead? What did he do with the rest of the Israelites after the final conquest of Israel?

13—Did Micah have a long term of service or a short one? Was he alive during the fall of Israel epic? Did he predict it?

14—Where did Micah say the Lord's house would be built in the last days? Explain the phrase, "the law shall go forth of Zion, and the word of the Lord from Jerusalem." What does this imply?

15—Did Micah say the Jews would be a weak people when they gathered in the last days? What did he say? How has this been verified in modern times?

16—Which prophet told where the birthplace of the Savior would be? How did this prophecy become important in the days of Herod?

17—When Micah spoke of the "remnant of Jacob" who would threaten the Gentiles in the last days, whom did he have in mind? How do we know this?

18—Is the fall of the American Gentiles inevitable? What did the Lord say about it? What responsibility does that place upon us?

19—Name the principal Gentile nations in North America; in South America. In which nations is the strain of Lamanite-Nephite blood the strongest?

20—What did Micah say the Lord requires of His people? Why did the prophets have to continually emphasize the simplicity of the Gospel's main objectives? Do we need to do this today?

CHAPTER NINETEEN

The Importance of Isaiah's Ministry

Now we are going to get better acquainted with a man living in the last half of the eighth century B.C. who recorded the important details of human history for the next 2,700 years. This is Isaiah. He left us the longest prophetic book in the entire canon of the Bible, yet there are indications that he knew a great deal more than he ever told.[1]

This was not the first time the Lord had pulled aside the mammoth curtain of the future but it seems to have been the first time the Lord allowed so much of it to be put in writing for the general public. Adam, for example, saw a history of the world, but no details are given.[2] Enoch also saw the panorama of the future but described only the highlights such as the Great Flood,[3] the crucifixion,[4] the resurrection[5] and the second advent of Christ.[6] Shortly after the Tower of Babel epic, the Brother of Jared (Mahonri-Moriancumr) saw the history of the world from the Creation to the end of the Millennium, but this was hidden up in the

---

1. This becomes entirely obvious as we study Nephi's commentary on Isaiah.
2. Doctrine and Covenants 107:56. Verse 57 says, "These things were all written in the Book of Enoch, and are to be testified in due time." As yet, we do not have the full text of this scriptural treasure.
3. Moses 7:48-51
4. Moses 7:54-56
5. Moses 7:56-59
6. Moses 7:60-67

sealed portion of the plates of Mormon and the Lord said it was never to be revealed until a time of righteousness finally prevailed upon the earth.[7]

Cnly a Book of Mormon prophet, the magnificent Nephi, was allowed to record and disseminate anywhere near the amount of details concerning the future as did Isaiah. Other prophets saw portions of the future and recorded what they saw, nevertheless, it remained for Isaiah to dip deeply into practically every aspect of the colorful spectrum of the coming centuries. In fact, excluding Nephi, the prophet Isaiah recorded for public distribution specific reference to more historical highlights of the future than practically all the other prophets combined.

Why Isaiah Is Difficult to Read

The rich and colorful eloquence of Isaiah makes his writings a brilliant literary treasure but when it comes to the reader's comprehension authorities agree that the book of Isaiah is one of the most difficult segments of the whole Bible. Why is this so?

In the first place, Isaiah, like all of the prophets, was under certain divine restrictions. It is obvious in many places that he was deliberately obscure. To many of His children the Lord cannot reveal too many details concerning the future without debilitating their free agency and thereby destroying the learning process in the second estate. However, to His righteous servants who can endure it, He disseminates this knowledge either obscurely or in parable form and then gives them a "key" which unlocks the full meaning. Jesus emphasized that this sometimes frustrating obscurity is by heavenly design and is intended to give knowledge to those it will help while withholding it from those it will hurt. Here is the way He explained it to His disciples, "Unto you it is given to know the mysteries of the kingdom of God; but to others in parables; that seeing they might not see, and hearing they might not understand."[8]

---

7. Ether 4:4-7; 3:25-28
8. Luke 8:10

This careful discrimination in giving to mankind only the quantity and quality of spiritual food they are capable of absorbing is repeatedly emphasized by Paul. Said he, "For every one that useth milk is unskilful [as yet] in the word of righteousness: for he is a babe [in the kingdom]. But strong meat belongeth to them that are of full age, even those who by reason of use have their senses exercised to discern both good and evil."[9] And when Paul was writing to the new converts in Corinth he had no compunction about telling them they were still "babes in Christ" and capable of receiving nothing but the milk of the Gospel. Said he, "And I, brethren, could not speak unto you as unto spiritual [mature Saints], but as unto carnal, even as unto babes in Christ. I have fed you with milk, and not with meat: for hitherto ye were not able to bear it, neither yet now are ye able."[10]

So, much of Isaiah was made deliberately obscure for those that "were not able to bear it." As we shall see in Nephi's commentary on Isaiah, his writings require a "key" to permit full comprehension by the student. The reader will immediately appreciate the priceless value of this key as we study Isaiah in detail. Were it not for modern revelation we would be as much in the dark on Isaiah as anyone else.

A second factor which makes Isaiah difficult to read is his poetic treatment of what he saw. Such an approach was the natural expression of his unusually brilliant mind and it reflects itself both in his literary style and in his presentation of the subject matter. Isaiah's mind was quick, sensitive and scintillating. Apparently his mental muscles flexed themselves by perpetually leaping about with lightning speed, and while this was merely an intellectual exercise in psychological gymnastics for Isaiah, it often presents his humble readers with a continuous series of fantastic strides forward, backward, skyward and sideways. This is because he takes the poet's approach of sweeping excitedly and impressionistically through the heights and depths of his visions rather than methodically recording each phase of the revelation the way most prophets have done. Isaiah thought nothing of taking a problem current in his own time and then,

---

9. Hebrews 5:13-14
10. 1 Corinthians 3:1-2

without the slightest warning to his reader, using it as an excuse for immediately discussing an identical problem which he knew would arise in the "latter days." And just to make it more of a riddle to the uninitiated, he deliberately identified God's enemies of the latter days by the names, nationalities and geographical locations with which God's enemies were known in Isaiah's day! Hence, the terms Assyria, Babylon, Edom, and Idumea which were familiar to his own generation, are freely used by Isaiah to identify wicked and rebellious nations which he knew would arise in our time.

Furthermore, to the modern reader, Isaiah leaves the impression that while he knew it was his duty to warn his own generation, he would have ten-thousand-times rather been spending all his energy talking about God's great day of triumph incidental to the Second Coming of Christ. Thus, his mind whirls from verse to verse in tantalizing dizziness, touching a point of historical reality in his own day, and then leaping joyously down the corridor of time 2,700 years to dwell with relish on events far in the future. It is no wonder that Isaiah takes more than the average amount of careful, prayerful analysis in order to understand what he is talking about.

A third factor which makes Isaiah a challenging writer is his extremely advanced skill in the art of literary expression. Isaiah was no rustic bumpkin who just happened to be handy when the Lord needed a spokesman. He apparently was raised right in Jerusalem and had spent his entire life attempting to refine his capacity to serve the Lord. The available text implies that he told the sneering skeptics of his own day that they dare not reject his words as being those of an ignorant numbskull, nor excuse themselves from recognizing the Lord's servant on the ground that he appeared before them as a hermit, mystic, or odd-ball denizen of the desert. He was one of their own, a city prophet, with all the advantages of education and refinement which Judah's civilization could bestow upon him. Cried he:

"The Lord . . . hath made my mouth like a sharp sword . . . and made me a polished shaft."[11] Then he added, "The

---

11. Isaiah 49:1-2

Lord God hath given me the tongue of the learned, that I should know how to speak a word in season to him that is weary."[12] Nephi verifies that the people of Jerusalem were sufficiently "learned" so that Isaiah's sermons did not go over their heads,[13] nevertheless it is Isaiah's "tongue of the learned" which makes his complex eloquence additionally difficult when translated into a modern language. In fact, Nephi tells us that within 200 years after Isaiah's time a branch of his own people were complaining that Isaiah's writings were already too difficult for them to comprehend. They therefore demanded that Nephi, their own prophet, interpret Isaiah for them.[14] This brings us to the most valuable and sacred treasure of knowledge concerning the book of Isaiah which has come into man's possession.

NEPHI RECEIVES A REVELATION AND WRITES THE ONLY AUTHENTIC COMMENTARY ON ISAIAH IN EXISTENCE

By way of background we should mention that around 600 B.C. when Lehi and his colony left Jerusalem for the long, treacherous migration to the Western Hemisphere, they brought along with them the precious Brass Plates which contained the Hebrew canon of scripture including the writings of Isaiah. Apparently it was following their settlement in America that they had time to scrutinize the scriptures more closely. Naturally, they turned to Isaiah whose writings, along with Jeremiah, were among the most recently recorded revelations from God.

But, as we have already noted, the study of Isaiah turned out to be a baffling mirage of illusive complexity for them. That is when they turned to Nephi and asked him to interpret this scripture for them. Nephi responded enthusiastically for we learn that NEPHI HAD SEEN MOST IF NOT ALL OF THE SAME REVELATIONS ISAIAH HAD SEEN.[15] Nephi therefore told the people that he would

---

12. Isaiah 50:4
13. 2 Nephi 25:5
14. 2 Nephi 25:1
15. Even before this time, Nephi refers to his revelations in general terms (see 1 Nephi, chapters 11 to 14), but as he proceeds to explain Isaiah it is obvious that he had received broad and penetrating insights into the most intimate details of the period with which Isaiah seemed the most concerned.

comment on Isaiah "according to the spirit of prophecy which is IN ME; wherefore I shall prophecy ACCORDING TO THE PLAINNESS which hath been with me from the time that I came out of Jerusalem with my father; for behold my soul DELIGHTETH IN PLAINNESS unto my people, that they may learn."[16]

Nephi prefaces his commentary by saying, "Isaiah spoke many things which were hard for many of my people to understand; for they know not concerning the manner of prophesying among the Jews."[17] Then Nephi says he wanted to address his commentary on Isaiah to all Israel, both ancient and modern. Said he, "Wherefore, hearken, O my people, which are of the house of Israel, and give ear unto my words; for because the words of Isaiah are not plain unto you, nevertheless, THEY ARE PLAIN TO ALL THOSE THAT ARE FILLED WITH THE SPIRIT OF PROPHECY . . . Yea, my soul delighteth in the words of Isaiah, for I came out from Jerusalem, and mine eyes have beheld the things of the Jews, and I know that the Jews DO UNDERSTAND the things of the prophets, and THERE IS NONE OTHER PEOPLE THAT UNDERSTAND the things which were spoken unto the Jews like unto them, save it be that THEY ARE TAUGHT AFTER THE MANNER OF THE THINGS OF THE JEWS."[18]

Nephi then identifies his own prophecies which he is about to relate in great plainness as being identical with those given by Isaiah. He says men will recognize their fulfillment when they come to pass in the last days.[19] "Wherefore they are of worth unto the children of men, and he that supposeth that they are not, unto him will I speak particularly, and confine the words unto [matters involving] mine own people; for I know that they shall be of great worth unto them in the last days; for in that day shall they understand them, wherefore, for their good have I written them."[20]

Nephi then proceeds to unfold his many brilliant and illuminating comments on the Book of Isaiah. In doing so, he bluntly states, "I proceed with mine own prophecy, ac-

---

16. 2 Nephi 25:4   19. 2 Nephi 25:7
17. 2 Nephi 25:1   20. 2 Nephi 25:8
18. 2 Nephi 25:3-5

cording to my plainness; in the which I KNOW THAT NO MAN CAN ERR."[21]

THE BOOK OF MORMON SETTLES THE QUESTION AS TO WHETHER THE BOOK OF ISAIAH WAS WRITTEN BY ONE AUTHOR OR SEVERAL

There is no doubt but what the Book of Isaiah has been one of the casualties of modern scholasticism. Certain Biblical "authorities" have undertaken the task of shredding and fragmenting it until it would seem to be a heap of literary shambles rather than a unified pillar of prophecy, exhortation and faith as Isaiah intended.[22]

Many of the objections to the book in its present form center around the contention that Isaiah just could not have anticipated events so far in the future. These self-appointed critics thereupon perform surgery on the text to accommodate this theory. Other critics make an internal analysis of the book itself and have lopped off whatever they deemed to be non-Isaiah text. The results of all this secular cynicism, abstracting and subtracting has been to destroy confidence in practically the entire prophetic panorama which Isaiah left us as a legacy for mankind.

Dr. Sidney B. Sperry of Brigham Young University classifies this whole school of Isaiah critics into the moderates and the radicals. The moderates claim that out of 66 chapters in Isaiah, they believe 44 were not written by Isaiah. The radicals go further. They say that out of 1292 verses in the Book of Isaiah that Isaiah wrote only 262! Fortunately, there are many competent Bible scholars whom Dr. Sperry quotes, that see far more evidence of unity in the book of Isaiah than the critics can produce to prove disunity.

Nevertheless, it is commonplace today for Bible commentaries to go along with the moderates and accept only chapters 1 to 39 as being written by the prophet Isaiah. They attribute chapters 40 to 55 to a second author and chapters 56 to 66 to yet a third.

---

21. 2 Nephi 25:7
22. For a discussion of this fragmenting of Isaiah, see *The Old Testament Prophets,* by Dr. Sidney B. Sperry, Deseret Sunday School Union manual, 1965, chapters 15 and 16.

For those who have ears to hear and are not precluded by prejudice from hearing it, the Book of Mormon has a unique and satisfying answer to this whole problem. Since the Isaiah text on the Brass Plates was recorded sometime before 600 B.C., it seems highly significant that the contents of our present Isaiah in the Bible are almost identical with the wide samplings quoted in the Book of Mormon. Dr. Sperry points out that the Nephite records contain fully quoted texts from the following chapters of Isaiah:

Isaiah	*Book of Mormon*
Chapters 2 to 14	2 Nephi, chapters 12-24
Chapter 29	2 Nephi, chapter 27
Chapters 48 and 49	1 Nephi, chapters 20 and 21
Chapters 50 and 51	2 Nephi, chapters 7 and 8
Chapter 52	3 Nephi, chapter 20
Chapter 53	Mosiah, chapter 14
Chapter 54	3 Nephi, chapter 22
Chapter 55	2 Nephi 26:25

The last ten chapters of Isaiah include much that is treated in earlier chapters so there is a consistency in prophetic subject matter and theology between the last ten chapters and those cited above.

This unity of Isaiah as presented in the Book of Mormon received the full endorsement of the resurrected Christ. Speaking to the American Saints around 34 A.D., He declared, "And now, behold, I say unto you, that ye ought to search these things. Yea, a commandment I give unto you that ye search these things diligently; FOR GREAT ARE THE WORDS OF ISAIAH. For surely he spake as touching all things concerning my people which are of the house of Israel; therefore it must needs be that he must speak also to the Gentiles. And all things that he spake have been and shall be, even according to the words which he spake."[23]

From this we therefore conclude that the samplings of Isaiah in the Book of Mormon which were recorded before 600 B.C., prove the original unity of this book. Furthermore, the fact that the Savior endorsed the version of Isaiah which was then in the hands of the American Saints gives unprece-

---

23. 3 Nephi 23:1-3

dented credence to our own version because it is essentially the same.

What Is the Best Way to Study Isaiah?

At some time in his perusal of the Bible, every student should acquaint himself with Isaiah by reading each chapter consecutively. This will at least expose the reader's mind to the massive but penetrating perspective of Isaiah's writings. However, ultimately he will want to read Isaiah topically. Only when the subject matter is broken down into concise categories will the student fully appreciate the genuine quality and scope of Isaiah's prophetic power and the skillful incisiveness of his inspired writing.

For the student who wishes to read Isaiah by consecutive chapters I highly recommend the excellent correlation and commentary by Dr. Sidney B. Sperry as set forth in his book, *The Voice of Israel's Prophets*.[24] In this book Dr. Sperry takes each chapter of Isaiah and correlates it with both historical and scriptural material which will supplement the student's background and comprehension of the Biblical text.

In this present volume we shall take the second approach to the study of Isaiah which is a treatment of the subject matter in topical-digest form. In doing so we will often rely upon the commentary of the prophet Nephi who apparently saw the same revelations and who wrote "with plainness" so that we could not mistake the intent of either Isaiah or himself.

Isaiah, the Man

Before treating his writings, however, let us get better acquainted with Isaiah as a man.

From Isaiah 6:1 we learn that this prophet was receiving revelation and was well into his calling as a servant of the Lord by the time King Uzziah died of leprosy around 739 B.C. We presume, therefore that he was probably born around 780 B.C.[25] but there is nothing specific concerning his na-

---

24. Published by the Deseret Book Company, 1961, Salt Lake City, Utah.
25. This is deducted from the fact that Isaiah had a son old enough to accompany him on an assignment as of around 735 B.C. (Isaiah 7:3)

tivity. The Bible simply describes him as the "Son of Amoz" without elaborating on it. We know he was married and had a son named Shear-jashub (meaning the remnant shall return), and a son named, Maher-shalal-hash-baz (meaning spoil speedeth, prey hasteneth) both of which names were given by revelation as prophetic symbols.[26] It is interesting that Isaiah's wife was a noble woman of deep spirituality who held the distinction of being called a "prophetess."[27]

So far as we can tell, the ministry of Isaiah lasted at least 48 years.[28] It may have lasted considerably longer. In any event, we can safely say that Isaiah was alive and constituted a powerful religious force around Jerusalem during practically all of the last half of the eighth century before Christ (750 to 700 B.C.).

Isaiah was a man of the most profound humility. He attributed everything about himself to the goodness of God. Understandably, however, his non-believing audiences interpreted this professed humility to be the most blatant kind of pride and boasting. For Isaiah to present himself as "a servant of God" and proclaim that his visions, eloquence and political insights all came from Heaven, was counted almost as blasphemous as the humble testimony of another who came 750 years later and said He was the Son of God.

Nevertheless, Isaiah dared not do less than testify humbly as to his personal witness concerning what he had seen, what he had been told and how he had happened to get involved in this strenuous business of a "prophetic calling." He wanted people to understand that sometimes a man "has to do what he has to do" just simply because God has put him in that inescapable responsibility of performing a certain mission. It goes without saying, of course, that Isaiah COULD have rejected the calling but not without jeopardizing his salvation, and this he did not intend to do. Therefore he pressed forward and in the most resolute manifestation of his own humility, testified that he was only doing what God had required at his hand. Said he:

---

26. See Isaiah 8:3 to illustrate the basis for this conclusion. Isaiah himself said: "Behold, I and the children whom the Lord hath given me are for signs and for wonders in Israel FROM THE LORD OF HOSTS . . ." (Isaiah 8:18)
27. Isaiah 8:3
28. Clarke, *Bible Commentary*, Vol. 4, p. 19

". . . hearken, ye people, from far; The Lord hath called me from the womb; from the bowels of my mother hath he made mention of my name. And he hath made my mouth like a sharp sword; in the shadow of his hand hath he hid me . . . and said unto me, Thou art my servant, O soldier of God,[29] in whom I will be glorified."[30]

But Isaiah was much like Noah, Abraham, Jeremiah and Mormon. He was called to bear down in pure testimony against a people whom he already knew would reject his message. There are few callings in the Priesthood more desperately discouraging than this kind. It is hard enough when there is a chance that one will see the fruits of his labor, but what happens when it becomes repugnantly apparent that there are not going to be any fruits? This is what happened to Isaiah:

"Then I said, I have laboured in vain, I have spent my strength for nought, and in vain: yet surely my judgment is with the Lord, and my work with my God."[31]

We learn in the next chapter why he had become discouraged. Like the Christ who would follow him, Isaiah was subjected to all the abuse of the apostates then in power. Nevertheless, he says, "I was not rebellious, neither turned away. . . . I gave my back to the smiters, and my cheeks to them that plucked off the hair [of the beard]: I hid not my face from shame and spitting."[32]

And the Lord assured Isaiah that his labor was not in vain. He was told that even though Israel would not be gathered to the Lord in his day, none the less, Isaiah would be "glorious in the eyes of the Lord"[33] because he had fought a good fight and had done the work of the Lord valiantly.

---

29. In our text of Isaiah 49:3 this phrase, "soldiers of God" is translated as a proper name, "Israel," but since the salutation is addressed to Isaiah it is believed it should have been translated in its literal sense rather than as a name. The above rendition removes the confusion.

30. Isaiah 49:1-3. This passage is correctly interpreted by authorities as referring not only to Isaiah but also to the Christ. However, it would be a mistake, I believe, to say that it applied exclusively to the Christ and not to Isaiah. Verse 4 seems to make it very clear that this section of scripture is being addressed to Isaiah personally since this particular detail does not fit the Messiah's life at all.

31. Isaiah 49:4

32. Isaiah 50:5-6

33. Isaiah 49:5

Among other things, Isaiah had the calling of proclaiming the good news of Israel's gathering or salvation in the last days. The Lord said He would also give Isaiah a message which would be "a light to the Gentiles."[34] Christ is the light to the Gentiles[35] but Isaiah was given the privilege of being the one to announce for the first time (as far as available scriptures show) that in the latter days the Gospel would spring forth among the Gentiles. So Isaiah was allowed to announce this great promise of hope and encouragement as a "light to the Gentiles." We will be discussing this in full detail in the next chapter. The Lord also told Isaiah his writings would be like a "covenant" to Israel whereby they would know that in the latter days they would re-occupy their "desolate heritages,"[36] and that like prisoners of captivity they would be liberated to gather back to their homeland.[37]

With such promises ringing in his heart, Isaiah sang out his psalm of triumph: "For the Lord God will help me; therefore shall I not be confounded: therefore have I set my face like a flint, and I know that I shall not be ashamed."[38]

And because he knew his prophecies would cover nearly all of the remainder of the Second Estate, he was most anxious that the people record his promises so that as the centuries passed by, men would know that Isaiah had spoken the truth. Said he, "Now go, write it before them in a table, and note it in a book, that it may be for the time to come for ever and ever."[39] Apparently somebody of the house of Joseph took this instruction seriously and recorded the full text of Isaiah's words in the family canon of scripture which is known to us as the "Brass Plates."[40] This was the record in the hands of Laban which Lehi later brought to America.[41]

---

34. Isaiah 49:6
35. Luke 2:32
36. Isaiah 49:8
37. Isaiah 49:9-13
38. Isaiah 50:7
39. Isaiah 30:8
40. 1 Nephi 3:3. That these plates were the family scripture of the house of Joseph is made plain in 1 Nephi 5:16: "And Laban was also a descendant of Joseph, wherefore he AND HIS FATHERS had kept the records."
41. 1 Nephi 4:38; Alma 37:3-5

Isaiah Sees a Vision of the Lord

Isaiah appears to have lived in the middle or lower city of Jerusalem,[42] and nearly all of his prophetic activities appear to have centered around the capital of Judah.

It was approximately 739 B.C. or the year King Uzziah died, that Isaiah says, "I saw also the Lord sitting upon a throne, high and lifted up, and his train filled the temple."[43] Whether he was actually in the temple or seeing a vision of it, we are not certain. In any event, Isaiah was frightened by the glorious vision of the Lord and His heavenly hosts. He cried out, "Woe is me! for I am undone; because I am a man of unclean lips, and I dwell in the midst of a people of unclean lips: for mine eyes have seen the King, the Lord of hosts."[44] Immediately, one of the Lord's attendants (called a seraphim — or angel of consuming glory)[45] took a coal from off the golden altar of incense (the only altar with fire inside the temple) and touched it to Isaiah's lips. Then he said, "Lo, this hath touched thy lips; and thine iniquity is taken away, and thy sin purged."[46]

Isaiah then heard the Lord saying to his hosts, "Whom shall I send, and who will go for us?"[47] From these words the prophet could not tell where the messenger was going or what message he was to deliver, but this was of no consequence to this humble man. If the Lord needed an ambassador, Isaiah stood ready. Therefore, he volunteered for the assignment. Said he, "Here am I; send me."[48]

The Lord accepted Isaiah and told him to go forth and make a proclamation. Said the Lord, "Go, and tell this people, Hear ye indeed, but understand not; and see ye indeed, but perceive not. Make the heart of this people fat and make their ears heavy, and shut their eyes; lest they see

---

42. 2 Kings 20:4. Note that the text says middle "court" but the marginal text says "or city."
43. Isaiah 6:1. Nephi verifies this testimony and says, ". . . he [Isaiah] verily saw my Redeemer, even as I have seen him." (2 Nephi 11:2)
44. Isaiah 6:5
45. Clarke, *Bible Commentary*, Vol. 4, p. 51
46. Isaiah 6:7. The touching of a live coal to Isaiah's lips would suggest that this whole account is the description of a vision rather than a physical experience.
47. Isaiah 6:8
48. Ibid.

with their eyes and hear with their ears, and understand with their heart, convert, and be healed."[49]

This strange passage makes it sound as though the Lord was deliberately stultifying His people so they would not be converted and saved from the conquest and dispersion which lay ahead. Dr. Clarke believes the Hebrew idiom would be better rendered as follows: "Ye certainly hear, but do not understand; ye certainly see, but do not acknowledge. Seeing this is the case, make the heart of this people fat — declare it to be stupid and senseless; and remove from them the means of salvation, which they have so long abused."[50]

Based on what Isaiah subsequently said to the people, this version would appear to be the more accurate one.

Isaiah then asked the Lord how long Israel and Judah would be spiritually blind, spiritually deaf, and spiritually fat-hearted. The Lord replied, "Until the cities be wasted without [an] inhabitant, and the houses without man, and the land be utterly desolate. And the Lord have removed men far away, and there be a great forsaking in the midst of the land."[51]

Then the Lord told Isaiah that in "the tenth" or remnant that would be left from the dispersion there was "the holy seed" that had in them the "substance" of survival and that these would return in the due time of the Lord.[52]

ISAIAH'S ENCOUNTER WITH A FAT-HEARTED KING

Three or four years after the above vision the Syrians and Israelites prepared to attack Jerusalem as we related in the last chapter. By this time the king of Judah was Ahaz, grandson of Uzziah. For the sake of the people of Judah, the Lord sent Isaiah to meet this apostate monarch. The conference took place, as we have previously mentioned, "at the end of the conduit of the upper pool in the highway of the fuller's field."[53] The Lord told Isaiah to take his eldest son with him[54] and tell the king to rely upon the Lord and all

---

49. Isaiah 6:9-10
50. Clarke, *Bible Commentary,* Vol. 4, p. 52
51. Isaiah 6:11-12
52. Isaiah 6:13
53. Isaiah 7:3
54. Ibid.

would be well. He was not to form alliances with heathen nations or get all heated up for war because if he obeyed God's counsel, the war being planned by the Syrians and Israelites would never come off. To give confidence to the renegade king, Isaiah was even authorized to have Ahaz test the prophet's integrity by asking for some great sign as proof that God was indeed behind the promise. However, the king declined. In fact, he ignored the advice of the prophet altogether. He made an alliance with the Assyrians, immediately suffered a devastating assault by Syria and Israel, and escaped total defeat only after his enemies were drawn away by the Assyrian attack on Damascus which we have already described in the last chapter.

So much for the life of Isaiah up to this point of our story. We will cross his path again when we come to the reign of the good king Hezekiah. Meanwhile, let us examine a number of the subjects on which Isaiah (and Nephi) left authoritative statements. These are matters which every Bible student should thoroughly understand since a correct interpretation of prophecy and an appreciation of important principles of Gospel doctrine depend upon it.

Isaiah and Nephi Explain the Law of Moses

Many students of the scripture think of Isaiah as being purely a writer on prophecy rather than an expositor of doctrine, but he was both. One of the best examples of Isaiah's doctrinal insights is found in his explanation of the meaning of the Law of Carnal Commandments as given to Moses. Probably no part of the Bible has been more universally misunderstood than these ordinances and precepts. Therefore Isaiah opens his writings by setting forth one of the finest explanations available on the purpose and meaning of the so-called Law of Moses.

To begin with, it is important to realize that Moses received two different canons of law. He first received the Ten Commandments and the Law of the Covenant which have always been a permanent part of the Gospel.[55] It was

---

55. A detailed discussion of this subject is presented in chapters 14 and 15 of *The Third Thousand Years.*

only after the open rebellion of Israel and the Golden Calf incident that the Lord saddled the people with a whole mass of additional detailed ritual and sacrifices ordinarily referred to as the "Law of Moses" or the "Law of Carnal Command-ments." However, Paul points out that these were "added because of transgressions,"[56] and did not typify the procedures which the Lord really desired. They were merely a "school-master" to teach the people the rhythm of obedience. They were temporary, emergency measures to keep the people from exploding to the four winds until after they had brought forth the Christ. Paul says they were laws "which stood only in meats and drinks, and divers washings, and carnal ordi-nances, imposed on them until the time of reformation [the coming of Christ].[57]

All of this was thoroughly understood by Isaiah. He therefore told the people of his own day (whom he compared to the exterminated cities of Sodom and Gomorrah) that all their multitudinous sacrifices contained no intrinsic virtue whatever. He wanted them to know that these were merely teaching devices and did not accomplish one iota of good unless they were accompanied by repentance and a firm resolve to obey God's commandments. Quoting the Lord's own words, he proclaimed:

"To what purpose is the multitude of your sacrifices unto me? saith the Lord: I am full of the burnt offerings of rams, and the fat of fed beasts; and I delight not in the blood of bullocks, or of lambs, or of he goats. . . . Bring no more vain oblations; incense is an abomination unto me; the new moons and sabbaths, the calling of assemblies, I cannot [en-dure them]. . . . Your new moons and your appointed feasts my soul hateth: they are a trouble unto me; I am weary to bear them. And when ye spread forth your hands, I will hide mine eyes from you: yea, when ye make many prayers, I will not hear: YOUR HANDS ARE FULL OF BLOOD!"[58]

Of course, the Lord himself had set up all these pro-cedures, sacrifices, assemblies and ceremonies, but when they

56. Galations 3:19
57. Hebrews 9:10
58. Isaiah 1:10-15

were performed as "vain oblations" without being accompanied by repentance and obedience, God hated them all. As Paul later said, they were a schoolmaster to bring Israel to Christ.[59] If they didn't bring Israel to Christ then all this bleeding, burning, praying and pontificating was nothing more than a meaningless hodgepodge of ritualistic rigmarole. It was taking the name of the Lord their God in vain. It was much to-do about nothing. Therefore, through Isaiah, the Lord cried out to His people:

"Wash you, make you clean; put away the evil of your doings from before mine eyes; cease to do evil; learn to do well; seek judgment, relieve the oppressed, judge the fatherless, plead for the widow. COME NOW, AND LET US REASON TOGETHER, saith the Lord: THOUGH YOUR SINS BE AS SCARLET, THEY SHALL BE AS WHITE AS SNOW; THOUGH THEY BE RED LIKE CRIMSON, THEY SHALL BE AS [white as] WOOL. IF YE BE WILLING AND OBEDIENT, YE SHALL EAT THE GOOD OF THE LAND."[60]

It is interesting that all of Isaiah's prophetic contemporaries — Amos,[61] Hosea[62] and Micah[63] — were preaching exactly this same doctrine, but none as completely and eloquently as Isaiah.

Over in America a few centuries later, the great prophet Nephi was saying to his people, ". . . ye must keep the performances and ordinances of God until the law shall be fulfilled which was given unto Moses."[64] And he left no

---

59. Galations 3:24
60. Isaiah 1:16-19
61. Amos 5:21-24: "I hate, I despise your feast days, and I will not smell in your solemn assemblies. Though ye offer me burnt offerings and your meat offerings, I will not accept them: neither will I regard the peace offerings of your fat beasts. Take thou away from me the noise of thy songs; for I will not hear the melody of thy viols. BUT LET JUDGMENT RUN DOWN AS WATERS, AND RIGHTEOUSNESS AS A MIGHTY STREAM."
62. Hosea 6:6: "For I desired mercy, and not sacrifice; and the knowledge of God more than burnt offerings."
63. Micah 6:6-8: "Wherewith shall I come before the Lord, and bow myself before the high God? shall I come before him with burnt offerings, with calves of a year old? Will the Lord be pleased with thousands of rams, or with ten thousands of rivers of oil? shall I give my firstborn for my transgression, the fruit of my body for the sin of my soul? He hath shewed thee, O man, what is good; and WHAT DOTH THE LORD REQUIRE OF THEE, BUT TO DO JUSTLY, AND TO LOVE MERCY, AND TO WALK HUMBLY WITH THY GOD?"
64. 2 Nephi 25:30

doubt as to the reason. Said he, "And, notwithstanding we believe in Christ, we keep the law of Moses, and look forward with steadfastness unto Christ, until the law shall be fulfilled. For, for this end was the law given; wherefore THE LAW HATH BECOME DEAD UNTO US, and we are made alive in Christ because of our faith; YET WE KEEP THE LAW BECAUSE OF THE COMMANDMENTS.

"And we talk of Christ, we rejoice in Christ, we preach of Christ, we prophesy of Christ, and we write according to our prophecies, that our children may know to what source they may look for a remission of their sins.

"Wherefore, we speak concerning the law that our children may know of the deadness of the law; and they, by knowing the deadness of the law, may look forward unto that life which is in Christ, and KNOW FOR WHAT END THE LAW WAS GIVEN. And after the law is fulfilled in Christ, that they need not harden their hearts against him WHEN THE LAW OUGHT TO BE DONE AWAY.

". . . wherefore I have spoken plainly unto you, that ye cannot misunderstand. And the words which I have spoken shall stand as a testimony against you; for they are sufficient to teach any man the right way; FOR THE RIGHT WAY IS TO BELIEVE IN CHRIST AND DENY HIM NOT; for by denying him ye also deny the prophets and the law."[65]

Thus spoke the prophet Nephi around 550 years before Christ was born. And 200 years before that, Isaiah was preaching the same doctrine to the Israelites!

How Much Did Isaiah Know About Jesus Christ?

We have seen earlier that King David had an astonishing amount of knowledge concerning the life of the Savior, particularly with reference to His crucifixion, even describing some of the words He would say. Isaiah also had a remarkably intimate knowledge concerning the life and mission of Jesus Christ.

---

65. 2 Nephi 25:24-29

For example, one of the most popular Old Testament scriptures referring to the Christ, is Isaiah's famous statement, "For unto us a child is born, unto us a son is given: and the government shall be upon his shoulder: and his name shall be called Wonderful, Counseller, The mighty God, The everlasting Father, The Prince of Peace."[66]

Isaiah, like Nephi[67] and Alma,[68] knew that the Savior would be born of a virgin.[69] The Revised Version of the Bible changes the word, "virgin," to read, "a young woman," but this will not do. The translators of the Septuagint (the most ancient Greek version) understood the word to mean "virgin" and Matthew quoted it for the purpose of demonstrating that this miraculous birth of a child by a virgin had been fulfilled in Jesus.[70] It will be recalled that Isaiah made this prophecy as a "sign" to King Ahaz to prove his prophetic integrity.[71] The only thing which made the prophecy a unique and significant "sign" was the fact that a *virgin* would bear a child. To simply say that "a young woman" would bear a child would be virtually absurd and carry no distinction whatever as "a sign." Thanks to the Book of Mormon, we now have an independent scripture which corroborates the fact that "virgin" is the correct word.[72]

Isaiah also said that this special child, born of a virgin, would be identified as "Immanuel,"[73] which means, "God is with us."[74] John specifically speaks of Jesus in this sense,[75] and early Christian writers often referred to the Savior as "Immanuel."[76]

---

66. Isaiah 9:6
67. 1 Nephi 11:13. Note that Nephi knew from an open vision that the virgin would be "exceedingly fair" and that Nazareth would be her home.
68. Alma 7:10. Note also that Alma was able to reveal what the virgin's name would be, the English transliteration of which is, "Mary." Mosiah gives the same information in Mosiah 3:8.
69. Isaiah 7:14
70. Matthew 1:23
71. Isaiah 7:11-14
72. 1 Nephi 1:13, 15, 18. Note especially Alma 7:10: "And behold, he shall be born of Mary, at [the land of] Jerusalem which is the land of our forefathers, SHE BEING A VIRGIN, a precious and chosen vessel, who shall be overshadowed and conceive by the power of the Holy Ghost, and bring forth a son, yea, even the Son of God."
73. Isaiah 7:14
74. Peloubet's *Bible Dictionary*, under "Immanuel."
75. John 1:14
76. Peloubet's *Bible Dictionary*, also under "Immanuel."

Isaiah knew that Jesus would be a direct descendant of Jesse, the father of King David. However, until modern revelation clarified it, the reference was somewhat obscure. Isaiah simply refers to the term, "stem of Jesse,"[77] incidental to his discussion of a "rod" and a "branch" and a "root."[78] When the Gospel was restored the question was asked concerning the identity of the "stem of Jesse," and the answer came as follows, "Verily, thus saith the Lord: It is Christ."[79] Isaiah therefore knew whereof he spoke when he called the Savior a stem or descendant of Jesse.

Isaiah knew that the ministry of the Savior would be preceded by that of John the Baptist. Isaiah is the source for the scripture which speaks of "The voice of him that crieth in the wilderness, Prepare ye the way of the Lord, make straight in the desert a highway for our God."[80] Both Matthew and John verify that it was John the Baptist whom Isaiah had in mind.[81]

Isaiah knew that during the Savior's ministry, He would reside in the territory originally occupied by the tribe of Zebulun and Naphtali, and that his message of Gospel light would spring from there.[82] Here again, the Bible reference in our modern version of Isaiah is somewhat obscure but Matthew quotes it in a much clearer form and says it was fulfilled when Jesus began his ministry in Capernaum.[83]

ISAIAH'S MESSIANIC CHAPTER

All of chapter fifty-three in the book of Isaiah is about Jesus Christ. Isaiah says He will "grow up" before God as a "tender plant" and as a root sprouting up out of dry ground.[84] Surprisingly, however, Isaiah says the Savior would not be particularly handsome or striking in size and appearance. Isaiah wrote as though he were looking at Jesus in mortality at that very moment and said, "he hath no form nor comeliness; and when we shall see him, there is no beauty that we should desire him."[85] Isaiah also saw how Jesus would be treated:

---

77. Isaiah 11:1
78. Isaiah 11:1, 10
79. Doctrine and Covenants 113:2
80. Isaiah 40:3
81. Matthew 3:3; John 1:23

82. Isaiah 9:1-2
83. Matthew 4:12-16
84. Isaiah 53:2
85. Ibid.

"He is despised and rejected of men; a man of sorrows, and acquainted with grief: and we hid as it were our faces from him: he was despised, and we esteemed him not."[86]

Continuing as though he were watching a vision of Christ's ministry, Isaiah could not help exclaiming:

"Surely he hath borne our griefs, and carried our sorrows: yet we [children of Judah] did esteem him stricken, smitten of God, and afflicted. But he was wounded for our transgressions, he was bruised for our iniquities: the chastisement of our peace was upon him; and with his stripes we are healed."[87]

When Isaiah uses the word "we" he is speaking of the whole human race. He says, "All we like sheep have gone astray; we have turned every one to his own way; and the Lord [the Father] hath laid on him [the Son] the iniquity of us all."[88]

Speaking of the illegal trial and execution of Jesus, Isaiah comments, "He was oppressed, and he was afflicted, yet he opened not his mouth: he is brought as a lamb to the slaughter, and as a sheep before her shearers is dumb, so he openeth not his mouth.[89] He was taken from prison[90] and from judgment:[91] and who shall declare his generation?[92] for he was cut off out of the land of the living: for the transgression of my people was he stricken.[93] And he made

---

86. Isaiah 53:3
87. Isaiah 53:4-5
88. Isaiah 53:6
89. At his trial false witnesses were used against Jesus and when they brought their charges Jesus would not even dignify them with a comment or reply. The High Priest tried to force Him to say something about these charges but "Jesus held his peace." (Matt. 26:63) Finally, the High Priest cried out, "I adjure thee by the living God, that thou tell us whether thou be the Christ, the Son of God." This was not a charge but a question, therefore Jesus condescended to reply. Said He: "Thou hast said [meaning 'it is so']: nevertheless, I say unto you, Hereafter shall ye see the Son of Man sitting on the right hand of power, and coming in the clouds of heaven." (Matt. 26:64)
90. Jesus was in a state of incarceration from the time of His arrest until He was "taken from prison" to be crucified.
91. Pilate gave a judgment which would have set Jesus free but He was taken from that judgment "when Pilate saw that he could prevail nothing" (Matt. 27:24) and turned over to the Roman guard for execution.
92. Jesus had no offspring by which his generation could be perpetuated, therefore He was "cut out of the land of the living."
93. The Septuagint says "smitten to death." (Clarke, *Bible Commentary,* Vol. 4, p. 207)
94. His burial place was near the base of the hill of execution where bodies of criminals were no doubt interred.

his grave with the wicked,[94] and with the rich in his death;[95] because he had done no violence, neither was any deceit in his mouth."[96]

Isaiah knew that the suffering and tribulation of the Savior involved a problem of infinite and profound significance and that by divine necessity His cruel death was an "offering for sin,"[97] which would "justify many; for He shall bear their iniquities."[98] He was also aware that after this terrible ordeal He would receive a great reward and then He would "see his seed."[99] Isaiah closes by quoting the declaration of the Father: "Therefore will I divide him a portion with the great, and he shall divide the spoil with the strong; because he hath poured out his soul unto death: and he was numbered with the transgressors; and he bare the sin of many, and made intercession for the transgressors."[100]

ISAIAH KNEW JEHOVAH WAS THE COMING MESSIAH

No writer of the Old Testament is as clear as Isaiah in addressing the great Jehovah of the Old Testament as the coming Messiah. Many people forget that the God of the Old Testament was the same as the God of New Testament. The Almighty Father, Elohim, did His great work in both ages through His Son. The name of the Son in the Old Testament was Jehovah but after His eternal spirit was born into mortality He became known as Jesus Christ. This is what John was talking about when he said that the Word which was with God [the Father] from the beginning was none other than the Savior: "And the Word was made flesh, and dwelt among us (and we beheld his glory, the

95. Jesus was fortunate in that "a rich man of Arimathaea, named Joseph . . . went to Pilate, and begged for the body of Jesus." (Matt. 27:57-58) This same scripture says Joseph was a disciple of Jesus and he laid the body "in his own new tomb, which he had hewn out in the rock: and he rolled a great stone to the door of the sepulchre and departed." (Matt. 27:60) We learn from John that "in the place where he was crucified there was a garden; and in the garden a new sepulchre, wherein was never man yet laid. There laid they Jesus . . ." (John 19:41-42) No doubt this tomb was at the foot of Golgotha, the place of the skull, where Jesus was crucified. (John 19:17-18)
96. Isaiah 53:7-9
97. Isaiah 53:11
98. Ibid. Anyone desiring to pursue the thrilling ramifications of the Atonement, is referred to a discussion entitled, "Why Was the Atonement Necessary?" which can be found in *The First 2,000 Years*, pp. 352-362.
99. Isaiah 53:10
100. Isaiah 53:12

glory of THE ONLY BEGOTTEN OF THE FATHER) full of grace and truth."[101]

But even recognizing this to be so, certain passages in the patriarchal writings are confusing because they imply that it is the Father, Elohim, who is talking instead of Jehovah, His Son. Take for example, the revelation to Moses. Moses saw a vision of God's vast creation and then asked how it had all been done. The divine personage with whom he was talking "face to face"[102] replied, ". . . by the word of my power, have I created them, which is MINE ONLY BE-GOTTEN SON, who is full of grace and truth."[103] Certainly this sounds like the Father talking.

It turns out that the key to this problem is found in the fact that heavenly messengers, including Jehovah, often deliver a message in the first person, so that there will be no mistake in the mind of the listener as to its source. Therefore, it would be perfectly correct for Moses to say that the Father told him His creations were by His Only Begotten Son. But if Moses testified that it was the Father who appeared before him and gave him this message, he would be in error. This kind of erroneous conclusion was reached by John the Beloved on the Isle of Patmos. A glorious being appeared before him and after showing John great visions of the future, John concluded that this personage standing in glory before him was none other than the Savior. He therefore bowed down to worship him, but the heavenly messenger was horrified and said, "See thou do it not: for I am thy fellowservant, and OF THY BRETHREN THE PROPHETS, and of them which keep the sayings of this book: worship God."[104] This was the second time John had become confused and tried to worship this glorious personage.[105] After John was restrained the second time, the angel who had described himself as one of the prophets started delivering his message in the first person and one can easily see why John kept getting the idea that this was his glorified Friend and Master. Listen to this amazing statement by the angel right after he had rebuked John the second time, ". . . behold, I come quickly;

---

101. John 1:14
102. Moses 1:31
103. Moses 1:32

104. Revelations 22:9
105. The first occasion is referred to in Revelations 19:10.

and my reward is with me, to give every man according as his work shall be. I am Alpha and Omega, the beginning and the end, the first and the last."[106] No person in his right mind who has had any experience with God's work would mistake the full implications of this statement. These are clearly the words of Jesus Christ and they fit no one else! However, it was not Jesus Christ who was standing before John reciting these words of Jesus. This is what the angel was trying to make clear to John. The angel was simply delivering a message from Jesus but doing it in the first person.

Now it will be more readily appreciated why Isaiah constantly addressed Jehovah in the Old Testament as his Redeemer and Savior. Even though Jehovah sometimes spoke as though He were the Father, Isaiah knew it was the Son, Jehovah, the coming Redeemer of Israel, who was delivering the Father's message in the first person. Twelve different times he refers to Jehovah as the Redeemer,[107] and on eight occasions he identifies Him as the Savior.[108] Notice such clear-cut statements as these which demonstrate Isaiah's knowledge that he was dealing with the future Jesus Christ:

"I, even I, am the Lord; and beside me there is no Saviour."

". . . O God of Israel, the Saviour."

"I the Lord am thy Saviour and thy Redeemer."

"And the Redeemer shall come to Zion."

"Thus saith the Lord, thy redeemer, and he that formed thee from the womb."

Of course, it would be legitimate to inquire whether Isaiah may not have been using the words "Redeemer" and "Savior" in their political sense rather than a religious sense. It could be argued that ultimately the Lord was going to be their Savior from political captivity and their Redeemer from further exploitation and conquest. Isaiah, however, left no doubt as to his true meaning. He had seen the Savior (Isaiah 6:1, 5) and Nephi verifes it (2 Nephi 11:2). He

---

106. Revelations 22:12-13. Note that in talking to Isaiah the Lord also used this final phrase: "Hearken unto me, O Jacob . . . I am he; I am the first, I also am the last." (Isaiah 48:12)
107. Isaiah 41:14; 43:14; 44:6; 44:24; 47:4; 48:17; 49:7; 54:5; 54:8; 59:20; 60:16; 63:16.
108. Isaiah 19:20; 43:3; 43:11; 45:15; 45:21; 49:26; 60:16; 63.8.

wanted it understood that he was talking about the very Redeemer who "was wounded for our transgressions, he was bruised for our iniquities . . . and with his stripes we are healed."[109] Isaiah said he was talking about the Man of Sorrows who "poured out his soul unto death" as an "offering for sin."[110] Even Paul could not have been plainer!

After the death and resurrection of the Savior, His disciples were anxious that Jesus be recognized and appreciated as the Jehovah of the Old Testament. We have already cited John's declaration that "the Word" had been made flesh and "dwelt among us." Jesus, himself, made emphatic reference to His former status on a number of occasions. At the Last Supper He prayed, "And now, O Father, glorify thou me with thine own self with the glory which I had with thee before the world was."[111] Later He prayed, "Father, I will that they also, whom thou hast given me, be with me where I am; that they may behold my glory . . . for thou lovedst me before the foundation of the world."[112] Even to the apostate Pharisees Jesus boldly declared, "Verily, verily, I say unto you, Before Abraham was, I am."[113]

Early Christian writers emphasized the role Jesus had formerly occupied as the Jehovah of the Old Testament. In his *Church History,* Eusebius called his second chapter, "Summary View of the Pre-existence and Divinity of Our Saviour and Lord Jesus Christ." In paragraph 8 of his fourth chapter Eusebius says, "But they [the prophets] also clearly knew the very Christ of God; for it has already been shown that he appeared unto Abraham, that he imparted revelations to Isaac, and he talked with Jacob, that he held converse with Moses and with the prophets that came after." This, of course, has reference to the days when He was known to the patriarchs and prophets as Jehovah. But, as we have seen in our study of Isaiah, Enoch, Joseph, Moses and David, those great men were well aware that this glorious being who ministered to them was the Messiah, the coming Jesus Christ.

---

109. Isaiah 53:5
110. Isaiah 53:10-12
111. John 17:5
112. John 17:24
113. John 8:58

Isaiah Anticipates Christ's Missionary Work
to the Dead

In one extremely choice passage, Isaiah deals with a perplexing problem which has tantalized the minds of men down through the ages: What happens to the wicked when they die?

Glorious hope has always been held out for the righteous and obedient, but what about the wicked? Doesn't God have any hope for them? The Greeks pondered this question as though it were something of most profound significance. So did the Babylonians and Egyptians. Plato's last "book" or chapter of his *Republic* deals almost exclusively with this question and fragments of truth will be found sprinkled here and there even though the bulk of it is man-made fiction. But Isaiah knew more about this question than Plato even though he wrote less.

Isaiah's reference to this question is raised in connection with his description of events which will occur at the time of the Second Coming. This discussion involves the entire twenty-fourth chapter. He describes how the earth will "reel to and fro like a drunkard"[114] and the destruction of mankind will be so universal that it will leave the planet virtually emptied"[115] and "few men left."[116]

But what happens to all of these? What happens to the kings, the "high ones"[117] as well as to the hosts of common people who are thus destroyed for their wickedness? Isaiah had the answer. Said he, "And they shall be gathered together, as prisoners are gathered in the pit (dungeon[118]), and shall be shut up in the prison, AND AFTER MANY DAYS THEY SHALL BE VISITED."[119]

We learn from another scripture that the wicked who were destroyed at the time of the Great Flood were also held in such a prison until they could be visited.[120] David knew that his spirit would spend some time in this prison because of his disobedience. (Psalms 16:9-10) Alma was

114. Isaiah 24:20
115. Isaiah 24:3
116. Isaiah 24:6
117. Isaiah 24:21

118. Marginal reading says "dungeon."
119. Isaiah 24:22
120. 1 Peter 3:19-20

told by an angel that this is where all of the unrighteous go and their condition is exactly what you would expect in a vast assembly of habitually violent and reprobate people.[121] Undoubtedly is this the very condition which helps humble them and prepare them to welcome the messengers of the Gospel when they finally come. In fact, this is probably the very reason why they are left in this state for "many days" before relief is offered to them. They must develop eyes that can see and ears that can hear before they are visited.

Isaiah knew that it would be the Savior who would initiate the program of teaching the Gospel to the dead. Isaiah recorded that an important part of the Savior's role as "a light to the Gentiles," would be to visit these rebellious souls in their spirit-world prison in order "To open the blind eyes, to bring out the prisoners from the prison, and them that sit in darkness out of the prison house."[122] In other words, He would seek to have them accept the Gospel, discontinue their rebellion against God, and agree to embrace the great plan of salvation designed for man's eternal joy and progression.

It is interesting that when Jesus came to earth and commenced His ministry among men, He quoted Isaiah to show that He knew His mission included the preaching of the Gospel to both the living and the dead. Standing up in the synagogue of His own hometown in Nazareth, Jesus read this passage from the book of Isaiah:

"The Spirit of the Lord God is upon me; because the Lord hath anointed me to preach good tidings unto the meek; he hath sent me to bind up the brokenhearted, TO PROCLAIM LIBERTY TO THE CAPTIVES, AND THE OPENING OF THE PRISON TO THEM THAT ARE BOUND; to proclaim the acceptable year of the Lord. . . ."[123]

When Jesus had read this passage to the people he told them He had come to fulfill it.[124] He first preached the Gospel to the living but after He had been crucified His disembodied spirit crossed over into the spirit world. There He found the

---

121. Alma 40:14
122. Isaiah 42:6-7
123. Isaiah 61:1-2. Note that the Isaiah text is clearer concerning the preaching of the Gospel to those in prison than the briefer version given in Luke 4:18-19.

righteous in a state of supreme happiness and joyful activity[125] while the unrighteous were being held back in a place of confinement or imprisonment (which is what "damnation" means) until they could be taught to behave in some degree or other like sons and daughters of God.[126]

As Jesus entered the spirit world the time for His preaching to the dead had arrived. Peter says, "For Christ . . . being put to death in the flesh, but quickened by the Spirit: by which also he went and preached to the spirits in prison."[127] Apparently as of that time (around 33 A.D.) the vast majority of those who made up the inhabitants of the spirit-world prison were the massive throngs who had been destroyed at the time of the Great Flood. Peter therefore makes special reference to them,[128] thereby implying that in spite of the many millions of wicked humans who had died since the Flood, nevertheless, the great hosts who populated the earth in the days of Noah and were drowned in the Flood, still constituted the dominant population in the spirit-world prison when Christ first visited there.

And these had waited "many days" indeed — over 2,300 years! Surely they must have been almost frantic with anticipation as they waited with voracious appetites for the meat of the Gospel. And excitement must have run equally high among the righteous Saints as Jesus organized His Priesthood and prepared to launch the gigantic project of preaching His message of liberty and hope to the dead.[129]

---

124. Luke 4:21
125. Alma 40:12. Jesus sought to demonstrate the separation of the righteous from the wicked and their respective circumstances in the spirit world when He related the parable of Lazarus and the rich man. (Luke 16:19-31)
126. And the degree of their response determines the degree of glory they will receive. (Doctrine and Covenants, Section 76)
127. 1 Peter 3:18-19
128. 1 Peter 3:20
129. The mammoth undertaking which was necessary to preach the Gospel to the dead is described by a modern prophet, Joseph F. Smith: "And as I wondered, my eyes were opened, and my understanding quickened, and I perceived that the Lord went not in person among the wicked and the disobedient who had rejected the truth, to teach them; but behold, from among the righteous he organized his forces and appointed messengers, clothed with power and authority, and commissioned them to go forth and carry the light of the gospel to them that were in darkness, even to all the spirits of men. And thus was the gospel preached to the dead. And the chosen messengers went forth to declare the acceptable day of the Lord, and proclaim liberty to the captives who were bound; even unto all who would repent of their sins and receive the gospel. Thus was the gospel preached to those who had died in their sins, without a

The news of their coming must have been electrifying. What an acclamation of thanksgiving and rejoicing must have echoed through the dismal darkness of that awful hell-milieu as the cry passed in all directions, "They are coming! They are coming!"

Peter said, "For for this cause was the Gospel preached also to them that are dead, that they might be judged according to men in the flesh, but live according to God in the spirit."[130] This, then, was the glorious event the prophet Isaiah had promised.

---

knowledge of the truth, or in transgression, having rejected the prophets. These were taught faith in God, repentance from sin, vicarious baptism for the remission of sins, the gift of the Holy Ghost by the laying on of hands, and all other principles of the gospel that were necessary for them to know in order to qualify themselves that they might be judged according to men in the flesh, but live according to God in the spirit." (*Gospel Doctrine*, Salt Lake City: Deseret Book, 1961, p. 474)

130. 1 Peter 4:6

Scripture Readings and Questions on Chapter Nineteen

Scripture Reading: Isaiah, chapters 1 to 39 inclusive.

1—Over approximately how many years do the prophecies of Isaiah refer? What other prophet is comparable in his prophetic writings to Isaiah?

2—Name the three things which make Isaiah difficult to read.

3—What made Nephi the ideal person to write a commentary on Isaiah? What motivated him to write it? What did he say was his main purpose in recording his commentary?

4—Why have some scholars attributed the book of Isaiah to several authors? How does the Book of Mormon clarify this problem?

5—Approximately how long was Isaiah active as a prophet? What part of what century?

6—Why was Isaiah's humility mistaken by his adversaries as evidence of pride and boasting? Did the same thing happen to Jesus?

7—To whom did Isaiah attribute his gift of eloquence? What did Isaiah mean when he described himself as a polished shaft in the quiver of the Lord?

8—Why did Isaiah get discouraged? What did the people do to him? What did he have in common with prophets like Noah, Abraham, Jeremiah and Mormon?

9—What did Isaiah tell the people about writing down his words? Why? What tribe recorded his words on the Brass Plates? What happened to them?

10—What were the details of the occasion when Isaiah saw a vision of the Lord in the temple?

11—Moses received two sets of laws. What were they? How were they different?

12—What was the attitude of the Nephites toward the Law of Moses?

13—Name two reasons why the mother of Jesus should have been referred to as a "virgin" rather than merely "a young woman"?

14—Who is the "stem of Jesse"? Who was Jesse? Who was his most outstanding son?

15—Which is the great "Messianic Chapter" in Isaiah? What does the word "Messianic" mean?

16—What deduction can be drawn from Isaiah's frequent reference to Jehovah as "Redeemer," and "Savior"? Could this possibly have been referring just to political and military blessings?

17—Give two proofs that Jehovah of the Old Testament is identical with Jesus Christ of the New Testament.

18—What did Isaiah say the Lord had in mind for the wicked and rebellious of the earth? What happens to them in the spirit world?

19—About how long had the majority of the wicked been waiting for the Gospel to be preached to them? What was the Lord's purpose in keeping them waiting?

20—Who initiated the program for the preaching of the Gospel to the dead? Who actually went in among the wicked to give them Christ's message?

CHAPTER TWENTY

The Closing Years of Isaiah's Ministry

Once the Bible reader grasps the scope of Isaiah's prophesies he cannot help being amazed at the vast, encyclopedia of foreknowledge which the Lord entrusted to this one man. In fact, it is so extensive that it has completely baffled the credulity of some modern scholars. They have ended up refusing to believe that Isaiah could have had such extensive powers.[1] Imagine, being able to name Cyrus 200 years before he was born! They explain such remarkable prophecies by saying that some scheming scribes inserted these passages *after* the event had happened and thereby gave Isaiah credit for something he did not do.[2] This is pure assumption, of course, and they admit they have no proof for this charge. However, to them it seems unreasonable to assume otherwise.

Fortunately, those who have access to the Book of Mormon possess an independent scripture which completely corroborates the fact that Isaiah did have this remarkable prophetic power. It further discloses that he possessed an addi-

---

1. See "The Predictive Element in Prophecy," in Dr. Sidney B. Sperry's *The Old Testament Prophets*, p. 8-9.
2. Ibid.

tional quantity of information which is not even included in the Bible.[3]

In order to best appreciate the prophecies of Isaiah, we will treat them chronologically. In other words, we will start with the prophecies concerning his own day and then follow through each major event he mentions until we reach our own day. Isaiah was one of those who knew a great deal about this marvelous age of miracles in which we now live. Isaiah also knew the devastating disasters which could summarily sweep us into oblivion if we failed to do our part. In some ways, Isaiah knew us better than we know ourselves, and that is why he addressed so many vigorous warnings to our dispensation. We shall commence, however, by examining the warnings which he gave to his own people.

Isaiah Itemizes the Sins of Israel

It will be recalled that Isaiah's ministry was well on its way by 739 B.C., and therefore we know he was proclaiming his message of pleading and warning for more than twenty years before Israel fell in 721 B.C. All during that time he was denouncing the violence, immorality and criminal dishonesty of the people and predicting what would happen if they did not repent.

When it came to excoriating and peeling off the hides of the apostate Israelites, none of the prophets was more specific or articulate than Isaiah. Note, for example, his denunciation of the widespread problem of alcoholism:

"Woe to the crown of pride, to the drunkards of Ephraim, whose glorious beauty is a fading flower . . . the priest and the prophet[4] have erred through strong drink, they are swallowed up of wine, they are out of the way through strong drink; they err in vision, they stumble in judgment. For all tables are full of vomit and filthiness, so that there is no place clean."[5]

---

3. This is made clear in Nephi's commentary on Isaiah which we shall consider shortly.
4. We have already seen that the heathen priests of Baal were called "prophets" in Israel even though "false prophets" would have been more apt. (1 Kings 18:22)
5. Isaiah 28:1, 7-8

Sorrowfully, Isaiah exclaimed, "Ah sinful nation, a people laden with iniquity, a seed of evildoers, children that are corrupters: they have forsaken the Lord, they have provoked the Holy One of Israel unto anger, they are gone away backward."[6]

In all Israel he tried to find some level of society, or some corner in the nation where righteousness still prevailed, but he said, ". . . the whole head is sick, and the whole heart faint. From the sole of the foot even unto the head there is no soundness in it; but wounds, and bruises, and putrifying sores. . . ."[7] He accused them of beating the people to pieces,[8] grinding the face of the poor,[9] taking away their land,[10] indulging in pomp, pride and agnosticism.[11] In addition, they had turned the world upside down by destroying all moral standards and the means of measuring excellence. He said they called "evil good, and good evil," they put "darkness for light, and light for darkness . . . bitter for sweet, and sweet for bitter!"[12] He said even the widows and orphans had been corrupted.[13] The great display of temporary prosperity had given many of the people a sense of security but Isaiah said it was a mirage which would fade away. He said the people had "multiplied the nation" with their conquests but not "increased the joy."[14] Instead of genuine, wholesome joy which comes from righteousness, the people were living in a drunken dream world. Cried Isaiah, "Woe unto them that rise up early in the morning, that they may follow strong drink; that continue until night, till wine inflame them! And the harp, and the viol, and tabret, and pipe, and wine, are in their feasts: but they regard not the work of the Lord, neither consider the operation of his hands."[15]

THE WOMEN OF ISRAEL

A particularly sharp and cutting barb was aimed by Isaiah at the female population of Israel.

". . . the daughters of Zion are haughty and walk with stretched forth necks and wanton eyes, walking and mincing

---

6. Isaiah 1:4
7. Isaiah 1:5-6
8. Isaiah 3:15
9. Ibid.
10. Isaiah 5:8

11. Isaiah 5:14, 18-23
12. Isaiah 5:20
13. Isaiah 9:17
14. Isaiah 9:3
15. Isaiah 5:11-12

as they go, and making a tinkling with their feet: therefore the Lord will smite with a scab the crown of the head of the daughters of Zion. . . . In that day the Lord will take away the bravery of their tinkling ornaments about their feet, and their cauls and their round tires like the moon, the chains, and the bracelets, and the mufflers, the bonnets, and the ornaments of the legs, and the headbands, and the tablets, and the earrings, the [finger] ring, and the nose jewels, the changeable suits of apparel, and the mantles, and the wimples, and the crisping pins, the glasses, and the fine linen, and the hoods, and the vails. And it shall come to pass, that instead of sweet smell there shall be stink; and instead of a girdle a rent; and instead of well set hair baldness; and instead of a stomacher a girding or sackcloth; and burning instead of beauty."[16]

It is interesting to contemplate how the debutantes of Samaria (not to mention their mothers) reacted to a shin-barking sermon like that one!

ISRAELITES ACCUSED OF IGNORING COVENANTS
MADE AT BAPTISM

From the earliest times, the Lord had emphasized the importance of baptism and the necessity of keeping the covenants made at the time this sacred ordinance is performed. In chapter 48 of the book of Isaiah, the Lord restates His great controversy with Israel. One of the more prominent charges is the fact that Israel had taken oaths in the name of the Lord and made covenants through baptism but had afterwards broken them.

The Book of Mormon version of this chapter is more correct than the one appearing in the Bible, and we shall therefore use it to present the Lord's point of view on this problem. The capital letters indicate significant words which appear only in the Book of Mormon version.

"Hearken, and hear this, O house of Jacob, who are called by the name of Israel, and are come forth out of the waters of Judah, OR OUT OF THE WATERS OF BAP-TISM, who swear by the name of the Lord, and make men-

---

16. Isaiah 3:16-24

tion of the God of Israel, yet they swear not in truth, nor in righteousness. Nevertheless, they call themselves of the holy city, BUT THEY DO NOT stay themselves upon the God Israel, who is the Lord of Hosts; yea, the Lord of Hosts is his name."[17]

The Lord states in this same chapter that He has always told Israel what He intended to do long in advance "lest thou shouldest say, Mine idol hath done them, and my graven image, and my molten image hath commanded them."[18] Through Isaiah He now puts Israel on notice that a whole debacle of calamity is about to be unleashed upon the people because of their stubborn, perverted and diabolical wickedness.

ISAIAH PREDICTS THE FALL OF ISRAEL

Isaiah was well acquainted with the haughty sneers which these egotistical sychophants focused on him whenever he had tried to get them to abandon their swill-barrel lives. Said he, "Woe unto them that are wise in their own eyes, and prudent in their own sight."[19] Then looking into the immediate future, he spoke as though the events were happening right before his eyes. Said he, "Your country is desolate, your cities are burned with fire: your land, strangers devour it in your presence, and it is desolate. . . ."[20] All that the prudent and the wise of Israel had believed impossible would suddenly sweep in on them like a flood.[21] It would wipe out most of them in a single day, particularly the leaders.[22] No foreign aid or alliance could possibly save them.[23] Those who resisted (and were put under siege) would eat their own dead.[24]

Quoting the Lord further, Isaiah said, "Upon the land of my people shall come up thorns and briers; yea, upon all the houses of joy in the joyous city: because the palaces shall be forsaken; the multitude of the city shall be left [gone]; the forts and towers shall be for dens for ever, a joy of wild asses, a pasture of flocks."[25]

---

17. 1 Nephi 20:1-2; Isaiah 48:1-2
18. Isaiah 48:5
19. Isaiah 5:21
20. Isaiah 1:7
21. Isaiah 8:7-8
22. Isaiah 9:14
23. Isaiah 8:9-10, 12
24. Isaiah 9:20
25. Isaiah 32:13-14

Isaiah made no secret of the source of all this destruction. He quoted the Lord who had said, "O Assyrian, the rod of mine anger, and the staff in their hand is mine indignation. I will send him against an hypocritical nation, and against the people of my wrath will I give him a charge, to take the spoil, and to take the prey, and to tread them down like the mire of the streets."[26]

In that hour "shall Ephraim be broken, that it be not a people!"[27]

The terrifying king of Assyria who performed this task of obliterating the last vestiges of Israel in 721 B.C., was Sargon II, son of Shalmaneser V. Among the ruins of Sargon's magnificent palace at Khorasbad were found these engraved words: "At the beginning of my rule, in the very first year I reigned . . . I set siege to and conquered Samaria."[28]

Isaiah, himself, lived to see all of this come to pass. He witnessed the nation of ten tribes which Jeroboam had launched in 922 B.C. come to its inglorious demise 201 years later. Of course, Sargon II gloried in what he had accomplished, but he had no idea that this victory would have never occurred had not the Lord stepped aside and allowed it. Sargon therefore gave credit to Assur, his heathen deity, and boasted in the strength of his own mighty arm as well as the heroism of his massive hosts encased in armors of brass. Had he consulted with Isaiah he would have learned that in a little more than a century, Assyria would be drowning in its own blood and the majestic city of Nineveh would be disintegrating into a multitude of huge, brown, mud mounds. Isaiah knew all about it.

THE STATE OF AFFAIRS IN JUDAH

Isaiah, of course, maintained his headquarters in Jerusalem, not in the precincts of the beleaguered Samaria. While Isaiah's troubled mind had been dwelling upon the ravaging conquest going on in Israel, a much more pleasant development was taking place in Jerusalem. In fact, some six years[29] before the fall of Israel, Jerusalem had seen the

---

26. Isaiah 10:5-6   28. Keyes, *Story of the Bible World*, p. 83
27. Isaiah 7:8   29. 2 Kings 18:10-11

end of the wicked and apostate King Ahaz. His place had been taken by his son, Hezekiah, who turned out to be one of the most notable cases in history of an unusually righteous son coming from the home and environment of an extremely wicked father. If all the facts were known we might discover that much of the credit for this righteous son belonged to the careful tutoring of his mother, but of this we are not sure. Certainly someone deserves a lot of credit. The Bible says that Hezekiah replaced his father, Ahaz, and immediately initiated a universal reform with a crash program to restore the true worship of God. Any physical object which Hezekiah found the people worshiping, he immediately ordered destroyed. This included one of the most sacred relics handed down from the days of Moses — the "Brasen Serpent." Hezekiah discovered the people offering incense to it, so he commanded that it be broken to pieces.[30]

There was such a contrast between Hezekiah and his father that the scripture is glowing in its praise of this new king. The Bible says, "And he did that which was right in the sight of the Lord, according to all that David his father [forefather] did. . . . He removed the high places, and brake the images, and cut down the groves. . . . He trusted in the Lord God of Israel; so that after him was none like him among all the kings of Judah nor any that were before him."[31] This is high praise, indeed.

Hezekiah Repairs, Sanctifies and Re-dedicates the Temple

To Isaiah, the coming of Hezekiah must have seemed almost too good to be true. From the cold, wretched days of apostasy and persecution under Ahaz, Judah suddenly emerged into the warm springtime of a glorious re-birth.

Barely were the coronation ceremonies over before the twenty-five-year-old Hezekiah began "in the first month" to repair the temple so that its doors could be opened once more to regular worship of Jehovah.[32] During the years of neglect under Ahaz the sacred precincts of the house of the

---

30. 2 Kings 18:4
31. 2 Kings 18:3-5
32. 2 Chronicles 29:1-3

Lord had become cluttered with rubble. But no more so than the lives of the people, including the priests. Therefore, as soon as the temple was repaired, Hezekiah began the most extensive program of repentance, reformation and sanctification the land had known in several generations. He called the apostate and lazy Levites in a conference and said unto them:

"Hear me, ye Levites, sanctify now yourselves, and sanctify the house of the Lord God of your fathers, and carry forth the filthiness out of the holy place. For our fathers have trespassed, and done that which was evil in the eyes of the Lord our God. . . . Also they have shut up the doors of the porch [of the temple], and put out the lamps, and have not burned incense nor offered burnt offerings. . . . Wherefore the wrath of the Lord was upon Judah . . . our fathers have fallen by the sword, and our sons and our daughters and our wives are in captivity for this. Now it is in mine heart to make a covenant with the Lord God of Israel, that his fierce wrath may turn away from us."[33]

Then he made a direct appeal to these custodians of the lesser Priesthood: "My sons, be not now negligent: for the Lord hath chosen you to stand before him, to serve him, and that ye should minister unto him. . . ."[34] A certain percentage of these Levites responded to the call, but we gain the impression from later statements that it was only the more valiant who responded and therefore a minority of the tribe.[35] The scripture continues:

"And they gathered their brethren, and sanctified themselves, and came, according to the commandment of the king. . . . And the priests[36] went into the inner part of the house of the Lord, to cleanse it, and brought out all the uncleanness that they found in the temple of the Lord into the court of

33. 2 Chronicles 29:5-10
34. 2 Chronicles 29:11
35. Both the scriptures and secular history clearly demonstrate that in a time of crisis those who respond to the need of the hour have nearly always been merely a valiant minority. It seems to be a social-political rule of life as well as a spiritual phenomenon.
36. The Priests were those Levites who were direct descendants of Aaron. The remainder of the Levites held offices comparable to Teacher and Deacon today. Only the Priests could go inside the Temple.

the house of the Lord. And the Levites took it, to carry it out abroad into the brook Kidron."[37]

Once everything had been cleaned up, the priests prepared for the re-dedication of the temple. As at the time of the original dedication, this ritual required eight days of extremely laborious and precise procedure.[38] On the eighth day Hezekiah came with all "the rulers of the city" and had the priests make a special sacrifice as an atonement for the wickedness of the whole people "for the king commanded that the burnt offering and the sin offering should be made for all Israel."[39]

Then the king had the choirs and orchestras assemble themselves. All the people "sang praises with gladness, and they bowed their heads and worshipped."[40] In fact, from the time that the burning of the sacrifice commenced until it was completely consumed "the singers sang, and the trumpeters sounded."[41] It was a most glorious time of rejoicing.

Then the king invited the people to bring forth their burnt offerings, peace offerings, and oblations just as Solomon had done at the first dedication.[42] But there were immediate complications. As the people brought forth seventy bullocks, a hundred rams and two hundred lambs THERE WERE NOT ENOUGH WORTHY PRIESTS TO TAKE CARE OF THE OFFERING. This was not really a great many animals compared to the original dedication but it was too many for the number of worthy priests. The scripture says, "the priests were too few, so that they could not flay all the burnt offerings: wherefore their brethren the Levites did help them, till the work was ended, and UNTIL THE OTHER PRIESTS HAD SANCTIFIED THEMSELVES: FOR THE LEVITES WERE MORE UP-

37. 2 Chronicles 29:15-16. Note that the Levites could only help dispose of the rubbish after it was brought out of the Temple by the Priests.
38. 2 Chronicles 29:17. This procedure is described in more detail in chapter 9 of this book where we discuss the original dedication of Solomon's Temple.
39. 2 Chroncles 29:24
40. 2 Chronicles 29:27, 30
41. 2 Chronicles 29:28
42. 2 Chronicles 29:31-33

RIGHT IN HEART TO SANCTIFY THEMSELVES
THAN THE PRIESTS."[43]

When the former King Ahaz had closed the temple
in order to initiate heathen practices, it had left the sons of
Aaron (the Priests) and the Levites with practically nothing
to do. In one generation they had gone back into secular
life and lost themselves in the mundane affairs of the people.
It was therefore quite a revolutionary undertaking to have
them all called on missions to once more function in their
Priesthood offices. As we shall see, this calling caught the
sons of Aaron or Priests especially off guard. The scripture
says "the thing was done suddenly."[44]

HEZEKIAH'S GREAT FEAST OF THE PASSOVER

Since the re-dedication of the Temple took place in
the first month of the year, it came into Hezekiah's heart to
immediately prepare the people for a great Feast of the
Passover which was always supposed to be celebrated in
the second month. However, the Bible says "they had not
done it of a long time,"[45] and it gives the following reasons
why: "For they could not keep it at that time [in the former
days], BECAUSE THE PRIESTS HAD NOT SANCTI-
FIED THEMSELVES SUFFICIENTLY, neither had the
people gathered themselves together to Jerusalem."[46]

Hezekiah was so enthused about the possibility of restoring the Passover to its former prominence as the principle
feast of the year that he sent invitations to every part of
ancient Israel. Not only were letters on royal parchment
dispatched to all sections of Judah but he ventured to invite
any fragments of the other tribes that might be found "from
Beer-sheba [in the south] even to Dan [in the north]."[47] His
invitation was specifically designed to appeal to those who
were remnants of the other tribes. It must be kept in mind
that these events happened just before the fall of Samaria,
but several years following the conquest of northern and

---

43. 2 Chronicles 29:34. Whenever there were not enough Priests, the Levites were
    asked to help with the arduous work of skinning, cleaning and washing the
    sacrificial animals. It is in this same spirit that Deacons and Teachers assist
    the Priests today.
44. 2 Chronicles 29:36   46. 2 Chronicles 30:3
45. 2 Chronicles 30:5   47. 2 Chronicles 30:5

eastern Israel by Assyria. Hezekiah's appeal was therefore to King Hoshea and the remnants around the capital city of Samaria. He wrote:

"Ye children of Israel, turn again unto the Lord God of Abraham, Isaac, and Israel, and he will return to the REM- NANT OF YOU, THAT ARE ESCAPED OUT OF THE HAND OF THE KINGS OF ASSYRIA. And be not like your fathers, and like your brethren, which tres- passed against the Lord God of their fathers, who therefore gave them up to desolation, as ye see." (2 Chron. 30:6-7.)

Since Hezekiah knew that King Hoshea of Israel and most of the "remnants" were practicing heathens his appeal focussed primarily on one of their most sensitive sentiments — their concern for their loved ones in captivity. He therefore said, "Now be ye not stiffnecked, as your fathers were, but yield yourselves unto the Lord, and enter into his sanctuary. . . . FOR IF YE TURN AGAIN UNTO THE LORD, [then] YOUR BRETHREN AND YOUR CHILDREN SHALL FIND COMPASSION BEFORE THEM [the Assyrians] THAT LEAD THEM CAPTIVE, so that they shall come again into this land: for the Lord your God is gracious and merciful, and will not turn away his face from you, IF YE RETURN UNTO HIM."[48]

As might have been expected, when Hezekiah's messen- gers delivered these invitations to King Hoshea and to the few remaining fragments of the apostate northern tribes, "they laughed them to scorn, and mocked them."[49] But the effort was not entirely in vain. The scripture says a "divers" few heeded the call, "humbled themselves, and came to Jeru- salem."[50] There they found that the people of Judah had come together in a mammoth congregation. They were united with "one heart to do the commandment of the king . . . by the word of the Lord."[51]

"Then they killed the passover on the fourteenth day of the second month: AND THE PRIESTS AND THE LEVITES WERE ASHAMED, AND SANCTIFIED

---

48. 2 Chronicles 30:8-9
49. 2 Chronicles 30:10
50. 2 Chronicles 30:11
51. 2 Chronicles 30:12

THEMSELVES. . . ."[52] We interpret this to mean that many who had been holding back came forward to perform their duties for the scripture continues, "And they stood in their place after their manner, according to the law of Moses. . . ."[53]

It will be recalled that the first Passover was eaten the night before the Children of Israel fled out of Egypt. In connection with it they also commenced eating unleavened bread because they had to bake their dough without having time to leaven it. Therefore the Feast of Unleavened Bread was supposed to be celebrated each year for a period of seven days, commencing with the Feast of the Passover. Hezekiah ordered that this be done. However, the scripture says that the people who assembled in Jerusalem on this notable occasion had such a magnificent time of rejoicing during the first seven days that "the whole assembly took counsel to keep [or celebrate] other seven days!"[54] So altogether they were united in celebrating this great occasion of feasting and covenant-making for a period of approximately half-a-month.

So many new converts had swarmed in upon the Priests during this conference that Hezekiah was fearful lest some small technicalities might have been overlooked in the mass-sanctification of so many people. He was also concerned lest the exact procedure would not have been followed by all of the people in connection with the Passover. Hezekiah therefore made a special appeal to the Lord to overlook such technicalities. He prayed, "[May] the good Lord pardon every one that prepareth his heart to seek God, the Lord God of his fathers, though he be not cleansed according to the purification of the sanctuary."[55] The Lord had emphasized to his prophets from earliest times that the main part of a sacrifice was the heart or attitude of the individual making the offering. Technicalities are incidental. Therefore, "the Lord hearkened to Hezekiah, and healed the people."[56]

So the scripture concludes, "And all the congregation of Judah, with the priests and the Levites, and all the con-

---

52. 2 Chronicles 30:15
53. 2 Chronicles 30:16
54. 2 Chronicles 30:23

55. 2 Chronicles 30:18-19
56. 2 Chronicles 30:20

gregation that came out of Israel, and the strangers [non-Israelite converts] that came out of the land of Israel, and that dwelt in Judah, rejoiced. So there was great joy in Jerusalem: for since the time of Solomon the son of David king of Israel there was not the like in Jerusalem."[57]

One final note should be mentioned concerning the generosity of Hezekiah during this period of public feasting and celebrating. Much of it was made possible because the king, like Solomon before him, was willing to contribute thousands of head of sheep and cattle to feed them. His princes also joined in this manifestation of generosity so that altogether the people had 2,000 bullocks and 17,000 sheep to feed upon during this gigantic general conference in Jerusalem.[58]

THE FRUITS OF RIGHTEOUSNESS

Once the people had followed their king back into the channels of righteous living, it was only a short time before the fruits of prosperity began to manifest themselves.

The king set the example by offering to contribute all of the sacrificial animals necessary for feast days and for the temple services each night and morning.[59] He then "commanded the people that dwelt in Jerusalem to give the portion of the priests and the Levites, THAT THEY MIGHT BE ENCOURAGED IN [administering] THE LAW OF THE LORD."[60]

As a result of this appeal the people began paying their tithes and they brought the abundance of their "first fruits" into the house of the Lord as required by the law of Moses.[61]

Within a month such great "heaps" of grain and other supplies began to accumulate in the courts of the temple that Hezekiah ordered "chambers" to be prepared so that these supplies might be safely stored.[62]

It is hard to believe that all of this revitalization of righteousness in Judah was going on right while Samaria and the remnants of the ten tribes were in their last throes

---

57. 2 Chronicles 30:25-26
58. 2 Chronicles 30:24
59. 2 Chronicles 31:3
60. 2 Chronicles 31:4
61. 2 Chronicles 31:5
62. 2 Chronicles 31:7-11

of dissipated apostasy. It was just two or three years after the dedication of the temple in Jerusalem that Assyrian officers arrived in the northern kingdom and placed the king of Samaria under arrest. A short time later the army of Assyria arrived to place the city under siege. The siege extended over a period of time and when Hezekiah was in the sixth year of his reign[63] the northern capital of the ten tribes crumbled in defeat as we have previously described. It will be recalled that the conquest of the northern tribes was completed under Sargon II. It was only a matter of eight years until his son, Sennacherib, was back in Palestine threatening to do the same thing to Judah!

The Assault of Assyria on Judah

The scripture says that it was in the fourteenth year of the reign of Hezekiah that the thousands of Assyrian infantry and charioteers arrived in Palestine. Their main objective was Egypt but Sennacherib was taking everything in his sweep to be certain there would be no resistance on his flank or in the rear. Judah was on his eastern flank since his main battle between Assyria and Egypt was being fought on the maritime plain with Sennacherib's principal siege being laid against Lachish, a city lying almost directly west of Hebron.

Although King Ahaz, Hezekiah's father, had paid tribute to Assyria, the current king of Judah felt the strength of Judah's new independence made it possible to remain aloof. Sennarcherib promptly dispatched some of his troops against Judah's military outposts and "fenced cities" with devastating results.[64] Hezekiah therefore prepared for the siege of Jerusalem which thereafter appeared inevitable. It was expected just as soon as the Assyrians had completed their siege of Lachish. Hezekiah "set captains of war over the people, and gathered them together to him in the street of the gate of the city, and spake comfortably to them, saying, Be strong and courageous, be not afraid nor dismayed for the king of Assyria, nor for all the multitude that is with him: for there be more with us than with him: with him is an arm of flesh;

---

63. 2 Kings 18:10
64. 2 Kings 18:13

but with us is the Lord our God to help us, and to fight our battles."[65]

Hezekiah cut a new channel in the limestone rock which allowed the water of Gihon Spring to run inside the city and then he blocked it off from the outside.[66] Said he, "Why should the kings of Assyria come, and find much water?"[67] Hezekiah put the people to work rebuilding the great wall and he also constructed a defensive wall beyond it.[68] He strengthened the fortress of Millo just in case there had to be a last stand.[69] Then he settled back to examine his position. This would have been a good time for him to have sent for Isaiah but apparently he did not. As he considered all the factors involved, Hezekiah suddenly realized he was subjecting his people to an impossible task. No doubt his spies brought in daily reports of the strength and deployment of troops and Hezekiah knew that once the Assyrians had finished with Lachish they could flatten Jerusalem. In a moment of realistic panic he apparently forgot his own courageous words to his troops and sent the following humble petition to Sennacherib at Lachish:

"I have offended," said he, "return from [being against] me: that which thou puttest on me will I bear."[70]

This was the kind of talk Sennacherib liked. He promptly assessed Judah with a tribute of three hundred talents of silver and thirty talents of gold.[71] Hezekiah knew this was a terrible price to pay for peace but he determined to pay it even if he had to strip the kingdom to achieve it. And this is literally what happened. The scripture says, "And Hezekiah gave him all the silver that was found in the house of the Lord, and in the treasures of the king's house." But it was still not enough. In order to meet the assessment Hezekiah had to "cut off the gold from the doors of the temple of the Lord, and from the pillars which Hezekiah king of Judah had overlaid."[72] All this was then sent to

---

65. 2 Chronicles 32:6-8
66. 2 Chronicles 32:30. Note that this channel ran down the "west side of the city of David," so it was not the same as the channel used today which runs into the Pool of Siloam on the east side.
67. 2 Chronicles 32:4
68. 2 Chronicles 32:5
69. Ibid.
70. 2 Kings 18:14
71. Ibid.
72. 2 Kings 18:15-16

the king of Assyria. However, the treacherous Assyrians did not take off the pressure.

Having impoverished Judah, Sennacherib next tried to subvert the people against their king.

THE ASSYRIANS ATTEMPT TO PROVOKE AN INSURRECTION AGAINST HEZEKIAH

Although the king of Assyria was deeply involved with his siege at Lachish, he released "a great host"[73] and sent them with a delegation to parley with the people of Judah. The Assyrian delegates took up a position by "the conduit of the upper pool, which is in the highway of the fuller's field."[74] From this spot they could be seen and heard by all the people standing on top of the nearby city wall. However, Hezekiah was anxious to create a truly diplomatic atmosphere while negotiating with the Assyrians and therefore he did not have his delegates shout down from the wall but sent them out into the public space where the Assyrian nobles were waiting.[75] But it was soon apparent that there was nothing to negotiate. The Assyrians were rude, bellicose and vindictive.

Hezekiah's representatives were embarrassed by the blatant demands of the Assyrians and like typical diplomats feared lest the people of Judah would realize how serious things had become. They therefore said to the Assyrians, "Speak, I pray thee, to thy servants IN THE SYRIAN LANGUAGE [Aramaic]: FOR WE UNDERSTAND IT: AND TALK NOT WITH US IN THE JEWS' LANGUAGE [which can be understood] IN THE EARS OF THE PEOPLE THAT ARE ON THE WALL."[76]

However, the disdainful Assyrians not only ignored the request but began shouting "with a loud voice,"[77] so that the people on the wall might hear even better. Previously they had accused the people of Judah of being a suspect ally of Egypt since they had not been willing to fight with Assyria.[78] Now, however, they made a direct attack on the king. Cried the Assyrian spokesman:

---

73. 2 Kings 18:17
74. Ibid.
75. 2 Kings 18:18

76. 2 Kings 18:26
77. 2 Kings 18:28
78. Isaiah 11:1, 10

"Hear the word of the great king, the king of Assyria.
. . . Let not Hezekiah deceive you: for he shall not be able
to deliver you out of his [Sennacherib's] hand: Neither let
Hezekiah make you trust in the Lord, saying, The Lord
will surely deliver us, and this city shall not be delivered
into the hand of the king of Assyria."[79] Then followed an
extremely significant statement. Said he, "Make an agreement with me by a present, and come out to me [away from
your king], and then eat ye very man of his own vine. . . .
UNTIL I COME AND TAKE YOU AWAY TO A
LAND LIKE YOUR OWN LAND, A LAND OF CORN
AND WINE . . . that ye may live and not die: and hearken
not unto Hezekiah, when he persuadeth you, saying, The
Lord will deliver us."[80]

Obviously Sennacherib was planning to eventually haul
the people of Judah back to Assyria precisely the way his
father, Sargon II, had hauled off the ten tribes!

This was enough for the delegates from Jerusalem. They
rushed back into the city, tore their fine robes as a token
of distress, and went in to report to the king. But Hezekiah
was not one whit less distressed than they were. He tore
his own clothes, put on sackcloth and went to the temple.[81]
It was not until he had been reduced to this abject level of
complete desperation that he finally thought of sending for
Isaiah. It was obvious that the material fortifications on which
Hezekiah had been instinctively relying were not enough. If
God would not save them, nothing would.

THE LORD TESTS THE FAITH OF HEZEKIAH

The king's servants all dressed in sackcloth and went
as a large delegation to see Isaiah. It is amazing that some
contact had not been made with this great spiritual leader
long before. Isaiah heard their plea and then bluntly told
them, ". . . say ye to your master, Thus saith the Lord, Be
not afraid of the words which thou hast heard, with which
the servants of the king of Assyria have blasphemed me.
BEHOLD, I WILL SEND A BLAST UPON HIM, AND

---

79. 2 Kings 18:28-30
80. 2 Kings 18:31-32
81. 2 Kings 19:1

HE SHALL HEAR A RUMOUR, AND SHALL RE-
TURN TO HIS OWN LAND; AND I WILL CAUSE
HIM TO FALL BY THE SWORD IN HIS OWN
LAND."[82]

It was a fantastic promise, almost unbelievable in its
fullest implications, but there it was. Hezekiah found the
strength to rely upon it, and therefore apparently sent the
Assyrian delegates away without any satisfaction whatever.[83]

But barely had Hezekiah received what he thought was
going to be certain relief from Assyria's monstrous threat
when a whole new cloud of catastrophe settled down upon
him. As far as we can tell it was right at this juncture that
Hezekiah came down with a deadly illness caused by a lethal
infection or abscess in his body.[84] He became so ill that he
asked Isaiah to visit him and disclose what his expectations
might be. Isaiah had bitter news for the king. Said he, "Set
thine house in order; for thou shalt die, and not live."[85] Even
under normal circumstances this would have come as a terrible shock to the king, but in view of the national crisis
sweeping down on Judah it seemed completely irrational that
the Lord would take him just now.

As soon as Isaiah had left the room, Hezekiah turned
his face to the wall and sobbed out a special pleading to
the Lord. Said he, "I beseech thee, O Lord, remember now
how I have walked before thee in truth and with a perfect
heart, and have done that which is good in thy sight. And
Hezekiah wept sore."[86]

By this time Isaiah was just leaving the middle court
of the palace.[87] Suddenly the Spirit stopped him and said,
"Turn again, and tell Hezekiah the captain of my people,

---

82. 2 Kings 19:6-7
83. The fact that "the great host" was not used by the delegates to immediately
    attack Jerusalem would indicate that the Assyrians were not anxious to become
    involved militarily until aftter the termination of the siege of Lachish.
84. Although the compiler of 2 Kings puts this incident in the next chapter, it
    obviously happened before the fall of Sennacherib's army as evidenced by 2
    Kings 20:6. We are therefore inserting it in the account where it appears to
    belong chronologically.
85. 2 Kings 20:1
86. 2 Kings 20:3. Hezekiah afterwards wrote down just how he felt on this tragic
    occasion. See Isaiah 38:9-20.
87. 2 Kings 20:4. The marginal notes says this may have been the middle of
    "the city."

Thus saith the Lord, the God of David thy father [fore-father], I have heard thy prayer, I have seen thy tears: behold, I will heal thee: on the third day thou shalt go up unto the house of the Lord. AND I WILL ADD UNTO THY DAYS FIFTEEN YEARS; AND I WILL DE-LIVER THEE AND THIS CITY OUT OF THE HAND OF THE KING OF ASSYRIA; and I will defend this city for mine own sake, and for my servant David's sake."[88]

Isaiah returned to the palace with this magnificent news. However, lest the healing of the king be taken too much for granted, Isaiah determined to require something at the hands of the king's servant. Just as Naaman, the leper, had been required to dip in the Jordan seven times, so now Isaiah required that a poultice of figs be spread over the king's abscess.[89]

But when King Hezekiah heard all that Isaiah had to say it soon became apparent that he was not taking any part of this message for granted. These prophecies were all so thrilling to contemplate that he did not dare believe them! Perhaps Isaiah was just trying to make him feel good in his last hours. The king therefore begged for some kind of confirmation, saying, "What shall be the sign that the Lord will heal me, and that I shall go up into the house of the Lord the third day?"[90]

Isaiah could have said, "Be still and wait patiently on the Lord," but the Spirit apparently authorized Isaiah to demonstrate to Hezekiah that the power of God was behind his words. The prophet therefore referred to the famous sun-dial which had been built by Ahaz, the father of Heze-kiah, and asked, "Shall the shadow [on the dial] go forward ten degrees, or go back ten degrees?"[91]

This was a rather fantastic proposition since the chang-ing of the shadow on the dial would apparently involve some dramatic change in the working relationship between the earth and the sun, and Hezekiah so interpreted it. Said he, "It is a light thing for the shadow to go down ten de-

---

88. 2 Kings 20:5-6
89. 2 Kings 20:7

90. 2 Kings 20:8
91. 2 Kings 20:9

grees [since it would only involve the speed up of existing processes] . . . but let the shadow RETURN BACKWARD ten degrees."[92]

The scripture continues, "And Isaiah the prophet cried unto the Lord: and he brought the shadow ten degrees backward, by which it had gone down in the dial of Ahaz."[93] It was a phenomenal miracle and must have impressed the king deeply not only because of its spectacular implications but also by giving comfort to his tormented mind. Someday the Lord will no doubt reveal whether this was done by direct intervention in the mechanics of stellar dynamics or whether He achieved it by the more simple and direct device of manipulating the rays of light and thereby causing the shadow to be shifted backward. Whatever the explanation, Hezekiah knew it required the power of the Almighty to achieve it, and that was enough.

The Miraculous Defeat of the Assyrian Army

Shortly after Hezekiah had gone through the above experience and recovered his health, something occurred which was enough to send him back to his sick bed. It was a letter from Sennacherib, king of the Assyrians.

Sennacherib had just learned that Tirhakah,[94] king of Ethiopia, was heading north with a fresh army. To the Assyrians, this meant that the issue in Judah must necessarily be resolved immediately lest Hezekiah be tempted to join the Egyptian-Ethiopian alliance. The rough letter which Sennacherib sent to Hezekiah was recognized by the king of Judah as an ultimatum. It greatly frightened him. In spite of the previous assurance of the Lord, this seemed to be a whole new development. The Assyrian letter told Hezekiah how the fighting men from Nineveh utterly and ruthlessly destroyed all who refused to collaborate. "And shalt thou be delivered?" the letter asked sarcastically.

---

92. 2 Kings 20:10
93. 2 Kings 20:11
94. Commentators describe Tirhakah as "an Ethiopian who was at first the general and then the successor of the Egyptian king Shabako. He was contemporary not only with Sennabcherib but with his two successors Essarhaddon and Asshurbanipal." (See Dummelow's *Bible Commentary* under 2 Kings 19:9)

Hezekiah took the letter and hurried to the temple where he spread out the epistle "before the Lord."[95] Then he prayed fervently, "O Lord God of Israel . . . bow down thine ear and hear. . . . Of a truth, Lord, the kings of Assyria have destroyed the nations and their lands. . . . Now therefore, O Lord our God, I beseech thee, save thou us out of his hand, that all the kingdoms of the earth may know that thou art the Lord God, even thou only."[96]

The Lord answered the king through his chosen spokesman, Isaiah. In the answer the Lord itemized the offenses of the Assyrians and then concluded by saying, "Therefore thus saith the Lord concerning the king of Assyria, He shall not come into this city, nor shoot an arrow there, nor come before it with shield, nor cast a bank against it. By the way that he came [along the coast], by the same shall he return, and shall not come into this city, saith the Lord."[97]

The Bible declares that the destruction of the Assyrian army came about that very night. The destruction came as a "blast" against the Assyrian hosts. It was massive annihilation of 185,000 soldiers if the record is accurate. Or if a cipher has been added as some authorities attribute to certain sections of the Bible, it was still a frightening loss. Whether the "blast" was by plague or by storm we are not told. The Bible simply says, "And it came to pass THAT NIGHT, that the angel of the Lord went out, and smote in the camp of the Assyrians an hundred fourscore and five thousand: and when they [the survivors] arose early in the morning, behold, they were all dead corpses."[98]

Sennacherib forgot all about attacking Judah. And he certainly was not going to stay around to be trapped by the powerful Ethiopian-Egyptian forces moving up from the south. We do not know whether he even dared stay long enough to dispose of his dead. However, the record does say that he departed abruptly for Nineveh with all that remained of his once great army. So far as is known, he never returned. Nevertheless, the shadow of Isaiah's prophecy followed him to his Tigris capital. The Lord had not

---

95. 2 Kings 19:14   97. 2 Kings 19:32-33
96. 2 Kings 19:15-19   98. 2 Kings 19:35

only said that Sennacherib would be compelled to return home but that after he arrived there, he would be murdered.

The fulfillment of this dark prediction took place many years later. While the king was in his chapel praying to his idol-image, two men crept up behind him unawares. They were two of the king's sons. For reasons history has not completely disclosed, they had come to assassinate their father. In an instant they struck him down with their swords and then fled for their lives to Armenia, the country located just north of Assyria.[99] A third son, named Esarhaddon, promptly seized the throne[100] and became the new king of Assyria around 780 B.C.

ISAIAH'S LAST APPEARANCE IN BIBLICAL HISTORY

But we must go back to events right after Sennacherib was compelled to flee out of Palestine following the destruction of the major segment of his army. Shortly after this miraculous escape from the terrors of an Assyrian massacre, it seems that delegates arrived from the king of Babylon. They had come to congratulate the king of Judah on his marvelous recovery from a well-nigh fatal sickness.[101] The Babylonian monarch had sent his own son as the principal ambassador and in his hand was a substantial gift.

We need to remind ourselves that Babylon was at this time a vassal of Assyria but she was nevertheless most anxious to build up an alliance against Nineveh. It is very likely, therefore, that this visit by the crown prince of Babylon had highly significant political overtones. The text would indicate that there were overtures of alliance by the Babylonians since the scripture says, "And Hezekiah *hearkened unto them,* and shewed them all the house of his precious things, the silver, and the gold, and the spices, and the precious ointment, and all the house of his armour, and all that was found in his treasures: there was nothing in his house, nor in all his dominion, that Hezekiah shewed them not."[102] Apparently the Assyrians who had stripped Judah of all her wealth as a tribute were compelled to abandon most of it when they

---

99. 2 Kings 19:37
100. Ibid.

101. Isaiah 39:1
102. 2 Kings 20:13.

began their hasty retreat. From such spoils Judah could have enriched herself once more. This is the only way to account for the fact that Hezekiah had such an abundance of treasure to display to the Babylonians during their visit.

One thing Hezekiah had not learned apparently was that alliances with heathen nations were repugnant to the Lord. These Babylonian heathens, for example, came as friends, but once they were taken on a tour they never forgot the treasures they saw in Jerusalem.

The scripture says that the Babylonians had scarcely departed when Isaiah came striding into the royal palace. He asked, "What said these men? and from whence came they unto thee?"[103] Isaiah was full of questions. When Hezekiah said they were from Babylon, Isaiah inquired further, "What have they seen in thine house?"[104] Hezekiah replied, ". . . there is nothing among my treasures that I have not shewed them."[105] That was just what Isaiah feared he might say. Things were just as serious as the Spirit had apparently been telling him. Isaiah therefore declared to Hezekiah, "Behold, the days come, that all that is in thine house, and that which thy fathers have laid up in store unto this day, shall be carried into Babylon: nothing shall be left, saith the Lord."[106] Then he added a more sinister note by saying, "And of thy sons [descendants] that shall issue from thee, which thou shalt beget, shall they [the Babylonians] take away; and they shall be eunuchs in the palace of the king of Babylon."[107]

What could a man do with a prophecy like that hanging over his head? Hezekiah decided that since this captivity was scheduled for his posterity and was some distance in the future he would spend the rest of his life making conditions as favorable as possible.

So, during the final years of his reign, "Hezekiah had exceeding much riches and honour: and he made himself treasuries for silver, and for gold, and for precious stones, and for spices, and for shields, and for all manner of pleasant

---

103. 2 Kings 20:14
104. 2 Kings 20:15
105. Ibid.

106. 2 Kings 20:17
107. 2 Kings 20:18

jewels; storehouses also for the increase of corn, and wine, and oil; and stalls for all manner of beasts, and cotes for flocks. Moreover he provided him cities, and possessions of flocks and herds in abundance: for God had given him substance very much."[108]

Thus the reign of Hezekiah finally came to a close. After his fifteen years of extended life were finally consumed, "Hezekiah slept with his fathers, and they buried him in the chiefest of the sepulchres of the sons of David: and all Judah and the inhabitants of Jerusalem did him honour at his death. And Manasseh his son reigned in his stead."[109] This transfer of the throne from Hezekiah to Manasseh is believed to have occurred about 699 B.C.

The End of Isaiah's Ministry

And sometime during these latter years of Hezekiah's reign the great prophet, seer and revelator, Isaiah, passed from the scene of history. He was indeed one of the most singular personalities in the Bible. He held the Melchizedek Priesthood[110] and, from all we can tell, he was never involved in any of the administrative functions of the lesser Priesthood. His entire adult life appears to have been devoted exclusively to teaching, preaching and writing and panoramic visions which were revealed to him with such amazing frequency. He was the Lord's official spokesman to several of Judah's kings and appears to have maintained an active public ministry during more than half a century. He wrote practically nothing about himself. Even the four historical chapters (36, 37, 38 and 39) which pertained to Isaiah and events of his days are believed by most scholars to have been borrowed and inserted from the 2 Book of Kings.[111] The language is practically identical.[112] It is thought that some

---

108. 2 Chronicles 32:27-29
109. 2 Chronicles 32:33
110. This is based on the statement of Joseph Smith that, "All the prophets [of Israel] had the Melchizedek Priesthood and were ordained by God himself." (*Teachings of Joseph Smith* compiled by Joseph Fielding Smith, pp. 180-181)
111. Sperry, *The Old Testament Prophets*, pp. 73-74
112. It must not be overlooked that Isaiah might have written these chapters and that later they were borrowed and incorporated in 2 Kings. This possibility is strongly hinted in 2 Chronicles 32:32. However, the reader will find no difficulty in observing that these four chapters are sharply different in style from the rest of Isaiah.

well-meaning scribe included them so that readers would
have at least a part of Isaiah's fascinating story incorporated in his own writings. Nevertheless, we must still depend
upon 2 Kings and 2 Chronicles for most of what is known
about Isaiah today.

We know nothing for certain of Isaiah's final days. We
learn from his own writings that in his earlier ministry he
suffered bitter persecution,[113] but since his ministry seems to
have terminated during the latter part of Hezekiah's reign
it is likely that he was honored and blessed by the people
as he came to the close of his life. Of course, his life on
earth could not endure forever, but his writings did. They
became a significant treasure in the scriptural canon because
they contained predictions of many important events from
then until now. We will therefore complete our study of
Isaiah by once more returning to a topical study of his
prophecies. As we shall see, these have thus far been fulfilled to the very letter as the scroll of history has unfolded.

THE FALL OF ASSYRIA

Although he never lived to see it, Isaiah knew that the
downfall of the mighty Assyrian empire was imminent. Even
while Isaiah was predicting that it would be Assyria which
would carry off the northern tribes and make a vassal of
Judah, he announced the Lord's coming revenge upon
Assyria. Through Isaiah the Lord said, "I will punish the
fruit of the stout heart of the king of Assyria, and the glory
of his high looks. For he saith, By the strength of my hand
I have done it, and by my wisdom; for I am prudent. . . ."[114]
The Lord went on to declare that none of these things would
have come to pass had not the Lord stepped aside and permitted it for purposes best known to Himself. One day,
however, He said the rich fields and possessions of Assyria
would be swept away and her cities would become a total
desolation.[115]

Actually, during the years immediately following the
ministry of Isaiah Assyria became more powerful than ever

---

113. Isaiah 50:5-6
114. Isaiah 10:12-13
115. Isaiah 10:16-18

before. Sennacherib's son, named Esarhaddon, conquered Egypt in 671 B.C., and his son, who was named Ashurbanipal, completely devastated all opposition by 640 B.C. In fact the manifest might of Nineveh's tyrants might be said to have reached its zenith at that time. A religious cynic could have certainly poked fun at Isaiah's prophecies during these years. Nevertheless, Assyria's days were numbered. Within thirty years she was virtually annihilated as a nation. In 612 B.C., "a force made up of Medes, Babylonians and their allies fell upon Nineveh, the fabulous Assyrian capital. While it was under siege the Tigris flooded and carried away parts of its walls, rendering it indefensible. The city was laid waste with such thoroughness that for ages it was completely lost sight of and became something of a myth."[116]

But something equally devastating was awaiting the wicked in Judah.

THE FALL OF JUDAH

As we shall see later, Judah succeeded in surviving as a nation for over a century after the capture of the ten tribes, and this was achieved in spite of Assyrian pressure and badgering. Isaiah knew that it would not be the Assyrians who would destroy Judah and carry her people away but the nation which would replace them. It would be Babylon. Remember the words which Isaiah declared to King Hezekiah, "Hear the word of the Lord. Behold, the days come, that all that is in thine house, and that which thy fathers have laid up in store unto this day, shall be carried into Babylon: nothing shall be left, saith the Lord."[117]

Addressing himself to the city of Jerusalem in her hour of total depravity, Isaiah said, "How is the faithful city become an harlot! it was full of judgment; righteousness lodged in it; but now murderers. Thy silver is become dross, thy wine mixed with water: thy princes are rebellious and companions of thieves: every one loveth gifts, and followeth after rewards: they judge [consider] not the fatherless, neither doth the cause of the widow come unto them."[118]

---

116. Keyes, *Story of the Bible World*, p. 89
117. 2 Kings 20:16-17
118. Isaiah 1:21-23

Isaiah saw Judah's day of siege and famine,[119] he saw the "people robbed and spoiled . . . snared in holes . . . hid in prison houses."[120] Just prior to their collapse he saw that no one would wish to govern. He said "a man shall take hold of his brother . . . saying, Thou hast clothing, be thou our ruler, AND LET THIS RUIN BE UNDER THY HAND [for correction]:" but he would refuse saying, "I will not be a binder up;[121] for in my house is neither bread nor clothing: make me not a ruler of the people."[122] When evil men have corrupted a country it becomes well nigh impossible to get men to take office, even good men.

Isaiah accused Judah of making a covenant with Hell in order to escape the wrath which was coming.[123] Nevertheless, he said the people of Judah would find their bed too short and their covers too narrow.[124] He said the conquest of Judah would be so terrible it would be a vexation to read about it, let alone endure it.[125] It would come suddenly, unexpectedly, like a flood from a bursting dam.[126]

Isaiah said Judah had been told from the beginning what to expect but except for brief periods of repentance, she had taken no heed.[127] He called them "children of transgression," who were guilty of "enflaming yourselves with idols [in connection with fertility worship] under every green tree, slaying the children in the valleys under the clifts of the rocks. . . ."[128] They revelled in false prophets and deliberately demanded lies of them, saying, "Prophesy not unto us right things, speak unto us smooth things, prophesy deceits."[129] They refused to hear the Gospel or teachings concerning the Messiah, but cried out, "Get you out of the way, turn aside out of the path, CAUSE THE HOLY ONE OF ISRAEL TO CEASE FROM BEFORE US."[130]

Isaiah anticipated the warnings of Jeremiah by a full century. He told the people of Judah that their attempt

---

119. Isaiah 1:30
120. Isaiah 42:22
121. The standard version says "an healer" but the marginal translation gives "a binder up" which appears more appropriate.
122. Isaiah 3:6-7
123. Isaiah 28:14-15
124. Isaiah 28:20
125. Isaiah 28:19
126. Isaiah 30:13-15
127. Isaiah 48:3-8
128. Isaiah 57:4-5
129. Isaiah 30:10
130. Isaiah 30:11

to escape the wrath of Babylon by forming an alliance with Egypt would be a catastrophic political trap.[131] "Woe to the rebellious children, saith the Lord, that take counsel, but not of me . . . that . . . strengthen themselves in the strength of Pharaoh . . . to trust in the shadow of Egypt! Therefore shall the strength of Pharaoh be your shame, and the trust in the shadow of Egypt your confusion. . . . For the Egyptians shall help in vain, and to no purpose: therefore have I cried concerning this, THEIR STRENGTH IS TO SIT STILL."[132]

And sit still they did. By 600 B.C., approximately a hundred years after Isaiah's ministry, the rulers of Judah rejected the warnings of both Isaiah and Jeremiah by entering into sticky alliances with Egypt. This amounted to an open defiance of the rulers of Babylon and was aggravated by their refusal to pay further tribute to Babylon. From this distance, the historical circumstances make the alliance appear so absurd as to border on stupidity. And when the Babylonians declared war, the last king of Judah learned to his abject sorrow that the strength of the Egyptians was indeed "to sit still." In 587 B.C., the city of Jerusalem was literally levelled to the ground, its temple and buildings burned and its king dragged off to the Babylonian camp where he was forced to watch each of his sons butchered and then have his own eyes both blinded. These were the terrible scenes envisioned by Isaiah which he struggled for half-a-century to help the people of Judah escape through repentance. But they would not.

THE FALL OF BABYLON

Isaiah also had a message for Babylon. Here was a people who had descended from those ancient rebels who built the Tower of Babel but who had remained in this area after the general dispersion. The city of Babylon had been built and destroyed in regular cycles extending clear back to the first generations. after the Flood. Sometimes she had ruled Assyria but more recently Assyria had ruled her. Then in 612 B.C. Babylon combined with the Medes to destroy

---

131. Isaiah 30:1-7
132. Ibid.

Nineveh and immediately rose to the position of supremacy in Mesoptamia. Under King Nebuchadnezzar Babylon was completely rebuilt and its fabulous hanging gardens became one of the seven wonders of the ancient world. But a hundred years before all of these things had become a reality, Isaiah was talking about them. In chapters 13, 14 and 47 Isaiah sets forth the Lord's great controversy with mighty Babylon of the future.

The Lord said his own people (Judah) would require chastising and He was going to allow Babylon to impose the punishment.[133] However, the Lord knew the kind of Babylonians who would inhabit the land in that day and said they would revel in excesses of horrible cruelty, particularly against the aged.[134] Therefore, the Lord said He would avenge Himself on them because they did not have the common sense or decency to restrain themselves from atrocities. To that future generation of Babylonians, Isaiah declared: "Therefore hear now this, thou that art given to pleasures, that dwellest carelessly, that sayest in thine heart, I am, and none else [exist] beside me; I shall not sit as a widow, neither shall I know the loss of children. But [on the contrary] these two things shall come to thee in a moment in one day, the loss of children, and widowhood. . . . Thy wisdom and thy knowledge, it hath perverted thee. . . . Therefore shall evil come upon thee; thou shalt not know from whence it riseth: and . . . thou shalt not be able to put it off: and desolation shall come upon thee suddenly. . . ."[135]

As though he were looking upon it, Isaiah cried, "Come down, and sit in the dust, O virgin daughter of Babylon, sit on the ground, there is no throne . . ."[136] He said, "Thou shalt no more be called, The lady of kingdoms."[137] He rebuked them for their "enchantments," and "multitude of sorceries." Said he to the people of that day, "Let now the astrologers, the star-gazers, the monthly prognosticators, stand up, and save thee from these things that shall come upon thee."[138]

Isaiah left no question as to the extent of their calamity. "Every one that is found shall be thrust through; and every

133. Isaiah 47:5-6
134. Ibid.
135. Isaiah 47:8-11

136. Isaiah 47:1
137. Isaiah 47:5
138. Isaiah 47:13

one that is joined unto them shall fall by the sword. Their children also shall be dashed to pieces before their eyes; their houses shall be spoiled, and their wives ravished. . . . Their bows also shall dash the young men to pieces; and they shall have no pity on the fruit of the womb; their eye shall not spare children."[139]

And just as Babylon would leave Nineveh a mound of desolated ruins, so it eventually would be with Babylon. It would be as desolate as Sodom and Gomorah. Isaiah declared, "And Babylon, the glory of kingdoms, the beauty of the Chaldees' excellency, shall be as when God overthrew Sodom and Gomorah. It shall never be inhabited, neither shall it be dwelt in from generation to generation. . . . But wild beasts of the desert shall lie there; and their houses shall be full of doleful creatures; and owls shall dwell there, and satyrs shall dance there. And the wild beasts of the islands shall cry in their desolate houses, and dragons in their pleasant palaces. . . ."[140]

Isaiah even told the future rulers of Babylon who was going to do all of this: "Behold, I will stir up the Medes against them, which shall not regard silver; and as for gold, they shall not delight in it."[141] In other words, no amount of bribery will induce them to desist. Like a tornado of destruction, they will go through them. Isaiah also knew that Elam or Persia would be joined with the Medes in attacking Babylon.[142] The whole terrible scene was shown to him. He wrote, "I was bowed down at the hearing of it; I was dismayed at the seeing of it."[143]

What he was seeing took place in 539 B.C. The Medes and Persians beseiged Babylon and then dug a deep trench which circumnavigated the entire city. One night they turned the Euphrates river into this trench. Before the Babylonians

---

139. Isaiah 13:15-18. Both Herodotus and Xenophon mention that the Persians and Medes used long bows and Xenophon says they were 3 cubits long or somewhere around five feet. This is also the period when we begin to hear of steel bows. Nephi had one (1 Nephi 16:18). "A bow of steel" is mentioned in Psalms 18:34 and "a bow of steel" is mentioned in Job 20:24. Dr. Clarke suggests that the superiority of the Medes and Persians may also have resulted from this advanced type of weapon. (Clarke, *Bible Commentary*, Vol. 4; p. 81)
140. Isaiah 13:19-22   142. Isaiah 21:2
141. Isaiah 13:17   143. Isaiah 21:3

knew what was happening the attacking troops were able to enter the city through the dry bed of the river which ran under the massive city walls. It was ingenius military strategy and Babylon fell like an over-ripe fruit and never rose again.

Isaiah likened the fall of the king of Babylon to the fall of Lucifer after the War in Heaven, and he gave the following as a comfort to the Jews and others who would be captives of the Babylonians at the time of her fall:

"And it shall come to pass in the day that the Lord shall give thee rest from thy sorrow, and from thy fear, and from the hard bondage wherein thou wast made to serve, that thou shalt take up this proverb against the king of Babylon, and say, How hath the oppressor ceased! the golden city ceased! The Lord hath broken the staff of the wicked, and sceptre of the rulers. He who smote the people in wrath with a continual stroke, he that ruled the nations in anger, is persecuted, and none hindereth. The whole earth is at rest, and is quiet: they break forth into singing. . . . How art thou fallen from heaven, O Lucifer, son of the morning! how art thou cut down to the ground, which didst weaken nations! For thou hast said in thine heart, I WILL ASCEND INTO HEAVEN, I WILL EXALT MY THRONE ABOVE THE STARS OF GOD: I WILL SIT ALSO UPON THE MOUNT OF THE CONGREGATION, IN THE SIDES OF THE NORTH: I WILL ASCEND ABOVE THE HEIGHTS OF THE CLOUDS; I WILL BE LIKE THE MOST HIGH. Yet thou shalt be brought down to hell, to the sides of the pit."[144]

ISAIAH KNEW THE CONQUEROR OF BABYLON WOULD BE CYRUS

Isaiah said that the military genius who would succeed in leading the Medes and Persians in their conquest of Babylon would be named Cyrus. The first several verses of chapter 45 are addressed to this noble pagan approximately 200 years before he came to power! Here they are:

---

144. Isaiah 14:3-7, 12-15

"Thus saith the Lord to his anointed, to Cyrus, whose right hand I have holden, to subdue nations before him; and I will loose the loins of kings, to open before him the two leaved [double] gates; and the gates shall not be shut; I will go before thee, and make the crooked places straight: I will break in pieces the gates of brass, and cut in sunder the bars of iron: and I will give thee the treasures of darkness, and hidden riches of secret places, that thou mayest know that I, the Lord, which CALL THEE BY THY NAME, AM THE GOD OF ISRAEL. For Jacob my servant's sake, and Israel mine elect, I have even called thee by thy name: I have surnamed thee, THOUGH THOU HAST NOT KNOWN ME. I am the Lord, and there is none else, there is no God beside me: I girded thee, though thou hast not known me."[145]

Certain modern scholars have found this alleged capacity of Isaiah to anticipate Cyrus by almost two centuries as being impossible to accept.[146] They refuse to believe it. In reality, though many of them are professional ministers, they are rejecting the power of God to reveal the distant future to His servants. They are denying the divine gift of prophecy. Nevertheless, there are mountains of evidence to clearly support the opposite position.[147]

Actually, the prophetic naming of individuals long before they were born occurred in a number of cases beside that of Cyrus. For example:

Moses was known by name to Joseph, son of Jacob, at least 65 years before he was born.[148]

---

145. Isaiah 45:1-5
146. See Dr. Theophile J. Meeks *The Interpreter's Bible*, Vol. 5, p. 383, where he rejects the capacity of Isaiah to see beyond his own day. This is why he and others of the same school insist that Isaiah, chapters 40-66 must have been written by some person of a later date. Dr. Meek says, "Attempts to show that chs. 40-66 are the projection of the prophet's vision into the distant future have led to the most tortuous kind of reasoning and are at variance with the whole nature of Hebrew prophecy where the oracles, however predictive in character, ARE ALWAYS RELATED TO CONCERNS AND ISSUES OF THE TIMES IN WHICH THE PROPHET IS LIVING." Jesus and the Apostles clearly repudiate Dr. Meek's thesis when they state that some of these very chapters were fulfilled clear up to their time! (See Matthew 3:3; 4:14-16; 8:17; 12:17-21; 13:14; Luke 3:4; 4:17; John 1:23; 12:38-39.)
147. See chapter 16 in *The Old Testament Prophets* by Sperry.
148. 2 Nephi 3:10

Aaron was also known to Joseph by name at least 65 years before he was born.[149]

Mary was known by name a 100 years before she was born.[150]

John the Beloved was known by name 550 years before he was born.[151]

Joseph Smith was known by name around 3,450 years before he was born.[152] So was his father.[153]

It certainly was nothing unusual for Isaiah to speak of Cyrus the way he did.

Cyrus was a remarkable man. Though a pagan, he had a deep respect for basic human values comparable in many ways with those trained in the discipline of the Gospel. Among the cruel and vicious heathen tyrants of the ancient world, Cyrus stands out like a pillar of light. For example, his defeat of the Babylonian capital was brilliant, ingenious and totally successful. But note what happened: "To the astonishment of the conquered, there was no mass slaughter of the inhabitants, no herd of unfortunate people marched away into captivity. Even the gods of Babylon were left undisturbed. With great tolerance, Cyrus allowed life to proceed without violent alteration, in marked contrast to the ways of the Assyrians and the Babylonians themselves had practiced toward conquered peoples. His vision of empire was completely different from that of others, for Cyrus hoped for a common wealth of self-governing dominions, under the beneficent control of a clement emperor. Trade and the advantages of peace throughout the world were to be enjoyed by all."[154]

It was in later rulers that the predictions of Isaiah concerning Babylon found their final fulfillment. As the Lord had said, he raised up Cyrus, the benevolent pagan, to help the remnant of Jacob return to Jerusalem, but after him there

---

149. Inspired Version, Genesis 50:35
150. Mosiah 3:8
151. 1 Nephi 14:27
152. 2 Nephi 3:6, 15
153. Ibid.
154. Keyes, *Story of the Bible World*, pp. 97-98

came others, first Persian and then Greek, who finally left the majestic, massive monument of mighty Babylon a heap of rubble and ruins.

ISAIAH'S HISTORICAL PERSPECTIVE

We have therefore seen enough of Isaiah's prophetic powers to appreciate that indeed the Lord had shared with this one man a virtual mountain of knowledge. Even so, we have passed over his tremendous and accurate predictions which are equally impressive concerning Egypt,[155] Moab,[156] Phoenicia (Tyre and Sidon),[157] and Syria.[158]

As for that great event which marked the meridian of time, we have already seen how much Isaiah knew concerning the birth, ministry, death and resurrection of Jesus Christ.

This, then, leaves us with the last remaining segment of Isaiah's prophecies, those relating to modern times. In many ways these were the most exciting of all for Isaiah. He considered everything which happened before our own modern times as being merely a great prelude. What he anticipated with the most exhilarating exuberance was the great day of the Lord's power when He would restore the Gospel among the gentiles, gather the Jews, recover the Ten Tribes, and then bring to pass the Second Coming of Jesus Christ which is the thrilling spectacle designed to open the mighty Millennial reign.

This latter-day panorama of Isaiah's prophecies will be the subject matter for our next chapter.

Scripture Readings and Questions on Chapter Twenty

Scripture Reading: Isaiah, chapters 40 to 55; 2 Kings, chapters 18 and 19; 2 Chronicles, chapters 29 to 32.

1—Cite three situations in our day when misguided people have called "good, evil" or "evil, good." Is this deliberate or through ignorance?

2—Name three things for which Isaiah criticized the women of Israel. Do any of them apply today? It is possible to be beautiful and "in style" and still be humble?

---

155. Isaiah, chapter 19
156. Isaiah, chapters 15 and 16
157. Isaiah, chapter 23
158. Isaiah, chapter 17

3—Did the ancient Israelites practice baptism? What had happened to their baptismal covenants? Their sacred oaths?

4—Describe in general terms what Isaiah said would happen when Israel fell. Did he say who would destroy the Ten Tribes?

5—What was the name of the king who took Israel? About how long had the kingdom of Israel been in existence since King Jeroboam?

6—While Israel was being destroyed through apostasy and conquest, what was happening in Judah?

7—How do you account for a righteous king like Hezekiah coming from a most vicious and apostate father such as Ahaz?

8—What had happened to the Priesthood during the days of Judah's apostasy? Which responded the most quickly, the Priests or the Levites, when Hezekiah called them back into service?

9—Who did Hezekiah invite to the celebration of the Passover? Did any come from the other tribes? What was Hezekiah's chief appeal?

10—When Sennacherib came from Assyria to fight Egypt, why did he feel compelled to subjugate Judah? What happened when Hezekiah offered to pay tribute? Were the Assyrians satisfied?

11—How did the Assyrians attempt to provoke insurrection against Hezekiah? What did Isaiah tell him to do? What did the Lord promise?

12—Was Hezekiah ill before or after the destruction of Sennacherib's army? What was the Lord's first message concerning the king's illness? What was the king's reaction? What made the Lord change His mind?

13—Why do you think Hezekiah required a sign before he would believe this new message from the Lord? Did he get one? What was it?

14—Do we know what destroyed the Assyrian army? What does the Bible call it? What did Sennacherib do afterwards? Did he ever return? What ultimately happened to him?

15—Why did the Babylonians come to see King Hezekiah? Did they have any other reasons? What did Hezekiah show them? What did Isaiah say?

16—Describe briefly the fall of Assyria.

17—Describe briefly the fall of Judah.

18—Describe briefly the fall of Babylon.

19—Why did the Lord speak kindly of Cyrus? Was he a "noble pagan"?

20—List three people in addition to Cyrus whose names were revealed long before they were born.

CHAPTER TWENTY-ONE

Isaiah and Nephi Write About America and Modern Times

Isaiah became so pre-occupied with the magnificent triumph of God's power in the latter days that he literally saturated his writings with references to events in modern times. Many of these prophecies have been fulfilled within the last several generations and many more will be fulfilled in this and the next generation. This present chapter will deal primarily with Isaiah's predictions about the latter days which have already been fulfilled. The next chapter will cover Isaiah's predictions which are immediately before us.

To appreciate the extent of Isaiah's knowledge concerning our days we rely heavily upon the supplementary material furnished by the great prophet Nephi. As we have already mentioned, Isaiah's writings were brought to America by migrating Israelites in the sixth century B.C., and comprised an important part of their scripture. When these people had difficulty understanding Isaiah they had the supreme good fortune to be living under Nephi, who appears to have seen just about everything Isaiah had seen. He therefore wrote his commentary on Isaiah with this opening declaration:

"Wherefore, hearken, O my people, which are of the house of Israel, and give ear unto my words; for because the words of Isaiah are not plain unto you, nevertheless they are plain unto all those that are filled with the spirit of prophecy. But I give unto you a prophecy, ACCORDING TO THE SPIRIT WHICH IS IN ME; wherefore I shall prophesy according to the plainness which hath been with me from the time I came out from Jerusalem with my father . . . [therefore] I proceed with mine own prophecy, according to my plainness; in the which I know that no man can err; nevertheless, in the days that the prophecies of Isaiah shall be fulfilled men shall know of a surety . . . when they shall come to pass."[1]

Because Nephi had such depth of understanding concerning the things which Isaiah saw, we will include his inspired writings right along with Isaiah. But even with this help it is important to appreciate how difficult it was for these ancient servants of the Lord to describe what they saw. Consider, for example, the great upheaval of events during the past three centuries. Imagine the task of describing them without being able to use any specific names, places or dates. The task of a prophet is not an easy one. Nevertheless, Nephi was confident that when these great events transpired, no honest student would have any difficulty recognizing what he and Isaiah were trying to describe.

Prophecies Concerning America

Between Isaiah and the Book of Mormon, the whole vista of early American history was anticipated, and its most significant and dramatic epics carefully chronicled centuries before they happened.

For example, Nephi's father knew as early as 600 B.C. that the American continent would be hidden for many centuries through the specific design of the Lord. Said he, "And behold, it is wisdom that this land should be kept as yet from the knowledge of other nations; for behold, MANY NATIONS WOULD OVERRUN THE LAND, THAT THERE WOULD BE NO PLACE FOR AN INHERITANCE."[2]

He said America was being saved to become a wellspring of liberty in the latter days: "Wherefore, this land

1. 2 Nephi 25:4, 7
2. 2 Nephi 1:8

is consecrated unto him whom he shall bring. And if it so be that they shall serve him according to the commandments which he hath given, it SHALL BE A LAND OF LIBERTY UNTO THEM; wherefore, they shall never be brought down unto captivity; if so, IT SHALL BE BECAUSE OF INIQUITY; for if iniquity shall abound cursed shall be the land for their sakes, but unto the righteous it shall be blessed forever."[3]

Isaiah spent a whole chapter describing a land "shadowing [literally 'buzzing'] with wings" which he said was far away "beyond the rivers of Ethiopia."[4] (How else would you tell the people of 700 B.C. about a great land west of their westernmost boundaries?) Isaiah knew a great work would be done in this land. He said here is where the Lord would take His rest.[5] It would be the land from which He would send forth swift messengers to gather His people who had been "scattered and peeled."[6] It would be the place where the name of the Lord of Hosts could be found for it would be the latter-day "Mount Zion."[7]

Therefore, Isaiah said, "All ye inhabitants of the world, and dwellers on the earth, SEE YE [pay attention], WHEN HE LIFTETH UP AN ENSIGN ON THE MOUNTAINS; AND WHEN HE BLOWETH A TRUMPET, HEAR YE."[8]

In anticipation of this great work which the Lord would do in America, Nephi spelled out the discovery and settling of the Western Hemisphere. He saw Columbus and said, "I beheld the Spirit of God, that it came down and wrought upon the man;[9] and he went forth upon the many

3. 2 Nephi 1:7
4. Isaiah 18:1
5. Isaiah 18:4
6. Isaiah 18:7
7. Ibid.
8. Isaiah 18:3
9. One of the foremost authorities on Columbus is Dr. Samuel Eliot Morison of Harvard University. He summarizes what all biographers of Columbus say concerning his faith in God: "Men may doubt this, but there can be no doubts that the faith of Columbus was genuine and sincere, and that his frequent communion with forces unseen was a vital element in his achievement. It gave him confidence in his destiny, assurance that his performance would be equal to the promise of his name. *This conviction* that God destined him to be an instrument for spreading the faith was far more potent than the desire to win glory, wealth and worldly honors, to which he was certainly far from indif-

waters."[10] He knew that when Columbus reached America he would find a native people whom Nephi identified as the descendants of his two brothers, Laman and Lemuel.[11]

In treating the history of the Western Hemisphere we often say that the fifteenth and sixteenth centuries belonged to the Spanish, the seventeenth century belonged to the French, and the eighteenth century belonged to the English. Nephi saw these multitudes of Gentiles sweeping across the continent.[12] He saw the millions of natives whom he knew to be apostate Israelites, fleeing before them and being smitten on every hand even though they greatly outnumbered the newcomers.[13] Nevertheless, he saw that in spite of this devastating conquest by the Gentiles, they would not annihilate the native peoples completely.[14]

With this kind of background, it will be readily seen why Nephi made such a competent commentator on Isaiah's writings concerning America. In addition to the above, he knew that many of the Gentiles who would migrate to America would be motivated by religious ideals,[15] and that they would come forth from the land of the mother Gentiles in order to escape "out of captivity."[16] He said they would be "white, and exceeding fair and beautiful" and that they would "prosper and obtain the land [from the natives] for their inheritance."[17]

Nephi saw the United States war of independence in the late 1700's and the wars of independence in the Latin American countries during the 1800's. He said, "I beheld that their mother Gentiles were gathered together upon the waters, and upon the land also, to battle against them. AND I BEHELD THAT THE POWER OF GOD WAS WITH THEM and also that the wrath of God was upon

---

ferent." (*Admiral of the Ocean Sea*, by Dr. Samuel E. Morison, Little, Brown & Co., Boston, 1942. p. 47)
    When Columbus wrote his report concerning the settlement of the New World he expressed the hope that none but devout Christians would be used as settlers, "since this was the end and the beginning of the enterprise, that it should be fore the enhancement and glory of the Christian religion, nor should anyone who is not a good Christian come to these parts." (Ibid., p. 279)

10. I Nephi 13:12
11. Ibid.
12. I Nephi 13:13-14
13. I Nephi 13:14
14. I Nephi 13:30-31

15. I Nephi 13:13
16. I Nephi 13:16
17. I Nephi 13:15

all those that were gathered against them to battle."[18] Nephi predicted the outcome of these mighty struggles, saying, "I, Nephi, beheld that the Gentiles that had gone out of captivity [from Europe] were DELIVERED BY THE POWER OF GOD OUT OF THE HANDS OF ALL OTHER NATIONS."[19]

---

18. I Nephi 13:17-18
19. I Nephi 13:19

The determination of the early American settlers to live the lives of practicing Christians, brought some rather amazing blessings.

In October of 1746 France assembled the largest fleet ever to be sighted from American soil and headed for Boston to avenge the defeat at Louisburg. There was no hope of matching the fleet either in cannon fire or manpower, so the Governor assembled what men and resources he could and then called for a universal day of fasting and prayer. One writer says, "everywhere men observed it, thronging to the churches. In Boston the Reverend Thomas Prince from the high pulpit of the Old South Meetinghouse, prayed before hundreds. The morning was clear and calm, people had walked to church through sunshine. 'Deliver us from our enemy!' the minister implored. 'Send Thy tempest, Lord, upon the waters to the eastward! Raise Thy right hand, Scatter the ships of our tormentors and drive them hence. Sink their proud frigates beneath the power of Thy winds!'

"He had scarcely pronounced the words when the sun was gone and the morning darkened. All the church was in a shadow. A wind shrieked around the walls, sudden, violent, hammering at the windows with a giant hand. No man was in the steeple — afterward the sexton swore it — yet the great bell struck twice, a wild, uneven sound. Thomas Prince paused in his prayer, both arms raised. 'We hear Thy voice, O Lord!' he thundered triumphantly. 'We hear it! Thy breath is upon the waters to the eastward, even upon the deep. Thy bell tolls for the death of our enemies!' He bowed his head; when he looked up, tears streamed down his face. 'Thine be the glory, Lord. Amen and amen!'

". . . All the Province heard of this prayer and this answering tempest. Governor Shirley sent a sloop, the *Rising Sun*, northward for news . . . she brought news so good it was miraculous — if one could believe it . . . The whole fleet was nearly lost, the men very sick with scurvy, or some pestilential fever. Their great admiral, the Duc d'Anville, was dead.

"A week later the news was confirmed by other vessels entering Boston from the northeastward. D'Anville was indeed dead; it was said he had poisoned himself in grief and despair when he saw his men dying round him. Two thousand were already buried, four thousand were sick, and not above a thousand of the land forces remained on their fleet. Vice-Admiral d'Estournelle had run himself through the heart with his sword. The few remaining ships, half-manned, were limping off to the southwestward, headed it was thought for the West Indies.

"Pestilence, storm and sudden death — how directly and with what extraordinary vigor the Lord had answered New England prayers!

"The country fell on its knees . . . A paper with d'Anville's orders had been found, instructing him to take Cape Breton Island, then proceed to Boston — 'lay that Town in Ashes and destroy all he could upon the Coast of North America; then proceed to the West Indies and distress the Islands.'" (Quoted from *John Adams*, by Catherine Drinker Bowen, Grosset & Dunlap, N.Y., 1950. pp. 5, 10-11)

Had the French Armada burned Boston, New York, Philadelphia and Charleston, the history of early America might have been changed completely.

Nephi knew that the Bible, "which is a record of the Jews" would "be of great worth to the Gentiles," and the foundation of the Gentile culture in America.[20]

With what appears to have been a specific reference to the United States, Nephi describes a Gentile nation which would prosper in the American promised land until it had "been lifted up by the power of God above all other nations."[21] Nephi said that among these Gentiles the Lord would commence His "marvelous work and a wonder" spoken of by Isaiah.[22] According to Nephi, the Lord said, "I will be merciful unto the Gentiles in that day, insomuch that I will bring forth unto them, in mine own power, MUCH OF MY GOSPEL, which shall be plain and precious, saith the Lamb."[23]

Nephi knew that in connection with this great restoration of the Gospel in our times the Lord would raise up a choice prophet. Isaiah was also aware of the mission of this latter-day seer.

JOSEPH SMITH IN PROPHECY

It would appear from everything we have available that some 2,500 years before he was born, Joseph Smith was the man Isaiah had in mind when he wrote about the "root of Jesse" in the eleventh chapter of his book. Isaiah quoted the Lord as saying, "And in that day there shall be a root of Jesse, which shall stand for an ensign of the people; TO IT SHALL THE GENTILES SEEK: and his rest [message of peace and salvation] shall be glorious."[24] The Lord then went on to say that in connection with the raising up of this servant "the Lord shall set his hand again the second time to recover the remnant of his people. . . . And he shall set up an ensign for the nations, and shall assemble the outcasts of Israel, and gather together the dispersed of Judah from the four corners of the earth."[25]

It was Joseph Smith who was given this precise responsibility when the keys "for the gathering of Israel" were conferred upon him and Oliver Cowdery April 3, 1836.[26]

---

20. I Nephi 13:23
21. I Nephi 13:30
22. Isaiah 29:14
23. I Nephi 13:34

24. Isaiah 11:10
25. Isaiah 11:11-12
26. Doc. & Cov. 110:11

Joseph Smith was once asked who this "root of Jesse" was, and he gave a most interesting but impersonal reply. Perhaps it would be more accurate to describe it as an extremely modest reply. In any event, this is what he said, "Behold, thus saith the Lord, it is a descendant of Jesse as well as of Joseph, unto whom RIGHTLY BELONGS THE PRIESTHOOD, AND THE KEYS OF THE KINGDOM, FOR AN ENSIGN, AND FOR THE GATHERING OF MY PEOPLE IN THE LAST DAYS."[27]

To identify this person, all one needs to do is ask, "Who was it in this dispensation who received the Priesthood, the Keys of the Kingdom, and finally, the Keys of the Gathering?" If we are correct in concluding that only Joseph Smith fits these specifications then it becomes completely obvious why Moroni recited this entire chapter of Isaiah to the 17-year-old Joseph Smith when he came to announce that the Lord's great latter-day program was about to commence.[28] Moroni told Joseph that the things mentioned in this chapter of Isaiah were about to be fulfilled[29] and of course if Joseph was the Lord's instrument to bring it about, Moroni would have a most significant reason in quoting this chapter to him.

Other prophets also talked about the latter-day seer. As we have mentioned in an earlier chapter, Joseph, who was sold into Egypt, knew that the prophet of the latter days would be a namesake as well as a descendant of his.[30] He said the father of this prophet would also be named Joseph.[31] Note that Joseph who was sold into Egypt was proud that Joseph Smith would be one of his lineage, but Isaiah was proud that he would be of Jewish lineage! Isaiah wanted to emphasize that this great servant of the Lord in our times would carry in his veins the same pure blood of Judah as that which flowed in the veins of King David and Jesus. Therefore, Isaiah called him "a root of Jesse," and Jesse, of course, was David's father, a Jew of Bethlehem, who was also the ancestor of Mary, mother of Christ.[32]

---

27. Doc. & Cov. 113:6
28. Pearl of G.P., p. 51:40
29. Ibid.
30. 2 Nephi 3:15
31. Ibid.
32. Luke 3:23-32. It should be noted that this is believed to have been the ancestoral line of *both* Mary and Joseph but of course Jesus would have partaken of it only through his mother.

Now, if Joseph Smith is indeed the "root of Jesse" spoken of by Isaiah, could he also be an Ephraimite? According to the modern revelation quoted above, the answer is yes. The Lord said the "root of Jesse" was "a descendant of Jesse AS WELL AS JOSEPH. . . ." When the genealogy of Joseph Smith is finally tabulated we may very well discover that in him the two great houses of Judah (through Jesse) and of Joseph (through Ephraim) have been brought together in symbolic harmony. We say "symbolic" since this very same chapter of Isaiah says that in this era when the "root of Jesse" will "stand for an ensign of the people" it will be noted that "Ephraim shall not envy Judah, and Judah shall not vex Ephraim" any more.[33] How appropriate, therefore, that the blood lines of these former antagonists should be blended together in the great prophet who would proclaim the message and commence the gathering which in due time would bring about the reconciliation of these two great peoples.

ISAIAH ADDRESSES HIMSELF TO THE ISRAELITES IN AMERICA

Isaiah, more than any other prophet, addresses himself on a number of occasions to the isles of the sea. Nephi's brother, Jacob, said this partly referred to the Israelites in America. He said, ". . . for the Lord has made the sea our path, and we are upon an isle of the sea."[34] From the point of view of the Eurasian land mass, the Western Hemisphere could be looked upon as a vast continental island. At least we know both Isaiah and the Nephites so considered it.

Isaiah invited those great Israelite explorers who had gone down to the sea in ships and become inhabitants of the isles to join him in a new song. He wrote, "Sing unto the Lord a new song, and his praise from the end of the earth, ye that go down to the sea, and all that is therein; the isles, and the inhabitants thereof."[35] He knew the American Israelites and those on other "isles" would be cut off from the Lord during a long period of apostasy, but he said that

33. Isaiah 11:10, 13
34. 2 Nephi 10:20
35. Isaiah 42:10

God would raise up his servant to "bring judgment to the Gentiles," and therefore he said "the isles shall wait for his law."[36]

Isaiah frequently had the inhabitants of those distant "isles" in mind. In his great 49th chapter which speaks of the latter-day redemption of Israel, he begins with, "Listen, O isles, unto me; and hearken, ye people, from far. . . ."[37] And later the Lord referred to the same period and said, "Hearken unto me, my people. . . . My righteousness is near; my salvation is gone forth, and mine arms shall judge the people; THE ISLES SHALL WAIT UPON ME, AND ON MINE ARM SHALL THEY TRUST."[38]

What were the people on the "isles" waiting for? Isaiah devotes a whole chapter to the redemption of the Israelites on the continental isle of America, and because he was talking about Nephi's own people, that inspired servant of the Lord could not resist devoting several chapters to this part of Isaiah's writings.[39] This, of course, is a scriptural treasure-chest for the modern student of Isaiah.

By placing the Isaiah text on one side of the page and the pertinent passages of Nephi's commentary on the other side we get a whole new insight into the extent of Isaiah's knowledge concerning both ancient and modern America. He knew about the fall of the Lamanite-Nephite civilization through apostasy, he knew of the occupation of the American continent by the Gentiles and he knew an amazing quantity of detailed information about the coming forth of the Book of Mormon. A careful reading of the following parallel scriptures will prove most profitable.

Isaiah and Nephi on the Coming Forth of the Book of Mormon

ISAIAH, Chapter 29	2 NEPHI, Chapter 25
1. Woe to Ariel, to Ariel, the city where David dwelt! add ye year to year; let them kill sacrifices.	9. And as one generation hath been destroyed among the Jews because of iniquity, even so have they been destroyed from generation to generation according to their iniquities; and never hath any of them been destroyed save it were foretold them by the prophets of the Lord.
2. Yet I will distress Ariel, and there shall be heaviness and sorrow: and it shall be unto me as Ariel.	

36. Isaiah 42:1, 4
37. Isaiah 49:1

38. Isaiah 51:4-5
39. Isaiah chapters 25-27

10. Wherefore, it hath been told them concerning the destruction which should come upon them, immediately after my father left Jerusalem; nevertheless, they hardened their hearts; and according to my prophecy they have been destroyed, save it be those which are carried away captive into Babylon.

11. And now this I speak because of the spirit which is in me. And notwithstanding they have been carried away they shall return again, and possess the land of Jerusalem; wherefore, they shall be restored again to the land of their inheritance.

12. But, behold, they shall have wars, and rumors of wars; and when the day cometh that the Only Begotten of the Father, yea, even the Father of heaven and of earth, shall manifest himself unto them in the flesh, behold, they will reject him, because of their iniquities, and the hardness of their hearts, and the stiffness of their necks.

13. Behold, they will crucify him; and after he is laid in a sepulchre for the space of three days he shall rise from the dead, with healing in his wings; and all those who shall believe on his name shall be saved in the kingdom of God. Wherefore, my soul delighteth to prophesy concerning him, for I have seen his day, and my heart doth magnify his holy name.

14. And behold it shall come to pass that after the Messiah hath risen from the dead, and hath manifested himself unto his people, unto as many as will believe on his name, behold, Jerusalem shall be destroyed again; for wo unto them that fight against God and the people of his church.

15. Wherefore, the Jews shall be scattered among all nations; yea, and also Babylon shall be destroyed; wherefore, the Jews shall be scattered by other nations.

ISAIAH, Chapter 29

3. And I will camp against thee round about, and will lay siege against thee with a mount, and I will raise forts against thee.

2 NEPHI, Chapter 26

14. But behold, I prophesy unto you concerning the last days; concerning the days when the Lord God shall bring these things forth unto the children of men.

15. After my seed and the seed of my brethren shall have dwindled in unbelief, and shall have been smitten by the Gentiles; yea, after the Lord God shall have camped against them round about, and shall have laid siege against them with a mount, and raised forts against them; and after they shall have

4. And thou shalt be brought down, and shalt speak out of the ground, and thy speech shall be low out of the dust, and thy voice shall be, as of one that hath a familiar spirit, out of the ground, and thy speech shall whisper out of the dust.

5. Moreover the multitude of thy strangers shall be like small dust, and the multitude of the terrible ones shall be as chaff that passeth away: yea, it shall be at an instant suddenly.

6. Thou shalt be visited of the LORD of hosts with thunder, and with earthquake, and great noise, with storm and tempest, and the flame of devouring fire.

7. And the multitude of all the nations that fight against Ariel, even all that fight against her and her munition, and that distress her, shall be as a dream of a night vision.
8. It shall even be as when an hungry man dreameth, and, behold, he eateth; but he awaketh, and his soul is empty: or as when a thirsty man dreameth, and, behold, he drinketh; but he awaketh; and, behold, he is faint, and his soul hath appetite: so shall the multitude of all the nations be, that fight against mount Zion.

been brought down low in the dust, even that they are not, yet the words of the righteous shall be written, and the prayers of the faithful shall be heard, and all those who have dwindled in unbelief shall not be forgotten.
16. For those who shall be destroyed shall speak unto them out of the ground, and their speech shall be low out of the dust, and their voice shall be as one that hath a familiar spirit; for the Lord God will give unto him power, that he may whisper concerning them, even as it were out of the ground; and their speech shall whisper out of the dust.
17. For thus saith the Lord God: They shall write the things which shall be done among them, and they shall be written and sealed up in a book, and those who have dwindled in unbelief shall not have them, for they seek to destroy the things of God.
18. Wherefore, as those who have been destroyed have been destroyed speedily; and the multitude of their terrible ones shall be as chaff that passeth away — yea, thus saith the Lord God: It shall be at an instant, suddenly —
19. And it shall come to pass, that those who have dwindled in unbelief shall be smitten by the hand of the Gentiles.

2 NEPHI, Chapter 27

1. But, behold, in the last days, or in the days of the Gentiles — yea, behold all the nations of the Gentiles and also the Jews, both those who shall come upon this land and those who shall be upon other lands, yea, even upon all the lands of the earth, behold, they will be drunken with iniquity and all manner of abominations —
2. And when that day shall come they shall be visited of the Lord of Hosts, with thunder and with earthquake, and with a great noise, and with storm, and with tempest, and with the flame of devouring fire.
3. And all the nations that fight against Zion, and that distress her, shall be as a dream of a night vision; yea, it shall be unto them, even as unto a hungry man which dreameth, and behold he eateth but he awaketh and his soul is empty; or like unto a thirsty man which dreameth, and behold he drinketh but he awaketh and behold he is faint, and his soul hath appetite; yea, even so shall the multitude of all the nations be that fight against Mount Zion.

9. Stay yourselves, and wonder; cry ye out, and cry: they are drunken, but not with wine; they stagger, but not with strong drink.

10. For the Lord hath poured out upon you the spirit of deep sleep, and hath closed your eyes: the prophets and your rulers, the seers hath he covered.

11. And the vision of all is become unto you as the words of a book . . .

. . . that is sealed . . .

4. For behold, all ye that doeth iniquity, stay yourselves and wonder, for ye shall cry out, and cry; yea, ye shall be drunken but not with wine, ye shall stagger but not with strong drink.

5. For behold, the Lord hath poured out upon you the spirit of deep sleep. For behold, ye have closed your eyes, and ye have rejected the prophets; and your rulers, and the seers hath he covered because of your iniquity.

6. And it shall come to pass that the Lord God shall bring forth unto you the words of a book, and they shall be the words of them which have slumbered.

7. And behold the book shall be sealed; and in the book shall be a revelation from God, from the beginning of the world to the ending thereof.

8. Wherefore, because of the things which are sealed up, the things which are sealed shall not be delivered in the day of the wickedness and abominations of the people. Therefore the book shall be kept from them.

9. But the book shall be delivered unto a man, and he shall deliver the words of the book, which are the words of those who have slumbered in the dust, and he shall deliver these words unto another;

10. But the words which are sealed he shall not deliver, neither shall he deliver the book. For the book shall be sealed by the power of God, and the revelation which was sealed shall be kept in the book until the own due time of the Lord, that they may come forth; for behold, they reveal all things from the foundation of the world unto the end thereof.

11. And the day cometh that the words of the book which were sealed shall be read upon the house tops; and they shall be read by the power of Christ; and all things shall be revealed unto the children of men which ever have been among the children of men, and which ever will be even unto the end of the earth.

12. Wherefore, at that day when the book shall be delivered unto the man of whom I have spoken, the book shall be hid from the eyes of the world, that the eyes of none shall behold it save it be that three witnesses shall behold it, by the power of God, besides him to whom the book shall be delivered; and they shall testify to the truth of the book and the things therein.

13. And there is none other which shall view it, save it be a few according to the will of God, to bear testimony

. . . which men deliver to one that is
learned, saying, Read this, I pray thee . . .

. . . and he saith, I cannot; for it is
sealed:

12. And the book is delivered to him
that is not learned, saying, Read this,
I pray thee: and he saith, I am not
learned.

13. Wherefore the Lord said, Forasmuch

of his word unto the children of men;
for the Lord God hath said that the
words of the faithful should speak as if
it were from the dead.

14. Wherefore, the Lord God will proceed to bring forth the words of the
book; and in the mouth of as many witnesses as seemeth him good will He establish his word; and wo be unto him
that rejecteth the word of God!

15. But behold, it shall come to pass
that the Lord God shall say unto him
to whom he shall deliver the book: Take
these words which are not sealed and
deliver them to another, that he may
show them unto the learned, saying:
Read this, I pray thee. And the learned
shall say: Bring hither the book, and I
will read them.

16. And now, because of the glory of
of the world and to get gain will
they say this, and not for the glory of
God.

17. And the man shall say: I cannot
bring the book, for it is sealed.

18. Then shall the learned say: I cannot read it.

19. Wherefore it shall come to pass,
that the Lord God will deliver again
the book and the words thereof to him
that is not learned: and the man that is
not learned shall say: I am not learned.

20. Then shall the Lord God say unto
him: The learned shall not read
them, for they have rejected them, and
I am able to do mine own work; wherefore thou shalt read the words which I
shall give unto thee.

21. Touch not the things which are sealed, for I will bring them forth in
mine own due time; for I will show unto
the children of men that I am able to do
mine own work.

22. Wherefore, when thou hast read
the words which I have commanded
thee, and obtained the witnesses which
I have promised unto thee, then shalt
thou seal up the book again, and hide
it up unto me, that I may preserve the
words which thou hast not read, until
I shall see fit in mine own wisdom to
reveal all things unto the children of men.

23. For behold, I am God; and I am a
God of miracles; and I will show
unto the world that I am the same yesterday, today, and forever; and I work
not among the children of men save it
be according to their faith.

24. And again it shall come to pass that
the Lord shall say unto him that
shall read the words that shall be delivered him:

as this people draw near me with their mouth, and with their lips do honour me, but have removed their heart far from me, and their fear toward me is taught by the precept of men:

14. Therefore, behold, I will proceed to do a marvellous work among this people, even a marvellous work and a wonder: for the wisdom of their wise men shall perish, and the understanding of their prudent men shall be hid.

15. Woe unto them that seek deep to hide their counsel from the Lord, and their works are in the dark, and they say, Who seeth us? and who knoweth us?

16. Surely your turning of things upside down shall be esteemed as the potter's clay: for shall the work say of him that made it, He made me not? or shall the thing framed say of him that framed it, He had no understanding?

17. Is it not yet a very little while, and Lebanon shall be turned into a fruitful field, and the fruitful field shall be esteemed as a forest?

18. And in that day shall the deaf hear the words of the book, and the eyes of the blind shall see out of obscurity, and out of darkness.

19. The meek also shall increase their joy in the Lord, and the poor among men shall rejoice in the Holy One of Israel.

20. For the terrible one is brought to nought, and the scorner is consumed, and all that watch for iniquity are cut off:

21. That make a man an offender for a word, and lay a snare for him that reproveth in the gate, and turn aside the just for thing of nought.

22. Therefore thus said the LORD, who redeemed Abraham, concerning the house of Jacob, Jacob shall not now be ashamed, neither shall his face now wax pale.

23. But when he seeth his children, the work of mine hands, in the midst of him, they shall sanctify my name, and sanctify the Holy One of Jacob, and shall fear the God of Israel.

24. They also that erred in spirit shall come to understanding, and they that murmured shall learn doctrine.

25. Forasmuch as this people draw near unto me with their mouth, and with their lips do honor me, but have removed their hearts far from me, and their fear towards me is taught by the precepts of men —

26. Therefore, I will proceed to do a marvelous work among this people, yea, a marvelous work and a wonder, for the wisdom of their wise and learned shall perish, and the understanding of their prudent shall be hid.

27. And wo unto them that seek deep to hide their counsel from the Lord! And their works are in the dark; and they say: Who seeth us, and who knoweth us? And they also say: Surely your turning of things upside down shall be esteemed as the potter's clay. But behold, I will show unto them, saith the Lord of Hosts, that I know all their works. For shall the work say of him that made it, he made me not? Or shall the thing framed say of him that framed it, he had no understanding?

28. But behold, saith the Lord of Hosts: I will show unto the children of men that it is yet a very little while and Lebanon shall be turned into a fruitful field; and the fruitful field shall be esteemed as a forest.

29. And in that day shall the deaf hear the words of the book, and the eyes of the blind shall see out of obscurity and out of darkness.

30. And the meek also shall increase, and their joy shall be in the Lord, and the poor among men shall rejoice in the Holy One of Israel.

31. For assuredly as the Lord liveth they shall see that the terrible one is brought to naught, and the scorner is consumed, and all that watch for iniquity are cut off;

32. And they that make a man an offender for a word, and lay a snare for him that reproveth in the gate, and turn aside the just for a thing of naught.

33. Therefore, thus saith the Lord, who redeemed Abraham, concerning the house of Jacob: Jacob shall not now be ashamed, neither shall his face now wax pale.

34. But when he seeth his children, the work of my hands, in the midst of him, they shall sanctify my name, and sanctify the Holy One of Jacob, and shall fear the God of Israel.

35. They also that erred in spirit shall come to understanding, and they that murmured shall learn doctrine.

Twenty Prophecies in These Texts Have Already Been Fulfilled

It is astonishing that the prophecies of Isaiah in the eighth century B.C., and the parallel prophecies of Nephi in the sixth century B.C., should have been so completely, literally and immaculately fulfilled in the nineteenth century A.D. A careful analysis of the above texts will disclose at least twenty separate conditions which had to be met in order to make these prophecies come true. Between Isaiah and Nephi we find the following:

1 — People originating in Jerusalem were to become a corrupted and afflicted segment of humanity who would go into a deep sleep of apostasy.[40]

In his commentary Nephi says this applied to all the people from Jerusalem but especially to his own people who came to America in the sixth century B.C. and whom Isaiah particularly had in mind. These people were the so-called Indian aborigines who numbered in the millions when America was first discovered by Europeans. That they had apostatized and lost what was once a magnificent civilization is borne out by the gigantic ruins which can still be seen.

2 — Both Isaiah and Nephi said these people would record their history and through it these people would "speak out of the ground, and . . . whisper out of the dust" and it would have a "familiar spirit."[41]

This was fulfilled when the Plates of Mormon were taken from the stone box buried on the side of Hill Cumorah.

3 — They said this history of the ancient American Israelites would go forth to the world in the form of a book.[42]

This commenced with the publication of the Book of Mormon in 1830. It has since been translated and published

---

40. Isaiah 29:1-2
41. Isaiah 29:4; 2 Nephi 26:16-17
42. Isaiah 29:11; 2 Nephi 27:6

in practically every major language and a number of minor ones.

    4—They said part of this record would be sealed and that this portion would contain a prophetic revelation of human history from the beginning to the end.[43]

A substantial amount of the plates was sealed.[44] Joseph Smith was allowed to translate only the unsealed portion. The sealed portion contained the revelation given to the Brother of Jared (Mahonri-Moriancumr). Concerning this revelation Moroni said, "Behold, I have written upon these plates the very things which the brother of Jared saw; and there never were greater things made manifest than those which were made manifest unto the brother of Jared."[45]

    5—The timing for the coming forth of this record was set for "the last days" when both "the Gentiles and also the Jews . . . will be drunken with iniquity and all manner of abominations."[46]

The Lord has verified that the age in which we now live is indeed the last days.[47] It was in this age that the Book of Mormon came forth just as Isaiah and Nephi said it would. It caught the world in a state of rebellion against God with agnosticism, cynicism, immorality, crime, violence and war characterizing the cultural pattern in much of the world.

    6—The book (or plates) were to be delivered into the hands of a man who was not learned.[48]

Many years after Joseph Smith had been martyred, a statement was obtained from his wife, Emma, concerning her recollection of earlier days. Commenting on the inability of Joseph Smith to have produced a volume like the Book of Mormon, she said: "Joseph Smith [as a young man] . . . could neither write nor dictate a coherent and well-worded letter, let alone dictate a book like the Book of Mormon, and though I was an active participant in the scenes that trans-

---

43. Isaiah 29:11; 2 Nephi 27:7-10
44. George Q. Cannon, *Life of Joseph Smith*, (new edition), p. 45.
45. Ether 4:4
46. 2 Nephi 27:1 and Isaiah 29:9-10
47. Doc. & Cov. 1:4; 29:1-26; 27:6; 39:11
48. Isaiah 29:12; 2 Nephi 27:19

pired, was present during the translation of the plates, and had cognizance of things as they transpired, it is marvelous to me — a marvel and a wonder — as much as to anyone else."[49]

In bearing her testimony of the divine origin of the Book of Mormon, she said, "My belief is that the Book of Mormon is of divine authenticity — I have not the slightest doubt of it . . . when acting as his scribe, your father [she was being interrogated by her son] would dictate to me hour after hour; and when returning after meals, or interruptions, he would at once begin where he had left off, without either seeing the manuscript or having any portion of it read to him. This was an unusual thing for him to do. It would have been improbable that learned man could do this, and FOR ONE SO IGNORANT AND UNLEARNED AS HE WAS, IT WAS SIMPLY IMPOSSIBLE."[50]

7 — Nephi said this unlearned man would not give the actual book to anyone (which Isaiah's more general statement implies) but that he would take the "words which are not sealed" and deliver them to a second man who would then present these words to the learned for examination.[51]

This second man turned out to be a well-to-do citizen farmer from Palmyra, named Martin Harris. Joseph Smith was instructed by the Lord to make a facsimile of some of the characters on the plates and have some of the learned men in New York City determine if they could translate them. Joseph made two facsimiles. One he translated, the other he did not.[52] Martin Harris took both of these to New York to find the most eminent linguists of ancient languages to examine them and read "the words" if possible.

8 — Both Nephi and Isaiah said that the words of the book[53] would be delivered to some learned or scholarly man for examination.[54]

---

49. Quoted in Preston Nibley's *The Witnesses of the Book of Mormon*, pp. 28-29.
50. Ibid.
51. 2 Nephi 27:10, 15; Isaiah 29:11
52. Doc. His. of the Church, Vol. 1, p. 19
53. Isaiah says "the book" but "WORDS of the book" would be more accurate as pointed out in 2 Nephi 27:10, 15.
54. Isaiah 29:11; 2 Nephi 27:15

This turned out to be Professor Charles Anthon of Columbia College, now Columbia University. The facsimiles and translation were also shown to Dr. Samuel L. Mitchell. Here is what occurred according to Martin Harris: "I went to the city of New York, and presented the characters which had been translated, with the translation thereof, to Professor Charles Anthon, a gentleman celebrated for literary attainments. Professor Anthon stated that the translation was correct, more so than any he had before seen translated from the Egyptian.[55] I then showed him those which were not yet translated, and he said that they were Egyptian, Chaldaic, Assyric, and Arabic; and he said they were true characters. He gave me a certificate certifying to the people of Palmyra that they were true characters, and that the translation of such of them as had been translated was also correct. I took the certificate and put it into my pocket, and was just leaving the house, when Mr. Anthon called me back, and asked me how the young man found out that there were gold plates in the place where he found them. I answered that an angel of God had revealed it unto him.

"He then said to me, 'Let me see that certificate.' I accordingly took it out of my pocket and gave it to him, when he took it and tore it to pieces, saying, that there was no such thing now as ministering of angels, and that if I would bring the plates to him, he would translate them. I informed him that part of the plates were sealed, and that I was forbidden to bring them. He replied, 'I cannot read a sealed book.' I left him and went to Dr. Mitchell, who sanctioned what Professor Anthon had said respecting both the characters and the translation."[56]

9—Nephi said the learned man would say, "Bring hither the book, and I will read them" (i.e., the words of the book).[57]

---

55. If Martin Harris is completely accurate in quoting the professor, then Dr. Anthon was extending himself professionally. As R. C. Webb says in his book, *Joseph Smith As a Translator,* p. 4: "It is difficult to understand how Professor Anthon could have stated that the translation was correct from the fact that, at that time (1828), the science of Egyptology, or the knowledge of the Egyptian language, had not advanced sufficiently to warrant the supposition that he, or any other scholar, could read a given inscription off-hand. In addition, so far as it is known, Anthon had not devoted sufficient attention to the subject to enable him to give authoritative utterance to such a verdict."

56. Doc. His. of the Church, Vol. 1, p. 20

57. 2 Nephi 27:15

As we have seen in the above statement of Martin Harris, Professor Charles Anthon said to him "that there was no such thing now as ministering of angels, AND THAT IF I WOULD BRING THE PLATES TO HIM HE WOULD TRANSLATE THEM."

10—Nephi said this statement would be made to get fame and money rather than because of his anxiety to help in the work of the Lord.[58]

Dr. Anthon's unfortunate role in these important events was a source of great embarrassment to him in later years and this would tend to verify the statement of Nephi that his motives were not entirely sincere. For example, he wrote a letter to E. D. Howe on February 17, 1834, verifying the visit of Martin Harris but ridiculing the claim that he had given Mr. Harris a certificate vouching for the accuracy of the translation or the authenticity of the writings. Said Professor Anthon, "He [meaning Martin Harris] requested an opinion from me in writing, which, of course, I declined to give, and he then took his leave, taking his paper with him."[59] Seven years later, April 3, 1841, Professor Anthon wrote a letter to Dr. T. W. Coit in which he said, ". . . he requested me to give him my opinion in writing about the paper which he had shown me. I DID SO WITHOUT HESITATING, partly for the man's sake, and partly to let the individual 'behind the curtain' see that the trick was discovered. THE IMPORT OF WHAT I WROTE WAS, AS FAR AS I CAN NOW RECOLLECT, SIMPLY THIS, that the marks in the paper appeared to be merely an imitation of various alphabetical characters, and had, in my opinion, no meaning at all connected with them."[60] At this point the duplicity of Dr. Anthon becomes fully evident as he verifies the very thing which he had formerly denied, all of which lends great credence to the simple and direct statement of Martin Harris as to what really happened.

At the time of the above visit, neither Martin Harris nor Joseph Smith were aware that the Book of Mormon

---

58. 2 Nephi 27:16
59. E. D. Howe, *Mormonism Unveiled*, Painesville, Ohio, 1834, chapter 18, and quoted by Berrett and Burton in *Readings in L.D.S. History*, Salt Lake City, Deseret Book Co., 1953, p. 46.
60. Ibid., p. 49

contained a commentary on Isaiah, chapter 29, nor that it impuned the motives of Dr. Anthon. In later years when Professor Anthon was told that he had been identified as the "learned" scholar in Isaiah 29:11, he was intellectually horrified. Martin Harris became aware of this when he made a special trip to New York a second time to personally present a copy of the newly published Book of Mormon to him. Professor Anthon would not even allow Martin Harris to leave a copy in the house![61]

11—Both Isaiah and Nephi said that this learned man would declare that he could not read a "sealed" book.[62]

Nephi described in considerable detail the circumstances which would lead to this strange statement[63] and in the above quotation Martin Harris says, "He then said to me, 'Let me see that certificate.' I accordingly took it out of my pocket and gave it to him, when he took it and tore it to pieces, saying, that there was no such thing now as ministering of angels, and that if I would bring the plates to him, he would translate them. I INFORMED HIM THAT PART OF THE PLATES WERE SEALED, AND THAT I WAS FORBIDDEN TO BRING THEM. He replied, 'I CANNOT READ A SEALED BOOK.'"

12—Both Isaiah and Nephi verified that the unlearned man who was given the "book" would have the gift and power of God to read or translate it.[64]

Once Joseph Smith had learned how to use the Urim and Thummim and once he had procured Oliver Cowdery to write down the translation, Joseph Smith was able to translate the Book of Mormon at the phenomenal rate of nearly

---

61. Ibid.
62. Isaiah 29:11 and 2 Nephi 27:17-18
63. 2 Nephi 27:7-18
64. Isaiah 29:12, 14, 18 (also 2 Nephi 27:19-20) — The verses in Isaiah are somewhat obscure and must be read carefully. Note, however, that when the man says "I am not learned" the Lord says He will "do a marvelous work" which will cause the wisdom of the wise to perish, and in verse 18 He says the words of the book will be sent forth. All of this implies that the man who is not learned will translate the book through the power of God. Nephi verifies that this is a correct deduction. (2 Nephi 27:20).

5,000 words per day.[65] No doubt he could have gone even faster, but apparently that was about as rapid as the scribe could write it down. The frantic haste of the scribe is indicated in the original manuscript by the frequent lack of punctuation and sometimes of capitalization. These defects had to be corrected later.

13—Both Isaiah and Nephi indicated that the sacred record of the American Israelites would not be allowed to go forth to the public but, as Isaiah says, "in that day shall the deaf hear the WORDS of the book."[66]

Nephi is much more explicit in explaining why the original record would not be placed on public exhibition. He said because it contained the "sealed" section containing the sacred revelation of world history which would be revealed at a later time, therefore the record was to be kept "hid from the eyes of the world," and none should see it save those to whom the unlearned man was told to show it."[67]

Joseph Smith verifies that even before he received custody of the record he was strenuously cautioned against showing it to anyone unless commanded of the Lord. Wrote Joseph Smith, "Again, he [Moroni] told me, that when I got those plates of which he had spoken — for the time that they should be obtained was not yet fulfilled — I should not show them to any person; neither the breastplate with the Urim and Thummim; only to those to whom I should be commanded to show them; if I did I should be destroyed."[68]

14—Nephi knew that there would be three special witnesses who would be permitted to see the sacred record.[69]

The three witnesses were Oliver Cowdery, David Whitmer and Martin Harris. They saw Moroni, they saw the sacred record, and in addition they saw the breastplate,

---

65. Joseph Smith worked from April 7, 1829, to the latter part of June, 1829, to translate all (but a few pages which were done earlier) of the Book of Mormon. An examination of Joseph Smith's history shows that this prodigious task was accomplished in approximately 65 working days. The manuscript is on foolscap sheets, 8 x 13 inches with approximately 647 words to a page. Joseph covered enough material to fill an average of seven pages per day, or an average of 4,615 words per day. (See *How did Joseph Smith Translate?* by Arch S. Reynolds, pp. 26-27.)

66. Isaiah 29:18; 2 Nephi 27:12   68. P. of G. P., p. 52:42
67. 2 Nephi 27:12-14, 21-22   69. 2 Nephi 27:12

the sword of Laban, the Urim and Thummim and the Liahona or "directors" by which Lehi and his family were directed to America by crossing Arabia and the Pacific Ocean in the sixth century B.C.[70]

15—Nephi knew the three witnesses would not only see the sacred records but that they would issue a declaration to the world in which "they shall testify to the truth of the book and the things therein."[71]

This statement is set forth in the front of the Book of Mormon. Even though each of these men subsequently had difficulty keeping up with the pressures and responsibilities involved in setting up the latter-day Kingdom, nevertheless, none ever wavered in the slightest degree in substantiating the integrity of this statement.[72]

16—Nephi knew there would be a "few" others who would see the sacred record in addition to the three witnesses. Said he, "And there is none other which shall view it, save it be a few according to the will of God. . . ."[73]

These "few" included the eight witnesses who were allowed to see and handle the plates prior to the time they were returned to the custody and safekeeping of Moroni.[74] They were not allowed to see anything else. The joint statement of these witnesses is also found in the front of the Book of Mormon.

17—Both Isaiah and Nephi predicted that the reason the Lord would elect to do His great work through an "unlearned" man in the latter days was because "this people draw near to me with their mouth, and with their lips do honour me, but have removed their heart far from me, and their fear toward me is taught by the precept of men."[75]

The Lord verified that this exact circumstance existed by 1820. When Joseph Smith received the First Vision in

70. See Doc. His. of the Church, Vol. 1, pp. 52-55
71. 2 Nephi 27:12
72. See *A New Witness for Christ in America,* by Francis W. Kirkham, Vol. 1, chapter 19, "Witnesses to the Book of Mormon".
73. 2 Nephi 27:13
74. Doc. His. of the Church, Vol. 1, pp. 57-58
75. Isaiah 29:13 and 2 Nephi 27:24-25

the spring of that year it so frightened him that at first he could not articulate. However, he says, "No sooner, therefore, did I get possession of myself, so as to be able to speak, than I asked the Personages who stood above me in the light which of all the sects was right — and which I should join. I was answered that I must join none of them, for they were all wrong; and the Personage who addressed me said that all their creeds were an abomination in his sight; that those professors were all corrupt; that 'they draw near to me with their lips, but their hearts are far from me; they teach for doctrines the commandments of men, having a form of godliness, but they deny the power thereof.' "[76] This is what Isaiah and Nephi had been talking about.

18—Both Isaiah and Nephi knew that in connection with the coming forth of the Book of Mormon the Lord would commence to do "a marvelous work among this people, even a marvelous work and a wonder: for the wisdom of their wise men shall perish, and the understanding of their prudent men shall be hid."[77]

Not only was the so-called "unlearned" Joseph Smith given the power to translate the "reformed Egyptian" of the Plates of Mormon, but he translated the writings of Abraham which were brought out of the Egyptian catacombs with 11 mummies in the early 1820's by Antonio Lebolo.[78] Joseph Smith was given enough revelations for the modern-day Saints to fill a whole volume.[79] He was given a missing chapter of the Bible describing how Moses happened to write Genesis.[80] By revelation he was given the English version of a lost manuscript written by John the Beloved while on the Isle of Patmos.[81] He received and recorded a vision concerning the different degrees of glory in Heaven which Paul felt reluctant to disclose.[82] He received the correct procedures and prayers for administering the ordinances of baptism and the Sacrament.[83] He was given the Aaronic Priesthood and

76. P. of G. P., p. 48:19
77. Isaiah 29:14; 2 Nephi 27:26
78. See P. of G. P., Book of Abraham
79. This is called, *The Doctrine and Covenants*
80. Moses, chapter 1
81. D. & C., Section 7
82. D. & C., Section 76 and 2 Cor. 12:2-5
83. D. & C., Sections 20:73 and 20:77-79

later the Melchizedek Priesthood.[84] He was taught how to construct temples and the proper ordinances to be performed in them.[85] He was shown how to organize and establish the true Church of Jesus Christ upon the earth.[86] He was told what the duties were among all the various ranks of office holders in the Kingdom.[87] Under his administration the marvelous gifts of the Spirit were restored and enjoyed.[88]

Who would deny that all of this was not truly a "marvelous work and a wonder"? It has been an astonishing enigma to the world's wise and prudent ever since it first began!

19—Isaiah and Nephi both knew that when the history of the American Israelites went forth many who had been both deaf and blind to the truthfulness of the Gospel would now respond.[89]

Since the restoration of the Gospel, several million Israelites have been gathered into the Gospel net and no single influence has had a greater missionary appeal in convincing men and women that God has spoken again than the Book of Mormon. It is a book which the Lord has promised to endorse through the Spirit of the Holy Ghost to all who will read it prayerfully and earnestly.[90] Thousands upon thousands can now testify that they whose eyes were blind are now able to see out of obscurity and darkness.

20—Isaiah and Nephi knew that the great and marvelous work which God would do among men in the latter days would be of particular significance to the poor and cause them to rejoice "in the Holy One of Israel."[91]

In one of the early revelations to the Church, the Lord said, "And the poor and the meek shall have the gospel

---

84. D. & C., Section 13 as also 27:12 — The latter scripture makes reference to the ordination but it had occurred sometime earlier.
85. During his lifetime, Joseph Smith built two temples (Kirtland and Nauvoo, the latter completed shortly after his death) and had the sites dedicated at Independence and Far West for two more. (See *Temples of the Most High,* by N. B. Lundwall, chapters 1, 2, 12 and 13.)
86. Joseph Smith saw a vision of the complete structure of the Church.
87. See as examples, D. & C. sections 20 and 107.
88. An excellent example of these powers being exhibited was at the dedication of the Kirtland Temple. See Doc. Hist. of the Church, Vol. 2, p. 428.
89. Isaiah 29:18; 2 Nephi 27:29
90. Moroni 10:4
91. Isaiah 29:19; 2 Nephi 27:30

peached unto them, and they shall be looking forth for the
time of my coming, for it is nigh at hand."[92] At a time when
churches were characterized by heavy assessments, extravagant vestments, pompous buildings, exploitation of the lowly,
God restored His Kingdom specifically designed to make the
Gospel free to all men. It was like the return of the fresh,
generous spirit of Paul when he said, "What is my reward
then? Verily that, when I preach the gospel, I may make
the gospel of Christ without charge, that I abuse not my
power in the gospel."[93]

Thus we conclude one of the most significant chapters
in the entire book of Isaiah. It reflected some of the most
important work the Lord would do in the latter days. Note
that Nephi thought it was so important he devoted the larger
segment of his commentary to it. Joseph Smith must have
been astonished as he went through this material and recognized how many details had been fulfilled during his own
administration. That the Lord revealed this information as
far back as 700 B.C. shows how important He considered it!

---

92. D. & C. sec. 35:15
93. I Cor. 9:18

Scripture Reading and Questions on Chapter Twenty-One

Scripture Reading: 3 Nephi, chapters 21 to 27 relating to Isaiah.

1—How did Nephi happen to write his inspired commentary on Isaiah? Did he depend upon the context of Isaiah or independent revelations?

2—Prior to the discovery of America, was the ignorance of the world concerning the Western Hemisphere accidental or to fulfill a divine purpose?

3—Do we have any reason to believe that Isaiah knew about America?

4—As far as we can tell, whom did Isaiah have in mind when he referred to the "root of Jesse"? According to modern revelation, what three things would characterize this person?

5—When Isaiah spoke of "the isles of the sea" did he intend to include America? How do we know?

6—What new ideas did you get as you read the parallel between Isaiah and Nephi's writings? Can you list at least three?

7—How was the prophecy fulfilled which said certain Israelites would "speak out of the ground"? Would they have a "familiar spirit"?

8—When did Isaiah and Nephi indicate that the Book of Mormon would come forth? What did Nephi say the status of the Gentiles and Jews would be at that time?

9—Just how "unlearned" was Joseph Smith at the time he received the plates?

10—What did the "sealed" portion of the plates contain? Did Joseph Smith try to translate any of that portion?

11—Why do you think Professor Anthon was so quick to change his attitude about the plates when Martin Harris said an angel had revealed their location?

12—Did the Three Witnesses get to see anything besides the plates? What did the Eight Witnesses get to see?

13—What did the Lord mean when He said, "Their fear toward me is taught by the precept of men"?

14—Why would the Lord tell Joseph Smith that the formalized creeds of the various churches were an abomination in His sight?

15—In what way did Joseph Smith commence a "marvelous work and a wonder"?

16—Approximately how many words did he translate per day? Have you ever tried to write that many words in your own language in a single day? How many have you written?

17—List five outstanding things Joseph Smith contributed or accomplished as a result of his calling as a servant of the Lord.

18—Where, in modern revelation, does the Lord tell how Moses happened to get the material in the opening portion of Genesis?

19—How important has the Book of Mormon been in converting people to the latter-day work of the Lord?

20—Why do you think the Lord specifically commanded that the Gospel should be preached to the poor? Did this exclude the rich?

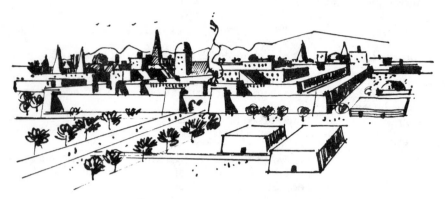

CHAPTER TWENTY-TWO

Prophecy and Modern Times

Now we turn to those prophecies of Isaiah which extend from the present to the distant future. First, however, let us make an observation concerning certain patterns in prophecy.

As each of the ancient prophets scanned the prophetic visions of the future, they must have been astonished as well as impressed by the fact that history tends to continually repeat itself. And this is true for individuals as well as nations. Therefore, Isaiah, David and a number of other scriptural writers, sometimes wrote their prophecies in such a way that their readers could apply them to a variety of situations, times and places AND BE CORRECT IN ALL OF THEM!

We have already seen a number of cases where Isaiah described his own experiences as being a type of the Savior's persecution and suffering which would come 700 years later.[1] We have noted David doing the same thing.[2]

Isaiah follows the same pattern when he makes his declarations concerning the isles of the sea. Nephi and his brother, Jacob, said these statements included the Israelites

---

1. Isaiah 50:5-6; 49:1-3; see marginal references to the New Testament
2. Psalm 22 is a typical example.

in America.[3] However, they were both quick to point out that there are Israelites scattered in other parts of the earth and therefore Isaiah's words would apply to them also.[4]

Isaiah promised that in connection with the great latter-day gathering of Israel the desert would "blossom as a rose." Here again we have multiple applications. It will be fulfilled when the Ten Tribes come down from the north to overflow the land, but it is already being fulfilled in the valleys of the Rockies and on the barren slopes and plains of Palestine. Micah and Isaiah both promised that the house of the Lord would be built in the tops of the mountains. This has already been fulfilled in the tops of the American mountains and will soon be duplicated when a great temple is built in the tops of the mountains of Israel. The gathering of Israel is taking place in America and also in the land of Judah. The Saints of God will be persecuted by the wicked in both places. They will be rescued by the Lord in both places. These are just a few examples of the pattern of "multiple fulfillments" which run through many prophecies found in the scriptures.

As we have previously noted, Isaiah's prophecies which were fulfilled in the past actually covered a tremendous sweep. The same can be said of his prophecies dealing with the future. It is not our purpose here to provide an exhaustive discussion of all of them but merely to present their scope. By this means we can appreciate the reason why Jesus told the American Israelites that Isaiah was one of the great writers of scripture who deserved careful and diligent analysis. He said: "And now, behold, I say unto you, that ye ought to search these things. Yea, a *commandment* I give unto you that ye search these things diligently; FOR GREAT ARE THE WORDS OF ISAIAH."[5]

Isaiah Speaks of the Two Great "Zions" of the Latter Days

One of the most significant terms in scriptural literature is the word, "Zion." Isaiah uses the word frequently. The Lord says the City of Enoch was first called "Zion" because "they were of one heart and one mind, and dwelt in righteous-

---

3. I Nephi 22:4-6; 2 Nephi 10:20-21   5. 3 Nephi 23:1
4. Ibid.

ness; and there was no poor among them.''[6] In modern times the Lord said, ''. . . let Zion rejoice, for this is Zion — THE PURE IN HEART. . . .''[7] Joseph Smith said both North and South America were intended by the Lord as ''Zion.''[8] The ancient prophets often referred to Jerusalem, especially Mount Moriah, as ''Zion.''[9]

Isaiah knew that in the latter days there would be a Zion in America and a Zion in Palestine. He therefore addresses both of them on a number of occasions but to distinguish one from the other he calls America ''Zion'' and Palestine ''Jerusalem.'' Here are typical examples:

''O Zion, that bringest good tidings, GET THEE UP INTO THE HIGH MOUNTAIN [the American Rockies to which the modern Church was led are about three times higher than the mountains of Judeah]; O Jerusalem, that bringest good tidings, lift up thy voice with strength.''[10]

''The first shall say to Zion, Behold, behold them: and I will give to Jerusalem one that bringeth good tidings.''[11]

''Awake, awake; put on thy strength, O Zion; put on thy beautiful garments, O Jerusalem, the holy city.''[12]

''For Zion's sake will I not hold my peace, and for Jerusalem's sake I will not rest, until the righteousness thereof go forth as brightness. . . .''[13]

''. . . princes shall be afraid of the ensign, saith the Lord, whose fire is in Zion, and his furnace in Jerusalem.''[14]

These are sufficient to show Isaiah's knowledge and concern for the two great centers of divine interest in the last days. As noted above, however, when he speaks of these two places together, Isaiah uses ''Zion'' for God's work in America and ''Jerusalem'' to designate the Lord's center of activity in Judeah. However, once we understand that ''Zion'' is a condition as well as a place, we are better able

---

6. Moses 7:18
7. D. & C. 97:21
8. *Teachings of the Prophet Joseph Smith,* p. 362
9. 2 Samuel 5:6-7; I Kings 8:1
10. Isaiah 40:9
11. Isaiah 41:27
12. Isaiah 52:1
13. Isaiah 62:1
14. Isaiah 31:9

to appreciate why Isaiah also calls Jerusalem a "Zion" on occasion. In one place he specifically talks about the people who "shall dwell in Zion at Jerusalem."[15]

As for the Zion in America, we have already seen that Isaiah was well aware that there was a country far off "beyond the rivers of Ethiopia" from which would go forth swift messengers to gather Israel which was once so strong, but had become trodden down, scattered and peeled.[16] He said these people would commence to gather and bring their presents to "the place of the name of the Lord of hosts, the mount Zion."[17] Isaiah admonished the whole world to listen when the trumpet blows and the ensign is set up "on the mountains" of this land.[18]

The Lord's purpose in setting up a "Zion" is to provide a haven of safety for the righteous. Therefore Isaiah says, "He that walked righteously . . . shall dwell on high: his place of defence shall be the munitions of rocks: bread shall be given him; his waters shall be sure."[19] Ultimately, this will apply to both Zions.

THE GREAT GATHERING

Isaiah knew that once the trumpet had sounded and the missionaries had gone forth to convert the righteous, they would flock to Zion in America. He also knew there would be a great gathering of the Jews to Jerusalem. Said he, "And it shall come to pass in that day, that the Lord shall set his hand again the second time to recover the remnant of his people. . . . And he shall set up an ensign for the nations, and shall assemble the OUTCASTS of Israel, and gather together the DISPERSED of Judah from the four corners of the earth."[20]

Isaiah said that as between the righteous Jews and the righteous descendants of Joseph there would no longer be the antagonism which existed in ancient times. Isaiah said,

---

15. Isaiah 30:19
16. Isaiah, chapter 18. Zephaniah helps identify America as the land "beyond the rivers of Ethiopia" by pointing out that it is from this land that the "daughter of my dispersed" (children of Israel) shall come to bring their offering in the last days. (Zephaniah 3:10)
17. Isaiah 18:7
18. Isaiah 18:3
19. Isaiah 33:15-16
20. Isaiah 11:11-12

"The envy also of Ephraim shall depart, and the adversaries of Judah shall be cut off: EPHRAIM SHALL NOT ENVY JUDAH, AND JUDAH SHALL NOT VEX EPHRAIM."[21]

The prophet saw that it would be a long time (over 2,500 years for the Israelites and 1,800 years for the Jews!) before they would get the call to rally and return again. Isaiah wanted the people to know this postponement or delay was all part of the plan: "And therefore will the Lord wait, that he may be gracious unto you, and therefore will he be exalted, that he may have mercy upon you: for the Lord is a God of judgment: BLESSED ARE ALL THEY THAT WAIT FOR HIM."[22]

Isaiah described a number of details concerning the gathering which are of special interest to those of us who are responsible for bringing it about. What foreign missionary, for example, could help but appreciate Isaiah's declaration that "with stammering lips and another tongue will he speak to this people."[23] And the Lord knew it would not be easy to overcome centuries of apostasy and ignorance. In order to "teach knowledge" and help them "understand doctrine" Isaiah said, ". . . precept must be upon precept . . . line upon line . . . here a little, and there a little."[24]

Although the call to the righteous would be world-wide, Isaiah declared that there would be a severe screening process. ". . . ye shall be gathered one by one, O ye children of Israel."[25]

THE RETURN OF THE LOST TEN TRIBES

Of course, as soon as the foundation of the Kingdom can be established by this extremely careful screening process, Isaiah indicated that great multitudes would suddenly flow into the Church through the arrival of the Ten Lost Tribes. Note that Isaiah specifically calls these tribes "outcasts" whereas the Jews are called "dispersed." Parley P. Pratt suggests that there is some deep significance behind the distinction in these two words.[26] From whence will the multi-

21. Isaiah 11:13
22. Isaiah 30:18
23. Isaiah 28:11

24. Isaiah 28:10
25. Isaiah 27:12
26. *Voice of Warning*, p. 30

tude of Ten Tribes come? It will be from that mysterious place to which they have been cast out, but its location is not known at the present time. But we do know that it will take a stupendous miracle to get them to America. Isaiah says, "And there shall be an highway for the remnant of his people, which shall be left, from Assyria [the last place the Ten Tribes were seen]; like as it was to Israel in the day when he came up out of the land of Egypt."[27]

Of course, the highway by which the Israelites came up out of Egypt was a most exciting thoroughfare, associated with a continuous series of miracles including the dividing of the Red Sea. Apparently the great transmission belt by which the Ten Tribes will return can be expected to be even more amazing. A modern scripture gives us some idea of its gargantuan proportions. Said the Lord, "And they who are in the north countries shall come in remembrance before the Lord; and THEIR PROPHETS[28] SHALL HEAR HIS VOICE [command], and shall no longer stay themselves; and they shall smite the rocks, and the ice shall flow down at their presence. And an highway shall be cast up in the midst of THE GREAT DEEP. Their enemies shall become a prey unto them, and in the barren deserts there shall come forth pools of living water . . . And they shall bring forth their rich treasures unto the children of Ephraim, my servants. And the boundaries of the everlasting hills shall tremble at their presence. And there shall they fall down and be crowned with glory, even in Zion, by the hands of the servants of the Lord, even the children of Ephraim."[29]

It is clear from this passage that the Ten Tribes will come in a great multitude from the north (the direction in which they disappeared), that the highway or means of returning will appear in the midst of "the great deep" (which could be either space or water), that neither the ice cap of

---

27. Isaiah 11:16
28. In June, 1831, Joseph Smith said that John the Revelator was already working among the Lost Ten Tribes. See Doc. His. of the Church, Vol. I, p. 176.
29. D. & C. 133:26-32. This spectacular event will be so marvelous that Jeremiah says: "Therefore, behold, the days come, saith the Lord, that they shall no more say, The LORD liveth, which brought up the children of Israel out of the land of Egypt; But, The LORD liveth, which brought up and which led the seed of the house of Israel out of the north country, and from all countries whither I had driven them; and they shall dwell in their own land." (Jeremiah 23:7-8)

the Arctic nor the mighty battlements of intervening mountains will deter them. They will overcome any manmade opposition which stands in their way, and they will come down the spine of the American continent to the modern headquarters of God's Priesthood where they can enter the temples and receive their sacred Endowments,[30] from the Ephraimite Saints who possess the keys to these great blessings.

When will the Ten Tribes come? The Savior gave the best clue when He was visiting the American Saints shortly after His resurrection. He said the New Jerusalem would be built on this, the American continent,[31] that the Savior, Himself, would make His appearance there,[32] "AND THEN shall the work of the Father commence . . . among all the dispersed of my people, yea, EVEN THE TRIBES WHICH HAVE BEEN LOST, which the Father hath led away out of Jerusalem."[33] So it would seem quite clear that the New Jerusalem must be built before the Ten Tribes return.

As this mammoth host marches in toward the City of Zion or the New Jerusalem, Isaiah described what it would be like: "They shall not hunger nor thirst; neither shall the heat nor sun smite them: for he that hath mercy on them shall lead them, even by the springs of water shall he guide them. And I will make all my mountains a way, and my highways shall be exalted. Behold, these shall come from far. . . ."[34] Nevertheless, after they have arrived, the impact of this overnight population explosion will be so great that the Ephraimite Saints will hardly know what to do with them. Isaiah said, "For thou shalt break forth on the right hand and on the left; and thy seed shall inherit the Gentiles, and

---

30. Wilford Woodruff stated in the *Journal of Discourses*, Vol. 4, pages 231-232: "Again, here are the ten tribes of Israel, we know nothing about them only what the Lord has said by His Prophets. There are Prophets among them, and by and by they will come along, and they will smite the rocks, and the mountains of ice will flow down at their presence, and a highway will be cast up before them, and they will come to Zion, receive their endowments, and be crowned under the hands of the children of Ephraim . . . They will receive their blessings and endowments, from under the children of Ephraim, who are the first fruits of the kingdom of God in this dispensation, and the men will have to be ordained and receive their Priesthood and Endowments in the land of Zion, according to the revelations of God."

31. 3 Nephi 21:23-24   33. 3 Nephi 21:26
32. 3 Nephi 21:25   34. Isaiah 49:10-12

make the desolate cities to be inhabited."[35] He indicates that the Ten Tribes will even be a greater host than the members of the Church, "for more are the children of the desolate than the children of the married wife, saith the Lord."[36]

The Lord will bless the desolate land in all the surrounding territory. "The wilderness and the solitary place shall be glad for them; and the desert shall rejoice, and blossom as the rose . . . for in the wilderness shall waters breaks out, and streams in the desert. And the parched ground shall become a pool, and the thirsty land springs of water: in the habitation of dragons [lizards, etc.] where each lay, shall be grass with reeds and rushes."[37] Isaiah saw that this wonderful blessing was by heavenly intervention. Said he, "For the Lord shall comfort Zion: he will comfort all her waste places; and he will make her wilderness like Eden, and her desert like the garden of the Lord; joy and gladness shall be found therein, thanksgiving, and the voice of melody."[38]

The surging crowds of newcomers will be carefully organized into orderly patterns that shall spread out in all directions from the center at New Jerusalem. Isaiah proclaimed, "Enlarge the place of thy tent, and let them stretch forth the curtains of thine habitations: spare not, lengthen thy cords, and strengthen thy stakes; For thou shalt break forth on the right hand and on the left; and thy seed shall inherit the Gentiles, and make the desolate cities to be inhabited."[39]

Eventually, when world conditions will permit it, these great hosts will joyfully move on to Palestine where they will be give a permanent inheritance and help the Jews build up a mighty kingdom. Ezekiel was especially impressed with this great day when the Lord would "take the children of Israel . . . and bring them into their own land: And I will make them one nation" saith the Lord, "in the land UPON THE MOUNTAINS OF ISRAEL; and one king shall be king of them all: and they shall be no more two nations,

---

35. Isaiah 54:3
36. Isaiah 54:1
37. Isaiah 35:1, 6-7
38. Isaiah 51:3
39. Isaiah 54:2-3. Verse 3 is repeated here, although previously quoted, in order to better appreciate its full intent.

neither shall they be divided into two kingdoms any more at all. . . . And David my servant shall be king over them."[40] And just as John the Revelator will have been instrumental in bringing these hosts of Israel to the American Zion[41] for their Priesthood Endowments, so also he will no doubt have an important responsibility in leading them back to the land of their original inheritance. According to modern revelation, this is the meaning of the little book which John was required to eat as mentioned in the tenth chapter of Revelations: ". . . it was a mission, and an ordinance, for him to gather the tribes of Israel."[42]

It is interesting to note that when the tribes return to Old Jerusalem they will take along with them any of the tribe of Joseph who wish to go. Even though America is the inheritance of Joseph,[43] Ezekiel says there will be a "portion for Manasseh"[44] and "a portion for Ephraim,"[45] when the permanent tribal inheritances are set up in Palestine.

Isaiah saw how marvelous it would be in Jerusalem when her temple had been rebuilt and all of the vast multitudes of Israel had been given their inheritances around her. He wrote, ". . . thine eyes shall see Jerusalem a quiet habitation, a tabernacle that shall not be taken down; not one of the stakes thereof shall ever be removed, neither shall any of the cords thereof be broken."[46]

The Building of the New Jerusalem in America

Let us now go back, however, and take a closer look at the great city of Zion or the New Jerusalem which is to be built on the American continent in these latter days.

The 54th chapter of Isaiah is devoted to the great gathering of Israel in America and the setting up of her magnificent capital. Jesus put this chapter in its proper context when He visited America after His resurrection. The

---

40. Ezekiel 37:21-24
41. See Doc. His. of the Church, Vol. I, p. 176, note.
42. D. & C. 77:14
43. Orson Pratt said that ". . . we are inheriting a land that was given to the remnant of Joseph, and God has said that we must be remembered . . . in the possession of this land." (*Journal of Discourses,* Vol. 12, p. 322) See also I Nephi 13:30.
44. Ezekiel 48:4   46. Isaiah 33:20
45. Ezekiel 48:5

Savior said that He would first bring the Gentiles to inhabit this continent, "For it is wisdom in the Father that they should be established in this land, and be set up as a free people by the power of the Father."[47] Then He said the Gospel would be restored among them, "For thus it behooveth the Father that it [the restored Gospel] should come forth from the Gentiles, that he may show forth his power unto the Gentiles, for this cause that the Gentiles, if they will not harden their hearts, that they may repent and come unto me and be baptized in my name. . . ."[48]

To accomplish this, Jesus said the Father would raise up an inspired servant in this day but many would not believe him: "there shall be among them those who will not believe it [the Gospel message] although a man shall declare it unto them."[49] Therefore the Lord's servant "shall be marred because of them. Yet I will heal him, for I will show unto them that my wisdom is greater than the cunning of the devil."[50]

At this point Jesus said the Gentiles would have to make a tremendous decision either to support the work of the Lord or be swept from the land. If they elected to fight the work of God, Jesus told them how terrible the consequences would be.[51] On the other hand, the Lord said, "if they will repent and hearken unto my words, and harden not their hearts . . . THEY SHALL ASSIST MY PEOPLE, the remnant of Jacob, and also as many of the house of Israel as shall come, THAT THEY MAY BUILD A CITY, WHICH SHALL BE CALLED THE NEW JERUSALEM. And then shall they assist my people that they may be gathered in, who are scattered upon all the face of the land, in unto the New Jerusalem."[52] In order to emphasize that it would be the place of great beauty, power and glory, Jesus declared, "And THEN shall that which is written [by Isaiah] come to pass."[53] He then went directly into the 54th chapter of Isaiah and quoted this scripture in its entirety.

What did Isaiah have to say about this great New Jerusalem which is to be built in America? It will be noted that

---

47. 3 Nephi 21:4
48. 3 Nephi 21:6
49. 3 Nephi 21:9
50. 3 Nephi 21:10

51. 3 Nephi 21:12-21
52. 3 Nephi 22:22-24
53. 3 Nephi 22:1

much that we have already said about the assembling of the Ten Tribes at the New Jerusalem was taken from this same chapter. In addition, Isaiah had this directly from the Lord concerning the New Jerusalem and its people:

"Behold, I will lay thy stones with fair colors, and lay thy foundations with sapphires. And I will make thy windows of agates, and thy gates of carbuncles,[54] and all thy borders of pleasant stones. And all thy children shall be taught of the Lord; and great shall be the peace of thy children. In righteousness shalt thou be established; thou shalt be far from oppression for thou shalt not fear, and from terror for it shall not come near thee. . . . No weapon that is formed against thee shall prosper; and every tongue that shall rise against thee in judgment thou shalt condemn. This is the heritage of the servants of the Lord, and their righteousness is of me, saith the Lord."[55]

So wrote Isaiah concerning America's future City of Zion or New Jerusalem.

The Gathering of the Jews and the Rebuilding of Old Jerusalem

Isaiah also was aware that during the same general period that the Lord was performing His great labor in America, He would be fulfilling His promises concerning the gathering of the Jews and the rebuilding of the Old Jerusalem.

Chapter 40 of Isaiah is the prophet's triumphant song of hope for Judah and Jerusalem. Isaiah's vision swept from the beginning of the city's restoration right on through to her glory in the millennium. Then he cried, "Comfort ye, comfort ye my people, saith your God. Speak ye comfortably to Jerusalem, and cry unto her that her warfare is accomplished, that her iniquity is pardoned: for she hath received of the Lord's hand double for all her sins. . . . O Jerusalem, that bringest good tidings, lift up thy voice with strength; lift it up, be not afraid; say unto the cities of Judah, BEHOLD YOUR GOD!"[56]

---

54. A carbuncle is "any of certain deep-red gems, especially a garnet with a smooth convex surface." (Webster's *New World Dictionary*)
55. 3 Nephi 22:11-17
56. Isaiah 40:1, 9

Actually, there will have to be many years of preparation before the Jews finally behold their God, but it will come. The first task of the Jews has been to establish a homeland in Palestine. This took three generations to accomplish.

The Lord's official program for the gathering of the Jews to Palestine was launched on October 24, 1841, when Orson Hyde, a Jewish disciple of the restored Church, stood on the brow of the Mount of Olives and poured forth his heart in a prayer which ended with the dedication of that land for the return of the Jews. During the past four centuries Palestine had been under the Ottoman Turks and it had become a land of total desolation just as the prophets had predicted. It had become the graveyard of a grandeur long since passed. Its terrain no longer boasted gardens, vineyards or fat flocks. Instead, barren, ragged rocks protruded from its mountains and hillsides while the fields and valleys lay largely neglected. Only the most primitive agricutural arts were practiced by the local Arabs.

An important part of the prayer of Orson Hyde, as he petitioned Heaven from the Mount of Olives, was as follows: "Grant, therefore, O Lord, in the name of Thy well-beloved Son, Jesus Christ, to remove the barrenness and sterility of this land, and let springs of living water break forth to water its thirsty soil. Let the vine and olive produce in their strength, and the fig tree bloom and flourish. Let the land become abundantly fruitful and possessed by its rightful heirs . . . let Thy great kindness conquer and subdue the unbelief of Thy people. Do Thou take from them their stoney heart, and give them a heart of flesh. . . . Incline them to gather in upon this land according to Thy word. Let them come like clouds and like doves to their windows. Let the large ships of the nations bring them from the distant isles; and let kings become their nursing father, and queens with motherly fondness wipe the tear of sorrow from their eye."[57]

In 1873, George A. Smith was sent by Brigham Young to re-dedicate the land and pray fervently that the work of the Lord might be expedited.[58] As of that time it is estimated that isolated pockets of Jews sprinkled among the Arab popu-

---

57. *Essentials of Church History*, pp. 312-313.
58. *Comprehensive History of the Church*, Vol. 5, pp. 474-75.

lation amounted to no more than 12,000 to 15,000. However, within five years two significant movements were established to encourage additional Jewish migration. One was set up among Russian Jews, called the "Lovers of Zion"; the other was mainly among Polish and Romanian Jews called the Bilu. This name was abbreviated from the Hebrew words meaning "House of Jacob, let us go!" These groups initiated the first wave of migration to Palestine, which is referred to as the "First *Aliyah*." They settled approximately 25,000 emigrants between 1882 and 1902.

Meanwhile, in 1897, the first conference of the World Zionist Organization was held in Basel, Switzerland. Its founder was Dr. Theodore Herzl, a Jewish journalist and lawyer from Vienna, who had been shocked by the anti-Jewish sentiment in France during the famous Dreyfus case. He had therefore written a dissertation in 1896 called, *The Jewish State*. He felt the Jews must shortly gather together or suffer severe persecution. His idea was to create a Jewish homeland in Palestine through diplomatic negotiation with the Turkish government and by purchase of the land from Arab landholders. This first Zionist congress discussed the erection of a Hebrew University in Jerusalem, the creation of a Jewish national fund, the setting up of a Jewish world bank in London to finance colonization, the design for a blue and white flag and the adoption of a national anthem for their country which did not yet exist.

In 1903, as Herzl had feared, a terroristic and brutal persecution of the Jews broke out in Russia. In Kishinev of Bessarabia, the Jewish dead were piled in the streets like cordwood. Herzl literally worked himself to death going from one world capital to another seeking support for his new Jewish state. He suddenly died July 3, 1904, at the age of 44, and today lies buried on a peak which is named after him, overlooking Jerusalem. By 1904 a new wave of migration had begun called the Second Aliyah and 40,000 more Jews, mostly young people, migrated between 1904 and 1914. These young people called themselves Halutzim, meaning "Pioneers." Among them was a frail, earnest lad from Western Russia named David Green. When he began writing he took the name of David Ben-Gurion (Son of the Young Lion). Another lad was Chaim Weizmann from a background similar to the Green boy. Later, David Ben-Gurion became the first Prime Minister of Israel. Chaim Weizmann became its first President.

In 1917 the British succeeded in capturing Palestine from the Turkish empire and was afterwards given a mandate over the territory by the League of Nations. The British issued the famous Balfour Declaration which made it possible for Jews to begin migrating to Palestine more freely. This brought about the Third Aliyah and about 34,000 additional Jews entered Palestine between 1919 and 1923.

The British then began placating the Arabs due to the discovery of Arabian oil and because of certain secret commitments which British officials had made to Arab leaders during the war. The threat of a possible restriction of Jewish migration caused a Fourth Aliyah, and 82,000 Jews migrated to Palestine between 1924 and 1931. By this time the stage was set for Hitler's massive reign of terror against the Jews. As of 1939 another 214,000 Jewish refugees or emigrants had entered Palestine.

Adolf Hitler and "The Protocols of the Learned Elders of Zion"

When Adolf Hitler wrote *Mein Kampf* (My Battle) he included a vitriolic attack against the Jewish race, and blamed most of Germany's problems on the German Jews. He said the Jews were out to take over the world and offered as his proof a publication called, *The Protocols [minutes of proceedings] of the Learned Elders of Zion*. This was supposed to have been the plans drawn up at a secret meeting by Jewish leaders for the complete domination of all nations and the building of a Jewish world-dictatorship.

The document Hitler was talking about was first published in Russia in 1903 and was subsequently published in a more extended form in Russia and later in Western Europe and America. It described all the techniques that could be used to destroy representative governments and western, Christian culture, thereby permitting the seizure of complete political power throughout the world. Being a highly inflammatory document, the *Protocols* made excellent propaganda for Hitler, but equally serious was the fact that it seemed to be accepted as evidence of Jewish duplicity even by many well-meaning people.[59]

Those who published the PROTOCOLS often wrote horrendous introductions so that the reader could not possibly miss the pointed implications which the publisher felt it contained. The copy in my own files is undated but appears to be of the early 1920 vintage and says, "It [Protocol XI] proves that the desire for a 'National Home' in Palestine is only camouflage and an infinitesimal part of the Jew's real object. It proves that the Jews of the world have no intention of settling in Palestine or any separate country, and that their annual prayer that they may all meet 'next year in Jerusalem' is merely a piece of their characteristic make-believe. It also demonstrates that the Jews are now a world menace, and that the Aryan races will have to domicile them permanently out of Europe."[60]

Imagine reading such an introduction and then finding lurid passages in the *Protocols* such as the following (which are supposed to be secret Jewish plans): "We are interested . . . in the diminuation, the killing out of the GOYIM [non-Jews]. Our power is in the chronic shortness of food and physical weakness of the worker because by all that this implies he is made the slave of our will, and he will not find in his own authorities either strength or energy to set against our will. . . . By want and the envy and hatred which it engenders we shall move the mobs and with their hands we shall wipe out all those who hinder us on our way."[61]

It can be readily seen why such a document would be spread all over Germany by someone like Hitler. It could not have been written to suit his purposes any better if he had composed it himself.

---

59. Henry Ford was one of these. He became extremely exercised after reading this document. The New York *World* of February 17, 1921, quotes him as saying, "The only statement I care to make about the PROTOCOLS is that they fit in with what is going on. They are sixteen years old, and they have fitted the world situation up to this time. They fit it now." A series of articles in Mr. Ford's *Dearborn Independent* were published weekly between May 22 and October 2, 1920, on the "international Jewish conspiracy." These were subsequently published by Mr. Ford in a pamphlet called *The International Jew*. According to the Universal Jewish Encyclopedia, under "Elders of Zion", the following appears: ". . . in a letter to Louis Marshall, dated June 30, 1927, Ford retracted and apologized for the publication, claiming that he had been duped by his assistants."
60. *Protocols of the Learned Elders of Zion*, p. 7
61. Ibid., p. 21

For many years it seemed that only the Jews themselves were anxious to run down the facts and discover where this so-called *Protocols of the Learned Elders of Zion* actually came from. However, the matter eventually ended up in the courts. In 1934, several Jewish societies in Switzerland brought suit against two Swiss Nazi's for distributing the *Protocols*. Based on the evidence Jewish scholars had collected, they charged that the *Protocols* were a complete forgery concocted by one of the Tsar's agents while in France and that it had nothing to do with the Jews. At the trial in Bern, which attracted wide attention, it was shown that most of the material was lifted or adapted from a French publication by Maurice Joly, who had written it as a satire against Napoleon III. It was designed to show how a clever fellow could organize a secret force to destroy democratic nations and set up a tyrannical world empire. The book was called "A Dialogue Between Machiavelli and Montesquieu." In this book it was not the learned Elders of Zion who were doing the plotting but Machiavelli. The author of the *Protocols* had obviously lifted words, phrases and ideas from this source.

The trial also brought out the origin of the publication of the *Protocols* and how it had been used by Russian officials to influence Tsar Nicholas II even before it was published. The author of the forgery was identified as a writer named Golovinskii who had done this work for a Tsarist agent in Paris named Rachkovskii. The date of its origin was put at around 1899-1901.

The trial at Bern accomplished much good by bringing before the scrutiny of a court the true origin and purpose of this spurious document. As a result, various reference works began warning students of the fraudulent nature of the *Protocols*. It is noted that the latest edition of Webster's College Dictionary has this to say: "PROTOCOLS OF THE ELDERS OF ZION: a set of forged writings created by Russian reactionaries in 1903 and circulated by anti-Semitic propagandists, purporting to be a record of a series of meetings in Basel in 1897 for plotting the overthrow of Christian civilization by Jews and Freemasons."

After hearing this evidence, the court at Bern reached a verdict that the *Protocols* were a forgery and therefore could not be distributed. Subsequently, a higher court held that under the broad and permissive laws of Switzerland, the fact that the *Protocols* were a forgery could not be the basis for banning them. Therefore this material continued to be circulated even in Switzerland.

It was brought out that in the very beginning the *Protocols* were circulated as something that *could* have been passed at some secret Jewish meeting. Only later was it specifically attributed to the World Zionist Congress of 1897. It was also discovered that at its inception the document was not presented as merely a Jewish document but as a conspiracy between Jews and Masons!

Adolf Hitler continued using the *Protocols* to justify the mass arrests of Jews on the ground that they were part of a racial conspiracy against Germany and the rest of the world. Once arrested, extermination soon followed for vast numbers of them while the remainder virtually starved to death in labor corps or concentration camps.

The Nazi terror against the Jews resulted in two migra- tions: one to Palestine where the Jewish population soon reached over a million, and one to the United States where the immigrants joined with the Jewish population which was already here and eventually rose to a total of over five mil- lion. The Jews in the United States then became the prin- cipal source of outside financial support for the Jews in Palestine. It was this combination of dedicated Jewish nation- builders in Palestine and the liberal financial support of the Jews in America that made much of Israel's success possible.

Back in 1879 Wilford Woodruff had written from the St. George Temple, "I wish in this testimony to say that the time is not far distant when the rich men among the Jews will be called upon to use their abundant wealth to gather the dispersed of Judah, and purchase the ancient dwelling places of their fathers in and about Jerusalem, and rebuild the holy city and temple."[62]

As for Hitler, a singular prophecy in Isaiah speaks of those Gentiles of the latter days who elect to make captives

---

62. M. F. Cowley, *Wilford Woodruff*, p. 509

of the Israelites rather than help them. This prophecy spelled the doom of Hitler even when he appeared to be at the height of his victories. Isaiah wrote to latter-day Israelites the following prophetic promise: "But thus saith the Lord, Even the captives of the mighty shall be taken away, and the prey of the terrible shall be delivered: for I will contend with him that contendeth with thee, and I will save thy children. AND I WILL FEED THEM THAT OPPRESS THEE WITH THEIR OWN FLESH; AND THEY SHALL BE DRUNKEN WITH THEIR OWN BLOOD, as with sweet wine: and all flesh shall know that I the Lord am thy Saviour and thy Redeemer, the mighty One of Jacob."[63]

THE CREATION OF A MODERN ISRAEL

By the commencement of World War II, the British, who had been given the responsibility of maintaining peace between Arabs and Jews, virtually terminated Jewish migration. After the war, however, the Jews insisted that since they had fought with the Allies, and the Arabs had lined up with the Axis, there now should be no question whatever as to their right to have a homeland of their own where the masses of refugees from Europe could find a haven. However, British policies against extensive migration continued in force and left the Jews with the conviction that they were being betrayed. As a result, the Jewish antagonism and reprisals grew so heated that the British finally became anxious to rid themselves of the whole problem. The matter came up in the United Nations for settlement, and there it was voted to create a separate Jewish state, a separate Arab state, and keep Jerusalem an open city. Therefore, as soon as the British forces withdrew the Jewish nation of Israel proclaimed itself a free and independent republic. This occurred May 14-15, 1948.

However, the Arabs did not declare themselves a republic. Instead, they declared war. In fact, six Arab nations joined together and attacked Israel on May 15, 1948. A fierce engagement resulted which for a few frantic weeks threatened to sweep the Jews into the Mediterranean. How-

---

63. Isaiah 49:25-26. Note that the 2 preceding verses identify the above quotations with the day when the Lord "will lift up mine hand to the Gentiles, and set up my standard to the people."

ever, the Israeli forces finally held. Furthermore, they succeeded in liberating a large population of Jews caught in a
pocket along the western suburbs of Jerusalem. They also
created sufficient resistance along all fronts so that the
Arabs agreed to join the Jews at a conference table where
a temporary truce was declared. After numerous incidents
of flash-fire skirmishes on both sides, the two forces were
finally brought to a permanent truce in July, 1949. Since
that time both the Arabs and Jews have had a number of
exchanges both in the United Nations and across their respective borders. On one of our visits to the Holy Land we
were not permitted to venture out on the Sea of Galilee because Syrian cannons on the eastern side were firing at boats
and settlements on the Israeli side.

Much as one would desire otherwise, prophecy indicates that the conflict in Palestine is not over. The Jews
are still restricted from Jerusalem and the possibility of rebuilding the temple is a very sensitive matter with the Arabs
since they have their own beautiful "Dome of the Rock"
Mosque covering the spot where the Jewish Holy of Holies
is believed to belong. The Arabs say this is the spot from
which Mohammed ascended into heaven so they feel it is
just as sacred to them as it is to the Jews. Many of us
who have close friends in both camps wish with all our hearts
that some ameliorating circumstance could avoid future conflict and that the sacred sentiments of both peoples could
be accommodated. Unfortunately, however, whole armies
have risen and fallen over the issue of who shall govern
Jerusalem and now the Lord has decreed that He, rather than
men, must move forward with His program which will be a
blessing to Arabs and Jews alike — in fact, to the whole
world. It requires that a temple be built in Jerusalem.

THE BUILDING OF A TEMPLE IN JERUSALEM

It was Micah who first talked about the fact that "In
the last days it shall come to pass, that the mountain of the
house of the Lord shall be established in the top of the
mountains. . . ."[64] This has seemed to refer to the temple in
the mountains of the American Zion. But Isaiah quotes this

---

64. Micah 4:1

same passage as applying to Jerusalem and Judah as well. In fact he specifically describes it as "The word of Isaiah the son of Amoz saw CONCERNING JUDAH AND JERUSALEM."[65]

At the present time there are severe political handicaps under which the modern Israelites must work. Nevertheless, the prophets of the Lord have indicated that the way will be opened up so that they can eventually accomplish their assigned task. Charles W. Penrose spoke of the time when they shall be in a position to build their temple:

"The work is moving on for the gathering of the Jews to their own land that they may build it up as it was in former times; that the temple may be rebuilt and the mosque of the Moslem which now stands in its place may be moved out of the way; that Jerusalem may be rebuilt upon its original site; that the way may be prepared for the coming of the Messiah."[66]

Joseph Smith also spoke of that day, saying, "Judah must return, Jerusalem must be rebuilt, and the temple, and water come out from under the temple, and the waters of the Dead Sea be healed. It will take some time to rebuild the walls of the city and the temple, etc.; and all this must be done before the Son of Man will make His appearance."[67]

It was Ezekiel who talked about this Jerusalem temple in greater detail than any of the ancient prophets. He had a vision of it and was allowed to walk through it, measuring it as he went.[68] There are enough details in the book of Ezekiel for a modern architect to go ahead and draw up the entire plan for the temple at Jerusalem without any further revelation!

Ezekiel mentions the fact that during his vision he was led around to the east gate of the temple, and noted a substantial stream which "issued out from under the threshold of the house eastward: for the forefront of the house stood toward the east, and the waters came down from under the right side of the house, at the south side of the altar."[69] The

---

65. Isaiah 2:1
66. *Journal of Discourses*, Vol. 24, p. 215
67. Doc. His. of the Church, Vol. 15, p. 337
68. Ezekiel, chapters 40 to 47
69. Ezekiel 47:1

famous Gihon spring is just below this location so there is good reason to believe there is considerable water in this temple mountain. According to Ezekiel's prophecy, the water would flow into the Brook Kidron and down toward the Dead Sea. Ezekiel says he saw that the river would increase in size and volume as it proceeded toward the Arabah Ghor wherein the Dead Sea is cradled. He saw that the sea had an outlet toward the greater sea, presumably the Red Sea at Akabah, and that as a result the waters of the Dead Sea were healed. In his vision Ezekiel said he perceived that the Dead Sea had become fresh-water with great schools of fish swimming about.[70] Only the surrounding marshes remained salty.[71] Anyone who has seen the Dead Sea and tasted of its extremely bitter, acrid water can appreciate what a miracle it would be to bring about such a change.

The Second Coming of Christ

Prophecy by its very nature, and especially the prophecies of Isaiah, usually compress whole vistas of future history into extremely limited digests so that much more is left out than is actually said. As we have pointed out earlier, this is by design and not by accident; too much knowledge concerning the future would destroy the educational and probationary aspects of the Second Estate. Nevertheless, the Second Advent was something which Isaiah anticipated with the greatest enthusiasm and he therefore referred to it frequently. Here we will merely reflect the highlights in order to show the extent of his knowledge.

Isaiah knew that incidental to the Second Coming there would be a most terrible destruction by earthquake, an upheaval of the sea, the churning of the crust of the earth, and a consuming fire of cleansing obliteration. It would be a time when special measures would have to be taken to protect the Saints during the preliminary violence and before they were "caught up." Through Isaiah the Lord said, "Come, my people, enter thou into thy chambers, and shut thy doors about thee: hide thyself as it were for a little moment, until the indignation be overpast. For, behold, the Lord cometh out of his place to punish the inhabitants of

---

70. Ezekiel 47:1-10   71. Ezekiel 47:11

the earth for their iniquity: the earth also shall disclose her blood, and shall no more cover her slain."[72]

Chapter 24 of Isaiah is devoted exclusively to the destruction which comes with the Second Advent of the Savior. He says it will be a time of ferocious wickedness. He saw that "The earth also is defiled under the inhabitants thereof; because they have transgressed the laws, changed the ordinance, broken the everlasting covenant. Therefore hath the curse devoured the earth, and they that dwell therein are desolate: therefore the inhabitants of the earth are burned, AND FEW MEN LEFT."[73]

Isaiah must have been both shocked and astonished with what he saw for he said, "Behold, the Lord maketh the earth empty, and maketh it waste, and turneth it upside down, and scattereth abroad the inhabitants thereof. And it shall be, as with the people, so with the priest; as with the servant so with his master; as with the maid, so with her mistress; as with the buyer, so with the seller. . . . The land shall be utterly emptied, and utterly spoiled; for the Lord hath spoken this word."[74]

So much for the destruction of people. Isaiah then turns to the vision of mankind's planetary home. He wrote, ". . . the foundations of the earth do shake. The earth is utterly broken down, the earth is clean dissolved, the earth is moved exceedingly. The earth shall reel to and fro like a drunkard, and shall be removed like a cottage; and the transgression thereof shall be heavy upon it; and it shall fall, and not rise again."[75]

It is at this point that Isaiah saw that all the multitudes and their rulers who were destroyed would be gathered together in the spirit world "as prisoners are gathered in the pit, and shall be shut up in the prison, and AFTER MANY DAYS SHALL THEY BE VISITED [just as those who were drowned in the Great Flood were visited after many days]."[76]

---

72. Isaiah 26:20-21
73. Isaiah 24:5-6
74. Isaiah 24:1-3

75. Isaiah 24:18-21
76. Isaiah 24:22

Then Isaiah closes the chapter with his note of triumph by saying that "Then . . . the Lord of hosts shall reign in mount Zion, and in Jerusalem, and before his ancients gloriously."[77]

Isaiah speaks of an amazing physical phenomenon which will accompany the Second Coming. It will be a removal of the veil which separates mortal men from the spiritual realities around them. In a modern revelation the Lord said, "And there shall be silence in heaven for the space of half an hour; and immediately after shall the curtain of heaven be unfolded, as a scroll is unfolded after it is rolled up, and the face of the Lord shall be unveiled; and the saints that are upon the earth, who are alive, shall be quickened and caught up to meet him. And they who have slept in their graves shall . . . be caught up to meet him in the midst of the pillar of heaven."[78]

Isaiah talks about these exact same events right after he has discussed the great destruction. Speaking as though he had seen the vision from the top of Mount Zion in Old Jerusalem (the site of the temple) he says, "And He will destroy in this mountain the face of the covering cast over all people, and the vail that is spread over all nations."[79] Then he talks about the resurrection saying, "He will swallow up death in victory; and the Lord God will wipe away tears from off all faces; and the rebuke of his people shall be taken away from off all the earth: for the Lord hath spoken it."[80] Later, he becomes very personal in speaking of the resurrection, saying, "Thy dead men shall live, together with my dead body shall they arise. Awake and sing, ye that dwell in dust: for thy dew is as the dew of herbs, and the earth shall cast out the dead."[81]

After Jesus appears in glory so that all surviving humanity sees Him together, He will have a great sacramental feast in Jerusalem with the prophets and Saints from the most ancient times. In the modern revelation He says, ". . . wherefore, marvel not, for the hour cometh that I will drink of the fruit of the vine with you on the earth, and with Moroni . . . Elias . . . John [the Baptist] the son of Zacharias

---

77. Isaiah 24:23
78. D. & C. 88:95-97
79. Isaiah 25:7
80. Isaiah 25:8
81. Isaiah 26:19

. . . Elijah . . . Joseph and Jacob, and Isaac, and Abraham . . . Michael, or Adam . . . and also with Peter, and James, and John . . . and also WITH ALL THOSE WHOM MY FATHER HATH GIVEN ME OUT OF THE WORLD."[82]

This will be a vast and glorious occasion. In Isaiah's song of joy over the magnificence of the Second Advent (which is all of chapter 25) Isaiah declares, "And in this mountain shall the Lord of hosts make unto all people a feast of fat things, a feast of wines on the lees, of fat things full of marrow, of wines on the lees well refined."[83]

He describes the thrilling reaction of the great throng which attends, "And it shall be said in that day, Lo, this is our God; we have waited for him, and he will save us: this is the Lord; we have waited for him, we will be glad and rejoice in his salvation."[84]

Isaiah has many other beautiful and powerful sentiments to express concerning the Second Coming but this will be sufficient to catch the breadth of his vision and the depth of his understanding concerning this sacred subject. He is also one of the foremost scriptural authorities on the subject of the Millennium.

THE MILLENNIUM

The Millennium is a perfect theme for a poet and therefore ideally suited to the interests and tastes of Isaiah. This theme will be found in his opening chapters, in his last chapter, and scattered all the way in between. His philosophic contemplation of the magnificence of the Millennial vision led him to exclaim, "For since the beginning of the world men have not heard, nor perceived by the ear, neither hath the eye seen, O God, beside thee, what he hath prepared for him that waiteth for him."[85] A short time later he records the word of the Lord as follows, ". . . the former troubles are forgotten . . . they are hid from mine eyes. For, behold, I create new heavens and a new earth: and the former shall not be remembered, nor come into mind. But be

---

82. D. & C. 27:5-14
83. Isaiah 25:6
84. Isaiah 25:9
85. Isaiah 64:4

ye glad and rejoice for ever in that which I create: for, behold, I create Jerusalem a rejoicing, and her people a joy."[86]

He says that during this period the earth will bring forth its strength. Great forests will grow up in the wilderness.[87] Rivers and springs will change deserts and wastelands into meadows and farmlands.[88] Noxious weeds, briars and thorns will give way to groves, orchards and profitable plant life.[89]

The physical and chemical nature of the earth will also be quickened. As mentioned above, the change will be so great that the Lord speaks of it as "a new earth" and says there will be so little to remind one of the deficient and fallen sphere which we now inhabit that "it shall not be remembered nor come to mind."

The refinement of the earth at that time will be so marked that the planet is described as being "transfigured." When the Apostles were together on the mount they were shown the vision of it and not at any time since then has the full account of its glory been revealed.[90]

Not only will the earth be transfigured, but among the righteous even human life will function on a more perfect and efficient scale than at any time since the Fall. In Section 101 of the Doctrine and Covenants, one of the most singular prophecies in all holy writ is recorded. Speaking of the time of the Millennium it says: "And there shall be no sorrow because there is no death."[91] The implications of this promise are tremendous. Such a condition would require strict self-discipline among all human beings and a sufficiently strong control over natural phenomena and secular circumstances so that there would be no accidents, no disease, no infant mortality, no senile old age, no congenital deformities. Such a condition would change many things in our mode of existence — no funerals, no cemeteries, no mortuaries, no insurance companies.

In saying that there will be no death, however, the Lord does not mean that people living during the Millennium

---

86. Isaiah 65:16-18
87. Isaiah 41:19
88. Isaiah 35:7
89. Isaiah 55:13
90. D. & C. 63:21
91. D. & C. 101:29

will be immortal. He goes on to explain that this promise simply means that among the righteous there will be no lengthy separation of the body from the spirit — no consignment of the body to the grave.[92] Men will live until they are a hundred years old[93] in the full strength of the antediluvian patriarchs; then they will be changed in the twinkling of an eye from mortal to resurrected beings.[94] Such persons will be "caught up" and their rest will be glorious.[95]

Nor does the Lord imply that this blessed promise of "no death" applies to everyone. It only applies to the righteous and obedient. During at least the early part of the Millennium there will be many who will survive the great destruction who are not members of Christ's Kingdom and these will have the opportunity to hear the Gospel and join the Church if they so desire.[96] If they do not, however, but choose to remain in their sins, Isaiah clearly indicates that the sorrows of death are still theirs.[97]

The scripture also indicates that among the righteous there will be no juvenile crime, no disobedient or disrespectful youth. For, says the Lord, "their children shall grow up without sin unto salvation."[98] In the same place He states that the Saints will "multiply and wax strong." It is highly possible that with the cessation of war, the eradication of infant mortality, the increase of the human life span to one hundred years and the marked increase in the arable land area, the number of individuals who will populate the earth during the thousand years of the Millennial reign will total more than all those who lived on the earth during the previous six thousand years.

Another of the rather startling predictions of changes to come during the Millennium is the prophecy that animals will lose their enmity one toward another. Isaiah twice describes this phenomenon and makes it definitely clear that "the wolf also shall dwell with the lamb, and the leopard shall lie down with the kid; and the calf and the young lion and the fatling together."[99] He even goes further and predicts that the animal species which have formerly been classi-

---

92. D. & C. 101:30-31; 63:51
93. Isaiah 65:20
94. D. & C. 63:51
95. D. & C. 101:31

96. D. & C. 77:11
97. Isaiah 65:20
98. D. & C. 45:58
99. Isaiah 11:6-9; 65:25; Hosea 2:18

fied as "carnivorous" because of their dependence on flesh from other animals will thereafter become herbivorous so that they can exist upon plant life rather than meat: "The lion shall eat straw like the bullock: and dust shall be the serpent's meat. They shall not hurt nor destroy in all my holy mountain saith the Lord."[100] In another place he again refers to this biological change when he says: "the lion shall eat straw like the ox."[101]

Not only will enmity between members of the animal kingdom disappear but fear and enmity between men and animals will likewise cease. Referring to it, Isaiah says: "And the sucking child shall play on the hole of the asp, and the weaned child shall put his hand on the cockatrice den. They shall not hurt nor destroy in all my holy mountain."[102]

Enmity between individuals will also be diminished. For centuries political scientists have dreamed of the unprecedented progress which mankind could make if their investments of money and materials could be directed exclusively toward peaceful pursuits. In the Millennium this will occur. Speaking of the relationship between individuals and nations, Isaiah says: "They shall beat their swords into plowshares, and their spears into pruning hooks: nation shall not lift up sword against nation, neither shall they learn war any more."[103]

Under such favorable circumstances the Saints of Israel will thrive and grow. Isaiah says, "He shall cause them that come to Jacob to take root: Israel shall blossom and bud, and fill the face of the world with fruit."[104] This will cause the people of Israel in that day to say to the Lord, "Thou hast increased the nation, O Lord, thou hast increased the nation: thou art glorified: thou hadst removed it far [extended it] unto all the ends of the earth."[105]

There will be no agnostics nor atheists in those days. Isaiah says, ". . . the earth shall be full of the knowledge of the Lord, as the waters cover the sea."[106]

---

100. Isaiah 65:25
101. Isaiah 11:7
102. Isaiah 11:8-9
103. Isaiah 2:4

104. Isaiah 27:6
105. Isaiah 26:15
106. Isaiah 11:9

Nor will the Saints have as much difficulty rising to the spiritual level where they can communicate with the Lord. Isaiah was told by the Lord "that before they call, I will answer; and while they are yet speaking, I will hear."[107]

Human relations will be on the highest level. Not only will there be peace and prosperity but all will have the security of their own inheritances and "none shall want her mate."[108] Malachi adds to this by saying children will be raised up as carefully as calves in a stall.[109] No wonder Isaiah surveyed this great era of the future and said, "Then judgment shall dwell in the wilderness, and righteousness remain in the fruitful field. And THE WORK OF RIGHTEOUSNESS SHALL BE PEACE: AND THE EFFECT OF RIGHTEOUSNESS QUIETNESS AND ASSURANCE FOR EVER. And my people shall dwell in a peaceable habitation, and in sure dwellings, and in quiet resting places."[110]

Thus we come to the end of our visit with the great prophet Isaiah. Reluctantly we lay his monumental book aside and confirm as we do so the pronouncement of Jesus when He said, "GREAT ARE THE WORDS OF ISAIAH!"[111]

---

107. Isaiah 65:24
108. Isaiah 34:16
109. Malachi 4:2
110. Isaiah 32:16-18
111. 3 Nephi 23:1

Scripture Readings and Questions on Chapter Twenty-Two

Scripture Reading: Isaiah, chapters 56 to 65.

1—Does prophecy tend to fulfill itself a number of times? Give two examples.

2—What does "Zion" mean? Is it a place or a condition?

3—Did Isaiah know there would be two "Zions" in the last days? Where were they to be located?

4—Why was it significant for Isaiah to say that when Israel is gathered, "Ephraim shall not envy Judah, and Judah shall not vex Ephraim"?

5—Did Isaiah anticipate that our generation would have difficulty communicating the Gospel to foreign countries? What did he say?

6—From which direction will the Lost Tribes come? Will they drift in a few at a time or come as a body?

7—Will they come before or after the New Jerusalem is built? Will their coming be very gradual and natural or will it be rather spectacular?

8—What impact will the coming the Lost Tribes have on the Church? Will they exceed the number of Church members? What does the scripture say about their food and water?

9—What great prophet and Apostle of ancient times will help bring the Lost Tribes to Zion?

10—Will the Lost Tribes first come to Palestine or America? Then where will they go? Will any of the tribe of Joseph go?

11—What chapter of Isaiah is about the New Jerusalem? In what other canon of scripture can it be found?

12—What year was the official launching of the great gathering of Judah to Palestine? Who dedicated the land? Who rededicated it? What year? How long afterwards did the "gathering" begin?

13—Who was the first Prime Minister of Israel? Where did he come from?

14—Recite briefly the history of the *Protocols of the Learned Elders of Zion*. Why were these useful to Hitler?

15—Who started the war between the Arabs and Israel in 1948? What was their objective? Was this to support or to overthrow what the United Nations had advocated?

16—What did Isaiah say would happen to those who held Israelites captive and refused to let them gather?

17—Where will the temple be built in Jerusalem? Who occupies this territory now?

18—What great catastrophe will occur just before the Second Coming? Will it be local or universal? What will it do to the population of the earth? What will happen to the righteous?

19—What will happen to the spirits of those who are slain during the great destruction? What is the purpose of this arrangement?

20—List five major changes which will occur when the Millennium comes.

CHAPTER TWENTY-THREE

Good and Evil in a Deadly Struggle

Now we turn from the exhilarating and marvelous prospects of the future as seen by Isaiah to the harsh and ugly realities of the past. And this is exactly what Isaiah was compelled to do over and over again. After the Lord would show him visions portraying His day of triumphant power, Isaiah would then have to return to the duties of his own calling which were to preach to a doomed people. No wonder he interrupted his writings so often to dwell with meditative delight on the great day of God yet to be!

Of course the latter part of Isaiah's writings was in the days of the good king Hezekiah and for this Isaiah must have been deeply grateful. But he knew that at best it was only a pleasant interlude. In fact, if Isaiah lived beyond the time of King Hezekiah (696 B.C.) he would have been under Manasseh, the most vicious and depraved king in the history of Judah. The Bible does not say exactly how long Isaiah lived, but according to Justin Martyr, writing around 150 A.D., it was the prevailing belief at that time that Isaiah not only lived under Manasseh but died by his order in a most horrible manner. Justin Martyr says he died by being "sawed asunder with a wooden saw!"[1] The Bible would seem to support the fact that Manasseh was indeed capable of such a thing.

KING MANASSEH OF JUDAH

It is almost incomprehensible that Manasseh should turn out to be such a reprehensible scoundrel after living for so many years under the righteous reign of his father, Hezekiah. For some reason which is not disclosed, Manasseh turned against the example of his father and emulated the debaucheries of his degraded grandfather, King Ahaz. Perhaps the answer to his behavior is the fact that he came to the throne when he was only 12 years of age[2] and his court counselors may have corrupted him. He endured as king from approximately 696 to 642 B.C. so he had plenty of time to impose his moral bankruptcy on Judah for over half-a-century. The scripture leaves very little to the reader's imagination as it catalogues his terrible crimes:

Manasseh rebuilt all the heathen altars which his father had so methodically broken down.[3]

He adopted every prevailing heathen cult from surrounding pagan nations. These included the worship of the fertility gods, Baal and Ashtoreth in the groves, the adoration of the sun, moon and stars at special shrines, and the reintroduction of the burning and sacrificing of children in the valley of Hinnom, which is on the southern border of Jerusalem.[4]

Manasseh not only made human sacrifices, including his own son,[5] but apparently took violent and vindictive reprisal against any who stood in his way or possessed something he wanted. The scripture says, "Moreover, Manasseh shed innocent blood very much, till he had filled Jerusalem from one end to another."[6]

---

1. *Dialogue With Trypho*, by Justin Martyr, chapter cxx. This appears in *The Ante-Nicene Fathers*, Vol. I, p. 259. Justin Martyr does not identify the executioner of Isaiah but simply refers to the incident. Bible authorities say the historical circumstances would have had to be during the days of Manasseh when he was persecuting the prophets of God. (Dummelow's *Bible Commentary*, p. 409)
2. II Chron. 33:1
3. II Chron. 33:3
4. II Chron. 33:3, 6
5. II Kings 21:6
6. II Kings 21:16

He also desecrated the temple by erecting in it "a graven image of the grove that he had made [these were usually obscene]."[7] He also "built altars for all the host of heaven [sun, moon and stars] in the two courts of the house of the Lord."[8]

Instead of encouraging the true prophets of God, he used "enchantments, and used witchcraft, and dealt with a familiar spirit, and with wizards."[9]

The names of the prophets who denounced these depraved activities are not given in scripture, but we are assured that the Lord poured verbal fire and brimstone down on the head of Manasseh and called him to repentance. In fact, the scripture says, "And the Lord spake by his servants the prophets, saying, Because Manasseh king of Judah hath done wickedly above all that the Amorites did, which were before him, and hath made Judah also to sin with his idols: Therefore, thus saith the Lord God of Israel, Behold, I am bringing such evil upon Jerusalem and Judah, that whosoever heareth of it, both his ears shall tingle."[10]

It would be one of Manasseh's grandsons, Zedekiah, who would see his sons killed before his face and then have his eyes blinded. And it would be other descendants of Manasseh who would be carried off with the princes of Judah to be slaves and peasants for the king of Babylon. Nevertheless, Manasseh who had done so much to corrupt these on-coming generations, tasted some of the bitterness of their punishment himself.

MANASSEH IS TAKEN CAPTIVE TO BABYLON

To appreciate what happened next it is necessary to bring ourselves up-to-date on what had been occurring recently in the great empire centers of Assyria and Egypt. It will be recalled that these two nations had been fighting each other when Sennacherib, king of Assyria, had decided to subjugate Judah in 701 B.C. At the time the Lord intervened and destroyed such a large percentage of the Assyrian army that Sennacherib was compelled to retreat back to

7. II Kings 21:7
8. II Chron. 33:5

9. II Chron. 33:6
10. II Kings 21:10-12

Nineveh and never returned. However, in 680 B.C., his son, Esarhaddon, launched a series of campaigns against Egypt and his available records show that he extracted heavy tribute from all vassal kingdoms of Assyria, including King Manasseh of Judah.[11]

Esarhaddon also determined to build a mighty palace and commandeered slave labor in great quantities from Assyria's tributary states, including Judah. The vassal kings were carried off as hostages along with their labor contingents to make certain that the work was done. Dr. Emil G. Kraeling thinks this was the occasion when the wicked Manasseh was taken captive and hauled off to Babylon.[12] The scripture describes Manasseh's arrest and deportation as follows, 'And the Lord spake to Manasseh, and to his people: but they would not hearken. Wherefore the Lord brought upon them the captain of the host of the king of Assyria, which took Manasseh among the thorns, and bound him with fetters, and carried him to Babylon.''[13] Babylon was the major vassal state of Assyria and was soon to challenge her overlord. There Manasseh saw the place where his own grandchildren and the greater part of Judah would one day be dragged or driven.

Although we have no details as to how Manasseh was treated, it must have been extremely harsh in spite of his regal status. And as a result of this treatment we discover that even a homicidal zealot of heathen ways such as Manasseh can find his better, humble self under the whiplash of adversity. The scripture says, "And when he was in affliction, he besought the Lord his God, and humbled himself greatly before the God of his fathers. And prayed unto him: and he [the Lord] was intreated of [by] him, and heard his supplication, and brought him again to Jerusalem into his kingdom. Then Manasseh knew that the Lord, he was God.''[14]

Just what circumstances led the Assyrian king to show this clemency toward Manasseh is not stated. Since we know that Esarhaddon had as one of his lifetime ambitions the total conquest of Egypt, it is possible that Manasseh

11. Keyes, Story of the Bible World, p. 88
12. See Rand McNally Bible Atlas, p. 306
13. II Chron. 33:10-11
14. II Chron. 33:12-13

was sent home in connection with one of these campaigns. Manasseh would be needed in Judah to rally support, tribute and perhaps even military manpower for the Assyrian conqueror. In any event, Manasseh returned home. He was so grateful to be back in Jerusalem that he immediately tried to undo some of the damage he had inflicted on Judah during his earlier apostate career. He attempted to clean up the heathen impedimentia by which he had cluttered and desecrated the temple precincts. He also tried to pull down the heathen altars and sanctuaries which he had previously erected.[15]

However, all of this proved relatively ineffective.[16] We find that the corrupted people rebuilt them so fast that the next generation had to cleanse the land all over again.[17]

Manasseh spent the energies of his last years attempting to strengthen the City of David or Ophel, just southeast and below the temple square. This may have been encouraged by the fact that about this time the Assyrians were extremely pre-occupied with the Lydians who were sweeping down out of Asia Minor, and the Babylonians who were on their way toward independence. Manasseh apparently thought this was a good time to re-fortify the land. It was one of the rare periods when he could do it without inviting immediate reprisal from the Assyrians. So the scripture says, "Now after this he built a wall without the city of David, on the west side of Gihon, in the valley, even to the entering in at the Fish Gate. And compassed about Ophel, and raised it up a very great height. and put captains of war in all the fenced cities of Jerusalem."[18]

Manasseh finally died around 642 B.C. after a reign of some 55 years — the longest in Judah's regal history.[19] He outlived by a number of years his Assyrian oppressor, Esarhaddon. The Assyrian king partially fulfilled his passion to rule Egypt when he captured the Lower Kingdom capital of Memphis (across the river from modern Cairo) in 671 B.C. Two years later he was on the way to conquer Thebes (capital of the Upper Kingdom 400 miles up-stream

---

15. II Chron. 33:15-16
16. II Chron. 33:17
17. II Chron. 34:3-4

18. II Chron. 33:14
19. II Chron. 33:1

from Cairo) when he died. Esarhaddon was then succeeded by his son Ashurbanipal in 669 B.C. and the latter carried on his father's campaign until Upper Egypt was brought to her knees in 667 B.C. Ashurbanipal was Assyria's last important ruler. By the time of his death in 626 B.C. the Assyrian empire was already tottering, soon to be replaced by Babylon. However, throughout the events covered by this chapter, Assyria remained the dominant political power of the earth with Egypt and Babylon both watching desperately for an opportunity to strike.

KING AMON OF JUDAH

When Manasseh died in 642 B.C., he was succeeded by his 22-year-old son, Amon. Apparently this crown prince was not at all impressed by his father's attempted reform in his old age. Therefore, as soon as Amon had gained possession of the throne he reversed the trend and went back to the abominations of his father's earlier years.

It gradually became apparent to the leading officers of the kingdom that the young king would eventually become just as reprobate as his father had been for "Amon trespassed more and more."[20] Therefore several of the king's officers finally decided to take matters into their own hands before the situation became unbearable. They formed a secret conspiratorial group to assassinate the king. This plot was successful and Amon, who was barely 24 years of age at the time, was slain "in his own house."[21]

But apparently the taint of corruption introduced by Manasseh and revived by Amon was still so popular with the people that they counted the death of Amon as a great tragedy. The scripture says "the people" formed into what must have been a mighty mob and the next thing the royal officers knew, they were not being hailed as heroes for their deed but were charged with being murderers who deserved to be lynched. And that is exactly what happened to them.[22] The mob then chose Amon's young son, Josiah, to rule in his stead.

---

20. II Chron. 33:23
21. II Chron. 33:24
22. II Chron. 33:25

KING JOSIAH OF JUDAH

Josiah was only 8 years of age when he ascended the throne to replace his murdered father.[23] We have no way of knowing who the kind and discerning tutor was that guided this boy away from the abominations and his father's practices and filled him with a zeal toward God. Perhaps it was his mother. In any event, the scripture says, that "... in the eighth year of his reign [when he was 16 years of age] while he was yet young, he began to seek after the God of David his father: and in the twelfth year [when he was 20] he began to purge Judah and Jerusalem. ... And they brake down the altars of Baalim in his presence; and the images, that were on high above them, he cut down; and the groves, and the carved images, and the molten images, he brake in pieces, and made dust of them, and strowed it [scattered it] upon the graves of them that had sacrificed unto them. And he burnt the bones of the priests [who had officiated at these shrines] upon their altars, and cleansed Judah and Jerusalem."[24]

JOSIAH CLEANSES THE TEMPLE AND A COPY OF THE ANCIENT LAW IS DISCOVERED

In connection with his national religious reform program, Josiah decided to duplicate the program of his great grandfather, King Hezekiah. He asked the presiding High Priest at the temple to take all the money which had been collected and give it into the hands of skilled workmen so that the temple might be restored.[25] This program was just getting under way when Hilkiah, the High Priest, stumbled on to a copy of the law which had been given to Moses.[26] This was turned over to Josiah and when the king saw what the Lord had said would happen if Israel apostatized, he was stirred to the depths of his soul. He could see that the people had done precisely what the Lord had warned them against. Now they stood ready to reap a devastating whirlwind.

The very fact that this book was counted such a spectacular find reflects the absolute bankruptcy of the sacred literature and historical resources which existed among the

---

23. II Chron. 34:1
24. II Chron. 34:3-5

25. II Kings 22:3-7
26. II Kings 22:8

Jews at this time. It meant that the king had not been given this important information in his training, and if the king did not get it, certainly the common people would not be likely to have access to it. No wonder the people were dwindling and perishing in unbelief![27] Things had degenerated amazingly since the days of the good king Jehoshaphat. At that time the king had emphasized religious education and had "sent Levites and priests"; and they went about through all the cities of Judah, and taught the people, having "THE BOOK OF THE LAW OF THE LORD WITH THEM."[28]

After reading the law, King Josiah feared lest the apostasy of the people had carried them to the "point of no return" and had made their punishment fixed and unavoidable. He therefore said to Hilkiah, the High Priest, "Go, inquire of the Lord for me, and for them that are left in Israel and in Judah, concerning the words of the book that is found: for great is the wrath of the Lord that is [likely to be] poured out upon us, because our fathers have not kept the word of the Lord, to do after all that is written in this book."[29]

Now Hilkiah, the High Priest, did a strange thing. Instead of getting out the Urim and Thummim which the High Priest customarily wore as part of his vestments, this High Priest had to find someone who enjoyed communications from Heaven *without* any Urim and Thummim. From this we conclude that these sacred instruments for revelation, translation and righteous judgment were no longer available, and without them Hilkiah apparently felt incapable of crossing the threshhold of that higher, spiritual realm where a revelation could be obtained. And where would he go to find someone who could cross that threshhold? Apparently the ruthless persecution of the prophets by Manasseh a few years earlier had left the people with practically no inspired guidance from the usual prophetic sources. Sometime during Josiah's reign Jeremiah appeared on the scene and so did Nahum and Zephaniah. But they must have come later, for the High Priest felt compelled to seek out of wife of Shallum, keeper of the temple wardrobe.[30] Her name was Huldah and

27. See I Nephi 4:13
28. II Chron. 17:7-9
29. II Chron. 34:21
30. II Chron. 34:22

she was known as a "prophetess." The High Priest came to her with the earnest request of the king that she attempt to learn the will of the Lord so Josiah would know what to expect in light of the things he had read in the book of the law.

This righteous woman responded to the request but the message she received turned out to be a profound, sobering and deeply discouraging pronouncement. Said she, "Thus saith the Lord, Behold, I will bring evil upon this place, and upon the inhabitants thereof, even all the curses that are written in the book which they have read before the king of Judah: Because they have forsaken me, and have burned incense unto other gods, that they might provoke me to anger with all the works of their hands; therefore my wrath shall be poured out upon this place, and shall not be quenched."[31]

This must have come as a shocking jolt to the hopeful and expectant servants of the king. Nevertheless, the prophetess said the Lord had a special message for Josiah the king. She told the messengers:

"And as for the king of Judah, who sent you to inquire of the Lord, so shall ye say unto him . . . Because thine heart was tender, and thou didst humble thyself before God, when thou heardest His words against this place . . . and didst rend thy clothes, and weep before me; I have even heard thee also, saith the Lord. Behold, I will gather thee to thy fathers, and thou shalt be gathered to thy grave in peace, neither shall thine eyes see all the evil that I will bring upon this place."[32]

To Josiah, this meant there was a little breathing space before Judah's final doomsday. Therefore there was no time to waste. He called a general conference and asked all the leaders and as many of the people as possible to attend. The meeting took place at the temple in Jerusalem. King Josiah presided and apparently spoke to the large audience from either the porch of the temple or the 8-foot brazen scaffold which Solomon had provided at the time of the temple's dedication.[33] In either case, the Bible says he stood by one of the great bronze pillars at the front of the temple and

---

31. II Chron. 34:24-25
32. II Chron. 34:26-28

33. II Chron. 6:13

"read in their ears ALL the words of the book of the covenant that was found in the house of the Lord."[34] One cannot help but wonder how long this conference session lasted!

Then the king "made a covenant before the Lord, to walk after the Lord, and to keep his commandments, and his testimonies, and his statutes, with all his heart, and with all his soul, to perform the words of the covenant which are written in this book."[35]

Now Josiah determined to demonstrate to the Lord that he really meant to keep his part of the agreement. In spite of the fact that the reform had been going on for a considerable period of time, it is obvious from the scripture that much remained to be done. Josiah set out to finish the job. The passages which follow are extremely valuable in demonstrating just how profligate and degenerate the people had become.

First, Josiah had the priests bring out all the paraphernalia which the heathens had installed in the holy temple.[36] This included the obscene Asherah, which was the object of worship in the fertility cult of the groves.[37]

"And he brake down the houses of the sodomites, THAT WERE BY THE HOUSE OF THE LORD, where the women wove hangings [partitions] for the grove."[38]

"And he put down the idolatrous priests, whom the kings of Judah had ordained to burn incense . . . unto Baal, to the sun, and to the moon, and to the planets, and to all the host of heaven."[39]

"And he defiled Topheth, which is in the valley of the children of Hinnom [the southern border of Jerusalem], that no man might make his son or his daughter to pass through the fire [as a sacrifice] to Molech."[40]

"And he took away the horses that the kings of Judah had given to the sun [probably a huge sculptured work] at the entering in of the house of the Lord. . . . And the altars that were on the top of the upper chamber of Ahaz, which the kings of Judah had made, and the altars which Manasseh

34. II Chron. 34:30
35. II Chron. 34:31
36. II Kings 23:4
37. II Kings 23:6 plus Clarke, *Bible Commentary*, Vol. 2, p. 562
38. II Kings 23:7
39. II Kings 23:5
40. II Kings 23:10

had made in the two courts of the house of the Lord, did the king beat down and brake them down from thence, and cast the dust of them into the brook Kidron. And the high places that were before Jerusalem, which were on the right hand of the mount of corruption [marginal note says Mount of Olives], which Solomon the king of Israel had builded for Ashtoreth the abomination of the Zidonians, and for Chemosh the abomination of the Moabites and for Milcom the abomination of the children of Ammon, did the king defile."[41]

Then Josiah went up to the northern territory from which the Ten Tribes had been largely evacuated. As he approached the heathen shrine of Bethel the spirit of prophetic fulfillment fell upon him. Whether consciously or not, Josiah now did what an unnamed prophet nearly 3 centuries earlier had predicted he would do. In the days of apostate Jeroboam, the first king of the northern tribes, this unnamed "man of God" had stood by this heathen altar while the king was officiating there and said to it, "O altar, altar, thus saith the Lord; behold, a child shall be born unto the house of David, JOSIAH BY NAME; and upon thee shall he offer the priests of the high places that burn incense upon thee, and men's bones shall be burnt upon thee."[42]

So when Josiah came to Bethel he burned the heathen shrine and then had his men dig up the bones of the apostate priests who had ministered at these shrines. Their bones were summarily burned upon this altar. But as they were emptying the sepulchres Josiah noticed one particular tomb and said, "What title [inscription] is that that I see? And the men of the city told him, It is the sepulchre of the man of God, which came from Judah, and proclaimed these things that thou hast done against the altar of Bethel. And he said, Let him alone; let no man move his bones."[43]

Then Josiah moved up into the ruined shambles of Israel's once proud capital of Samaria, where he found the shrines which symbolized all of the evil that had led the people of Israel down the pathway of degradation and apostasy. And he saw some of the heathen priests still lurking

---

41. II Kings 23:11-13
42. I Kings 13:2
43. II Kings 23:17-18

about their cesspools of vice, debauchery and infant sacrifice. The Bible says, "And all the houses [shrines] also of the high places that were in the cities of Samaria, which the kings of Israel had made to provoke the Lord to anger, Josiah took away, and did to them according to all the acts that he had done in Bethel. And he slew all the priests [heathen holy men][44] of the high places that were there upon the altars, and burned men's bones [from nearby sepulchres] upon them, and returned to Jerusalem."[45]

JOSIAH'S GREAT PASSOVER

Having followed the notable example of his righteous grandfather in cleansing the temple and removing the heathen cult centers, Josiah now set about to duplicate his grandfather's celebration of the annual Passover. For some reason the people just could not keep this pattern of Passover observance going. Hezekiah had resurrected the annual celebration of the Passover in his day, yet here was Josiah doing the same thing all over again just a few years later.

The scripture says, "And the king commanded all the people, saying, Keep the passover unto the Lord your God, as it is written in the book of this covenant."[46] Note the reference here to the book of the law as a "book of this covenant." It is for this reason that the Old Testament with its laws and commandments used to be called the Book of the Old Covenant, and the New Testament the Book of the New Covenant.[47] On the same basis, the modern compilation of God's commandments is called, "The Doctrine and Covenants."

Not only did Josiah initiate the law of the Passover again, but he studied the book of the covenant or commandments to see what else the Lord might require. Wherever there was a commandment, Josiah performed it. The scripture says, "Moreover the workers with familiar spirits, and the wizards, and the images, and the idols, and all the abomi-

---

44. These were often called "chemarims" or in the Hebrew, Kemarim. The word is said to have implied "black" and "howlers". They could therefore, with propriety, be called the "black-robed howlers." See Clarke, *Bible Commentary,* Vol. IV, p. 646.
45. II Kings 23:19-20
46. II Kings 23:21
47. See Peloubet's *Bible Dictionary* under "Covenant".

nations that were spied in the land of Judah and in Jerusalem, did Josiah put away, THAT HE MIGHT PERFORM THE WORDS OF THE LAW WHICH WERE WRITTEN IN THE BOOK THAT HILKIAH THE PRIEST FOUND IN THE HOUSE OF THE LORD."[48]

This is the kind of humble obedience which the very angels in Heaven rejoice to observe. And how much more so, the Lord, whose plan of salvation and program for happy living are supported by so few. The historian who compiled the Book of II Kings had this to say concerning Josiah:

"And like unto him was there no king before him, that turned to the Lord with all his heart, and with all his soul, and with all his might, according to all the law of Moses; neither after him arose there any like him."[49]

The Raising Up of Prophets in the Land

As we have already pointed out, the cruel persecution of the true prophets of God during the earlier part of Manasseh's reign seems to have destroyed or driven underground the servants of the Lord for a considerable period of time. Isaiah prophesied right up to approximately 700 B.C. but it is not until the middle of the reign of Josiah (around 620 B.C.) that prophets seem to have been generally available again. The very fact that Hilkiah, the High Priest, had to seek out a righteous woman in Judah to obtain the will of the Lord for the king, strongly supports the conclusion that even during the early part of Josiah's reign there were no prophets available.

We have reason to believe, however, that long before this, the Lord had been preparing certain chosen servants for the great climactic period into which Judah was now moving. One of these great prophets whom the Lord had been tutoring from his earliest youth was Jeremiah, whom we will be discussing more intimately in the next chapter. Another was the prophet Zephaniah and two others were Nahum and Habakkuk. These great men appear to have been the first trickle in a stream of prophetic forces which finally became a flood just before Judah fell.[50]

48. II Kings 23:24
49. II Kings 23:25

50. I Nephi 1:4; II Chron. 36:15-16

Although exact dating for each of the prophets during this period is impossible, at least it will be helpful to consider briefly what is known about each of them and what the contents of their messages were.

THE PROPHET ZEPHANIAH

Here was a great spirit who is described specifically as having received "the word of the Lord . . . in the days of Josiah, . . . king of Judah."[51]

He is described as being the "son of Cushi, the son of Gedaliah, the son of Amaria, the son of Hizkiah."[52] Some have thought this last name might be Hezekiah, great grandfather of King Josiah, but there is no additional data to support this position. If it were so it is more than likely that the ancient scribes would have made a real point of it. We therefore have nothing specific with which to equate the background or ancestry of Zephaniah. He appears to be very familiar with Jerusalem,[53] so we assume he probably was an inhabitant of the Jewish capital.

It is interesting that none of the contemporary prophets of any period take occasion to refer to one another. They each received their respective revelations, each bore faithful testimony of them, and each suffered the consequences without involving his fellow-believers. It was so with Zephaniah. He makes no reference to other workers in the vineyard, even though we have every reason to believe he was laboring in the field right along with Jeremiah, Nahum and Habakkuk.

Zephaniah denounced conditions in Judah during his day (which was during the reign of Josiah as noted above), so there has been a tendency to assume that his ministry was before the reformation of Josiah. However, as we have already pointed out, there does not appear to have been any prophets available to Josiah prior to the twentieth year of his reign. And Josiah's "reform" was not an enthusiastic and universal revival of the Gospel program insofar as the bulk of the people were concerned. If it had been they would not have been destroyed. Kings had launched great reforms

---

51. Zeph. 1:1
52. Ibid.
53. Zeph. 1:4, 10

before, and all of it to their credit, but the Bible reader is impressed with the fact that these royal edicts of repentance seldom got beneath the skin of the peoples' conscience unless they were accompanied by some national calamity. As of the time Zephaniah was preaching it is likely that the good king Josiah was right in the full tide of a great reform on his own level, but the national calamity which would humble the whole people was still ahead. In the light of all the known circumstances, we would therefore conclude that Zephaniah wrote his prophecies sometime after 620 B.C. and before the fall of Nineveh in 612 B.C. which he, himself, predicts.

The writings of Zephaniah, though short, are extremely stimulating reading. In many respects, he follows the format of Isaiah by first emphasizing the ugly facts of the present, the calamities of the immediate future, and then sweeping clear down the hallway of history to the threshhold of the Millennium to sing his song about God's great day of triumph. Here are some representative passages.

Speaking of the conquest of Jerusalem, he says, "And it shall come to pass in that day, saith the Lord, that there shall be the noise of a cry from the fish-gate, and a howling from the second, and a great crashing from the hills. Howl, ye inhabitants of Maktesh [the market place of Jerusalem], for all the merchant people are cut down; all they that bear silver are cut off. And it shall come to pass at that time, that I will search Jerusalem with candles, and punish the men that are settled on their lees: that say in their heart, The Lord will not do good, neither will he do evil."[54]

All the prophets have had trouble with self-styled "practical men" who are quite certain that God leaves men to their own devices and is neither deeply concerned nor intending to interfere with what goes on. These men of Maktesh were accustomed to wheeling and dealing, negotiating and manipulating. They would squeeze out of any crisis by some means. But Zephaniah declared, "Neither their silver nor their gold shall be able to deliver them in the day of the Lord's wrath; but the whole land shall be devoured by the fire of his jealousy; for he shall make even a speedy riddance of all

---

54. Zeph. 1:10-12

them that dwell in the land."[55] Speedy riddance, indeed! These men would live to see how literally prophecy can be fulfilled.

Zephaniah had words for the whole Philistine plain, as well. He also wanted to warn those who made their homes in the pleasant highland habitations of Moab (east of the Dead Sea) and Ammon (east of the Jordan). Concerning the sea-coast plains, Zephaniah said, "Wo unto the inhabi-- tants of the sea coast, the nation of the Cherethites [recent migrants of the isle of Crete]! the word of the Lord is against you; O Canaan, the land of the Philistines, I will even de- stroy thee, that there shall be no inhabitant [of these people]. And the sea coast shall be dwellings and cottages for shep- herds, and folds for flocks."[56] Not only was this literally ful- filled but it remained that way for many centuries. Only within the past generation has it begun to change with the return of the remnant of Judah.[57] Zephaniah anticipated this change in the last days and said, "And the coast shall be for THE REMNANT OF THE HOUSE OF JUDAH; they shall feed thereupon . . . for the Lord their God shall visit them, and turn away their captivity."[58] Every visitor to the Holy Land today sees the fulfillment of this prophecy before his very eyes!

The visitor to the Holy Land is also impressed by the abject sterility and desolation of the once lush highlands of Moab and Ammon. Listen to Zephaniah predict it: "There- fore, as I live, saith the Lord of hosts, the God of Israel, Surely Moab shall be as Sodom, and the children of Ammon

---

55. Zeph. 1:18
56. Zeph. 2:5-6
57. When the Jews began returning to Palestine, they found that the cheapest land available was the former luxurious plain of Sharon. This is the district which lies along the coast between Tel Aviv and Haifa. For some reason this once fertile area had been turned into deadly malaria-infested swamps. Dr. Howard S. Bennion advised the writer when we were together in Palestine that this was caused by silt from the Nile being swept along by the Mediterranean currents and deposited on the beaches of this area. The wind then blew the silt inland, creating great dunes which trapped the drainage water flowing down from the hills and mountains to the east. This is what had created the pestilent swamps so despised by the Arabs. Jewish engineers discovered the cause of the problem, and determined to solve it. They purchased the land at very cheap rates, initiated extensive drainage projects, planted the dunes with greenery so they would not move about, and then turned this into one of the richest sections of the eastern Mediterranean. Today it is covered with citrus groves, banana plantations, vegetable truck gardening, and prosperous settlements.
58. Zeph. 2:7

as Gomorrah, even the breeding of nettles, and saltpits, and a perpetual desolation. . . ."[59] Although it has not yet come to pass, Zephaniah said that ultimately these upland wastes would also be reclaimed by Judah and her fellow Israelites who would completely rehabilitate them just as the maritime plain is being turned into a garden of Eden today. The prophet said, ". . . the residue of my people shall spoil them, and the remnant of my people shall possess them."[60]

Pulling the focus of his vision down a little closer to his own time, Zephaniah took a hard look at the monumental political and military ferocity of Assyria and said, "And he will stretch out his hand against the north, and destroy Assyria, and will make Nineveh a desolation, and dry like a wilderness. And flocks shall lie down in the midst of her, all the beasts of the nations: both the cormorant and the bittern [the pelican and the porcupine][61] shall lodge in the upper lintels of it; their voice shall sing in the windows; desolation shall be in the threshholds; for he shall uncover the cedar work [meaning their beautiful interiors would be exposed when the roofs were gone]. This is the rejoicing city that dwelt carelessly, that said in her heart, I am, and there is none beside me: how is she become a desolation, a place for beasts to lie down in! every one that passeth by her shall hiss and wag his head."[62]

For Zephaniah to say this in his day was as fantastic in its implications as for someone in our day to say this was going to happen to New York or London. But the generation to whom Zephaniah preached these words lived to see them fulfilled.

Zephaniah's song of hope is just like that of his predecessor, Isaiah. He cried out, "Therefore, wait ye upon me, saith the Lord, until the day that I rise up to the prey . . . that I may assemble the kingdoms, to pour upon them mine indignation, even all my fierce anger: for all the earth shall be devoured with the fire of my jealousy."[63] This refers to the great consumption just before or incidental to the Second Advent.

---

59. Zeph. 2:9
60. Ibid.
61. Clarke, *Bible Commentary*, Vol. 4, p. 757
62. Zeph. 2:13-15
63. Zeph. 3:8

Zephaniah says a unique feature of the Millennial reign is that we will all be able to speak the same language and praise God "with one consent."[64]

Zephaniah then takes up the double-Zion theme, indicating that he, like Isaiah, knew about the Zion in America as well as the one in Jerusalem. Just as Isaiah does in his chapter 18 so Zephaniah refers to America as the land "from beyond the rivers of Ethiopia" and says this is the land from which the gathered people of "my dispersed" (Israel) will come to gain their inheritance in the ancient Promised Land of Palestine.[65]

Then he addresses the two world capitals of that great Millennial day — Zion in America and Zion in old Jerusalem — saying, "Sing, O daughter of Zion: shout O Israel; be glad and rejoice with all the heart, O daughter of Jerusalem. The Lord hath taken away thy judgments; He hath cast out thine enemy: the king of Israel, even the Lord, IS IN THE MIDST OF THEE: thou shalt not see evil any more."[66]

In the spirit of triumph he says, "In that day it shall be said to Jerusalem, Fear thou not: and to Zion, Let not thine hands be slack. . . . At that time will I bring you again, even in the time that I gather you: for I will make you a name and a praise among all people of the earth, when I turn back your captivity before your eyes, saith the Lord."[67]

And on this pleasant note, Zephaniah closes his book.

The Prophet Nahum

Nahum was a prophet who had an ideal assignment. His entire message is focused on one basic theme — the wicked Assyrians and the destruction of their capital city, Nineveh. This gave Nahum plenty to say, but he was allowed to say it from a safe distance — Jerusalem. What wouldn't Jonah have given to denounce the people of Nineveh from the battlements on the high walls of his own hometown! Instead, Jonah had to go right into the dragon's den and risk having himself subjected to torture, his body flayed alive,

---

64. Zeph. 3:9
65. Zeph. 3:10

66. Zeph. 3:14-15
67. Zeph. 3:16-20

his tongue torn out by the roots, and his limbs dismembered joint by joint.

Nahum, on the other hand, saw the vision of Nineveh's fall but wrote all about it for home consumption. Perhaps this is why he was able to reduce his inspired thoughts to some of the most powerful poetic expressions in the Old Testament.

We can only fix the dating for Nahum's writing by its internal context. Since he was predicting the downfall of Nineveh we know he was writing sometime before 612 B.C., and since he talks about the recent conquest of an Egyptian capital and treats it in the past tense we know he must have been functioning within the framework of the period we are presently discussing.

Nahum calls himself an Elkoshite but the significance of this term is lost. Some think this meant he came from a small village near Galilee, others fix his place of origin in Trans-Jordan. Unfortunately, we just don't know. We therefore accept Nahum's writings for the value of their contents and suspend our curiosity concerning the details of his life until such time as the Lord finds it propitious to reveal them.

The core of the Lord's controversy with Nineveh is in the third chapter. This depicts the depravity and the cruelty of the Assyrian culture: "Woe to the bloody city! it is all full of lies and robbery, the prey departeth not; The noise of a whip, and the noise of the rattling of the wheels, and of the pransing horses, and of the jumping chariots. The horseman lifteth up both the bright sword and the glittering spear: and there is a multitude of slain, and a great number of carcases; and there is none end of their corpses; they stumble upon their corpses: because of the multitude of the whoredoms of the well-favoured harlot, the mistress of witchcrafts, that selleth nations through her whoredoms, and families through her witchcrafts. Behold, I AM AGAINST THEE, SAITH THE LORD OF HOSTS. . . ."[68]

In these verses Nahum is comparing Assyria to a public and alluring prostitute who uses all her wiles to rule or

---

68. Nahum 3:1-5

ruin both families and nations. But Nahum assures Assyria (and her abused victims) that justice is coming. ". . . I will cast abominable filth upon thee and make thee vile, and will set thee as a gazingstock. And it shall come to pass, that all they that look upon thee shall flee from thee, and say, Nineveh is laid waste: who will bemoan her? Whence shall I seek comforters for thee?"[69]

Nahum then reminds the Assyrians what happened to a great Egyptian city when it fell. And he asks, "Art thou better than populous No,[70] that was situated among the rivers, that had the waters round about it, whose rampart was the sea, and her wall was from the sea? Ethiopia and Egypt were her strength, and it was infinite; Put and Lubim [nearby allies] were thy helpers. YET WAS SHE CARRIED AWAY, SHE WENT INTO CAPTIVITY: her young children also were dashed in pieces at the top of all the streets: and they cast lots for her honourable men, and all her great men were bound in chains."[71]

Nahum reminds the Assyrians that this should give them a good idea of what to expect since he knew that the conquerors of Diospolis — the Chaldeans from Babylonia — would be among the conquerors of Nineveh. He said the Assyrian strongholds would fall like figs from a figtree and their soldiers would be like women. Nineveh would go down and never rise again. Said he, "O king of Assyria: thy nobles shall dwell in the dust, thy people is scattered upon the mountains and no man gathereth them. There is no healing of thy bruise; thy wound is grievous: all that hear the bruit [report] of thee shall clap the hands [for joy] over

---

69. Nahum 3:6-7
70. It is currently popular to consider this "No" in Nahum to be Thebes since its downfall in 667 B.C. was one of the most notable events of that century. However, the description does not fit Thebes. It was not situated "among the rivers that had the waters round about it," but was on the straight bank of the Nile. Nor was her rampart the sea since it was several hundred miles north and therefore she scarcely could have a wall that "was from the sea". Dr. Adam Clarke, although writing a century ago, thinks it was Diospolis on the Delta which was destroyed about this time. Concerning it, Clarke says: "Being situated in the Delta, it had the fork of two branches of the Nile to defend it by land; and its barrier or wall was the sea, the Mediterranean, into which these branches emptied themselves: so that this city, and the place it stood on, were wholly surrounded by the waters." (*Bible Commentary*, Vol. 4, p. 739)
71. Nahum 3:8-10

thee: for upon whom hath not thy wickedness passed continually?"[72]

All of the material in chapter 3 is specific and tangible. Chapters 1 and 2, however, are more nebulous. Nahum begins by talking about the massive power of the Lord to destroy the wicked and the power he describes is that which is reserved for the Second Advent. The opening of chapter 2 almost sounds like an ancient writer who is attempting to describe modern conditions — in fact, some have so interpreted it. In any event, here is what he says: "The chariots shall rage in the streets, they shall jostle one against another in the broad ways: they shall seem like torches, they shall run like the lightnings."[73]

As we have mentioned earlier, prophets often wrote in this kind of language when their words applied to more than one situation. Note how Nahum concludes this description: "And Huzzab [not a proper name, but meaning "that which was established"][74] shall be led away captive, she shall be brought up, and her maids shall lead her as with the voice of doves, tabering upon their breasts."[75] None of this last phrase fits Nineveh. In fact, in the very next verse it is almost as though he were now changing the subject: Nahum says, "BUT Nineveh is of old like a pool of water."[76] This will help the reader understand why some authorities feel several passages in chapter 2 refer to conditions in modern times.

THE FALL OF NINEVEH AND THE ASSYRIAN EMPIRE

All that Nahum predicted concerning the great city of Nineveh and the fall of the Assyrian empire was fulfilled in that generation. To appreciate what happened let us summarize the last century of Assyria's history.

It will be recalled that for several generations the ferocious and aggrandizing Assyrians had determined to pass through the portals of hell if necessary to conquer Egypt. They conquered practically everything else in sight, but Egypt proved slippery and elusive. In 701 B.C. when Sen-

---

72. Nahum 3:18-19
73. Nahum 2:4
74. See Nahum 2:7, marginal note

75. Nahum 2:7
76. Nahum 2:8

nacherib was on his way to conquer Egypt, he offended the Lord by trying to besiege and massacre Jerusalem on the way. The Lord struck his army down with a "blast" which must have been some kind of plague and killed 185,000 troops overnight.[77] This compelled Sennacherib to return to Assyria, but his son, Esarhaddon (681-669 B.C.), came back in 674 and again in 671 when he finally subdued Egypt and took Memphis, which was the Egyptian capital of the Lower (Delta) Kingdom. Shortly afterwards, however, Egypt rebelled and Esarhaddon was on his way to reconquer her when he died in 669 B.C. He was succeeded by his son, the famous Ashurbanipal (669-626 B.C.) who reconquered Egypt and sacked Thebes, capital of the Upper Kingdom, which is 430 miles up the Nile from Memphis.

Native governors were appointed over the various districts of Egypt to collect tribute and maintain order. The governor for Memphis and district of Sais was named Necho, grandfather of Necho II of the Bible. Governor Necho died and was succeeded by his son, Psammetichus (664-610 B.C.) who successfully rebelled against Assyria, set up the 26th Dynasty, and ruled Egypt for 54 years. As Assyria was collapsing and breathing her last, it was his son, Necho II (610-593 B.C.), who drove up to the Euphrates to rescue Assyria from Babylon. But that is getting ahead of our story.

Assyria subjected the civilized world to a long and violent series of military atrocities before she went down. Shortly after Ashurbanipal lost Egypt in 660 B.C. he faced a rebellion at home. The principal province of Assyria was Babylon and at the moment it was ruled by Ashurbanipal's twin brother. This brother lined up with Elam in the east and the Arabians to the west and south so Ashurbanipal soon found his kingdom about to split asunder. However, he pooled all the resources at his command and after a series of costly battles finally put Babylon to the siege in 648 B.C. Babylon was starved into submission that year and Ashurbanipal's twin brother burned down the royal palace with himself inside of it to avoid falling into Ashurbanipal's hands. Ashurbanipal then wreaked vengeance on the Arabs and later upon Elam. His conquest of Elam was

77. Isaiah 37:36

particularly bitter and its capital of Susa was levelled to the ground around 640-639 B.C.

Much of this fighting was not carried on by Ashurbanipal, but was delegated to his various generals. Ashurbanipal, with a certain air of sophisticated disdain, went about the business of building beautiful palaces, collecting rich libraries, and decorating (and fortifying) the capital city. In the British museum today there are thousands of tablets taken from the Ashurbanipal library at Nineveh.

By the time of Ashurbanipal's death in 626 B.C. a whole new tidal wave of humanity was sweeping down from southern Europe and Asia called the Scythians. These were apparently descendants of Japheth (with whom fragments of the Ten Tribes later mixed) who had settled all of the region extending out from the northern side of the Black Sea. For some time some of them, called Cimmerians, had been filtering down west of the Black Sea to take over Asia Minor, while others had come around the east side of the Black Sea to attack Assyria. This latter group mixed in with the population of Media, a mountainous plateau just east of Assyria, where they established their capital at Ecbatana. Assyria, then, began to be boxed in by Babylon on the south, the Medes (and Scythians) on the northwest. It was just a question of time until these pressures exploded on Nineveh. This occurred in 612 B.C. and it was just as terrible as the Hebrew prophets had said it would be.

In 1923 a researcher discovered among the writings and artifacts in the British Museum a "Chronicle of the fall of Nineveh." This was published in 1923 by C. J. Gadd. It verifies the Biblical account and furnishes additional details. It tell how Kyaxares (Cyaxares) of Media came down to join King Nabopolassar of Babylonia and how they completely devastated the great city of Nineveh. We learn from other sources that every living thing in sight was put to the sword.[78] The terrors and vicious violence of unbridled human passion were loosed upon the city until its inhabitants were exterminated, its buildings burned, and its ruins left in a heap. It was exactly what Assyria had been doing to other people for several centuries.

---

78. Kraeling, Rand McNally *Bible Atlas*, p. 310

The conquest of Nineveh was apparently facilitated by a sudden flood of perhaps both the Choser river which ran through the city, and the Tigris river which ran past the city. The Greek historians say this flood made a serious breach in the walls through which the enemy poured.[79] No doubt this is what Nahum was talking about when he said, "The gates of the rivers shall be opened, and the palace shall be dissolved," or as the revised version says, "dismayed."[80]

A leading Assyrian who escaped from this devastating debacle established a new emergency capital for Assyria at Haran, which was Abraham's former headquarters, located over toward the Euphrates river to the west. This new leader of the Assyrian remnants called himself Ashur-uballit II. Suddenly our attention is directed away from this region toward Egypt. It seems that by this time the Egyptians, who had formerly resisted Assyria, now saw that the new threat was going to be Babylonia and so Egyptian armies were sent up to support Assyria and maintain the balance of power against King Nabopolassar of Babylon. This brings us back to King Josiah of Judah who was about to become entangled in this mammoth power struggle.

THE DEATH OF THE GOOD KING JOSIAH

It will be recalled that we left King Josiah at that stage of his career where he was doing everything in his power to eliminate the monstrous evil of idolatrous immorality and human sacrifices which his father and grandfather had inflicted upon the land. He had refurbished the temple and restored the true pattern of worship on the *official* level for all Judah. As we have already mentioned, he could scarcely be blamed for the fact that a great many of the people still longed for "the good old days!" Corruption is not easily rooted out, and therefore the prophets of this period continued to denounce the plague of apostasy which Josiah's predecessors had initiated.

It was at this stage of righteous endeavor, when his reform movement was just beginning to bear some promising fruits, that Josiah was killed. It was the result of his becoming

79. Ibid.
80. Nahum 2:6

involved in the tentacles of the power struggle between Egypt, Assyria and Babylon.

As previously mentioned, the decline of Assyria and the rise of Babylon, shocked the Egyptians into realizing that a whole new monopoly of power was gravitating toward Babylon. Pharaoh Necho II of Egypt therefore set out with a large army to head off the Babylonians who were marching on Assyria's emergency capital at Haran.[81] This is the setting for the last act in the life of Josiah. Dr. Keyes describes what happened:

"Although Josiah had reigned thirty-one years, he was only thirty-nine when Egyptian armies under Pharaoh Necho began to move north over the land bridge on their way to help their old enemies the Assyrians against a common enemy, the rising Babylonian state. Josiah, a vassal of Assyria like his father, grandfather and great grandfather before him, hated the Assyrians and wanted to see them destroyed. Hoping, therefore, to prevent the Egyptians from joining the Assyrians, he gathered together his small army and the two forces met the Meggido in 609 B.C."[82]

The sudden blocking of the pass at Meggido was all very disconcerting to Pharaoh Necho. When he saw what the King of Judah was attempting to do he looked upon it as strictly diversionary. It distracted him from the task at hand and he deeply resented being delayed from getting to the Euphrates where a whole series of great battles between Babylon and Assyria were shaping up. Necho therefore "sent ambassadors to him, saying, What have I to do with thee, thou king of Judah? I come not against thee this day, but against the house wherewith I have war: for God [of the Egyptians] commanded me to make haste: forebear thee from meddling with God, who is with me, that he destroy thee not."[83]

It perhaps appeared to Josiah that this was just a tactical device to prevent him from taking military action against

81. In II Kings 23:29 it says that Pharaoh Necho went up "against" the king of Assyria. Authorities now point out that this is the wrong word because Necho went up as an ally "to" the king of Assyria and fought with him against Babylon. (See Kraeling, Rand McNally *Bible Atlas*, p. 311)
82. Keyes, *Story of the Bible World*, p. 88
83. II Chron. 35:21

Necho at a time when the Egyptians might turn the tide for the Assyrians. Therefore Josiah decided to go ahead with his attack on Necho II. The scripture says he "disguised himself, that he might fight with him, and hearkened not unto the words of Necho from the mouth of [his] God, and came to fight in the valley of Meggido."[84]

But, for reasons best known to the Lord, Josiah's mission on earth was allowed to be terminated. The protective forces beyond the veil stepped aside and when the Egyptian archers launched their arrows into the charging chariots of Judah, one of them found its target in the vitals of King Josiah. He was taken from his heavy war chariot and placed in a lighter one which raced back toward Jerusalem. But somewhere along that rough, frantic, sixty-mile journey, the spirit of Josiah returned to his Maker and the chariot arrived at the capital with only a dead corpse.

The scripture leaves no doubt as to the impact of this great loss to Judah. It was especially felt among the more righteous contingent of the people. There was great lamentation everywhere and Jeremiah is specifically mentioned as being a principal mourner.[85]

But Pharaoh Necho rejoiced. For the moment it appeared as though the god of Egypt was overwhelmingly superior to the God of Judah. He therefore proceeded up the Mediterranean coast and then worked his way inland to Riblah where he set up military headquarters. This camp was located at the northern end of Becka Valley on the west bank of the Orontes river, not far from Hamath.[86] There Necho made preparations for his confrontation with the Babylonians. The series of battles which followed did not go well with Necho nor with the Assyrians. But neither was there a conclusive defeat. The massive and decisive conflict which would settle affairs did not come until the Battle of Carchemish in 605 B.C., four years thence.

Meanwhile, between engagements, Necho II undertook to strengthen his logistical supply lines coming out of Egypt and this brought his attention back to Judah. He now con-

---

84. II Chron. 35:22
85. II Chron. 35:25

86. Kraeling, Rand McNally *Bible Atlas*, p. 312

sidered Judah to be one of his own vassal states but he learned that the people of Judah had placed one of Josiah's younger sons on the throne. Necho immediately summoned Jehoahaz to his camp at Riblah.[87] For some reason Necho didn't like Jehoahaz and ordered him imprisoned. Later, he shipped him to Egypt and there he died.[88]

This fulfilled a sorrowful passage in Jeremiah's writings where he referred to this son of Josiah as Shallum and after his departure wrote the following, "Weep ye not for the dead [Josiah], neither bemoan him: but weep sore for him that goeth away: FOR HE SHALL RETURN NO MORE, NOR SEE HIS NATIVE COUNTRY. For thus saith the Lord touching Shallum the son of Josiah king of Judah, which reigned instead of Josiah his father, which went forth out of this place: He shall not return thither any more: but he shall die in the place whither they have led him captive, and shall see this land no more."[89]

Pharaoh Necho now selected another son of Josiah to rule in the place of his brother. His name was originally Eliakim but Necho changed it to Jehoiakim.[90] At the same time Necho made Jehoiakim king he placed Judah under an annual tribute of a hundred talents of silver and a talent of gold which was a veritable fortune.[91] Jehoiakim was 25 when he became king[92] which means he was older than his brother whom the people had preferred as king. The scripture says Jehoiakim not only dutifully collected the tribute for Necho but "he did all that was evil in the sight of the Lord, according to all that his fathers had done,"[93] meaning, of course, that he reversed the religious trend away from the prophets back toward idolatry and immorality.

But from here on events did not favor either Necho or Jehoiakim. After a series of major battles back and forth for Haran and other fortified positions in the region, the forces of Egypt and Assyria finally met Babylon in a decisive military contest at Carchemish in 605 B.C. By this time King Nabopolassar of Babylon had turned all of his military campaigns over to his son, the crown prince, Nebuch-

---

87. II Kings 23:33-34
88. 11 Chron. 36:4 and II Kings 23:34
89. Jeremiah 22:10-12
90. II Kings 23:34

91. II Kings 23:33
92. II Kings 23:36
93. II Kings 23:37

adnezzar, and this belicose and ambitious Chaldean[94] turned out to be more than a match for both the Egyptians and the Assyrians. At Carchemish, the Egyptians were cut to ribbons while the Assyrians were scattered and later fled to Hamath.

The following year, Nebuchadnezzar was in the midst of a mopping-up campaign against the last stronghold of the Egyptian-Assyrian alliance when his father died. He hurried to Babylon and was crowned king in 604 B.C. He then pushed his kingdom across Syria, down through Palestine and right up to the gateway of Egypt. By this time the Egyptian Pharaoh was completely terrified. The Bible says, "And the king of Egypt came not again any more out of his land: for the king of Babylon had taken from the river of Egypt unto the river Euphrates all that pertained to the king of Egypt."[95]

Of course, in the process of sweeping westward, Nebuchadnezzar had devoured Judah like a small morsel of nothing. For three years Jehoiakim paid tribute to Babylon. Then, in 601 B.C., the Babylonians attempted to conquer Egypt and were repulsed. This apparently encouraged Jehoiakim to rebel against the Babylonians in spite of vigorous warnings from Jeremiah. The king's decision had some disastrous consequences which we shall describe in the next chapter.

We have not reached the point in our story where we are ready to consider the writings of Jeremiah. Before passing to that exciting epic, however, we have one more prophet to cover briefly because his writings belong to this period.

THE PROPHET HABAKKUK

Although this prophet seems to have written after the fall of Assyria, it was before the captivity of Judah, so we insert his commentary here along with those prophets who seem to have been his contemporaries.

Once again we are dealing with a prophet who modestly excludes anything about himself or his ministry but who faithfully records the substance of the revelations he received.

---

94. Nabopolassar and his dynasty were from Chaldea, south of Babylon and this is why the Babylonians during this period are often referred to as "the Chaldeans".
95. II Kings 24:7

It requires extremely careful reading of Habakkuk to discern just what he is saying. His writings are in question and answer form, but it is not always immediately clear where the prophet leaves off and the Lord begins. Once this is understood, Habakkuk's writings become more comprehensible.

The two main questions which Habakkuk asked the Lord were undoubtedly the same questions many others must have been asking at this same time. For example, Habakkuk wanted to know when the Lord was going to take action. His prophets had been predicting the terrible consequences of Judah's crimes and the punishment she was about to receive, but nothing ever seemed to come of it. The human equation in prophets causes them to get impatient just like ordinary people, so Habakkuk cried out, "O Lord, how long shall I cry, and thou wilt not hear! even cry out unto thee of violence, and thou wilt not save!"[96]

The prophet said he was tired of having the Lord continually show him how wicked the people were. He knew that already. Always, he said, "spoiling and violence are before me: and there are [those] that raise up strife and contention."[97] He said nobody was paying attention to the law any more. ". . . the law is slacked, and judgment doth never go forth; for the wicked doth compass about the righteous; therefore wrong judgment proceedeth."[98] One of the most significant symptoms of a collapsing society is a nation's inability to protect its people from wrong-doers. The criminal and the perpetrators of fraud work through Gadianton webs of influence to cheat justice so as to deprive the injured of their remedy.

The Lord's answer to this complaint was to declare or confirm that Judah was going to be conquered by the new world power, the "Chaldeans, that bitter and hasty nation, which shall march through the breadth of the land. . . . They are terrible and dreadful: their judgment and their dignity shall proceed of themselves [without allies]. Their horses also are swifter than the leopards, and are more fierce than

96. Hab. 1:2
97. Hab. 1:3
98. Hab. 1:4

the evening wolves [when they come from their lairs ravenous with hunger]."[99]

But this reply immediately raised another question. How could a just God punish the Jews by having them conquered by a nation that is even more wicked? Or as Habakkuk put it, "Thou art of purer eyes than to behold evil, and canst not look on iniquity: wherefore lookest Thou upon them that deal treacherously, and holdest Thy tongue when the wicked devoureth the man [or people] that is more righteous than he?"[100] Having posed the question, Habakkuk said to himself, "I will . . . watch to see what He will say unto me, and what I shall answer when I am reproved."[101] Apparently he feared lest he had asked a silly question for which he might be rebuked for appearing to doubt the Lord's integrity. In any event, the Lord replied, ". . . Write the vision and MAKE IT PLAIN UPON TABLES, THAT HE MAY RUN THAT READETH IT."[102] (So much for publishers who put their books in small print!)

The revelation Habakkuk received announced God's attitude toward the wicked. While it was true that the Chaldeans would be allowed to punish Judah for her apostasy it was equally true that the Lord was going to allow the Chaldeans to be thoroughly punished for their own wickedness. Hence, the revelation proclaims the ultimate fall of Babylon.

"Wo to him," declared the Lord, "that coveteth an evil covetousness to his house, that he may set his nest on high, that he may be delivered from the power of evil!"[103] This was referring to Nebuchadnezzar who wished to build the Babylonian empire on his own family, but both empire and family collapsed in a remarkably short time.

"Wo to him, "continued the Lord, "that buildeth a town with blood, and stablisheth a city by iniquity!"[104] Babylon had become renowned for her magnificence, but she was built on the spoils and sufferings of surrounding nations. The Lord wanted her proud kings to know that in short order their mighty city would be melting into heaps of unorganized chaos

---

99. Hab. 1:6-8
100. Hab. 1:13
101. Hab. 2:1

102. Hab. 2:2
103. Hab. 2:9
104. Hab. 2:12

just like Nineveh. Said the Lord, "Because thou hast spoiled many nations, all the remnant of the people shall spoil thee. . . ."[105]

So Habakkuk had the answers to his two great questions. He closes his writings with a prayer. He knew from what he had seen that terrible times lay directly ahead. And he knew that in such extremities the Lord requires the righteous, especially his prophets, to suffer in the midst of the wicked. Habakkuk wanted the Lord to know that he had resolved to stay faithful no matter what happened. He ended his prayer with these words, "Although the fig tree shall not blossom, neither shall fruit be in the vine; the labour of the olive shall fail, and the fields shall yield no meat; the flock shall be cut off from the fold, and there shall be no herd in the stalls: YET I WILL REJOICE IN THE LORD, I WILL JOY IN THE GOD OF MY SALVATION. The Lord God is my strength, and he will make my feet like hinds' feet, and he will make me to walk upon mine high places."[106]

Thus Habakkuk set his face like flint to await the future.

Now we are ready to turn to the life and times of the greatest Old Testament personality since Isaiah. He was God's official mouthpiece in the days of Judah's downfall — Jeremiah.

---

105. Hab. 2:8
106. Hab. 3:17-19

Scripture Readings and Questions on Chapter Twenty-Three

Scripture Reading: 2 Chronicles, chapters 33 to 34; the Books of Nahum, Zephaniah and Habakkuk.

1—List four things which King Manasseh did to corrupt Judah.

2—What did the Lord say was the worst offense of all? Where did this occur?

3—Why do we think Manasseh was arrested and carried off to Babylon? What did he do? Did he ever return to Jerusalem?

4—Did King Amon improve conditions in Judah? What happened to him? What was the reaction of the people? Why?

5—How old was Josiah when he began to reign? After having a wicked father and grandfather, did he follow their example?

6—What procedure did Josiah follow to cleanse the land of idolatry?

7—What literary treasure was found during the cleansing of the temple? Since the king and his advisors were so excited over this discovery, what do we deduct concerning religious education at this time?

8—Why did the king ask Hilkiah, the High Priest, to get a revelation from the Lord? Where did Hilkiah go to get it? What does this imply?

9—What did the revelation say concerning Judah? What did it say concerning the king?

10—Why did the king dig up the bones of those buried near the heathen shrines? At Bethel there was one sepulchre he did not disturb — why?

11—What did Josiah do with the heathen priests who were still lurking about their shrines? Was this justified?

12—What did Zephaniah say the attitude of "practical men" would be in the day of Judah's destruction?

13—What did Zephaniah say would happen to Assyria? Was it fulfilled?

14—What did Zephaniah say about the language of the people during the Millennium?

15—Why is it suggested that the prophet Nahum had "an ideal assignment"? How did it contrast with the mission of Jonah?

16—Were the Assyrians ever successful in permanently conquering Egypt? Who were the Scythians?

17—How did King Josiah happen to get killed? Briefly outline the circumstances.

18—What did Necho do with Josiah's successor? What happened to him?

19—Who won the battle at Carchemish in 605 B.C.? How did this change the world picture?

20—What two questions did the prophet Habakkuk ask the Lord? What were the answers?

CHAPTER TWENTY-FOUR

The Prophet Jeremiah

Among all of the so-called "Latter Prophets" — from
Isaiah to Malachi — we know more about Jeremiah than any
of them.* From his extremely interesting biographical data

---

* THE BOOK OF JEREMIAH is one of the most interesting segments of scripture
ever written, but at the same time authorities agree that it is one of the most
mixed-up books in the Bible. Dr. Clarke believes that the sheets of an early manuscript were accidentally shuffled and then bound together in that unfortunate
arrangement. He suggests that respect for the sanctity of holy writ subsequently
forbade the rearrangment of the sheets in their correct order and that for this reason
even the King James translators left them just as they came to hand. Based on a
careful analysis of the text itself as well as a number of authoritative commentaries,
the following chapter arrangement is suggested as the one most likely to give the
reader the best chronological sequence of events for study. Certain chapters remain
somewhat dubious but most of them fit the following pattern without forcing.

Chapter	Est. Date B.C.	Principal Topic
1	626	Jeremiah receives his calling.
2	626-620	The Lord's controversy with Judah.
3	626-620	Gathering of Israel in the Latter Days.
4	626-620	Jerusalem's coming desolation.
5	620	Jeremiah rejected as he commences his ministry.
6	609	No peace, the Babylonians are on their way.
22	609	Weep for Jehoahaz, cursed is Jehoiakim.
7	608	The abominations of idolatry.
8	608	Bitterness of the coming desolation.
9	608	O that my head were water, and mine eyes fountain of tears.
10	607	Learn not the ways of the heathen.
11	607	Jeremiah's fellow townsmen seek his life.
12	607	Jeremiah's family turn against him.
13	607	Message to Jehoiakim and his queen.
17	607	Hallow the Sabbath day and be saved.
18	607	Plot to kill Jeremiah.
26	607	Jeremiah is saved but Urijah is killed.

we learn many things about the calling of a prophet which might otherwise be difficult or impossible to demonstrate from Biblical sources. For example, how did the ancient prophets receive and record their extensive revelations? As we shall see, only Jeremiah gives us the actual *modus operandi.*

Jeremiah was a Levite, born and raised, so far as we know, in Anathoth, a small community located about 2½ miles northeast of Jerusalem and very near the modern Arab town of Anata. In those days there lived at this place a whole colony of men and their families who were direct descendants of Aaron. They were therefore Priests. Jere-

19	607	Ye shall eat the flesh of your children.
20	607	Pashur abuses Jeremiah.
35	607	Jeremiah's visit to the Rechabites.
14	605	The great drouth.
15	605	Not even Moses or Samuel could save Judah now.
16	605	Jeremiah forbidden to marry during time when a curse is on the land.
25	605	All heathen nations to imbibe in the cup of war.
36	605	Jehoiakim burns Jeremiah's scroll but the prophet dictates another.
45	605	The Lord comforts Jeremiah's scribe.
46	604	Defeat of Egypt predicted.
23	598	Denunciation of apostate prophets.
24	598	Vision of the two baskets of figs.
29	597	Jeremiah's letters to the captives.
27	595	Jeremiah wears bonds and a yoke.
28	595	Hananiah publicly challenges Jeremiah and dies.
30	588	Latter-day glory of Judah.
31	588	Latter-day restoration of Israel.
33	588	Glory of Jerusalem when the Messiah comes.
21	588	Zedekiah seeks a revelation through Jeremiah as war threatens.
34	588	Zedekiah will be taken to Babylon as a captive.
37	588	Jeremiah is imprisoned for treason.
32	588	Jeremiah buys a field while in prison.
38	587	Jeremiah rescued from dungeon by negro servant of the king.
39	587	Jerusalem falls.
40	587	Jeremiah joins remnant at Mizpah.
41	587	Gedaliah assassinated at Mizpah.
42	587	Mizpah leaders reject Jeremiah's advice.
43	587	Mizpah remnant goes to Egypt.
44	584-571	Idolatrous Jews in Egypt to be completely destroyed.
47	584-571	Prophetic warning to the Philistines.
48	584-571	Prophetic warning to the Moabites.
49	584-571	Prophetic warning to the other nations bordering Israel.
50	584-571	Coming fall of Babylon.
51	584-571	Total desolation coming to Babylon.
52	584-571	Summary of the fall of Judah.

miah's father is specifically identified as Hilkiah, one of the Priests of this Anathoth colony.[1]

As our story unfolds, we discover the tragic fact that this settlement of Priests at Anathoth had apparently become a seriously corrupted and apostate colony of people. They became some of Jeremiah's worst enemies, and we do not find the slightest hint that Jeremiah's father made any attempt to either defend him or offer assistance. His own brothers also conspired against him. Like Abraham of old, Jeremiah's proclamation of repentance was directed as much toward his own family as it was toward the public.

In one respect Jeremiah was identical with Enoch, Abraham, Samuel, Nephi, Mormon and Joseph Smith. Like them, he received his prophetic assignment and was given his opening revelation from God while still a boy.

Jeremiah describes himself at the time of his call as "a child," and Dr. Adam Clarke suggests the probability that he was about fourteen.[2] This is very likely the approximate age of Enoch when he received his call as "a lad."[3] Abraham was an unmarried youth when divine revelations began illuminating his understanding,[4] and since Samuel is described as being age twelve when he was dedicated to the Lord,[5] he probably would be around fourteen or fifteen when his call first came. Nephi says he was "exceeding young" when the vista of revelation flooded down upon him,[6] and since he was the youngest of four unmarried brothers it is not likely

---

1. Jeremiah 1:1 — The chief priest at the temple during this period was also named Hilkiah, but there is nothing to suggest that this man was identical with Jeremiah's father. In fact, there are two factors which would imply the very opposite. *First,* Jeremiah's father is called "Hilkiah of the priests that were at Anathoth," whereas if Jeremiah could have been tied in with "Hilkiah, the chief priest of the temple," the writer of the introductory note would have no doubt done it. *Second,* five years after Jeremiah's call, but before he had commenced his public ministry, the chief priest (Hilkiah) at the temple tried to find someone who could get a revelation for the king. He went to Huldah, the prophetess. Had he been Jeremiah's father, he would have known of Jeremiah's gift and no doubt put it to the test.
2. Clarke, *Bible Commentary,* Vol. 4, p. 251
3. Moses 6:31
4. Abraham 1:16 describes his calling and Abraham 2:2 indicates that he married a considerable time afterwards.
5. Josephus, *Antiquities of the Jews,* Book 5, ch. 20:4
6. I Nephi 2:16

he would have been more than fifteen or sixteen.[7] Mormon when he received the magnificent and glorious visitation in says he was "fifteen years of age" when he saw the Savior,[8] and Joseph Smith says he was also in his "fifteenth year" when he received the magnificent and glorious visitation in the grove.[9] For most growing boys, age fifteen is the most uncomfortable and rebellious year of the entire teen-age maturation pattern. It is interesting that the Lord would seem to choose this particular year for the calling of so many of His choice servants!

The book of Jeremiah starts out with an introductory note which is believed to have been inserted by Ezra when he arranged the Hebrew canon of scripture.[10] It says, "The words of Jeremiah . . . to whom the word of the Lord came in the days of Josiah . . . in the thirteenth year of his reign."[11]

According to our table of chronology, this would place the calling of Jeremiah at 626 BC., and if he were fourteen at that date, then his birth would have been about 640 B.C. These are only estimates, of course, but for reasons indicated above, they are probably very close.

Jeremiah commenced his writing by describing how he was called by the Lord. He writes, "Then the word of the Lord came unto me, saying, Before I formed thee in the belly I knew thee; and before thou camest forth out of the womb I sanctified thee, and I ordained thee a prophet unto the nations."[12]

Some Bible commentaries have indicated that this means the Lord simply *anticipated* the calling of Jeremiah, but we now know from the writings of Abraham[13] and other sources[14] that Jeremiah was personally known to the Lord in the pre-existent estate. He existed in the spirit world before he came here just as Jesus did,[15] and just as we did also.[16] Therefore,

---

7. His older brothers were Laman, Lemuel and Sam (I Nephi 2:5). They all married daughters of Ishmael subsequent to Nephi's first revelation (I Nephi 16:7).
8. Mormon 1:15
9. Pearl of Great Price, p. 47:7
10. Clarke, *Bible Commentary*, Vol. 4, p. 255
11. Jeremiah 1:2
12. Jeremiah 1:4-5
13. Abraham 3:22
14. Doc. & Cov. 29:31-32
15. John 1:1-2, 14; 6:38; 8:58; 17:5
16. John 3:13; Abraham 3:24-26; Ephesians 1:3-6; Hebrews 12:9

the Lord wanted Jeremiah to realize that He knew him, chose him, and ordained him to be a prophet of God before he was ever born. He was foreordained to be a mouthpiece of the Lord to all who came within sound of his voice or in sight of his writings. He thereby became a prophet not only to the nations of his own day and time but to those which have followed.

Nevertheless, Jeremiah tried to get out of it. He pleaded with the Lord, "Ah, Lord God! behold, I cannot speak: for I am a child."[17] The Lord replied, "Say not, I am a child; for thou shalt go to all that I shall send thee, and whatsoever I command thee thou shalt speak."[18] He did not have to be a Demosthenes or a cultured orator. All he had to do was speak forth words which the Lord would instruct him to say. Jeremiah says: "Then the Lord put forth his hand and touched my mouth. And the Lord said unto me, Behold, I have put my words in thy mouth."[19]

However, the Lord knew that this divine commission, especially for a person called so early in his youth, would be frightening. He therefore gave Jeremiah special instructions as to just how he should carry out his mission.

First, he was to assert himself and confront the rich, powerful and wicked leaders of the people with boldness. Even though by training and natural inclination he might feel modest, retiring, and easily intimidated, he must stand before these people and forcefully present his message.[20]

Second, once he came before them, he was not to be "dismayed by their faces." The Lord knew it is an awesome thing for a young and ordinary person to project himself into the midst of the sophisticated and sometimes pompous leaders of the people. The Lord also knew Jeremiah had a humble, sensitive spirit, and in the presence of sneering, disdainful public prelates he might panic. Therefore the Lord said, "Thou therefore gird up thy loins, and rise, and speak unto them all that I command thee: be not dismayed at their faces, lest I confound thee before them."[21] In other words,

---

17. Jeremiah 1:6
18. Jeremiah 1:7
19. Jeremiah 1:9

20. Jeremiah 1:8
21. Jeremiah 1:17

throw off your timidity, seize the initiative and maintain it. Then the Lord gave Jeremiah a promise:

"For, behold, I have made thee this day a defenced city, and an iron pillar, and brasen walls against the whole land, against the KINGS of Judah, and the PRINCES thereof, against the PRIESTS thereof, and against the PEOPLE of the land."[22]

Jeremiah Passes Through a Period of Intensive Preparation

Although Jeremiah received his calling while "a child," we have strong indications that he had a substantial period of preparation before he was allowed to deliver his message publicly.

It will be noted that he spends three chapters describing all the various revelations and instructions he received and then up in the fourth chapter he indicates that he cannot hold his peace much longer. After a particularly moving vision of the terrible trouble awaiting Jerusalem if she did not repent, he cried:

"My bowels, my bowels [my inward parts]! I am pained at my very heart; my heart maketh a noise in me; I CAN-NOT HOLD MY PEACE, because thou hast heard, O my soul, the sound of the trumpet, the alarm of war. Destruction upon destruction is cried; for the whole land is spoiled."[23]

There is no doubt but what Jeremiah was being filled to overflowing with the power of his calling. And the fact that he found it difficult to hold his peace would strongly imply that up to this time he had been under some type of divine restriction while he was being prepared for his mission. This is further borne out by the fact that while he was told way back in the beginning to "Go and cry in the ears of Jerusalem," it is way up in chapter 5 that he finally refers to his going forth and describes the reception he received.

A similar pattern of extensive preparation occurred with Joseph Smith. He received the first of a series of magnificent revelations beginning when he was fourteen, but while he

---

22. Jeremiah 1:18
23. Jeremiah 4:19-20

shared these with his family and a few intimate friends, he did not launch forth into any type of public ministry until April, 1830. By that time he was 24. A year earlier, Joseph's older brother, Hyrum, was so thrilled with the avalanche of new knowledge which Joseph had been receiving that he, like Jeremiah, became restless with anxiety and wanted to go forth immediately to spread the good news. But the Lord said to Hyrum:

'Seek not to declare my word, but FIRST SEEK TO OBTAIN MY WORD, and THEN shall your tongue be loosed; THEN, if you desire, you shall have my Spirit and my word, yea, the power of God unto the convincing of men. But now HOLD YOUR PEACE; STUDY MY WORD . . .''[24]

In the light of what we know about Jeremiah, he also was required to hold his peace and study what the Lord had revealed. The Lord needed time in which to tutor him, and Jeremiah needed time in which to grow up. This would help account for the fact that even though Jeremiah received his first revelation in 626 B.C., he was still apparently unknown to the public five years later when the King was starting his great reform and wanted someone who could get him a revelation from the Lord.[25] It will be recalled that the chief priest, Hilkiah, went to Huldah, the prophetess,[26] when Hebrew discipline would have ordinarily required him to seek out and utilize a Priesthood holder if one had been available. Apparently Jeremiah was still unknown.

THE LORD'S CONTROVERSY WITH JUDAH

Now let us turn to the early chapters of Jeremiah and see what the Lord revealed to him.

Jeremiah was told that the people had committed a double offense against the Lord. It was bad enough for them to drift away from the Lord into agnostic materialism (the principal sin of modern man), but these people had compounded the sin by replacing their Creator and Father with synthetic gods, clumsily fashioned after their own absurd

---

24. Doc. & Cov. 11:21-22
25. 2 Kings 22:12-13
26. 2 Kings 22:14

and childish notions. It was irrational and ridiculous. So the Lord said, ". . . they have forsaken me the fountain of living waters, and hewed them out cisterns, broken cisterns, that can hold no water."[27]

The Lord told Jeremiah the people were like a bronco, female pack-camel, swiftly lumbering out across the desert "traversing her [misguided] ways."[28] He also compared Judah to the snorting capers of "a wild ass used to the wilderness, that snuffeth up the wind at her pleasure. . . ."[29] The Lord said this wild, rebellious people were guilty of the following charges:

1—They had attributed their creation to stumps of wood (no doubt referring to the phallic symbols of fertility worship) and to idols of stone.[30]

2—They had duplicated the religious stupidity of the heathens by creating a god for every town and city.[31]

3—They had put true prophets of God to the sword.[32]

4—They had shed innocent blood by numerous murders.[33]

5—They had shed more innocent blood by offering their children up as human sacrifices to Moloch, god of Ammon, in the valley of Hinnom, just outside Jerusalem.[34]

6—The people had become addicted to gross immorality: ". . . they . . . committed adultery, and assembled themselves by troops in the harlot's houses. They were as fed horses in the morning: every one neighed after his neighbour's wife."[35]

7—The people had attempted to achieve political security by no longer depending on God's protection but substituting alliances with Egypt.[36]

8—The Priests of Aaron had apostatized and no longer said, "Where is the Lord,"[37] but taught for commandments the doctrines of men.

---

27. Jeremiah 2:13
28. Jeremiah 2:23
29. Jeremiah 2:24
30. Jeremiah 2:27
31. Jeremiah 2:28
32. Jeremiah 2:30

33. Jeremiah 4:31
34. Jeremiah 7:31
35. Jeremiah 5:7-8
36. Jeremiah 2:36
37. Jeremiah 2:8

9—The judges had corrupted themselves so that they no longer depended upon the Lord or His law to provide equity and righteous judgment among the people.[38]

10—The people depended upon prophets who were not prophets at all, but hirelings who were servants of Satan.[39] As the Lord said later concerning these men who called themselves "prophets":

"They commit adultery and walk in lies: they strengthen also the hands of evildoers, that none shall return from his wickedness. . . ."[40] Their prophecies are simply "wind,"[41] because "they speak a vision of their own heart, and not out of the mouth of the Lord."[42] When they lack sufficient imagination to concoct delusions by themselves they borrow from the evil imaginations of their deluded associates.[43] The Lord concludes by saying, ". . . I sent them not, nor commanded them: therefore they shall not profit this people AT ALL, saith the Lord."[44]

11—The people prided themselves in their acquisition of much learning and sophisticated intellectualism. However, the Lord said their brainpower was being used to contrive clever schemes for criminal machinations against their neighbors, immoral seduction of the young, the perversion of the innocent. For religious truths, they had substituted philosophical speculations. All through Jeremiah's writings these elements of pseudo-intellectualism are continually denounced. Apparently this is what the Lord therefore had in mind when He said, "THEY ARE WISE TO DO EVIL, BUT TO DO GOOD THEY HAVE NO KNOWLEDGE."[45]

Judah's Coming Calamity

Mixed in with the Lord's charges against Judah were clear predictions of an early judgment which would come in the form of violent conquest and catastrophic desolation.

Jeremiah was shown the rod of an almond tree which the Lord used to symbolize the fact that this, the earliest

---

38. Ibid.
39. Ibid.
40. Jeremiah 23:14
41. Jeremiah 5:13

42. Jeremiah 23:16
43. Jeremiah 23:30
44. Jeremiah 23:32
45. Jeremiah 4:22

blossoming tree, would provide a limber whip or rod by which Judah would be thrashed.[46] In other words, the Lord would use the first available instrument to bring about this punishment.

Then Jeremiah was shown a "seething pot," with its vapor and fumes pouring down "from the face of the north."[47] Ezekiel would also see a boiling pot representing the forces of war,[48] and this was exactly what was going to descend on Jerusalem. Although Babylon and her vassals (called in Jer. 1:15, "families of the kingdoms of the north") were located more to the east, their attack on Jerusalem did indeed come out of the north.

So this was the message Jeremiah was to take to the leaders of Judah and the people: War and desolation were coming unless the people reformed.

We should perhaps mention that during this period the forces of war came to the Mediterranean Near East from two sources. One source was the Scythians, the other the Babylonians. As we have mentioned earlier, the Scythians were descendants of Japheth who had settled all around the upper side of the Black Sea and had spread into Europe and Asia. Between 630 and 624 B.C., they came streaming back down across Asia Minor to attack the Mediterranean kingdoms. However, these reckless hosts appear to have concentrated mostly on the maritime plain while leaving the less attractive mountain kingdoms for some future conquest. Before this could be achieved, they were turned back.

By the time Jeremiah was ready to take his message to the people the Scythian threat was fading and it was King Nabopolassar of Babylon who loomed large on the horizon. He had started a series of conquests which his son, Nebuchadnezzar, would finish. Jeremiah knew that during these campaigns the forces of Babylon would grind rebellious Judah to powder. Therefore the Lord said, "The lion is come up from his thicket, and the destroyer of the Gentiles is on his way; he is gone forth from his place to make thy land deso-

---

46. Jeremiah 1:11-12
47. Jeremiah 1:13 — marginal reading which is now believed to be the correct translation.
48. Ezekiel 24:3

late; and thy cities shall be laid waste, without an inhabitant."[49]

THE LORD'S MESSAGE OF HOPE

But in spite of this dark prospect for the future, Jeremiah was told by the Lord that he could give the people two promises. The first was that even now, regardless of the past, if they would truly repent the destruction of Jerusalem could be averted.[50] After all, if the wicked city of Nineveh found it possible to be saved by repentance, why not Jerusalem? The Lord specifically said it was possible.

The second promise was given as a message of hope in case the people elected to follow their present path of destruction and ultimately go into dispersion. It will be noted that instead of emphasizing the temporary return to Jerusalem and the occasional moments of Judah's respite from suffering, the revelation sweeps down to the last days and God's great era of manifest power. The Lord said to Jeremiah:

"Go and proclaim these words toward the north, and say, Return, thou backsliding Israel. . . . I am married unto you: and I will take you one of a city, and two of a family, and I will bring you to Zion: and I will give you pastors according to mine heart, which shall feed you with knowledge and understanding."[51]

The Lord said it would be a day in which He would personally rule in Jerusalem so that no longer would they need the Ark of the Covenant for they would have the very presence of the Lord.[52]

The Lord assured Jeremiah that in that day there would not only be a gathering of Judah but the hosts of Israel would be gathered as well. Said He, "In those days the house of Judah shall walk with the house of Israel, and they shall come together out of the land of the north to the land that I have given for an inheritance unto your fathers."[53]

Jeremiah was also shown a vivid panoramic vision of what the face of the earth would look like when "the presence

---

49. Jeremiah 4:7
50. Jeremiah 4:14
51. Jeremiah 3:12, 14-15

52. Jeremiah 3:16-17
53. Jeremiah 3:18

of the Lord" came to cleanse the earth at the time of the Second Advent:

"I beheld the earth, and, lo, it was without form, and void; and the heavens, and they had no light. I beheld the mountains, and, lo, they trembled, and all the hills moved lightly. I beheld, and, lo, there was no man, and all the birds of the heavens were fled . . . the fruitful place was a wilderness, and all the cities thereof were broken down AT THE PRESENCE OF THE LORD,[54] and by his fierce anger. For thus hath the Lord said, The whole land shall be desolate; yet will I not make a full end."[55]

Young Jeremiah Pleads the Cause of Judah Before the Lord and Suffers a Rude Awakening

At the end of Jeremiah's extensive period of preparation, one would have thought he would gird on his sandals and charge into the multitudes at Jerusalem with a message of fire and brimstone. But he didn't. He took issue with the Lord. He actually attempted to convince the Lord that He was too harsh!

This was the same mistake Moses had made. It will be recalled that very often when the Lord would pronounce a righteous judgment on Israel, Moses would commence to defend the evil-doers and ask that affairs be managed a different way. Out of respect for Moses, the Lord often granted his wish, but IN EVERY CASE, MOSES TURNED OUT TO BE WRONG. Now Jeremiah had the same experience. He later confessed what he had done:

"Therefore I said, Surely these are poor; they are foolish: for they know not the way of the Lord, nor the judgment of their God. I WILL GET ME UNTO THE GREAT MEN, AND WILL SPEAK UNTO THEM; for they have not known the way of the Lord, nor the judgment of their God. . . ."[56]

---

54. Here is the key phrase which signals to the reader the fact that this whole passage has reference to a time far in the future and not the pending destruction of Jerusalem. It was the presence of the Babylonians, not the presence of the Lord, which was to destroy Judah and Jerusalem. At no time was the Babylonian conquest accompanied by any physical disturbance which made the crust of the earth "without form and void." This was a great event far in the future which Jeremiah was allowed to see.

55. Jeremiah 4:23-27   56. Jeremiah 5:4-5

Jeremiah even went further. At one time he openly excused the people for what they had done. The modern Bible is believed by Dr. Clarke to have distorted the original intent of this passage so we use the Jewish *Targum* which quotes Jeremiah as writing, "And I said, Receive my supplication, O Lord God; for, behold, the false prophets deceive this people and the inhabitants of Jerusalem, saying Ye shall have peace."[57]

Apparently the Lord did not argue with Jeremiah. He let him find out the hard way. Certainly the false prophets had been a debasing influence, but let Jeremiah now go to all these "poor," "foolish," "great men" he was so certain he could convert. We have no details concerning the woeful and revolting treatment which young Jeremiah received, but we have his shocked conclusion after it was all over: ". . . THESE HAVE ALTOGETHER BROKEN THE YOKE, AND BURST THE BONDS!"[58]

And this was only the beginning. Before his mission was far along, Jeremiah suddenly realized he would be extremely fortunate if he filled this assignment and lived to tell about it. It turned out that his problem in dealing with these people was not merely having the patience to endure their insults and abuse, but possessing the genius to escape being murdered.

JEREMIAH GETS A MORE REALISTIC PERSPECTIVE

From here on, everything the Lord said about the poor, foolish great men of Judah was apparently accepted by Jeremiah with a loud "Amen." One can almost hear the Lord's declaration and Jeremiah's response:

"But this people hath a revolting and rebellious heart."[59]

AMEN!

"For among my people are found wicked men. . . ."[60]

AMEN!

---

57. Clarke, *Bible Commentary*, Vol. 4, p. 266. This has reference to Jeremiah 4:10.
58. Jeremiah 5:5
59. Jeremiah 5:23
60. Jeremiah 5:26

"They lay [in] wait, as he that setteth snares; they set a trap, they catch men."[61]

AMEN!

"As a cage is full of birds, so are their houses full of deceit . . . [thereby] they are become great, and waxen rich."[62]

AMEN!

"They are waxen fat, they shine: yea, they overpass the deeds of the wicked. . ."[63]

AMEN!

"They judge not the cause, the cause of the fatherless, yet they prosper; and the right of the needy do they not judge."[64]

AMEN!

"A wonderful and horrible thing is committed in the land."[65]

AMEN!

"The prophets prophesy falsely, and the priests bear rule by their means; AND MY PEOPLE LOVE TO HAVE IT SO. . . ."[66]

AMEN AND AMEN!

Here was the key phrase to the whole situation: *"My people love to have it so!"*

THE REIGN OF KING JOSIAH, KING JEHOAHAZ AND KING JEHOIAKIM

By this time King Josiah was well along in his program of reform and while the people attended his Feast of the Passover and went through the motions of token reform, it is obvious that it was no more than skin deep. Had it been otherwise, the Lord would have rescued the people from their impending destruction just as He promised He would.[67] The

---

61. Jeremiah 5:26
62. Jeremiah 5:27
63. Jeremiah 5:28
64. Ibid.
65. Jeremiah 5:30
66. Jeremiah 5:31
67. Jeremiah 4:14

fact that He did not proves that Josiah's reform was mostly on the surface or on the "policy level." Nevertheless, Jeremiah rejoiced in what the king was trying to accomplish and supported the reform as best he could. In fact, he greatly mourned the death of Josiah in 609 B.C. when the king of Judah was unexpectedly killed while trying to stop the passage of Pharaoh Necho II at Meggido.[68] During the following years Jeremiah had many occasions to long for the return of a righteous reign like the one provided by the good king Josiah. Upon the death of Josiah, the people installed as their new king a young son of Josiah named Jehoahaz.[69] However, he only reigned for 3 months. Necho summoned him to his military headquarters in Syria, disapproved of him and placed him under arrest. While the people were still in mourning over Josiah, Jeremiah declared, "Weep ye not for the dead [Josiah], neither bemoan him: but weep sore for him that goeth away [his son, Jehoahaz]: for he shall return no more, nor see his native country. . . . But he shall die in the place whither they have led him captive, and shall see this land no more."[70] This is exactly what happened. Jehoahaz was deported to Egypt and there he eventually died.[71]

Meanwhile, Necho II imposed on Judah an older, and, as it turned out, more wicked son of Josiah, named Eliakim. Necho re-named him Jehoiakim and he reigned 11 years.[72] But Jeremiah had a word for this Jehoiakim. The prophet said that he would go to his grave unmourned,[73] and would be thrown beyond the gates of Jerusalem with about as much ceremony as "the burial of an ass."[74] He also said that the king's son and his mother would be dragged off to another country and die there and that he would leave no heir to the throne of David, but it would pass to another.[75] As we shall see, all of these things came to pass with painful exactness.

The writings of Jeremiah from chapter 7 on, make it apparent that a wicked king is on the throne. Jeremiah is

68. 2 Chron. 35:25
69. 2 Chron. 36:1
70. Jeremiah 22:10-12
71. 2 Kings 23:34

72. 2 Chron. 36:4-5
73. Jeremiah 22:18
74. Jeremiah 22:19
75. Jeremiah 22:24-30

specifically told to call the king and his queen to repentance.[76]
We thereby know that by this time the good King Josiah
was gone, and that Jeremiah's denunciation of the current administration is aimed at Jehoiakim. The scripture says that
unlike Josiah, this Jehoiakim "did that which was evil in the
sight of the Lord his God."[77] This means that he once more
brought back the idolatry, heathen sacrifices, astrologist su-
perstitions, wizardry and all the other things his dead father
had tried to exterminate.

JEREMIAH FLOUNDERS IN THE MIRE OF PERSECUTION

Beginning with chapter 7, we find Jeremiah under orders from the Lord to "stand in the gate of the Lord's house,
and proclaim. . . ."[78] His sermons extend up through chapter
11. Then the pressures of hate, murder, persecution, and betrayal by friends and family began to take their toll. In the
11th chapter, Jeremiah speaks of the Priests and people from
his own hometown who seem to have initiated much of the
opposition against him. Referring to the men of Anathoth,
Jeremiah exclaims with surprise, "I knew not that they had
devised devices against me, saying, Let us destroy the tree
with the fruit thereof [the prophet and his prophecies], and
let us cut him off from the land of the living, that his name
may be no more remembered."[79]

These men came to him with murderous threats, saying,
"Prophesy not in the name of the Lord, that thou die not
by our hand."[80] And in the next chapter the Lord refers to
Jeremiah's own family, saying, "For even thy brethren, and
the house of thy father, even they have dealt treacherously
with thee; yea, they have called a multitude after thee: believe them not, though they speak fair words unto thee."[81]

Perhaps to get Jeremiah's mind off his troubles, the
Lord told him to take a fine girdle which he was wearing
and carry it to the banks of the Euphrates. There he
was to hide it among the rocks.[82] After this was accomplished
and many days had passed, Jeremiah was told to return to

---

76. Jeremiah 13:18
77. 2 Chron. 36:5
78. Jeremiah 7:2
79. Jeremiah 11:19

80. Jeremiah 11:21
81. Jeremiah 12:6
82. Jeremiah 13:4

the Euphrates and retrieve the girdle. Naturally, it had seriously deteriorated. The Lord said, "After this manner will I mar the pride of Judah, and the great pride of Jerusalem."[83]

Thus the Lord continued to assure Jeremiah that in spite of the persecution he was suffering, and the abominations of the people (who were prospering!) the justice of God would one day prevail.

JEREMIAH NEARLY LOSES HIS LIFE

Nowhere is the desperate character of Jeremiah's ministry better demonstrated than in chapter 26. Shortly after Jehoiakim had become king[84] and lifted the ban on idolatry, and right while feelings were running so bitterly against Jeremiah, the word of the Lord came to him saying, "Stand in the court of the Lord's house, and speak unto all the cities [citizens] of Judah . . . all the words that I command thee to speak unto them; DIMINISH NOT A WORD."[85] He was told to tell the people they would choose either hope or horror. If they would repent, Jerusalem and the people still would be saved. If they did not, the Lord said it would become like the city of Shiloh, 25 miles north, which was once Israel's great center of worship until it had been totally desolated during the Philistine wars.

The reaction to the speech was sudden and violent. The apostate priests, hireling "prophets" and dissolute people formed a mob and began screaming, "Thou shalt surely die!"[86] It caused such a commotion that the princes and governors of the people came rushing up from the nearby palace to sit in judgment on whomever had caused this riot. Jeremiah was dragged before them and a spokesman for the mob said, "This man is worthy to die; for he hath prophesied against this city. . . ."[87] The charge was treason. Jeremiah was giving "aid and comfort to the enemy" by destroying the confidence of the people in their great city.

The delicacy of Jeremiah's position may be better appreciated if we recall that Jehoiakim was put on his throne by appointment of Pharaoh Necho II of Egypt, and

---

83. Jeremiah 13:9
84. Jeremiah 26:1
85. Jeremiah 26:2

86. Jeremiah 26:8
87. Jeremiah 26:11

Necho was at that moment up in Syria preening his forces for the great battle at Carchemish, which would take place just a short time hence in 605 B.C. However, Jeremiah had already predicted the downfall of the Egyptians![88] Now he was predicting the overthrow of Jerusalem. Such talk was easily twisted around to sound like a deliberate attempt to demoralize the people from resisting Babylon, Necho's enemy.

After this volatile charge against him, Jeremiah was allowed to speak, and he used the opportunity to deliver the Lord's message a second time. Said he, "The Lord sent me to prophesy against this house and against this city all the words that ye have heard. Therefore now amend your ways and your doings, and obey the voice of the Lord your God; and the Lord will repent him [turn back from] the evil that he hath pronounced against you. AS FOR ME, BE-HOLD, I AM IN YOUR HAND: DO WITH ME AS SEEMETH GOOD AND MEET UNTO YOU."[89]

This last sentence was no display of grand-stand bravado. Jeremiah was literally offering his life for the work of the Lord. The scripture says Jeremiah's fellow prophet, Urijah, had been recently caught in a situation very similar to this and had fled to Egypt to save his life! However, King Jehoiakim had used his influence with Pharaoh Necho to have Urijah captured and extradited back to Judah. The Bible account demonstrates the murderous mood of the people against God's prophets during this dark period by saying, "And they fetched forth Urijah out of Egypt, and brought him unto Jehoiakim the king; who slew him with the sword, and cast his dead body into the graves of the common people."[90]

This is precisely what could have happened to Jeremiah, and he knew it. Fortunately, however, one of the great men of Jerusalem, a man named Ahikam who had been a top advisor to King Josiah,[91] cried out in Jeremiah's defense and saved the prophet's life. Ahikam pointed out that when the prophet Micah came with a message identical with Jeremiah's, the good king Hezekiah did not kill Micah but had the people repent and the city was saved. Therefore, he said if they

---

88. Jeremiah, chapter 46
89. Jeremiah 26:12-14

90. Jeremiah 26:23
91. 2 Kings 22:12, 14

killed Jeremiah they would be committing a great offense against Jerusalem and their own souls.

This speech was sufficiently persuasive so that Jeremiah was released and Ahikam and the prophet became fast friends. In fact, they may have been good friends even before this time. Some twenty years later, when Jerusalem fell, we find the son of Ahikam taking Jeremiah into his protection and care.[92]

THE LONELY LIFE OF A PROPHET

As the years swept by, we catch a hint here and there of the drudgery and dreariness of Jeremiah's lot during these days of poverty, persecution and loneliness. It was during a particularly severe period of famine that Jeremiah thought he might use his good offices to intercede for the wretched, wicked, but suffering people. However, the Lord did not want simpering or slushy sentimentality at a time when the circumstances called for parental firmness, needed discipline and warranted retribution. He wanted Jeremiah to attempt to catch the larger view which God must maintain; namely, that God must determine what is good for mankind in the long run, what is good for the millions yet unborn, for the civilizations yet to be. These lessons are taught in chapters 14 and 15 of Jeremiah. The Lord said:

"Though Moses and Samuel stood before me, yet my mind could not be [moved] toward this people: cast them out of my sight and let them go forth."[93] The Gods in the eternal heavens are intelligent beings. They can become so weary of perpetual murder, perversion, lying, stealing, robbery, and the sacrifice of children to idols, that their faces can become as flint. The Father is a God of love. Jesus is a God of love. So is the Holy Ghost. But all three are Gods of justice, equity and common sense. So the Lord declared that this reprobate, debauched generation of corrupted human beings was headed down four paths: "Such as are for death, to death; and such as are for the sword, to the sword; and such as are for the famine, to the famine; and such as are for captivity to the captivity."[94]

---

92. Jeremiah 39:14
93. Jeremiah 15:1

94. Jeremiah 15:2

By this time Jeremiah was getting up around thirty to thirty-five years of age. However, his mission had been so tempestuous, dangerous and difficult that he had not followed the normal pattern of getting married and raising a family. Apparently he had begun thinking of taking this important step but the Lord told him in effect that there is a time to marry and a time not to marry. And this was NOT the time to marry. Therefore the Lord said, "Thou shalt not take thee a wife, neither shalt thou have sons or daughters in this place."[95]

The Lord explained why. Said He, ". . . concerning the sons and concerning the daughters that are born in this place . . . they shall die of grievous deaths . . . neither shall they be buried; but they shall be as dung upon the face of the earth: and they shall be consumed by the sword, and by famine; and their carcases shall be meat for the fowls of heaven, and for the beasts of the earth."[96] In other words, the judgment has gone forth, this place is now accursed, let your marriage be later when this great woe has passed over.

Day after day, month after month, Jeremiah plodded on with the burden of his message. He stood in the main gate and promised them an escape from their woes if they would start obeying the Sabbath day;[97] he went to the pottery factory where marred vessels were rebuilt and used it as a symbol of how the Lord would perfect Judah if she would repent;[98] he took an earthen vessel from the pottery factory and went down to the Valley of Hinnom where children were burned alive as a sacrifice to Moloch, and said if this abominable practice were not stopped these diabolical parents would one day eat the flesh of their own dead children (during the terrible siege that would be put upon them);[99] then he smashed the piece of pottery to dramatize what would happen to Judah and Jerusalem.

JEREMIAH IS ABUSED BY PASHUR, SON OF A PRIEST

It will be recalled that Jeremiah was a Levite and one of those Levites who happened to be a direct descendant of Aaron. Therefore he was entitled to the dignity and respect

---

95. Jeremiah 16:2
96. Jeremiah 16:3-4
97. Jeremiah 17:19-27

98. Jeremiah 18:1-8
99. Jeremiah 19:9

of a Priest. But the Priests in control of affairs in those days were generally apostate and they hated Jeremiah. Though they scarcely would have acknowledged it, they would have been amazed to learn that this relative of theirs had more Priesthood than all the rest of them put together. By receiving his calling directly from the Lord, Jeremiah held the highest authority or the Melchizedek Priesthood. Joseph Smith says this was true with each of the prophets thus raised up.[100]

The Priest who was governor of the temple at this time, had a son named Pashur. When Pashur heard Jeremiah prophesy such great evil against Jerusalem, he decided to make an example of him. Of course, by this time King Jehoiakim was openly encouraging the widespread practice of idolatry so Pashur knew that many of the things Jeremiah was denouncing constituted the most popular fads of the day. Pashur was therefore certain that he would have the backing of the king and all the leaders of Jerusalem in taking direct action against this thorny mouthpiece of doom. He would teach Jeremiah not to collect crowds in the temple with his prophecies; he would make him the laughing stock of the city so he could no longer stir up strife by denouncing the accepted culture of the day! The scripture says:

"Then Pashur smote Jeremiah the prophet, and put him in the stocks that were in the high gate of Benjamin, which was by the house of the Lord."[101] Pashur left him there, bruised, beaten and apparently without food or water until the next day. Then he released him. Jeremiah was no doubt weak, stiff and hungry, but he had something to say to this apostate priest appropriate to the occasion. He looked upon Pashur and said, "The Lord hath not called thy name Pashur, but Magor-missabib [fear on every side]."[102] Then Jeremiah poured down on Pashur and all those who stood around, the Lord's decree. No longer did he talk obscurely about the evil from out of the north, nor use a parable to make his point. He declared, "Thus saith the Lord . . . I will give all Judah into the hand of the king of Babylon [nothing obscure about

---

100. As previously pointed out, Joseph Smith declared that "all the prophets [Israel] had the Melchizedek Priesthood and were ordained by God him (*Teachings of Joseph Smith*, pp. 180-181)
101. Jeremiah 20:2   102. Jeremiah 20:3

that!]. . . . And thou, Pashur, and all that dwell in thine house shall go into captivity: and thou shalt come to Babylon, and there thou shalt die, and shalt be buried there, thou, and all thy friends, to whom thou hast prophesied lies."[103]

From this last statement it would appear that Pashur was not only the son of a Priest, but one of the self-appointed false prophets who so vehemently hated Jeremiah.

Jeremiah recorded some of his own thoughts which boiled within him while these events were transpiring. He was frank to admit that the ability of his enemy to overpower him and abuse him as Pashur had done was something for which he was not at all prepared. He complained to the Lord,[104] and even lamented the day he was born.[105] At one point he resolved to stop preaching for awhile, but the spirit of prophetic zeal within him would not allow it. He says, "But his word was in mine heart as a burning fire shut up in my bones, and I was weary with forbearing, and I could not stay."[106]

So Jeremiah continued his mission with plodding, grinding, painful determination.

THE RECORDED REVELATIONS OF JEREMIAH ARE BURNED BY KING JEHOIAKIM

The plots against the life of Jeremiah thereafter became so intensive that from around 605 B.C. to the end of Jehoiakim's reign in 598 B.C. we find Jeremiah in almost continuous hiding. This enforced seclusion was not only miserable and personally inconvenient to the prophet, but far more important, it silenced him. With his prophetic calling virtually burning in his bones, Jeremiah found this situation intolerable. It was equally objectionable to the Lord and so the dramatic events recorded in chapter 36 now took place. The scripture says:

". . . in the fourth year of Jehoiakim [605 B.C.] . . . this word came unto Jeremiah from the Lord, saying, Take thee a roll of a book, and write therein all the words that I have spoken . . . from the days of Josiah, even unto this day. It may be that the house of Judah will hear all the evil which

103. Jeremiah 20:4-6   105. Jeremiah 20:14-18
104. Jeremiah 20:7   106. Jeremiah 20:9

I purpose to do unto them; that they may return every man from his evil way; THAT I MAY FORGIVE THEIR INIQUITY AND THEIR SIN."[107]

So Jeremiah called in his scribe, a man named Baruch, and told him to write down the revelations which the Lord had given His prophet during the past twenty years. To the undoubted amazement of Baruch, Jeremiah *dictated* these revelations to his scribe as the spirit of God rested upon him. There were no papers, notes or previous transcriptions. It was a phenomenal gift. The scripture says, "and Baruch wrote from the mouth of Jeremiah all the words of the Lord. . . ."[108]

Jeremiah then said, "I am shut up; I cannot go into the house of the Lord; Therefore go thou, and read in the roll . . . in the ears of all Judah. . . ."[109] Baruch obeyed this instruction and many of the more honest elders and scribes of the people were much impressed. Out of sheer curiosity they asked Baruch, "Tell us now, How didst thou write all these words at his mouth? Then Baruch answered them, HE PRONOUNCED ALL THESE WORDS UNTO ME WITH HIS MOUTH, AND I WROTE THEM WITH INK IN THE BOOK."[110] They promptly took the sacred scroll to the king, but with catastrophic results. When the wicked Jehoiakim heard these powerful words of warning, he had the entire scroll burned![111] Some of the elders tried to intervene and pleaded with him, but to no avail.[112]

The king not only burned the precious scroll of scripture but sent out an order that Jeremiah and Baruch should

---

107. Jeremiah 36:1-3
108. Jeremiah 36:4
109. Jeremiah 36:5-6
110. Jeremiah 36:17-18. It is interesting in view of this scripture to observe an identical *modus operandi* followed by the prophet Joseph Smith in our own times. Parley P. Pratt, an early associate of Joseph Smith, describes how revelations were dictated under the power of the Holy Spirit:

"Each sentence was uttered slowly and very distinctly, and with a pause between each, sufficiently long for it to be recorded by the ordinary writer, in long hand. This was the manner in which all his written revelations were dictated and written. There was never any hesitation, reviewing, or reading back, in order to keep the run of the subject; neither did any of these communications undergo revisions, interlinings, or corrections. As he dictated them so they stood, so far as I witnessed and I was present to witness the dictation of several communications of several pages each." (*Life of Parley P. Pratt*, pp. 65-66)

111. Jeremiah 36:23   112. Jeremiah 36:25

both be captured. They both immediately hid themselves and somehow escaped arrest. But these were miserable days. Nevertheless, to their dismal hideaway came the word of the Lord, saying, "Take thee again another roll, and write in it all the former words that were in the first roll, which Jehoiakim the king of Judah hath burned."[113] This was glorious news. So the scriptural treasure would not be lost after all. Jeremiah took another scroll and as the Spirit of revelation descended upon him he began to dictate once more. And Baruch, the scribe, "wrote therein from the mouth of Jeremiah all the words of the book which Jehoiakim king of Judah had burned in the fire: and there were added besides unto them many like words."[114]

It is from this scroll that we have the book of Jeremiah today. Chapter 45 indicates that Baruch, the scribe, perhaps had some doubts as to whether this business of being clerk to a prophet was quite as glamorous as his professional talents called for. It was bad enough to work for a fugitive master, but when Baruch had to find a hole to hide in, it was too much. Said he: "Woe is me now! for the Lord hath added grief to my sorrow: I fainted in my sighing, and I find no rest."[115]

In a revelation through Jeremiah the Lord indirectly reprimanded Baruch by saying, "And seeketh thou great things for thyself?"[116] The Lord said all material things and possessions in Jerusalem would be smashed and destroyed. These Baruch would not have. Nevertheless, Baruch's life would be saved and that would be more precious than all his possessions no matter where he went.[117]

THE FIRST BABYLONIAN CAPTIVITY — 598 B.C.

Beginning about 601 B.C., after Nebuchadnezzar had failed in his attempt to conquer Egypt, King Jehoiakim began refusing to pay his tribute to Babylon and commenced mov-

---

113. Jeremiah 36:27-28
114. Jeremiah 36:32
115. Jeremiah 45:3
116. Jeremiah 45:5
117. Jeremiah 45:5 — This is the meaning of the passage as rendered by Dr. Clarke. (See *Bible Commentary*, vol. 4, p. 370)

ing back toward his original patron, Pharaoh Necho. Babylon immediately bristled but was too busy getting ready for another Egyptian campaign to punish Jehoiakim, so it was two or three years before the Babylonians got around to settling scores with Judah.

Eventually, however, Nebuchadnezzar did send over a contingent of Babylonian troops and ordered his nearby tributaries to join them in attacking Judah. Thus, the Bible says, there came up "bands of the Chaldees [Babylonians], and bands of the Syrians, and bands of the Moabites, and bands of the children of Ammon, and sent them against Judah to destroy it, according to the word of the Lord. . . ."[118]

The details are sketchy, but the record is clear that Jehoiakim firmly rejected Jeremiah's advice to cooperate with Nebuchadnezzar. Rather than pay further tribute or ally himself with the Babylonians, Jehoiakim was determined to expose Jerusalem to the terrors of a siege and the wholesale destruction which was likely to follow. This might have seemed somewhat heroic on the part of the king and his counselors had it not been for the fact that Jehoiakim had been repeatedly informed that it was God's desire that he remain, for the time being at least, under the Babylonian confederation. His position was therefore one of stubborn rebellion against God rather than a heroic resistance to oppression. What Jehoiakim was electing to do would not only bring oppression but desolation as well. This is what the Lord was trying to tell him.

In fact, as the defense of Jerusalem began to stiffen, the king of Babylon ordered that the attack on the city be severely intenstified. All food and other supplies needed in Jerusalem were completely choked off and it was only a question of time until the fall of the city became inevitable. In the final stages an incident occurred which accelerated the surrender of the city. We have no details so it is impossible to tell how it happened but somehow king Jehoiakim either tried to escape or otherwise exposed himself at a point where his defenses were weak, and the Babylonians captured him.

---

118. 2 Kings 24:2

The scripture says, ". . . Nebuchadnezzar king of Babylon . . . bound him in fetters to carry him to Babylon."[119]

But the trip never took place because Jehoiakim, who was only 36 years of age at this time,[120] unexpectedly died or was killed. As one authority puts it, "Either in a skirmish or by assassination by some of his own oppressed subjects Jehoiakim came to a violent end in the eleventh year of his reign. His body was cast out ignominiously on the ground, and then was dragged away and buried 'with the burial of an ass,' without pomp or lamentation, 'beyond the gates of Jerusalem.' "[121]

Thus, this wicked son of the good king Josiah, a man who had killed Urijah the prophet, who had burned the scroll of Jeremiah and who had brought back the curse of heathen idolatry to Judah, came to his predicted fate. Time and again the Lord had warned him, even pleaded with him, but he would not listen.

The dead king's eight-year-old son[122] began to reign in his stead under the guidance of a regency, but his 3-month reign did not last long enough to even allow him to actually rule over Judah. This boy-king is known to us generally as JehoiaCHIN (do not confuse with his father, JehoiaKIM), but he is also referred to by other names in scripture such as Jeconiah, Joachin and Coniah.

After the death of King Jehoiakim in 598 B.C., the city of Jerusalem only survived the siege three more months and then the leaders of the people decided to cease resisting in order to save the city from ravaging and the people from starving. Therefore, "Jehoiachin the king of Judah went out to the king of Babylon, he, and his mother, and his servants, and his princes, and his officers. . . ."[123] The young king was carted off to Babylon and held in some type of imprisonment for 37 years before a later king of Babylon finally

---

119. 2 Chron. 36:6
120. 2 Chron. 36:5
121. Peloubet's *Bible Dictionary* under "Jehoiakim". All of this was just as Jeremiah had predicted it. See Jeremiah 22:18-19; 36:30.
122. 2 Chron. 36:9. In 2 Kings 24:8 it says he was 18 years old but this is obviously an error since his father was only 36 when he died. (2 Chron. 36:5)
123. 2 Kings 24:12

brought him out and allowed him the relative freedom of other Jews.[124]

As a result of the surrender of Jerusalem in 598 B.C. there was no general destruction of the city by the Babylonians at this time. That did not occur until 11 years later following another rebellion by Jerusalem. This first conquest in 598 was simply to keep Judah on the Babylonian team. The idea was to impose some kind of punishment but not extermination. The punishment consisted of limited looting and the taking of hostages. Nebuchadnezzar took only the smaller gold and silver vessels from the temple, then he rounded up and carried away "all the princes, and all the mighty men of valour, even ten thousand captives, and all the craftsmen and smiths. . . ."[125] Ezekiel is believed to have been in this group, but not Daniel. Daniel had been taken 8 years earlier.[126]

Since Nebuchadnezzar was taking the 8-year-old boy-king with him, he left as ruling governor of the land a man who is known to us as Zedekiah. This man's Jewish name was Mattaniah,[127] but the king of Babylon changed it.[128] Zedekiah, we discover, was the younger son of the good king Josiah, and therefore the third son of Josiah to sit on the throne. He was the brother of Jehoahaz and Jehoiakim and therefore the uncle of the deposed boy-king, Jehoiachin. Actually, many of the Jews still continued to count the boy-king as the legitimate ruler of Judah and in many cases continued measuring their chronicle of events in terms of his reign rather than Zedekiah's. Zedekiah, they felt, was the puppet of Nebuchadnezzar and the enemy of the people. He collected Babylonian tribute and ruled by the grace of the Babylonian king. How Zedekiah hated this role! He did not mind being a puppet so much, but he wanted Egypt to be his master, not Babylon. He was about to launch Judah into the mainstream of political strategy which not only violated the commandments of the Lord but repeated all the monumental blunders of his older brother, King Jehoiakim. These led to the second conquest of Judah which is the subject of our next chapter.

---

124. Jeremiah 52:31-34
125. 2 Kings 24:14
126. Daniel 1:1, 6

127. 2 Kings 24:17
128. *Ibid.*

Scripture Reading and Questions on Chapter Twenty-Four

Scripture Reading: Jeremiah, chapters 1 to 26 inclusive.

1—To what tribe did Jeremiah belong? By right of birth was he entitled to the Levitical Priesthood or the Aaronic Priesthood?

2—What was Jeremiah's home town? About how old does he appear to have been at the time of his calling?

3—Name three other prophets who were called at about the same age as Jeremiah and describe the first revelation given to each.

4—What does it mean to be "chosen" before a person is born?

5—Why do we think that Jeremiah went through an intensive period of preparation prior to his public ministry? Is there any scriptural evidence?

6—Name five offenses the Lord accused Judah of committing. Which would you consider the worst? Why?

7—What did the Lord say would happen to Judah if she did not repent?

8—What message of hope did the Lord give if the people repented? What message of hope did He give even if they did not repent and were conquered?

9—Why do you think Jeremiah believed the Lord was a little too harsh on the people? How did he excuse them? What did he discover when he went out to preach to them?

10—Is there any indication that King Josiah's reform was never genuinely accepted by the people? What is the evidence?

11—What was the reaction of the people from his own hometown when he began preaching? What was the reaction of his own family?

12—Explain why Jeremiah's advice to collaborate with Babylonia would be considered treason. What does "treason" mean? Were the leaders of Judah committing treason against the Lord?

13—Why did the Lord counsel Jeremiah not to marry at this time?

14—What were Jeremiah's circumstances when he was commanded to write down all the revelations he had received?

15—How did he record his revelations? How does this compare with the manner in which Joseph Smith did it?

16—What was the king's reaction to the revelations which Jeremiah had recorded? What did he do about it? How did the Lord remedy the situation?

17—What was Baruch's reaction to the persecution he now received? What did the Lord tell him?

18—What brought on the "First Captivity" of Judah? Could this have been avoided? Was the king of Judah heroic or rebellious?

19—What happened to King Jehoiakim? How long afterwards was the city surrendered?

20—Was Jerusalem desolated at this time? What kind of punishment was imposed on Judah? About how many hostages or captives were carried away?

CHAPTER TWENTY-FIVE

Jeremiah Sees the Fall of Jerusalem 587 B. C.

The great burden of a prophet of God is three-fold. *First,* he is given the foreknowledge of disaster which awaits the people if they do not repent; *second,* he is shown the magnificent blessings of happiness and prosperity which will come if they do repent; and *third,* he has to often watch in helpless amazement as the people elect to follow the forbidden path of wicked and defiant rebellion which ends in violent catastrophe. Such was the trend of events when Zedekiah became king of Judah. Jeremiah had to watch him as he deliberately chose to follow the pathway of rebellion even though he was warned repeatedly that it would lead to the ultimate downfall of Judah.

JEREMIAH RECEIVES A REVELATION FOR THE CAPTIVES

Meanwhile, however, Jeremiah had his extremely important revelation known as the vision of the two baskets of figs. One basket was filled with fruit that was sweet to the taste. The other was bitter as gall. Jeremiah learned to his great satisfaction that these 10,000 or more who had just gone into captivity were going to have a very profitable experience. They would be treated kindly in Babylon.[1] Some

---

1. Jeremiah 24:5

would become top officials in government. Others would become wealthy merchants. They would become humble and obedient to the laws of God,[2] and in due time this group or their descendants would be allowed to return to Jerusalem.[3]

The bitter figs, on the other hand, represented Zedekiah and all the people who would rebel and bring upon themselves the coming conquest of Judah. They would be scattered, persecuted, enslaved and never allowed, as a group, to return.[4]

As soon as Jeremiah had this extremely important information, he sat down and wrote to the exiles who had just gone over to Babylon. He told them:

1—Build houses and cultivate fields.[5]

2—Encourage large families so as to multiply the population of God's people.[6]

3—Do not create a rebellion or insurrection but "seek the peace of the city."[7]

4—Completely ignore the false prophets and diviners who will try to deceive the captives into thinking they will be returning immediately.[8]

5—It will be 70 years before the Lord will bless the Jews in redeeming Jerusalem.[9]

6—Contrary to what the false prophets are preaching, Zedekiah is going to be dethroned, and Jerusalem is going to be destroyed.[10]

Two of the false prophets in Babylon who were trying to deceive the people were named Ahab and Zedekiah. Jeremiah quoted the Lord as saying they were both committing adultery with their neighbor's wives and were preaching lies for prophecies.[11] He said the Lord had revealed that they were both going to be killed by Nebuchadnezzar and "roasted in the fire."[12]

Jeremiah's letters brought immediate retaliation from these self-appointed holy men in Babylon. One of them, named Shemaiah, claimed to be under the prophetic power which permitted him to speak in the name of God. He wrote

---

2. Jeremiah 24:7
3. Jeremiah 24:6
4. Jeremiah 24:8-10
5. Jeremiah 29:5
6. Jeremiah 29:6
7. Jeremiah 29:7
8. Jeremiah 29:8-9
9. Jeremiah 29:10-14
10. Jeremiah 29:15-19
11. Jeremiah 29:23
12. Jeremiah 29:22

a letter to Zephaniah, the number-two Priest at the temple in Jerusalem, saying it was God's will that Zephaniah should now be the chief priest with the special assignment of punishing Jeremiah for telling the captives of Babylon they would be there for a number of years. However, Zephaniah immediately called in Jeremiah and let him read the letter from Babylon, whereupon the Lord told Jeremiah to tell Zephaniah that the message from Shemaiah was without authority and a lie.[13]

THE FALSE PROPHETS AND POLITICAL LEADERS COMBINE AGAINST JEREMIAH

However, these false prophets were a nasty lot with which to tangle. They were in league with the Egyptian party at Jerusalem, the counselors to the king, and many of the most influential and avaricious leaders among the people. Their impact on the 21-year-old King Zedekiah was also prodigious. Because he was a weak character they succeeded in both persuading and frightening him. His natural inclination was to agree with their major objectives anyway, but, as we shall see, even when he might have taken a different course he was completely intimidated by these powerful Gadianton forces around him.

Only a year or so after the first captivity the official policy of Jerusalem began to swing away from Babylon as the king and his counselors openly espoused an alliance with the Egyptians. All of this was in violation of a sacred oath King Zedekiah had taken in which he had promised to remain loyal to Babylon.[14] Zedekiah, however, was not at all adverse to taking the name of the Lord in vain if it suited his purposes. This, he was now prepared to do.

In order for Jeremiah to try to prevent the king from making a tragic blunder, the Lord's prophet ran the risk of being accused of meddling in politics. Like all of the prophets, however, a principal part of his calling had been to denounce or expose prospective political bungling by the leaders of the people, so the accusation of "meddling" in politics would be nothing new. And there was no doubt about it, Jeremiah

---

13. Jeremiah 29:31-32
14. 2 Chron. 36:13

was about to meddle in Zedekiah's politics on a monumental scale.

The word of the Lord came to Jeremiah, telling him to go boldly forth among the people with bands on his arms and feet, and a yoke about his neck and send bonds and yokes to nearby nations to dramatically symbolize the fact that for the time being it was in their own best interest to remain subject to Babylon.[15]

Jeremiah did exactly as he was told, but his pro-Babylon policy brought him into immediate polemic conflict with the apostate priests, the hireling prophets, and the pro-Egyptian politicians at court. Right while King Zedekiah was negotiating with the Egyptians, Jeremiah was parading through the streets wearing his yoke and bonds while crying out, "Be ye subject to Nebuchadnezzar and live!"[16]

He proclaimed that the departure of Nebuchadnezzar after the subjugation of Judah in 598 B.C. was only a temporary respite, that he would be back, that all the big vessels at the temple, the brazen sea, the brass oblation bases and everything else of value would be carried away unless Judah remained tractable.[17] Furthermore, the city would be laid waste, the people would flee in all directions and would be butchered while the few survivors would be hauled off into slavery. In other words, the Egyptian alliance was a trap — therefore, "Be ye subject to Nebuchadnezzar and live!"

With this hue and cry going up and down the streets of Jerusalem there was no doubt but what Jeremiah was making a genuine mess of King Zedekiah's politics.

One could have safely predicted that some fatuous priest or hireling prophet would take upon himself the task of putting Jeremiah in his place. It turned out to be Hananiah who was a second-generation pseudo-holy man, his father being a prophet-pretender named Azur from Gibeon.[18] Whether Hananiah was relying upon the message of some "familiar spirit," astrological reading, or just his own wishful thinking, we do not know. But whatever it was, he presumed to

---

15. Jeremiah 27:2-9
16. An abbreviated version of Jeremiah 27:12

17. Jeremiah 27:18-22
18. Jeremiah 28:1

do a most radical and dangerous thing. He gained a vast audience of people and cried out:

"Thus speaketh the Lord of hosts, the God of Israel, saying, I have broken the yoke of the king of Babylon. WITHIN TWO FULL YEARS WILL I BRING AGAIN INTO THIS PLACE ALL THE VESSELS OF THE LORD'S HOUSE, that Nebuchadnezzar king of Babylon took away from this place, and carried them to Babylon: And I will bring again to this place Jeconiah [the boy-king, Jehoiachin] . . . with all the captives of Judah, that went into Babylon, saith the Lord: for I will break the yoke of the king of Babylon."[19]

It was great news — and exactly what the people were waiting to hear. At last the people had an authoritative word of encouragement from the Lord. But it completely repudiated what Jeremiah had been saying. No doubt there was a great sense of eager anticipation as they watched Jeremiah step forward to speak. With the symbolic bonds hanging on his limbs and a yoke about his neck, the prophet of God stood before them and said:

"AMEN: [let] the Lord do so: the Lord perform thy words which thou hast prophesied. . . . Nevertheless hear thou now this word that I speak in thine ears, and in the ears of all the people; The prophets that have been before me and before thee of old prophesied both against many countries, and against great kingdoms, of war, and of evil, and of pestilence. . . . WHEN THE WORD OF THE PROPHET SHALL COME TO PASS, THEN SHALL THE PROPHET BE KNOWN, THAT THE LORD HATH TRULY SENT HIM."[20]

Jeremiah was simply saying that time would tell whether he or Hananiah were right. Hananiah had said these great things would come to pass in two years. Very well, let them wait. They would see. Moses had said this was the way to test a true prophet[21] and Jeremiah was perfectly willing to have the people apply that test to decide the issue. But Hananiah impetuously stepped forward to have a final word.

---

19. Jeremiah 28:2-4
20. Jeremiah 28:6-9
21. Deut. 18:22

Roughly he dragged the wooden yoke off Jeremiah's neck and smashed it. Then he shouted, "Thus saith the Lord, Even so will I break the yoke of Nebuchadnezzar king of Babylon from the neck of all nations within the space of two full years."[22]

So be it. The scripture says Jeremiah did not remain to quarrel about it. He simply "went his way."[23] Time would tell.

However, the Lord knew that much damage might be done if the people relied upon Hananiah for two full years and then used his prophecy to excuse themselves for rejecting Jeremiah. Therefore the Lord decided to give a much earlier sign as to who was His true prophet. He told Jeremiah that henceforth a yoke of iron should be used as a symbol in his message to the Jews and the nearby nations.[24] Then He gave Jeremiah a prophecy for Hananiah. It was a death sentence.

At the appropriate time, and no doubt in some public gathering, Jeremiah approached the professional holy man and declared aloud, "Hear now, Hananiah; The Lord hath not sent thee; but thou makest this people to trust a lie. Therefore, THUS SAITH THE LORD: BEHOLD, I WILL CAST THEE FROM OFF THE FACE OF THE EARTH: THIS YEAR THOU SHALT DIE, BECAUSE THOU HAST TAUGHT REBELLION AGAINST THE LORD."[25]

The people did not have long to wait. Within two months he was dead.[26] If ever the king and the masses of the people had the slightest inclination to repent, this should have brought it to the surface. But, amazingly, it did not. Matters continued very much as they had before.

THE PROPHET LEHI, CONTEMPORARY OF JEREMIAH

It was right at this precise time in the historical setting described by the Bible that the Book of Mormon branches

---

22. Jeremiah 28:11
23. Ibid.
24. Jeremiah 28:13-14
25. Jeremiah 28:15-16
26. Jeremiah 28:17. Note that Hananiah died in the seventh month after having made his prophecy in the fifth month (Jeremiah 28:1).

off. The ominous cloud of calamity about to descend on Jerusalem made it a good time for the Lord to lead away a group of choice servants and shepherd them to the Western Hemisphere where the Lord had been planning to start a whole new civilization. The Lord had told Joseph (who was sold into Egypt) all about it centuries before.

Jeremiah does not mention by name his fellow-prophets who labored with him. Nevertheless, he refers to them collectively. He reminded the people of Judah that "the Lord hath sent unto you all his servants the prophets" to confirm the message which he had been preaching, "but ye have not hearkened. . . ."[27] One of these prophets had been Urijah who was slain.[28]

And now the Lord was about to raise up another valiant servant whom the people would also try to kill. His name was Lehi. The Book of Mormon commences with the history of this prophet. He was given his divine commission the first year that Zedekiah became king of Judah.[29]

Lehi was not a Jew, but a descendant of Joseph through Manasseh.[30] His life's work had not been that of a religious leader, even though by natural inclination he was a very religious man. Lehi's professional career had been that of a merchant and trader.[31] Through this means he had become very wealthy.[32] We learn from the Book of Mormon that Lehi was married, that he had a wife named Sariah and four sons named Laman, Lemuel, Sam and Nephi.[33] Lehi and his family were living in Jerusalem throughout the period we have just discussed.[34] They were apparently there when

---

27. Jeremiah 25:4-5
28. Jeremiah 26:20-23
29. I Nephi 1:4-6. It is interesting that the Book of Mormon fixes the first year of King Zedekiah's reign at precisely 600 B.C. This was the year that Lehi left Jerusalem and he was told by revelation that the Messiah would be born 600 years from that time (I Nephi 10:4; 19:8). This means that the chronology we are presently using for the Bible is just two years off, but Bible chronology being what it is, the wonder is that it is so close! The only reason for using 598 B.C. for Zedekiah in this present study is so that the student may keep the dating in correlation with other standard reference works. He should keep in mind, however, that revelation fixes the true date as 600 B.C.
30. Alma 10:3
31. See Dr. Hugh Nibley, *An Approach to the Book of Mormon*, chapter 4.
32. I Nephi 2:4
33. I Nephi 2:5
34. I Nephi 1:4

Nebuchadnezzar swept down on Jerusalem, raided the temple and carried off more than 10,000 hostages. Like the rest of the inhabitants Lehi and his family undoubtedly wondered if the young King Zedekiah could keep the peace with the Babylonians or whether he would follow policies which would bring Nebuchadnezzar back for revenge later on. The answer to that question suddenly came direct from Heaven through a sudden upsurge of many prophetic voices.

The Book of Mormon says Lehi was very impressed by the great number of prophets who came forth that very year, each one testifying, as did Jeremiah, that Jerusalem was about to be destroyed.[35] Lehi became extremely agitated over these prophetic declarations and therefore prayed to the Lord on behalf of this doomed people. As a result, he received a marvelous revelation. In this open vista of revealed knowledge it was verified to him that Jerusalem would indeed be destroyed. He also saw the Savior and His Twelve Disciples.[36]

Being a man of affairs and accustomed to dealing with all classes of people, Lehi immediately went throughout Jerusalem telling his friends and anyone else who would listen that he had a personal, scientific, tangible witness of what was about to happen to Jerusalem. He warned them that unless there was repentance on a broad and penetrating scale there was certainly going to be a terrible destruction of both the city and the people.[37] For his trouble, Lehi almost lost his life.[38] In fact, he was forced to flee into hiding in order to save himself. For a practical, hard-headed businessman, it must have seemed incomprehensible that all of his former friends and associates could be so blind.

Lehi was next commanded to leave Jerusalem with his family and move down by the Red Sea in the wilderness, preparatory to being led to a distant, choice land.[39] This he did, moving, as we suppose, somewhere along the east side of the Gulf of Akabah where he made his first permanent camp. Then the Lord told him to send his sons back for the sacred record which the house of Joseph had preserved

---

35. Ibid.
36. I Nephi 1:8-13
37. I Nephi 1:19

38. I Nephi 1:20
39. I Nephi 2:2, 5

throughout the centuries because it contained the Hebrew canon of scripture from Adam to the prophet Jeremiah.[40] At the moment this record, inscribed on brass plates, was in the custody of another wealthy citizen of Jerusalem, a man named Laban — who, like Lehi, was a direct descendant of Joseph.[41] However, this man Laban did not respond to the Lord's commandment to deliver the record to Lehi and so the plates were obtained only after much difficulty. In fact, during the negotiation Laban tried to murder Lehi's sons,[42] and in the final round, lost his own life.[43]

Once the plates were obtained, the Lord told Lehi to send back for a family living in Jerusalem belonging to a man named Ishmael.[44] He had two married sons and a number of unmarried daughters about the same age as Lehi's sons.[45] The Lord said that the intermarriage of these two families would form the foundation for a great new people in the "choice land" to which they would be led.[46] Ishmael turned out to be a descendant of Joseph through Ephraim,[47] and the "choice land" turned out to be the great western hemisphere which today we call the American continent.

How Lehi and his colony traveled for eight years before finally constructing the vessel by which they made the trans-oceanic voyage is a thrilling epic which belongs to a study of the Book of Mormon rather than here. Nevertheless, it was felt desirable to refer to this important incident of the prophet Lehi since it relates significantly to the life and times of Jeremiah. Now we return to Jeremiah, Zedekiah and the final phase of Jerusalem's downfall.

---

40. I Nephi 3:2-3, 5:10-13
41. I Nephi 5:14, 16
42. I Nephi 3:12-13, 25
43. I Nephi 4:10, 12, 18
44. I Nephi 7:1-4
45. I Nephi 7:6
46. I Nephi 7:1
47. "The Prophet Joseph informed us that the record of Lehi, was contained on the 116 pages that were first translated and subsequently stolen, and of which an abridgement is given us in the first Book of Nephi, which is the record of Nephi individually, he himself being of the lineage of Manasseh; but that Ishmael was of the lineage of Ephraim, and that his sons married into Lehi's family, and Lehi's sons married Ishmael's daughter. . . ." (From a discourse by Apostle Erastus Snow in the Journal of Discourses, Vol. 23, p. 184)

THE GREAT FINAL SIEGE OF JERUSALEM COMMENCES

From this far away in history, the mentality of King Zedekiah seems difficult to comprehend. It would have seemed elementary that in light of all the tangible evidence of Jeremiah's divine calling, Zedekiah would have gratefully taken his proffered advice. But Zedekiah did not. In spite of all Jeremiah had said, the young king deliberately supported an Egyptian plot to start a rash of rebellions among the vassal kingdoms in the Near East. Judah rebelled,[48] so did Tyre,[49] and Egypt backed them both.[50]

Egypt may have triggered or encouraged these rebellions as a result of a new, ambitious Pharaoh coming to the throne. It will be recalled that Necho II was Pharaoh the last time we mentioned Egypt, but in 594 he was succeeded by Psammetichus II (Psamtik for short) who reigned until 588 B.C. Now a new Pharaoh was on the throne named Hophra or Apries, and his military blustering is believed to have been the occasion for Ezekiel's prophecy against Egypt.[51]

In any event, regardless of what might have triggered it, Zedekiah's announced rebellion against Babylon was soon answered with military thunder and lightning brought to the Mediterranean by Nebuchadnezzar in person. He mass-marched his troops across the great land bridge from Mesopotamia and literally swarmed over the land. As Zedekiah heard of their coming he virtually suffered political apoplexy. He excitedly sent his chief advisors to Jeremiah to see if the Lord Jehovah might save the people. With the Lord it was an old story — the return of the unfaithful wife. The spokesman for the king's advisors pleaded with Jeremiah, saying, "Inquire, I pray thee, of the Lord for us; for Nebuchadnezzar king of Babylon maketh war against us; if [it] so be that the Lord will deal with us according to all his wondrous works . . . [Nebuchadnezzar] may go up from us."[52]

Jeremiah received the word of the Lord immediately but it descended on the heads of the king's messengers like an

48. 2 Kings 24:20
49. Kraeling, Rand McNally *Bible Atlas*, p. 315
50. Ibid.
51. Ezekiel, chapter 29
52. Jeremiah 21:2

avalanche of overwhelming disappointment. The Lord declared, ". . . I myself will fight against you with an outstretched hand and with a strong arm, even in anger, and in fury, and in great wrath. And I will smite the inhabitants of this city, both man and beast: they shall die of a great pestilence."[53] He then said to tell King Zedekiah that he was going to lose this war and become a captive of Nebuchadnezzar."[54]

The king's messengers must have found it difficult to believe that the Lord, who had forgiven His people so often and so freely in the past, would now turn His face against them like carved flint. Nevertheless, the Lord did offer the people a last minute means of escape if they dared use it. He said: "Behold, I set before you the way of life, and the way of death. He that abideth in this city shall die by the sword, and by the famine, and by the pestilence; but he that goeth out, and falleth to the Chaldeans that besiege you, he shall live, and his life shall be unto him for a prey [a precious prize]."[55]

Apparently, Zedekiah not only rejected this divinely endorsed procedure to save the city and its people, but he considered it treason for anyone to attempt to carry out this instruction of the Lord. One of the first to be trapped by this policy was Jeremiah.

Jeremiah is Arrested and Charged With Treason

The siege of Jerusalem is dated in the record as commencing in January, 588 B.C., and ending in the hot midsummer of 587 B.C.[56] In the midst of the siege the Egyptians sallied forth to give token support to the members of its alliance and most of the Babylonian battalions had to be hurriedly diverted from the siege to confront them. To Zedekiah this meant that maybe Judah's pro-Egyptian policy would pay off after all! He sent messengers to see if Jeremiah would now agree with him. The prophet received the following revelation for the messengers, "Thus shall ye say to

---

53. Jeremiah 21:5-6
54. Jeremiah 21:7. Later the Lord told Jeremiah to take this message to Zedekiah in person (Jeremiah 34:1-7).
55. Jeremiah 21:8-9
56. Kraeling, Rand McNally *Bible Atlas*, p. 315

the king of Judah that sent you unto me to inquire of me; Be
hold, Pharaoh's army, which is come forth to help you,
shall return to Egypt into their own land. And the Chaldeans
shall come again, and fight against this city, and take it, and
burn it with fire. Thus saith the Lord; Deceive not yourselves,
saying, The Chaldeans shall surely depart from us: for they
shall not depart."[57]

But the stubborn Zedekiah, influenced heavily by his
conniving pro-Egyptian counselors, determined to firm up
their resistance in spite of all they had been told. To Jeremiah
it was insane. He had done his best to save Zedekiah and
this people from Babylon but he could not save them from
themselves. Under the divine principle of free agency, neither
could the Lord. So Jeremiah prepared to abandon the city.

As the Babylonians moved out from Jerusalem to join
battle with the Egyptians, Jeremiah saw an opportunity to
leave the city and go up to Anathoth, his nearby home in
Benjamin.[58] But he never made it.

The captain of the gate-guard intercepted Jeremiah and
accused him of falling away to the Babylonians. Jeremiah
denied it but to no avail. He was charged with treason and
thrown into prison.[59] During his trial the judges "smote"
him.[60]

Apparently, an improvised prison for political offenders
had been set up in the courtyard of the private residence of
Jonathan, the scribe.[61] There cabin-cells had been constructed
in the courtyard and dungeons or pits were provided for the
more dangerous prisoners. Jeremiah was confined in both
types from time to time during his "many days" in that miserable place.[62]

Eventually, Jeremiah was allowed to see the king. Zedekiah still stubbornly wondered if the Lord might not bless
his nefarious political strategy and therefore he had Jeremiah secretly brought "in his house" where he confidentially
said to him, "IS THERE ANY WORD FROM THE
LORD?"[63] Jeremiah rallied what little strength he had and

---

57. Jeremiah 37:7-9
58. Jeremiah 37:11-12
59. Jeremiah 37:13-15
60. Jeremiah 37:15

61. Ibid.
62. Jeremiah 37:16
63. Jeremiah 37:17

replied, "There is . . . thou shalt be delivered into the hand of the king of Babylon"[64] — unless, of course, the king would follow the advice the Lord had given him. But this, Zedekiah still refused to do. Jeremiah nevertheless improved his condition a little during this visit by pleading with the king not to let them put him back into the dungeons at Jonathan's house "lest I die there."[65] The king ordered that he be kept above ground in one of the courtyard cabin-cells and that he be given one piece of bread per day as long as there were any rations left.[66]

Then certain counselors or "princes" of the king picked up the earlier story about Jeremiah claiming to have received a revelation saying the people should surrender themselves to the Babylonians and save their lives.[67] This was the revelation Jeremiah had received on the request of the king himself,[68] but the king never mentioned this fact to his counselors. He sat there silently as his princes made their demands for Jeremiah's life. "Let this man be put to death," they said, "for thus he weakeneth the hands of the men of war that remain in this city, and the hands of all the people, in speaking such words unto them: for this man seeketh not the welfare of this people, but the hurt."[69]

If ever there had been an ideal opportunity for Zedekiah to redeem himself by reflecting some spark of character and virile decency, this was it. But it wasn't in him. Like a cowering whelp from beneath the king's own table, he mumbled, "Behold, he is in your hand: for the king is not he that can do any thing against you."[70]

Triumphantly, the counselors dragged Jeremiah back to his place of incarceration at Jonathan's place. In the courtyard was an extremely deep hole which some time in the past had been dug to imprison a man named Malchiah. There the king's counselors decided to entomb Jeremiah until he died. They lowered him down into the dark pit with ropes and when the prophet had reached its final depth he sunk into the deep mud which lay at the bottom.[71] There they left him with neither food nor water, to die.

---

64. Ibid.
65. Jeremiah 37:20
66. Jeremiah 37:21
67. Jeremiah 38:1-3

68. Jeremiah 21:8-9
69. Jeremiah 38:4
70. Jeremiah 38:5
71. Jeremiah 38:6

It was a Negro eunuch in the household of Zedekiah, whose love and appreciation for the Lord's prophet saved Jeremiah's life. While the king was sitting as judge at one of the main gates, this humble house-boy from the king's palace came saying, "My Lord the king, these men have done evil in all that they have done to Jeremiah the prophet, whom they have cast into the dungeon; and he is like to die for hunger in the place where he is: for there is no more bread in the city."[72]

Being in a public place, the king apparently wished to appear generous, therefore he did what he had previously said he did not dare to do. He crossed his "princes" and saved Jeremiah's life. Zedekiah authorized the Negro servant to get thirty men and haul Jeremiah up. The servant ran and found some old rags which he threw down to Jeremiah to put under his arm-pits, then a rope was tied around him and he was hauled up. We later learn that there were still some meager rations available and no doubt the eunuch secured some of these to feed the famished prophet. From then on Jeremiah was kept in one of the cabin-cells which had been constructed in the courtyard, and he was there when Jerusalem finally fell.[73]

Before that happened, however, Jeremiah had one more contact with the king. In the last desperate months of the siege, when the Babylonians had returned in full force, Zedekiah ordered the emaciated prophet-prisoner secretly brought to one of the gates of the temple. Between these two men there then occurred one the most amazing conversations to be found in the entire Bible. First, Zedekiah asked Jeremiah to tell him the absolute, naked truth as to what was about to happen.[74] Jeremiah said he feared that if he did, the king would kill him, and that if he told the king how to escape what was going to happen, the king would not hearken unto him.[75] Zedekiah took an oath in the name of the Lord that he would not kill Jeremiah, no matter what he told him, and the king also promised he would not allow the princes to kill

---

72. Jeremiah 38:9. This last phrase illustrates how desperate the siege had become and even with many of the Babylonians gone to fight the Egyptians, the surrounding territory was so ravaged that few resources could be obtained.
73. Jeremiah 38:28
74. Jeremiah 38:14
75. Jeremiah 38:15

him.[76] However, he made no commitment as to whether he would follow Jeremiah's advice. Jeremiah said:

"If thou wilt assuredly go forth [surrender] unto the king of Babylon's princes, then thy soul shall live, and this city shall not be burned with fire; and thou shalt live, and thine house. But if thou wilt not go forth to the king of Babylon's princes, then shall this city be given into the hand of the Chaldeans, and they shall burn it with fire, and thou shalt not escape out of their hand."[77]

Zedekiah replied that he was afraid to surrender to Babylon. His reason was rather fantastic. He said he was afraid that Nebuchadnezzar would ship him to Babylon and turn him loose among the Jewish captives who would then "mock" or abuse him for being such an incompetent king.[78] Jeremiah assured him that the Babylonians would not "deliver" him to the captives for any such abuse if the king would surrender instead of waiting to be captured. Jeremiah then pleaded with all his might to persuade the king to use a little common sense and thereby save both himself and the people. Zedekiah listened to the prophet but any semblance of common sense was neutralized by the fearful cowardice which seemed abnormally prevalent in this man's personality. At the end of the conversation the king had aroused no genuine fortitude in himself whatever. His last words to Jeremiah were both a plea and a threat. He said, "Let no man know of these words, AND THOU SHALT NOT DIE."[79] He then told Jeremiah that when the "princes" tried to worm out of him what he had discussed with the king he should merely emphasize the part of their conversation which related to his own situation in prison and not mention the political matters.[80] The princes did indeed try to drain from Jeremiah a detailed account of what had happened, but the prophet owed them nothing and told them nothing. Then Jeremiah was shuffled back to prison and "he was there when Jerusalem was taken."[81]

---

76. Jeremiah 38:16
77. Jeremiah 38:17-18
78. Jeremiah 38:19
79. Jeremiah 38:24
80. Jeremiah 38:25-26
81. Jeremiah 38:28

JERUSALEM IS CONQUERED AND LEVELED — 587 B.C.

It was July, 587 B.C., when Jerusalem was finally starved into a state of total collapse.[82] Even so, however, the decisive factor was a Babylonian break-through of the outer wall.[83] This is believed to have occurred on the north side "where the depression dividing the western and eastern ridges, the Tyropoeon Valley, begins."[84]

Zedekiah knew Nebuchadnezzar had only the weaker, inner wall to surmount and then the city would be inundated with blood. He therefore rallied his officers and army together and they fled. The scripture says they "went forth out of the city by night by the way of the gate between the two walls, which was by the king's garden [at the southeast corner, bordering on the Kidron Valley]."[85]

Having left the women, children, and other civilians to the ravages of the conquering army, Zedekiah and his troops fled down toward Jericho, apparently hoping to escape into Trans-Jordan. But they never reached it. ". . . the army of Chaldeans pursued after the king, and overtook Zedekiah in the plains of Jericho; and all his army was scattered from him."[86] Zedekiah was taken up to Riplah near Hamath where Nebuchadnezzar had his campaign headquarters.[87]

Meanwhile, in Jerusalem the frightened populace waited for the inevitable victory shout as the Babylonians finally smashed down the gates or made a breach in the second wall. It was perhaps in this critical hour of pending massacre that the Negro eunuch in the king's palace who had saved Jeremiah's life received a thrilling message of comfort from the imprisoned prophet. It said the city was indeed about to fall but "I will deliver thee in that day, saith the Lord: and thou shalt not be given into the hand of the men of whom thou art afraid. For I will surely deliver thee, and thou shalt not fall by the sword, but thy life shall be for a prey [a precious prize] unto thee: because thou hast put thy trust in me, saith the Lord."[88]

---

82. Jeremiah 52:6; Kraeling, Rand McNally *Bible Atlas,* p. 316
83. Jeremiah 52:7
84. Kraeling, Rand McNally, *Bible Atlas,* p. 316
85. Jeremiah 52:7
86. Jeremiah 52:8
87. Jeremiah 52:9
88. Jeremiah 39:17-18

The horrors of the final weeks of the siege are spared the Bible reader, but a prophecy of Ezekiel gives some idea of what went on. Ezekiel wrote of Jerusalem, "Therefore the fathers shall eat the sons in the midst of thee [those who had already died of the famine], and the sons shall eat their fathers; and I will execute judgments in thee. . . . A third part of thee shall die with the pestilence, and with famine shall they be consumed in the midst of thee: and a third part shall fall by the sword round about thee; and I will scatter a third part into all the winds, and I will draw out a sword after them."[89] This meant that two thirds of the population would die during or immediately after the siege from starvation and disease, while the remaining third would flee to all the surrounding nations seeking to escape the vengeance of Babylon. Therefore, of the total number, only a fragmentary few would ever be taken to Babylon as captives.[90]

When the fall of Jerusalem came it was accompanied by all of the horrors of rapine, burning, looting and killing which characterized the techniques of conquest in those blood-thirsty days. For weeks the fires of Jerusalem filled the air with the pungent odor of destruction and death. The Babylonian troops spread violence and terror in every direction and then herded together the few survivors to be marched off toward Mesopotamia.[91] Among the prisoners were found many of the leaders of the city, enemies of Jeremiah, who guided the weak King Zedekiah into adopting his catastrophic and tragic policies. These were taken up to Nebuchadnezzar's headquarters in Riplah and summarily executed.[92]

Included among the prisoners were also found several of Zedekiah's sons. These were brought before the imprisoned king and killed before his very eyes.[93] Then Zedekiah was blinded and thrust into chains ready to be hauled off to Babylon.[94] Jeremiah had said Zedekiah would be carried to Babylon,[95] but Ezekiel (a captive already in Babylon) had prophesied that Zedekiah would never see Babylon even though he would die there.[96] It was a confusing prophecy. When the wretched Zedekiah was carried off to Babylon

---

89. Ezekiel 5:10-12
90. Ezekiel 5:3
91. Jeremiah 39:8-9
92. Jeremiah 52:24-27

93. Jeremiah 39:6
94. Jeremiah 39:7
95. Jeremiah 32:5
96. Ezekiel 12:13

without eyes to see that land, both of these apparently contradictory prophecies were literally fulfilled.

As already mentioned, however, before Zedekiah was
blinded he saw his sons brought in before him to be executed.
Zedekiah must have secretly rejoiced to observe that one
of them was not there. Of course he probably had no way
of knowing with certainty whether the boy were even alive,
but at least he was not there to be executed. Zedekiah undoubtedly went to his grave not knowing whatever happened
to this son. The boy's name was Mulek. We now know
that one of the bands which escaped from Jerusalem took
this son of Zedekiah with them and eventually made their
way to the western hemisphere![97]

Jeremiah Escapes With the Aid of the Babylonians

When Jerusalem first fell, the Babylonian officers had
certain instructions which were methodically carried out.
They completely looted the city of all precious commodities
including the remaining temple vessels and utensils, the braz-
en sea, the massive brass pillars and every other source of
wealth.[98] Most of the metal objects were melted down.[99] The
great Ark of the Covenant, the most magnificent and sacred
treasure of all Israel was destroyed or stolen at this time.
The Bible makes no reference to it but the Apocryphal book
of 2 Esdras 10:22 mentions the plundering of the Ark during
the destruction of Jerusalem. This ancient and beautiful relic
from the days of Moses is never heard of again.

---

97. We find the following in the Book of Mormon: ". . . and the land north was
   called Mulek, which was after the son of Zedekiah; for the Lord did bring
   Mulek into the land north, and Lehi into the land south." (Helaman 6:10)
   These people eventually settled in Zarahemla and were discovered by the
   descendants of Lehi about three centuries later. The record says, "Behold, it
   came to pass that Mosiah discovered that the people of Zarahemla came out of
   Jerusalem at the time that Zedekiah, king of Judah, was carried away captive
   into Babylon. And they journeyed in the wilderness, and were brought BY
   THE HAND OF THE LORD across the great waters, into the land where
   Mosiah discovered them; and they had dwelt there from that time forth. And
   at the time that Mosiah discovered them they had become exceeding numerous.
   Nevertheless, they had had many wars and serious contentions, and had fallen
   by the sword from time to time; and their language had become corrupted; and
   they had brought no records with them; and they denied the being of their
   creator; and Mosiah, nor the people of Mosiah, could understand them. But
   it came to pass that Mosiah caused that they should be taught in his language."
   (Omni, verses 15-18) The Book of Mormon verifies that no other sons of
   Zedekiah escaped save Mulek. (Helaman 8:21)
98. Jeremiah 52:17-20
99. This is taken to be the meaning of Jer. 52:19.

As for the general desolation accompanying the conquest of Jerusalem, the Bible says the Babylonians "... burned the house of the Lord, and the king's house; and all the houses of Jerusalem, and all the houses of the great men. ... And all the army of the Chaldeans, that were with the captain of the guard, brake down all the walls of Jerusalem round about. Then Nebuzar-adan the captain of the guard carried away captive ... the rest of the multitude. But ... [he] left certain of the poor of the land for vine-dressers and for husbandmen.''[100]

But while all this destruction was going on, the Babylonians saw to it that Jeremiah was saved from injury. Apparently, Nebuchadnezzar had somehow learned of Jeremiah's teachings which advocated friendly relations with the Babylonians. In fact, the captain of the guard even knew that Jeremiah had predicted a Babylonian victory over Jerusalem as a punishment from Israel's God.[101] The scripture says that Nebuchadnezzar had told his commanding general, "Take him, and look well to him, and do him no harm; but do unto him even as he shall say unto thee.''[102] So the Babylonian leaders went in person to get Jeremiah out of his prison and make sure that no harm befell him.[103] They also seemed to have been looking out for Jeremiah's friends who had sympathized with his pro-Babylonian counsel. One of these was Gedaliah, the son of Ahikam, the same Ahikam who had courageously defended Jeremiah years before and saved the prophet from a mob.[104] All of these people were allowed to leave the ruined Jerusalem and remain in Judah instead of being deported. In fact, the Babylonians soon decided to make Gedaliah the governor over the farmers and vine-dressers who were being left behind.[105] Jeremiah was put into the hands of this colony.[106] It is also likely, though the scripture only infers it, that Jeremiah used his good offices to see that no harm befell his Negro friend, the eunuch at the king's palace, who had saved his life.[107]

In the chapter following the above events, we read that Jeremiah had somehow become separated from his colony of

100. Jeremiah 52:13-16
101. Jeremiah 40:2-3
102. Jeremiah 39:12
103. Jeremiah 39:13
104. Jeremiah 26:24
105. Jeremiah 40:5
106. Jeremiah 39:14
107. Jeremiah 39:16-18

protectors and was thereupon scooped up and made a captive in chains to be included among those woe-begotten survivors being dragged off to Babylon.[108] The commanding
general heard of it and stopped the prisoner exiles at Ramah
(Samuel's old home-town just a few miles north of Jerusalem). He ordered Jeremiah released. The commander said,
"And now, behold, I loose thee this day from the chains which
were upon thine hand. If it seem good unto thee to come
with me into Babylon, come; and I will look well unto thee: but
if it seem ill unto thee to come with me into Babylon, forbear:
behold, all the land is before thee: whither it seemeth good
and convenient for thee to go, thither go."[109]

A little later the commander urged Jeremiah to "Go back
also to Gedaliah the son of Ahikam the son of Shaphan,
whom the king of Babylon hath made governor over the cities
of Judah, and dwell with him among the people: or go where-
soever it seemeth convenient unto thee to go."[110] Jeremiah
was in such a poverty-stricken and weakened condition that
the Babylonians gave him "victuals and a reward" so that
he could make the short journey to Mizpah where Gedaliah
had set up his headquarters.[111]

THE CLOSING DAYS OF JEREMIAH

For Jeremiah, the lengthening shadows of life were
drawing to a close. He had fulfilled a monumental mission
but it would remain for future history to fix its greatness. At
the moment events were chaotic, running in a continuous scarlet tide of destruction and catastrophe. Even at Mizpah there
was little to comfort an old man whose back was bent with the
burden of many years of persecution in the Lord's service,
and whose body was emaciated by the bare-survival existence which he had endured in the Jerusalem prison throughout the last bitter months of the long siege. A terrible and
lonely dreariness of savage desolation displayed its grim visage across the valleys and mountains of all Judea. There
was a gaunt spectre of poverty and misery everywhere. The
most haunting aspect of it all was the cruel fact that none of it
needed to have happened. The Lord had described how to

108. Jeremiah 40:1   110. Jeremiah 40:5
109. Jeremiah 40:4   111. Jeremiah 40:5-6

escape the whole fatal disaster. But they would not listen. It was maddening.

Even in Mizpah, Jeremiah's friend Gedaliah, who was the governor of the remnant, suffered assassination at the hands of Ishmael, a member "of the seed royal."[112] Ishmael then fled to the Ammonites, while an ex-army officer named Johanan took over and tried to restore order.[113] Soon afterwards the people moved from Mizpah to a settlement near Bethlehem. Johanan came to Jeremiah to see if they should go on to Egypt where so many of the exiles had fled, but Jeremiah told them they should remain in Judah. He predicted that if they stayed, all would be well, but if they went down into Egypt, all of them would perish.[114] Johanan and his captains had previously sworn that no matter what the Lord told them to do they would obey,[115] but after all this suffering, destruction, terror and bloodshed, these brick-headed, defiant rebels clung to their stubborn ways and rejected the message. They accused Jeremiah of being influenced by his scribe, Baruch, and said he had prophesied falsely.[116] They moved down to Egypt and settled at Tahpanhes (Daphne) in the eastern Delta region. They dragged Jeremiah and Baruch along with them, so Jeremiah dictated all of his final revelations from there.[117]

Jeremiah prophesied that all these refugees from Judah who had come into Egypt would be consumed by sword, pestilence and famine because they had continued their idolatry in spite of all that happened to them.[118]

Jeremiah prophesied that the Pharaoh Hophra would go into the hands of his enemies just as Zedekiah had gone into the hands of the Babylonians.[119]

---

112. Jeremiah 41:1-2
113. Jeremiah 41:15,16
114. Jeremiah 42:1, 9-18
115. Jeremiah 42:5-6
116. Jeremiah 43:2-4
117. Jeremiah 43:5-7, 8-13
118. Jeremiah, chapter 44
119. Jeremiah 44:30. "In 569 B.C. Pharaoh Hophra went to aid the Libyans against the Greeks, who had established themselves on the African coast at Cyrene. He was defeated and a rebellion broke out in his army, a part of which elevated Amasis as Pharaoh. In a battle fought between the opposing groups in 569 B.C., Amasis prevailed over Hophra. The latter was able to co-exist for some time but then was put to death." (Kraeling, Rand McNally *Bible Atlas*, p. 318)

He also predicted the fall of Babylon and described the great calamities that would come upon that mighty nation.[120]

THE PROPHET OBADIAH

It was at this time, during the latter part of Jeremiah's ministry, that the Prophet Obadiah is believed to have made his scriptural contribution. We know nothing of his personal life but, like Jeremiah, he had a message for some of the surrounding heathen people, particularly those who were distant relatives of Israel.

The available writings of Obadiah are very short, barely a page and a half in the average Bible, but they tell of his "vision" and the message which he had for the Arab people who were descendants of Esau living in Edom.[121]

The Edomites had participated in the recent sacking of Jerusalem, apparently as an ally of Babylon, and for this Obadiah shamed them. He wrote:

"For thy violence against thy brother Jacob shame shall cover thee. . . . Thou shouldest not have entered into the gate of my people in the day of their calamity . . . nor have laid hands on their substance . . . neither shouldest thou have stood in the crossway, to cut off those of his that did escape; neither shouldest thou have delivered up those of his that did remain in the day of distress."[122]

Then he closes his prophecy against Edom by looking toward the great last day when Israel would return in triumph to this land and the "host of the children of Israel" shall possess all the territory round about this region.[123] He said it would be a time when "saviours shall come up on mount Zion to judge the mount of Esau; and the kingdom shall be the Lord's."[124]

THE LAMENTATIONS OF JEREMIAH

Now that we have reviewed the principal events in this disastrous period it is easier to comprehend the profound

---

120. Jeremiah, chapters 50 and 51. This was literally fulfilled when Cyrus conquered Babylon in 539 B.C. and subsequent events led to the complete dissolution of the city.
121. Obadiah, verse 1
122. Obadiah, verses 10-14
123. Obadiah, verses 20-21
124. Obadiah, verse 21

feelings of the prophet Jeremiah as we find them expressed in his Lamentations.

Jeremiah was somewhat like the prophet Noah after the Great Flood. He, himself, had asked that the wicked be destroyed but after witnessing the great destruction he was so touched by the suffering and pathos of it all that he found it difficult to endure the memory of it.

Jeremiah acknowledged that everything which had happened to Judah was the direct result of her own culpable and vicious rebellion against truth, righteousness, and human decency. The people and their leaders had insulted God, sacrificed their children, listened to false prophets, and degraded themselves with every type of immorality and crime. No amount of warning would turn them from their course, therefore they had reaped the whirlwind.

Nevertheless, Jeremiah could not forget the haunting memory of the starving children,[125] the famished multitudes of the common people,[126] the living feeding upon the remains of the dead.[127] He also recounted to himself the measure of his own personal suffering during this period. They had cast him in dungeons, and abused him even in his old age.[128] He also recalled the bitter sorrow of seeing Judah's distant relatives, the Edomites, joining in Jerusalem's destruction. He predicted that their judgment was eventually coming and they would regret deeply their betrayal of Judah.[129] He also lamented the perfidy of Egypt which had encouraged Judah's rebellion, and then failed to provide any substantial assistance as previously promised. This simply confirmed what Jeremiah had been saying about Egypt all his prophetic life. It made him despise her treachery all the more to see her hypocrisy in visible action.

Jeremiah closed his Lamentations with a prayer that the Lord would always remember these terrible sufferings of both the guilty and the innocent and help His people find their way back. Cried he, "Turn thou us unto thee, O Lord, and we shall be turned; renew our days as of old."[130]

---

125. Lamentations 2:11-13
126. Lamentations 4:5-9
127. Lamentations 4:10
128. Lamentations 3:1-20, 48-55
129. Lamentations 4:20-21
130. Lamentations 4:21

The Mighty Prophet Fades Into the Darkness
of an Unknown Oblivion

Finally the voice and pen of the great Jeremiah was stilled. Just how it happened no modern man can be certain. Some said he was killed, others that he died a natural death. All we know is that apparently the great Jeremiah died in Egypt, the land of Israel's ancient captivity. His ministry had lasted approximately 42 years. Time and again he had been required to offer his own life on the altar of sacrifice in order to fulfill God's commandment concerning the continuous warning of the people. He had forfeited marriage, family, parents, brothers, sisters and friends in order to function as the prophet of the Lord during this epic of chaos and continuous crisis which prevailed throughout his life. He had undergone punishment by physical beating and endured personal suffering through prolonged imprisonment. He had endured the shock and sorrow which came when the king executed his fellow-worker, Urijah, and mourned when his friend and protector, Gedaliah, was assassinated by a descendant of David who wanted to seize the only remaining fragment of power left in Judah. Even his last political master of the Mizpah colony, the ex-army leader Johanan, had asked for, but afterwards refused the prophet's advice concerning the means of avoiding disaster. All the company, including the prophet, therefore went into Egypt where the mysterious land of the Nile engulfed them and an unknown fate befell them.

We leave Jeremiah with a reluctance which comes with the feeling that we are parting from an old friend. Certainly here was one of the truly great shafts of polished hardwood in the quiver of the Lord Almighty. Even among the most faithful Saints of God throughout all the ages, there would be few who could equal Jeremiah.

Scripture Reading and Questions on Chapter Twenty-Five

Scripture Reading: Jeremiah, chapters 27 to 52, Book of Lamentations, Book of Obadiah.

1—What are the three burdens of a prophet? Which do you think is the most difficult to bear?

2—What was the main message in the vision of the two baskets of figs? Was this helpful to Jeremiah?

3—What did Jeremiah tell the captives in Babylon to do after he received this revelation? Who resisted it? What did they say?

4—Why are prophets of the Lord continually accused of "meddling" in politics? Are they able to fulfill their calling without passing on to the leaders of the people the inspiration God gives them?

5—What did Hananiah do to repudiate Jeremiah? Did Jeremiah offer to debate him? What test did he suggest the people use on Hananiah?

6—Why do you suppose the Lord wanted to give a more immediate sign? When did it come to pass?

7—What tribe did Lehi belong? Who was his fourth son? Had Lehi been a religious leader? What was his occupation?

8—What was the major message in the vision which Lehi saw? What reaction did he get when he told the people?

9—What caused Nebuchadnezzar to launch his attack on Jerusalem in 588 B.C.? What was one of the first things King Zedekiah did? What was the Lord's revelation to Jeremiah at this time?

10—What was the Lord's "escape" for Jerusalem? Was it used?

11—How did the Babylonians happen to leave Jerusalem temporarily? What was Jeremiah's advice? Did Zedekiah agree?

12—Why did Jeremiah abandon Jerusalem? Why was he arrested for treason?

13—What did Zedekiah do when Jeremiah was brought before him? What did the "princes" do with Jeremiah? Who saved his life?

14—What did Zedekiah do when he saw Jerusalem was about to fall? What happened to him? Where was Nebuchadnezzar's headquarters?

15—What happened to Zedekiah's sons? What happened to the one who escaped? What were the two contradictory prophecies about Zedekiah?

16—What was the attitude of the Babylonians toward Jeremiah? With whom did he go? Could he have gone to Babylon?

17—What happened to the colony at Mizpah? What did Jeremiah tell Johanan? Did he take the advice?

18—To whom did Obadiah address his prophecies? Whom did he say would ultimately possess the land around Palestine?

19—In Jeremiah's Lamentations what gave him the greatest cause for mourning? Did he mention his own suffering?

20—Do we know what happened to Jeremiah? Give your estimate of this prophet's character.

CHAPTER TWENTY-SIX

Ezekiel — Prophet of the Captivity

In 598 B.C. when the first body of 10,000 Jewish captives arrived in Babylon, they were scattered to different cities and settlements as bond servants and slaves. However, they were not common slaves. They were more like the famous Greek scholars, artists, architects, builders, engineers, and skilled workmen who became the slaves of the Romans. Culturally speaking, many of the Greeks became the masters of their own proprietors. The 10,000 captive Jews of the 598 B.C. contingent also represented the finest scholars, artisans, smiths and builders from Judah. In some respects their cultural level at the beginning was below that of the Babylonians. Nevertheless, the Lord knew what they could do if they would industriously apply themselves. The most important thing was to give these people something to strive for. They needed to be challenged. When they first arrived, these weary Exiles carried with them a miasma of total despondency. In fact, the heartbreak of these 10,000 displaced persons is caught in the 137th Psalm as the refugee Jews sang out their sorrows to the Lord.

> By the rivers of Babylon,
> There we sat down,
> Yea, we wept,
> When we remembered Zion.

We hanged our harps upon the willows
In the midst thereof.
For there they that carried us away captive
Required of us a song;
And they that wasted us
Required of us mirth, saying,
Sing us one of the songs of Zion.

How shall we sing the Lord's song
In a strange land?
If I forget thee, O Jerusalem,
Let my right hand forget her cunning.
If I do not remember thee,
Let my tongue cleave to the roof of my mouth. . .

JEREMIAH'S MESSAGE OF HOPE

To give these people renewed hope, the Lord revealed to Jeremiah the vision of the two baskets of figs. It will be recalled that one basket contained sweet figs, delicious to the taste. The other contained figs so bitter none of the fruit could be eaten. Jeremiah was told that the first basket represented the first contingent of Jewish captives — the Exiles of 598 B.C. The Lord said their stay in Babylon would be profitable and a satisfying experience. The next conquest, however, would bring down upon Jerusalem an experience almost too bitter to bear. This was symbolized by the second basket of figs. The people would die of famine and sword, and most of those who escaped would flee in all directions and become lost to Israel. Only a meager few would survive to join their brethren in Babylon.

It will be recalled that Jeremiah immediately wrote to the captives to give them the good news. A blessing awaited them in their new home. He encouraged them to settle down, build homes, raise large families, compete wherever possible for a place in the affairs of the nation, and stay close to the Lord.

It will also be recalled that certain self-appointed "prophets" who were living in adultery with their neighbor's wives and teaching the people lies, tried to sabotage the impact of Jeremiah's letters. However, in this they largely failed for the Lord exposed them as false prophets through a revelation to Jeremiah.

Jeremiah's instruction that the people repent and return to the Lord succeeded to a rather remarkable degree. The false prophets achieved less and less influence until by 593 B.C. the Lord was ready to give the Exiles a prophet of their very own. He was a righteous Priest who had been brought over in this first deportation. His name was Ezekiel.

THE GREAT ORACLE OF THE CAPTIVITY — EZEKIEL

The name Ezekiel means "God is strong" or "God doth strengthen."[1] In the first verse Ezekiel makes reference to "the thirtieth year," as being the time when he had his first vision. This is generally believed to refer to his own age at the time the heavens were opened to him. The next two verses explain that this was the fifth year since the Exiles and their boy-king, Jehoiachin, came into captivity. This would mean that Ezekiel was around 25 years of age when he first came to Babylon from Judah and, as already mentioned, 30 years old when he received his first vision.

Ezekiel, like Jeremiah, was a direct descendant of Aaron from the tribe of Levi. Therefore, he is described as a "Priest."[2] This would mean his father, Buzi, would be a Priest also.[3] Ezekiel was married but later lost his wife through what appears to have been a sudden, unforeseen stroke.[4] She died the day that the siege of Jerusalem commenced.[5] They had a home of their own[6] which became a center for conferences with the elders of the Jews.[7] This was located very near to the capital city of Babylon on a canal which is said to have connected the Tigris and Euphrates rivers. It was called the Chebar river,[8] or "Grand Canal,"[9] and the community along its banks where Ezekiel lived was called Tel-Abib.[10] It was here, in approximately 593 B.C., on the fifth day of the fourth month[11] (latter part of June or

---

1. Peloubet's *Bible Dictionary*, under Ezekiel.
2. Ezekiel 1:3
3. Ibid.
4. Ezekiel 24:16-18
5. Ezekiel 24:1-2; Dummelow's *Bible Commentary*, Vol. 4, p. 489
6. Ezekiel 3:24; 8:1
7. Ezekiel 8:1
8. Ezekiel 1:1
9. Dummelow's *Bible Commentary*, Vol. 4, p. 491
10. Ezekiel 3:15
11. Ezekiel 1:1

early July)[12] that Ezekiel says, "the heavens were opened, and I saw visions of God."[13]

EZEKIEL SEES THE PERSONAGE OF GOD

The opening vision began with a great whirlwind out of the north which came in a cloud of fire and glory. Out of the midst of this glory came four living creatures with astonishing powers and spectacular magnificence. They were accompanied by a nest of four wheels of gigantic dimensions which had many eyes and seemed alive. They followed the living creatures with the greatest precision wherever they moved.

The living creatures would seem to be identical with those seen by John the Revelator,[14] and modern revelation discloses that John's creatures actually represented four types of glorified animals as they exist in that exalted dimension of cosmic reality where God lives.[15] According to this revelation the eyes and wings of the creatures were to symbolize the "light and knowledge" as well as the powers of mobility which these various animal entities enjoy in their resurrected estate. In other words, just as man will be exalted above anything his mind might imagine, so also animal life is granted faculties and powers far beyond those which their earthly status would lead us to expect. The modern scripture says, "Their eyes are a representation of light and knowledge, that is, they are full of knowledge; and their wings are a representation of power, to move, to act, etc."[16] John even attributes to them the capacity to articulate themselves in praising God.[17]

No mention is made in this modern revelation concerning the meaning of the wheels which were full of eyes and could move through space with marvelous maneuverability. However, by taking the above modern scripture as a lead, we might assume that the wheels were to illustrate a principle well-known to the modern prophets; namely, that there are organized intelligences or the ingredients of "life" in matter — in the so-called inanimate objects, or in what are referred

---

12. Clarke, *Bible Commentary*, Vol. 4, p. 427
13. Ezekiel 1:1
14. Rev. 4:6-8
15. Doc. & Cov. 77:2
16. Doc. & Cov. 77:4
17. Rev. 4:9

to as inorganic materials — and that this body of organized intelligences is like the intelligences or the element of life in "living" creatures. These intelligences are filled with light and knowledge and have the capacity to move any material imbued with them as well as to articulate themselves. Thus, Enoch heard the earth speaking as though it were a living embodiment with sentiments, understanding and intelligent comprehension.[18] As a modern prophet has said, "There is life in all matter throughout the vast extent of all the eternities; it is in the rock, the sand, in water, air, the gases, and in short, in every description and organization of matter whether it be solid, liquid or gaseous, particle operating with particle."[19]

It might not be too unreasonable to suggest that the wheels which Ezekiel saw, represented four different segments of God's material, cosmic universe, each part of which — whether we are speaking of atoms, solar systems, galaxies, or super-galactic systems — operate on the principle of wheels within wheels. The eyes in the wheels would represent the light and knowledge of the intelligences with which the physical elements are imbued,[20] and the harmonious movement of the wheels could represent the capacity of organized cosmic creations to move in accordance with intelligent direction and not necessarily depend exclusively upon mechanical gravitational forces.

Such a concept fits in well with what the Lord has revealed concerning His operation of the cosmos; certainly better than the one-time popular mechanistic theory. In modern revelation the Lord equates "the light of truth" with "intelligence."[21] He says the individual intelligence is an eternal reality which "was not created or made, neither indeed can be."[22] He explained to Abraham that intelligences are individualistic. In other words, there are many different levels of these eternal intelligences, and the supreme intelligence of them all is God.[23] The infinite hosts of these graded intelligences

---

18. Moses 7:48-49
19. *Discourses of Brigham Young,* 1925 ed., p. 566; see also "The Nature and Extent of Organized Intelligence Throughout the Universe," on pp. 356-357 in *The First 2,000 Years.*
20. Doc. & Cov. 93:29-36
21. Doc. & Cov. 93:29
22. Ibid.
23. Abraham 3:16-19

voluntarily obey the Lord[24] and through their superlative obedience the work or glory of God is manifest.[25]

Now listen to the way the Lord says He operates the universe: He says this "light of truth" or obedient host of intelligences under the direction of the Lord is the means by which "he is in the sun, and the light of the sun, and the power thereof by which it was made. As also he is in the moon, and is the light of the moon, and the power thereof by which it was made; as also the light of the stars . . . and the earth also, and the power thereof, even the earth upon which you stand."[26] Then He says this light or host of organized intelligences which move out from God "to fill the immensity of space" is "the light [or intelligence] which is IN ALL THINGS, which giveth LIFE to all things, which is the LAW BY WHICH ALL THINGS ARE GOVERNED, EVEN THE POWER OF GOD. . . ."[27]

This gives us a whole new insight into what might be called, "God-science" or the great first causes of the universe which ancient philosophers were always seeking to comprehend but never could quite grasp. Nor could we, except as God has seen fit to reveal it.

Next, Ezekiel saw the supreme and most exalted vision which man can enjoy and still remain in mortality[28] — the personage of God in all His majesty and power. Ezekiel did his best to describe the vision, but it is obvious that ordinary words were inadequate and the most he could do was to testify that various aspects of the vision were "as the appearance" of things already known to his reader.[29] He saw the likeness of a throne with the appearance of brilliant sapphire stone.[30] On the throne was a Personage which had the figure and likeness of a man,[31] but Ezekiel soon learned that this was Jehovah, the Lord Almighty, in whose image (as well as that of His Father, Elohim) man was made.[32] Around Him

---

24. Doc. & Cov. 93:30
25. Doc. & Cov. 93:36
26. Doc. & Cov. 88:7-10
27. Doc. & Cov. 88:12-13
28. Moses 1:5
29. In some respects, John is a little more lucid in describing an identical vision given to him on the isle of Patmos (Rev., chapter 4).
30. Ezekiel 1:26
31. Ibid.   32. Moses 2:27

was a brilliant bow or halo of glory and His very being seemed to reflect a brightness of radiant effulgence.[33]

It was no wonder that Ezekiel fell upon the ground in shocked astonishment.[34]

Ezekiel Receives His Call

Ezekiel heard a voice speaking to him, which said: "Son of man, stand upon thy feet, and I will speak unto thee. And the spirit entered into me when he spake unto me, and set me upon my feet, that I heard him that spake unto me."[35]

The Lord then told Ezekiel that he was being called to preach to a rebellious people, "the children of Israel."[36] Note that his call was not merely to the Exiles but to the whole Twelve Tribes, wherever they might be. As it turned out, many of the Exiles responded to his message and prepared for their return, but the other scattered remnants went their abominable way and have remained dispersed until this dispensation when they are now beginning to be gathered, nearly 2,500 years later!

As for the Exiles, the Lord warned Ezekiel that they would reject him in the beginning, and some never would accept him, ". . . yet shall [they] know that there hath been a prophet among them."[37] As a symbol of the great message he was to preach, Ezekiel was given a scroll or book by the Lord, and told to eat it.[38] It was sweet to him in his mouth just as the book which was later given to John the Revelator.[39]

---

33. Ezekiel 1:27
34. Ezekiel 1:28
35. Ezekiel 2:1-2. Moses describes the impact which similar visions had upon him: "And the presence of God withdrew from Moses, that his glory was not upon Moses; and Moses was left unto himself. And as he was left unto himself, he fell unto the earth. And it came to pass that it was for the space of many hours before Moses did again receive his natural strength like unto man; and he said unto himself: Now, for this cause I know that man is nothing, which thing I never had supposed. But now mine own eyes have beheld God; but not my natural, but my spiritual eyes, for my natural eyes could not have beheld; for I should have withered and died in his presence; but his glory was upon me; and I beheld his face, for I was transfigured before him." (Moses 1:9-11) Joseph Smith says that following the vision in the grove it left him lying prone upon the ground. Then he says. "When the light had departed, I had no strength; but soon recovering in some degree, I went home." (P. of G. P., p. 48:20)
36. Ezekiel 2:3
37. Ezekiel 2:5
38. Ezekiel 2:9-10; 3:1-3
39. Rev. 10:8-11; Doc. & Cov. 77:14

But John says his book was bitter to digest. This is taken to mean that great missionary calls are received with rejoicing, but the Lord wants it understood that often these calls involve the most desperate and bitter kind of experiences, measured out in physical, mental and spiritual anguish.

The Lord said to Ezekiel that his over-all calling was "unto the house of Israel" and "not to many people of a strange speech and of an hard language, whose words thou canst not understand. . . . But," the Lord lamented, "the house of Israel will not hearken unto thee; for THEY WILL NOT HEARKEN UNTO ME: for all the house of Israel are impudent and hardhearted."[40] Ezekiel was therefore told to "go, get thee to them of the captivity, unto the children of thy people, and speak unto them, and tell them, Thus saith the Lord God. . . ."[41]

The Lord knew Ezekiel would receive a certain amount of persecution, especially in the beginning, so He strengthened him in the same way He had strengthened Jeremiah: "Behold, I have made thy face strong against their faces, and thy forehead strong against their foreheads . . . harder than flint . . . fear them not, neither be dismayed at their looks, though they be a rebellious house."[42]

THE RESPONSIBILITY OF A PROPHET

But Ezekiel was going to need more preparation than this. When this vision was over, it left the prophet-novice in a state of mental and spiritual shock. He obeyed the Lord by going out among the captives at Tel-Abib, but he just simply could not bring himself to start speaking to them. He later confessed, "I sat where they sat, and remained there astonished among them seven days."[43] But God's prophets are not like certain holy men of the orient who spend their time in religious retreats sitting cross-legged, staring at their navels. God's servants must be up and doing. Ezekiel says, "And it came to pass at the end of seven days, that the word of the Lord came unto me, saying, Son of man, I HAVE MADE THEE A WATCHMAN UNTO THE HOUSE OF ISRAEL: therefore hear the word at my mouth, and give

40. Ezekiel 3:4-7   42. Ezekiel 3:8-9
41. Ezekiel 3:11   43. Ezekiel 3:15

them warning from me. When I say unto the wicked, Thou shalt surely die; and thou givest him not warning, nor speakest to warn the wicked from his wicked way, to save his life; the same wicked man shall die in his iniquity; BUT HIS BLOOD WILL I REQUIRE AT THINE HAND. Yet if thou warn the wicked, and he turn not from his wickedness, nor from his wicked way, he shall die in his iniquity; BUT THOU HAST DELIVERED THY SOUL."[44]

Ezekiel was then told that he had an equal responsibility to continually warn the *righteous*. The prophet was told that if he failed to be diligent as a shepherd and constantly serve as a voice of warning to the righteous, then he would be held responsible if they fell.[45]

In order to further prepare Ezekiel, the Lord now said to him, "Go, shut thyself within thine house."[46] The Lord said that until such time as He sent Ezekiel forth again he was to be like a man in bonds whose tongue had grown to the roof of his mouth.[47] During this period of preparation the Lord said that for the time being, "thou . . . shalt not be to them a reprover. . . ."[48] However, at the proper time, he could go forth. The Lord said, "But when I speak with thee, I will open thy mouth, and thou shalt say unto them, Thus saith the Lord God. . . ."[49]

EZEKIEL'S PROPHECIES CAPTURED IN SYMBOLIC TEACHING DEVICES

To help Ezekiel conceptualize the literal reality of future events, the Lord now undertook to teach Ezekiel a great number of prophecies through symbolic images which, with the proper key, a child could understand. We find that all of Ezekiel's early prophetic lessons had to do with the wickedness of Judah and the fall of Jerusalem. He was instructed to take a tile and draw upon it a portrayal or picture of Jerusalem. He was to set up a number of things around it to represent a siege, and do a variety of emblematic things to represent the severity of the siege and the hardships which

---

44. Ezekiel 3:16-19
45. Ezekiel 3:20-21
46. Ezekiel 3:24
47. Ezekiel 3:26
48. Ibid.
49. Ezekiel 3:27

would follow. His food and water were to be austere.[50] He was to lie in bonds on one side for a period without turning over so as to represent the years of iniquity in Israel.[51] Then he was to lie in bonds on the other side to represent the years of iniquity in Judah.[52] He had to shave his head and beard, place the hair on a scale (representing divine justice) and then burn a third, cut up a third with a knife and scatter the other third to the wind.[53] A few hairs were to be collected and hidden in the lap of his robe.[54] The meaning was that one third of Jerusalem should die by famine and pestilence,[55] one third by the sword,[56] and one third by flight.[57] Only a few strands were to be retained which represented the tiny fragment of people who would be left and brought to Babylon after the fall of Jerusalem.

During September, 592 B.C.,[58] Ezekiel was allowed to see the Lord in glory once more[59] and then he was shown a servant of the Lord passing among the people of Jerusalem preparatory to its destruction. All those who still remained faithful were given a mark in the forehead[60] so they would be protected and saved, whereas all others were marked for death.[61]

In several additional revelations to Ezekiel the Lord denounced the idolatrous abominations in Judah just as He was doing at the same time and with equal vehemence through Jeremiah. Then suddenly, the Lord introduces some new names into the narrative. He said, "Though these three men, Noah, Daniel and Job were in it [the doomed city of Jerusalem], they should deliver but their own souls by their righteousness, saith the Lord God."[62] In other words, the presence of men even as great as these could not save Jerusalem now. They could save themselves but not the city.

---

50. Ezekiel 4:10-11
51. Ezekiel 4:5, 8. The figures in this passage are probably tampered with and do not fit any specific situation. A different figure is not given in the Septuagint. (See Dummelow's *Bible Commentary,* Vol. 4, p. 494)
52. Ezekiel 4:6. The figure of forty years is believed to represent the iniquity of Judah from the abominations of Manasseh to the fall of Jerusalem. (See Clarke, *Bible Commentary,* Vol. 4, p. 436)
53. Ezekiel 5:1-2
54. Ezekiel 5:3
55. Ezekiel 5:12
56. Ibid.
57. Ibid.
58. Ezekiel 8:1
59. Ezekiel 8:4
60. Ezekiel 9:4
61. Ezekiel 9:5-10
62. Ezekiel 14:14

The Lord was emphasizing how far Judah had gone toward the brink of destruction.

It is highly significant that the Lord would mention Daniel and Job along with the famous patriarch, Noah. The naming of Daniel gives clear evidence that this young man from Judah had already risen to great prominence in the palace of Nebuchadnezzar at Babylon, which was located just a short distance away. As for Job, this is the first time his name is mentioned in any of the prophetic books of the Bible. We therefore pause to briefly examine the place of this valiant personality in the scriptures.

THE EPIC OF JOB

Job is one of the great unknown quantities in the Bible. No one knows for certain the age to which he belongs. However, from this one statement by Ezekiel we knew that by this time he had become a national symbol of Godly integrity and patient endurance in suffering. Because the Book of Job is such an exquisite gem of Hebrew literature, some have suggested that Job was perhaps just an imaginary hero in a fictional story. However, the Apostle James refers to Job as though he were a real person[63] and so does the Lord in a modern revelation.[64]

The greatest single lesson to be learned from the Book of Job is the fact that a great war is being waged during this, the Second Estate. It is a war between Jehovah and Lucifer. It demonstrates that the worth of a human soul is so precious in the sight of both God and Satan that these competitive leaders are locked in a deadly struggle for the allegiance of the Father's children.[65] Lucifer knows that if he fails to destroy Jehovah's program, he will be cast forth into the limbo of outer darkness and death forever.[66] So the great contest is both terrible and real.

Lucifer's principal strategy is to use freedom to destroy freedom. His technique is to induce men to use their individual free agency in a way that will bring judgment upon

---

63. James 5:11
64. Doc. & Cov. 121:10
65. Moses 4:1-4; Isaiah 14:12-14; Rev. 12:7-17
66. Doc. & Cov. 88:113-114; Rev. 20:10

them and thereby limit their future power to choose. He knows that the Father's plan calls for the testing of mankind with both good and evil during the Second Estate so that each person can prove the degree of his integrity by the choices he makes. Lucifer's plan is to get human beings exposed to as much evil as possible. By this means he hopes to increase the percentage of those who will choose evil. The government of God through the Priesthood beyond the veil must curb this avalanche of evil, but they must be careful that in blessing the faithful they do not hedge them up against evil so completely that the temptations intended for the Second Estate become virtually non-existent. In fact, traditionally, the program of the Lord has been to chasten and test those whom He loves that they might better demonstrate their integrity and capacity for loyalty and faithfulness under distress. As the Lord said to the early Christians, "As many as I love, I rebuke and chasten: be zealous therefore, and repent."[67] Nevertheless, Lucifer watches for those who might have become insulated behind an over-abundance of blessings, so that he cannot easily get to them. When this happens he raises a hue and cry.

It is therefore in this framework of reference that the Book of Job has its setting:

While the Lord was attending a conference with certain members of the Priesthood[68] beyond the veil, Satan put in an appearance. "And the Lord said unto Satan, Whence comest thou? Then Satan answered the Lord, and said, From going to and fro in the earth, and from walking up and down in it. And the Lord said unto Satan, Hast thou considered my servant Job, that there is none like him in the earth, a perfect and an upright man, one that feareth God, and escheweth evil?"[69]

The person speaking to Satan was Jehovah, the future Jesus Christ, the one who had been chosen over Lucifer in the Pre-existence, and the one who had cast Lucifer out of the precincts of Heaven.[70] Lucifer's reply was therefore a

---

67. Rev. 3:19
68. The text says "sons of God" but note the Lord's declaration that those holding the Melchizedek Priesthood are those entitled to be referred to as "sons of God." See Doc. & Cov. 76:57-58
69. Job 1:7-8   70. Moses 4:1-4

biting accusation that Jehovah was violating the Father's plan by purchasing Job's loyalty with a super-abundance of blessings. In this sense Lucifer was accusing Jehovah of using "celestial bribery." Said he:

"Doth Job fear God for nought? Hast not thou made an hedge about him, and about his house, and about all that he hath on every side? thou hast blessed the work of his hands, and his substance is increased in the land."[71]

Having made his point, Lucifer now drove home the shaft. He challenged his former brother of the Pre-existence by shrewdly saying, "But put forth thine hand now, and touch [take away] all that he hath, and he will curse thee to thy face."[72]

The Lord said He would accept the challenge (in fact, the rules laid down for the Second Estate almost compelled this decision). He declared in effect that He would withdraw some of the protective care which surrounded Job so that this faithful servant might be further tested. "And the Lord said unto Satan, Behold, all that he hath is in thy power; only upon himself put not forth thine hand [take not his life]. So Satan went forth from the presence of the Lord."[73]

Job did not know it, but the Priesthood beyond the veil and of course the Lord, Himself, now watched him with the greatest sympathy and perhaps anxiety as they saw Job being threshed and wrung out by Satan's machinations of sorrow and suffering. They knew from their own experiences that a great human drama was unfolding before them.

This is sufficient to lay the foundation for a study of Job. It is an exciting and satisfying segment of scripture to read, and will fully demonstrate why the Lord would use the illustrious name of Job in association with the great prophet of the past, Noah, and the famous prophet of the present, Daniel, as examples of those whom God greatly loved. Now we return to our account of Ezekiel.

---

71. Job 1:9-10
72. Job 1:11
73. Job 1:12

Jerusalem Is Besieged and Ezekiel's Wife Dies

The history of the prophets will demonstrate that while they were loved of the Lord and showered with great blessings, they were required to suffer, learn and endure like the most humble of the Lord's multitudinous flock. One of Ezekiel's great trials came to him in January, 588 B.C., the very day the siege of Jerusalem commenced.[74] All that day the Lord had Ezekiel go through an assortment of symbolic patterns and procedures which illustrated in a tangible way the tragedies which were about to be enacted in Jerusalem. The Lord also forewarned Ezekiel that this day he would lose his beloved wife, "the desire of thine eyes."[75] But he was told not to weep or mourn for her loss because the hand of the Lord was in it, and all would be well. By the same token, he was told to tell the Exiles that the downfall of Jerusalem was imminent and they were not to mourn for its loss either. The Lord was determined that this desecrated and polluted center of His former sanctuary should be torn down to its foundations and rebuilt in another day. To the Lord it was the tragic loss of something He had dearly loved. Ezekiel writes, "So I spake unto the people in the morning: and at even my wife died; and I did in the morning as I was commanded."[76]

Here indeed was a choice, faithful servant of God!

Ezekiel's Prophecies Concerning the Immediate Future

As we have previously noted, Ezekiel dates each one of his revelations with the greatest precision, so that we can translate these dates with considerable accuracy into modern calendar terms. Altogether, he had twelve great spiritual experiences which he felt deserved to be identified by date. The first three were received before the siege of Jerusalem (593-591 B.C.),[77] and two were given while the siege was taking place (588-587 B.C.). Seven more dated revelations were given after the fall of Jerusalem.[78]

---

74. Ezekiel 24:1-2
75. Ezekiel 24:16
76. Ezekiel 24:18
77. See Ezekiel 1:2; 8:1; 20:1
78. See Ezekiel 26:1; 30:20; 33:21; 32:1; 32:17; 40:1; 29:17

As with Jeremiah, the Lord used Ezekiel to warn not only the Jews but all the nations in that whole surrounding region of the calamities which awaited them unless they turned from their idolatrous ways.

One revelation was to the children of Lot, called the Ammonites.[79]

One revelation included not only the Ammonites, but the Moabites, Edomites and the Philistines as well.[80]

Chapters 26, 27 and 28 are addressed to Tyre and Sidon of Phoenicia.

Chapters 29 to 32 constitute Ezekiel's warning to Egypt — and the coming overthrow of Pharaoh Hophra.

However, once Jerusalem had fallen and that great tragedy had become a part of history, Ezekiel's mind was turned by the Lord toward the same subject which had so thoroughly fascinated both Isaiah and Jeremiah — the great Last Days. From then on the mind of Ezekiel seemed to dwell intently and reverently on this one exclusive theme. He opens it up with a prophetic commentary on the rise of Israel in the latter days under a mighty political leader named David.

THE BUILDING OF A GREAT JEWISH KINGDOM
UNDER PRINCE DAVID

A number of ancient prophets as well as the Lord's modern servants have been aware that an outstanding descendant of David will be raised up in the latter days. His role has been considered so important that the Lord disclosed it to the prophets over 2,500 years ago.

Ezekiel devotes his thirty-fourth chapter to the life and time of this prince. Concerning the day of the calling up of this great servant, the Lord looked into the future and said, ". . . yea, my flock was scattered upon all the face of the earth, and none did search or seek after them. . . . Behold, I, even I, will both search my sheep and seek them out . . . and will deliver them out of all places where they have been scattered in the cloudy and dark day. And I will bring them out

---

79. Ezekiel, chapter 21   80. Ezekiel, chapter 25

from the people, and gather them from the countries, and will bring them to their own land, and feed them upon the mountains of Israel by the rivers, and in all the inhabited places of the country. . . . And I will set up one shepherd over them, and he shall feed them, even my servant David; he shall feed them, and he shall be their shepherd. And I the Lord will be their God, and my servant David a prince among them; I the Lord have spoken it."[81]

Many scholars, including the King James translators (who capitalized some references to this prince) thought these passages referred to the Savior at the time of His Second Coming. However, verse 23 of this chapter puts the situation in its proper perspective by saying this Prince David of the latter days will be a servant of God under the direction of the Lord.

Joseph Smith referred to this Prince David and said he would replace David, his great ancestor, for ". . . the throne and kingdom of David is to be taken from him [the ancient David] and given to another by the name of David in the last days, raised up out of his lineage."[82]

The administration of this outstanding leader will apparently last a long time and will extend over to the time when the Ten Tribes (who will first gather in America to receive their blessings)[83] are led back to Palestine to become one united nation with the Jews. The Lord referred to this time when He said, "And I will make them one nation in the land upon the mountains of Israel; and one king shall be king to them all: and they shall be no more two nations, neither shall they be divided into two kingdoms any more at all. . . . And David my servant shall be king over them. . . ."[84]

Ezekiel devoted much of chapter 46 to the days of this righteous David and his ministry of the kingdom. Jeremiah also had much to say of him. Writing at the Lord's dictation he said, "For it shall come to pass in that day, saith the Lord of hosts, that I will break his [Israel's] yoke from off thy neck, and . . . they shall serve the Lord their God, and David their king, whom I will raise up unto them."[85]

81. Ezekiel 34:6, 11-13, 23-24
82. Doc. His. of the Church, Vol. 6, p. 253
83. Doc. & Cov. 133:26-32

84. Ezekiel 37:22-24
85. Jeremiah 30:8-9

Isaiah said this "David" would be "a witness to the people, a leader and commander to the people."[86] Zechariah referred to him as The Branch who would build the temple of the Lord, "and shall sit and rule upon his throne; and he shall be a priest upon his throne. . . ."[87]

This "Branch" may be identical with the rod or limb growing "out of the stem of Jesse" which was referred to by Isaiah.[88] Concerning it a modern revelation identifies the stem of Jesse as Jesus Christ[89] and then states, "Behold, thus saith the Lord: It [the rod growing out of the stem of Jesse] is a servant in the hands of Christ, who is partly a descendant of Jesse as well as of Ephraim, or of the house of Joseph, ON WHOM THERE IS LAID MUCH POWER."[90] This could very well be the "Prince David" about whom the prophets wrote.

THE RESURRECTION OF ISRAEL AND JOINING OF THE TWO STICKS

Chapter 37 of Ezekiel is the famous vision of the resurrection which symbolized the resurrection of the nation of Israel which for so long had ceased to be a political entity. Ezekiel saw the dry bones come together in skeletons, and then flesh appeared on the bones, and finally they "stood up upon their feet, an exceeding great army."[91] The Lord said to Ezekiel, ". . . these bones are the whole house of Israel: behold, they say, Our bones are dried, and our hope is lost: we are cut off for our parts. Therefore prophesy and say unto them . . . [I] shall put my spirit in you, and ye shall live, and I shall place you in your own land: then shall ye know that I the Lord have spoken it, and performed it, saith the Lord."[92]

Not only would the house of Judah and the house of Israel become one again, but they would bring their histories together and form them into a single scripture to testify to the world. Ezekiel was told to take one stick "and write upon it, For Judah, and for the children of Israel his companions:

---

86. Isaiah 55:3-4
87. Zechariah 6:12-13
88. Isaiah 11:1
89. Doc. & Cov. 113:1-2

90. Doc. & Cov. 113:3-4
91. Ezekiel 37:10
92. Ezekiel 37:11-14

then take another stick, and write upon it, For Joseph, the stick of Ephraim, and for all the house of Israel his companions: and join them one to another into one stick; and they shall become one in thine hand."[93]

The Lord has verified in modern times that the term "stick" refers to books. The Book of Mormon is specifically identified by the Lord as "the stick of Ephraim."[94] In fact, we now know that within approximately twenty-five years after the Lord told Ezekiel about these two "sticks" the Lord was instructing His prophets from the house of Joseph (who had just come to America) to start preparing their record. This ultimately came forth as the Book of Mormon. We also know that only a short time after Ezekiel had recorded his own book (which became part of the stick of Judah), the Lord was saying this to His prophet-scholars in America:

"For behold, I shall speak unto the Jews and they shall write it; and I shall also speak unto the Nephites and they shall write it; and I shall also speak unto the other tribes of the house of Israel, which I have led away, and they shall write it. . . . And it shall come to pass that the Jews shall have the words of the Nephites, and the Nephites shall have the words of the Jews; and the Nephites and the Jews shall have the words OF THE LOST TRIBES OF ISRAEL. . . . And it shall come to pass that my people, which are of the house of Israel, shall be gathered home unto the lands of their possessions; and my word also shall be gathered in one."[95]

THE BATTLE OF ARMAGEDDON

Ezekiel knew that at a certain point following the return of the Jews to Palestine, and after they had built up the land and its cities, there would be a monumental military conflict which would precede the manifestation of the Messiah unto them.[96]

Ezekiel said a great conquering host would come out of the north. He identified them as a massive military coali-

---

93. Ezekiel 37:16-17
94. Doc. & Cov. 27:5
95. 2 Nephi 29:12-14
96. That the Jews would meet their Messiah immediately after this time is referred to in Ezekiel 39:22-29. Zechariah describes it in detail. See Zechariah 12:9-10.

tion of the people of Magog, Tubal and Meshech.[97] These are three of the sons of Japheth, father of the Gentiles,[98] whose descendants became the principal settlers of Europe and Asia. Their leader is identified by Ezekiel as "Gog," who is the dictatorial commander-general or "chief prince" over all these hosts.[99]

The Lord said this army would come over the land "like a cloud"[100] and that it would be an unprovoked assault against defenseless cities.[101] There would be savage fighting "throughout all my mountains," the Lord said.[102]

These Events as Seen by the Prophet Joel

It is at this point that we digress long enough to examine the writings of Joel. His entire vision pertained to this period of terrible warfare and struggle just prior to the manifestation of the Messiah.[103] We do not have any certain way of determining exactly when Joel wrote, but it is believed to have been long before this, probably in the eighth or ninth century B.C.[104]

The first two chapters of Joel have great significance for people living in an age of atomic warfare and mechanized cavalry. He describes what the war against Judah will be like and the modern reader may well be astonished at some of the details. He says seeds will not grow in the ground,[105] the land will be completely defoliated, ". . . for the fire hath devoured the pastures of the wilderness, and the flame hath burned all the trees of the field. The beasts of the field cry also unto thee: for the rivers of waters are dried up, and the fire hath devoured the pastures of the wilderness."[106]

Joel describes a great war-like people who use fire as a weapon of desolation. He says, "there hath not been ever

---

97. Ezekiel 38:2
98. Genesis 10:2
99. Ezekiel 39:1
100. Ezekiel 38:9
101. Ezekiel 38:10-11
102. Ezekiel 38:21
103. Joel 1:15; 2:1
104. See Sperry, *The Old Testament Prophets*, p. 265, for a discussion of the dating of Joel.
105. Joel 1:17
106. Joel 1:19-20

the like, neither shall be any more after it. . . . A fire devoureth before them; and behind them a flame burneth: the land
is as the garden of Eden before them, and behind them a
desolate wilderness; yea, and nothing shall escape them."[107]

Joel tried to describe what he saw: "The appearance
of them is as the appearance of horses; and as horsemen, so
shall they run."[108] But these were like no other horses he
had ever seen. Notice this bold attempt to describe the strange
mobile units which he saw: "Like the noise of chariots [not
horses] on the tops of mountains shall they leap, like the
noise of a flame of fire that devoureth the stubble . . . they
shall run like mighty men [once again the simile changes];
they shall climb the wall like men of war; and they shall
march every one on his ways, and they shall not break their
ranks: Neither shall one thrust another; they shall walk every
one in his path: and when they fall upon the sword, they
shall not be wounded. They shall run to and fro in the city;
they shall run upon the wall, they shall climb up upon the
houses; and they shall enter in at the windows like a thief.
The earth shall quake before them; the heavens shall tremble."[109] It sounds very much as though he were attempting to
describe a modern armored division rumbling across a city
with cannon and flame-throwers spreading destruction all
around.

Joel recommended that when the people of Judah see this
great Gentile juggernaut sweeping toward them they should
go into fasting and prayer, for without God's help they will
never survive. He cried, "rend your heart, and not your
garments, and turn unto the Lord your God. . . . Blow the
trumpet in Zion, sanctify a fast, call a solemn assembly:
gather the people, sanctify the congregation . . . let them
say, Spare thy people, O Lord, and give not thine heritage
to reproach. . . . Then will the Lord be jealous for his land,
and pity his people. Yea, the Lord will answer and say . . . I
will remove far off from you the northern army. . . ."[110]

Ezekiel was also told that in this hour of distress the
Lord would manifest His power. The Lord said divine judgments would issue forth for a considerable period of time to

---

107. Joel 2:2-3
108. Joel 2:4

109. Joel 2:5-10
110. Joel 2:13-20

keep His people from being immediately conquered. It was indicated that among these judgments there would be earthquake,[111] pestilence,[112] great hailstones,[113] and eventually a sweeping manifestation of fire and brimstone.[114]

Before treating the fiery destruction of Gog and his hosts, however, we should mention that John the Revelator was shown a vision of this great war, particularly as it came to its climax at Jerusalem. He said the hosts of the Gentiles would get to the outer court of the new temple and there would be continuous assault upon the city for $3\frac{1}{2}$ years.[115] The Lord told Zechariah, who wrote a generation after Ezekiel (520 B.C.), that at this critical moment half of Jerusalem would fall: "For I will gather all nations against Jerusalem to battle; and the city shall be taken, and the houses rifled, and the women ravished; and half of the city shall go forth into captivity, and the residue of the people shall not be cut off from the city [in other words, they will continue fighting]."[116]

During the $3\frac{1}{2}$ years of violent warfare John was told that two ordained servants of God would be prophesying to the Jews and helping to resist the assault of the Gentiles.[117] They would be given miraculous powers to shut the heavens against rain, to turn water to blood, to smite the earth with plagues and command consuming fire to destroy their enemies until the $3\frac{1}{2}$ years were completed.[118] John said that at the end of their prophesying, Gog and his hosts would succeed in killing these two prophets,[119] this apparently being at the time they took half the city captive. He said the bodies of the two men would lie in the streets $3\frac{1}{2}$ days and then a voice would call to them from the heavens and they would rise up as resurrected, exalted beings, whereupon they would ascend to Heaven in the sight of Gog and all his forces.[120] Then a great earthquake would rumble through these mountains and a tenth of the city would fall.[121]

This is probably the same earthquake as the one described by Zechariah who saw the Lord appear on the Mount

---

111. Ezekiel 38:19-20
112. Ezekiel 38:22
113. Ibid.
114. Ibid., also Ezekiel 39:6
115. Rev. 11:2
116. Zechariah 14:2

117. Rev. 11:2-3
118. Rev. 11:5-6
119. Rev. 11:7
120. Rev. 11:11-12
121. Rev. 11:13

of Olives. He saw that immediately afterwards the mountain would split in twain, forming a great valley through which the beleaguered people of Jerusalem could flee.[122] At the same time he said there would be a massive destruction of Gog and his forces. This destruction would be achieved in a great measure by the fiery plague which Ezekiel had said would destroy all but one sixth of the Gentile hosts.[123] And Joel said the remnant sixth would flee to the "east sea" to escape.[124] Zechariah described the fiery annihilation of the other five-sixths of the army: "Their flesh shall consume away while they stand upon their feet, and their eyes shall consume away in their holes, and their tongue shall consume away in their mouth."[125] (Shades of Hiroshima!)

Meanwhile, Zechariah had previously seen what would be happening to the Jews who had escaped. They would joyfully gather around their Messiah for whom they had waited so long and rejoice in the glory of His presence. Then an exciting thing would happen. "And one shall say unto him, What are these wounds in thine hands? Then he shall answer, Those with which I was wounded in the house of my friends."[126] What a traumatic impact that will have on these suffering refugees of Judah who suddenly realize that their ancient ancestors did indeed crucify the great Jehovah when He was manifest among them in the flesh! ". . . and they shall look upon me whom they have pierced, and they shall mourn for him, as one mourneth for his only son, and shall be in bitterness for him. . . . In that day shall there be a great mourning in Jerusalem."[127]

But after that there will be rejoicing. At last the people of Judah and the Saints of the Lord in America will see "eye to eye" [Isaiah 52:8]. The people of Judah will go

---

122. Zechariah 14:4-5
123. Ezekiel 39:2
124. Joel 2:20
125. Zechariah 14:12. An eye-witness of the Hiroshima bomb came across a group of Japanese soldiers who had been exposed during the explosion and later said, "their faces were wholly burned, their eye-sockets were hollow, the fluid from their melted eyes had run down their cheeks. . . Their mouths were mere swollen, pus-covered wounds, which they could not bear to stretch enough to admit the spout of the teapot [from which they were trying to drink some water]." (John Hersey, *Hiroshima,* Bantam Books, 1959, p. 67)
126. Zechariah 13:6
127. Zechariah 12:10-11

forth to cleanse the land and repair the great destruction which will have resulted from the war. Ezekiel was told the Jews will need seven months before the bodies and bones of all the dead can be buried.[128] The removal and burning of all the weapons and debris left by the war will require seven years.[129]

The greatest blessing of all will be the fact that now, at last, their great Messiah will be a reality among them. His great temple which they will have built years before and which they will have preserved during the battle of Armageddon, will now become the Lord's true sanctuary. The Lord told Ezekiel, "So the house of Israel shall know that I am the Lord their God from that day and forward. . . . Neither will I hide my face any more from them. . . . "[130]

Ezekiel closes his writings by describing the great temple which will be the glory of Jerusalem in these days. We therefore turn to this final segment of Ezekiel's revelations.

THE BUILDING OF A MODERN TEMPLE IN JERUSALEM

Because the latter-day gathering of Judah will take place prior to the time of their conversion, it was essential that the Lord place in the custody of one of their ancient prophets the complete architectural specifications for their temple, which was to be built prior to the manifestation of the Messiah unto them. This honor and responsibility fell to Ezekiel.

To fulfill this mission of recording the technical information necessary for such a structure, Ezekiel was taken in vision to Jerusalem.[131] There he saw the structure the way it would apear when it was completed and embellished. He saw the courts, the porches, the annexes, and the sacred precincts for the occupation of the Priests. He was allowed to walk through the rooms of the temple, through the courtyards and all the related area, measuring and recording every important dimension as he went. This was done with such careful consideration for detail that modern architects have been able to sketch the dimensions of the temple which the Jews will soon be in a position to build. In these last chap-

128. Ezekiel 39:11-14
129. Ezekiel 39:9
130. Ezekiel 39:22, 29
131. Ezekiel 40:1-2

ters of Ezekiel the Lord has given the Jews everything they need to go forward and build their temple when the time is right. There are also sufficient instructions so that the Sons of Levi can then begin offering unto the Lord an offering in righteousness.

The dimensions and specifications given for the modern temple of Jerusalem are identical with those used in the temple of Solomon. However, there are numerous details in Ezekiel's writings which fill in many parts of the descriptive data which are missing from the available data on Solomon's temple. This is why Ezekiel's writings are so important now that the Jews are nearing the time when their temple can be built.

Chapters 40 to 42 of Ezekiel contain most of the descriptive information referred to above. Chapters 43 and 44 describe the ordinances and procedures in the temple. Chapter 45 deals with the division of the land among the priests, the people and the prince who will rule over them. Chapter 46 is primarily addressed to the ruling prince and the procedures he is to follow. Chapter 47 describes the borders of Israel as they will exist when the kingdom is finally established. Chapter 48 describes the districts of inheritance for the various tribes and the beauty of the gates of Jerusalem. This is where the book ends.

So, after a period of some 22 years, the writings of Ezekiel come to a close. There is no doubt but what he was one of the major prophets of the Lord no matter how we measure him. He modestly left out nearly every scrap of biographical data on his own life except as it related to his revelations. We therefore do not know what association he may have had with Daniel in nearby Babylon, nor of his relations with any of the other inspired men of God who were his contemporaries. Nor do we know how he died, or whether he left any posterity. All that he left is his book, but that is a treasure.

Now we turn to the amazing career of a man whom the Lord said he especially loved. This is Ezekiel's fellow-prophet in exile, Daniel.

Scripture Reading and Questions on Chapter Twenty-Six

Scripture Reading: The Book of Ezekiel and the Book of Joel.

1—What type of "slaves" did the Babylonians take from Judah in 598 B.C.? About how old was Ezekiel when this happened?

2—What did Ezekiel see in his first great vision? Was it easy for him to describe? What does this vision tell us about the "image" of God?

3—What did the eyes and wings in the four animals represent? How do we know this?

4—When Ezekiel first went forth to preach, what happened to him? What did the Lord do about it?

5—What visual aids did the Lord use in further preparing Ezekiel for his ministry?

6—In one revelation the Lord mentioned Noah, Daniel and Job. What does this imply concerning Daniel as of this time?

7—What do we learn from the opening portion of the Book of Job with reference to the contest between Satan and Jehovah?

8—On what important date did Ezekiel's wife die? Why did the Lord tell him not to mourn?

9—Did the Lord want His people to mourn over the loss of Jerusalem? What was the reason?

10—Why do you think Ezekiel was extremely careful to date each of his revelations? Did any of the other prophets do this?

11—Briefly describe what both ancient and modern prophets have said about the raising up of a certain "David" in the Last Days.

12—Describe the resurrection scene set forth in one of Ezekiel's visions. What did this represent besides the resurrection?

13—What is a "stick"? What did the Lord decribe as "The stick of Ephraim"?

14—What other record must come forth before the joining of the two sticks will be complete?

15—Under what peculiar circumstances will the great Battle of Armageddon take place? How long will it last? Who will win?

16—When Joel was shown the combatants in modern warfare, did he have difficulty describing some of them? What do some of his prophecies appear to be representing?

17—What did Joel tell the Jewish people to do when they were besieged by Gog and Magog? Will they have any prophets among them at that time?

18—How long will the final siege of Jerusalem last? Will any of the city be conquered? What will rescue the people?

19—Will the Jews be told who their Messiah is when He first appears among them? What will be their reaction?

20—Could the Jews build a temple in Jerusalem at the present time? Do they have enough revealed specifications?

CHAPTER TWENTY-SEVEN

The Prophet Daniel —
Counselor to Kings

We now come to one of the best-loved but nevertheless amazing biographies in the Old Testament.

Daniel was the second principal prophet during the Exile. He was the "prophet in the palace," while his fellow-laborer, Ezekiel, was a "prophet among the people." In the biography of Daniel we discover the remarkable career of a talented and spiritual son of Judah who left Jerusalem as a young hostage and lived to become a principal government official, first in the king of Babylon and later in the kingdom of Persia.

Daniel arrived in Babylon eight years before the migration of the 10,000 Exiles who came in 598 B.C. This was because he was selected while still a youth to be a personal protege of King Nebuchadnezzar. Bible story books usually describe Daniel as merely a child when he was first brought to Babylon, but we now have reason to believe he was probably in his late teens and already a very promising young man to be tutored under the king's own patronage.[1] Here is the story:

---

1. The text calls them "children" (Daniel 4:1) but Dr. Clarke points out that *yeladim* means "youths" or "young men" and should be so translated throughout the first chapter of Daniel instead of "children." (See Clarke, *Bible Commentary*, Vol. 4, p. 565)

It was in the year 606 B.C.,[2] while Nebuchadnezzar was still acting as co-regent with his father and serving as general of the Babylonian army, that he pushed Egypt back sufficiently far to place Judah under tribute. During this operation he took a few of the vessels from the temple as a token of conquest.[3] He also decided to take a small body of hostages. This was how it happened that Ashpenaz, governor of the king's palace, was told to select a number of young Jews who could be trained in the language and courtly ways of the Babylonians.[4] Among others, the steward selected Daniel, Hananiah, Mishael, and Azariah, all of whom were given new names: Belteshazzar to Daniel; Shadrach to Hananiah; Meshach to Mishael; and Abed-nego to Azariah.[5] The king said they were to be nourished and trained for three years and then brought before him for examination.

After being taken to Babylon the four young Jews frightened the wits out of their custodial officer by refusing to eat or drink the rich rations furnished to them on orders of the king. This officer had already gained a great affection for young Daniel,[6] but when this sudden stubborn streak appeared he frankly told the young Jews that if they persisted in this reluctant attitude, "then shall ye make me endanger my head to the king!"[7] Daniel did not wish to appear stubborn. He simply asked that they be fed wholesome vegetables or the kind of "pulse" to which they were accustomed. He said the steward could judge for himself after a ten-day trial whether or not this was better for them than the king's fine wines and rich foods. The test was conducted and sure enough it proved to be a tremendous success. The steward agreed that if Daniel and his friends continued looking as healthy and robust as they did at the end of the test, then there would be no reason for him to be criticized or punished.

During the three years of training prescribed for these four Jewish youths they demonstrated phenomenal capacities, aptitudes and skills. When they were brought before the king in 603 B.C., Nebuchadnezzar personally examined

---

2. Daniel 1:1 identifies the date as the third year of Jehoiakim, king of Judah, who began his reign in 609 B.C.
3. Daniel 1:2
4. Daniel 1:3-4
5. Daniel 1:7

6. Daniel 1:10
7. Ibid.

them and was astonished. He found them far superior in factual knowledge, wit and wisdom to his magicians and astrologers.[8] Nebuchadnezzar therefore assigned these four young men to be counted among his "wise men."[9] This was supposed to be the highest possible compliment, but the next thing the young Jews knew, their apparent good fortune was about to cost them their lives.

The Lord Saves Daniel and His Associates from Execution

The scripture says that "in the second year of the reign of Nebuchadnezzar . . . [he] dreamed dreams."[10] Since his father had died in 604 B.C., and Nebuchadnezzar had ascended the throne that year, this incident we are about to relate would have occurred in 602 B.C., just a year or so after the Jewish young men had graduated into "wise men."

It would seem from the Bible account that Nebuchadnezzar was troubled by some sort of nightmare which he could not remember after he had awakened. He called in the astrologers, sorcerers, and wise men, but they told him they obviously could not interpret the king's dream until he told them what it was. He challenged them to conjure up the dream for him, and when they could not, he was so enraged that he sentenced all of them to execution. So the scripture says, "And the decree went forth that the wise men should be slain; AND THEY SOUGHT DANIEL AND FELLOWS TO BE SLAIN."[11]

When the captain of the guard came to arrest the young Jews Daniel asked him what was charged against them. Apparently he was completely unaware of what had happened. As soon as Daniel learned the reason for the king's wrath he hurried in before Nebuchadnezzar and petitioned the king to delay the execution until Daniel could ask the Lord about it.

It is interesting that Daniel took this action exclusively on faith. The scripture says, "Then Daniel went to his house, and made the thing known to Hananiah, Mishael, and Azar-

---

8. Daniel 1:20
9. This becomes apparent from the fact that they were lumped with the other wise men in the later execution decree (Daniel 2:13).
10. Daniel 2:1   11. Daniel 2:13

iah, his companions."[12] All four of them immediately began praying to the Lord in the greatest anxiety hoping He would hear their plea. In due time Daniel had the thrilling experience of crossing the threshhold of the spirit. Suddenly he was shown both the king's dream and also its meaning. The Bible student cannot read Daniel's psalm of animated praise and thanksgiving which followed without sensing the profound depth of relief and the exalted jubilation which was produced by this marvelous revelation.

Once he had the information, Daniel hurried to the captain of the guard and said: "Destroy not the wise men of Babylon: bring me in before the king, and I will show unto the king the interpretation!"[13]

Daniel Reveals the Highlights of the Future History of the World

As he was brought before the king, Daniel's opening speech is a classic expression of humble self-confidence, well worth repeating. Said he, "The secret which the king hath demanded cannot the wise men, the astrologers, the magicians, the soothsayers, show unto the king; but there is a God in heaven that revealeth secrets, and maketh known to the king Nebuchadnezzar what shall be in the latter days. Thy dream, and the visions of thy head upon thy bed, are these . . . thy thoughts came into thy mind . . . what should come to pass hereafter . . . [so now] he that revealeth secrets maketh known unto thee what shall come to pass. But as for me, this secret is not revealed to me for any wisdom that I have more than . . . [other people] but for their sakes [the condemned men, including the four young Jews]. . . . Thou, O king, sawest, and beheld a great image. This great image, whose brightness was excellent, stood before thee; and the form thereof was terrible. This image's head was of fine gold, his breast and his arms of silver, his belly and his thighs of brass, his legs of iron, his feet part of iron and part of clay. Thou sawest till that a stone was cut out without hands, which smote the image upon his feet that were of iron and clay, and brake them to pieces. Then was the iron, the clay, the brass, the silver, and the gold, broken to pieces together,

---

12. Daniel 2:17
13. Daniel 2:24

and became like the chaff of the summer threshing-floors; and the wind carried them away . . . and the stone that smote the image became a great mountain, and filled the whole earth."[14]

From the king's subsequent behavior it would appear that as Daniel spoke, the memory of his troublesome night vision returned to him, and he knew for a certainty that Daniel was imbued with a most marvelous and miraculous power. Daniel proceeded immediately to interpret the dream. He told the king the head of gold was his own kingdom, magnificent and glorious in all its dimensions. He said the silver breast and arms represented a second kingdom, the belly and thighs of brass a third kingdom, and the iron legs a fourth kingdom which would disintegrate into many kingdoms represented by the feet and toes of iron and clay. But in the "latter days"[15] — in the days when all these rulers of the splintered kingdoms should prevail — then "shall the God of heaven set up a kingdom, which shall never be destroyed: and the kingdom shall not be left to other people, but it shall break in pieces and consume all these kingdoms, and it shall stand for ever."[16]

So that was it! As Nebuchadnezzar heard this swift, incisive interpretation of what he had dreamed, he was overwhelmed with amazement. Without any compunction whatever, he came down from his magnificent throne and fell to his knees before the young foreigner. Said he, "of a truth it is, that your God is a God of gods, and a Lord of kings, and a revealer of secrets, seeing thou couldest reveal this secret."[17] And he commanded his attendants to offer Daniel an oblation and sprinkle his hair and clothes with sweet perfume.[18] At this time or shortly thereafter Nebuchadnezzar ordered that Daniel should be given extravagant gifts and he appointed him ruler over the city of Babylon and the surrounding district. He also placed him in charge of the so-called "wise men" of Babylon whose lives he had saved.[19]

---

14. Daniel 2:27-35
15. Daniel 2:28
16. Daniel 2:44
17. Daniel 2:47
18. Daniel 2:46
19. The fact that this honor came to Daniel and his associates just four years after their arrival in Babylon clearly proves they were mature youths and not "children" when they first came.

Once again, Daniel displayed his great faith. With such an overwhelming responsibility, he did not plead his incapacity because of youthfulness or inexperience. He once more relied upon God to give him sufficient wisdom to administer these complicated affairs with the zeal of Joseph in Egypt. In fact, he wisely asked the king to let his three young Jewish associates perform the actual management duties while he "sat in the gate of the king."[20] This was where the king rendered judgments each day and therefore this last phrase is interpreted to mean that henceforth Daniel served as "the confident and counsellor of the king."[21]

HISTORICAL ACCURACY OF NEBUCHADNEZZAR'S DREAM

For many centuries scholars tried to force the meaning of this dream so that it would seem to be fulfilled in the meridian of time with the first coming of Christ.[22] They thought the stone was the setting up of God's kingdom by the Savior and the Apostles. Had this been the true intent of the prophecy then the previous kingdoms would have to be accounted for in the events of earlier centuries. What they overlooked was Daniel's statement that this vision pertained to the things God would do in the "latter days." He was referring to the occasion when God would establish His great kingdom for the last time, never again to be uprooted, and when it would gradually move out across the earth to eventually replace every government on the face of the earth with a divinely inspired theocracy.[23] This will not be achieved until the Millennial reign but the foundation for it is being established right now. In fact, at our present stage of history, the entire prophetic implication of Nebuchadnezzar's dream is in the final phase of its fulfillment. Like all prophecy it has been fulfilled literally so far, and will continue to be fulfilled literally as it unfolds. For example, consider the following suggested application of the dream as interpreted by Daniel:

---

20. Daniel 2:49
21. Clarke, *Bible Commentary*, Vol. 4, p. 571
22. Dr. Adam Clarke stumbled into this unfortunate error in his commentary (Vol. 4, pp. 574-577), and his labored attempts to justify it only demonstrate its manifest fallacy.
23. See Hyrum Andrus: *Joseph Smith and World Government*, Salt Lake City: Deseret Book Co., 1958.

THE HEAD OF GOLD: The Babylonian Empire, 605-539 B.C.

THE SILVER BUST: The Persian Empire, 539-331 B.C.

THE BELLY OF BRASS: The Macedonian-Greek Empire, 331-161 B.C.

THE LEGS OF IRON: The Roman Empire, 161 B.C. to 395 A.D., then it was divided into the Eastern Roman Empire (with a capital at Constantinople) and the Western Roman Empire (with a capital at Rome). The Eastern Empire came to an end in 1453 with its conquest by the Ottoman Turks. It subsequently disintegrated into many independent countries. The Western Roman Empire tried to delay its disintegration by launching the Holy Roman Empire which may be dated with the crowning of Charlemagne in 800 A.D. or, as some prefer, with the crowning of Otto I as emperor by the Pope in 962 A.D. In either event, the attempt failed, and what fragments of power remained were abandoned by the last holder of the title, Francis II of Austria, in 1806.

THE FEET AND TOES OF IRON AND CLAY: Since the days of the Roman Empire no attempt to unite all nations has succeeded though many ambitious rulers have attempted it. This remains true today. The process is toward fragmentation and the setting up of numerous independent nations. Daniel later saw a temporary but fierce dictator of many nations rise up to smash God's adherents, but that too, will pass.

THE STONE CUT WITHOUT HANDS: This represents the restored Kingdom of God in 1830 which is presently flourishing. It is laying the foundation for a Millennial world-wide theocracy. The Lord specifically identified it as the "stone" of Nebuchadnezzar's dream when He made the following statement in a modern revelation: "The keys of the kingdom of God are committed unto man on the earth, and from thence shall the gospel roll forth unto the ends of the earth, AS THE STONE WHICH IS CUT OUT OF THE MOUNTAIN WITHOUT HANDS SHALL ROLL FORTH, UNTIL IT HAS FILLED THE WHOLE EARTH." (Doc. and Cov. 65:2.)

DANIEL SERVES NEBUCHADNEZZAR AS A LEADING GOVERNMENT OFFICIAL

Nebuchadnezzar had his famous dream in 602 B.C.[24] Therefore, when the first Exiles arrived in Babylon from Judea in 598 B.C., Daniel and his three Jewish companions

---

24. This was the second year of his reign (Daniel 2:1).

already had been administering the capital district of Babylon for four years. This may account for the rather liberal treatment the Exiles received. Even though Babylon probably had the largest brick-making factories in the ancient world,[25] we have no indication that the 10,000 Jewish Exiles were ever employed in them as they had been when they were slaves in Egypt. Archaeologists have discovered clay records from a Jewish firm set up in Babylon about this time indicating that some of the Exiles were allowed to establish business operations and carry them out on an extensive scale.[26] This particular firm endured for 150 years so its founders did not return to Jerusalem when the opportunity came. Business was just too good!

It will be recalled that after Nebuchadnezzar conquered Jerusalem in 598 B.C. he appointed Zedekiah king and returned home thinking peace would now prevail in that troubled land. When we consider the prominent positions of Daniel and his friends in Babylon, it can be seen that the Lord had everything beautifully arranged for a fair and generous treatment of the vassal kingdom of Judah if Zedekiah and his counselors had just possessed the good sense to listen to God's inspired prophets. How Daniel must have prayed that the foolish Zedekiah would listen to the words of Jeremiah as that prophet paraded the streets of Jerusalem with a yoke about his neck, crying, "Be ye subject to Nebuchadnezzar and live!" But Zedekiah behaved himself like the wild ass in the wilderness referred to by Jeremiah."[27] He went braying off toward Egypt, and the second devastating siege of Jerusalem soon followed.

In 587 B.C. a forlorn fragment of Exiles came straggling in from a completely subjugated Judah. They had come to the precincts of Babylon for assignment to the various provinces as servants of the State. By this time Daniel was in his early thirties and undoubtedly the supreme pride of the various Jewish colonies already in Exile. It must have been obvious to Daniel and others who saw them that these bedraggled refugees had eaten indeed the bitter figs seen by Jeremiah!

---

25. Werner Keller, *The Bible As History*, p. 294.
26. Ibid., p. 295
27. Jeremiah 2:24

TRIAL BY FIRE

The next incident we wish to relate did not involve Daniel personally but it was a life-and-death crisis for his three good friends, Shadrach, Meshach and Abed-nego. Nebuchadnezzar, like most ancient monarchs was accustomed to having his commands obeyed without the slightest hesitation and he was quick to mete out death sentences to any who resisted his edicts. To achieve complete religious unity in Babylon, Nebuchadnezzar and his officers erected a huge gold-plated image 90 feet in height[28] and placed it in the center of the great plain of Dura near Babylon where all could come and worship it.

The dedication of this image was a major affair of state. All the dignitaries of the kingdom were called in. These, of course, would include the three Jewish administrators of the Babylon district. When they were all assembled, a herald cried aloud, "To you it is commanded, O people, nations, and languages, that at what time ye hear the sound of the cornet, flute, harp, sackbut, psaltery, dulcimer, and all kinds of musick, ye fall down and worship the golden image that Nebuchadnezzar the king hath set up: AND WHOSO FALLETH NOT DOWN AND WORSHIPPETH SHALL THE SAME HOUR BE CAST INTO THE MIDST OF A BURNING FIERY FURNACE."[29]

It was not at all unusual for monarchs to seek to impose national religious unity on the people by techniques such as this and usually, if the facts were known, the whole scheme was engineered by some cadre of ambitious heathen priests seeking to elevate their own station in life. In any event, the inevitable happened. When the music began to play and all the people grovelled in the dust moaning and chanting their devotion to this brick and metal monstrosity, the three Jewish administrators stood perfectly erect.

Then certain "Chaldeans" — meaning they were from Nebuchadnezzar's party — accused the Jews of committing a capital crime. The three men were dragged before the king and accused to their faces of deliberately violating a sacred

---

28. Daniel 3:1
29. Daniel 3:4-6

edict of the king. It was one of those moments when men have to choose between violation of conscience and death. The minds of these men were already made up. In fact, they were probably made up before they ever went to the dedication. The profound faith of Shadrach, Meshach and Abednego is caught in the following statement:

"If it be so [that you decide to cast us into the fiery furnace], our God whom we serve is able to deliver us . . . and he will deliver us out of thine hand, O king. BUT IF NOT [if the Lord does not elect to save us], BE IT KNOWN UNTO THEE, O KING, THAT WE WILL NOT SERVE THY GODS, NOR WORSHIP THE GOLD IMAGE WHICH THOU HAST SET UP."[30]

The violent reaction of the king to this courageous declaration was exactly what one might have expected under the circumstances. The scripture says, "Then was Nebuchadnezzar full of fury, and the form of his visage was changed against Shadrach, Meshach, and Abed-nego: therefore he spake, and commanded that they should heat the furnace one seven times more than it was wont to be heated."[31]

Where Daniel was all of this time we are not told. Undoubtedly he was close at hand and either lacked the power to stop the tragic proceedings or had been told by the Lord not to interfere.

So the decree was carried out. The three Jews were bound tightly in their robes[32] and thrown into the furnace. Whoever had charge of fueling the furnace had taken the king's order literally. The roaring conflagration had created such an intense heat that when the "mighty men" hauled the hapless Jews to its entrance the blast of furious flames leaped out and burned them alive the instant they had tossed their human burdens through the furnace door.[33]

Nebuchadnezzar was right on hand and even though a number of his own veterans from the ranks of the army had been killed carrying out his order, at least he had the satisfaction of being avenged on these obstinant Jews. But unexpectedly something happened. The Bible says:

30. Daniel 3:17-18   32. Daniel 3:21
31. Daniel 3:19   33. Daniel 3:22

"Then Nebuchadnezzar the king was astonished, and rose up in haste, and spake, and said unto his counsellers, Did not we cast three men bound into the midst of the fire? They answered and said unto the king, True, O king. He answered and said, Lo, I see four men loose, walking in the midst of the fire, and they have no hurt; and the form of the fourth is like the Son of God. Then Nebuchadnezzar came near to the mouth of the burning fiery furnace, and spake, and said, Shadrach, Meshach and Abed-nego, ye servants of the most high God, come forth, and come hither. Then Shadrach, Meshach and Abed-nego, came forth of the midst of the fire. And the princes, governors, and captains, and the king's counsellers, being gathered together, saw these men, upon whose bodies the fire had no power, nor was an hair of their head singed, neither were their coats changed, nor the smell of fire had passed on them. Then Nebuchadnezzar spake, and said, Blessed be the God of Shadrach, Meshach, and Abed-nego, who hath sent his angel, and delivered his servants that trusted in him, and have changed the king's word [revoked their sentence of death by burning], and yielded their bodies, that they might not serve nor worship any god, except their own God . . . there is no other God that can deliver after this sort!"[34]

So this story had an exceedingly happy ending. And the three faithful Jews were all restored to their high administrative posts in the district of Babylon.[35]

THE END OF NEBUCHADNEZZAR'S DYNASTY

Nebuchadnezzar is best remembered in secular history as the flamboyant and fabulous builder of mighty Babylon. Its extravagant and magnificent hanging gardens became one of the seven wonders of the ancient world. He was also a shrewd strategist and commanding general in the field of battle. He pushed the boundaries of his empire westward until they included the conquest of all of Egypt in 572 B.C. However, the life of Nebuchadnezzar finally came to a close in 562 B.C., and he was replaced by his son, Amil-Marduk (Evil-Merodach of the Bible). It was he who allowed the

---

34. Daniel 3:24-29
35. Daniel 3:30

former boy-king of Judah (Jehoiachin, who was now around 37) to come out of his imprisonment and enjoy the freedom enjoyed by other Jews.[36]

After a reign of only two years, Evil-Merodach was killed in 560 B.C. by his ambitious brother-in-law, Neriglissor. This former army officer in Nebuchadnezzar's army had married the king's daughter sometime earlier and now he murdered his son. Neriglissor ruled until 556 B.C., when he died and was replaced by his young son, Labashi-Marduk. This unfortunate boy lasted only nine months when he was assassinated and one of the conspirators took over the throne. His name was Nabonidus and he ruled Babylon until its fall in 539 B.C.

All of these political upheavals were probably witnessed by Daniel since he was a prominent personality at the king's great Babylonian palace. If we had his full biography it would undoubtedly disclose many exciting chapters during this period. Unfortunately, these details are missing from his writings and the story of his life does not continue until the reign of Nabonidus was well on its course. At this point we come to an important contribution to the Bible which has been made by modern archaeology.

Who Was the King That Went Insane?

In the fourth chapter of Daniel we read that the king of Babylon had a dream in which he saw a beautiful tree that represented the king himself. He saw that it was hewn down until only a stump was left. The Bible says the stump was given the heart of a beast instead of a man and it was left with the dew falling upon it amid the tender grass of the open field. The king asked Daniel to interpret the dream for him but when Daniel was told by the Lord what it meant he was deeply troubled in his heart and it was a full hour before he could bring himself to tell the king what it represented.[37] Finally he said the tree symbolized the king and that he would be cut down from his pinnacle of power for a time. Daniel told the king he would lose his mind for seven years; he would become like a beast of the field eating grass as an ox

36. Jeremiah 52:31   37. Daniel 4:19

and sleeping in the open where the dew would fall upon him. Nevertheless, Daniel said the stump represented the fact that during his mental illness the kingdom would be preserved unto him. Daniel said to the king, "Wherefore, O king, let my counsel be acceptable unto thee, and break off thy sins by righteousness, and thine iniquities by showing mercy to the poor; if it may be a lengthening of thy tranquility."[38]

But the king failed to do so and 12 months later he became insane.[39] Not until 7 years later did his reason return.

In our modern Bible, all of this is attributed to Nebuchadnezzar, but historians were puzzled because these facts do not fit into the known records concerning Nebuchadnezzar's life. What they do fit, however, is the life history of King Nabonidus. He was the last king of Babylon, and scholars have discovered that he was absent from the throne for a period of seven years while his son, Belshazzar, the crown prince (but sometimes called "king") served in his stead. One of the Dead Sea scroll fragments completely supports the proposition that it was Nabonidus and not Nebuchadnezzar who went insane. Scholars assume that the more famous name of Nebuchadnezzar was deliberately inserted in the fourth chapter of Daniel in place of Nabonidus by some ancient scribe.

The Dead Sea scroll fragment contains a testimonial by King Nabonidus which says, "The words of the prayer which Nabonidus (*Nbny*), king of Assyria and king of Babylon, the great king spoke when he was smitten with a severe inflammation by the command of the Most High God in the city of Teiman (error for Tema): I was smitten for seven years and I was put far from men. But when I confessed my trespasses and sins he left me a seer. HE WAS A JEW FROM THE EXILES OF BABYLONIA. He gave his explanation and wrote that honor should be given and glory to the name of the Most High God."[40]

This would seem to completely sustain the conclusion that chapter 4 in the Book of Daniel is talking about Naboni-

---

38. Daniel 4:27
39. Daniel 4:28-33
40. Quoted by Kraeling, in Rand McNally *Bible Atlas*, p. 325

dus and this would explain why his son, Belshazzar, had to rule in his stead for seven years.

This conclusion fits in appropriately with the fact that the very next chapter of Daniel deals with the famous Belshazzar incident. However, before telling of that fateful night which ended the Babylonian Empire, let us mention two visions which Daniel received during the reign of Belshazzar.

THE VISION OF THE FOUR BEASTS AND THE GREAT CONFERENCE AT ADAM-ONDI-AHMAN

One of the most ingenious ways of describing future political kingdoms in prophecy is to have them represented in the vision by various animals. This is what the Lord did for Daniel in the first years of Belshazzar's reign (while he was regent during his father's 7-year illness). In Daniel, chapter 7, we learn that this prophet was shown a lion (Babylon), a bear (Persia), and Leopard (Greece) and a "diverse" beast with iron teeth (Rome). Out of the last beast grew ten horns representing the fragmentation of Rome into many separate nations[41] just like the ten toes of the image in Nebuchadnezzar's dream. Then the scripture says that Daniel saw the Ancient of Days (Adam)[42] with millions of people surrounding him. The Son of God came to this great conference and received back from Adam the keys of dominions over the kingdoms of the earth which Adam had been given in the early ages of human history.[43] Joseph Fielding Smith explains the significance of this great conference:

"Joseph, the Prophet, in speaking of this event, said: 'Daniel in his seventh chapter speaks of the Ancient of Days; he means the oldest man, our father Adam, Michael; he will call his children together and hold a council with them TO PREPARE THEM FOR THE COMING OF THE SON OF MAN. He (Adam) is the father of the human family, and presides over the spirits of all men, and all that have had the keys must stand before him in this grand council. . . .'[44]

---

41. Daniel 7:24
42. Doc. His. of the Church, Vol. 3, pp. 386-387; Vol. 4, pp. 207-209
43. Daniel 7:13-14
44. Doc. His. of the Church, Vol. 3, pp. 386-387

"It was in the night vision that all this was shown to Daniel, and he saw the Son of Man come to the grand council, as he did to the first grand council in the valley of Adam-ondi-Ahman, and there he received the keys from Adam 'and there was given him dominion, and glory, and a kingdom, that all people, nations, and languages, should serve him: his dominion is an everlasting dominion, which shall not pass away, and his kingdom that which shall not be destroyed.'[45] In this council Christ will take over the reigns of government, officially, on this earth, and 'the kingdom and dominion, and the greatness of the kingdom under the whole heaven, shall be given to the people of the Saints of the most High, whose kingdom is an everlasting kingdom, and all dominions shall serve and obey him,'[46] even Jesus Christ.

"This council in the valley of Adam-ondi-Ahman is to be of the greatest importance to this world. At that time there will be a transfer of authority from the usurper and impostor, Lucifer, to the rightful King, Jesus Christ. Judgment will be set and all who have held keys will make their reports and deliver their stewardships, as they shall be required. Adam will direct this judgment, and then he will make his report, as the one holding the keys for this earth, to his superior officer, Jesus Christ. Our Lord will then assume the reigns of government; directions will be given to the Priesthood; and he, whose right it is to rule, will be installed officially by the voice of the Priesthood there assembled. This grand council of Priesthood will be composed, not only of those who are faithful who now dwell on this earth, but also of the prophets and apostles of old, who have had directing authority. Others may also be there, but if so they will be there by appointment, for this is to be an official council called to attend to the most momentous matters concerning the destiny of this earth.

"When this gathering is held, THE WORLD WILL NOT KNOW OF IT; THE MEMBERS OF THE CHURCH AT LARGE WILL NOT KNOW OF IT, yet it shall be preparatory to the coming in the clouds of glory of our Savior Jesus Christ as the Prophet Joseph said. The world cannot know of it. The Saints cannot know of it —

---

45. Daniel 7:13-14   46. Daniel 7:27

except those who officially shall be called into this council —
for it shall precede the coming of Jesus Christ as a thief in
the night, unbeknown to all the world.''[47]

Daniel was told that there would be a great persecution
of the Saints right up to the time of this conference.[48] However, Daniel was told that the conference at Adam-ondi-
Ahman would mark the ending of that persecution and the
Saints would thereafter serve as stewards of the Lord in
preparing a righteous government for the whole earth.[49]

Later, Daniel saw a vision in the third year of Belshazzar portraying a ram and a he-goat. The ram represented
the Medes and Persians,[50] while the he-goat represented
Greece.[51] He was told precisely what would (and did!)
happen to those two empires. Then he saw "in the latter
time"[52] a person with a fierce countenance whom the scripture describes as follows:

"And through his policy also he shall cause craft to
prosper in his hand; and he shall magnify himself in his heart,
and BY PEACE SHALL DESTROY MANY."[53]

In these latter days we have had a number of ingeniously
evil men who have risen up in the earth proclaiming peace
while preparing for devastating war.

Now, back to Belshazzar.

THE FEAST OF BELSHAZZAR AND THE FALL OF BABYLON

Belshazzar, it turns out, was the son of Nabonidus and
not the son of Nebuchadnezzar in Daniel 5:2. Therefore
the same scribe who mutilated chapter 4 by inserting Nebuchadnezzar for Nabonidus, must have done the same in chapter 5.

Belshazzar held a feast for 1,000 of his lords and it was
during this festive occasion that the ghostly spectre of a

---

47. Joseph Fiedling Smith, *The Way to Perfection*, chapter 40
48. Daniel 7:21-22   51. Daniel 8:21
49. Daniel 7:27   52. Daniel 8:23
50. Daniel 8:20   53. Daniel 8:25

human hand was seen writing on the wall: Mene, Mene,
Tekel Upharsin.[54] The king was badly frightened and when
none of the king's wise men could interpret what it meant the
queen suggested that the king send for the famous Daniel.
Belshazzar was not acquainted with Daniel except by reputation, but that was enough to persuade him to do as the
queen suggested. Belshazzar, who was crown prince acting
as regent or second in command during his father's mental
illness, offered Daniel great rewards and the office of "third
ruler in the kingdom" (i.e. immediately under Belshazzar),
if he would interpret the meaning of the words. Daniel rejected all rewards but told Belshazzar he would interpret the
writing. The meaning was given as follows:

MENE: God hath numbered thy kingdom and finished
it.

TEKEL: Thou art weighed in the balance and found
wanting.

PERES: Their kingdom is divided, and given to the
Medes and Persians. ("Upharsin")

Obviously, Daniel took much more out of these words
than they meant by themselves. In other words, they were
couched in a sort of celestial code with a secret meaning for
which Daniel was given the necessary key. If anyone had
any doubt as to its authenticity, he had only a short time
to wait. Belshazzar was murdered that very night[55] by two
of his lords[56] and Cyrus was within their walls with all his
hosts before the sun was up!

KING CYRUS — A PAGAN IN PROPHECY

As we have previously pointed out, the prophet Isaiah
knew that the conqueror of Babylon would be Cyrus. The
opening portion of chapter 45 is specifically addressed to him

---

54. Daniel 5:25. The alternative for the last word is PERES.
55. Daniel 5:30
56. According to the Greek general and historian, Zenophon, Belshazzar was killed
by two lords, Gadatas and Gobrias, because of wrongs allegedly committed
against them. (See Clarke, *Bible Commentary*, Vol. 4, p. 588)

and was written nearly 150 years before Cyrus came to power.[57]

Daniel 5:31 gives Darius credit for overthrowing Babylon, but this was probably erroneously added to chapter 5 by a scribe who knew that Darius had overthrown a later resurgency of Babylon when she tried to get her independence two or three decades later. However, Isaiah was speaking of the original conqueror of Babylon in 539 B.C., and that was Cyrus.

Cyrus was a remarkable personality just as Isaiah had predicted he would be. His father was Cambyses, king of Persia who ruled from 600 to 559 B.C. However, Persia was then a vassal state of the Medes, and as so often happened in those days the king of the Medes (named Astyages) gave his daughter in marriage to Cambyses, the young king of Persia. Cyrus was born of this marriage. There had been an earlier Cyrus so he is referred to as Cyrus II. In 550 B.C. he went up and conquered his grandfather's kingdom of Media, his victory being facilitated by the Medes, who made Astyages a prisoner and allowed Cyrus to take over with very little bloodshed. Cyrus then rumbled across the northern region of the old Assyrian empire and entered Asia Minor where he conquered the Lydian kingdom in 546 B.C., and also brought the Greek colonies along the coast into the Persian Empire. He returned to his home base in Persia greatly strengthened and by 539 B.C. was prepared to conquer Nabonidus, king of Babylon, as well as his son and co-regent, Belshazzar.

According to the Chronicle of Nabonidus, that king was out of circulation from the eleventh to the seventeenth year of his reign.[55] However, he returned just in time to meet Cyrus in battle in 539 B.C. Nabonidus was defeated at Opis that year but managed to escape and was later made a governor of one of the provinces under Cyrus.

---

57. The Lord said of him: "Thus saith the Lord to his anointed, to Cyrus, whose right hand I have holden, to subdue nations before him; and I will loose the loins of kings, to open before him the two leaved gates; and the gates shall not be shut. . . . For Jacob my servant's sake, and Israel mine elect, I have even called thee by thy name: I have surnamed thee, though thou hast not not known me." (Isaiah 45:1, 4)

58. This fits perfectly with the 7 years of insanity mentioned in Daniel 4:33.

Meanwhile Cyrus prepared to enter the great city of Babylon. It will be recalled that this was achieved by digging a huge trench around the city and then diverting the river through the canal during the night so that his army could march through the regular channel which went under the massive city walls. With Belshazzar freshly murdered by his own people, there was little resistance and Cyrus was able to enter the city and restore order almost immediately.[59] Most of the desolation of Babylon which Isaiah had seen in vision came in the following decades under other rulers.

As we shall see in the next chapter, Cyrus displayed a spirit of warm tolerance toward the Jews. He issued an edict authorizing those who wished to do so, to return to Jerusalem and rebuild the temple. To encourage the project, he gave the Jewish leaders 5,400 gold and silver vessels which had been taken from the temple. These no doubt came from the raids of 506[60] and 598 B.C.[61] since the vessels taken in 587 B.C. were apparently melted down.[62]

THE MINISTRY OF DANIEL IN HIS LATTER DAYS

When Cyrus issued his edict to the Jews about 538 B.C., Daniel did not return to Jerusalem but continued his ministry among the remaining Exiles where the future still held many exciting experiences in store for him.

It was in the third year of the reign of Cyrus that Daniel received the vision recorded in chapter 10. By this time he had probably been removed to the Persian capital of Susa or Shushan. The vision mentioned in this chapter is the occasion when Daniel fasted and prayed for three weeks before he received the heavenly visitation he needed.

Now, to appreciate the principal events in this latter part of Daniel's life, we should mention that Cyrus died in 529 B.C. He was killed while fighting the Scythian tribes on his northern frontier. The Persian throne then passed to his son Cambyses II who re-conquered Egypt in 525 B.C. but died before he could return in 522 B.C.

---

59. The Babylonian Chronicles fix the date as October 29, 539 B.C. (Kraeling, in Rand McNally *Bible Atlas,* p. 328)
60. Daniel 1:2
61. 2 Chronicles 36:7
62. 2 Kings 25:15

As soon as word reached Babylon that Cambyses was dead, a pagan priest, named Gaumata, rose up pretending to be Smerdis, the younger son of Cyrus and the brother of Cambyses. Actually, Smerdis had long since been secretly executed by Cambyses, so the pretender was not exposed for seven months. Then a distant cousin of Cyrus, named Darius, succeeded in killing the false Smerdis (Gaumata) and laid claim to the throne himself. By 519 B.C. he had become Darius I of Persia and was fully entrenched in power. This is Darius the Great, who ruled until 486 B.C. He was the man under whom Daniel spent the latter part of his life.

Darius Issues a Decree Which Almost Gets Daniel Killed

When Darius first set up his new administration there was more than the usual amount of intrigue in the air. The recent death of Cambyses followed by seven months of deceit by the priest Gaumata, had left a train of distrust and dark suspicion in its wake. During this time of perilous crisis Daniel received the supreme compliment of being placed in a top position of responsibility. The scripture says:

"It pleased Darius to set over the kingdom an hundred and twenty princes, which should be over the whole kingdom; And over these three presidents; of whom Daniel was first: that the princes might give account unto them, and the king should have no damage. Then this Daniel was preferred above the presidents and princes, because an excellent spirit was in him; and the king thought to set him over the whole realm."[63]

As one might suspect, the native princes of the kingdom developed a jealous hatred of this Jew whom Darius had so highly honored, and they attempted to find fault with him. But Daniel was not only highly spiritual in nature, but also a practical man of affairs. He gave them no excuse to accuse him. They therefore conspired to entrap him. The amazing extent of this conspiracy is demonstrated by the statement that it included Daniel's two associate presidents, all of the governors, the princes, the counselors and military captains

---

63. Daniel 6:1-3

of the whole kingdom.[64] They induced Darius to issue a decree that no one but Darius could make a prayer or petition to any god for thirty days.[65] It was well known that Daniel had private prayers three times a day and even though Daniel knew of the decree he continued his usual practice. This was exactly what the Babylonian officials hoped he would do so it was easy to bring charges against him and have him arrested. King Darius was greatly grieved when he discovered how Daniel had been ensnared by the devious machinations of these men, particularly since the penalty for violating the decree had been written right into the statute and required that Daniel be thrown into a den of lions. The king argued with his whole regal court until sundown trying to save Daniel, but they were not to be cheated of their prey. The Lords of Babylon reminded the king that under Persian law, no royal decree could be altered. If so, the king would forfeit his throne.[66]

Now a rather astonishing thing happened. In his desperate state of mind Darius decided to depend on the power of Daniel's God to save him. He had heard that Jehovah was a God of powerful miracles and so he came to the place where Daniel was in custody and said, "Thy God whom thou servest continually, he will deliver thee."[67] This bold statement was made by Darius as a matter of hope rather than certainty. An abject fear chilled him to the marrow of his soul as he watched the soldiers lead Daniel away to be delivered to the lions. The scripture says the king hastened to his palace and immediately went into a state of "fasting" and stayed awake all night apparently imploring the God of Daniel to save his servant's life.

Meanwhile Daniel had suffered a chilling and traumatic experience of his own. What would it be like to be thrown into a menagerie of deliberately starved, half-mad lions? If one has watched a number of these huge flesh-eating beasts mangle and tear apart the carcass of an antelope or zebra they have slain, he will have some idea of the nightmare that awaited Daniel as his guards held him above the pit ready to cast him in. By this time Daniel was an extremely old

64. Daniel 6:7
65. Ibid.
66. Daniel 6:15
67. Daniel 6:16

man. Even the rough handling involved in throwing him into the lion's den could have had serious consequences. But the guards as well as Daniel must have been amazed at what happened. Not only did the beasts fail to tear the prophet apart but they apparently went meekly about as though he were one of them. It would appear that not until Daniel had gone through the shock of being thrown bodily among the beasts did he know for certain whether the Lord had answered his desperate plea for help. It would be impossible to measure the feelings of this man of God as he sat there watching these man-eating beasts throughout the night.

As soon as the early dawn light would permit it, Darius rushed to the lion pit to see what had happened to the faithful servant of Jehovah. When Darius found Daniel was still alive, his joy knew no bounds. In fact, he expressed his relief and happiness by ordering his soldiers to seize Daniel's accusers and throw them to the lions. The Bible says, "and the lions had mastery of them, and brake all their bones in pieces or ever [even before] they came at the bottom of the den."[68]

Darius issued another decree that in all the kingdom of Babylon the God of Daniel should be respected. This did not mean Darius was a convert to Jehovah. He just wanted the pagan pan-theism of many gods to make room for another deity. The record closes by saying, "So this Daniel prospered in the reign of Darius. . . ."[69]

THE LAST RECORDED VISION OF DANIEL

It was in this first year of the reign of Darius that Daniel learned from the study of the Book of Jeremiah that the Lord had fixed the date of the Jews' return as 70 years.[70] Since the first contingent of immigrants which returned under the edict of Cyrus had not been able to start the temple, Daniel now prayed mightily that the Lord would lift the curse of desolation from Jerusalem and bless the people in redeeming their ruined city.

Daniel was visited by Gabriel — whom we now know was Noah[71] — the same angelic personage who later an-

---

68. Daniel 6:24
69. Daniel 6:28

70. Daniel 9:1-2
71. Doc. His. of the Church, Vol. 3, p. 386

nounced the birth of John the Baptist[72] and Jesus.[73] He told Daniel that the city would be redeemed[74] and survive until the ministry of the Savior,[75] following which it would be desolated again and remain in that forlorn condition until the great day of the Lord's power.[76] Just as Lehi was told the exact year when Jesus would be born,[77] so Daniel was told the number of years until the time of His ministry.[78] It is interesting that Daniel says the new covenant would be confirmed unto many by the Savior for seven years.[79] This would seem to include the ministry of John the Baptist. Since Jesus taught 3½ years, this would leave 3½ years for the ministry of John, making a total of seven.

It was this same year that Daniel received the visions recorded in chapters 11 and 12. In the latter chapter he saw the universal resurrection. Actually, the series of resurrections which will bring forth the just will be spread over the whole length of the Millenium, but the wicked will have to wait until the last.[80] Summarily speaking, the overall effect will be as Daniel described it: "And many of them that sleep in the dust of the earth shall awake, some to everlasting life, and some to shame and everlasting contempt."[81]

At the very close of Daniel's divine manifestations the visions came faster than he could comprehend them. Therefore he says, "And I heard, but I understood not: then said I, O my Lord, what shall be the end of these things?"[82] The heavenly messenger was not the Lord, but an angel[83] and he said to Daniel, "Go thy way, Daniel [don't be concerned about it]: for the words are closed up and sealed till the time of the end. . . . But go thou thy way till the end be; for thou shalt rest, and stand in thy lot at the end of the days."[84]

This concludes the known history and writings of one of the most impressive and spectacular personalities in the Old Testament scripture.

72. Luke 1:13-20
73. Luke 1:26-38
74. Daniel 9:24
75. Daniel 9:24-27
76. Daniel 9:27
77. I Nephi 10:4
78. Daniel 9:24. Unfortunately the text appears to have been tampered with. For an interesting analysis and possible solution to this problem see Duane Crowther's, *Prophets and Prophecies of the Old Testament*, Salt Lake City: Deseret Book Co., 1966, pp. 515-516.
79. Daniel 9:27. "Weeks" in this Chapter are equated with years. See Verse 24.

80. Doc. & Cov. 88:97-101
81. Daniel 12:2
82. Daniel 12:8
83. Daniel 12:7
84. Daniel 12:9, 13

Scripture Reading and Questions on Chapter Twenty-Seven

Scripture Reading: The Book of Daniel.

1—How did Daniel happen to be taken to Babylon before the conquest of Jerusalem? Does he appear to have been a child or a 'teenager'?

2—What were the names of Daniel's three friends who went with him? Did any others go?

3—When the four young Jews had been trained for three years, how did they compare with other intellectuals in Babylon? Where did the king assign them?

4—Relate the circumstances of Nebuchadnezzar's dream.

5—Give the interpretation of Nebuchadnezzar's dream. How has it been fulfilled thus far?

6—Describe how Daniel's three friends came to be sentenced to death by burning. What happened?

7—Who was the king of Babylon who went insane? What leads us to believe this?

8—What will be the circumstances when the great Priesthood conference is called at Adam-ondi-Ahman? Will all the Priesthood attend?

9—Who will be given the keys at Adam-ondi-Ahman to rule and reign over the whole earth?

10—What happened at the Feast of Belshazzar? What did the words mean?

11—Describe the fall of Babylon. What happened to Belshazzar?

12—What kind of a personality was Cyrus? Why do you think the Lord mentioned him in prophecy 150 years before he came to power?

13—What did Darius do for Daniel that made the other Persian officials jealous? How did they ensnare Daniel?

14—Describe the details of Daniel's experience when he was thrown to the lions. What did Darius do afterwards?

15—Why did Daniel seek a special blessing from the Lord for Jerusalem about this time?

16—Who brought Daniel the answer? Do we know the name of this person when he lived on earth? To what other people did he later appear as an angel?

17—Did Daniel know about the resurrection? Who did he say would be resurrected?

18—At the very close of Daniel's ministry something happened to which he objected. What was his problem?

19—What was Daniel told? Was it by the Lord or an angel?

20—Give your impression of Daniel the prophet.

CHAPTER TWENTY-EIGHT

The Rebuilding of Jerusalem

Cyrus, the Persian king who conquered Babylon, issued a proclamation almost immediately after he came to power which was strange indeed for a pagan monarch. It was dated 538 B.C. Said he:

"Thus saith Cyrus king of Persia, The Lord God of heaven hath given me all the kingdoms of the earth; and he hath charged me to build him an house at Jerusalem, which is in Judah. Who is there among you of all his people? his God be with him, and let him go up to Jerusalem, which is in Judah, and build the house of the Lord God of Israel, (he is the God), which is in Jerusalem."[1]

At first glance it would almost seem as though Cyrus had become a convert to Jehovah, the God of Abraham, Isaac and Jacob. But such was not the case. We know Cyrus was honoring heathen deities with equal fervor about this same time. But at least he was honest about it — honest enough to include the true God Jehovah, along with whatever others he had been taught to accept. It was a typical pagan approach to pan-theism.

The king invited Jews from all regions to contribute to the temple fund and also to the financial support of the temple

---

1. Ezra 1:2-3

builders.[2] Cyrus, himself, brought forth 5,400 vessels of gold and silver which were captured during the earlier conquests of Judah, and turned them over to the Jewish leaders in charge of the expedition to Jerusalem.[3] He also ordered that the expenses for the restoration of the temple should be paid out of the king's personal account.[4]

The temporal leader of the Jewish people at this time was a man named Zerubbabel[5] (meaning "born in Babylon"), but he is referred to on at least two occasions as Sheshbazzar,[6] so it is assumed that this latter designation is his Persian name.[7] Zerubbabel was a direct descendant of David, being the grandson of Jehoiachin, the former boy-king who came out of Jerusalem with the first captives in 598 B.C. He became known as "Governor of Judah"[8] but remained a vassal of Persia, of course, so he never achieved the title of "king" of Judah. Zerubbabel is a name to be remembered since he was the last person of any prominence in Old Testament history who was a descendant of the illustrious David. After Zerubbabel the Davidic line drifts down into complete obscurity and remains there until the birth of the Savior.

The spiritual leader of the Jewish Exiles at this time was their High Priest, Joshua, grandson of the High Priest Seraiah, whom Nebuchadnezzar had executed at Riblah when Jerusalem fell.[9]

Ezra, chapter 2, describes the great throng of approximately 50,000[10] Jews who made the long trek back to Jerusalem under the edict of Cyrus. Of the twenty-four Aaronic Priesthood "courses" which David had set up, only four had representatives, but these totalled over 4,000.[11] By way of contrast, we discover that the Levites which greatly outnumbered the Priests in earlier times, now sent back only 74 men who could prove they were Levites from their genealogical records. There was another large group who claimed this right but the scripture says: "These sought their register among those that were reckoned by genealogy, but they

2. Ezra 1:4
3. Ezra 1:11; 5:14
4. Ezra 6:4
5. Ezra 2:2
6. Ezra 1:11; 5:14
7. That the two names belong to the same man may be deducted from Ezra 5:16.
8. Haggai 1:1
9. I Chronicles 6:14; 2 Kings 25:18
10. Ezra 2:64-65
11. Ezra 2:36-39

were not found: therefore were they [considered], as polluted, PUT FROM THE PRIESTHOOD. And the Tirshatha [governor] said unto them, that they should not eat of the most holy things, till there stood up a priest with Urim and with Thummim [to verify their true lineage]."[12] Unfortunately, the Urim and Thummim, like the Ark of the Covenant, were never heard of again following the destruction of Jerusalem, so these unfortunate claimants to the right of ordination apparently remained outside the pale of the Priesthood. And the Levitical Priesthood from this point on remained in constant competition with the Aaronic Priesthood (Priests) because of their comparatively few numbers.

The returning Exiles had with them 736 horses, 235 mules, 435 camels, 6,720 asses.[13] No doubt the aged and sick were carried on some of these animals, but the majority would be forced to walk since the remaining animals would be required for baggage. The caravan had to make its way up along the west side of the Euphrates river and then cross the desert portion of the Fertile Crescent toward Hamath or Damascus. The pilgrims then made their slow, tedious way down toward the mountains of Judah. Authorities estimate from various sources that such a trek probably took four months.[14]

The scripture is clear that this band of immigrants was not rich but neither was it poor. It went back with a considerable treasure collected as donations for the temple.[15] They also had the great spiritual treasure of their sacred scriptures, although the ravages of persecution and idolatry had already destroyed many of the most precious writings of the past.

As we have briefly mentioned earlier, they also took back with them a great quantity of vessels, chargers, knives, basins, tankards, salvers, cups, fire pans, dishes, spoons, and so forth, which belonged to the temple. All of these were made of gold and silver and were rescued from the king's treasury by Cyrus, himself. Originally, they had been seized

12. Ezra 2:62-63
13. Ezra 2:66-67
14. Geikie, *Hours With the Bible*, Vol. 6, p. 415. This was the exact time consumed by Ezra and his party. (Ezra 7:9)
15. Ezra 2:68-69

by Nebuchadnezzar in his raids on the temple in 606 and 509 B.C.[16] Cyrus ordered that they all be turned over to the custody of Zerubbabel (Sheshbazzar) for use in the new temple.[17] Altogether there were 5,400 of these gold and silver utensils![18]

RETURN TO THE "PROMISED LAND"

What the pilgrims found when they returned to Judah was anything but inspiring. Perhaps only a few were old enough to remember the glories of Jerusalem before the Babylonians practically levelled this once proud capital of Judah to the ground. Since that had been done after the Exiles were removed from the area it must have been especially shocking to these elderly people to come upon the scene of the former citadel of David and the sanctuary of the Lord, and see them both lying in desolated ruins. The great high walls which protected the city were all pulled down and the former homes of the people lay strewn about in heaps of fire-gutted rubble.

What had once been a rather substantial territory belonging to the tribe of Judah had been whittled down to a sliver. The Edomites who helped the Babylonians destroy Jerusalem had seized Hebron and all of Judah down to the Philistine Plain. There were other heathen or mixed nationalities crowding around them in every direction. The Jews therefore found themselves restricted to Jerusalem and a small region immediately adjacent to it which they secured through the good offices of Cyrus. The district went only as far down as Bethlehem (7 miles south) and as far up as the northern borders of Benjamin (7 miles north). It would be nearly a century before the pilgrims would successfully recover a significant part of their lost heritage.

However, once Zerubbabel and his 50,000 "Zionists" had returned to their ancient capital, it was the signal for many other Jewish colonies to pull up roots and join them. There were also the remnants of the peasantry who had been left by Nebuchadnezzar to dress the vineyards and farm

---

16. Ezra 6:5. Note that the vessels seized in 587 B.C. were apparently melted down (Jeremiah 52:19).
17. Ezra 1:11   18. Ibid.

the land. From all of these sources, the Jewish population once more began to congeal into the substance of a nation. But it was not a return to glory. It was merely the existence of a remnant which was sufficiently cohesive to give visible evidence of a national entity. Never again would this nation of Jews be independent during the Old Testament epic other than for a brief interval during the Maccabean revolt. They would remain permanent vassals to each of the great powers as they came along — Persia, Greece, Syria and Rome. Then their national light would be extinguished, never to shine again until almost 1900 years later. The prophets had written all about it.

THE FIRST STEP IS TAKEN IN REBUILDING THE TEMPLE

Meanwhile, however, their prophets had written about the immediate requirement to rebuild the temple. The future would have to take care of itself. So Zerubbabel called a great conference within a few weeks after their arrival. Even though they did not have a temple, they could at least offer sacrifices and keep the feasts in proper order. Therefore, the temple block was cleared of the mountains of wreckage which had been stacked upon it and an altar was built exactly where its predecessor had stood.[19] It must have been a glorious occasion as these returning exiles stood on the sacred ground of the ancient sanctuary and offered up their oblations to the Lord. It was also the season for the Feast of the Tabernacles, so the people celebrated that great festival.[20] Of course, the foundation of the temple was not yet laid,[21] so that was the next thing to commence.

The preparations alone involved strenuous effort and great expenditures of what little wealth they possessed. The scripture says, "They gave money also unto the masons, and to the carpenters; and meat, and drink, and oil, unto them of Zidon, and to them of Tyre, to bring cedar trees from Lebanon to the sea of Joppa, according to the grant that they had of Cyrus king of Persia."[22]

It was not until the second month of the year that they were prepared to commence the laying of the foundation for

---

19. Ezra 3:2-3
20. Ezra 3:4

21. Ezra 3:6
22. Ezra 3:7

the second temple.[23] The new stones were squared and ready, and the old stones had been recut where necessary; the shiploads of cedars had arrived and were turned into beams and boards; the debris had been removed from the temple site. All was ready. The laying of the first stone was accompanied by as much pageantry as the leaders could provide under the circumstances. They used both orchestra and choirs, and all of the people concluded the ceremony with a great shout.[24]

For the older people, however, the memories of the ancient temple and the sadness of its destruction caused greater sorrow than the prospect of the new one. So while some of the people were shouting for joy, others were weeping.[25] It was quite an occasion.

Zerubbabel Is Offered Help from the Heathens

As soon as the surrounding tribes, towns and cities heard that the Jews were actually about to commence the rebuilding of the famous temple of Solomon, they did a peculiar thing. They set aside their former hostilities and came marching up to Zerubbabel with an astonishing proposition. Said they, "Let us build with you: for we seek your God, as ye do; and we do sacrifice unto him since the days of Esarhaddon king of Assur, which brought us up higher."[26]

All of this was most embarrassing to the governor of Judah. There was probably nothing he would have liked better than to take some conciliatory step which would reduce the tensions between the Jews and their neighbors. But they had offered him one of the few things he could not accept. It may be recalled that these were the people from Samaria and other nearby Gentile settlements who worshipped Jehovah one moment and heathen deities the next. They were hybrid Israelites, partly by intermarriage with the remnant of the various tribes of Israel, and partly by giving token devotion to the God of Israel while remaining practicing pagans. They were about the most mixed-up people in the Persian empire. Zerubbabel knew that if he allowed them to help build the temple they would insist upon offering their unclean sacrifices which would immediately pollute the new temple.

23. Ezra 3:8
24. Ezra 3:11

25. Ezra 3:12-13
26. Ezra 4:2

He therefore decided to deal with the problem immediately rather than later. He turned his heathen neighbors down.[27] As one would have expected, they never forgave him for it. The scripture says:

"Then the people of the land weakened the hands of the people of Judah, and troubled them in building. And hired counselors against them, to frustrate their purpose, all the days of Cyrus king of Persia, even until the reign of Darius king of Persia."[28]

This campaign was effective. It took the whole momentum out of the temple-building project. Hostile skirmishes by night and day plus political pressures from unsympathetic officers of the king soon had Zerubbabel preoccupied with survival rather than temple-building. Cyrus was deeply involved in continuous warfare himself, and therefore not available for the emergency support which was so badly needed. In fact, as we have pointed out earlier, he was killed while fighting the Scythians in 529 B.C., and his son, Cambyses II continued these military campaigns until his death in 522 B.C. This was followed by the hoax king, it will be recalled, who rose up pretending he was Cambyses' brother. It was only after seven months that he was finally exposed and killed. The Persian hero of that episode was Darius, a true, though distant relative of Cyrus and Cambyses.

During such a hectic period of continuous warfare and palace intrigue it is understandable why Zerubbabel received no particular help from the ruling monarchs of Persia. With Darius, however, things began to change. Daniel and two other new prophets (Haggai and Zechariah) helped to bring about a change.

It seems that Daniel was reading the book of scripture left by Jeremiah and he noted that the land of Jerusalem was to be redeemed after 70 years.[29] This promise was made right after the first captivity in 598 B.C.[30] so Daniel decided the time was up. During the first year of the reign of Darius (522 B.C.) Daniel undertook to obtain a commitment from the Lord. He prayed, "Now therefore, O our God, hear the

---

27. Ezra 4:3
28. Ezra 4:4-5

29. Daniel 9:2
30. Jeremiah 29:1, 10

prayer of thy servant, and his supplications, and cause thy face to shine upon thy sanctuary that is desolate . . . defer not, for thine own sake, O my God: for thy city and thy people are called by thy name."[31]

It was Gabriel (or Noah), as pointed out in the last chapter, who answered this petition and assured Daniel that the time indicated by Jeremiah was correct,[32] and that the promises of the Lord would all be fulfilled. At almost exactly the same time Daniel was receiving this revelation in Babylon, the Lord was raising up two inspired prophets in Jerusalem. The first was Haggai.

THE PROPHET HAGGAI

All we know of this inspired man is that he was called, "the prophet unto Zerubabbel."[33] In the second year of King Darius, Haggai received five dated revelations which are compiled together in two chapters of scripture comprising all that we have of the Book of Haggai.

On the first day of the sixth month of that year (around September 1, 520 B.C.), Haggai was told that the people were erroneously preaching to one another that this was no longer the time to consider building the temple.[34] The Lord said He was fully aware that they were discouraged by poor crops and drouth, but He said the reason for all this hardship was their failure to step forward and rebuild the temple.[35] They were told that if they went to work on this project again they would most assuredly be blessed.[36]

Three weeks later,[37] the people had repented sufficiently to rally around Zerubbabel and Joshua again. The temple project was being reactivated. The Lord encouraged them, saying, "I am with you."[38]

During the next month the Lord revealed that the glory of this "latter house" could be greater than the original tem-

---

31. Daniel 9:17-19
32. Daniel 9:24
33. Haggai 1:1
34. Haggai 1:2
35. Haggai 1:3-6, 9-11
36. Haggai 1:7-8
37. Haggai 1:15
38. Haggai 1:13

ple of Solomon.[39] That, of course, depended upon how valiant the people proved themselves to be.

Two months later, the Lord told Haggai that the people must continually realize that the building of a temple is a very special blessing afforded only to the righteous. Offerings from those who are unclean will not be acceptable.[40] This verified what Zerubbabel had told his heathen neighbors. By this time the hard-working people had finished the foundation;[41] therefore the Lord said that if they would continue to persevere, He would bless them abundantly.[42]

Another revelation was directed to Zerubbabel which told him to take courage, for the Lord had chosen him.[43]

We next learn that the Lord had chosen another prophet to work with Haggai.

THE PROPHET ZECHARIAH

Zechariah, who labored alongside Haggai during these same years, was the son of Berechiah, the son of Iddo, the prophet.[44]

Zechariah prophesied in the second[45] and fourth years[46] of King Darius and saw a comprehensive history of future events, though the writings which he left us are much more brief than those recorded by Isaiah, Jeremiah and Ezekiel. In a single night Zechariah had eight visions which are set forth in his first six chapters.

The first vision was to assure the Saints of Judah that the Lord was mindful of them and fully intended to restore the land and the people to a stronger position.[47]

The second vision was to assure them that their enemies would be punished.[48]

The third vision concerned the day of the Lord's power when He would come and dwell in Jerusalem.[49]

---

39. Haggai 2:9. Wickedness and rebellion prevented this from being realized.
40. Haggai 2:11-14
41. Haggai 2:18
42. Haggai 2:18-19
43. Haggai 2:23
44. Zechariah 1:1; Ezra 5:1; 6:14
45. Zechariah 1:1
46. Zechariah 7:1
47. Zechariah 1:8-17
48. Zechariah 1:18-21
49. Zechariah 2:1-12

The fourth vision compared the High Priest, Joshua, of Zechariah's day, with Prince David who would build and sanctify the temple of Jerusalem in the latter-days.[50]

The fifth vision assures Zerubbabel that he will yet finish the temple[51] and makes reference to the two prophets whom God will raise up to Judah in the last days, just before the Battle of Armageddon.[52]

The sixth vision showed a huge scroll whereon the names were written of those who had committed crimes and should be punished.[53]

The seventh vision was symbolic of the abundance of sin which would be attributed to Shinar or Babylon.[54]

The eighth vision was like the fourth, in that it compared Joshua, the High Priest of that day with the Priest and king of the last days who would be called the Branch (believed to be Prince David) and who would build the latter-day temple, rule from his throne and establish peace among the people.[55]

All the remainder of Zechariah's writings pointed toward the distant future. He left two notable prophecies concerning the coming of the Savior in the meridian of time. He spoke of the king of Israel coming, "riding upon an ass, and upon a colt the foal of an ass."[56] There is also the prophecy concerning the betrayal of the Lord for thirty pieces of silver.[57]

In an earlier chapter we have already treated the last vision received by Zechariah which relates to the Battle of Armageddon and the coming of the Savior to Jerusalem in the great day of the Lord's power.

THE FINAL ATTEMPT TO DISRUPT THE BUILDING OF THE TEMPLE

The sudden burst of energy by the Jewish people in reviving their temple-building project after many years of neglect soon attracted the attention of their old enemies. The

50. Zechariah 3:1-10
51. Zechariah 4:5-10
52. Zechariah 4:1-14; Revelations 11:4
53. Zechariah 5:1-4

54. Zechariah 4:5-11
55. Zechariah 6:1-15
56. Zechariah 9:9; Matthew 21:1-9
57. Zechariah 11:12-13

next thing Zerubbabel knew the Persian governor or satrap of all Syro-Palestine was calling on him.[58] He challenged the authority of Zerubbabel to use all these resources and man-power to construct this temple. He wanted to know just who was involved in this nefarious business.[59] When Zerubbabel claimed they had authority direct from King Cyrus, the Persian governor decided to clear the matter with headquarters. He wrote a rather elaborate letter setting forth the situation and concluded by saying, "Now therefore, if it seem good to the king, let there be search made in the king's treasure house, which is there at Babylon, whether it be so, that a decree was made of Cyrus the king to build this house of God at Jerusalem, and let the king send his pleasure to us concerning this matter."[60]

This letter apparently stirred up a hornet's nest at the hub of the empire. No such edict could be found in Babylon, but it was located in a royal palace clear up in one of the provinces of the Medes. This indicates that an exhaustive search was conducted. Persian kings took the greatest pride in honoring to the tiniest jot and tittle every regal decree. But it turned out that this particular decree by King Cyrus had not been honored. It had been lost and forgotten. Therefore Darius was determined to make up for it. He wrote back to the governor of Syro-Palestine stating that the edict was found and in it Persia had made the following positive commitments to the Jews: authority had been granted to build the temple; it was to be built well, with its stones "strongly laid"; the cost of the building was to come from the treasuries of Persia (the edict had said, "LET THE EXPENSES BE GIVEN OUT OF THE KING'S HOUSE");[61] all vessels taken by Nebuchadnezzar from the old temple were to be returned.

Motivated no doubt by a passion to maintain the honor of Persia, Darius wrote to his governor general and those in Palestine who had brought up this whole ugly issue, saying, "Let the work of this house of God alone; let the governor of the Jews and the elders of the Jews build this house of God in his place. Moreover I make a decree what ye shall do

---

58. Ezra 5:3
59. Ezra 5:9-10
60. Ezra 5:17
61. Ezra 6:4

to the elders of these Jews for the building of this house of God: THAT OF THE KING'S GOODS, EVEN OF THE TRIBUTE BEYOND THE RIVER [Euphrates], FORTHWITH EXPENCES BE GIVEN UNTO THESE MEN, THAT THEY BE NOT HINDERED. And that which they have need of, both young bullocks, and rams, and lambs, for the burnt offerings of the God of heaven, wheat, salt, wine, and oil, according to the appointment of the priests which are at Jerusalem, let it be given them day by day without fail: That they may offer sacrifices of sweet savours unto the God of heaven, AND PRAY FOR THE LIFE OF THE KING, and of his sons."[62]

Darius ended on a rather ominous note, saying that any man or woman who failed to carry out this decree would have a scaffold built from the boards of his own home and then be hanged thereon![63]

As soon as the governor of Syro-Palestine received this letter his puckish ears picked up the signal immediately. This Jewish project was nothing for a politician to be fooling around with. The scripture says he rallied his officers around him and whatever King Darius had told them to do, "so they did speedily."[64] Thinking about that scaffold was enough to give a man a crimp in the neck.

THE TEMPLE IS COMPLETED

As for the temple project, the whole political climate changed immediately. Opposition disappeared. The people went to work with new zeal. Stockpiles of supplies came pouring in. The thought must have occurred to Zerubbabel more than once that there is nothing like having the exchequer of the Persian empire to draw from and the backing of a life-and-death potentate like Darius to lean upon when a person is trying to complete a major building project.

The scripture says that by the sixth year of Darius (516 B.C.), after a lapse of only four years, this great structure was completed. The temple of Solomon took longer but most of the time was consumed in the creative artistry of its elab-

62. Ezra 6:7-10
63. Ezra 6:11
64. Ezra 6:13

orate decorations and embellishments which the temple of Zerubbabel did not have. We have no description of this temple, but it no doubt followed the basic pattern of its predecessor just as Herod's temple did. There was a huge square enclosing the temple block and the wall consisted of three courses of hewn stone, capped with planed cedar beams.[65]

However, not only did this temple lack embellishments, it lacked the testimony of God's covenant — the Ark. The Holy of Holies was empty and the only object of sacred significance was the outcropping of natural rock where the fire of the Lord had consumed David's sacrifice, and other events had occurred which made it a most venerated spot. Today, the famous Moslem mosque called "The Dome of the Rock" protects this sacred place. In addition to all of the other important events which transpired here, the Moslem faith believes this is the rock from which Mohammed was taken into heaven.

In connection with the temple there was a palace or castle built in the north-west precincts of the temple block. This became the residence of the governor and, when necessary, the headquarters for a military post.[66] It is thought that this was the same building as that which was known during the Roman domination as the Fortress Antonia.[67]

We are not told when Zerubbabel's temple was actually dedicated, but no doubt he made it just as magnificent and beautiful as the circumstances and talents of the people would allow. The completion of this second temple marked a great historical milestone for the Jews. Not only did it stand as a mark of important material achievement, but it restored their ethnical and religious confidence. It provided a sanctuary for the holy ordinances revealed from Heaven. It also fulfilled God's promises that one day this second temple would rise on the ruins of the famous temple built by Solomon.

QUEEN ESTHER

The reign of Darius came to an end around 486 B.C. Not only had it been an era of peace and prosperity for the

---

65. Ezra 6:4
66. Nehemiah 2:8; 7:2
67. Geikie, *Hours With the Bible*, Vol. 6, p. 449

Jews, but it became an epic of monumental historical consequence for the rest of the world. This was the age in which the Persians were led by Darius clear up to the Danube River in Europe, but were finally turned back forever from further encroachment on the West when the Greeks defeated Darius at Marathon in 490 B.C. Four years later when Darius died he was succeeded by Xerxes (pronounced ZURK-seez). Xerxes was a young son of Darius who was appointed before his father's death.[68] He reigned for 21 years and is believed by authorities to be identical with Ashasuerus of the Bible; Xerxes is the name given to him by Greek historians.[69] He practically exhausted his empire trying to defeat the Greeks and avenge the disgrace at Marathon, but he only added three additional military cemeteries to Persia's history. His armies and naval forces were soundly routed at Salamis, Thermopylae and Plataea. Nevertheless, the grandeur of the rest of the empire remained well-stabilized from Asia Minor to India and the center of all its glory was at Susa (Shushan), the main residence of the so-called Great King. The city of Susa was located about 150 miles north of the head of the Persian Gulf, and nestled in the uplands of a mountainous region east of the Tigris river. Here had been the home of Daniel the latter part of his life and here was to be the scene for another exciting episode in Jewish history, the comet-like career of a daughter of Judah who became the famous Queen Esther of the Bible.

To appreciate the setting for this story we turn to Dr. Geikie who says, "The river Choaspes flowed brightly through the valley on the east of the city (Susa), while the Eulaus, the Ulai of Daniel, with the Shapur, and other streams, spread a network of shining waters round it, making the region a proverb for its luxuriance and fertility. The capital was famous for its palace fortress, one of the residences of the Great King; each monarch, apparently, adding a house for himself to the vast piles already built by his predecessors. . . . At Shushan (Susa), the palace stood on three distinct platforms of earth, the mounds formed by which cover a space of three-and-a-half miles round, and rise to a height of from fifty to sixty feet. The side of these immense

---

68. Kraeling, Rand McNally *Bible Atlas*, p. 333
69. Geikie, *Hours With the Bible*, Vol. 6, p. 454

elevations shone with a casing of enameled bricks, displaying in vivid colours a long succession of military splendour,
in life-sized figures of the different services that made up
the armies of the empire. . . . Above this, stretched through
its whole length, a frieze of lions, drawn with wonderful
skill, each about six feet high, and more than eleven feet
from the mouth to the end of the outstretched tail. . . . The
great audience hall of Xerxes stood on one of the three arti-
ficial platforms, and was approached, on the south-west, by
a grand staircase, wide enough, as it seems, to let an army
ascend its stately steps. The audience hall, itself, was nearly
three hundred and fifty feet broad, and about two hundred
and fifty feet deep, its roof being supported by thirty-six
columns, the size of which may be estimated by that of those
in the smaller audience at Persepolis, which are over eighteen
feet in diameter [and 60 to 76 feet in height]. . . . The walls
of the audience chamber were eighteen feet thick, to keep out
the heat, while the three great ante-chambers measured each
200 feet in width and 65 in depth. . . . But this was only the
lower story. Overhead, the building rose to a height of from
100 to 120 feet, so that it must have towered, in all, 170 to
180 feet above the ground. Spreading far on every side
from this amazing structure were gardens, well called a
'paradise.' . . .

"The table of the Great King was proverbial for its
splendid appointments and its luxury. Vast numbers of oxen,
game, and fowl, were consumed each day; for not only the
king, his court and harem, but his whole life-guard, consisting
of 2,000 cavalry, 2,000 mounted lancers, and 10,000 infantry,
were fed in the palace."[70]

In between military campaigns Xerxes held the most
extravagant and elaborate banquets at the palace. Dignitaries from the entire empire were invited to attend. During
one of these festive occasions, Xerxes desired to show off
the beauty of his queen whose name was Vashti. However,
she threw some kind of tantrum and refused to come into
the banquet hall. This embarrassed Xerxes in front of this
great crowd of dignitaries so that government officials around
the king suggested that he punish Vashti by replacing her

70. Ibid., pp. 454-457

as queen. Consequently, a sort of Persian beauty contest was held in all the provinces of the empire to discover the best candidate for a new queen.

Working in the place at the time was a Jew named Mordecai and he had adopted a young cousin, an orphan girl, who had developed into a most beautiful and personable young woman. This was Esther. He brought her forward for the consideration of the palace officials and she was immediately included among the candidates. All of the virgins, including Esther, were prepared for twelve months before being presented to the king. When Esther was brought into the presence of Xerxes it was apparently love at first sight. Not only did she receive the immediate approbation of the king but the scripture says, "And the king loved Esther above all the women, and she obtained grace and favour in his sight more than all the virgins; so that he set the royal crown upon her head, and made her queen instead of Vashti."[71]

Shortly after this Mordecai learned through his palace contacts that two of the king's chamberlains had become angry with Xerxes and were plotting his assassination. Mordecai immediately gave the information to Esther and she passed it on to the King. An investigation was conducted which verified the reality of the plot and both men were hanged. The king was so grateful to Mordecai that he had his name and details of the incident written into the official chronicle of the empire.[72]

But Esther and Mordecai knew of another secret which they held back from the king. This was the fact that Esther was a descendant from the families of the Jewish captives who were seized by Nebuchadnezzar in 598 B.C. Mordecai had told Esther to keep her ancestry and religion to herself. However, a series of events soon transpired which brought her ancestry and religion to the forefront and triggered an international crisis for the Jews.

The scripture says that the Grand Vizier or first minister of the empire was a man named Haman. According to the Bible, he was from among the Agagites[73] or better known

---

71. Esther 2:17
72. Esther 2:21-23

73. Esther 3:1

in Israel's history as the Amalekites,[74] one of the bitterest enemies of the Jews through the centuries. When the king first elevated Haman to the second position in the realm he issued an edict that all should bow down to this man as the chief minister of the king. For some reason best known to himself, Mordecai did not bow down or "make reverence" to Haman. Haman's assistants demanded that he do so, but he would not. Without knowing it, Mordecai was exposing his entire people to the possibility of massacre.

It seems that Haman decided that not only Mordecai but that all Jews held his authority in contempt. He therefore presented a proposal to the king. Said he, "There is a certain people scattered abroad and dispersed among the people in all the provinces of thy kingdom; and their laws are diverse from all people; neither keep they the king's laws: therefore it is not for the king's profit to suffer them. If it please the king, let it be written that they may be destroyed: and I will pay ten thousand talents of silver to the hands of those that have the charge of the business, to bring it [the confiscated wealth of the Jews] into the king's treasuries."[75]

So the edict was written and sealed with the king's signet and sent to all the provinces declaring that on the thirteenth day of a certain month the rulers were "to destroy, to kill, and to cause to perish, all Jews, both young and old, little children and women, in one day . . . and to take the spoil of them for a prey."[76]

When the Jews heard this fantastic news they went into the most awful mourning and public lamentation throughout the whole empire. Mordecai dressed himself in sack cloth and ashes and began to wail and mourn in front of the palace gate. This attracted the attention of Queen Esther, so she sent out her messengers to learn what on earth was wrong. Mordecai sent back a message describing what had happened. He also told Esther that she must immediately go before the king, disclose her nationality, and make deepest supplication to the king on behalf of her people.

---

74. Geikie, *Hours With the Bible*, Vol. 6, pp. 460-461
75. Esther 3:8-9
76. Esther 3:13

Esther was deeply frightened. The penalty for going in before the king unbidden was death and Esther had her messengers tell Mordecai that she had not seen the king in thirty days and knew not, of course, how long before she would see him again. Mordecai sent back instructions that no matter what the personal risk, she must go in unto the king. He said, ". . . who knoweth whether thou art come to the kingdom for such a time as this?"[77] In other words, it may be for this very crisis that the Lord had brought her to such a highly favored position. Esther finally sent back word that she would like to have all the Jews in the city fast for her during the next three days and that she, herself, would fast also. After these three days Esther said she would force her way into the great private hall of the king to make her petition. She said, "And if I perish, I perish!"[78]

But as soon as the king saw Esther he was not offended at all but beckoned to her to approach the throne. When he asked what she wished Esther said she would like to have a private dinner with only the king and his chief minister present. The king was agreeable and called in Haman. However, as they later sat down to dine Esther's courage failed her and she asked that they dine together again when she would reveal what was on her mind. Once more the king consented.

As Haman was proceeding home from this pleasant meeting, he passed Mordecai in the gate and, as usual, the Jew made no obeisance to him whatever. Haman was so angry by the time he reached home that he told his wife and friends that all his honors were as nothing so long as this contemptible Mordecai remained alive. They suggested that a high tower of fifty cubits be erected with a gallows on top and that he obtain permission from the king to hang Mordecai. So the gallows was erected.

Late that night Haman went to the king to get permission to hang Mordecai. However, the king was at that moment thinking of Mordecai and wondering how to reward him for saving his life by revealing the recent assassination plot. As Haman came in the king abruptly asked him, "What

---

77. Esther 4:14   78. Esther 4:16

shall be done unto the man whom the king delighteth to honour?"[79] The egotistical Haman of course thought the king was referring to him, so he suggested that the man be dressed in regal robes and that after being honored with a crown upon his head, he should be led through the streets of the city on the king's horse.

The king thought this was a splendid idea. He told Haman to personally see that this was immediately done for Mordecai the Jew who had saved the king's life. Haman could hardly believe his ears! He would rather have taken a beating than perform this abominable task. Nevertheless, he bitterly went forth to do as he was told. The next day Haman led the king's horse through the streets with the honored Mordecai, nobly dressed, seated in the saddle. Haman proclaimed on every side, "Thus shall it be done to the man whom the king delighteth to honour."[80] When it was all over, Haman went home weeping with "his head covered."[81]

But later that day Haman once more kept the appointment to sit at the festive table of the king where Esther had promised to make her special petition. When the king asked what was troubling her, she said that she had come to plead for the life of herself and her people. Esther said they had been condemned to be killed. The king could not believe it and asked who under heaven would attempt such an infamous thing. Esther then revealed that she was a Jewess and that Haman had induced the king to issue an edict that all Jews should be killed on a certain date which was now drawing very close.

As soon as the king saw the full implication of what had happened he was so enraged that he had to walk in the garden to cool his temper before he spoke. As he was returning one of his chamberlains added to the fuel of his fury by telling the king that Haman was planning to hang Mordecai, the very man whom the king had just honored for saving his life! That did it. The king immediately made two sweeping decisions. First he ordered Haman hanged on his own gallows. Then he ordered Mordecai to be brought into the palace and installed in Haman's place as chief minister.

---

79. Esther 6:6
80. Esther 6:9

81. Esther 6:12

Such a rapid and sensational reversal of circumstances was almost unbelievable. This now made it possible for Esther to press her original petition to have the king revoke the extermination order which had been issued against the Jews. The date was drawing near when this order would be executed in every one of the 127 provinces of the empire. However, the king sadly admitted that he had no authority to revoke the order under Persian law. A king was not permitted to reverse an edict. However, he said he would issue a new edict authorizing the Jews to arm and defend themselves. This was all Mordecai needed.

Couriers on camels or mules were sent in every direction to proclaim that the Jews were authorized to defend themselves when the day for the scheduled execution arrived. It was very apparent to the politically sensitive satraps throughout the empire that the once despised Jews had just left their position at the bottom of the totem pole and had suddenly escalated to the top. To these "practical" men of affairs such sudden switches in Persian policy disturbed neither their manners nor their morals. They did not ask who was right but who was on top. So now an amazing thing happened. The scriptures say, "AND MANY OF THE PEOPLE OF THE LAND BECAME JEWS; for the fear of the Jews fell upon them."[82] As pragmatic politicians of the same stripe in modern times are heard to say, "If you can't beat them, join them!" It was so even in ancient times.

But in spite of the shift in the government's Jewish policy, there were still some who had built up enough hatred to make them look forward to the designated doomsday of Jewry with blood-thirsty anticipation. There would be a glorious massacre — men, women and children! But when the fatal day arrived, a surprising turn of events transpired. Everywhere the mobsters engaged in pitched battles against the Jews, they were badly beaten. One such street battle occurred in the capital of Susa. When it was over the zeal of the Jewish defenders had wiped out 500 members of the mob. The next day there was great rejoicing in every Jewish colony throughout the 127 provinces of the entire Persian empire.

---

82. Esther 8:17

And the heroine of it all was Esther. In the coming centuries millions of Jews would tell their children about the wonderful girl-queen. She was made the central figure in one of the annual Jewish festivals. Never would they forget this beautiful young Jewess who risked her life to save her people, saying, "And if I perish, I perish!"

Xerxes remained king until 465 B.C. but we have no further mention of Esther or Mordecai. Mordecai may have died some time after the exciting events we have just related for we know that the last few years of Xerxes' administration were dominated by a chief minister of state named Artabanus. In fact, it was Artabanus who murdered Xerxes. He assassinated the king and then elevated one of Xerxes' younger sons to the throne. He is known in history as Artaxerxes (pronounced Arta-ZURK-seez). However, after a few months the new king discovered that Artabanus had murdered his father. He angrily slew the Vizier and his sons during a hand-to-hand combat in the great palace. Thereafter, the reign of Artaxerxes progressed rather smoothly. He continued his father's policy of toleration for the Jews and had as his official cupbearer the famous Nehemiah of the Bible. Because a cupbearer was in the most logical place to poison a king, only the most trusted servants were allowed to occupy this assignment.

It was in the seventh year of his reign or 458 B.C. that a learned scribe and well-known Priest of the Jewish colony in Babylon asked the king for permission to lead a group of his people to Jerusalem. This brings us to the distinguished servant of the Lord named Ezra.

EZRA GOES TO JERUSALEM

With the passing years many of the families of the Jews in Persia grew wealthy. They had time to devote to the arts and to literature. But nothing meant more to them than the canon of the Law as given to Moses on Mount Sinai. Men devoted their whole lives to its study and began writing commentaries on each verse. These finally became the twelve folio volumes of the famous Talmud.

Among the scribes in Persia, none was more famous than Ezra. The scribes were the copyists, custodians and expositors of the scriptures. Ezra was not only a scribe but a man of priestly rank. He was a direct descendant of Aaron, and could list among his ancestors many outstanding priestly dignitaries. One of them was the High Priest, Hilkiah,[83] contemporary of Jeremiah, who had found the Book of the Law during the rehabilitation of the temple under King Josiah. He was also a descendant of Seraiah, the Chief Priest whom Nebuchadnezzar had put to death at Riblah.[84] He traced his lineage back through Zadok of David's day to Eleazar, the oldest surviving son of Aaron.[85] So this learned disciple of Moses and the prophets was no casual up-start who had suddenly been taken up with the zeal of religion. Ezra was practically bred and born to the strict observance of God's commandments.

Having been born in Babylon under Persian rule, Ezra had never been allowed to see the great temple in Jerusalem. But his fervor for the strengthening of God's kingdom pulled him like a magnet toward that sacred edifice. He went to the king to ask permission to lead a party back to Jerusalem.[86]

Artaxerxes not only gave him permission but waxed enthusiastic about the project. He was most anxious to become worthy of the blessings of the God of the Jews. He therefore took up a collection of gold and silver from his chief administrators and added substantially to it himself.[87] He sent up additional vessels for the temple and not only made all of those who ministered in the temple immune from taxes and tributes, but authorized Ezra to call on the chief satrap of Syria and Palestine to furnish the money to buy the necessary animals to make the daily sacrifices or other oblations. Equally important, the king authorized Ezra to set up judges to enforce the laws of Moses. He even authorized Ezra's judges to impose the death penalty in prescribed cases — an extremely unusual concession."[88]

---

83. Ezra 7:1
84. Ibid. plus 2 Kings 25:18-21
85. Ezra 7:2-5
86. Certain scholars in recent years have suggested that perhaps the ministry of Ezra was during the reign of Artaxerxes II instead of Artaxerxes I. However, at the present time the preferred evidence for such a conclusion is so tenuous that it is felt that the traditional setting should be presented as the one most compatible with the many historical facts set forth in the Biblical narrative. For a discussion of the other view see Dr. Kraeling, Rand McNally *Bible Atlas*, pp. 335-336.
87. Ezra 7:15   88. Ezra 7:25-26

Ezra took a very substantial group of people with him including some of the "chief men" of Israel in Babylon.[89] Altogether, 1,500 men of the better classes assembled at the rendezvous point which was at Ahava in Babylon. Ezra was very particular about who went up with him and spent several days checking every person's genealogy. Then he proclaimed a fast to ask for God's protection on the journey. He had boasted to the king that God always blessed His people. Afterwards he said, "I was ashamed to require of the king a band of soldiers and horsemen to help us against the enemy in the way.[90] He therefore asked the people to fast and pray that they might indeed be worthy of the blessings about which he had boasted to the king.

The pilgrimage departed from Babylon on New Year's day and arrived four months later.[91] Ezra delivered all the gold and silver to the temple and turned over the king's letter to the satrap. He then set about to put things in order.

The Priests and Levites in Jerusalem had allowed the temple service to seriously deteriorate and many of them had gone out to make a living because the temple was not supported sufficiently to allow them to serve full-time. In the process some of them had also taken wives of the pagan nations, all of which horrified Ezra. He had come to Jerusalem to preach the law of the Lord straight from the book. Where there were deviations he meant to put things straight. He saw immediately that unless this unequal yoking of believers with non-believers was drastically terminated the whole Jewish culture would gradually become corrupted and the purposes of God frustrated just as they had been in the past. He therefore called a great conference at the temple to put the people under a new covenant. Among other things he proposed to launch a great reform program which would summarily eliminate the heathen elements from all Jewish families.

On the appointed day of the conference a downpour drenched the congregation as they sat in their places. The scripture says they were "trembling" both because of their sense of guilt and also on account of the chilling effect of "the great rain."[92] During the conference it was decided that

---

89. Ezra 7:28
90. Ezra 8:22

91. Ezra 7:9
92. Ezra 10:9

the judges of the people should consider each case individually rather than summarily separate the men from their alien wives and children. In many cases there were important mitigating circumstances. Apparently some of the wives were seeking to become converted and others were obedient to their husbands in religious matters and therefore deserving of further consideration. Actually, the law of Moses required the literal adoption of any converts regardless of lineage, but apostasy and prejudice had narrowed much of the generosity originally intended by the law. At this stage lineage may have been particularly stressed because of the Canaanite elements which were so prevalent all around.

Ezra continued his program with the greatest dedication and energy but he had observed in the very beginning that Jerusalem still represented a scene of ugly desolation. The situation would have been particularly objectionable to Ezra, who had lived his entire life in the majestic centers of population around Babylon. He therefore wrote about repairing the desolation of Jerusalem and rebuilding the walls and fortifications which were so desperately needed for its protection.[93]

It would seem reasonable to assume that Ezra would seek in every way possible the arousing of interest among those back at the great centers in Babylon and Persia for his favorite project. He needed voluminous help to rebuild Zion. One day a marvelous source of support arrived.

THE COMING OF NEHEMIAH

Fourteen years after Ezra had first departed for Jerusalem there came to this same city the king's royal cupbearer, Nehemiah. He not only brought a commission from the king to build up the land but also an appointment as governor of Judah! Since the Bible places this incident in the twentieth year of the reign of Artaxerxes,[94] it would be approximately 445 B.C.

Nehemiah states that he was motivated to seek this appointment and undertake the journey because of a report

93. Ezra 9:9
94. Nehemiah 1:1

he received from some of his "brethren" who had just recently returned from Jerusalem. Their description of the broken down walls and other desolations which so deeply distressed Ezra also distressed Nehemiah. Just hearing this oral report of the conditions of disrepair in the Holy City caused Nehemiah to weep. Then he went into a season of fasting and prayer.[95] The king noticed that his exceptionally pleasant cupbearer[96] was morosely sad and he asked if Nehemiah were sick. Nehemiah responded by telling the king exactly what was troubling him. The king felt this was nothing to mourn about. The city of Jerusalem should be rebuilt or repaired and refurbished. He promptly gave Nehemiah a letter authorizing him to rebuild the walls of Jerusalem. He also sent along a military guard to see that no harm befell his faithful cupbearer while crossing the treacherous Syrian desert enroute to Judah.[97]

The trip was made without incident until Nehemiah reached Samaria. Nehemiah then noticed that when he showed his letter of authorization to the governing satraps they were greatly displeased. They expressed open hostility toward the Jews.[98] Nehemiah therefore proceeded quietly into Jerusalem without fanfare and stayed three days without even making himself known to the local authorities.[99] Then he made a secret night inspection of the entire city of Jerusalem and mapped out in his mind just what must be done to repair its walls![100] He also figured out how it could be done in sections if he could induce leading princes of Judah to assume responsibility for one section apiece.

Only after all of this did Nehemiah disclose his identity. He called upon the leaders of Jerusalem to rally behind him in rebuilding the walls.[101] This must have seemed like manna from Heaven to Ezra who had been waiting 14 years for just such a development. Eliashib, the High Priest, was also enthusiastic and gradually the contagion spread until the people "strengthened their hands for this good work."[102]

The miracle of cooperation and team-work soon manifested itself. The High Priest set the example by gathering

95. Neheimah 1:4
96. Nehemiah 2:1
97. Nehemiah 2:9
98. Nehemiah 2:10
99. Nehemiah 2:11-12
100. Nehemiah 2:12-16
101. Nehemiah 2:17
102. Nehemiah 2:18

the Priests together and starting the reconstruction of the Sheep Gate.[103] The wall section next to them was built by the men of Jericho. Other sections were taken on by the various guilds — the goldsmiths, the apothecaries, the merchants. Some communities such as Gibeon and Mizpah each took on a section. One individual, a man named Shallum who ruled half of Jerusalem, said that he and his daughter would be responsible for a section. Altogether thirty-five volunteers are named who accepted and completed their parts of this great project.[104] One group, however, stands out in ignoble disgrace. The Bible says the men of Tekoa "put not their necks to the work of the Lord."[105]

All of the most important landmarks around Jerusalem are described by Nehemiah in connection with the assignments he gave these volunteer labor forces. This description has been extremely valuable to archaeologists in locating the foundations of these original walls and gates of the old city.

Labors Performed in the Shadow of the Sword

Nehemiah soon found, however, that this massive building program had to be undertaken without the help of any Persian authorities. In fact, it had to be done in spite of them. The letter from the king had little effect on them. They began organizing military parties to harass the builders and attack the workers when they were caught in small groups or working without the protection of their arms. To achieve their hostile objective, several of the native satraps united together and formed an alliance. This alliance represented the people of Samaria on the north, the Ammonites across the Jordan to the east, the Arabians on the south, and the Philistines in the west. The higher the walls grew, the more determined these pagan forces grew to smash them down. Finally Nehemiah had to divide the work force in two parts with half standing guard to repell attacks while the remainder did the work.[106]

Morale of the workers was further damaged by certain unscrupulous sons of Judah who had taken out mortgages on

---

103. Nehemiah 3:1   105. Nehemiah 3:5
104. Nehemiah, chapter 3   106. Nehemiah 4:16

practically everything the people owned. In addition, they had charged such outrageous usury that the people could not possibly pay them back. Many of the temple workers were therefore losing all their property by foreclosures. It should be mentioned that the voluntary workers were not being paid for their services and many had been compelled to borrow in order to pay their taxes and Persian levies.[107]

When Nehemiah realized what some of the corrupt and immoral money-lenders were doing he was outraged and immediately called them into a conference.[108] He unleashed such a tongue-lashing that he soon shamed them into canceling all their claims on the people and delivering back to the wretched workmen the property they had confiscated. This speech was so effective that the money-lenders not only capitulated to Nehemiah's demands but agreed to put it in the form of an oath administered by the Priests.[109] As the conference ended, the wrathful Nehemiah looked at these men and then shook his robe at them saying, "So God shake out every man from his house, and from his labour, that performeth not this promise, even thus be he shaken out, and emptied."[110] The guilty money-lenders wished to assure Nehemiah that they were back of him four-square. They all piously chanted a loud "Amen," meaning "So be it!"[111]

The principal leaders of Judah's enemies at this time included Sanballat from Samaria and Tobiah the Ammonite. Tobiah was especially hostile and had all kinds of agents operating inside Jerusalem against Nehemiah.[112] They told Tobiah everything Nehemiah said.[113] The enemy forces also had false prophets and agent provocateurs within the city to stir up strife.[114] At one point Sanballat and a man named Geshem did everything possible to lure Nehemiah outside the city to parley with them. Nehemiah refused to go, however, fearing they would assassinate him.[115] Thus the struggle went precariously on from day to day and week to week. Finally, however, in spite of traitors within and enemies without, the walls were finished in 52 days.[116] Nehemiah now in-

---

107. Nehemiah 5:3
108. Nehemiah 5.6-7
109. Nehemiah 5:12
110. Nehemiah 5:13
111. Ibid.

112. Nehemiah 6:17-18
113. Nehemiah 6:19
114. Nehemiah 6:10-12
115. Nehemiah 6:1-2
116. Nehemiah 6:15

augurated a program for the protection of the city. Regular guards were appointed for both night and day. The city gates were not to be opened until the day shift had taken over. At night there was a citizens' patrol and every citizen was expected to take his "watch" or tour of duty. When off duty he was to guard his own house.[117]

NEHEMIAH STRENGTHENS THE PEOPLE

Having fortified the city and set up a security police, Nehemiah now set about to strengthen the people. His object was to have them keep the commandments of the Lord so that the city and temple would receive whatever divine approbation was necessary to preserve them in the crises of the future.

The first thing he did was to take a census of the people in order to add the recent immigrants to the lists of genealogical records set up by the first arrivals.[118] The next step was to educate the people in the laws and ordinances of God's Kingdom.

All through this part of the scripture it is apparent that Ezra was working in the closest alliance with Nehemiah, the indefatigable governor of Judah. At the first opportunity a huge conference was held where Ezra could read the law of Moses to all the people. No doubt Ezra was grateful for the chance. He had always felt that the biggest problem in Judah was ignorance. The people just simply did not know what the Lord required of them. Ezra therefore took advantage of this great conference in the Kidron valley (near the Water Gate) to read the law of the Lord to this large public gathering. This "public reading of the law" is the basis for the instituting of the synagogue[119] which has prevailed ever since among the Jews wherever they are found.

Of course Ezra's problem under these circumstances was allowing all to hear the law as it was read. He therefore set up a unique device which might be called a decentralized broadcasting system. He erected a high platform on which he stood. His plan was to read a few passages of scripture

117. Nehemiah 7:3
118. Nehemiah 7:5
119. Geikie, *Hours With the Bible*, Vol. 6, p. 527

and then have the thirteen Priests and a number of Levites (who were apparently scattered throughout the audience) provide a brief but illuminating commentary on each of the verses. Ezra would then read a few more passages and the procedure would be repeated.

It is interesting that when Ezra first took out the copy of the Law which he had brought from Babylon, the people who had been sitting cross-legged on the ground immediately stood up out of respect for these sacred writings given to Moses by the Lord.[120] Ezra began the proceedings with a brief prayer. Then he started reading out of the books of Moses — the Law. As Ezra read the text and the Priests and Levites explained it to the people, there suddenly began to be widespread weeping among the people. Many of them realized for the first time how much they had offended God. They began to weep and mourn but Ezra told them it was a time to rejoice.[121] After reading and interpreting the scripture for about 6 hours, [122] Ezra dismissed the people and told them to come the next day.

The next day they heard about the Feast of the Tabernacles which was due at that very moment.[123] So they gathered the people together and celebrated this feast by living in booths or tabernacles just as the children of Israel had done over a thousand years earlier.[124] At subsequent meetings Ezra read the law for three hours instead of six, and then the congregation spent the remaining three hours teaching, confessing, and worshipping God.[125] As the people became better acquainted with what was expected of them, Nehemiah felt they should enter into a new covenant with the Lord. A document was therefore prepared, committing each one who signed it to a life of obedience to the Lord. The covenant specifically committed the signatory to obey the Law of Moses, not to intermarry with the heathens, not to buy or sell on Sunday, to fallow (refrain from cultivating) the land every seventh year, and to release and forgive all indebtedness every seventh year. The supplying of wood for the altar was delegated, so was the gathering of the first-

---

120. Nehemiah 8:5
121. Nehemiah 8:9
122. Nehemiah 8:10-13
123. Nehemiah 8:14
124. Nehemiah 8:16
125. Nehemiah 9:3

fruits and the garnering of temple supplies. In order to prevent the Priests and Levites from leaving their temple duties
to earn a living, provision was made so that the tithes would
be collected and distributed regularly to the full-time servants
of the Lord.

Nehemiah now had one last ambition to fulfill before
he held the dedication ceremonies for the new city walls and
defenses. He wanted to fill up the city. Strangely, most
everyone seemed anxious to live in the country. They wanted
to be where they could do a little farming and enjoy the freedom of rural life in spite of the risk involved. Practically all
of the rulers of Judah lived inside Jerusalem but the people
remained aloof. In order to make the city sufficiently strong
to resist an attack the people drew lots. Every tenth family
was asked to move into Jerusalem.[126]

Now Nehemiah was ready for the dedication of the
newly fortified city of Jerusalem. He assembled choirs and
orchestras of the Levites and then called the people together.
After being divided into two groups, they were invited to
mount the broad battlements of the high wall and march
around them; one division (led by Ezra) went one way while
the other celebrants (led by Nehemiah) went the other. They
met at the opposite side of the city where the prayer of dedication was pronounced.

All of this was carried out according to Nehemiah's
plan and afterwards they offered a multitude of sacrifices
in thanksgiving for all that the Lord had made possible for
them to accomplish.

This is the last recorded event before Nehemiah returned
to the capital of Persia. He had been in Jerusalem 12 years
and besides being weary he perhaps felt the need to re-
establish his good offices with the king. In any event he
went back. Barely was he out of sight before the ravages
of apostasy began to take hold again. It was fantastic. It
demonstrated that even with a zealous and strict scriptorian
like Ezra to teach true precepts, the people still needed a
forceful temporal leader to continually induce them to practice those precepts. It is not sufficient for most people to

126. Nehemiah 11:1

merely know the truth. To live the truth they almost invariably require strong, inspired leadership.

Nehemiah states that when he returned from his Persian vacation he found the payment of tithes already badly neglected. As a result, the Levites and Priests felt compelled to abandon the temple and find a way to earn a living. Nehemiah also found that many of the people were mixing once more with their pagan neighbors. They bought and sold on the Sabbath day. Worst of all, the High Priest had actually provided a furnished apartment for Tobiah in the temple annex! Here was the abominable Tobiah, Nehemiah's enemy, being treated like a Priest! But the king's former cupbearer was accustomed to dealing with such obstreperous creatures. He ousted Tobiah, flung his furniture out, and ordered the ceremonial purification of the whole area which Tobiah had occupied.[127] He also lashed out at the sabbath-breakers, verbally blasted the men who had married pagans, scolded the Priests and Levites who had abandoned the temple, and bristled with fury at the people that had robbed God of an honest tithe. Nehemiah was a supremely valiant servant in the vineyard of the Lord. It was tragic that Judah had not produced more like him.

The people did not know it, but Judah was about to slip into another 400 years of dismal dark ages. It would be a period where qualities of leadership like those of Nehemiah would be horribly conspicuous by virtue of their total absence. Perhaps a long dynasty of Nehemiahs could have saved Judah. She certainly was not able to save herself. The next time Judah came up for light she would be staring at the noble personage of the very Son of God. But for the most part the people of Judah would not even know Him. He would come before them lowly, riding on the foal of a donkey. He would be a light shining in darkness.

So this brings us to the great last sweeping epic of Jewish history — the blackout which preceded the coming of the Messiah.

---

127. Nehemiah 13:4-9

Scripture Reading and Questions on Chapter Twenty-Eight

Scripture Reading: The Books of Ezra, Nehemiah, Haggai, Esther and Zechariah.

1—Name three things Cyrus did to encourage the Jews to rebuild Jerusalem.

2—What does the name Zerubbabel mean? What famous king was his ancestor? What happened to his descendants?

3—About how many Jews returned to Jerusalem in the migration of 538 B.C.? Why did some of them need to have the High Priest check their lineage for them through the Urim and Thummim? Was it any longer available?

4—In what condition did the pilgrims find Jerusalem? Were there any Jews in the vicinity who had not gone into captivity?

5—Did Zerubbabel build the altar of sacrifice or the temple first? When he built the altar where was it located?

6—Why did Zerubbabel turn down the proffered help from the heathen nations? In your opinion was he right? Why?

7—What happened to stop the building of the temple even before the foundation was built?

8—What ruler did the Prophet Haggai serve as a prophet? Identify two of his revelations.

9—When did Zechariah live? Where? Briefly identify two of his prophecies.

10—When the governor of Palestine challenged the authority of the Jews to build a temple, why did he feel compelled to write to the Persian capital about it? What was the reply?

11—In what year was the second temple finished? Was it as fully decorated as Solomon's temple?

12—What was in the Holy of Holies? Why do the Moslems consider this spot sacred?

13—Briefly relate the story of Esther.

14—What happened to Xerxes? Who replaced him?

15—Was Ezra entitled to the Levitical Priesthood or the office of Priest in the Aaronic Priesthood? What was a scribe?

16—Where did Nehemiah come from? What office did he hold? Why did he want to come to Jerusalem?

17—What were the two major handicaps for Nehemiah when he was rebuilding the walls of Jerusalem? How did he solve each one?

18—What happened during Nehemiah's day which laid the foundation for the institution of the Jewish Synagogue?

19—When the city walls were dedicated, where did the people march? Why was the completion of the walls a cause for celebration? How long did it take to build the walls?

20—What was the condition in Jerusalem after Nehemiah returned from his Persian vacation? What did this demonstrate?

CHAPTER TWENTY-NINE

Judah Awaits the Messiah

Except for one final flash of prophetic light in the person of Malachi, Judah now passed into a treacherous period of dismal dark ages which lasted for more than four centuries. This final phase of the Fourth Thousand Years was to be one of continuous travail for Judah. Having lost her status as an independent people Judah became just another of the many pawns in the hands of the imperialistic political gladiators who now maneuvered about the Mediterranean basin seeking to rule the world. In these vast, violent struggles, huge military juggernauts moved out across the Fertile Crescent land bridge and plowed Palestine from Dan to Beersheba.

Little did the Jews realize that their long awaited Messiah stood poised ready to minister to them at the other end of this night of sorrows. And certainly they would never have guessed that He would come and leave without most of them knowing He had ever been there.

However, before plunging into the exciting but distressing period of Judah's dark ages, let us examine what little is known of that last prophetic voice to be heard in Judah prior to the coming of John the Baptist.

The Prophet Malachi

Somewhere around 400 B.C. and shortly after Ezra and Nehemiah had disappeared from the scene,[1] Malachi administered to the Jews at Jerusalem. His name means, "My Messenger" and some scholars have wondered if the book of Malachi might not belong to some unknown individual who was a messenger of the Lord.[2] However, we know from the Book of Mormon that Jesus told the Nephites to "write the words which the Father had given unto Malachi,"[3] so from this it seems quite apparent that the name of Malachi belongs to a real person and was not just a title or designation.

During his ministry Malachi stressed three major themes. All of them echoed the pleas of Ezra, Nehemiah and Haggai so we assume that Malachi was not far behind them, perhaps even a contemporary for a short time. Malachi first accused the people of neglecting and perverting the proper Priesthood functions. Secondly, he chastised them for offending the wives of their youth by taking heathen women in marriage. Finally, he said the people were robbing God by refusing to pay their tithes. This is the basic message of Malachi.

Concerning the degeneration of the Priestly function the Lord said the Priests "despise my name."[4] They "offer polluted bread upon mine altar" so that "the table of the Lord is contemptible."[5] Instead of securing prime animals for sacrifice to appropriately represent the sacrifice of the very Son of God, the Priests had been offering the cheapest and poorest from their domestic flocks, keeping the best for themselves. The Lord said, "ye brought that which was torn, and the lame, and the sick; thus ye brought an offering: should I accept this of your hand?"[6] The rest of the people were no better. They, too, brought to the Lord the worst of their flock for sacrifice. So the Lord said, "But cursed by the deceiver, which hath in his flock a male and voweth, and sacrificeth unto the Lord a corrupt thing. . . ."[7]

---

1. Some authorities think Malachi was their contemporary.
2. For a discussion of this problem, see Dr. Sperry, *The Old Testament Prophets*, pp. 321-322.
3. 3 Nephi 24:1
4. Malachi 1:6
5. Malachi 1:7
6. Malachi 1:13
7. Malachi 1:14

As we have pointed out earlier, the Lord had given the law of carnal commandments to teach the people a pattern of obedience. But now the Priests were rebelling against it, saying, "Behold, what a weariness is it!"[8] If the Priests held the word of the Lord in contempt, no wonder it was reflected in the common people.

Malachi emphasized that the Priests and Levites were supposed to be teaching the people the Law and inspiring them to do good. Then he said they deserved to have dung spread across their faces for the contemptible job they were doing.[9] The Lord said that when He originally adopted the tribe of Levi for the Priesthood function, He had intended to give the people exemplary men to follow, men of "life and peace,"[10] men who had "the law of truth" in their mouths and renounced sin wherever they found it.[11] He said the earlier custodians of the Priesthood were men who "walked with me in peace and equity, AND DID TURN MANY AWAY FROM INIQUITY."[12] He wanted a ministry of righteous servants who prepared themselves for their work, who were filled with a knowledge of the law of the Gospel and who had it on their lips for instant use in delivering God's message to the people.[13]

But now what were the Aaronic and Levitical Priesthood holders doing? The Lord said, ". . . ye are departed out of the way; YE HAVE CAUSED MANY TO STUMBLE AT THE LAW; ye have corrupted the covenant of Levi!"[14]

One of the worst things they had done was to divorce the wives of their youth to take unto themselves women of the abominable heathen cultures. The Lord said that when such men came with an offering and a sacrifice it was abhorrent and void for the altar had already been covered with the tears of their wives whom they had betrayed. Malachi declared:

". . . the Lord hath been witness between thee and the wife of thy youth, against whom thou hast dealt treacherously: yet is she thy companion, and the wife of thy cove-

---

8. Malachi 1:13
9. Malachi 2:3
10. Malachi 2:5
11. Malachi 2:6
12. Ibid.
13. Malachi 2:7
14. Malachi 2:8

nant."[15] Then he admonished them, "Therefore take heed to your spirit, and let none deal treacherously against the wife of his youth. For the Lord, the God of Israel, saith that he hateth putting away [divorcing of wives]."[16]

THE PRINCIPLE OF TITHING

All through the Old Testament we find the Lord promising the Saints abundant blessings if they will faithfully demonstrate that they are willing to share a tenth of their increase to further the Kingdom of God. It is in Malachi that we find the most comprehensive statement of this proposition. Through Malachi the Lord issued His mighty challenge and warm invitation to those who claim to love Him:

"Even from the days of your fathers ye are gone away from mine ordinances, and have not kept them. Return unto me, and I will return unto you, saith the Lord of hosts. But ye said, Wherein shall we return?

"Will a man rob God? Yet ye have robbed me. But ye say, Wherein have we robbed thee? IN TITHES AND OFFERINGS.

"Ye are cursed with a curse: for ye have robbed me, even this whole nation.

"Bring ye all the tithes into the storehouse, that there may be meat in mine house, and prove me now herewith, saith the Lord of hosts, if I will not open you the windows of heaven, and pour you out a blessing, that there shall not be room enough to receive it."[17]

Those who hearkened to the word of the Lord in Malachi's day received a double reward. Not only were they blessed spiritually and materially, but their names were inscribed in a "book of remembrance" as those who "feared the Lord, and thought upon his name."[18] Concerning them the Lord said, "And they shall be mine, saith the Lord of hosts, in that day when I make up my jewels; and I will spare them, as a man spareth his own son that serveth him."[19]

---

15. Malachi 2:14
16. Malachi 2:14-16
17. Malachi 3:7-10
18. Malachi 3:16
19. Malachi 3:17

The Lord said the time was coming when there would be a complete separation "between him that serveth God and him that serveth him not."[20] For some it will be the separation incidental to the Second Coming: "For, behold, the day cometh, that shall burn as an oven; and all the proud, yea, and all that do wickedly, shall be stubble: and the day that cometh shall burn them up, saith the Lord of hosts, that it shall leave them neither root nor branch. But unto you that fear my name shall the Sun of righteousness arise with healing in his wings; and ye shall go forth and grow up as calves of the stall."[21]

It will be immediately seen that this promise pertains to our own day rather than Malachi's. In a modern revelation the Lord made specific reference to the Malachi scripture and said, "Behold, now it is called today until the coming of the Son of Man, and verily it is a day of sacrifice, and a day for the tithing of my people; for he that is tithed SHALL NOT BE BURNED AT HIS COMING. For after today cometh the burning — this is speaking after the manner of the Lord — for verily I say, tomorrow all the proud and they that do wickedly shall be as stubble; and I will burn them up, for I am the Lord of Hosts; and I will not spare any that remain in Babylon. Wherefore, if ye believe me, ye will labor while it is called today."[22]

And just as the people of the Lord kept books of remembrance to record the sacrifice and righteous obedience of the Saints in ancient times, so it is done today. The tithing records of the Church are part of the books of remembrance. Some people rationalize that they are doing good with their money and counting it as tithing without making it available to the servants of the Lord's kingdom. These may find that what they think is generosity on their part is actually embezzlement. They are being generous with money that belongs to the Lord. The Lord asks that resources intended as tithes be brought to His "storehouse" and not squandered to gratify some personal sense of philanthropy. Those who are recorded in the Lord's book of remembrance are those who do these things the Lord's way.

---

20. Malachi 3:18
21. Malachi 4:1-2

22. Doc. & Cov. 64:23-25

MALACHI IS QUOTED TO A MODERN PROPHET

It is interesting that when Moroni appeared to Joseph Smith on the evening of September 21, 1823, the very first scripture which was quoted to him from the Old Testament was from Malachi. Joseph states, "After telling me these things [about the work Joseph was called to do], he commenced quoting the prophecies of the Old Testament. He first quoted part of the third chapter of Malachi; and he quoted also the fourth or last chapter of the same prophecy, though with a little variation from the way it reads in our Bibles."[23]

Joseph Smith did not specify which part of the third chapter of Malachi was quoted by Moroni. It is thought to have been verses 1 to 6 which reads as follows: "Behold, I will send my messenger,[24] and he shall prepare the way before me: and the Lord, whom ye seek, shall suddenly come to his temple, even the messenger of the covenant, whom ye delight in: behold, he shall come, saith the Lord of hosts.

"But who may abide the day of his coming? and who shall stand when he appeareth? for he is like a refiner's fire [excessively hot], and like fullers' soap [containing caustic lye].

"And he shall sit as a refiner and purifier of silver: and he shall purify the sons of Levi, and purge them as gold and silver, that THEY MAY OFFER UNTO THE LORD AN OFFERING IN RIGHTEOUSNESS.

"Then shall the offering of Judah and Jerusalem be pleasant unto the Lord, as in the days of old, and as in former years.

"And I will come near to you to judgment; and I will be a swift witness against the sorcerers, and against the

---

23. Documentary History of the Church, Vol. 1. p. 12
24. John the Baptist was identified by the Savior as the "messenger" who came to prepare the way for the Lord in connection with his first coming (Matt. 11:10). So also John the Baptist initiated the preparatory work of the Priesthood when he ordained Joseph Smith and Oliver Cowdery to the Aaronic Priesthood, May 15, 1829. (Doc. & Cov. 27:8) Joseph Smith, himself, then became a "messenger" in the calling of an Elias or forerunner. (Teachings of Joseph Smith, p. 335) Joseph Smith says this was specifically explained to him by John the Baptist when the work first started: Joseph says he was told "that my ordination was a preparatory work, or a going before, which was the spirit of Elias." (Ibid.)

adulterers, and against false swearers, and against those that oppress the hireling in his wages, the widow, and the fatherless, and that turn aside the stranger from his right, and fear not me, saith the Lord of hosts.

"For I am the Lord, I change not; therefore ye sons of Jacob [the faithful ones, worthy of the name] are not consumed."

Joseph Smith was told that all of these things were going to come to pass in the not too distant future.[25] Therefore the Gospel was to be restored to fulfill God's purposes in the latter days.

Joseph Smith says Moroni also quoted the fourth chapter of Malachi to him. However, Moroni made certain significant changes in the first verse and last two verses. We will set them forth in parallels so the reader may analyze the differences:

BIBLE	AS QUOTED BY MORONI
Verse 1: For, behold, the day cometh, that shall burn as an oven; and all the proud, yea, and all that do wickedly, shall be stubble: and the day that cometh shall burn them up, saith the Lord of hosts, that it shall leave them neither root nor branch.	Verse 1: For behold, the day cometh that shall burn as an oven, and all the proud, yea, and all that do wickedly shall burn as stubble; FOR THEY THAT COME shall burn them, saith the Lord of Hosts, that it shall leave them neither root nor branch.
Verse 5: Behold, I will send you Elijah the prophet before the coming of the great and dreadful day of the Lord.	Verse 5: Behold, I will REVEAL UNTO YOU THE PRIESTHOOD, by the hand of Elijah the prophet, before the coming of the great and dreadful day of the Lord.
Verse 6: And he shall turn the heart of the fathers to the children, and the heart of the children to their fathers lest I come and smite the earth with a curse.	Verse 6: And he shall PLANT IN THE HEARTS OF THE CHILDREN THE PROMISES MADE TO THE FATHERS, and the hearts of the children shall turn to their fathers. If it were not so, the whole earth WOULD BE UTTERLY WASTED AT HIS COMING. (Pearl of Great Price, p. 51)

Joseph Smith explained the great mission of Elijah to be as follows: "The spirit, power and calling of Elijah [when conferred upon a person] is, that ye have power to hold the key of the revelations, ordinances, oracles, powers and en-

---

25. Documentary History of the Church, Vol. 1, pp. 13-14

dowments of the fulness of the Melchizedek Priesthood and of the Kingdom of God on the earth; and to receive, obtain, and perform all the ordinances belonging to the Kingdom of God, even unto the turning of the hearts of the fathers unto the children, and the hearts of the children unto the fathers, even those who are in heaven. . . . I wish you to understand this subject, for it is important and if you will receive it, this is the spirit of Elijah, that we redeem our dead, and connect ourselves with our fathers which are in heaven, and seal up our dead to come forth in the first resurrection; and here we want the power of Elijah to seal those who dwell on earth to those who dwell in heaven. This is the power of Elijah and the keys of the Kingdom of Jehovah."[26]

Elijah restored the keys in modern times and literally fulfilled the prophecy of Malachi. This occurred on April 3, 1836, at the Kirtland Temple. Joseph Smith states, "After this vision had closed, another great and glorious vision burst upon us; for Elijah the prophet, who was taken to heaven without tasting death, stood before us, and said: Behold, the time has fully come, which was spoken of by the mouth of Malachi — testifying that he [Elijah] should be sent, before the great and dreadful day of the Lord come — to turn the hearts of the fathers to the children, and the children to the fathers, lest the whole earth be smitten with a curse — Therefore, the keys of this dispensation are committed into your hands; and by this ye may know that the great and dreadful day of the Lord is near, even at the doors."[27]

Modern Jews are Awaiting Elijah

Even since the days of Malachi, some 2,300 years ago, the Jewish faithful have been patiently waiting for Elijah to manifest himself. They know that when he does come, the appearance of the Messiah will soon follow. Did not Malachi say that the revealing of Elijah would precede the "dreadful day of the Lord"?

Most of the Jews did not believe in Jesus when He came the first time and therefore they never knew that Elijah had appeared in the meridian of time on the Mount of Transfigur-

---

26. *Teachings of Joseph Smith,* pp. 337-338
27. Doc. & Cov. 110:13-16

ation. And only those Jews who have accepted the Gospel in modern times are aware that Elijah has already brought his commission to the earth and as of April 3, 1836, turned it over to two of the Lord's servants at the Kirtland Temple.

All other Jews are still patiently waiting for Elijah to reveal himself.

A great Jewish scholar, Joseph Klausner of the Hebrew University in Israel, has written a book entitled, *The Messianic Idea of Israel*. He has a whole chapter on the Elijah theme. It is called "Elijah, the Forerunner of the Messiah." Dr. Klausner says there has always been a great deal of discussion as to just what Elijah will do as the forerunner of the Messiah and just how he will turn the hearts of the children to the fathers. He points out that the concensus among Hebrew scholars seems to be that he will: 1—"certify the ritual cleanness of families that had suffered at one time or another from mixed marriages or even forbidden unions, and to grant permission to hitherto excluded peoples to intermarry with the Jews . . ."[28]; 2—restore "the flask of manna"; 3—restore "the flask of water for purification"; and 4—restore "the flask of oil for anointing."[29] Some extend Elijah's functions further to include 5—restoring "Aaron's rod, with its ripe almonds and blossoms,"[30] and 6—"having a part in the resurrection of the dead."[31]

But the Jews believe the most important function of all the many things Elijah must do, will be to anoint the Messiah as King of Kings. Dr. Klausner says that according to Talmudic sources, Elijah was a "Righteous Priest" or even "Melchizedek." He says, "It was the custom of the high priests and prophets to anoint the kings. The political and spiritual king, the King-Messiah, will be anointed by Elijah who is both prophet and high priest."[32]

These Talmudic suppositions are correct concerning Elijah's great powers as a High Priest after the Order of Melchizedek. However, the other suppositions are merely the expressions of animated hope coming from a people who

---

28. Joseph Klausner, *The Messianic Idea in Israel,* New York, Macmillan, 1955, p. 454
29. Ibid., p. 455
30. Ibid.
31. Ibid., p. 456
32. Ibid.

have temporarily lost the light of prophetic leadership. Nevertheless, they are faithfully waiting out the time when God's will can be manifest in their behalf, as the Lord has promised it will be.

And we can appreciate from Dr. Klausner's carefully documented presentation how completely Malachi's last two verses closed the age of oracles for the Jews. Nevertheless, it has remained for them their last bright promise of a coming Messiah. Down through the centuries they have expectantly waited and longed for Elijah and the Lord.

But with the fading of revelation and prophetic power from the vista of Jewish affairs, a curtain of darkness settled down on the people. An example of the passionate Jewish anxiety for the return of divine guidance is reflected in an incident which happened in 142 B.C., three centuries after Malachi. During one bright but brief period of independence and hope the people appointed a man named Simon to be their new high priest and governor. But this man-made attempt to fill both the political and spiritual vacuum in Judah was done with the specific reservation that it should only prevail with Simon and his descendants "until the faithful prophet should arise."[33] Unfortunately, one never came, and high priests and governors continued to rule under man-made appointments right up until the coming of Christ. By that time Jewish leaders could not recognize a prophet when they saw one. They plunged right on through to 70 A.D. when their political and religious life was blown to the four winds following the conquest of Jerusalem by the Romans.

But now we return to the period following the days of Malachi when the Persian kings still dominated the civilized world.

THE RISE OF GREECE — THE BRASS KINGDOM OF NEBUCHADNEZZAR'S DREAM

The life of the Old Testament Jews during their final period of dark ages can best be appreciated within the framework of world history which now rolled back and forth across them as the great empires violently struggled for supreme

---

33. I Maccabees 14:41

domination of all mankind. A major conflict was building up between Greece and Persia. Had not Greece become anemic from a century or more of civil war, she might have confronted Persian power long before the days of Alexander the Great.

It is interesting that the famous golden age of Grecian culture occurred right about the time the Jews were returning to Jerusalem from Babylon in 438 B.C. These were the days of Athenian democracy under Pericles. Today, as the visitor views the remnants of world-famous architectural beauty which grace the Acropolis of Athens, it is hard to believe that practically all of this came into being during the 30-year administration of this one man, Pericles. The Persian wars had destroyed most of Athens and so there was an ideal opportunity to do some creative planning for the new city. The Parthenon was erected as a temple to Athena. Across the way the famous Erechtheium temple still stands, and at the top of the magnificent marble stairway leading up to the main entrance of the Acropolis is the famous temple of the Wingless Victory.

This was the age of Herodotus and Thucydides, the famous Greek historians. It was the age of Socrates the philosopher, Hippocrates the physician, Phidias the sculptor, Aristophanes, the satyrical dramatist, and Sophocles and Euripedes and classical Greek dramatists. Sculpture, architecture, painting, drama, science, philosophy, history, commerce and political stability all flourished during this amazing period. It has truly been called "the Golden Age of Pericles."

It will be recalled that the Lord had originally intended to make Israel the great cultural anchor of the world by purging Palestine and setting up a City-of-Enoch civilization which would eventually become the dominant political, moral, economic and cultural force among all mankind. Its purpose would have been to spread universal peace and universal prosperity throughout the world. Tragically, the Israelites bungled their opportunity and left the world leadership task to far less competent hands. Now, in the fifth century before Christ, the Greeks had experimentally discovered the formula for a brief but majestic way of life not at all alien to the program which the Lord had originally projected for Israel.

In a funeral address designed to honor Athenian warriors who had died fighting Sparta, Pericles gave this choice oratorical declamation on the Athenian way of life as it then existed. Said he:

"Our government is called a democracy because it is in the hands of the many and not of the few. Our laws secure equal justice for all in their private disputes, and our public opinion welcomes and honors talent in every kind of achievement, not for any sectional reason, but on grounds of excellence alone. And as we give free play to all in our public life, so we carry the same spirit into our daily relations among ourselves. We are not angry with our neighbor if he does what he likes, nor do we put on sour looks at him which, though harmless, are unpleasant.

"Open and friendly in our private relations, in our public acts we keep strictly within the law. We recognize the restraint of reverence; we are obedient to officials and laws, especially to the laws that protect the oppressed and to the unwritten laws whose violation brings admitted shame.

"Yet ours is no work-a-day city only. No other provides so many recreations for the spirit — contests and sacrifices all year round, and beauty in our public buildings to cheer the heart and delight the eye day by day. Moreover, this city is so large and powerful that the wealth of the whole world flows into her, so that our own products seem no more homelike to us than those of other nations.

"We love beauty without extravagance, and wisdom without unmanliness. We employ wealth, not as a means to vanity and ostentation, but as an opportunity for service. To acknowledge poverty is no disgrace; the true disgrace is in making no effort to overcome it.

"An Athenian citizen does not neglect public affairs because he is too concerned with his private business. We regard a person who takes no interest in public affairs, not as 'quiet' but useless.

"If few of us are originators, we are all sound judges of a policy. The great impediment to action is, in our opinion, not discussion, but the lack of full information which is gained by discussion prior to action."[34]

How Moses would have thrilled to hear the leader of an Israelite commonwealth make such a speech!

But this spectacular breakthrough which was achieved by Pericles lasted no longer than he did. In 429 B.C., right while Ezra and Nehemiah were struggling for survival in Jerusalem, Pericles died. Greece was soon involved once more in the suicidal civil war slug-fest which is known as the Peloponnesian Wars. The golden age of Athens promptly began to fall apart. The greatest single opponent of this absurd policy was Isocrates who established an academy around 390 B.C. and began advocating political unity for all Greece. For fifty years Isocrates tried to find some Greek with enough sense to lead out in such a movement. He finally settled on a new young king in Macedonia named Philip. In 346 B.C. Isocrates gave his famous *Philippus* oration inviting Philip to assume leadership and unite Greece. Philip responded and by the time Isocrates died in 338 B.C., Philip had defeated the Athenian armies and united the warring states.

But in 336 B.C. Philip was assassinated by one of his own courtiers and his 20-year-old son, Alexander, suddenly found himself in possession of a volatile but united military machine capable of carving up the Persian empire.

Fortunately for Alexander, the new Persian capital at Persepolis was in an uproar. The king of Persia (Artaxerxes III) had just been poisoned by his vizier or prime minister. The king's son was placed on the throne but after two years the vizier poisoned him. He then put the incompetent Darius III on the throne. The first thing Darius III did was to poison the vizier! It was Darius III whom young Alexander eventually confronted and attacked.

Alexander had studied under Aristotle, the famous Greek philosopher, political scientist, and naturalist. This son of Philip was handsome, persuasive and well-trained for a career of building empires. His plan of strategy was, "unite

---

34. William Ebenstein, *Two Ways of Life*, New York: Holt, Rinehart and Winston, 1962, pp. 10-11

and conquer." Alexander first started out by uniting the dissident forces of Greece, then of Asia Minor and Syria. Finally he took Egypt in 332 B.C. and was crowned king of Pharaohland. Then he was ready to march eastward.

In 331 BC., Alexander's mammoth war machine captured Babylon. He then entered Persia and chased Darius III up into Media. However, Darius was murdered by his own nobles, so Alexander pronounced himself the ruler of the whole Persian domain. Additional military action was required for a time to subdue the eastern Persian territory but when that was completed Alexander proceeded on to India. This became his easternmost boundary. He returned to the coast in due time but suddenly became ill and died there on June 13, 323 B.C. Alexander had not yet reached his thirty-third birthday.

Judah in the Cross-fire of Quarreling Greek Generals

As soon as Alexander had died, there was a mad scramble among his generals to seize the territories where they happened to be assigned at the time. All of them set up separate kingdoms. Greece and Macedonia went to the one-eyed general named Antigonus Cyclops, who also had the western part of Asia Minor and hoped to take Syria and the rest of the former Persian empire. However, the other generals stopped him and the Asiatic holdings of the empire ended up in the hands of a general named Seleucus Nicator.

Seleucus did not use Damascus for his capital but established himself at Antioch on the Orontes river. This became the most important city along the eastern Mediterranean and Seleucus finally expanded his holdings until they extended from India to Thrace. This became known as the Seleucid empire.

Meanwhile, another general named Ptolemy had taken over Egypt and the African holdings of the Greek empire. Ptolemy established a dynasty that lasted 300 years. A new capital for Egypt was built at Alexandria and Ptolemy and his descendants took on the title of Pharaoh. Not until 30 B.C. when Cleopatra, the last of the Ptolemys, committed suicide, did this dynasty lose its grip on Egypt.

In the partitioning of the Greek empire there were long years of war and political maneuvering. Members of Alexander's own family were among the victims. His mother, half-brother, wife and son, were all murdered.

As the years wore on, Judah also frequently found herself in the cross-fire of these frenzied military contests. In 320 B.C. Ptolemy I attacked Jerusalem and carried off many captives. In 314, the Greek ruler Antigonus came down and took Palestine. In 312 B.C. Ptolemy grabbed it back. Things then took a rather stable turn. During these days many Jews migrated to Cyrene, one of the Mediterranean ports of north Africa lying about 300 miles west of Alexandria. Other colonies of Jews preferred Alexandria itself and settled themselves there where a rich Greek culture was rapidly taking root.

Around 275 B.C. Ptolemy II, known as Philadelphus, undertook to make the library at Alexandria the most famous in the world. He wanted to include the sacred literature of the Jews but he felt it should be translated into Greek so the local scholars could read it. Ptolemy II therefore imported a body of Jewish scholars who assembled at Pharos, an island just offshore from Alexandria, and there they completed the translation of the Torah (or Hebrew scripture) in 72 days. This seventy-two day miracle gave the translation its name — the Septuagint version.

In 223 B.C., about fifty years after the above event, the house of Seleucus put Antiochus III on the Syrian throne. He immediately attempted to seize nearby Phoenicia and Palestine from Egypt. He thought he could get away with this because Egypt had then come under one of the most depraved rulers since the Ptolemys took over. His name was Ptolemy IV or Philopator. He was believed to have killed his father to gain the throne, and then his first act as Pharaoh was to murder his own mother and younger brother. It was thought that the public hostility toward this despised ruler would make him easy to defeat. But when the Seleucid armies met the Egyptian hosts at Raphia, some 20 miles below Gaza in 217 B.C., the Egyptians beat the Syrians unmercifully and sent them streaming back up toward the north.

Judah was directly involved in this conflict because the moment Ptolemy IV (or Philopator) had won this victory he visited the famous city of Jerusalem and compelled the Jews to allow him to offer pagan sacrifices at the temple. The people finally developed a resistance movement and Ptolemy IV became so enraged that he went back to Egypt and started a Nazi-type liquidation of all Jews.

Ptolemy IV died in 203 B.C., and Antiochus III of Syria promptly invaded the Holy Land again. This time he was successful and after the battle of Panias in 198 B.C. he added Palestine to the Seleucid empire. Antiochus then pressed forward to take Greece and push into Europe, but at the Thermopylae Pass he met the westward march of the Romans and after being thoroughly defeated, was pushed back. This was one of the early symptoms of a new rising power soon to be reckoned with. In fact, in 190 B.C., just a few years after Antiochus III returned to the mainland of Asia Minor, he was attacked by another Roman army at Magnesia (near Ephesus) where the Roman general, Scipio, beat him badly. The Romans then dictated severe terms and demanded an enormous tribute. The Syrians were forced to send hostages to Rome, including the son of Antiochus III named Antiochus Epiphanes. The name of this infamous personaltiy is one to be remembered. He spent 15 years in Rome to pledge the performance of those promises made by his father and later by his brother. Not until the death of his brother would the Romans allow Antiochus Epiphanes to return home and take over the throne of Syria. Even then, he ruled as a vassal of Rome.

Judah Under the Heel of Antiochus Epiphanes

It became the zealous passion of this new Syrian ruler from the house of Seleucid to unify Syria and her tributaries in every way possible. He wished to make the Greek culture universal so as to form a resistance to the encroachments of the Roman culture. One of his foremost ambitions was to unite his empire along religious lines. He therefore issued edicts which not only created an impossible situation for the Jews but was almost as revolting to the other Syrian tributaries. However, in spite of all resistance, Antiochus was doggedly determined to carry out his project.

The Syrian king sent agents to Jerusalem with specific instructions to annihilate Judaism.

Right while massive pagan temples were being built in Baalbeck to honor Zeus, the supreme deity of the Greeks (but known to the Romans as Jupiter), the agents of Antiochus Epiphanes were desecrating the temple in Jerusalem by erecting an image of Zeus in the Holy of Holies. They plundered the temple of its wealth, burned the sacred books, forbade circumcision or the sanctifying of the Sabbath day on pain of death. To further mortify the feelings of the people, the Greeks sacrificed a sow in the temple to honor Zeus. From then on the strict observance of every heathen festival became compulsory for all Jews.

To prevent a revolt in Jerusalem, many of the Jews were sold into slavery and the walls of the city were demolished. What a heartbreak that would have been for the faithful Nehemiah!

In fact, Antiochus Epiphanes was guilty of practically everything he could have concocted to provoke a violent revolution on the part of these people. And that is exactly what happened.

The Revolt of the Maccabees

About 17 miles northwest of Jerusalem in a small town called Modin, there lived an aged Priest named Mattathia ("Gift of God"). He watched what was happening in Jerusalem with the greatest abhorrence. In fact, when the Syrian official came to Modin and prepared to offer a heathen sacrifice, the old man killed him. Mattathias had five sons and they knew there would be immediate retribution by Antiochus Epiphanes, so they took their father and fled to the hills. The following year (in 166 B.C.) the courageous old Priest passed away, but his five sons rallied behind Judas (the third brother) to raise up a national revolt against the Syrians. The family name of these brothers was Hasmonaeans, but Judas took upon himself the name of Maccabaeus — the Hammer — and soon the whole family was known by that name.

Now a long series of struggles commenced which eventually led to the violent death of each of the five brothers, but left their heirs in charge of a more vigorous and united people than had existed since the days of Nehemiah.

Two factors were primarily responsible for the more or less successful revolt of the Maccabees — a power struggle

among the leaders of Syria and significant though not decisive interference from Rome. Rome was not ready to throw
her whole weight into the contest until a century later, but
she did officially recognize the independence of Judah, and
distracted Syria with military forays along her borders.

The first of the heroic Maccabees to be killed was Judas,
but not until he had provided six years of outstanding leadership. In 165 B.C. Judas defeated the Syrian army under
Lysias, while Antiochus Epiphanes was on an eastern scav-
enger campaign trying to raise enough money to pay his
tribute to Rome. A Jewish victory made it possible for Judas
to then recapture Jerusalem. He immediately pulled down
all of the heathen shrines, cleansed the temple and prepared
it for a new dedication. This was one of the highlights in
Jewish history and is called the Hanukkah, or the Feast of
Dedication, which became an annual celebration.[35]

In 162 B.C. the Syrians besieged Jerusalem and tried to
make the Jews knuckle down again, but strife at Antioch
over the Syrian throne forced the siege to be lifted and the
Jews were granted complete religious liberty if they would
keep the peace. However, the Syrians insisted on their right
to choose the person who would be high priest. They had
selected a Hellenistic-minded priest named Alcimus which
finally led to a Jewish revolt. This is when Judas Maccabaeus
first sent envoys to Rome to get support. Meanwhile he had
his brother, Jonathan, take over the office of High Priest.

VIOLENT DEATHS OF JUDAS, JOHN, ELEAZAR AND JONATHAN

In 160 B.C., a sudden Syrian attack required the most
extreme exertion on the part of Judah to ward off the enemy.
It was in this campaign that Judas Maccabaeus was killed
at Elasa, north of Jerusalem. His brother, Jonathan, who had
been serving as High Priest immediately took charge of the
army as well. Jonathan not only lost Judas at this time but
two of his other brothers also. John, the eldest of the brothers,
was captured and shortly thereafter killed. Eleazar, the next
to the youngest, was crushed to death during a battle, by an
elephant which he had wounded.

---

35. This is referred to in John 10:22.

Syria continued to have stormy quarrels and power struggles at home, so this gave Judah some respite for several years. Then Rome finally conquered Carthage in north Africa and Jonathan sent delegates to Rome, to encourage their further intervention in Palestine to enforce Judah's independence. But before this project had borne any fruit, Jonathan was murdered in 142 B.C. by a pretender to the Syrian throne, named Tryphon. Now the one remaining brother was Simon. He took over and resisted Tryphon so that the Syrian throne fell into the possession of Demetrius II. Demetrius was so grateful for the help of the Jews in getting rid of Tryphon that he granted the Jews independence and freedom from further tribute. This is when the Jews held their famous "solemn assembly" and proclaimed Simon and his descendants High Priests and ethnarchs (provincial governors) "until a faithful prophet should arise."[36]

DEATH OF SIMON AND RISE OF JOHN HYRCANUS

Judah enjoyed peace until 138 B.C. when a new king of Syria, Antiochus VII, felt hard pressed for funds and appeared on the northern border of Judah with a good sized army, demanding that they pay up for each of the years they had missed under Demetrius. Simon was too old to lead a resistance so his two sons, John Hyrcanus and Judas, did it for him. While this war was a success it was followed by a tragedy. A man named Ptolemy had married one of Simon's daughters and had ambitions to seize the throne of Judah. He therefore murdered Simon, the last of the original Maccabees. Ptolemy failed to seize the throne as he had hoped, for John Hyrcanus disposed of him and took his father's place. Barely was this accomplished when the Syrians were back with the biggest enemy force Judah had seen in a long time. John Hyrcanus was forced to retreat within the city of Jerusalem where the people were subjected to a desolating siege before they finally surrendered. A harsh tribute was then laid upon them, and the city's defenses were demolished. Nevertheless, as the years went by, it became apparent to Jewish officials that a resolute leadership with a fairly substantial army could

---

36. I Maccabees 14:41

restore Judah to a respectable position once more. John Hyrcanus decided that the situation justified the hiring of mercenaries. His own people were not soldiers but herdsmen,
farmers, domestics. They were capable of defending their
homes, but what John Hyrcanus had in mind was the recovery of Israel's territory which had been lost down through
the centuries. So he set up a personal honor guard of valiant
men and paid them a fixed salary to help spread the territories of Judah back to the original boundaries of all Israel.
First, Samaria was defeated and the heathen temple on Mount
Gerizim was destroyed. Then Idumea, the Arab kingdom to
the south, was conquered. Syria tried to interfere occasionally
but her own deterioration and involvement with Roman ha-
rassment prevented her from being effective.

With the expansion of Judah to these remarkable dimensions, one would have thought the reign of John Hyrcanus
would have been very popular. However, he had made one
serious mistake. When he first started on his campaign the
country was so poor that he could not pay the mercenaries
who had to do the fighting. In desperation he burrowed
into the tomb of David and expropriated the extent of his
needs from the valuable jewelry and articles of gold and
silver which had been preserved there for nearly 900 years!
The people never forgave him for that.

Nevertheless, when John Hyrcanus died in 104 B.C.,
he left Judah in a more prosperous and contented state than
she had been since these terrible dark ages first began.

John Hyrcanus was succeeded by his son, Judas Aristobulus, who was the first of the Maccabees to assume the
title of king. However, he only survived a year when he was
replaced by his brother, Alexander Jannaeus. Alexander
ruled for 27 years and sought to further his father's policy
of recovering the lost territory of Israel. His campaigns resulted in the recovery of considerable territory east of the
Jordan.

It was during the reign of Alexander that civil war broke
out between the Sadducees and the Pharisees. The Sadducees
were the wealthy and influential Priests whose functions at
the temple kept them united in mutually agreeable doctrines
and party objectives. On the other hand, the Pharisees in-

cluded many of the Levites and Rabbis. They were much more numerous and believed that the Sadducees had apostatized by denying the resurrection, angels, spirits, and the need to follow the strict requirements of the law. The Sadducees, however, were zealots when it came to administering the law of an eye for an eye and a tooth for a tooth. They did not want to allow a person the privilege of redeeming his offense through the payment of money or working out the damages as a bond servant the way Moses had taught. The Pharisees supported the more tolerant view taken by Moses.

Difficulties between the Sadducees and Pharisees frequently occurred during this period. Their arguments went all the way from controversial polemics to the outright shedding of blood.

When Alexander Jannaeus died in 76 B.C., the reigns of government passed to his wife, Salome Alexandra. She ruled until 67 B.C., and appointed one of her sons, Hyrcanus II, to serve as High Priest. The actual administration of the government was turned over to high officials among the Pharisees and thereafter Salome functioned principally as queen at the social affairs of state.

When Salome died in 67 B.C., her son, Hyrcanus, held the throne for three months but was challenged by his younger brother, Aristobulus II. Now we come to the famous quarrel which ultimately took the whole Kingdom of Judah into the Roman lion's den. When Hyrcanus was forced to relinquish the throne, it was obvious that perpetual civil war was likely to ensue. The Arabs had good offices with the Romans and therefore Hyrcanus began using them to negotiate for Roman support in ousting Aristobulus. The Arab who did the negotiating was one whose family would influence the affairs in this region for a long time to come. His name was Antipater, the Idumean, whose son became king of Judah and infamous in history as Herod the Great.

However, the Romans elected to support Artistobulus instead of Hyrcanus so Antipater quickly retired from the scene temporarily.

The people of Judah would never have believed it but they were now just three years away from being taken over

by the Romans. The quarrel between these two brothers facilitated the final collapse. To appreciate just how it happened
we now turn briefly to the history of Rome.

THE RISE OF ROME — THE IRON KINGDOM IN NEBUCHADNEZZAR'S DREAM

As we have previously noted, the Roman legions had
been battering and badgering their way toward the east and
coming into direct conflict with the masters of the Middle
East for over 150 years. Up to this point, however, everything that had happened was merely prelude. The Romans
were now about to take over the whole theater of civilization from England to India.

The Romans were of a different temperament than the
Greeks but equally ambitious. They had experimented with
limited democracy, and developed a flare for the most rigid
kind of military discipline. They had also exercised the greatest delight in building thousands of miles of roads together
with equally impressive aqueducts, amphitheaters, coliseums,
palaces, temples and race tracks. They were methodical per-
fectionists but the Romans had imbued themselves with one
non-conformist quality which distinguished them from practically all other empire builders. They generaly practiced religious tolerance. Establishing a universal system of worship
was not among the ambitions of the Romans. Their passion
was for peace, order, and the Latin version of law and justice.

Anyone standing on the sidelines might never have
guessed that the pagan Roman legions which strictly enforced
their doctrine of Pax Romana, also brought with them the
framework of indispensible circumstances required for the
ministry of Jesus Christ! Yet such was the case, and the
Heavens knew it. The orderly timetable for the succession
of kingdoms which Nebuchadnezzar had seen in his dream
was right on schedule.

For 400 years the Romans relied on a Republican form
of government but by the first century B.C. they had evolved
into a series of military dictatorships. Even when they passed
laws prohibiting their generals from seizing power, the very
next emergency would find the Senate violating its own rules

and giving almost unlimited authority to one or more of its most trusted military leaders. Thus it was that by 63 B.C. the famous generals, Julius Caesar and Gnaeus Pompey, both found themselves in virtual control of the Roman empire.

While Caesar was on a campaign in Spain, Pompey undertook the conquest of the old Seleucid empire. He came sweeping across Asia Minor and down the Orontes valley toward Palestine, devouring provinces and kingdoms as he came. When he reached Judah the quarrel between the two brothers, Hyrcanus and Aristobulus II, made Roman intervention inevitable. Each of the men had eagerly pleaded with the Roman general to intervene. Pompey intervened, but on behalf of Rome. In 63 B.C. the iron-shod wheels of Roman chariots rumbled through the streets of Jerusalem and Roman eagles were implanted on top of Mount Zion. It was the end of the Maccabees, and the end of any semblance of Jewish independence. Now Judah was assigned to a Roman governor.

Shortly afterwards the three leading generals of Rome formed a triumvirate and divided administrative and military responsibility for the empire into three parts. Julius Caesar took Gaul, a general named Crassus took Syria, and Pompey took Greece, Asia Minor, Phoenicia and Palestine. At first Caesar and Pompey were very closely allied. Pompey married a daughter of Caesar in 56 B.C. but she died in 54 B.C. and the next year Crassus was killed in the Parthian campaign. The natural result was an open split between the two men who now began manuevering for exclusive control of the empire. The Senate backed Pompey so he had them order Caesar, who was then in Gaul, to disband his army. Instead, Caesar cried out, "The die is cast," and marched his army across the Rubicon toward Rome. Pompey fled to Greece but Caesar followed and defeated him. In final desperation Pompey fled to Egypt seeking refuge.

At Alexandria, Egypt, the last of the Ptolemys were then in power — a 21-year-old girl named Cleopatra and her 15-year-old brother (Ptolemy XIV) to whom she was "married" after the custom of the Egyptians. At the moment, the two were fighting each other in a struggle for the Egyptian throne. Upon hearing that Pompey was sailing to Egypt, young Ptolemy saw an opportunity to curry favor with Caesar by assassinating his enemy. Therefore, when Pompey came to Egypt seeking refuge he was stabbed to death before he even reached shore. Caesar soon followed but instead of being pleased to learn of Pompey's murder he was outraged. He would teach pompous foreigners to assassinate Roman generals! But the next thing Caesar knew he was surrounded by Ptolemy's Egyptian army which threatened the extinction of the smaller Roman task force. The thing which turned the tide for Caesar was the arrival of several thousand men under the command of the Idumean, Antipater. This man had an uncanny capacity to be in the right place at the right time. After fierce fighting the Romans were saved. Antipater's part in saving Caesar's reputation and perhaps his life, resulted in his being made the governor of Judah. The irony of it all was the fact that he had once been a vassal of Judah.

It was during this Egyptian excursion that Caesar, who was now 54, became associated with Cleopatra. The Egyptian queen's first child was born in consequence of this union. In 44 B.C., while Caesar was back in Rome he was assassinated on the 14th of March. A new triumvirate was formed with Mark Antony and Caesar's successor, Octavian, being the principal parties. Cleopatra, however, for reasons best known to herself, induced Mark Antony to come to Egypt where she bore him two sons. Mark Antony's loss of prestige at home permitted Octavian to begin building sufficient strength so that he could oppose Mark Antony in a new struggle for power.

At the famous battle of Actium in Greece during 31 B.C., Octavian succeeded in defeating the forces of both Cleopatra and Mark Antony. This settled the question of who would rule Rome during the next 41 years. Mark Antony and Cleopatra fled to Alexandria, and in 30 B.C. both of them committed suicide.

Octavian now took over the Roman empire and had himself named "first citizen." He did not wish to be called "emperor," though he did take the title of Augustus, meaning the "revered one."

So here was the Augustus Caesar of the New Testament ready to play his role in an epic far greater than the empire itself. He would establish a long era of peace and stability so that a babe could be born in Bethlehem and accomplish a mission for which righteous men and women had been waiting nearly 4,000 years.

Meanwhile, in Judah. the Idumean (known as Antipater) had been poisoned, and after a long series of narrow escapes his son, Herod, received the approval of Rome and finally became the governor of the entire territory.

Up in Nazareth a beautiful young girl and a carpenter had recently become betrothed. They were both descendants of King David and were living with their families in relative poverty and complete obscurity. The young girl was known by the Hebrew name of Miryam, but it has come down to us through the Greek as Mary. The young man was called Joseph.

Down near Jerusalem there lived a very aged Priest named Zacharias who was married to one of Mary's cousins, a woman named Elizabeth. Elizabeth had always wanted a child but she was now too old to have one. It seemed too bad.

This was the year of the Romans, 752. None of these people could have guessed what was about to happen to them.

In less than a year John the Baptist would be born to Elizabeth, and six months later the Son of God would be born to Mary in Bethlehem.

Questions and Scripture Reading on Chapter Twenty-Nine

Scripture Reading: Book of Malachi

1—In Malachi's day, what were the Priests doing which so displeased the Lord?

2—In the Book of Malachi what does the Lord promise those who pay their tithing — everything else being equal?

3—What did the Lord say in modern times concerning tithe-payers?

4—Who, in your opinion, is "the messenger" referred to in Malachi chapter 3? Any special reason?

5—Who are the modern Jews waiting for besides their Messiah? Has he already come?

6—Approximately when was the golden age of Athens? Who was the ruler of Athens? What happened when he died?

7—Name four things in the funeral oration given by the ruler of Athens which we enjoy in our own society.

8—What did Isocrates want to have the Greeks do? Did they achieve it?

9—Who trained Alexander the Great in his youth? Was Alexander a good military strategist or just lucky?

10—About when was the Septuagint version of the Old Testament translated into Greek? Why does it bear that name?

11—List four of the things which Antiochus Epiphanes did to the Jewish people to make them revolt.

12—What does the word "Maccabee" mean? How many Maccabee brothers were there? Concerning their deaths, what did they share in common?

13—When Simon, the last of the Maccabee brothers, was made governor or ruler of Judah, what reservation did the Jews attach to his appointment?

14—Did the Sadducees and Pharisees ever get mixed up in politics? Name two differences in their respective beliefs.

15—Who was Antipater? What nationality? What reward did he receive for saving Julius Caesar at Alexandria?

16—What year did the Romans conquer Jerusalem? Who was the general? What happened to him?

17—To whom was Cleopatra married? What do you think she was trying to do for Egypt by this marriage?

18—What was the "iron kingdom" seen in Nebuchadnezzar's dream? Why does that appellation fit?

19—What was the one thing about which the Romans were very tolerant at this stage of their history?

20—What was Mary's Hebrew name? What famous person was her ancestor? Who was her aged cousin?

Index

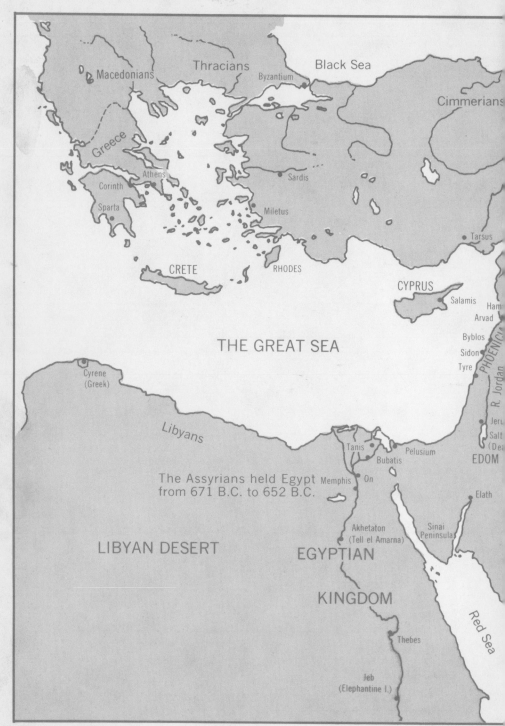

Macedonians
Thracians
Black Sea
Byzantium
Cimmerians
Greece
Sardis
Athens
Corinth
Sparta
Miletus
Tarsus
CRETE
RHODES
CYPRUS
Salamis
Ham
Arvad
Byblos
Sidon
Tyre
PHOENICIA
R. Jordan
THE GREAT SEA
Cyrene
(Greek)
Libyans
Jeru
Salt
(Dea
Tanis
Pelusium
EDOM
Bubatis
The Assyrians held Egypt
from 671 B.C. to 652 B.C.
Memphis
On
Elath
Akhetaton
(Tell el Amarna)
Sinai
Peninsula
LIBYAN DESERT
EGYPTIAN
KINGDOM
Red Sea
Thebes
Jeb
(Elephantine I.)